Ordnance Survey

STREET ATLAS
Hertfordshire

Contents

III	*Key to map symbols*
IV-V	*Key to map pages*
VI	*Administrative and post code boundaries*
1	*Street maps*
177	*Explanation of street index reference system*
177	*Key to town, village and rural locality abbreviations in index*
178	*Index of hospitals, railway stations, schools, shopping centres, street names and universities*

PHILIP'S

First edition published 1986
Fourth edition published 1994
First colour edition published 1996
Reprinted in 1996, 1997 by

Ordnance Survey®   and   George Philip Ltd
Romsey Road,   an imprint of Reed Consumer Books Ltd
Maybush,   Michelin House, 81 Fulham Road,
Southampton SO16 4GU   London SW3 6RB
                                        and Auckland and Melbourne

ISBN 0-540-06174-3 (hardback)
ISBN 0-540-06175-1 (wire-o)

To the best of the Publishers' knowledge, the information in this atlas
was correct at the time of going to press. No responsibility can be
accepted for any errors or their consequences.

The representation in this atlas of a road, track or path is no evidence
of the existence of a right of way.

**The mapping between pages 1 and 176 (inclusive) in this atlas is
derived from Ordnance Survey® OSCAR® and Land-Line® data,
and Landranger® mapping.**

Ordnance Survey, OSCAR, Land-Line and Landranger are registered
trade marks of Ordnance Survey, the National Mapping Agency of
Great Britain.

Printed and bound in Spain by Cayfosa

Key to map symbols

▬▬	Motorway
▬▬	Primary Routes (Dual carriageway and single)
▬▬	A Roads (Dual carriageway and single)
▬▬	B Roads (Dual carriageway and single)
▬▬	C Roads (Dual carriageway and single)
▬▬	Minor Roads
---	Roads under construction
·—·—·	County boundaries
▬▬	All Railways
········	Track or private road
▬┬▬	Gate or obstruction to traffic (restrictions may not apply at all times or to all vehicles)
········	All paths, bridleways, BOAT's, RUPP's, dismantled railways, etc.

The representation in this atlas of a road, track or path is no evidence of the existence of a right of way

174	Adjoining page indicator

Abbr	Full	Abbr	Full
Acad	Academy	Mon	Monument
Cemy	Cemetery	Mus	Museum
C Ctr	Civic Centre	Obsy	Observatory
CH	Club House	Pal	Royal Palace
Coll	College	PH	Public House
Ex H	Exhibition Hall	Resr	Reservoir
Ind Est	Industrial Estate	Ret Pk	Retail Park
Inst	Institute	Sch	School
Ct	Law Court	Sh Ctr	Shopping Centre
L Ctr	Leisure Centre	Sta	Station
LC	Level Crossing	TH	Town Hall/House
Liby	Library	Trad Est	Trading Estate
Mkt	Market	Univ	University
Meml	Memorial	YH	Youth Hostel

⇄	British Rail station
🚂	Private railway station
●	Bus, coach station
◆	Ambulance station
◆	Coastguard station
◆	Fire station
◆	Police station
✚	Casualty entrance to hospital
✝	Churches, Place of worship
H	Hospital
i	Information Centre
P	Parking
□	Post Office
●	Public Convenience
�	Important buildings, schools, colleges, universities and hospitals
River Soar	Water Name
········	Stream
▬ ▬	River or canal (minor and major)
	Water Fill
	Tidal Water
	Woods
	Houses

The scale of the maps is 5.52 cm to 1 km (3½ inches to 1 mile)

The small numbers around the edges of the maps identify the 1 kilometre National Grid lines

Scale bar:
0 — ¼ — ½ — ¾ — 1 mile
0 — 250m — 500m — 750m — 1 Kilometre

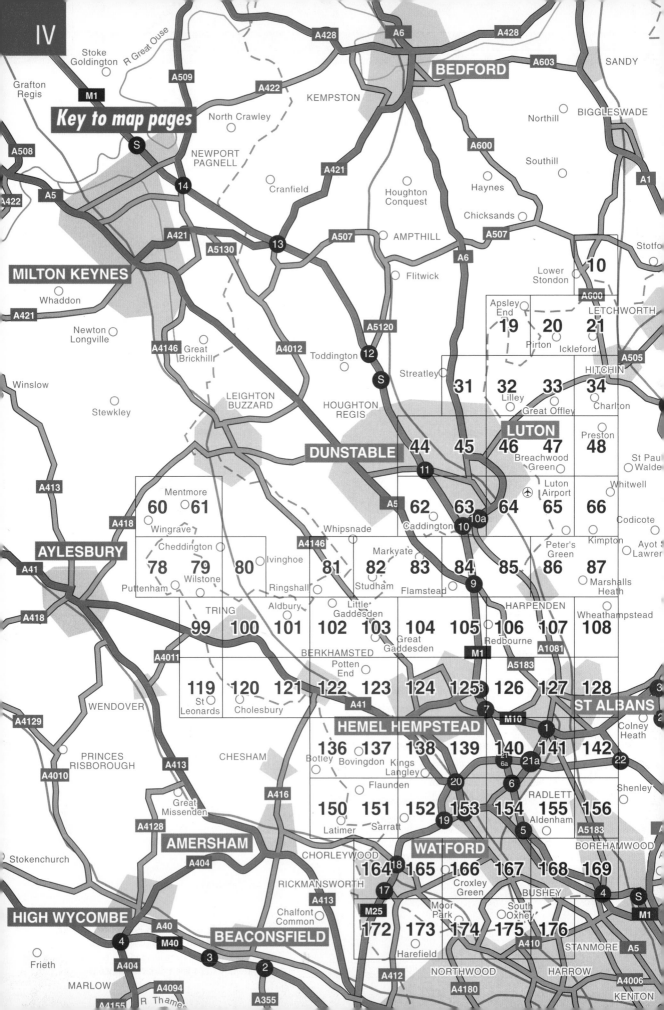

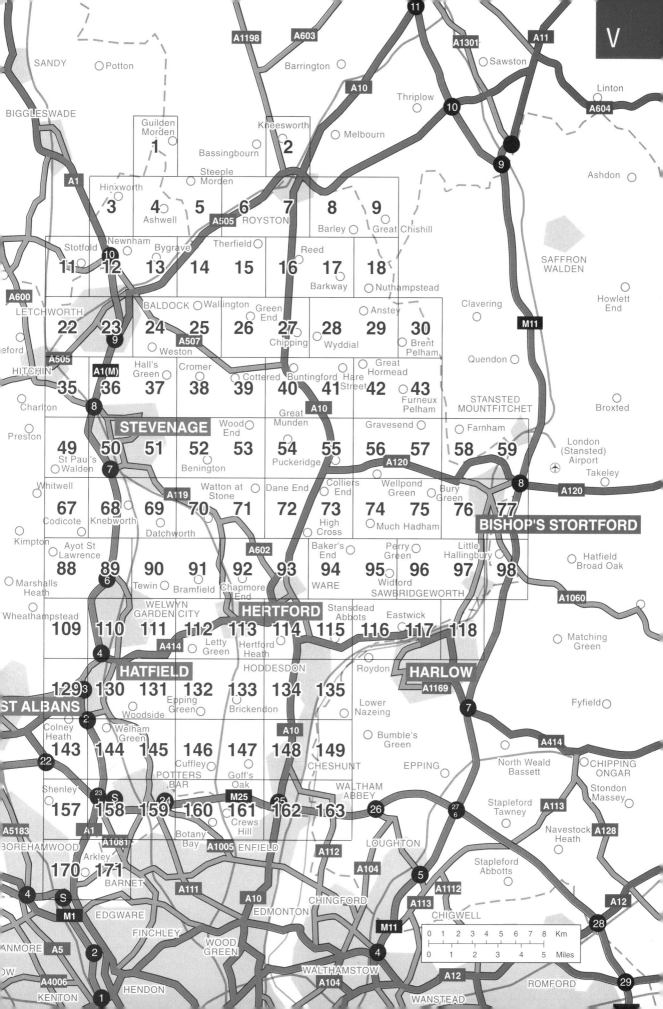

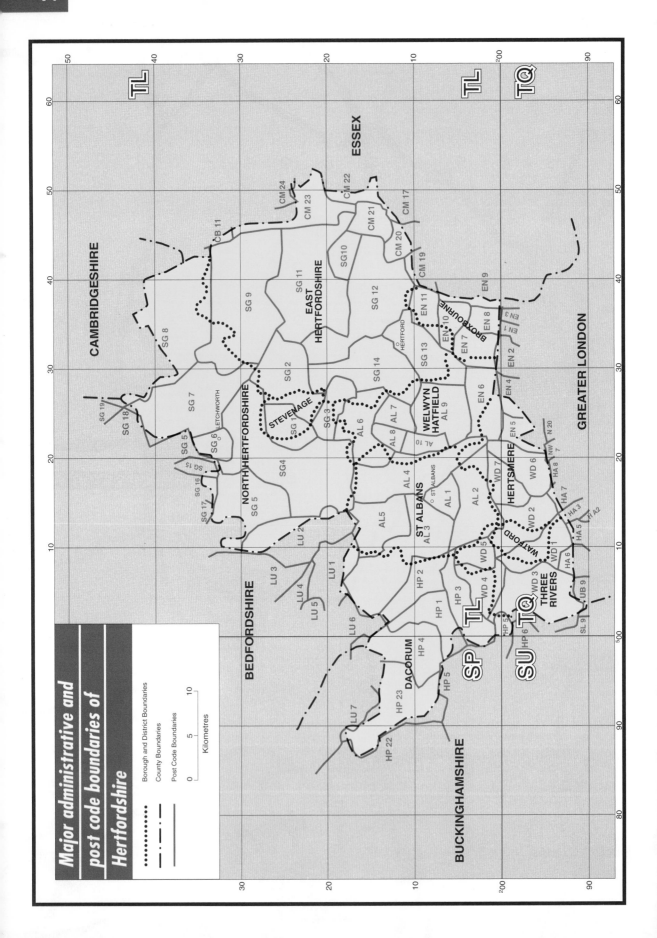

Major administrative and post code boundaries of Hertfordshire

Borough and District Boundaries

County Boundaries

Post Code Boundaries

Kilometres

0   5   10

CAMBRIDGESHIRE

ESSEX

BEDFORDSHIRE

BUCKINGHAMSHIRE

GREATER LONDON

EAST HERTFORDSHIRE

NORTH HERTFORDSHIRE

STEVENAGE

WELWYN HATFIELD

ST ALBANS

DACORUM

HERTSMERE

WATFORD

THREE RIVERS

BROXBOURNE

TL

TQ

SP

SU

TL

TQ

SG 8
SG 7
SG 9
SG 11
SG 10
SG 12
SG 2
SG 14
SG 13
SG 3
SG 1
SG 4
SG 5
SG 6
SG 18
SG 19
SG 15
SG 16
SG 17

CB 11
CM 24
CM 23
CM 22
CM 21
CM 20
CM 19
CM 17

AL 6
AL 7
AL 8
AL 9
AL 10
AL 4
AL 1
AL 2
AL 3
AL 5

EN 11
EN 10
EN 9
EN 8
EN 7
EN 6
EN 5
EN 4
EN 3
EN 2
EN 1

WD 7
WD 6
WD 3
WD 2
WD 1
WD 4
WD 5

HA 8
HA 7
HA 6
HA 5
HA 3
HA 2

N 20
NW 7

LU 1
LU 2
LU 3
LU 4
LU 5
LU 6
LU 7

HP 2
HP 1
HP 3
HP 4
HP 5
HP 6
HP 23
HP 22

SL 9
UB 9

LETCHWORTH
HERTFORD
HERTFORD
ST ALBANS

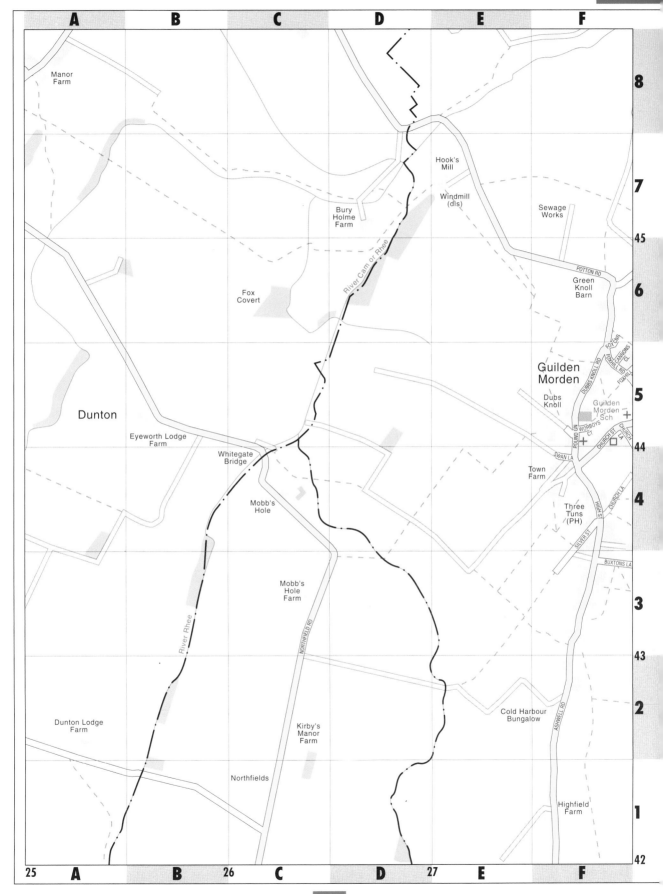

Manor Farm

Hook's Mill

Windmill (dis)

Sewage Works

POTTON RD

Bury Holme Farm

River Cam or Rhee

Green Knoll Barn

Fox Covert

FOX LNR

FOSHILL RD CL

CANNONS

DUBBS KNOLL RD

FOXHILL

Guilden Morden

Dubs Knoll

Guilden Morden Sch

Dunton

WORBOYS

POUND GN

CHURCH ST

CHURCH

Eyeworth Lodge Farm

SWAN LA

Whitegate Bridge

Town Farm

Mobb's Hole

Three Tuns (PH)

SILVER ST

HIGH ST

CHURCH LA

BUXTONS LA

Mobb's Hole Farm

River Rhee

NORTHFIELD RD

Cold Harbour Bungalow

ASHWELL RD

Dunton Lodge Farm

Kirby's Manor Farm

Northfields

Highfield Farm

25   A   B   26   C   D   27   E   F

A   B   C   D   E   F

A1198
CAMBRIDGE CRES
CARDIFF PL

8

Dyer's
Green

BRIDGE ST

Mettle Hill
Farm

KNEESWORTH RD

Mettle
Hill

Bassingbourn
Barracks

Ermine
Farm

Frog
Hall

7

OXFORD CL

Danger
Area

45

Harcamlow Way

6

Danger
Area

Resr

Melbourn

NIGHTINGALE
AVE
WELLINGTON PL
CHESTNUT LA

TOWER
CL
ORCHARD
CL
THE CAUSEWAY
CANBERRA CL
PH
PH
SWINNELL CL
TOWER CL

5

Kneesworth

H
Kneesworth
House

44

OLD NORTH RD
TUDOR CL

4

Beauval
Farm
TUDOR CT

Harcamlow Way

3

Bury
Farm
ASHWELL ST

Nurseries

43

Holland
Hall

A10

2

Highfield
Farm

Sewage
Works

New
Farm

A1198

WORDSWORTH
CL
THACKERAY
CL
TENNYSON
CL

1

KEATS CL
TEASDALE CL
CRISPEN CL
BURNS RD
SPENSER
SHELLEY CL

A505
OLD NORTH RD
MILTON CL
LINDSAY
AVE
HOLLISDAY AVE
KEATS
CL
Schs
SWINBURNE CL 1
SCOTT CL 2
SWIFT CL
HARTSLANDS
CAMPKING RD
MELBOURNE RD
A10
A505

42

34   A   B   35   C   D   36   E   F

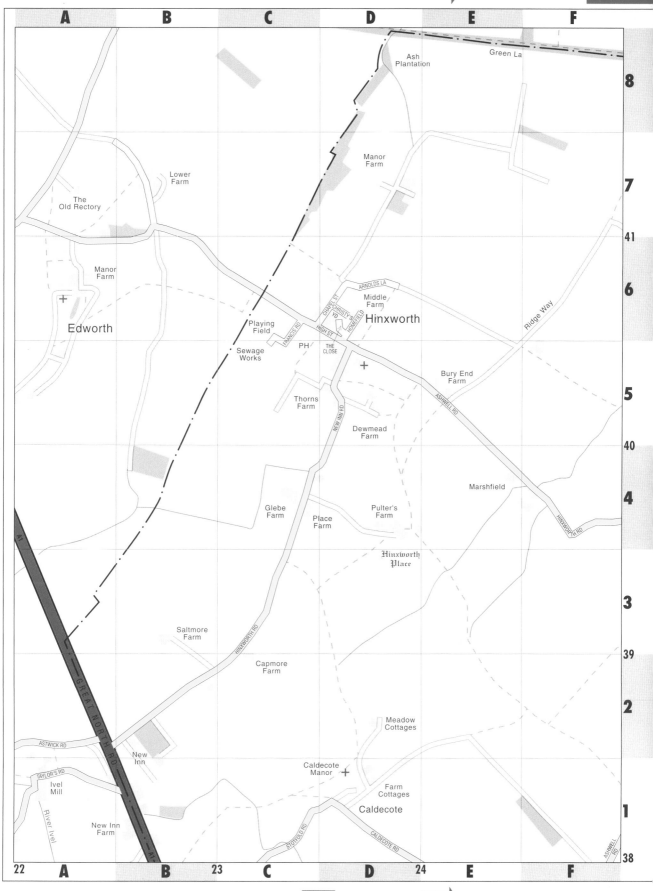

A B C D E F

8

7

41

6

5

40

4

3

39

2

1

38

Ash
Plantation

Green La

Manor
Farm

Lower
Farm

The
Old Rectory

Manor
Farm

Edworth

ARNOLDS LA

Middle
Farm

Hinxworth

Ridge Way

CHAPEL ST

CHRISTY S

YO

HOMEFIELD

Playing
Field

FRANCIS RD

HIGH ST

PH

THE
CLOSE

Sewage
Works

Bury End
Farm

Thorns
Farm

ASHWELL RD

NEW INN RD

Dewmead
Farm

Glebe
Farm

Place
Farm

Pulter's
Farm

Marshfield

HINXWORTH RD

Hinxworth
Place

Saltmore
Farm

HINXWORTH RD

Capmore
Farm

Meadow
Cottages

A1

GREAT NORTH RD

ASTWICK RD

New
Inn

TAYLOR'S RD

Ivel
Mill

River Ivel

New Inn
Farm

Caldecote
Manor

Farm
Cottages

Caldecote

STOTFOLD RD

CALDECOTE RD

ASHWELL RD

22 A B 23 C D 24 E F

A   B   C   D   E   F

Green La
Barrowsford Bridge
Ridge Way
NORTHFIELD RD
ASHWELL RD
ASHWELL RD

8

Cold Harbour

7

41

Sewage Works
COMMON LA

6

Bluegates Farm
River Rhee

Ashwell End

Bluegates Dairy
Elbrook House

5

Cemy
Baldwin's Corner
GREEN LA

40

Love's Farm
LOVE LA
Ashwell Bury
FORDHAM CL
MILL ST
SPRINGHEAD
LUCAS LA

Quarry Hills Farm
ROLLYS LA
ALMS LA
Hotel
Ashridge Farm

4
ALMS LA
CHURCH LA
GARDINERS LA
HODWELL
STATION RD

Whittington Farm
THE RICKYARD
BACON'S
SWAN ST
HIGH ST
SILVER ST
KINGS LAND WAY
WOODFORDE CL

HINXWORTH RD
Farrow's Farm
WEST END
WILSONS LA
BACK ST
DIXIES CL
BEAR LA
ANGEL'S MDW
MNTX EV
ASHWELL
Ashwell Junior Mixed Infants Sch
CLAYBUSH RD

3
PARTRIDGE HILL

39
Newnham Hill

Claybush Hill

NEWNHAM WAY

2
Arbury Banks

Ashwell

ASHWELL RD

1
Ash Hill

38
25   A   B   26   C   D   27   E   F

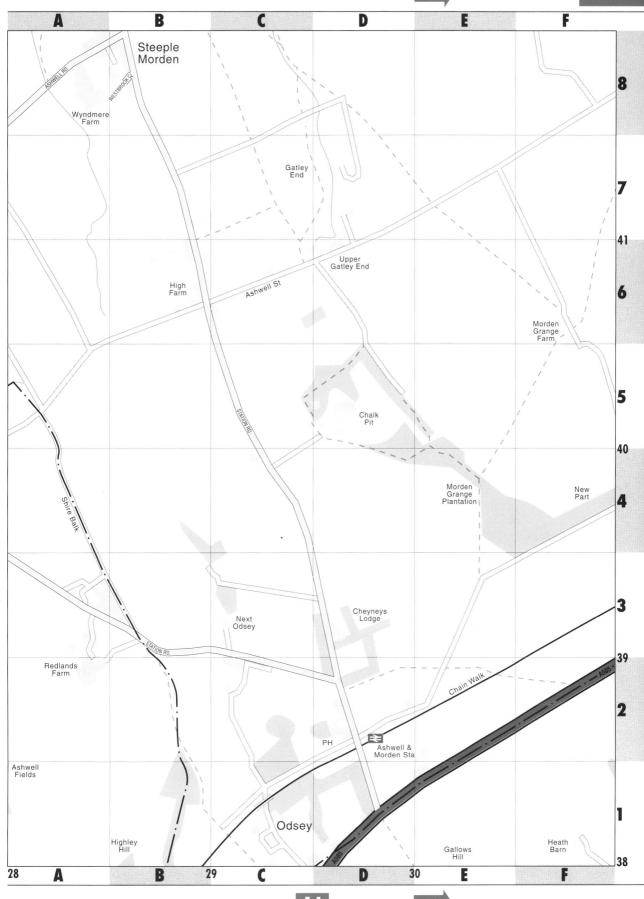

A B C D E F

Steeple
Morden

ASHWELL RD

WESTBROOK CL

Wyndmere
Farm

Gatley
End

Upper
Gatley End

High
Farm

Ashwell St

Morden
Grange
Farm

STATION RD

Chalk
Pit

Shire Balk

Morden
Grange
Plantation

New
Part

Cheyneys
Lodge

Next
Odsey

STATION RD

Redlands
Farm

Chain Walk

A505

PH

Ashwell &
Morden Sta

Ashwell
Fields

Odsey

Highley
Hill

A505

Gallows
Hill

Heath
Barn

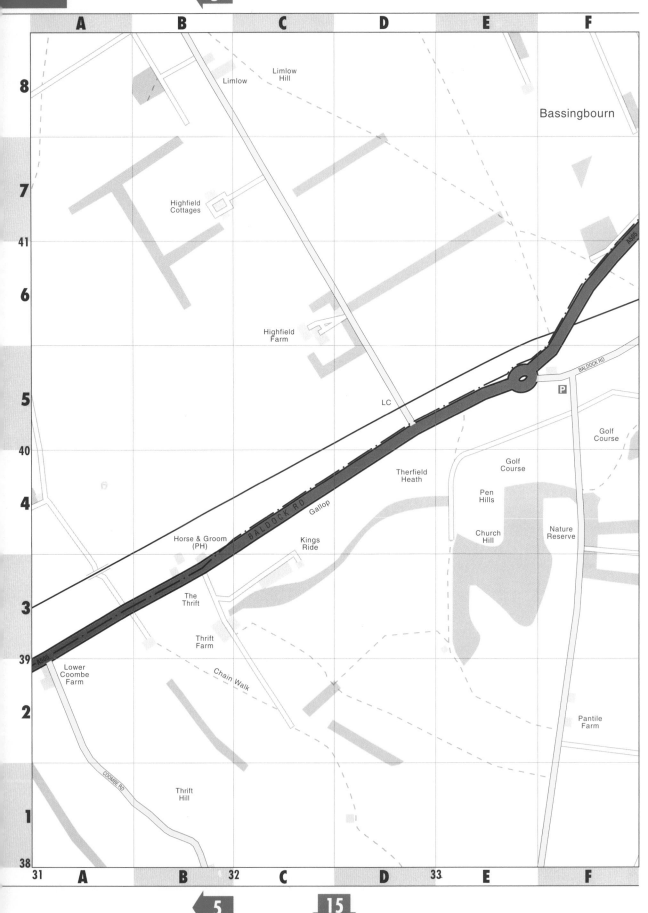

A B C D E F

8

Limlow
Limlow
Hill

Bassingbourn

7

Highfield
Cottages

41

A505

6

Highfield
Farm

BALDOCK RD

5

LC

P

Golf
Course

40

Therfield
Heath

Golf
Course

4

BALDOCK RD Gallop

Pen
Hills

Nature
Reserve

Horse & Groom
(PH)

Kings
Ride

Church
Hill

3

The
Thrift

Thrift
Farm

A505

39

Lower
Coombe
Farm

Chain Walk

2

Pantile
Farm

COOMBE RD

Thrift
Hill

1

38

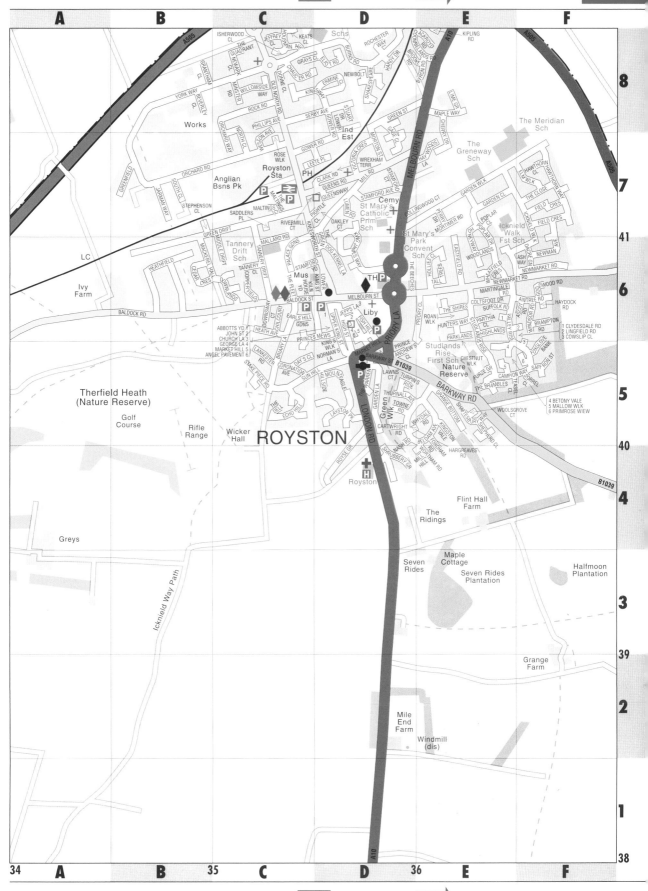

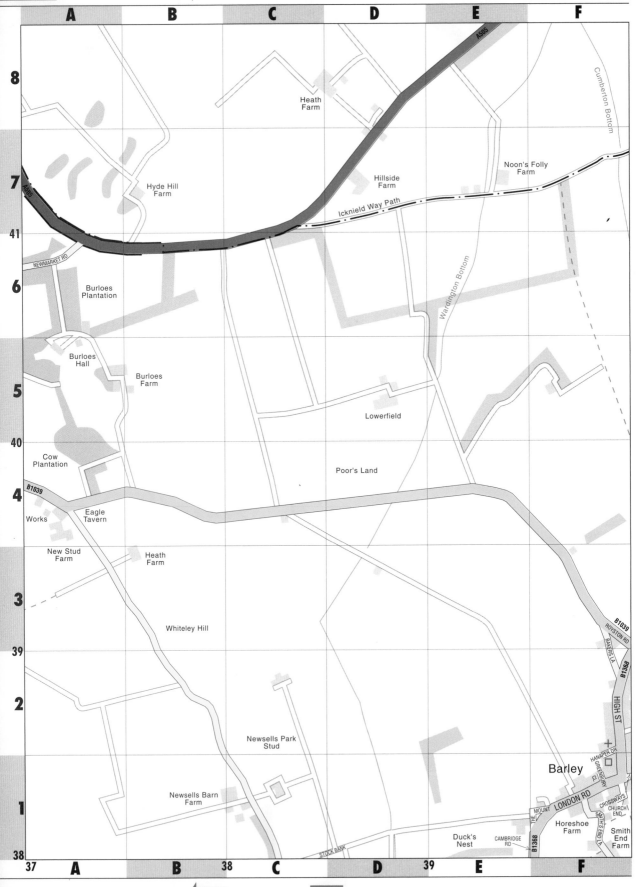

A   B   C   D   E   F

8

Heath
Farm

7

Hillside
Farm

Noon's Folly
Farm

Cumberton Bottom

A505

Hyde Hill
Farm

Icknield Way Path

41

NEWMARKET RD

Wardington Bottom

6

Burloes
Plantation

Burloes
Hall

Burloes
Farm

Lowerfield

5

40

Cow
Plantation

Poor's Land

B1039

4

Works

Eagle
Tavern

New Stud
Farm

Heath
Farm

B1039

ROYSTON RD

BAKERS LA

B1368

3

Whiteley Hill

39

HIGH ST

2

Newsells Park
Stud

Barley

HANAPER DR

GREENBURY CL

1

Newsells Barn
Farm

THE MOUNT

LONDON RD

CROSSWAYS

CHURCH
END

SMITH'S END LA

Horeshoe
Farm

Smith
End
Farm

38

Duck's
Nest

CAMBRIDGE
RD

B1368

STOCK BANK

37   A   B   38   C   D   39   E   F

A	B	C	D	E	F

North Hall Farm

B1368

Harcamlow Way

Icknield Way Path

Sells Close Farm

BARLEY RD

Harcamlow Way

Icknield Way Path

FOWLMERE RD

Green Ditch

8

7

41

New Buildings Farm

Clay Hill

NEW RD

6

Rectory Farm

5

40

Cumberton Bottom

4

CAMBRIDGE RD

New Hill

Lynchets Farm

CHISHILL RD

Lime Farm

3

HEYDON RD

REEVES PIGHTLE

39

PICKNAGE RD

BARLEY RD

THE PUDDELL

PLAISTOW WAY

PH

Great Chishill

HALL LA

2

Chishill Windmill

Hill Farm

MAY ST

MALTINGS LA

COATS CROFT

WALLER CLO

Barley Voluntary Primary Sch

B1039

CHISHILL RD

PICKNAGE CNR

May Street Farm

The Hall

B1039

CHURCH END

SCHOOL LA

PUDDING LA

CHURCHFIELD

SHAFTENOE END RD

Standard Hill

BOGMOOR RD

LITTLE CHISHILL RD

1

38

40	A		B	41	C		D	42	E		F

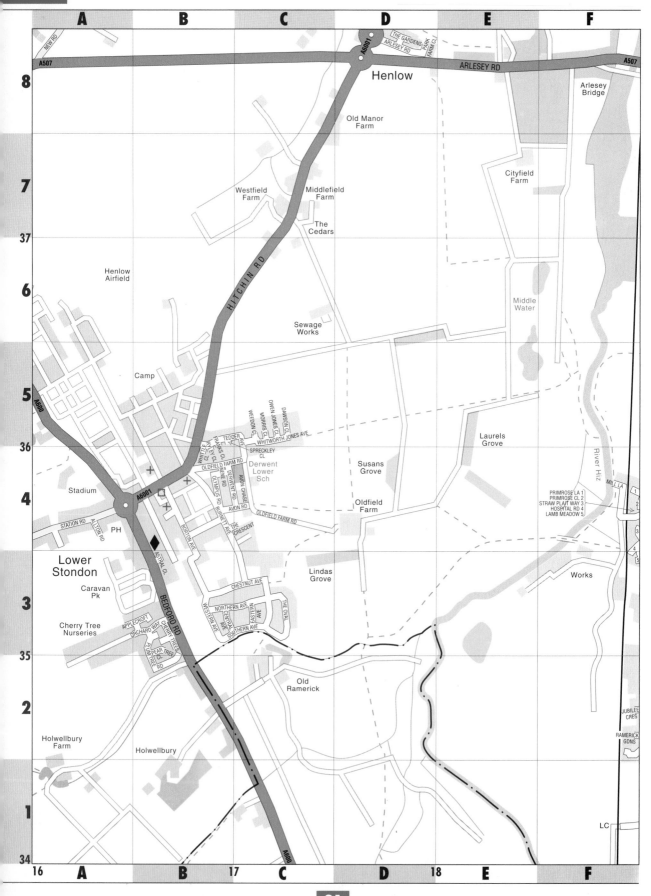

A   B   C   D   E   F

8

Henlow

7

37

6

5

36

4

3

35

2

1

34

16   A   17   B   C   18   D   E   F

A507   NEW RD   A507
ARLESEY RD
THE GARDENS
ARLESEY RD
PARK FARM CL 1
A6001
Old Manor Farm
Arlesey Bridge
Cityfield Farm
Westfield Farm
Middlefield Farm
The Cedars
HITCHIN RD
Middle Water
Henlow Airfield
Sewage Works
Camp
River Hiz
MILL LA
Laurels Grove
WEEDON CL
OWEN JONES CL
MORRIS CL
DAWSON CL
WHITWORTH JONES AVE
SPRECKLEY CL
TEDDER AVE
WHITTLE
FRANKS CL
HURLEY CL
CHENNE RD
OLDFIELD FARM RD
OLYMPUS RD
DERWENT RD
AVON CHASE
AVON RD
Derwent Lower Sch
Susans Grove
PRIMROSE LA 1
PRIMROSE CL 2
STRAW PLAIT WAY 3
HOSPITAL RD 4
LAMB MEADOW 5
A600
Stadium
A6001
BURNET AVE
THE CRESCENT
OLDFIELD FARM RD
Oldfield Farm
Works
STATION RD
ALLTON RD
PH
ASTRAL CL
BORTON AVE
Lindas Grove
Lower Stondon
Caravan Pk
CHESTNUT AVE
THE OVAL
Cherry Tree Nurseries
APPLECROFT
ORCHARD WAY
NORTHERN AVE
WESTERN AVE
CENTRAL AVE
EASTERN AVE
SOUTHERN AVE
BEDFORD RD
CHERRY TREE
PEAR TREE CL
PLUM TREE RD
JUBILEE CRES
RAMERICK GDNS
Old Ramerick
Holwellbury Farm
Holwellbury
A600
LC

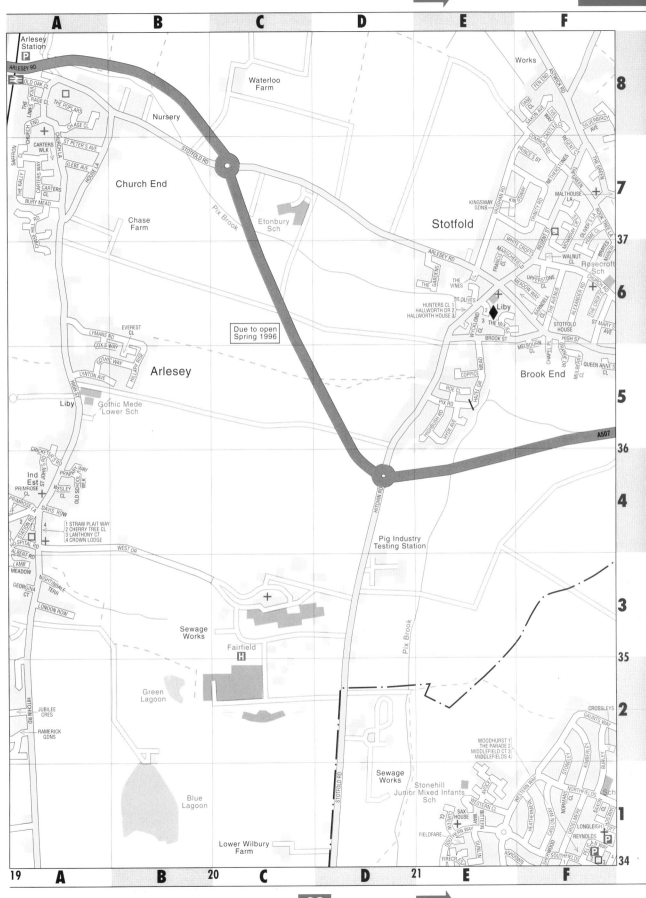

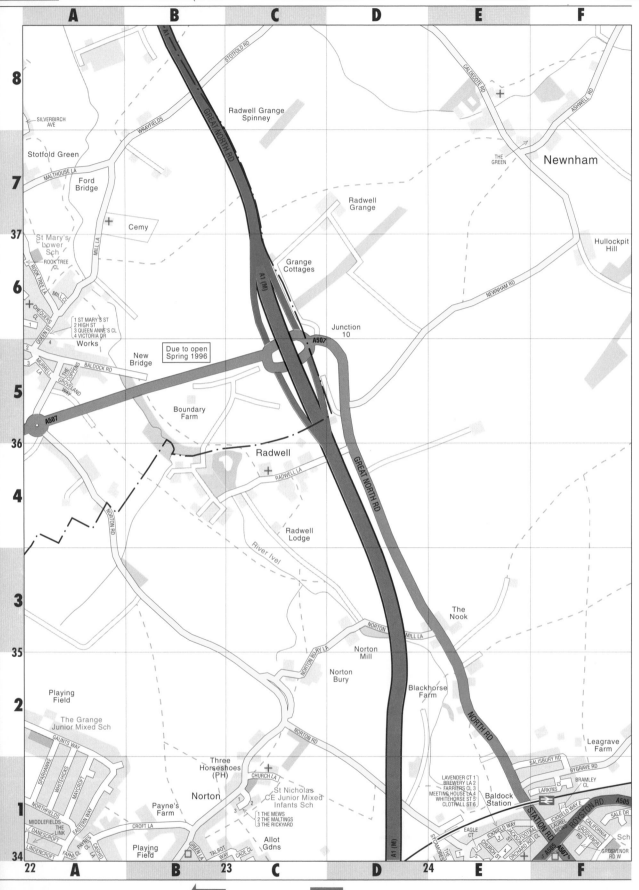

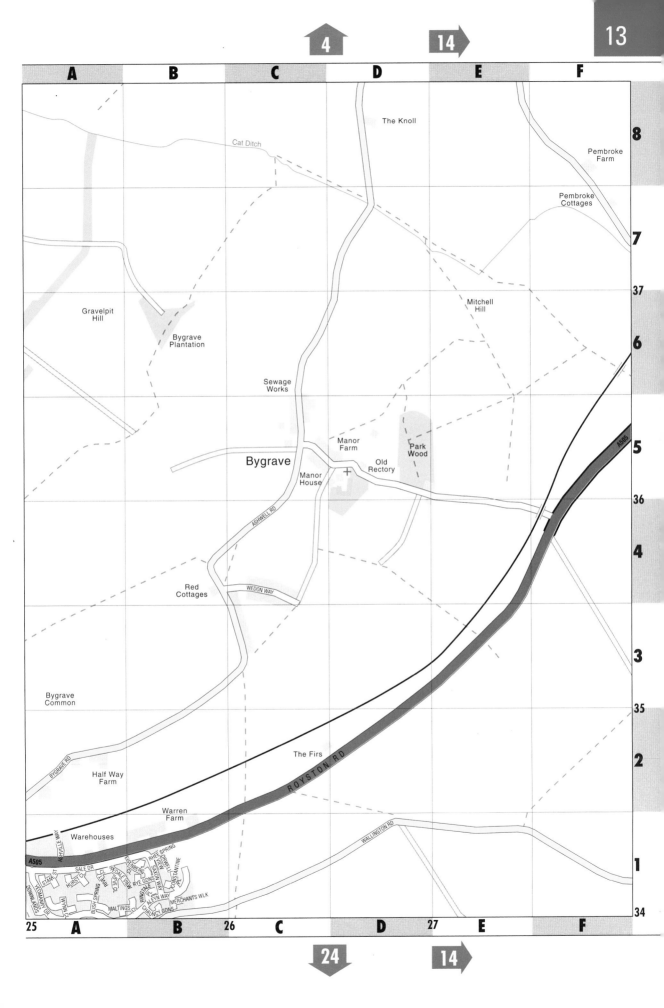

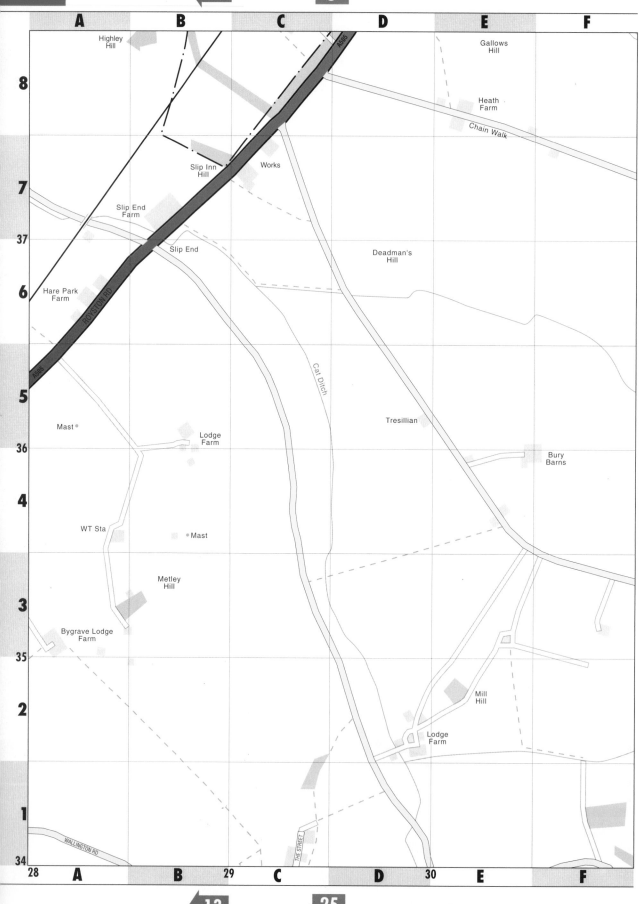

A   B   C   D   E   F

Coombe
Farm

Park Farm

8

MILL LA

Hill Farm

Therfield

Slipes
Wood

Therfield
First Sch

Gatleyway
Farm

Tuthill
Farm

THE CAUSEWAY

PEDLARS LA

FOX LA

POUND ROW

The Fox & Duck
(PH)

7

Crouch Hill

Chain Walk

Stump
Cross

North
End

Wtr
Twr

Hall

CHURCH LA

Hay Farm

Recn
Gd

37

ROOKS NEST LA

Mount Hill

Hay
Green

HOOPS LA

6

Fox
Hall

Hagger's
Farm

Duck's Gn

Hay Green
Farm

Grange
Farm

Pott's Hill

Manor
Farm

KELSHALL ST

Chain Walk

Kelshall

5

36

Rain Hill

Chain Walk

4

Kelshall La

Woodcotes

Wheat
Hill

Gannock
Farm

Lords
Wood

3

Gannock
Green

Little Sark

35

Philpott's
Wood

Drift Way

Icknield
Path Way

Hawkins
Wood

2

Chestnut
Hill

Partridge
Hall Farm

Park
Lane

The
Mount

Notley La

PAYNE END

Sandon
Bury

Notley
Green

DARK LA

ASHWELL RD

Sandon

Roe
Wood

The Chequers
(PH)

Sandon
Junior Mixed
Infants Sch

Cock's
Lodge

1

Icknield Path Way

A B C D E F

8

7

37

6

5

36

4

3

35

2

1

34

Icknield Path Way

Hatchpen

Meadow Way

Washingditch Green

HAYWOOD LA

River Rib

Mardleybury

Mast

THE JOINT

Reed End

Holborn Farm

BRICKYARD LA

JACKSON'S LA

WILLOW CL

BLACKSMITH'S LA

Reed Junior Mixed Infants Sch

CROSS LA

Wisbridge Farm

Reed

ROOKS NEST LA

Southview

HIGH ST

The Cabinet (PH)

CHURCH LA

DRIFTWAY

Queenbury

Dane End

Mast

Rooksnest Farm

Reed Hall

Gannock Grove

Kelshall La

Chapel Green

River Rib

Reed Wood

Southfield Grove

Sewage Works

Hilly Wood

Brandish Wood

Slate Hall Farm

34 A B 35 C D 36 E F

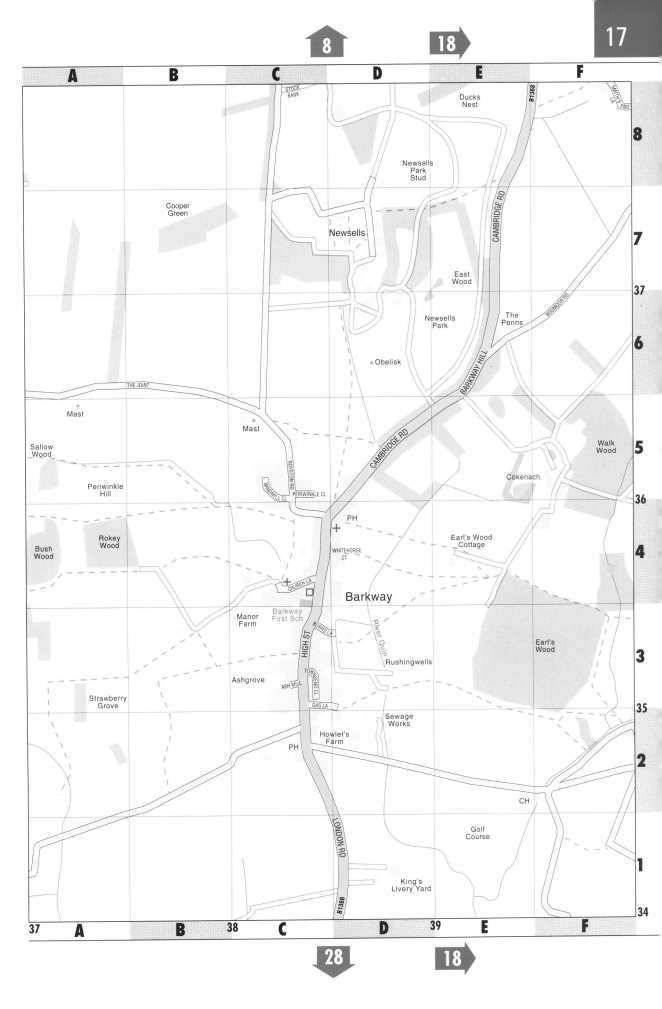

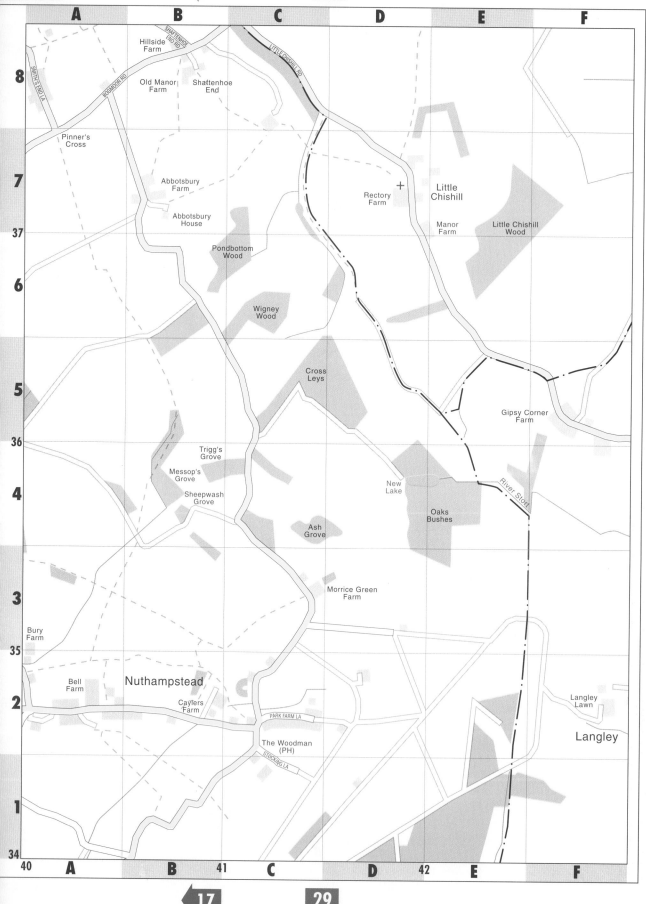

A B C D E F

8

Hillside
Farm

Old Manor
Farm

Shaftenhoe
End

SHAFTENHOE END RD

BOGMOOR RD

SMITH'S END LA

LITTLE CHISHILL RD

Pinner's
Cross

7

Abbotsbury
Farm

Abbotsbury
House

Rectory
Farm

Little
Chishill

Manor
Farm

Little Chishill
Wood

37

Pondbottom
Wood

6

Wigney
Wood

5

Cross
Leys

Gipsy Corner
Farm

36

Trigg's
Grove

Messop's
Grove

New
Lake

River Stort

4

Sheepwash
Grove

Ash
Grove

Oaks
Bushes

3

Morrice Green
Farm

Bury
Farm

35

Bell
Farm

Nuthampstead

Caylers
Farm

Langley
Lawn

2

PARK FARM LA

Langley

The Woodman
(PH)

STOCKING LA

1

34

40 A B 41 C D 42 E F

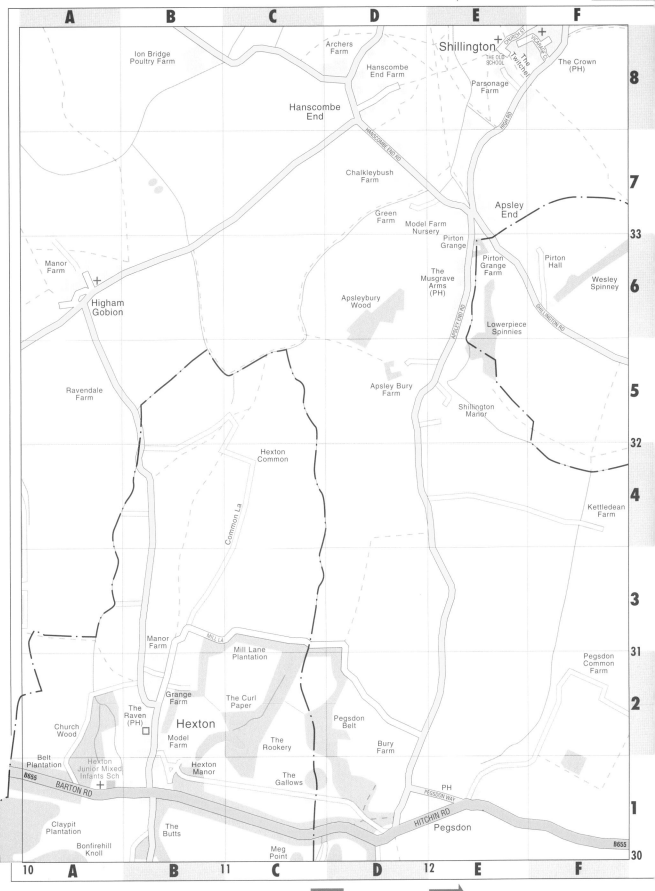

A | B | C | D | E | F

Ion Bridge
Poultry Farm

Archers
Farm

Hanscombe
End Farm

Shillington

THE OLD SCHOOL

The Twitchel

The Crown
(PH)

Hanscombe
End

Parsonage
Farm

HANSCOMBE END RD

HIGH RD

CHURCH ST

VICARAGE C.

Chalkleybush
Farm

Apsley
End

Green
Farm

Model Farm
Nursery

Pirton
Grange

Pirton
Grange
Farm

Pirton
Hall

Manor
Farm

The
Musgrave
Arms
(PH)

Wesley
Spinney

Higham
Gobion

Apsleybury
Wood

Lowerpiece
Spinnies

SHILLINGTON RD

APSLEY END RD

Ravendale
Farm

Apsley
Bury
Farm

Shillington
Manor

Hexton
Common

Kettledean
Farm

Common La

Pegsdon
Common
Farm

MILL LA

Manor
Farm

Mill Lane
Plantation

Grange
Farm

The Curl
Paper

Pegsdon
Belt

The
Raven
(PH)

Hexton

Church
Wood

Model
Farm

The
Rookery

Bury
Farm

Belt
Plantation

Hexton
Junior Mixed
Infants Sch

Hexton
Manor

PH

B655

BARTON RD

The
Gallows

PEGSDON WAY

HITCHIN RD

Pegsdon

Claypit
Plantation

The
Butts

Meg
Point

B655

Bonfirehill
Knoll

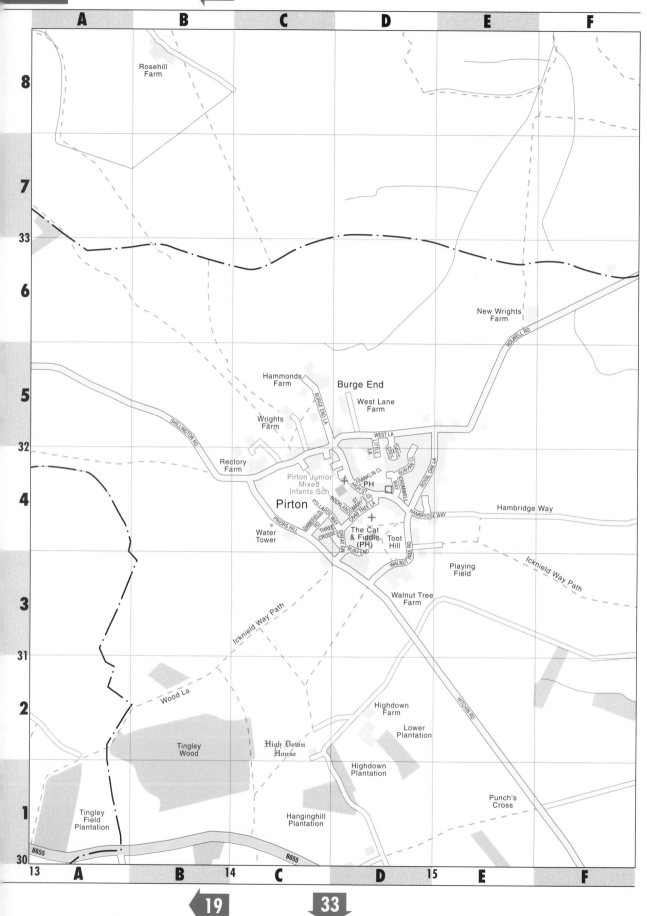

A   B   C   D   E   F

8

7

33

6

5

32

4

3

31

2

1

30

Rosehill
Farm

New Wrights
Farm

HOLWELL RD

Hammonds
Farm

Burge End

West Lane
Farm

Wrights
Farm

BURGE END LA

WEST LA

LITTLE
LA

DAVIS
CRES

SHILLINGTON RD

Rectory
Farm

Pirton Junior
Mixed
Infants Sch

FRANKLIN CL

PH

BUNYAN CL

CROMWELL WAY

ROYAL OAK LA

Pirton

HIGH ST

ST
MARY'S CL

CRAB TREE LA

Hambridge Way

Hambridge Way

DAMENFIELD
RD

POLLARDS WAY

BUCKLANDS WAY

THREE
CROSSES

GREAT GN

HAMBRIDGE WAY

PRIORS HILL

Water
Tower

BURY END

The Cat
& Fiddle
(PH)

Toot
Hill

WALNUT TREE RD

Playing
Field

Icknield Way Path

Icknield Way Path

Walnut Tree
Farm

HITCHIN RD

Wood La

Highdown
Farm

Lower
Plantation

Tingley
Wood

High Down
House

Highdown
Plantation

Punch's
Cross

Tingley
Field
Plantation

Hanginghill
Plantation

B655

B655

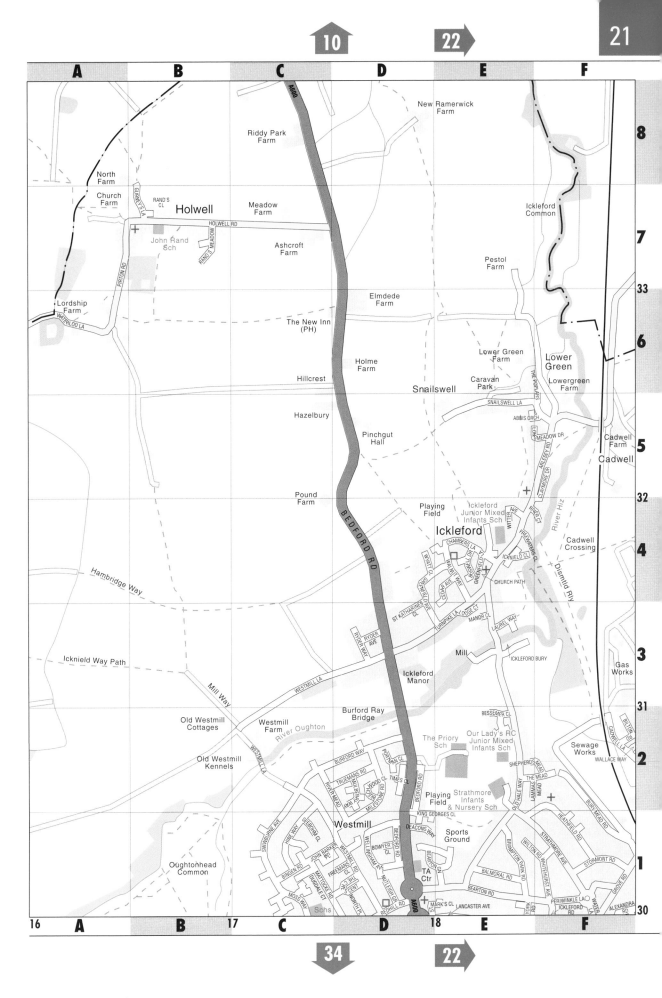

A B C D E F

8

7

33

6

North
Farm

Church
Farm

Holwell

Riddy Park
Farm

New Ramerwick
Farm

Meadow
Farm

RAND'S
CL

John Rand
Sch

HOLWELL RD

RAND'S MEADOW

GURNEY'S LA

PATON RD

A600

Ickleford
Common

Lordship
Farm

WATERLOO LA

Ashcroft
Farm

Elmdede
Farm

Pestol
Farm

The New Inn
(PH)

Holme
Farm

Lower Green
Farm

Lower
Green

THE POPLARS

Lowergreen
Farm

Hillcrest

Snailswell

SNAILSWELL LA

Caravan
Park

ABBIS ORCH

MEADOW DR

LONG CROFT

Hazelbury

Pinchgut
Hall

ARLESEY DR

CLAYMORE DR

RIVER CT

River Hiz

Cadwell
Farm

Cadwell

5

32

Pound
Farm

BEDFORD RD

Playing
Field

Ickleford
Junior Mixed
Infants Sch

WITTER RD

FREEWATERS CL

Dismild Riv

Cadwell
Crossing

Ickleford

CHAMBERS LA

WYATT CL

WALNUT WAY

GREENFIELD

ICKNIELD CL

ICKNIELD AVE

4

Hambridge Way

33RD

SHEFFIELD AVE

CEDAR AVE

EDGE CT

CHURCH PATH

3

Icknield Way Path

RYDER AVE

RYDER WAY

Mill Way

WESTMILL LA

ST KATHARINE'S
CL

TURNPIKE LA

MANOR CL

LAUREL WAY

Mill

ICKLEFORD BURY

Gas
Works

Ickleford
Manor

31

Old Westmill
Cottages

Westmill
Farm

River Oughton

Burford Ray
Bridge

BESSEMER CL

Sewage
Works

BILTON

CADWELL LA

2

WESTMILL LA

BURFORD WAY

PORTMAN CL

TIMES CL

Our Lady's RC
Junior Mixed
Infants Sch

The Priory
Sch

SHEPHERDS

WALLACE WAY

BURY MEAD RD

Old Westmill
Kennels

RIVER MEAD

TRUEMANS RD

MILBERN

MILESTONE RD

WOOD CL

THE MEAD

OLD HALE WAY

LAMMAS MEAD

HEATHFIELD RD

Strathmore
Infants
& Nursery Sch

Playing
Field

Sports
Ground

KING GEORGES CL

BEDFORD RD

DEACONS WAY

BRAMPTON PARK RD

WILTON RD

STRATHMORE AVE

WHITEHURST AVE

STORMONT RD

1

Westmill

SWINBURNE AVE

HINE WAY

SEEBORN CL

BINGEN RD

JOHN BARKER PL

WESTMILL RD

THE CL

SIMONTH PL

WELLINGHAM

BOWYER CL

NUTLEIGH GR

BEARTON GN

TA
Ctr

BALMORAL RD

BEARTON RD

Oughtonhead
Common

MOSS WAY

DUGDALE CT

MATTOCKE RD

FREEMANS RD

Schs

REDHILL RD

A600

MARK'S CL

LANCASTER AVE

YORK RD

ICKLEFORD RD

PERIWINKLE LA

WATER

GROVE RD

ALEXANDRA RD

30

16 A B 17 C D 18 E F

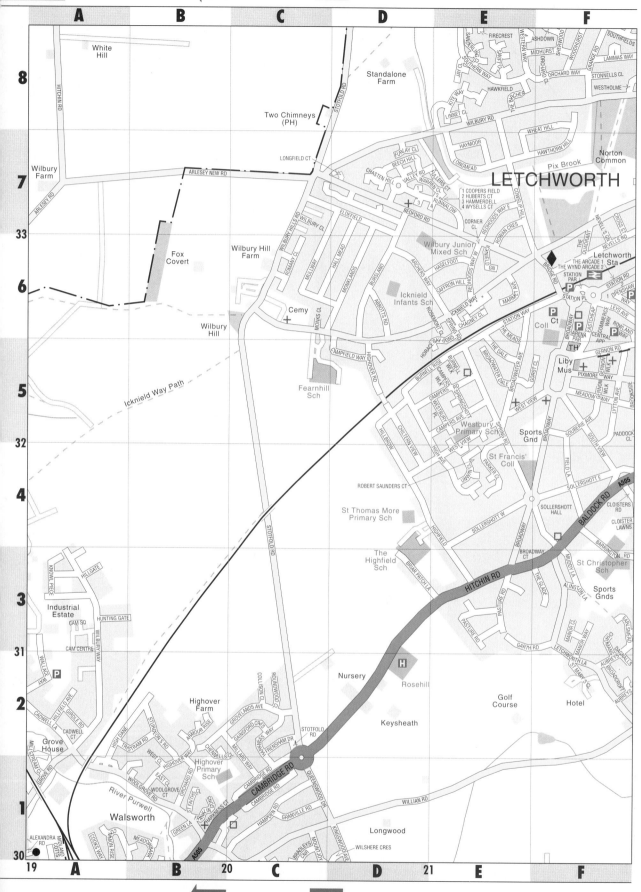

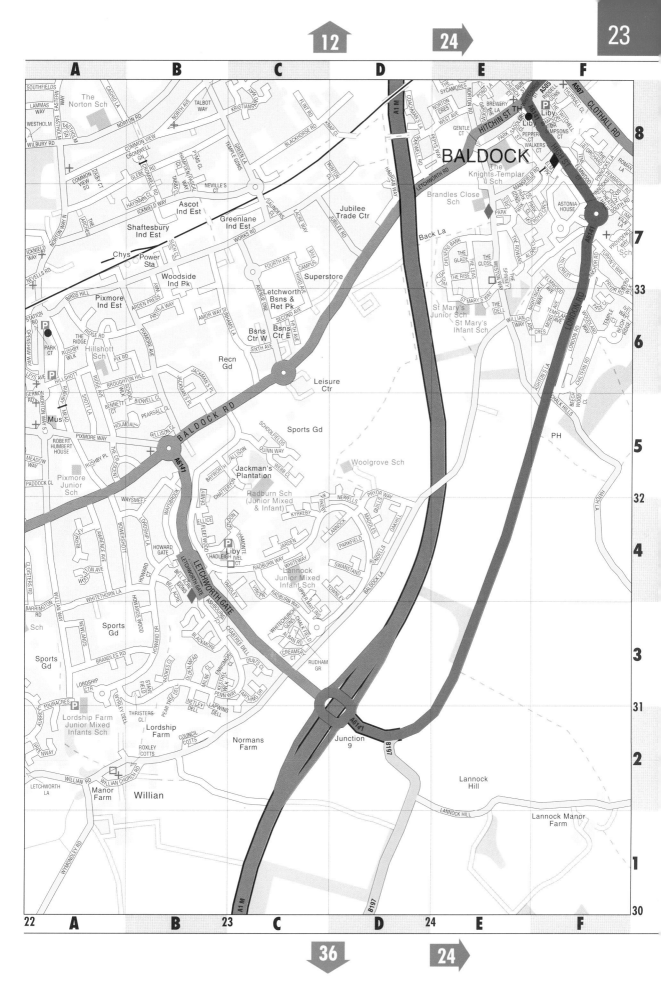

A   B   C   D   E   F

8

Clothall Common

Nursery
Home
Land

ROMAN A507

SOUTH RD

WALLINGTON RD

MERCIA RD

WESTELL CL

YEOMANRY DR

BARCLAY RISE

YEOMANRY DR

ALEYN WAY

WEAVERS WAY

7

Cambrai
Farm

WALK

JAY WALK

LAXTON GDNS

The
Homestead
Caravan Park

Sch

LIMEKILN LA

BYRD WLK

PRYOR RD

IVEL WAY

33

WARREN LA

Icknield Way Path

Cockpit

Quickswood

Icknield Way Path

CLOTHALL RD

Bird Hill

6

Welbury
Farm

Windmill Hill

5

Weston Hills

Clothall
Bury

32

Newfield Hill

Ashanger Hill

4

Clothall

ASHANGER LA

Green
Grove

Hickman's Hill

Bush Wood

The Barley Mow
(PH)

3

HATCH LA

31

Green End

2

Darnall's Hall
Farm

Mill
Farm

Weston Windmill
(dis)

PH

Old
Farm

MILL LA

FORE ST

Weston

Weston
Junior Mixed
Infant Sch

Weston
Bury

1

POST
OFFICE
ROW

Oakley's
Farm

CHURCH LA

THE SNIPE

FRIARS RD

HITCHIN RD

MAIDEN ST

BLUNTS
MEADOW

SCHOOL LA

CHURCH LA

Town
Farm

DAMASK
GREEN RD

Manor
House

Works

Recn
Gd

Church
End

30

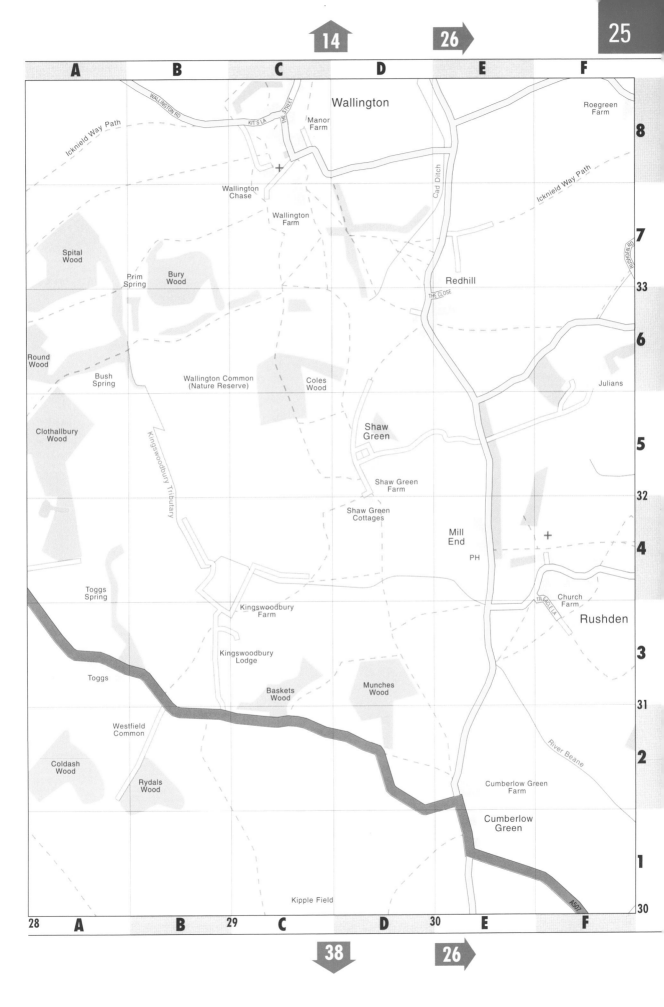

A B C D E F

WALLINGTON RD
KIT'S LA
THE STREET
Icknield Way Path
Wallington
Manor Farm
Roegreen Farm
Cad Ditch
Icknield Way Path
Wallington Chase
Wallington Farm
Redhill
RUSHDEN RD
THE CLOSE
Spital Wood
Prim Spring
Bury Wood
Round Wood
Bush Spring
Wallington Common (Nature Reserve)
Coles Wood
Julians
Clothallbury Wood
Kingswoodbury Tributary
Shaw Green
Shaw Green Farm
Shaw Green Cottages
Mill End
PH
Toggs Spring
Kingswoodbury Farm
Church Farm
TR EAGLE LA
Rushden
Toggs
Kingswoodbury Lodge
Baskets Wood
Munches Wood
Westfield Common
River Beane
Coldash Wood
Rydals Wood
Cumberlow Green Farm
Cumberlow Green
Kipple Field
A501

25
15

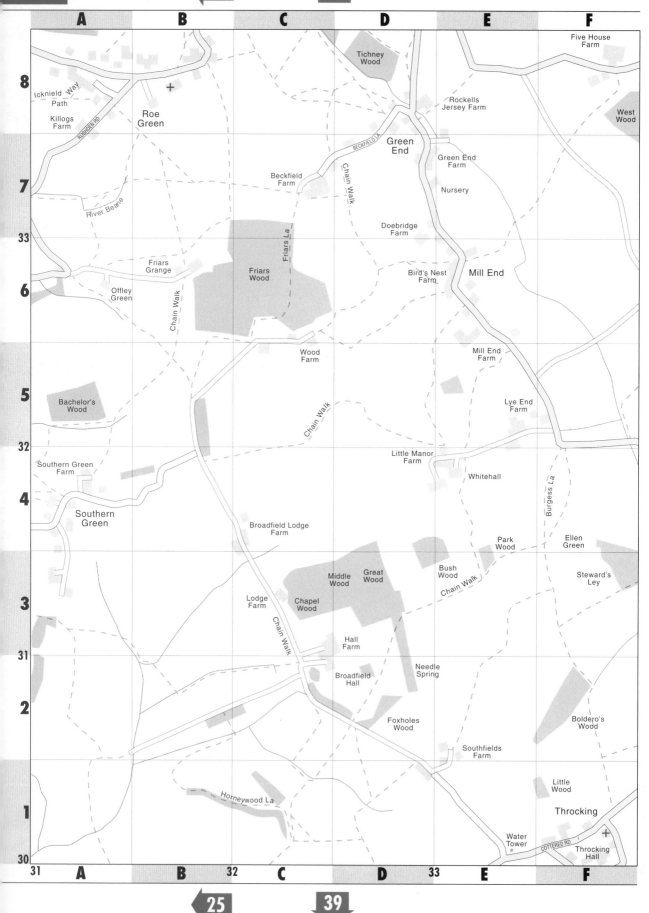

25
39

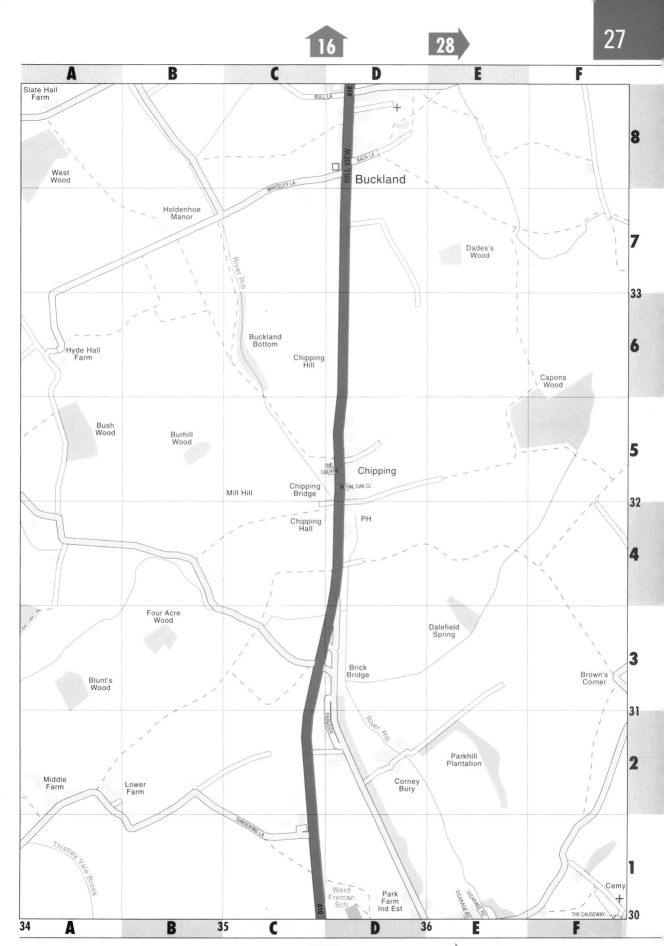

Slate Hall Farm

West Wood

Holdenhoe Manor

River Rib

BULL LA

A10

HILL VIEW

WHITELEY LA

BACK LA

Buckland

Dades's Wood

Hyde Hall Farm

Buckland Bottom

Chipping Hill

Capons Wood

Bush Wood

Burhill Wood

THE SQUARE

Chipping

Mill Hill

Chipping Bridge

ROYAL OAK CL

Chipping Hall

PH

Four Acre Wood

Dalefield Spring

Brown's Corner

Blunt's Wood

Brick Bridge

River Rib

PARKSIDE

Parkhill Plantation

Middle Farm

Lower Farm

Corney Bury

THROCKING LA

Thistley Vale Brook

Ward Freman Sch

A10

Park Farm Ind Est

VICARAGE RD

VICARAGE RD

Cemy

THE CAUSEWAY

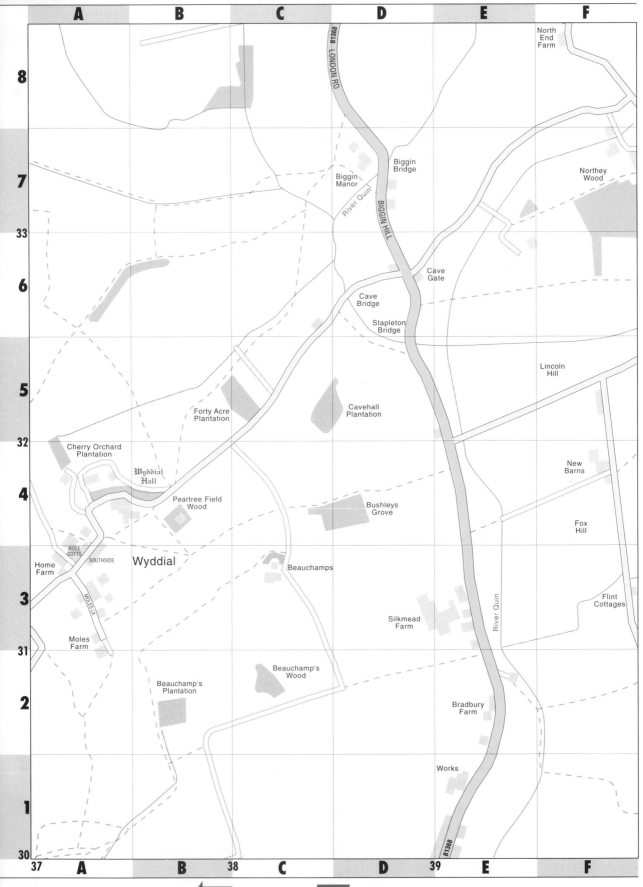

A   B   C   D   E   F

8

7

33

6

5

32

4

3

31

2

1

30

North End Farm

LONDON RD B1368

Biggin Bridge

Biggin Manor

River Quin

BIGGIN HILL

Northey Wood

Cave Gate

Cave Bridge

Stapleton Bridge

Lincoln Hill

Forty Acre Plantation

Cavehall Plantation

Cherry Orchard Plantation

Wyddial Hall

New Barns

Peartree Field Wood

Bushleys Grove

Fox Hill

ROSE COTTS

SOUTHSIDE

Wyddial

Home Farm

MOLES LA

Beauchamps

River Quin

Flint Cottages

Moles Farm

Silkmead Farm

Beauchamp's Plantation

Beauchamp's Wood

Bradbury Farm

Works

B1368

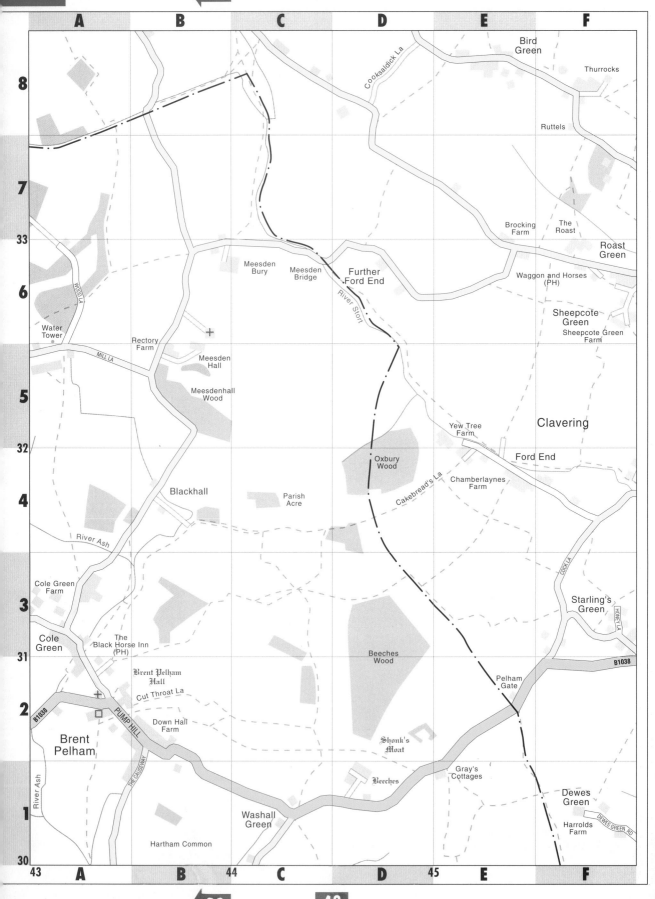

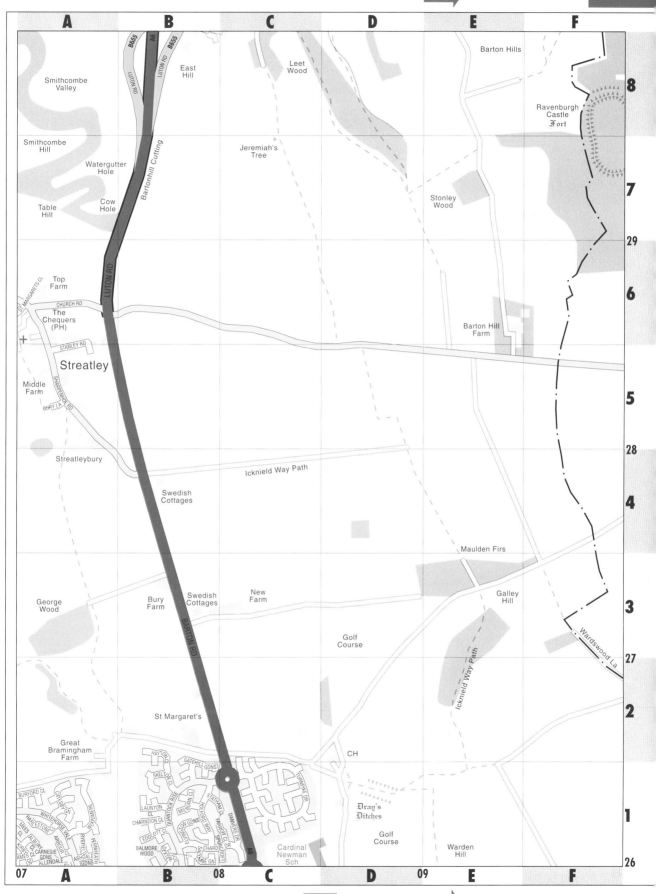

A   B   C   D   E   F

B655
LUTON RD
A6
LUTON RD
B655

Smithcombe
Valley

East
Hill

Leet
Wood

Barton Hills

8

Smithcombe
Hill

Watergutter
Hole

Bartonhill Cutting

Jeremiah's
Tree

Ravenburgh
Castle
Fort

Cow
Hole

Table
Hill

Stonley
Wood

7

29

LUTON RD

Top
Farm

ST MARGARET'S CL

CHURCH RD

6

The
Chequers
(PH)

STANLEY RD

Streatley

Barton Hill
Farm

+

Middle
Farm

SHARPENHOE RD

BURY LA

5

28

Streatleybury

Icknield Way Path

Swedish
Cottages

4

BARTON RD

Maulden Firs

George
Wood

Bury
Farm

Swedish
Cottages

New
Farm

Galley
Hill

3

27

Icknield Way Path

Wardswood La

St Margaret's

2

Great
Bramingham
Farm

HAYLING DR
GATEHILL GDNS
SKELTON CL
DAMTOCK RISE
MILBURN CL
STATHAM CL
FOXFORD WAY
DANVERS DR
FAIRGOLD CT
TURPYN DR

CH

Dray's
Ditches

1

BURFORD CL
CATESBY GN
WHITEHORSE DALE
HARLESTONE
ARBOUR CL
DOWEN CL
LAUNTON
CL
CHARNDON CL
EDGCOTT CL
ELMSTEAD
SACOMBE GN
CHARDCROFT
SPURCROFT
BALMORE
WOOD
ASHDALE
ALBURY
FERNWREATH
RYEHILLS
AMES CL
CARNEGIE
GDNS
ALLENDALE
KIRBY CL
TREES

Cardinal
Newman
Sch

Golf
Course

Warden
Hill

26

A6

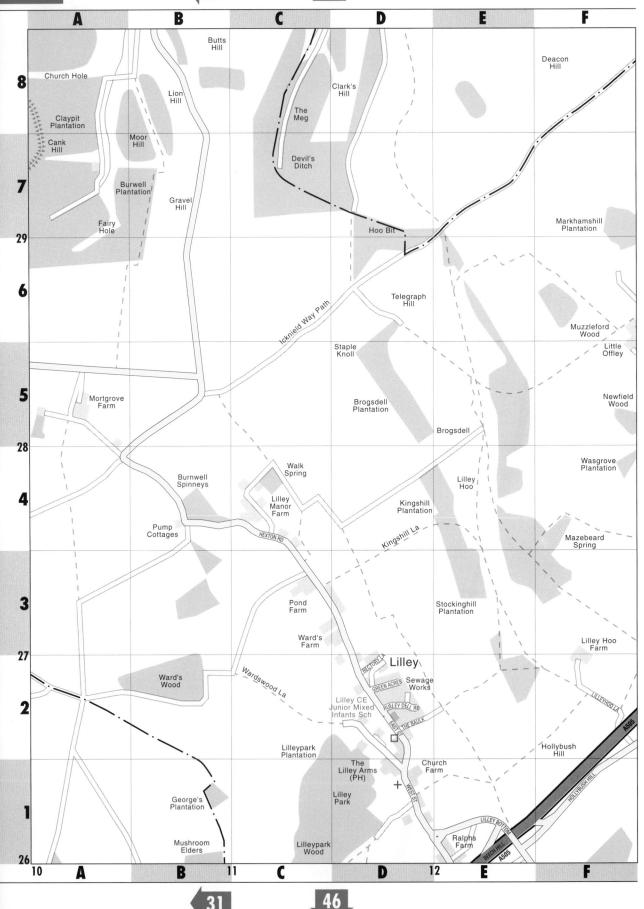

A   B   C   D   E   F

8 Church Hole

Butts
Hill

Lion
Hill

Clark's
Hill

Deacon
Hill

Claypit
Plantation

The
Meg

Cank
Hill

Moor
Hill

Devil's
Ditch

7 Burwell
Plantation

Gravel
Hill

Fairy
Hole

Hoo Bit

Markhamshill
Plantation

29

Telegraph
Hill

6

Icknield Way Path

Muzzleford
Wood

Staple
Knoll

Little
Offley

5 Mortgrove
Farm

Brogsdell
Plantation

Brogsdell

Newfield
Wood

28

Walk
Spring

Wasgrove
Plantation

Burnwell
Spinneys

Lilley
Hoo

4

Lilley
Manor
Farm

Kingshill
Plantation

Pump
Cottages

HEXTON RD

Kingshill La

Mazebeard
Spring

3

Pond
Farm

Stockinghill
Plantation

Ward's
Farm

Lilley Hoo
Farm

27

RECTORY LA

Lilley

Ward's
Wood

Wardswood La

GREEN ACRES

Sewage
Works

LILLEYHOO LA

2

RUELEY DELL RD

Lilley CE
Junior Mixed
Infants Sch

THE BAULK

A505

Lilleypark
Plantation

Hollybush
Hill

HOLLYBUSH HILL

The
Lilley Arms
(PH)

Church
Farm

WEST ST

BEECH HILL

1

George's
Plantation

Lilley
Park

LILLEY BOTTOM

Ralphs
Farm

A505

26 Mushroom
Elders

Lilleypark
Wood

10   A   B   11   C   D   12   E   F

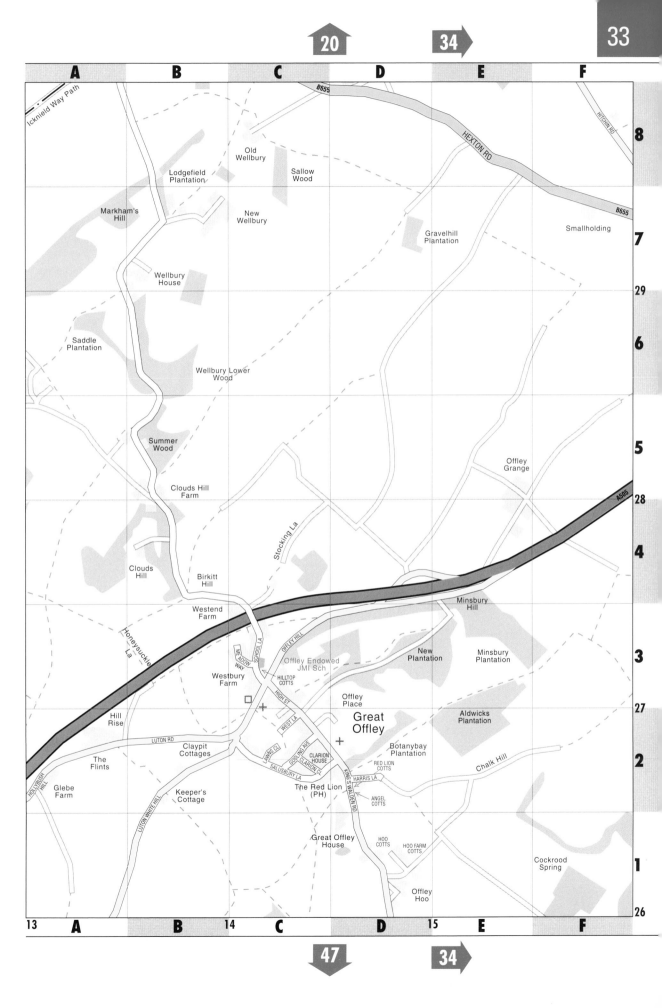

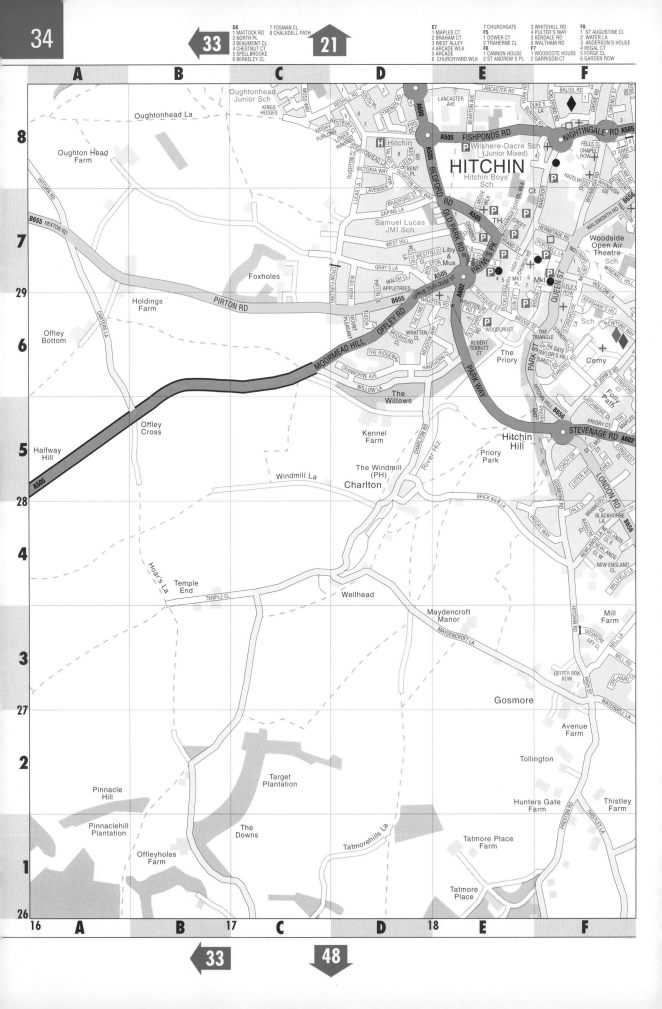

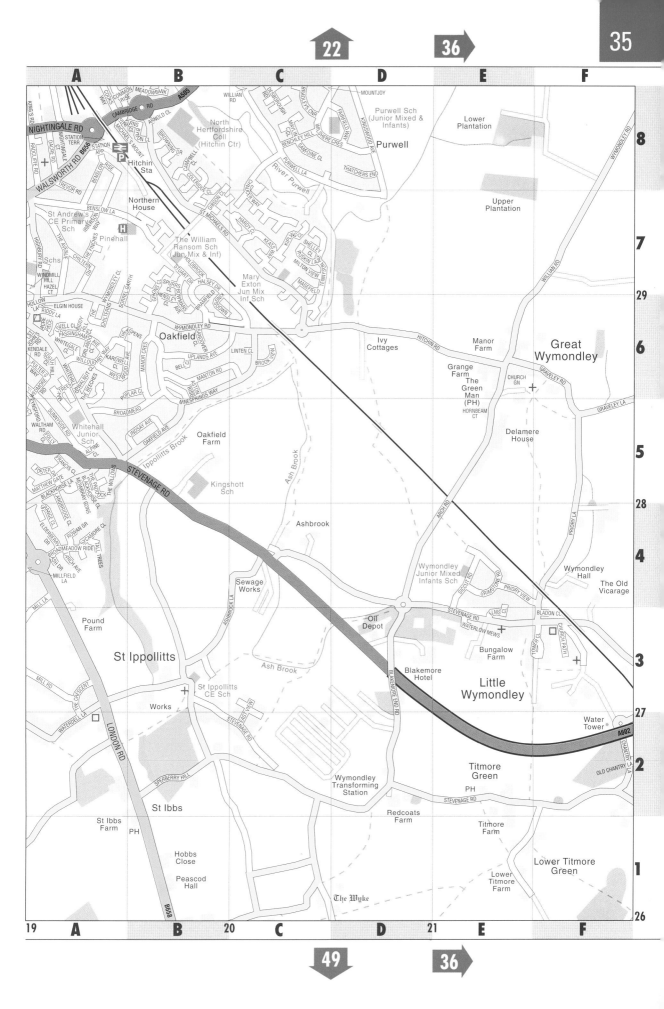

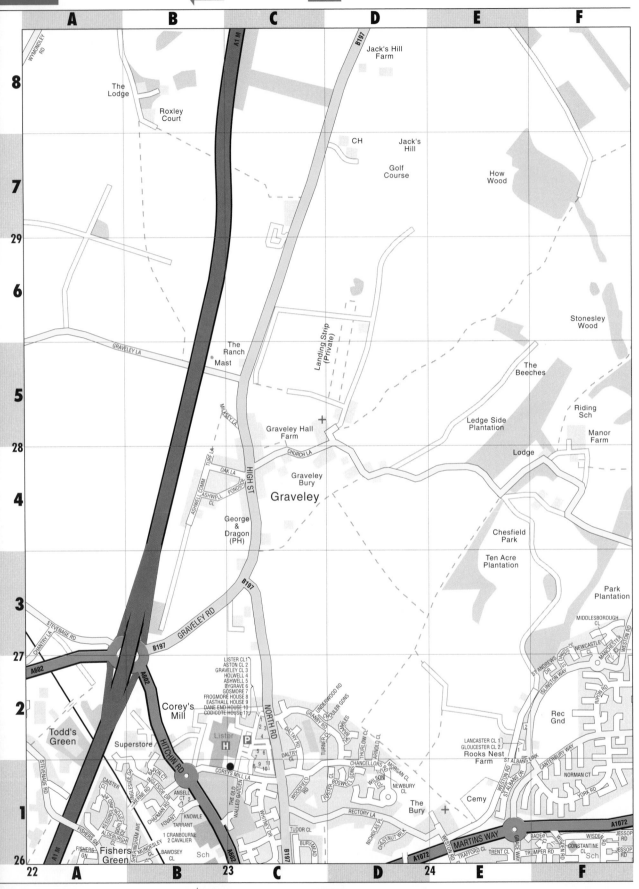

A   B   C   D   E   F

8

WYMONDLEY RD

The Lodge

Roxley Court

A1 M

B197

Jack's Hill Farm

CH

Jack's Hill

Golf Course

How Wood

7

29

6

Stonesley Wood

GRAVELEY LA

The Ranch
Mast

Landing Strip (Private)

The Beeches

Riding Sch

5

MILKSEY LA

Graveley Hall Farm

CHURCH LA

Ledge Side Plantation

Manor Farm

28

TURF LA

OAK LA

ASHWELL COMM

ASHWELL CL

PONDS CL

HIGH ST

Graveley Bury

Graveley

Lodge

4

George & Dragon (PH)

Chesfield Park

Ten Acre Plantation

3

B197

GRAVELEY RD

Park Plantation

MIDDLESBOROUGH CL

NEWCASTLE CL

WESTON RD

27

B197

A602

CHANTRY LA

STEVENAGE RD

A602

LISTER CL 1
ASTON CL 2
GRAVELEY CL 3
HOLWELL 4
ASHWELL 5
BYGRAVE 6
GOSMORE 7
FROGMORE HOUSE 8
EASTHALL HOUSE 9
DANE END HOUSE 10
CODICOTE HOUSE 11

ST ANDREWS DR

OMONDS CL

GUNSTON WAY

MANCHESTER CL

RIPON RD

A602

HITCHIN RD

Corey's Mill

UNDERWOOD RD

GRANBY RD

DALTRY RD

TURNER CL

SABLES

ST ALBANS LINK

CANTERBURY WAY

2

Todd's Green

NORTH RD

THURLOW CL

ARNOLD CL

MORGAN CL

NEWBURY CL

Rec Gnd

LANCASTER CL 1
GLOUCESTER CL 2

Rooks Nest Farm

Superstore

Lister

P

H

COREYS MILL LA

DALTRY CL

CHANCELLORS RD

WILSON

WESTON RD

NORMAN CT

YORK RD

1

STEVENAGE RD

CAISTER CL

INGLIS

ON CT

CHAPMAN RD

ANSELL CT

KNOWLE

WOODFIELD RD

FOSTER CL

BOSWELL GDNS

RECTORY LA

The Bury

Cemy

26

A1 M

FISHERS GN

Fishers Green

SHERINGHAM AVE

MUNDESLEY

BAWDSEY CL

FOVANT

TARRANT

1 CRANBOURNE
2 CAVALIER

Sch

THE OLD WALLED GARDEN

WHITNEY DR

TUDOR RD

BURY MEAD

B197

NICHOLAS PL

CHESTNUT WLK

A1072

MARTINS WAY

TRAFFORD CL

TRENT CL

BADER

GRACE WAY

TRUMPER RD

CONSTANTINE CL

WISDEN RD

JESSOP RD

Sch

A1072

22   A   B   23   C   D   24   E   F

A   B   C   D   E   F

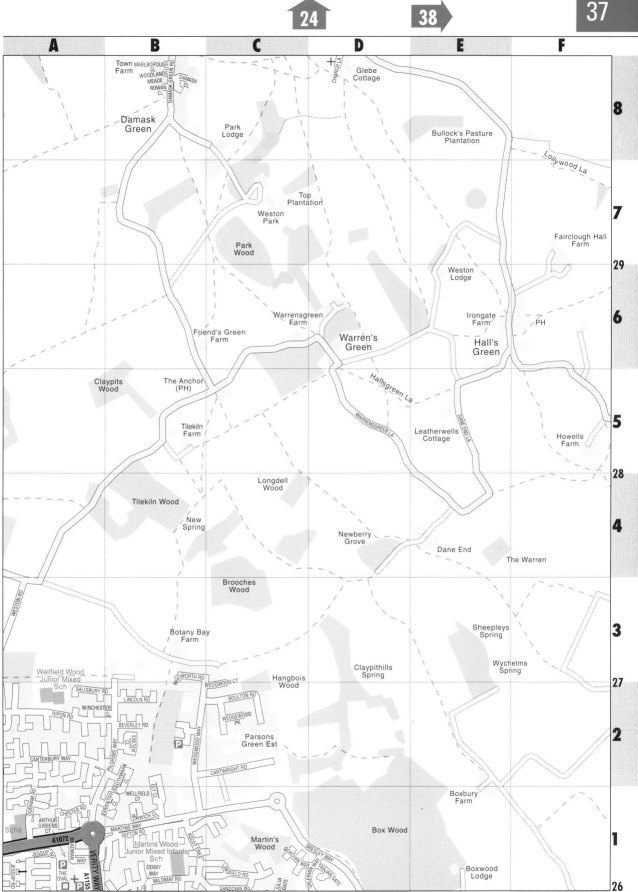

8
7
29
6
5
28
4
3
27
2
1
26

Town Farm
MARLBOROUGH CL
WOODLANDS MEADE
ROWAN CL
DAMASK GREEN RD
DAMASK CL
Damask Green
Park Lodge
Glebe Cottage
Bullock's Pasture Plantation
CHURCH LA
Lollywood La
Top Plantation
Weston Park
Park Wood
Fairclough Hall Farm
Weston Lodge
Warrensgreen Farm
Friend's Green Farm
Warren's Green
Irongate Farm
PH
Hall's Green
Claypits Wood
The Anchor (PH)
Haltsgreen La
Tilekiln Farm
WARRENSGREEN LA
Leatherwells Cottage
DANE END LA
Howells Farm
Longdell Wood
Tilekiln Wood
New Spring
Newberry Grove
Dane End
The Warren
Brooches Wood
Botany Bay Farm
Sheepleys Spring
Wychelms Spring
Wellfield Wood Junior Mixed Sch
WHITWORTH RD
WEDGWOOD CT
Hangbois Wood
Claypithills Spring
SALISBURY RD
LINCOLN RD
BOULTON RD
WEDGEWOOD PK
Boxbury Farm
RIPON RD
WINCHESTER CL
BEVERLEY RD
EXETER CL
WEDGWOOD WAY
Parsons Green Est
CANTERBURY WAY
PILGRIMS WAY
CARTWRIGHT RD
DURHAM RD
COVENTRY CL
SOUTHWARK CL
WELLFIELD CT
ELY CL
NORWICH CL
Box Wood
CHESTER RD
ARTHUR GIBBENS CT
MARTINS WAY
SEFTON RD
ASCOT CRES
Martin's Wood
GRESLEY WAY
Schs
A1072
JESSOP RD
VERITY WAY
BRADMAN WAY
Martins Wood Junior Mixed Infants Sch
DERBY WAY
GORDIAN WAY
TRAJAN GATE
Boxwood Lodge
JESSOP RD
THE OVAL
A1155
MILDMAY RD
LINGFIELD RD
VALFRIAN WAY
JULIA GATE
Boxwood Lodge
SANDOWN RD

25   A   B   26   C   D   27   E   F

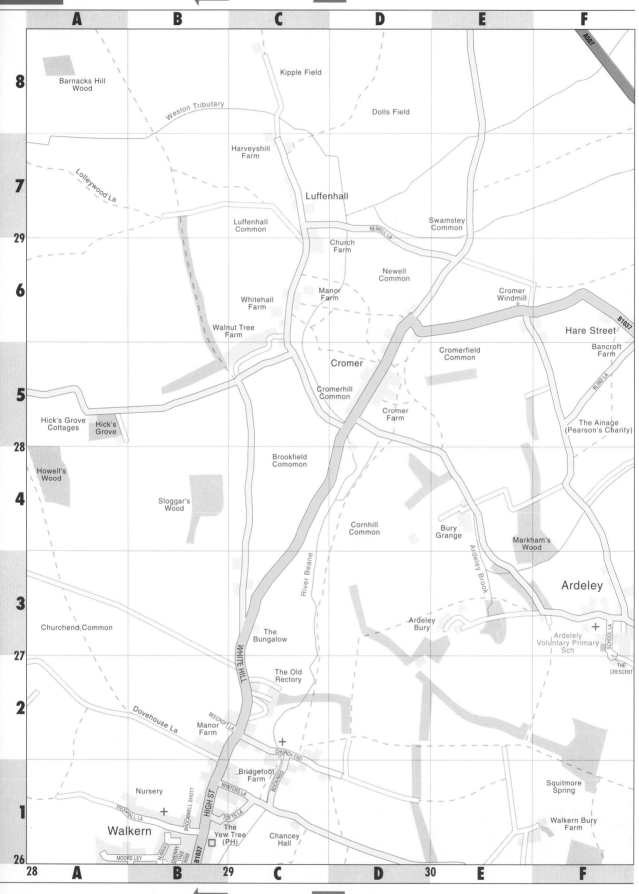
37

25

	A	B	C	D	E	F

8

Barnacks Hill Wood

Kipple Field

Weston Tributary

Dolls Field

A507

Harveyshill Farm

7

Lolleywood La

Luffenhall

29

Luffenhall Common

Swamstey Common

NEWELL LA

Church Farm

6

Newell Common

Cromer Windmill

Whitehall Farm

Manor Farm

B1037

Walnut Tree Farm

Hare Street

Cromerfield Common

Bancroft Farm

Cromer

BLIND LA

5

Cromerhill Common

The Ainage (Pearson's Charity)

Hick's Grove Cottages

Hick's Grove

Cromer Farm

28

Howell's Wood

Brookfield Comomon

4

Sloggar's Wood

Cornhill Common

Bury Grange

Markham's Wood

Ardeley

River Beane

Ardeley Brook

3

Churchend Common

Ardeley Bury

Ardelely Voluntary Primary Sch

SCHOOL LA

27

The Bungalow

WHITE HILL

THE CRESCENT

The Old Rectory

2

Dovehouse La

BEECROFT LA

Manor Farm

CHURCH END

BOCKINGS

Squitmore Spring

Bridgefoot Farm

Nursery

WINTERS LA

1

FROGHALL LA

HIGH ST

BROCKWELL SHOTT

TOTTS LA

Walkern Bury Farm

Walkern

The Yew Tree (PH)

Chancey Hall

N BRIES

CHERRY TREE RISE

B1037

26

MOORS LEY

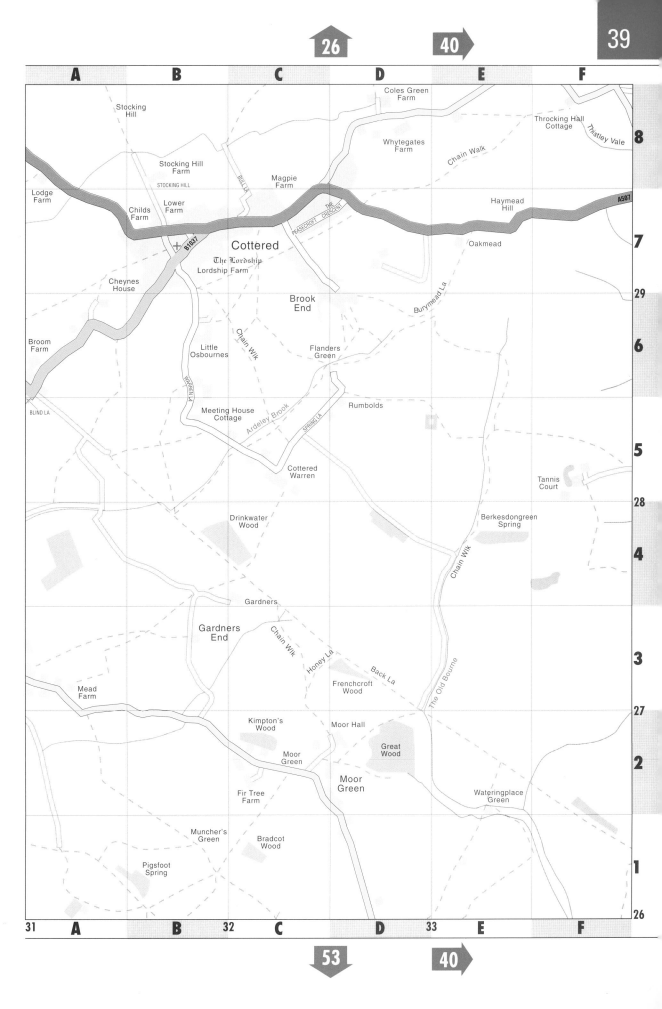

26
40

A   B   C   D   E   F

8

Stocking
Hill

Coles Green
Farm

Throcking Hall
Cottage

Thistley Vale

Stocking Hill
Farm

Whytegates
Farm

Chain Walk

STOCKING HILL

Magpie
Farm

BULL LA

Lodge
Farm

Childs
Farm

Lower
Farm

THE CRESCENT

Haymead
Hill

A507

7

PEASECROFT

Cottered

The Lordship
Lordship Farm

Oakmead

B1037

Cheynes
House

Brook
End

Burymead La

29

Broom
Farm

Little
Osbournes

Chain Wlk

Flanders
Green

6

BLIND LA

WARREN LA

Meeting House
Cottage

Ardeley Brook

SPRING LA

Rumbolds

Cottered
Warren

Tannis
Court

5

Drinkwater
Wood

Berkesdongreen
Spring

28

Chain Wlk

4

Gardners

Gardners
End

Chain Wlk

Honey La

Back La

The Old Bourne

3

Mead
Farm

Frenchcroft
Wood

27

Kimpton's
Wood

Moor Hall

Moor
Green

Great
Wood

2

Fir Tree
Farm

Moor
Green

Wateringplace
Green

Muncher's
Green

Bradcot
Wood

Pigsfoot
Spring

1

26

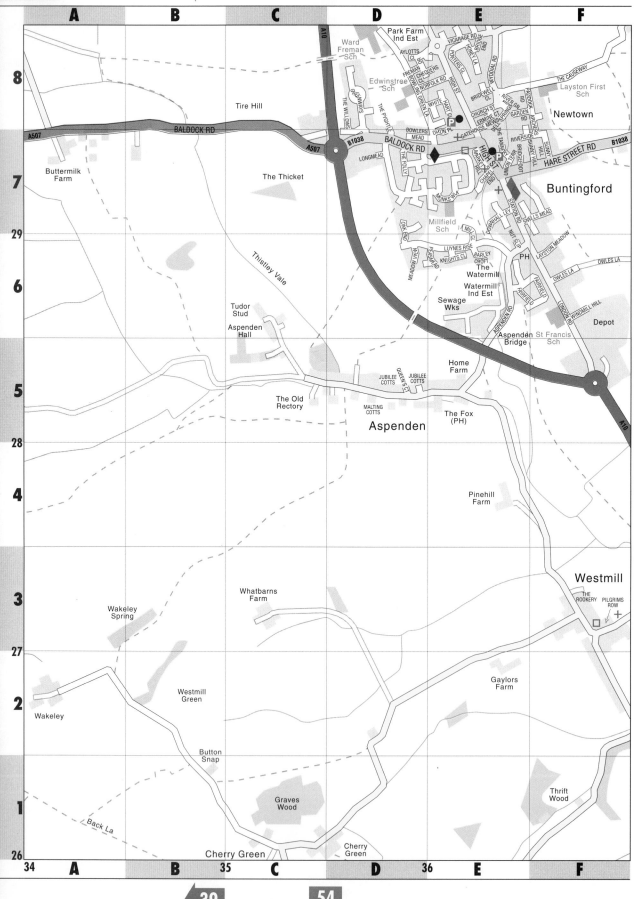

A · B · C · D · E · F

8

Park Farm
Ind Est
VICARAGE RD
Ward
Freman
Sch
AYLOTTS
CL
PORTERS CT
HONEY LA
WYDIAL RD
BRIDGE
END
THE CAUSEWAY
FREMAN
CHEQUERS
NORFOLK RD
HIGH ST
BRIDEWELL
CL
Layston First
Sch
Edwinstree
Sch

Tire Hill

GREENWAYS
WHITE HART ROW
CHURCH ST
LERMINE CT
PADDOCK CL
GARDEN
RD
Newtown
THE WILLOWS
THE PIGHTLE
BALDOCK RD
BOWLERS MEAD
DIXON PL
GATEHOUSE MEWS
RIVER GN
SPRINGLES LA
THE TANNERY
RIVERSIDE
SUNNY HILL
SUNNY
A507
A507
B1038
B1038
BALDOCK RD
LONGMEAD
THE FOLLY
HIGH ST
MARKET HILL
CHAPEL END
BRIDGEFOOT
HARE STREET RD
B1038

Buttermilk
Farm

7

The Thicket

MONKS VIA
CHAPEL END
STATION RD
SHELLS MEAD
Buntingford

29

Thistley Vale

OAK END
Millfield
Sch
MEADOW VW
LUYNES RISE
KNIGHTS CL
PEARMEAD
BARLEY
CROFT
MILL CL
DONKHALL LEY
INIT SLIP
LAYSTON MEADOW
OWLES LA
OWLES LA

6

Tudor
Stud
Aspenden
Hall
The
Watermill
PH
Watermill
Ind Est
FAIRFIELD
FAIRFIELD
ASPENDEN RD
LONDON RD
WINDMILL HILL
Depot

Sewage
Wks

Aspenden
Bridge
St Francis
Sch

5

The Old
Rectory
JUBILEE
COTTS
QUEEN'S CT
JUBILEE
COTTS
MALTING
COTTS
Home
Farm
Aspenden
The Fox
(PH)

28

Pinehill
Farm

4

Westmill

3

Whatbarns
Farm
THE
ROOKERY
PILGRIMS
ROW

Wakeley
Spring

27

Westmill
Green
Gaylors
Farm

2

Wakeley

Button
Snap

Thrift
Wood

1

Graves
Wood

26

Back La

Cherry Green
Cherry
Green

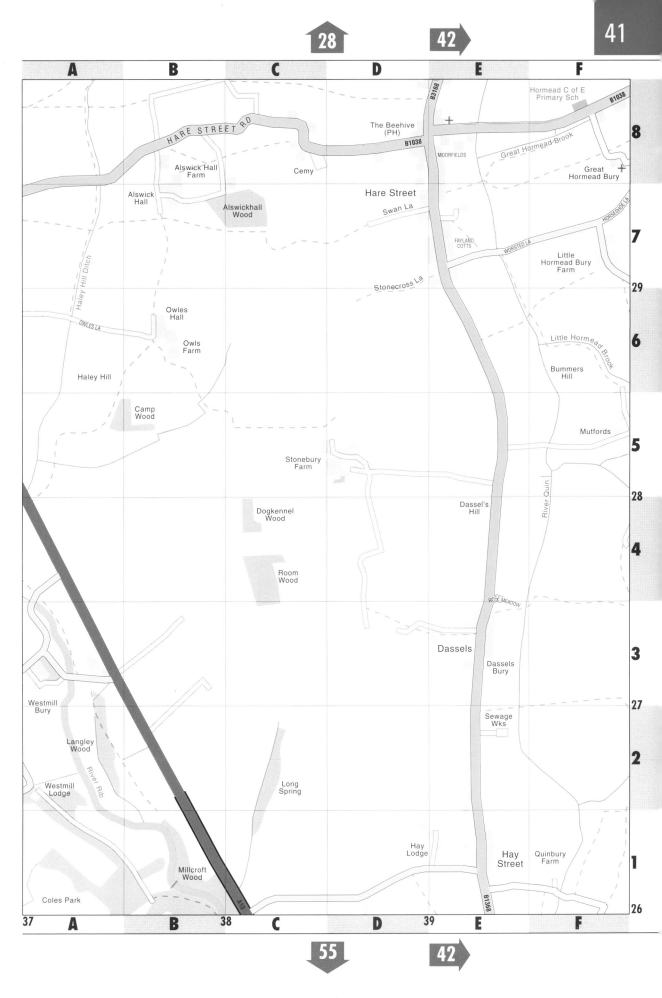

HARE STREET RD

Alswick Hall Farm

Cemy

Alswick Hall

Alswickhall Wood

The Beehive (PH)

B1038

Moorfields

Hormead C of E Primary Sch

B1038

B1038

Great Hormead Brook

Great Hormead Bury

Hare Street

Swan La

HORSESHOE LA

Fayland Cotts

WORSTED LA

Little Hormead Bury Farm

Stonecross La

Haley Hill Ditch

Owles Hall

OWLES LA

Owls Farm

Little Hormead Brook

Haley Hill

Bummers Hill

Camp Wood

Mutfords

Stonebury Farm

Dassel's Hill

River Quin

Dogkennel Wood

Room Wood

ROSE MEADOW

Westmill Bury

Dassels

Dassels Bury

Langley Wood

Sewage Wks

River Rib

Westmill Lodge

Long Spring

Hay Lodge

Hay Street

Quinbury Farm

Millcroft Wood

A10

Coles Park

B1368

41
29

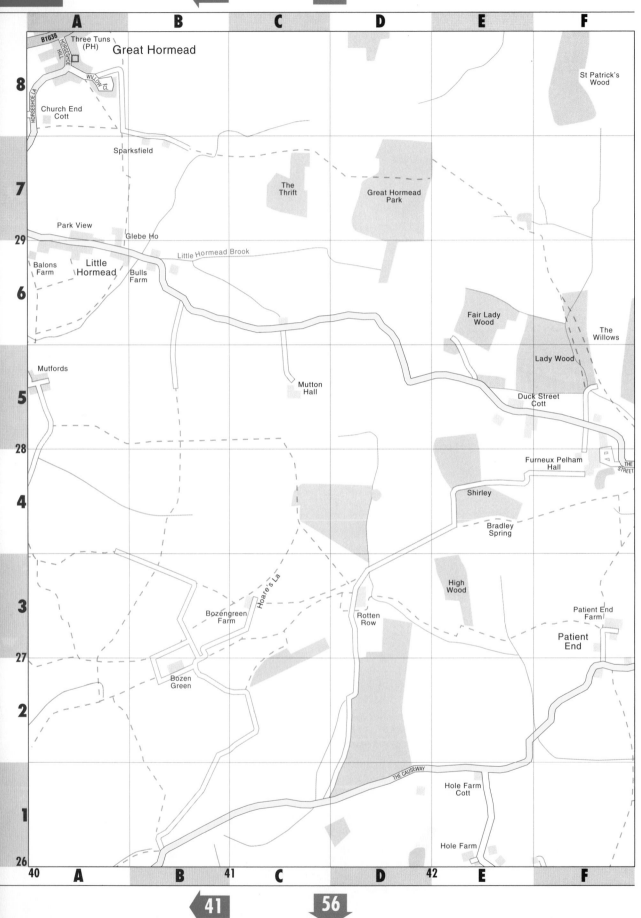

Great Hormead

Three Tuns (PH)

B1038

HORSESHOE HILL

WILLOW CL

HORSESHOE LA

Church End Cott

Sparksfield

The Thrift

Great Hormead Park

St Patrick's Wood

Park View

Glebe Ho

Little Hormead Brook

Balons Farm

Little Hormead

Bulls Farm

Fair Lady Wood

The Willows

Lady Wood

Mutfords

Mutton Hall

Duck Street Cott

Furneux Pelham Hall

THE STREET

Shirley

Bradley Spring

High Wood

Patient End Farm

Hoare's La

Bozengreen Farm

Rotten Row

Patient End

Bozen Green

THE CAUSEWAY

Hole Farm Cott

Hole Farm

41
56

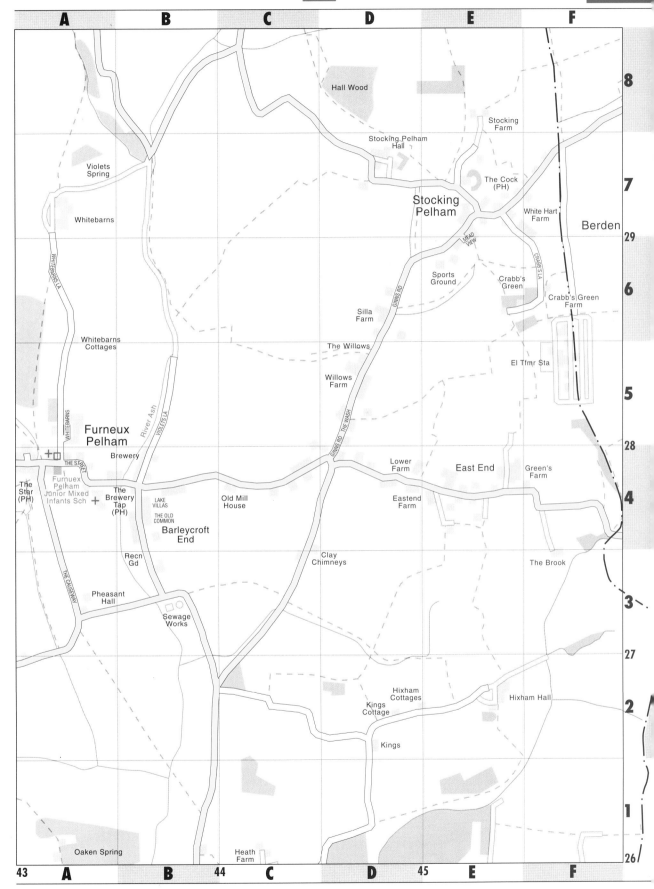

Hall Wood

Stocking
Farm

Violets
Spring

Stocking Pelham
Hall

The Cock
(PH)

Stocking
Pelham

White Hart
Farm

Berden

Whitebarns

MEAD
VIEW

29

WHITEBARNS LA

Sports
Ground

Crabb's
Green

CRABB'S LA

Crabb's Green
Farm

6

Silla
Farm

GINNS RD

Whitebarns
Cottages

The Willows

El Tfmr Sta

Willows
Farm

5

River Ash

VIOLETS LA

THE WASH

GINNS RD

28

WHITEBARNS

Furneux
Pelham

Brewery

Lower
Farm

East End

Green's
Farm

The Star
(PH)

THE STREET

Furnuex
Pelham
Junior Mixed
Infants Sch

The
Brewery
Tap
(PH)

LAKE
VILLAS

THE OLD
COMMON

Old Mill
House

Eastend
Farm

4

Barleycroft
End

The Brook

Recn
Gd

Clay
Chimneys

THE CAUSEWAY

Pheasant
Hall

3

Sewage
Works

27

Hixham
Cottages

Hixham Hall

2

Kings
Cottage

Kings

1

Oaken Spring

Heath
Farm

26

43 A   B   44   C   D   45   E   F

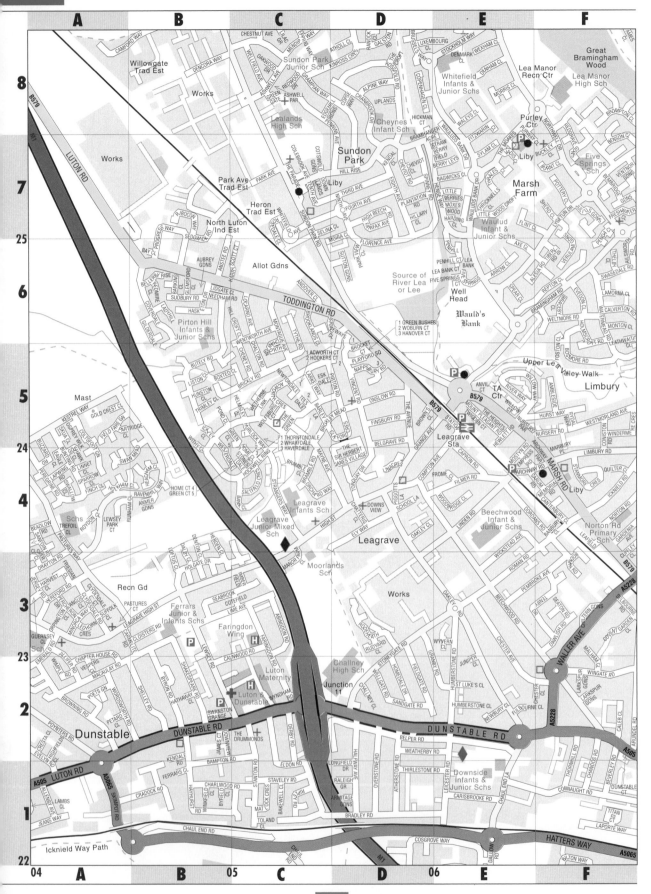

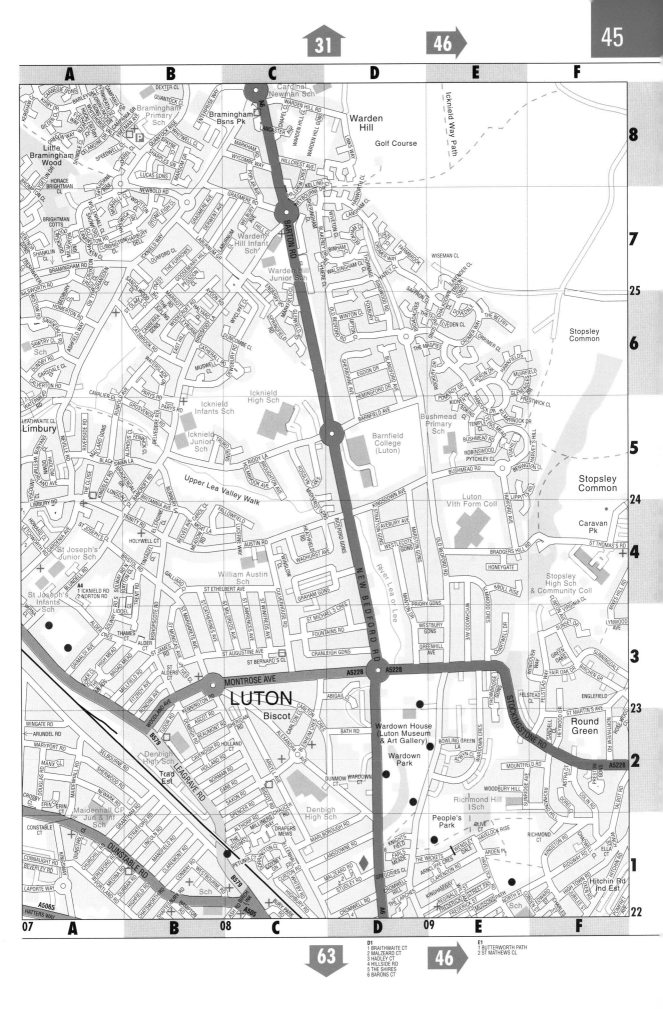

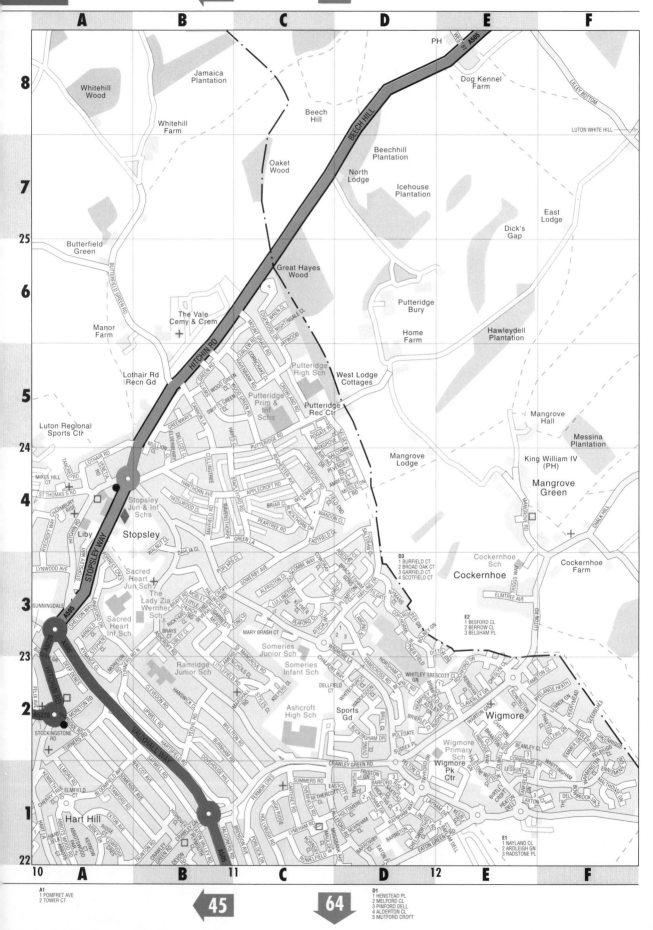

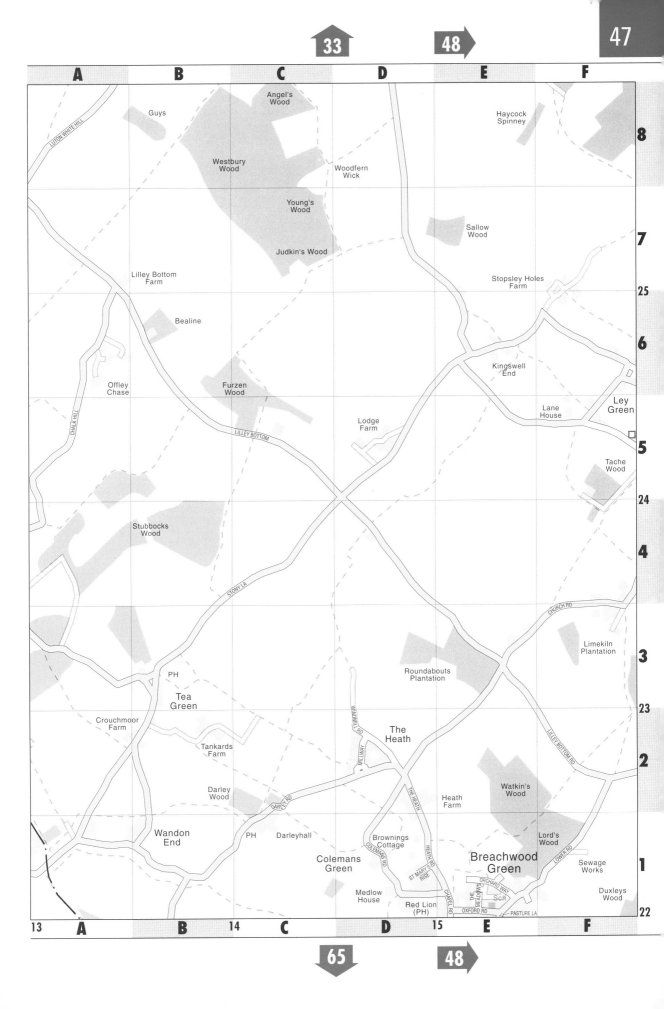

47
34

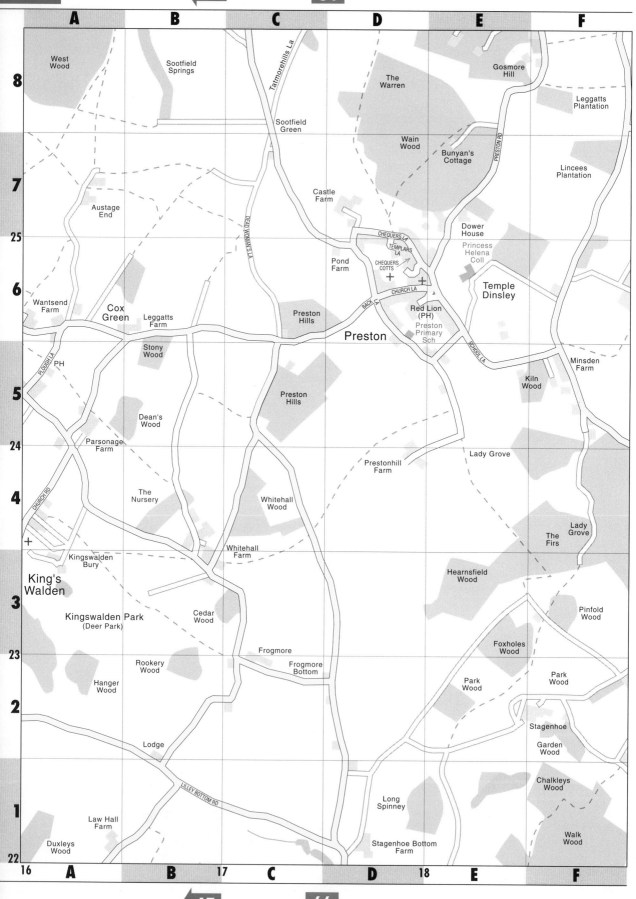

A   **B**   **C**   **D**   **E**   **F**

8

West Wood

Sootfield Springs

The Warren

Gosmore Hill

Leggatts Plantation

Sootfield Green

Wain Wood

Bunyan's Cottage

Lincees Plantation

7

Castle Farm

Austage End

25

CHEQUERS LA

TEMPLARS LA

Dower House

Princess Helena Coll

6

Pond Farm

CHEQUERS COTTS

CHURCH LA

Temple Dinsley

Wantsend Farm

Cox Green

Leggatts Farm

Preston Hills

BACK LA

Red Lion (PH)

Preston

Preston Primary Sch

SCHOOL LA

Minsden Farm

5

PLOUGH LA

PH

Stony Wood

Preston Hills

Kiln Wood

Dean's Wood

24

Parsonage Farm

Lady Grove

Prestonhill Farm

4

CHURCH RD

The Nursery

Whitehall Wood

The Firs

Lady Grove

Kingswalden Bury

Whitehall Farm

Hearnsfield Wood

King's Walden

3

Kingswalden Park (Deer Park)

Cedar Wood

Pinfold Wood

Frogmore

Foxholes Wood

23

Rookery Wood

Frogmore Bottom

Park Wood

Park Wood

Hanger Wood

2

Stagenhoe

Garden Wood

Lodge

Chalkleys Wood

LILLEY BOTTOM RD

1

Long Spinney

Law Hall Farm

Walk Wood

Duxleys Wood

22

Stagenhoe Bottom Farm

16   **A**   **B**   **17**   **C**   **D**   **18**   **E**   **F**

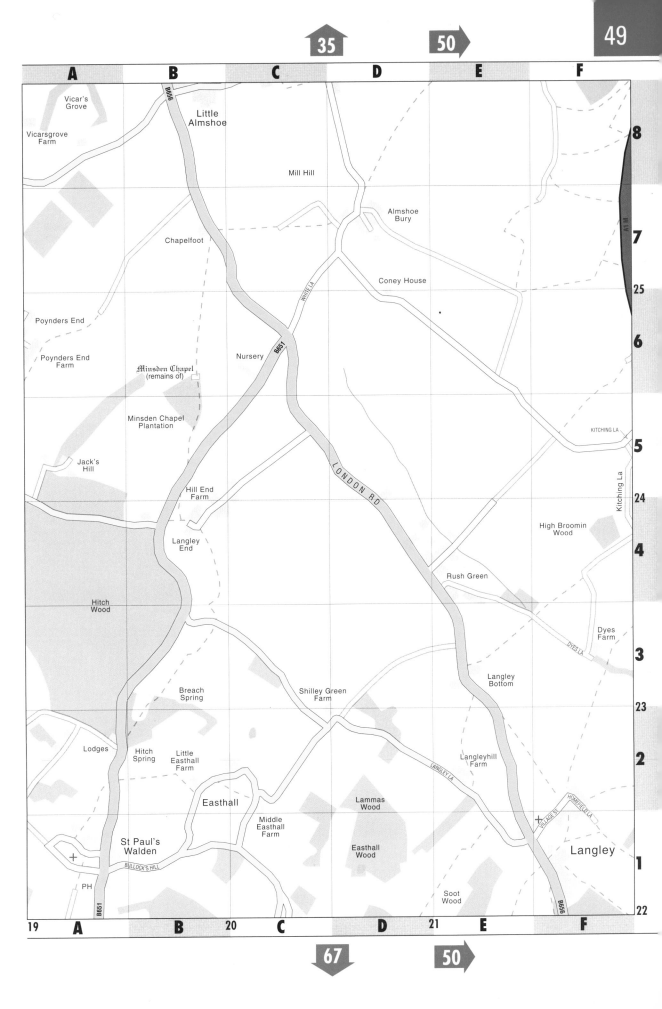

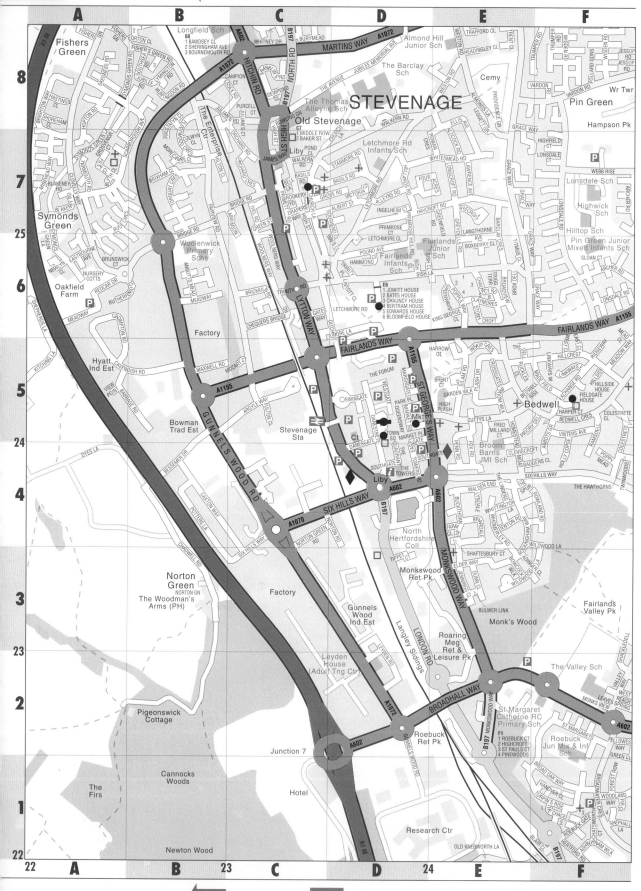

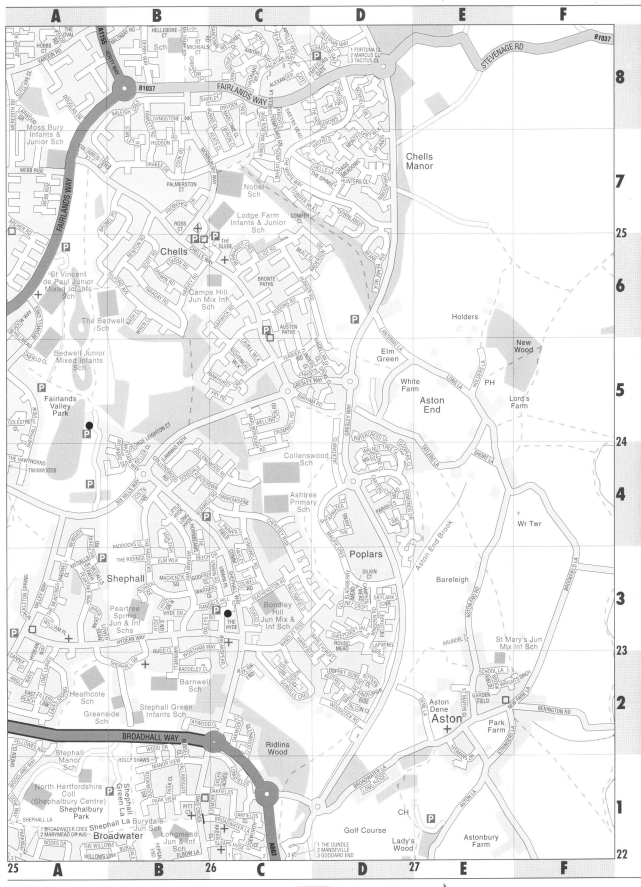

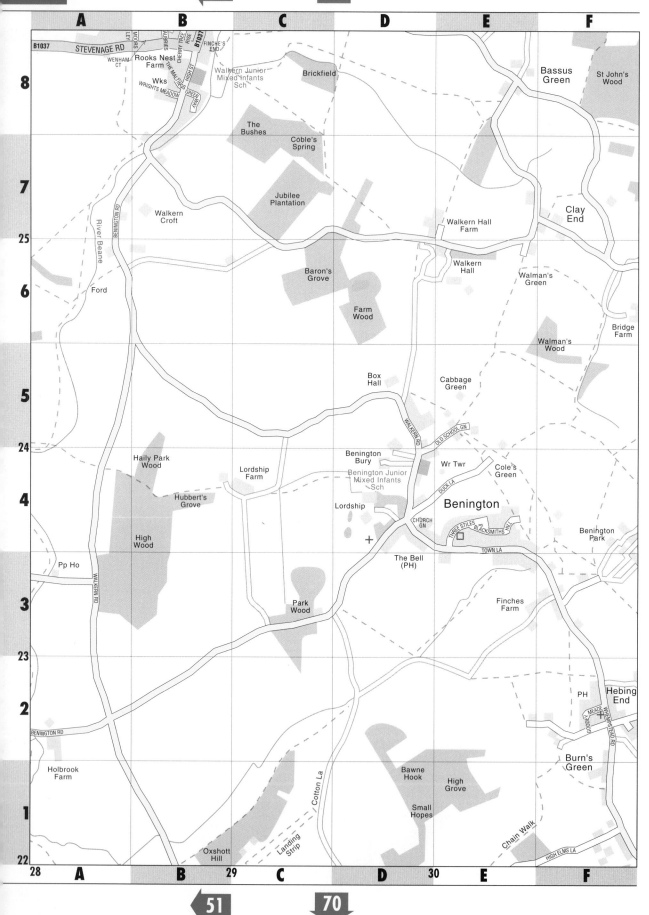

A   B   C   D   E   F

B1037

STEVENAGE RD

WENHAM CT

Rooks Nest Farm

Wks

WRIGHTS MEADOW

THE MALTINGS

MOORS LEY

AUBRIES

CHERRY TREE RISE

HIGH ST

GREEN WAY

FINCHE'S END

B1037

Walkern Junior Mixed Infants Sch

Brickfield

Bassus Green

St John's Wood

The Bushes

Coble's Spring

River Beane

BENINGTON RD

Walkern Croft

Jubilee Plantation

Walkern Hall Farm

Clay End

8

7

25

6

Ford

Baron's Grove

Farm Wood

Walkern Hall

Walman's Green

Walman's Wood

Bridge Farm

5

24

Box Hall

Cabbage Green

Haily Park Wood

Lordship Farm

Benington Bury

Benington Junior Mixed Infants Sch

WALKERN RD

OLD SCHOOL GN

Wr Twr

Cole's Green

4

Hubbert's Grove

Lordship

DUCK LA

Benington

CHURCH GN

THREE STILES

BLACKSMITHS HILL

Benington Park

High Wood

TOWN LA

3

Pp Ho

WALKERN RD

The Bell (PH)

Park Wood

Finches Farm

23

2

BENINGTON RD

PH

MEADE

GOODERS

WHEMPSTEAD RD

Hebing End

Holbrook Farm

Burn's Green

Bawne Hook

High Grove

Small Hopes

Chain Walk

1

COTTON LA

Landing Strip

HIGH ELMS LA

Oxshott Hill

22

28   A   B   29   C   D   30   E   F

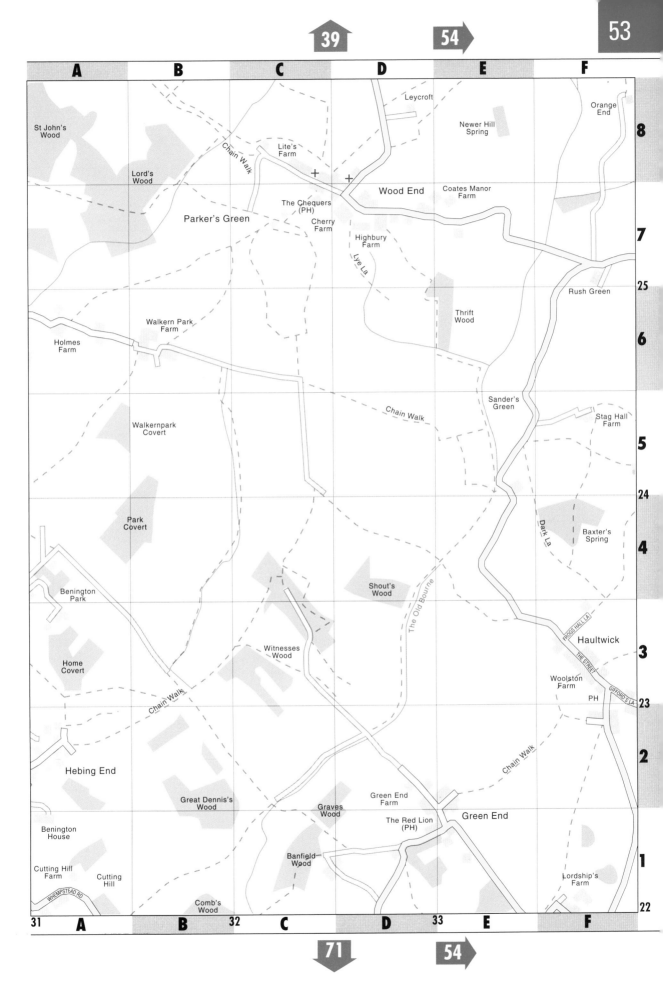

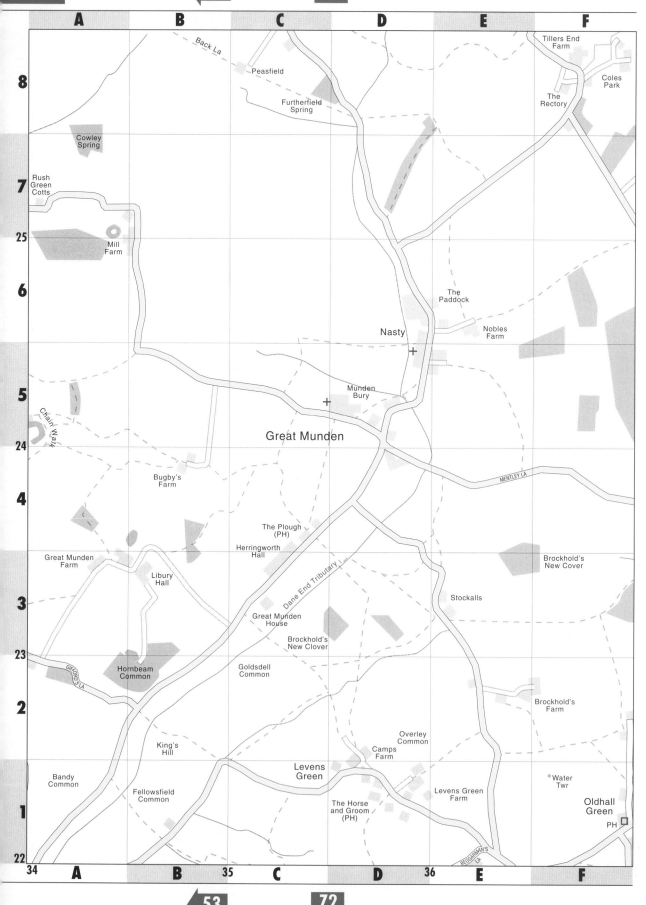

A   B   C   D   E   F

8

7

25

6

5

24

4

3

23

2

1

22

34   A   B   35   C   D   36   E   F

Back La

Peasfield

Furtherfield Spring

Tillers End Farm

Coles Park

The Rectory

Cowley Spring

Rush Green Cotts

Mill Farm

The Paddock

Nasty

Nobles Farm

Munden Bury

Chain Walk

Great Munden

Bugby's Farm

MENTLEY LA

The Plough (PH)

Herringworth Hall

Dane End Tributary

Brockhold's New Cover

Great Munden Farm

Libury Hall

Great Munden House

Stockalls

Brockhold's New Clover

GIFFORD'S LA

Hornbeam Common

Goldsdell Common

Brockhold's Farm

King's Hill

Overley Common

Camps Farm

Levens Green

Levens Green Farm

Water Twr

Bandy Common

Fellowsfield Common

The Horse and Groom (PH)

Oldhall Green

PH

BEGGARMAN'S LA

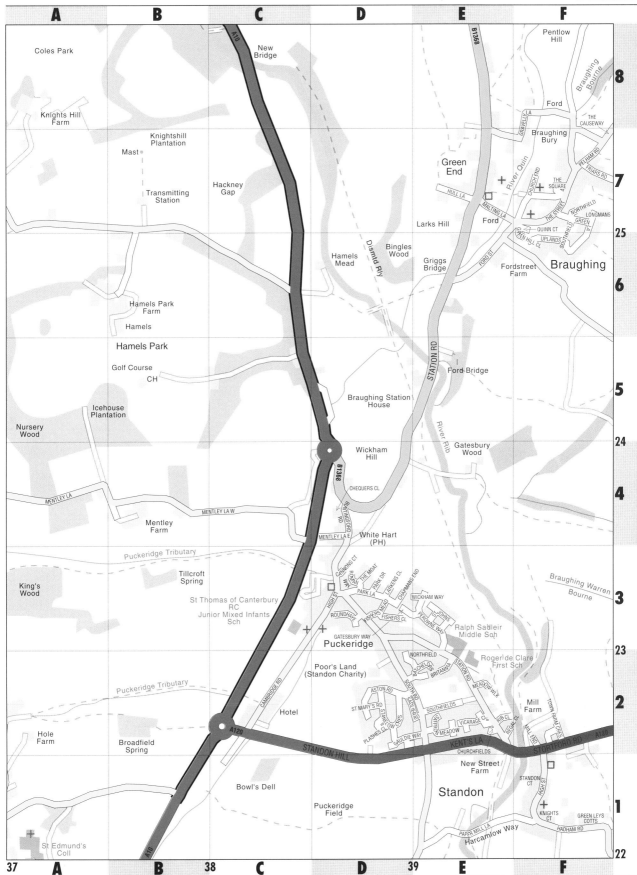

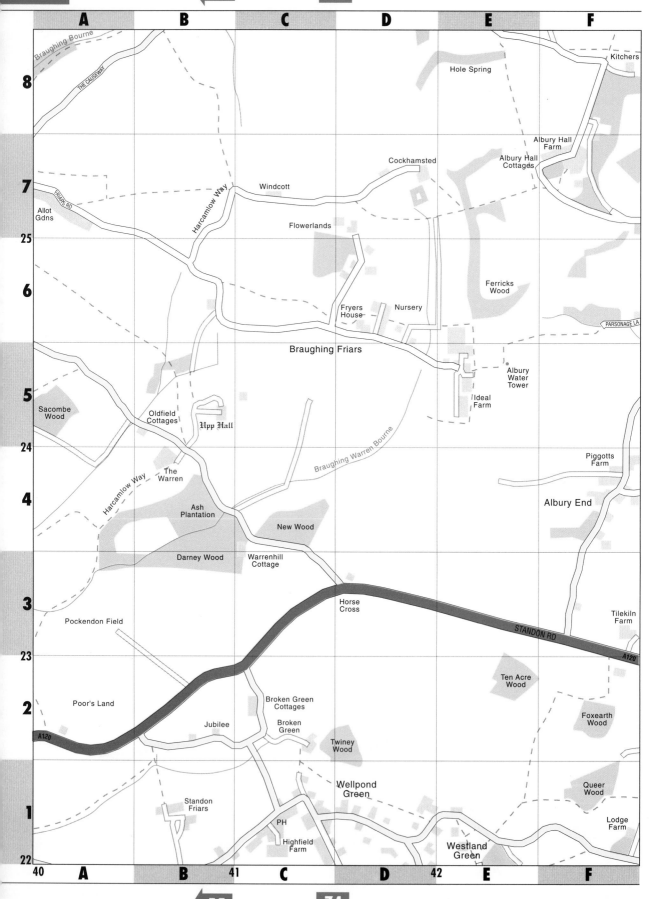

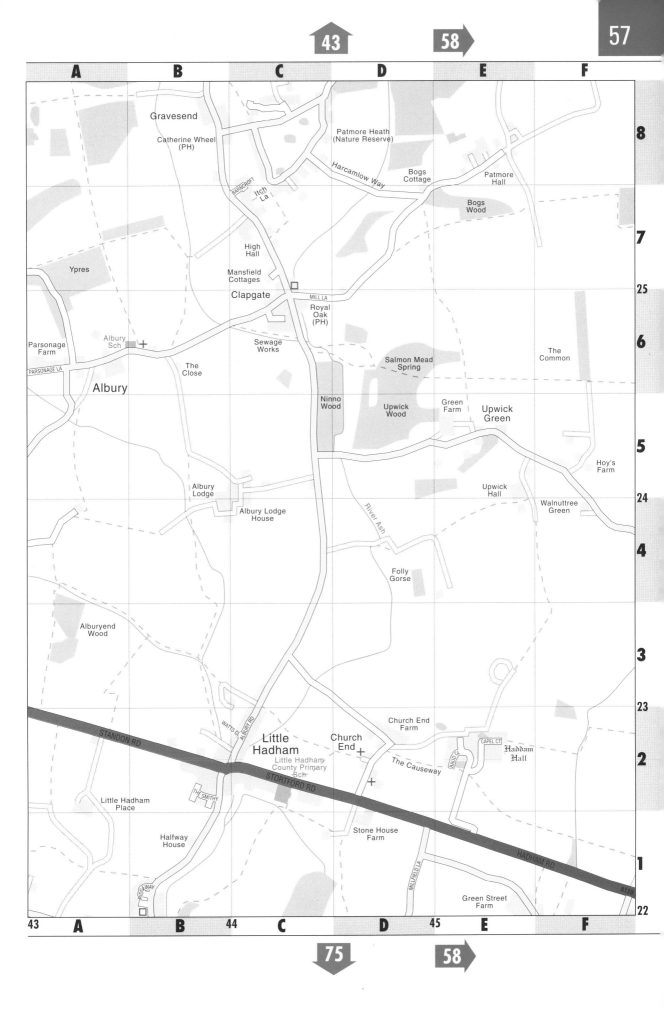

A | B | C | D | E | F

Gravesend

Catherine Wheel
(PH)

Patmore Heath
(Nature Reserve)

8

Harcamlow Way

BARNCROFT

Itch
La

Bogs
Cottage

Patmore
Hall

Bogs
Wood

High
Hall

7

Mansfield
Cottages

Clapgate

MILL LA

25

Ypres

Royal
Oak
(PH)

Parsonage
Farm

Albury
Sch

The
Common

6

PARSONAGE LA

Sewage
Works

Salmon Mead
Spring

Albury

The
Close

Ninno
Wood

Upwick
Wood

Green
Farm

Upwick
Green

5

Hoy's
Farm

Albury
Lodge

Upwick
Hall

24

Albury Lodge
House

River Ash

Walnuttree
Green

4

Folly
Gorse

Alburyend
Wood

3

23

STANDON RD

WATTS CL

ALBURY RD

Church End
Farm

CAPEL CT

Haddam
Hall

Little
Hadham

Church
End

BAUD CL

2

Little Hadham
County Primary
Sch

The Causeway

THE SMITHY

STORTFORD RD

Little Hadham
Place

Stone House
Farm

Halfway
House

HADHAM RD

RIDGEWAY

1

MILLFIELD LA

A4120

Green Street
Farm

22

43 | A | B | 44 | C | D | 45 | E | F

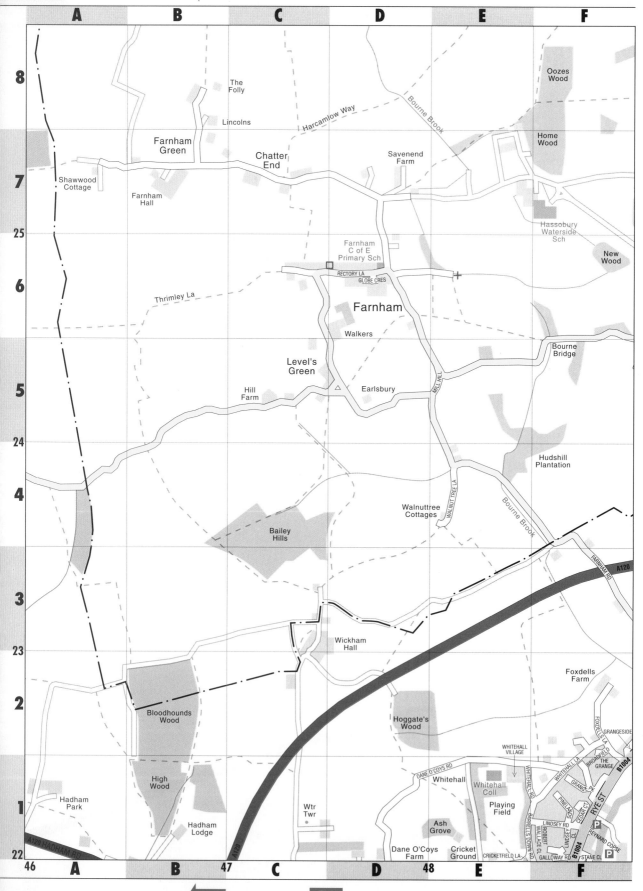

A B C D E F

8

7

25

6

5

24

4

3

23

2

1

22

46 A B 47 C D 48 E F

Oozes Wood

Home Wood

The Folly

Lincolns

Harcamlow Way

Bourne Brook

Savenend Farm

Hassobury Waterside Sch

New Wood

Farnham Green

Chatter End

Shawwood Cottage

Farnham Hall

Farnham C of E Primary Sch

RECTORY LA
GLOBE CRES

Thrimley La

Farnham

Walkers

Bourne Bridge

Level's Green

Hill Farm

Earlsbury

MILL HILL

Hudshill Plantation

Bourne Brook

Walnuttree Cottages

WALNUT TREE LA

Bailey Hills

FARNHAM RD

A120

Wickham Hall

Foxdells Farm

Bloodhounds Wood

Hoggate's Wood

GRANGESIDE

WHITEHALL VILLAGE

FOXDELLS LA

BROADFIELD

THE GRANGE

B1004

High Wood

Hadham Park

DANE O'COYS RD

Whitehall

Whitehall Coll

Playing Field

WHITEHALL RD

GRANGE PK

PINELANDS

RYE ST

Wtr Twr

Ash Grove

LINDSEY RD

ROBERT WALLACE CL

LINDSEY CL

CEDAR CT

REYNARD COPSE

P

Hadham Lodge

A120 HADHAM RD

A120

Dane O'Coys Farm

Cricket Ground

CRICKETFIELD LA

BARRELLS DOWN RD

GALLOWAY RD

B1004

STANE CL

P

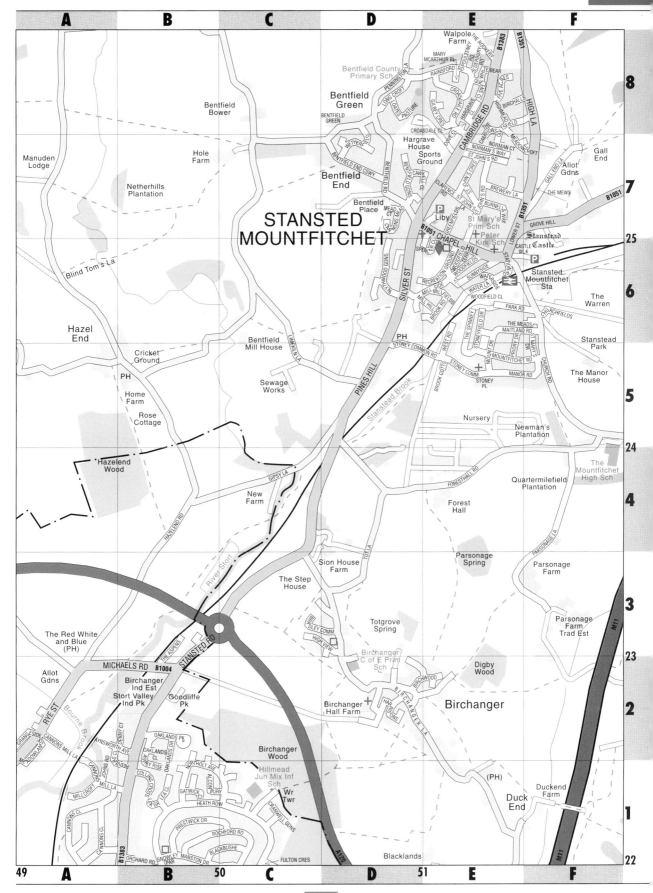

STANSTED MOUNTFITCHET

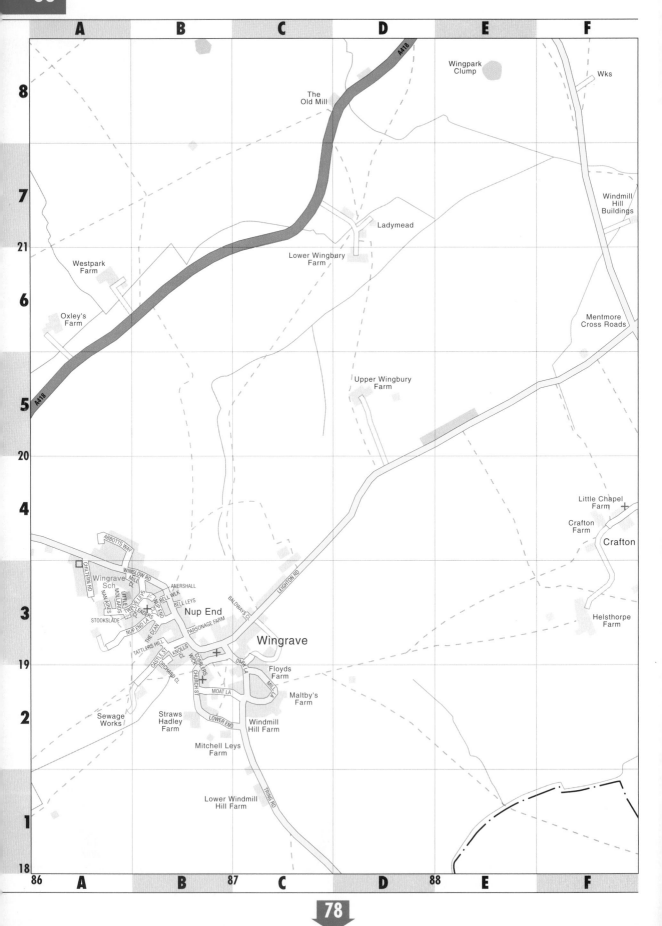

A B C D E F

8

The Old Mill

Wingpark
Clump

Wks

7

Windmill
Hill
Buildings

21

Ladymead

Westpark
Farm

Lower Wingbury
Farm

6

Mentmore
Cross Roads

Oxley's
Farm

A418

5

Upper Wingbury
Farm

20

Little Chapel
Farm

4

Crafton
Farm

Crafton

ABBOTTS WAY

Helsthorpe
Farm

WINSLOW RD

Wingrave
Sch

ANERSHALL
WLK

LEIGHTON RD

CHILTERN RD

MILL CL

BELL WLK

BALDWIN'S CL

3

NAM AIRES

MOLLARDS

TWP LE LEYS

NUP END

BELL LEYS

Nup End

STOOKSLADE

NUP END LA

THE BEAN

PARSONAGE FARM

Wingrave

19

TATTLERS HILL

CASTLE ST

KNOLLS CL

ORCHARD CL

WICK
CHURCH ST

COBBLERS
CL

OAK LA

MILL LA

Floyds
Farm

Maltby's
Farm

2

Sewage
Works

Straws
Hadley
Farm

MOAT LA

LOWER END

Windmill
Hill Farm

Mitchell Leys
Farm

TRING RD

1

Lower Windmill
Hill Farm

18

86 A B 87 C D 88 E F

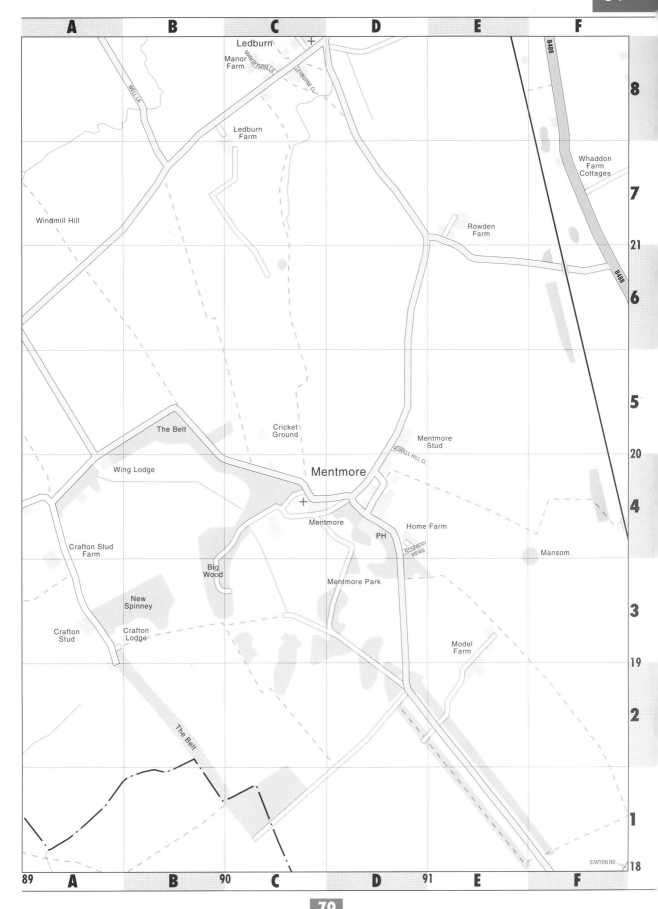

A B C D E F

8
7
21
6
5
20
4
3
19
2
1
18

Ledburn

Manor Farm

MANOR FARM LA

LEYBURNE CL

WELL LA

Ledburn Farm

B488

Whaddon Farm Cottages

Windmill Hill

Rowden Farm

B488

The Belt

Cricket Ground

Mentmore Stud

HOWELL HILL CL

Wing Lodge

Mentmore

Crafton Stud Farm

Mentmore

Home Farm

PH

ROSEBERY MEWS

Mansom

Big Wood

Mentmore Park

New Spinney

Crafton Stud

Crafton Lodge

Model Farm

The Belt

STATION RD

89 A B 90 C D 91 E F

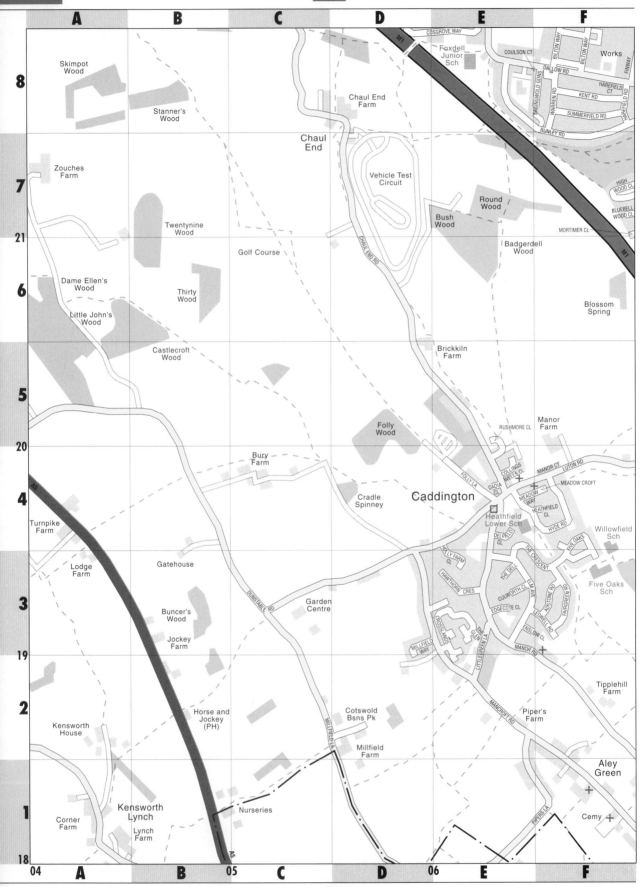

A B C D E F

8

7

21

6

5

20

4

3

19

2

1

18

04 A B 05 C D 06 E F

Skimpot Wood

Stanner's Wood

Chaul End Farm

Chaul End

Foxdell Junior Sch

Works

COSGROVE WAY

M1

COULSON CT

BILTON WAY

BILTON WAY

DALLOW RD

PASSINGWOLD GDNS

WARREN RD

KENT RD

COULSON CT

HAREFIELD CT

HAREFIELD RD

SUMMERFIELD RD

FINWAY

RUNLEY RD

Zouches Farm

Vehicle Test Circuit

Bush Wood

Round Wood

HIGH WOOD CL

BLUEBELL WOOD CL

MORTIMER CL

M1

Twentynine Wood

Golf Course

CHAUL END RD

Badgerdell Wood

Dame Ellen's Wood

Thirty Wood

Little John's Wood

Blossom Spring

Castlecroft Wood

Brickkiln Farm

Folly Wood

Manor Farm

RUSHMORE CL

Bury Farm

Cradle Spinney

Caddington

COLLINGS WELLS CL

CADIA CL

FOLLY LA

MANOR CT

LUTON RD

MEADOW CROFT

MEADOW WAY

HEATHFIELD CL

Willowfield Sch

Heathfield Lower Sch

HYDE RD

Turnpike Farm

DELFIELD CL

FIVE OAKS

THE CRESCENT

Five Oaks Sch

Lodge Farm

Gatehouse

HOLLY FARM CL

HAWTHORN CRES

THE DELL

ELM AVE

CULWORTH CL

ADSTONE RD

FAIRGREEN RD

DUNSTABLE RD

Buncer's Wood

Garden Centre

EDGECOTE CL

LEDWELL RD

Jockey Farm

CROSS LAWNS

THE GLEN

ENSLOW CL

MILLFIELD WAY

LITTLEGREEN LA

MANOR RD

Tipplehill Farm

Horse and Jockey (PH)

Cotswold Bsns Pk

MANCROFT RD

Piper's Farm

Kensworth House

MILLFIELD LA

Millfield Farm

Aley Green

PIPERS LA

Corner Farm

Kensworth Lynch

Nurseries

Cemy

Lynch Farm

A5

A5

D8
1 HILLSIDE RD
2 THE BARLEYCORN
3 DEACONS CT
4 THE MOUNT
5 BEDFORD GDNS
6 VILLA CT

45

7 ST NINIAN'S CT
8 DEACONS CT
E6
1 ROBERT ALLEN CT
2 ROCHDALE CT
3 KIRKDALE CT
4 ESSEX CT

64

5 CHOBHAM WLK
6 FLOWERS IND EST
7 HOLLY ST TRAD EST
8 LONGLEY TERR IND PK
9 JAMES CT
10 TRACEY CT
11 TELMERE IND EST

E8
1 ELGAR PATH
2 BUTTERWORTH PATH
3 BERKELEY PATH
4 HAVELOCK RD
5 ALBION CT

63

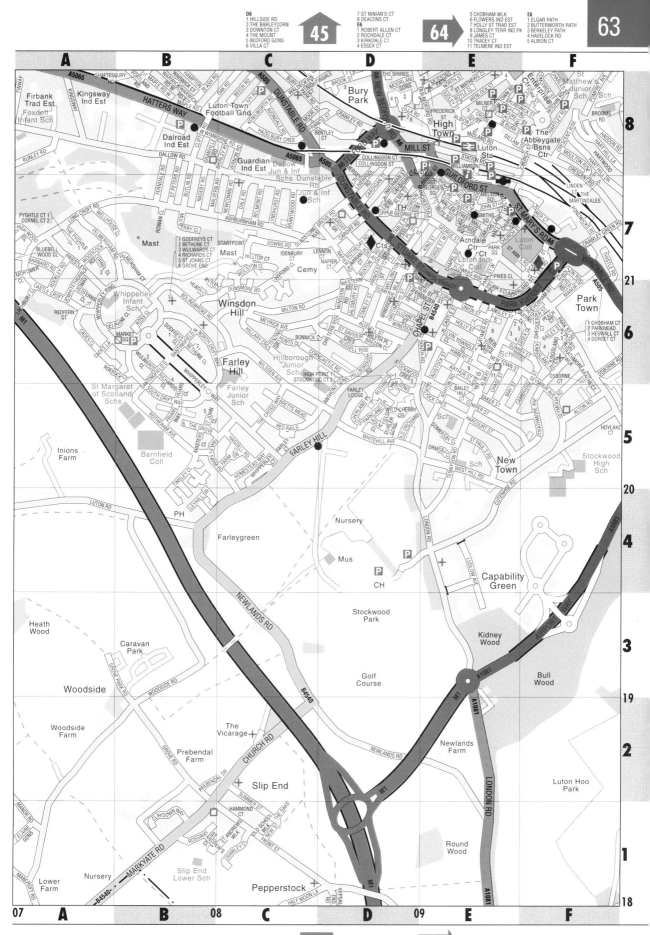

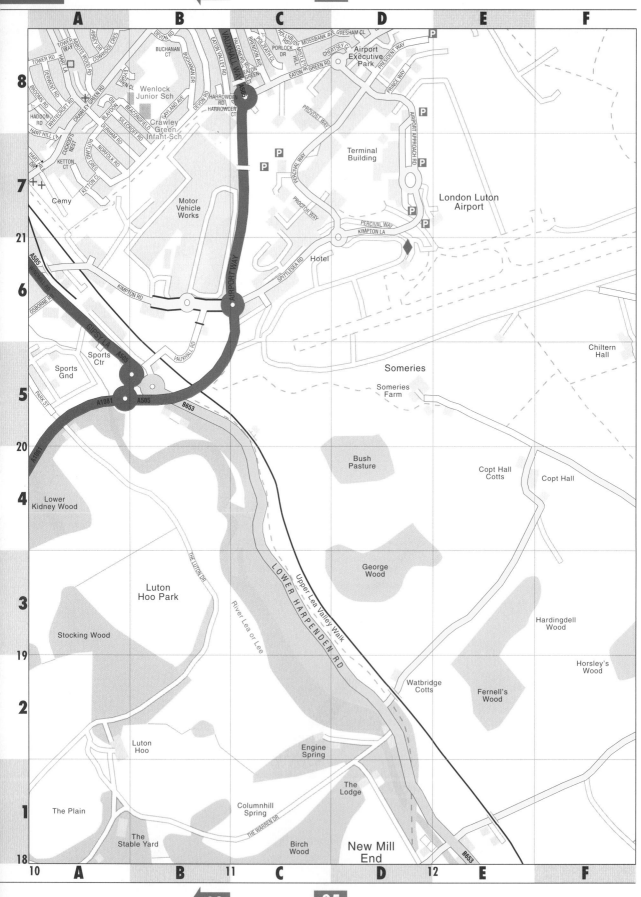

A B C D E F

8

7

21

6

5

20

4

3

19

2

1

18

10 A B 11 C D 12 E F

Tower Rd
Abbots Wood Rd
Cowridge Cres
Devon Rd
Eaton Valley Rd
Falconers Rd
Vauxhall Way
A505
Hollybush Rd
Mossbank Ave
Gresham Cl
Mistley Rd
Polzeath Cl
Porlock Dr
Cheatsey Cl
Airport Executive Park
President Way
P
Prince Way
Abbey Rd
Buchanan Ct
Gayland Ave
Eaton Green Rd
Brendon Ave
Eaton Rd
Eaton Green
Hart La
Derwent Rd
Brooms Rd
Haddon Rd
Whitecroft Rd
Cuckoos Nest
Cranley Green Rd
Dell
Blaydon Rd
Beaconsfield
Silencroft
Durham Rd
Buchanan Dr
Devon Rd
Harrowden Rd
Harrowden Ct
Provost Way
Airport Approach Rd
P
Wenlock Junior Sch
Crawley Green Infant Sch
Ketton Ct
Norfolk Rd
Rutland Cres
Ketton Ct
Terminal Building
P
P
London Luton Airport
Cemy
Hart Hill La
Hart Hill Dr
Motor Vehicle Works
Airport Way
Percival Way
Proctor Way
P
P
Percival Way
A505
Osborne Rd
Vauxhall Rd
Kimpton Rd
Gipsy La
A505
Spittlesea Rd
Hotel
Kimpton La
Chiltern Hall
Park St
A1081
A505
B653
Somaries
Someries Farm
Sports Ctr
Sports Gnd
A1081
Bush Pasture
Copt Hall Cotts
Copt Hall
Lower Kidney Wood
The Luton Dr
River Lea or Lee
Lower Lea Valley Walk
LOWER HARPENDEN RD
George Wood
Hardingdell Wood
Luton Hoo Park
Stocking Wood
Horsley's Wood
Watbridge Cotts
Fernell's Wood
Luton Hoo
Engine Spring
Columnhill Spring
The Lodge
The Plain
The Stable Yard
The Warren Dr
Birch Wood
New Mill End
B653

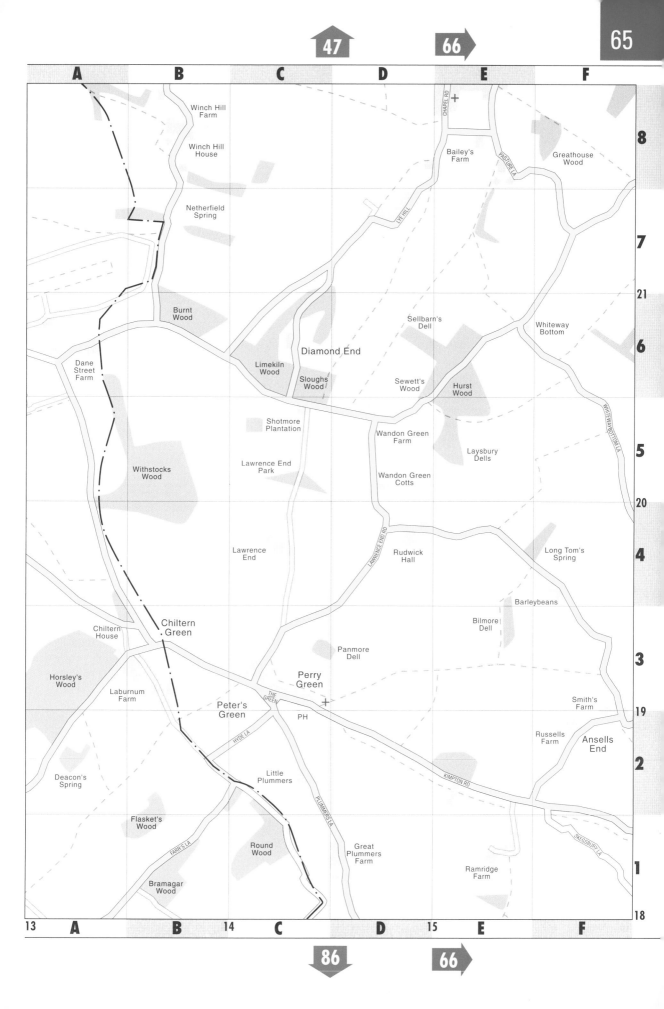

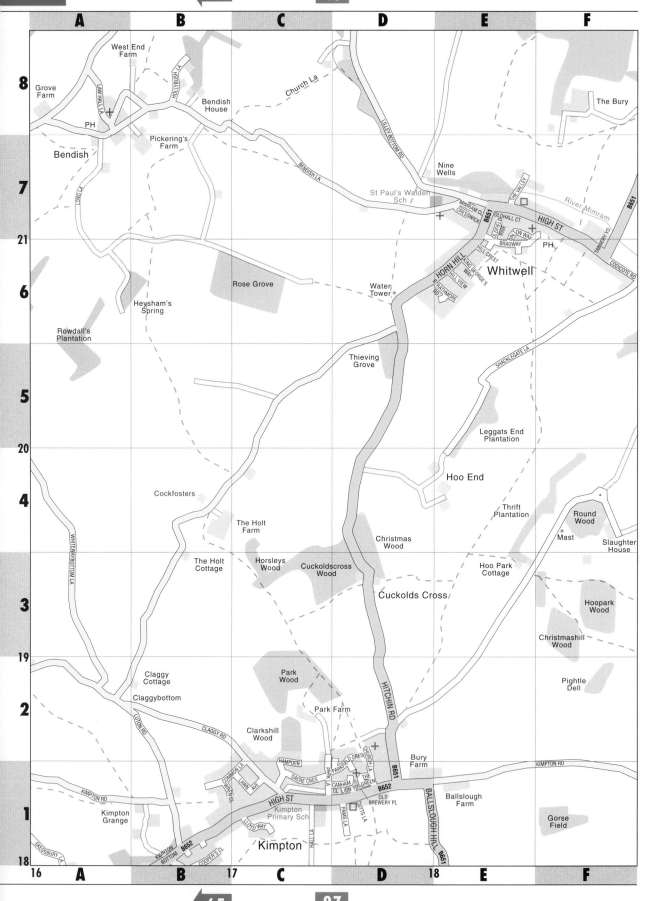

A B C D E F

8

Grove Farm

West End Farm

LAW HALL LA

HOLLYBUSH LA

Bendish House

Church La

The Bury

PH

Pickering's Farm

LILLEY BOTTOM RD

Bendish

LONG LA

BENDISH LA

Nine Wells

St Paul's Walden Sch

River Mimram

B651

7

MIMRAM CL

CRESSWICK

THE VALLEY

HIGH ST

21

OLDFIELD RISE

OLDHALL CT

BRADWAY

PH

TANNERY YD

CODICOTE RD

Rose Grove

HORN HILL

HILL CREST

KING GEORGE'S WAY

HILL VIEW

Whitwell

6

Heysham's Spring

Water Tower

STRATMORE RD

Rowdall's Plantation

Thieving Grove

SHACKLEGATE LA

5

Leggats End Plantation

20

Hoo End

Cockfosters

Thrift Plantation

Round Wood

4

The Holt Farm

Christmas Wood

Mast

Slaughter House

WHITEWAYBOTTOM LA

The Holt Cottage

Horsleys Wood

Cuckoldscross Wood

Hoo Park Cottage

Hoopark Wood

Cuckolds Cross

3

Christmashill Wood

HITCHIN RD

19

Claggy Cottage

Park Wood

Pightle Dell

2

LUTON RD

Claggybottom

Park Farm

CLAGGY RD

Clarkshill Wood

HAMPDEN

COMMON LA

DACRE CRES

PARKFIELD CRES

CHURCH LA

Bury Farm

KIMPTON RD

KIMPTON RD

LAWN AVE

PARK LA

CANHAM CL

THE GREEN

B651

Ballslough Farm

WREN CL

LION YD

B652

1

Kimpton Grange

LLOYD WAY

HIGH ST

Kimpton Primary Sch

HALL LA

PARIS LA

CUTTS LA

OLD BREWERY PL

BALLSLOUGH HILL

Gorse Field

SKEGSBURY LA

KIMPTON BOTTOM

B652

COOPER'S CL

Kimpton

B651

18

16 A B 17 C D 18 E F

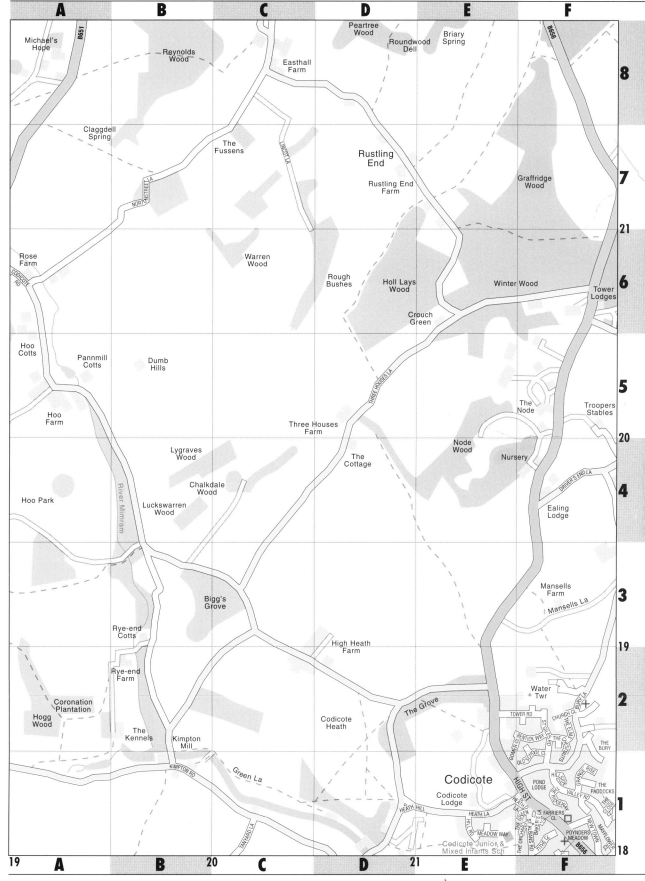

A B C D E F

8

7

21

6

5

20

4

3

19

2

1

18

22 A B 23 C D 24 E F

Burleigh Grove
Cowley's Corner Wood
North Lodges
Burleigh Farm
Wintergreen Wood
Knebworth Country Park
Mausoleum
Knebworth Ho
Miniature Rly
Manor Farm
Old Knebworth
Lodge Farm
Martlets
Knebworth Sta
Park Wood
Driver's End
Nup End
Lytton Arms (PH)
Homewood
The Bothy
Hogsnorton
New Wood
Hornbeam Spring
Thickney Wood
Plummer's Farm
Robin Hood & Little John (PH)
Deard's Wood
Rableyheath
Water Twr
The Iron House
Tagmore Green
Rableyheath Farm
Ashley Grove
Arnold's Farm
Ninning's Wood
Little Wood
Pottersheath
Mardley Heath
Heath Field
Ridge Farm
Little Bury Farm
Arnold's Spring
Nursery
Welwyn Heath
Mardley Wood
Golf Course

1 THE BIRCHES
2 THE PADDOCKS
3 MAYFLOWER CL

PARK LA
OLD KNEBWORTH LA
A1 M
STEVENAGE RD
B197
LONDON RD
HAZELMERE RD
DRIVER'S END LA
SLIP LA
BURY LA
B656
SALLY DEARDS LA
RABLEY HEATH RD
COXDOTE HEIGHTS
POTTERSHEATH RD
DANESBURY PARK RD
CANONSFIELD RD
HEATH RD
SPRINGS LA
DARBY DR
NINNING'S LA
NORMANS LA
WYCH ELM LA
GIPSY LA

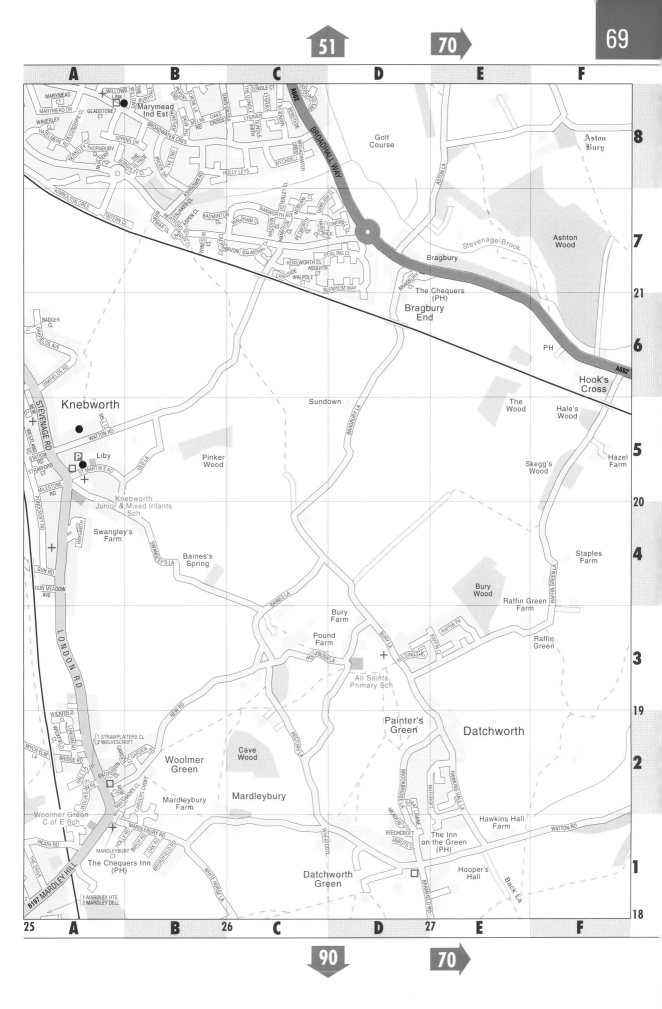

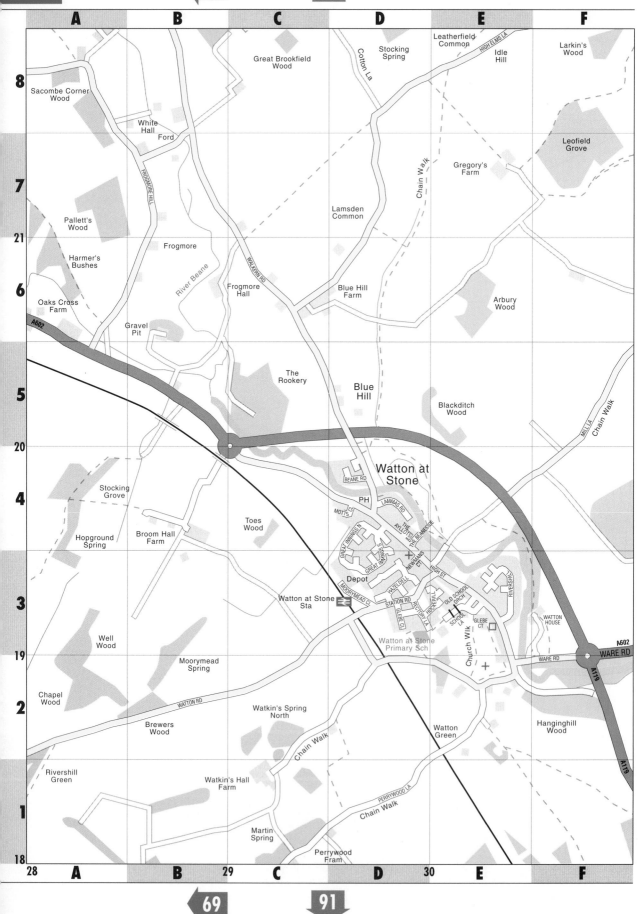

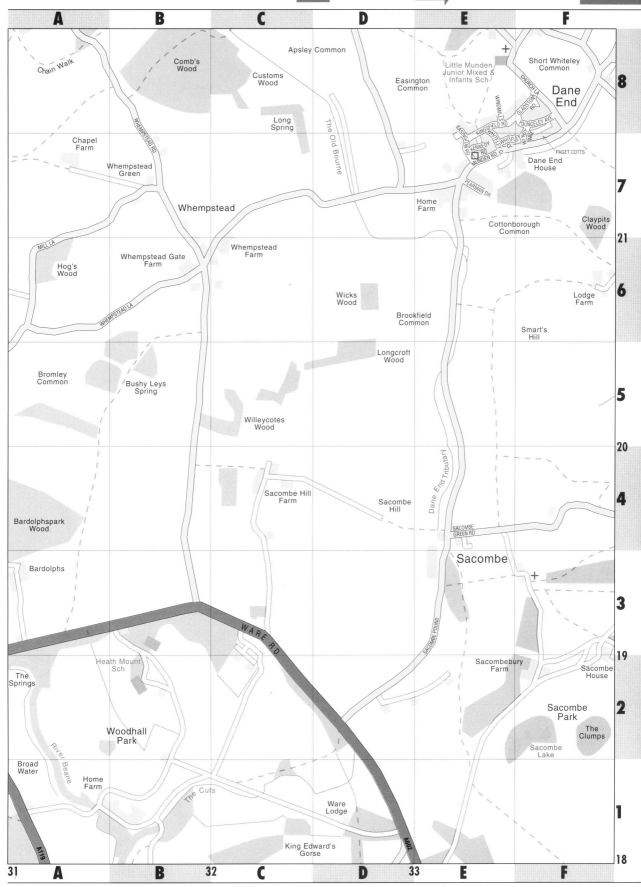

A **B** **C** **D** **E** **F**

Chain Walk

Comb's Wood

Apsley Common

Little Munden Junior Mixed & Infants Sch

Short Whiteley Common

Dane End

8

Customs Wood

Easington Common

CHURCH LA

Chapel Farm

Long Spring

The Old Bourne

WINDMILL RD
KINGSFIELD RD
EASINGTON RD
KENNEDY RD
MUNDEN RD
WHITLEY RD
GLADSTONE RD
WITNEY
PAGE
FOUNCELEY AVE

Whempstead Green

PAGET COTTS

Dane End House

7

Whempstead

Home Farm

PEARMAN DR

MILL LA

Whempstead Gate Farm

Whempstead Farm

Cottonborough Common

Claypits Wood

21

Hog's Wood

Wicks Wood

Lodge Farm

6

WHEMPSTEAD LA

Brookfield Common

Smart's Hill

Bromley Common

Bushy Leys Spring

Longcroft Wood

5

Willeycotes Wood

20

Dane End Tributary

Bardolphspark Wood

Sacombe Hill Farm

Sacombe Hill

4

SACOMBE GREEN RD

Bardolphs

Sacombe

3

The Springs

Heath Mount Sch

WARE RD

SACOMBE POUND

Sacombebury Farm

19

Sacombe House

Broad Water

Woodhall Park

River Beane

Sacombe Park

2

Home Farm

The Cuts

Ware Lodge

A602

Sacombe Lake

The Clumps

1

A119

King Edward's Gorse

18

A **B** **C** **D** **E** **F**

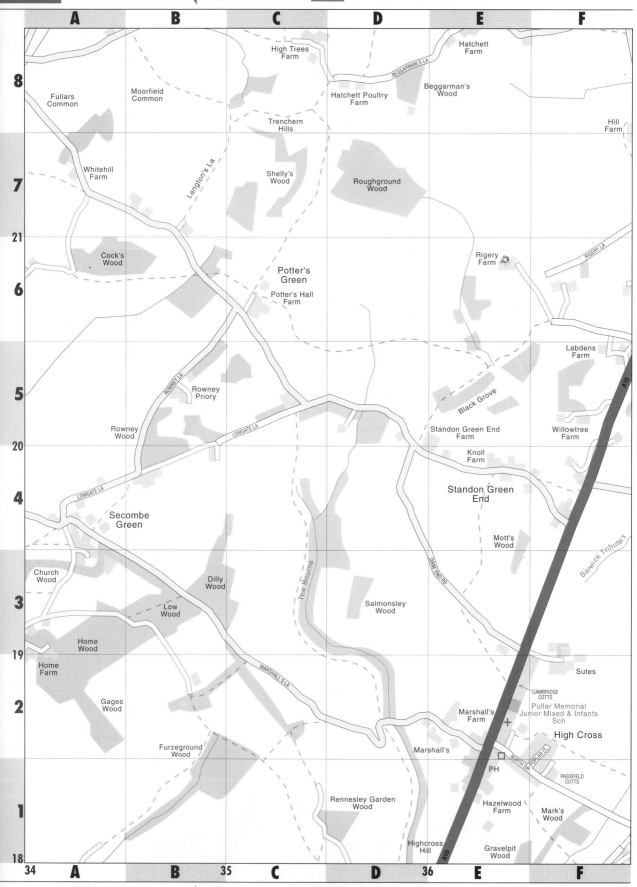

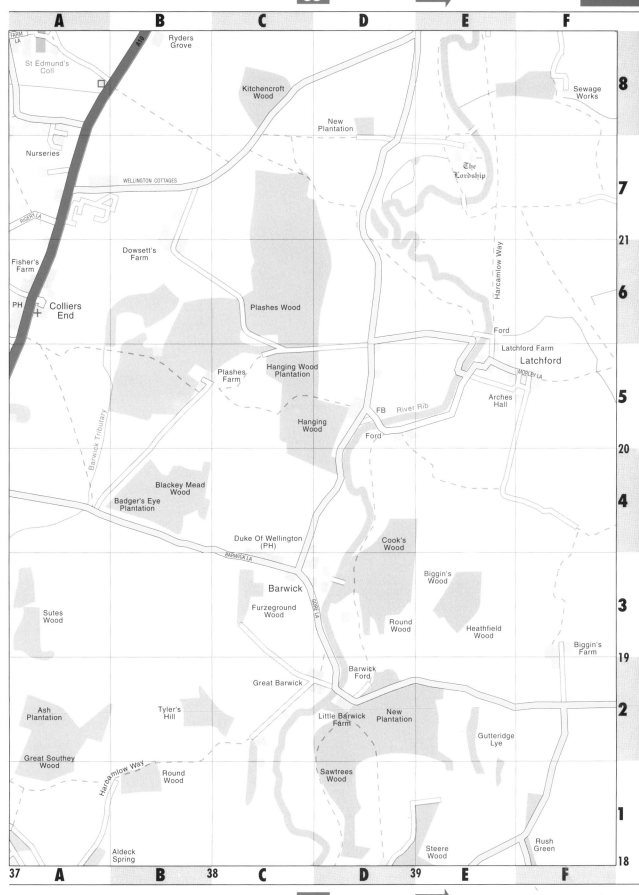

A   B   C   D   E   F

FARM LA

St Edmund's Coll

Ryders Grove

8

Kitchencroft Wood

New Plantation

Nurseries

The Lordship

WELLINGTON COTTAGES

7

RIGERY LA

21

Dowsett's Farm

Harcamlow Way

Fisher's Farm

6

PH
+ Colliers End

Plashes Wood

Ford

Latchford Farm

Latchford

Plashes Farm

Hanging Wood Plantation

MORLEY LA

Barwick Tributary

Arches Hall

5

FB   River Rib

Hanging Wood

Ford

20

Blackey Mead Wood

Badger's Eye Plantation

4

Duke Of Wellington (PH)

Cook's Wood

BARWICK LA

Biggin's Wood

Sutes Wood

Barwick

GORE LA

Furzeground Wood

Round Wood

Heathfield Wood

3

Biggin's Farm

19

Barwick Ford

Great Barwick

Ash Plantation

Tyler's Hill

Little Barwick Farm

New Plantation

2

Gutteridge Lye

Great Southey Wood

Harcamlow Way

Round Wood

Sawtrees Wood

1

Aldeck Spring

Steere Wood

Rush Green

18

37   A   B   38   C   D   39   E   F

73
56

A B C D E F

8
7
21
6
5
20
4
3
19
2
1
18

Balsams

Bromley

Alder Wood

Westfield Farm

Little Balsams

Caley Wood

Bowles Wood

Bromleyhall Farm

Damsel's Spring

The Wilderness

Cambercroft Spring

Standon Lodge Farm

Chaldean Farm

Rector's Springs

Vineyard Spring

Spindle Bridge

Bartram's Wood

WINDING HILL

B1004

New Barns

THE SQUARE

Dismtd Rly

Cox La

Much Hadham

HIGH ST

CHURCH LA

The Bull (PH)

PARK TERR

OUDLE LA

Brand's Farm

Moor Place

St Andrews C of E Junior Mixed Infants Sch

TOWER HILL

The Barn Sch

Nimney Bourne

FERNDALE

ASH MEADOW

Blackcroft Farm

Hadham Cross

WALNUT CL

MALTING LA

PH

KETTLE GREEN RD

Old Hall Farm

BROADFIELD CL

BROADFIELD

CULVER CT

Nursery

WIDFORD RD

WINDMILL WAY

LAURELDENE

Kettle Green Farm

MILL FIRST VIEW

STATION RD

B1004

Kettle Green

Moat Farm

40 A B 41 C D 42 E F

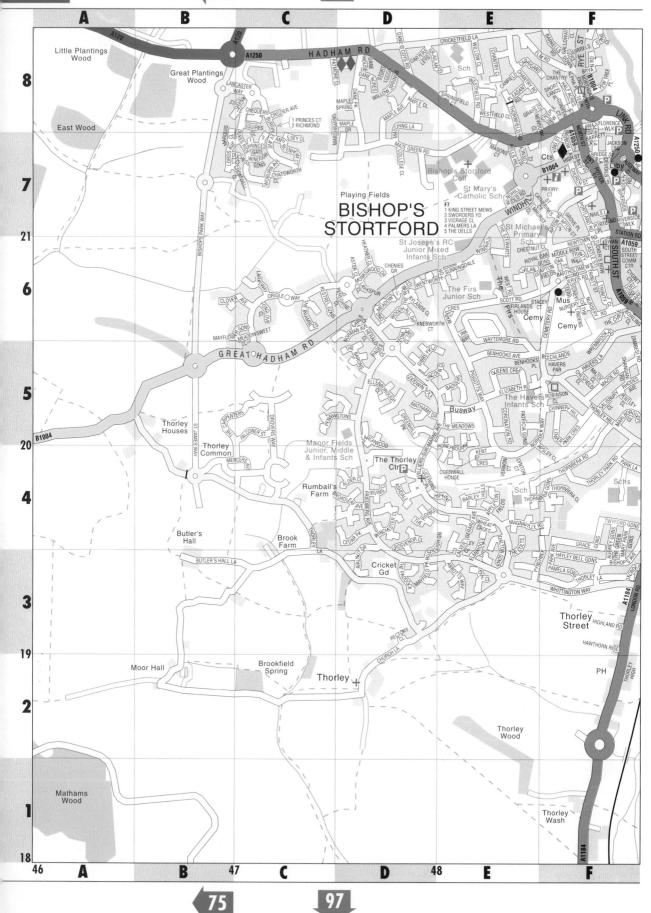

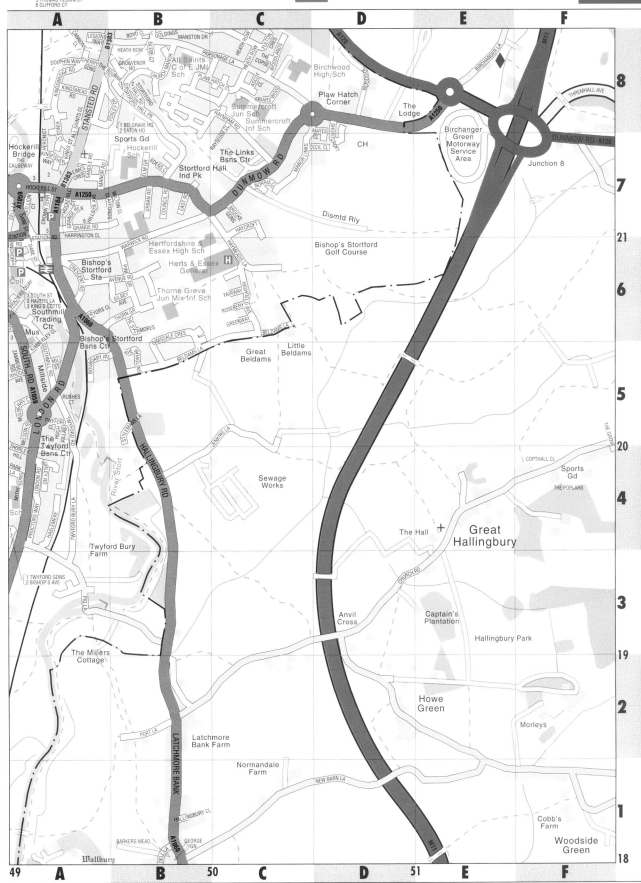

A7
1 FULLER CT
2 THE OLD MALTINGS
3 CASTLE VIEW
4 BAKERS CT
5 THOMAS HESKIN CT
6 CLIFFORD CT

60

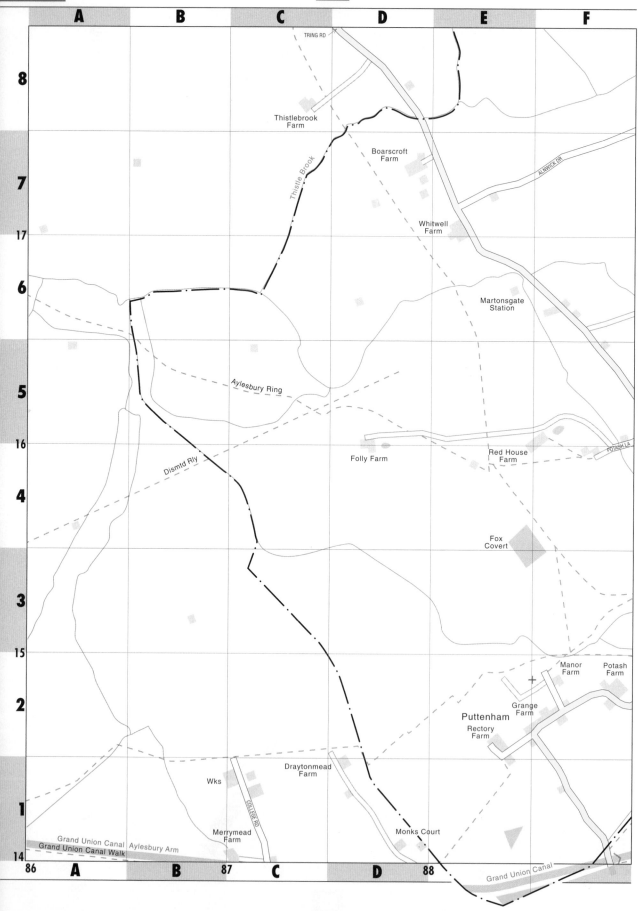

TRING RD

Thistlebrook
Farm

Thistle Brook

Boarscroft
Farm

ALNWICK DR

Whitwell
Farm

Martonsgate
Station

Aylesbury Ring

Dismtd Rly

Folly Farm

Red House
Farm

POTASH LA

Fox
Covert

Manor
Farm

Potash
Farm

Grange
Farm

Puttenham

Rectory
Farm

Draytonmead
Farm

Wks

COLLEGE RD

Monks Court

Merrymead
Farm

Grand Union Canal Aylesbury Arm
Grand Union Canal Walk

Grand Union Canal

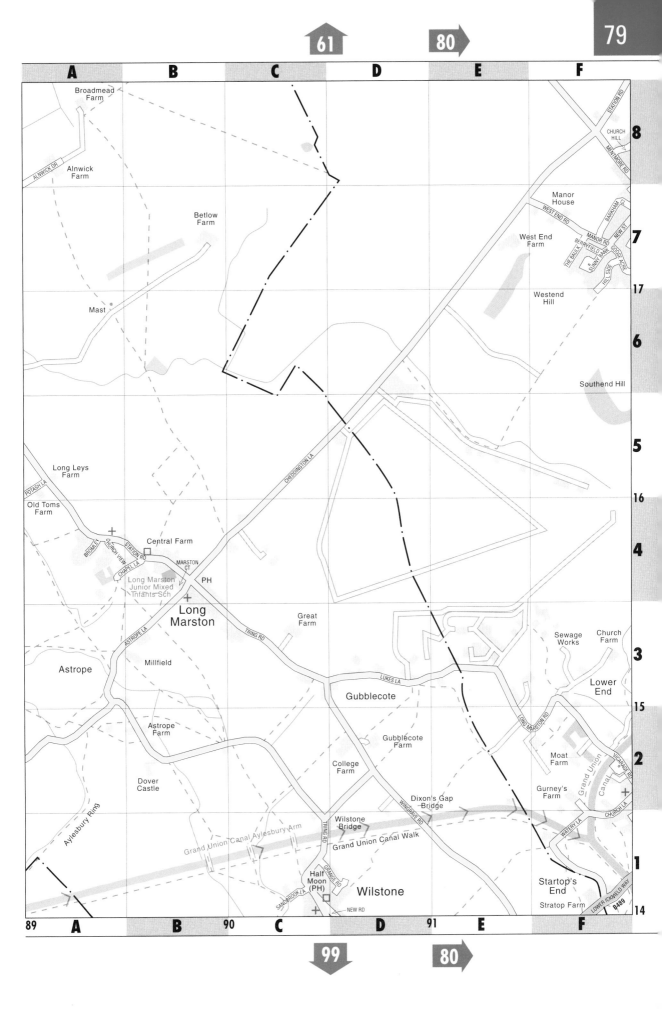

79

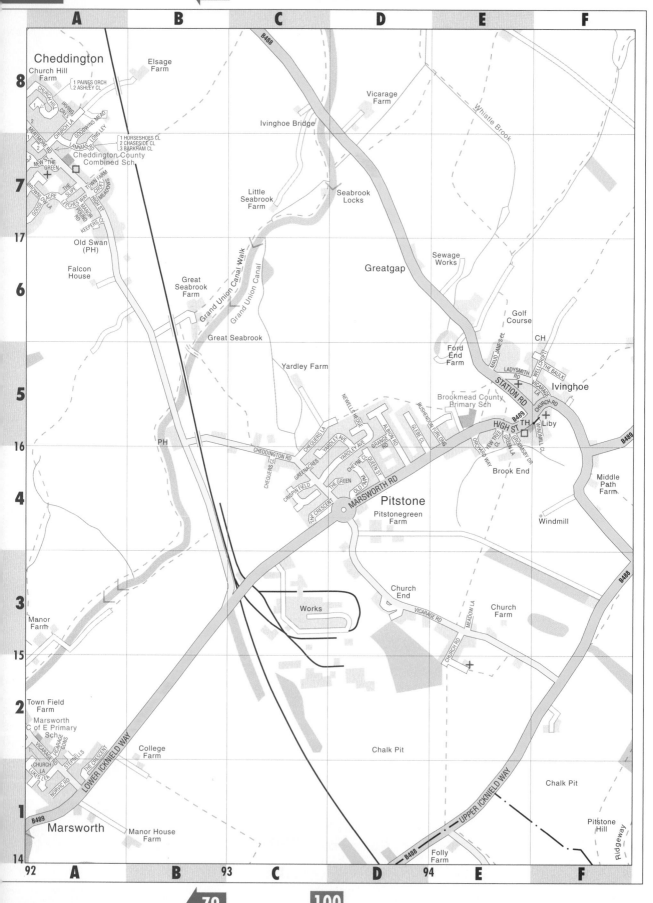

79
100

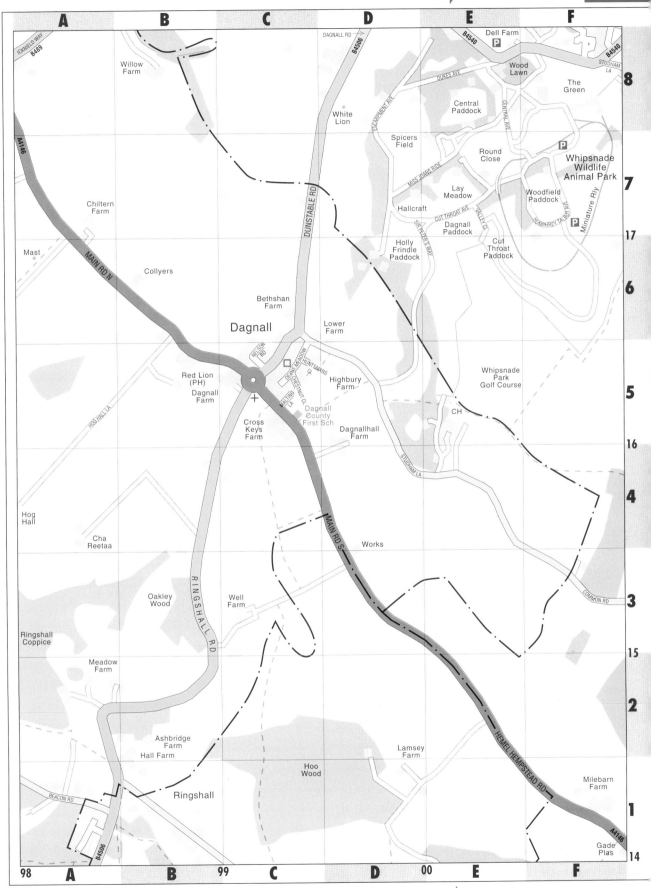

ICKNIELD WAY
B489
A4146
MAIN RD N
Chiltern Farm
Mast
Collyers
Hog Hall
Cha Reetaa
Ringshall Coppice
Meadow Farm
HOG HALL LA
RINGSHALL RD
BEACON RD
B4506
Ringshall
Ashbridge Farm
Hall Farm
Oakley Wood
Willow Farm
DAGNALL RD
White Lion
DUNSTABLE RD
B4506
Bethshan Farm
Dagnall
Red Lion (PH)
Dagnall Farm
NELSON RD
MALTING LA
DEANS MEADOW
CHESTNUT CL
HUNTSMANS CL
Cross Keys Farm
Dagnall County First Sch
Lower Farm
Highbury Farm
Dagnallhall Farm
Well Farm
MAIN RD S
Works
Hoo Wood
Lamsey Farm
HEMEL HEMPSTEAD RD
A4146
Milebarn Farm
Gade Plas
COMMON RD
STUDHAM LA
CH
Whipsnade Park Golf Course
Whipsnade Wildlife Animal Park
Miniature Rly
JINX LA
HUMPHREY LA BOX
P
Woodfield Paddock
Cut Throat Paddock
Dagnall Paddock
VALLEY CL
Holly Frindle Paddock
SIR PETER'S WAY
CUT THROAT AVE
Hallcraft
Lay Meadow
MISS JOAN'S RIDE
Spicers Field
ESCARPMENT AVE
CENTRAL AVE
Central Paddock
Round Close
DUKES AVE
B4540
Dell Farm
P
Wood Lawn
The Green
B4540
STUDHAM LA

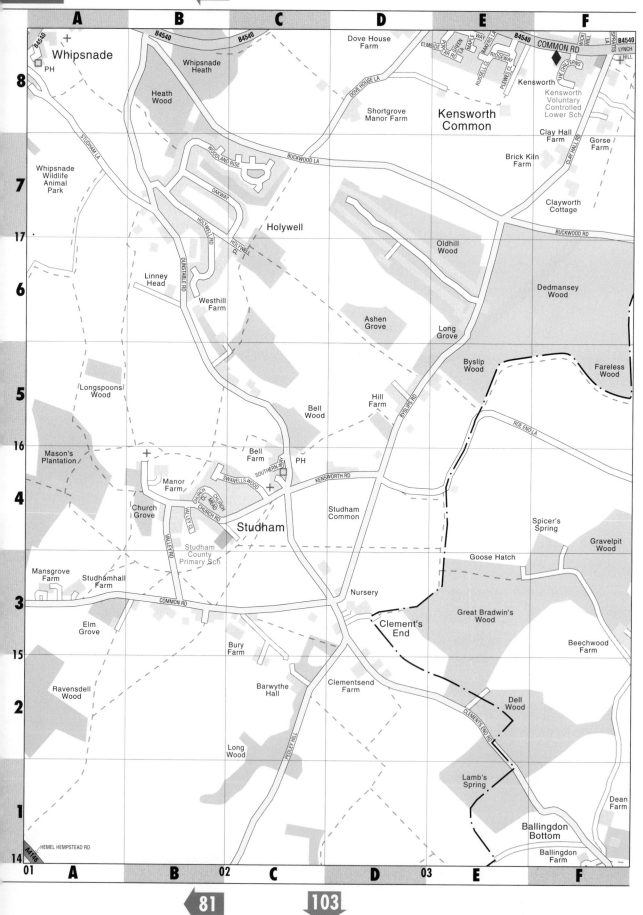

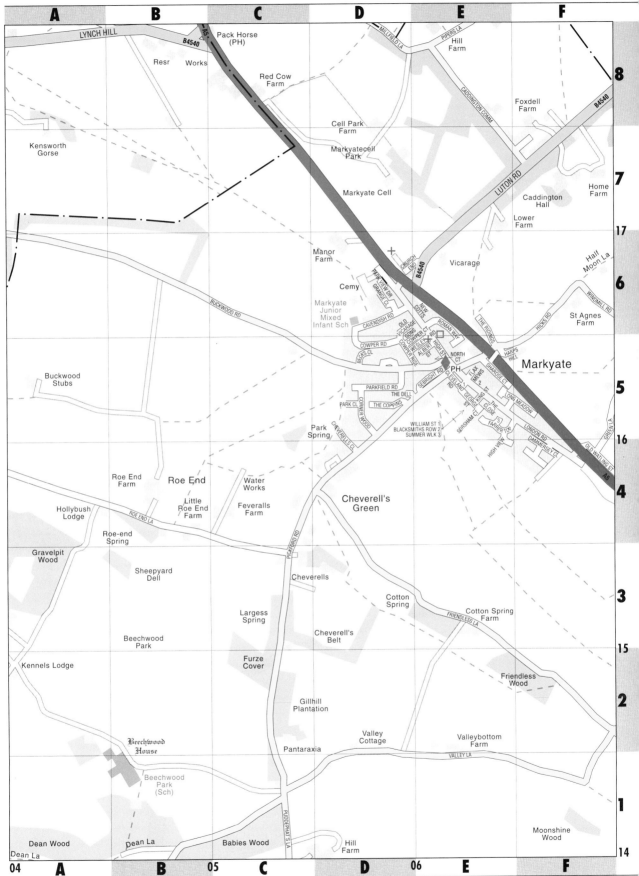

A   B   C   D   E   F

LYNCH HILL

B4540

Pack Horse (PH)

Resr   Works

Red Cow Farm

MILLFIELD LA

PIPERS LA

Hill Farm

8

Kensworth Gorse

Cell Park Farm

Markyatecell Park

Foxdell Farm

CADDINGTON COMM

LUTON RD

B4540

Markyate Cell

Home Farm

7

Caddington Hall

17

Lower Farm

Manor Farm

CHURCH END

B4540

Vicarage

Half Moon La

6

Cemy

PARK VIEW DR
GRANGE CL

NEW COTTS

ROMAN WAY

WINDMILL RD

HICKS RD

St Agnes Farm

Markyate Junior Mixed Infant Sch

CAVENDISH RD

OLD VICARAGE
COTTS
WESLEY CT
COWPER CT

ALBERT ST

HIGH ST

THE RIDINGS

BUCKWOOD RD

COWPER RD

BECKS CL

COPPER TREE

NORTH CT

PH

HARPS HILL

Markyate

Buckwood Stubs

PARKFIELD RD

THE DELL

THE COPPINS

SEBRIGHT RD

FLAX MEWS

CLEVELAND RD

GEORGE ST

KING ST

SHARPSE CT

LONG MEADOW

5

PARK CL

CORNER WOOD

THE CLOSE

16

Park Spring

CHEVERELL'S CL

WILLIAM ST 1
BLACKSMITHS ROW 2
SUMMER WLK 3

SURSHAM CT

HIGH WEST

FARPER LOS

LONDON RD

DAMMERSEY CL

OLD WATLING ST

GREEN LA

A5

Roe End Farm

Water Works

Cheverell's Green

4

Roe End

Little Roe End Farm

Feveralls Farm

Hollybush Lodge

ROE END LA

Roe-end Spring

Gravelpit Wood

Sheepyard Dell

PICKFORD RD

Cheverells

Cotton Spring

Cotton Spring Farm

3

Largess Spring

FRIENDLESS LA

Beechwood Park

Cheverell's Belt

15

Kennels Lodge

Furze Cover

Friendless Wood

2

Gillhill Plantation

Beechwood House

Valley Cottage

Valleybottom Farm

Pantaraxia

VALLEY LA

Beechwood Park (Sch)

PUDDEPHAT'S LA

1

Moonshine Wood

Dean Wood

Dean La

Dean La

Babies Wood

Hill Farm

14

04   A   B   05   C   D   06   E   F

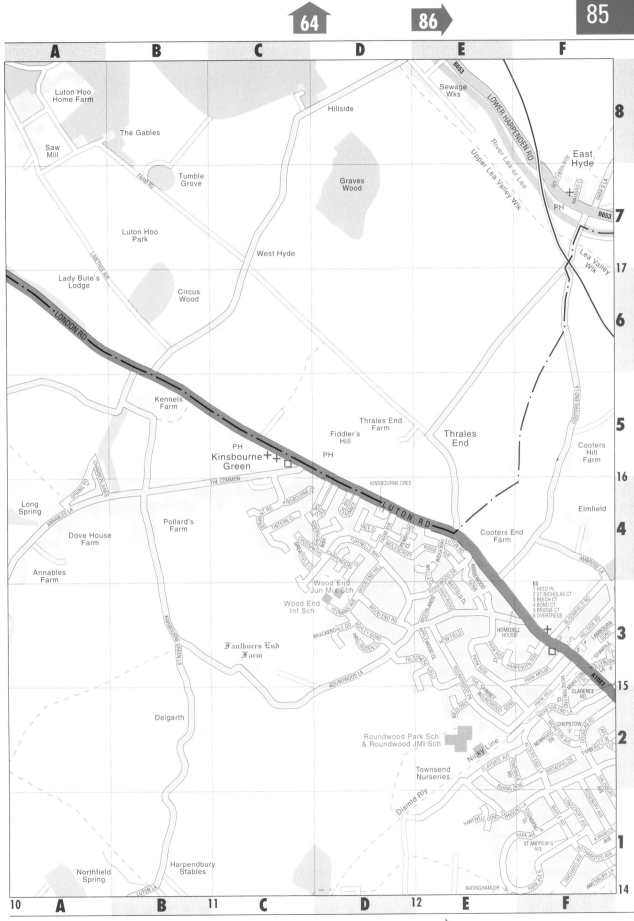

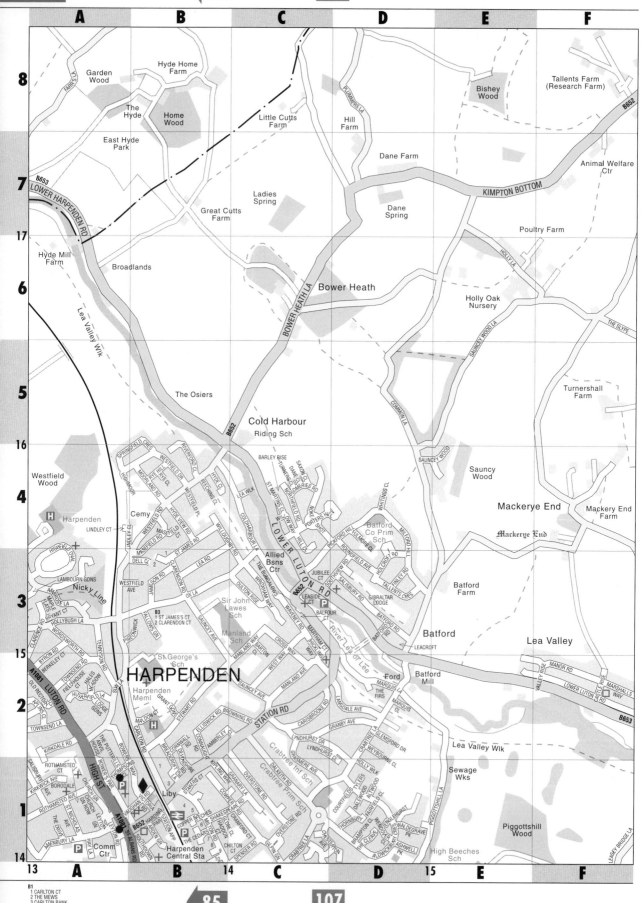

B1
1 CARLTON CT
2 THE MEWS
3 CARLTON BANK
4 COLERIDGE CT
5 BEAUMONT CT
6 MILTON CT
7 YARDLEY CT
8 SHELLEY CT
9 AVON CT
10 FURZEDOWN CT

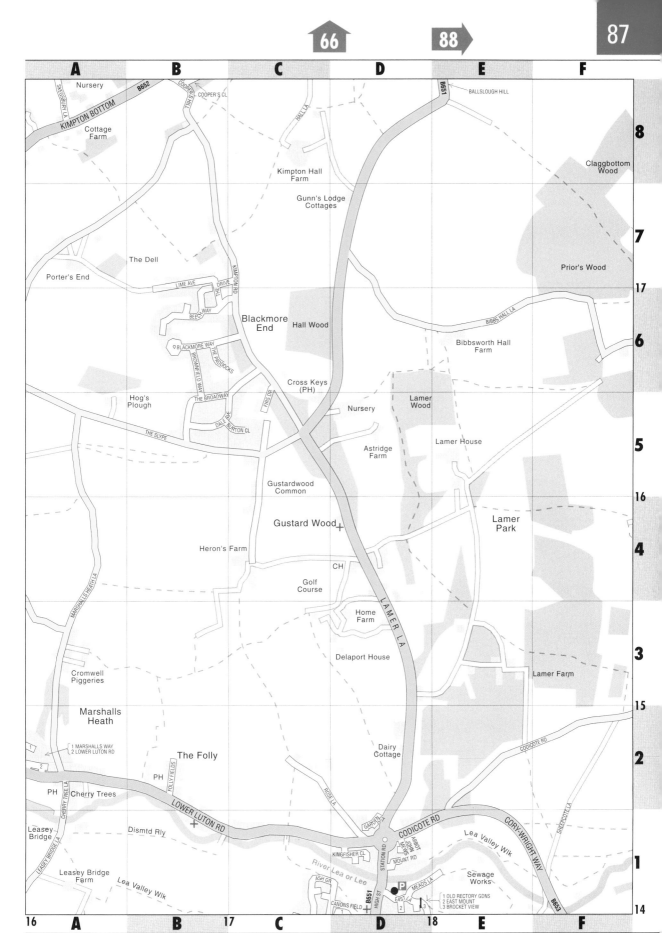

A B C D E F

8

7

17

6

5

16

4

3

15

2

1

14

19 A B 20 C D 21 E F

Codicote Bottom

POYNDERS MEADOW 1
THE OPENING 2
NEW TOWN 3

HIGH ST

B656

COWARDS LA

WINCH CL

THE RUDDY

Three Hills

Bottom Farm

Ayot Lodge

Long Valley

ST ALBANS RD

Chalk Pit

Abbotshay

Hollowdane Spring

TANYARD LA

Brimstone Wood

Ayot Park

LORD MEAD LA

River Mimram

Ayot House

HAMPTON RD

BIBBS HALL LA

PH

Ayot Farm

Shaw's Corner

Ayot St Lawrence

Pulmer Water

Harepark Spring

Norfolk Cottages

BRIDE HALL LA

HILL FARM LA

Hill Farm

Ryefield Farm

Bride Hall

Linces Spring

Hurstling's Wood

Round Spring

Little Norfolk Wood

Stocking Springs

CODICOTE RD

Dowdell's Wood

Ayot Bury

AYOT ST PETER RD

Great Norfolk Wood

Fish Wood

Ayot St Peter

War Meml

Scratching Grove

Threegroves Wood

Warren Wood

Ayot Place

Saul's Wood

Cherrytree Spring

Coneydell Spring

Bladder Wood

Ayot Greenway

Robinson's Wood

Hunter's Bridge

Manor Farm

AYOT LITTLE GREEN LA

WATEREND LA

River Lea or Lee

Lea Valley Wlk

Sparrowhall Bridge

Sparrowhall Farm

James's Wood

Bowle's Wood

Ayot Little Green

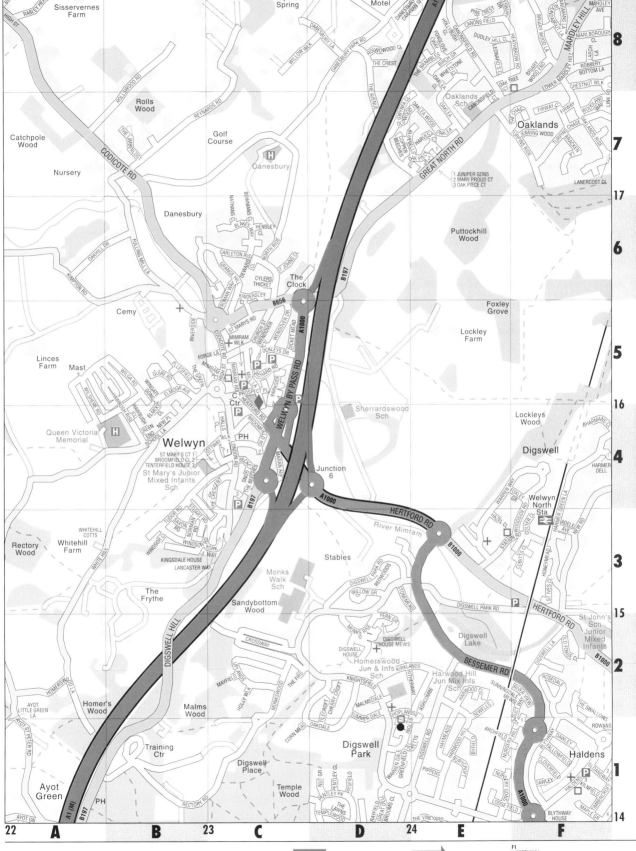

F1
1 NORTHWAY
2 FLEXLEY WOOD
3 HALDENS HOUSE
4 RUNSLEY

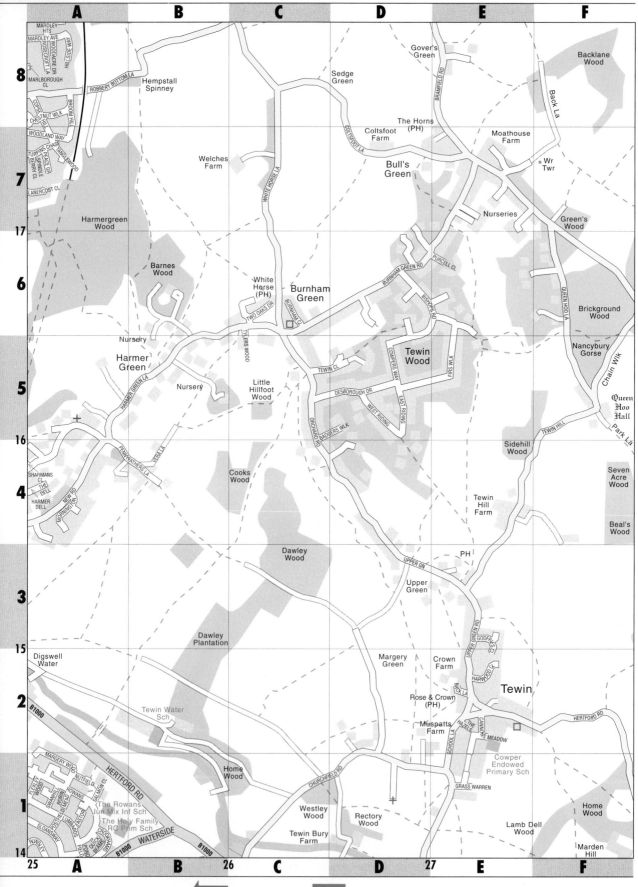

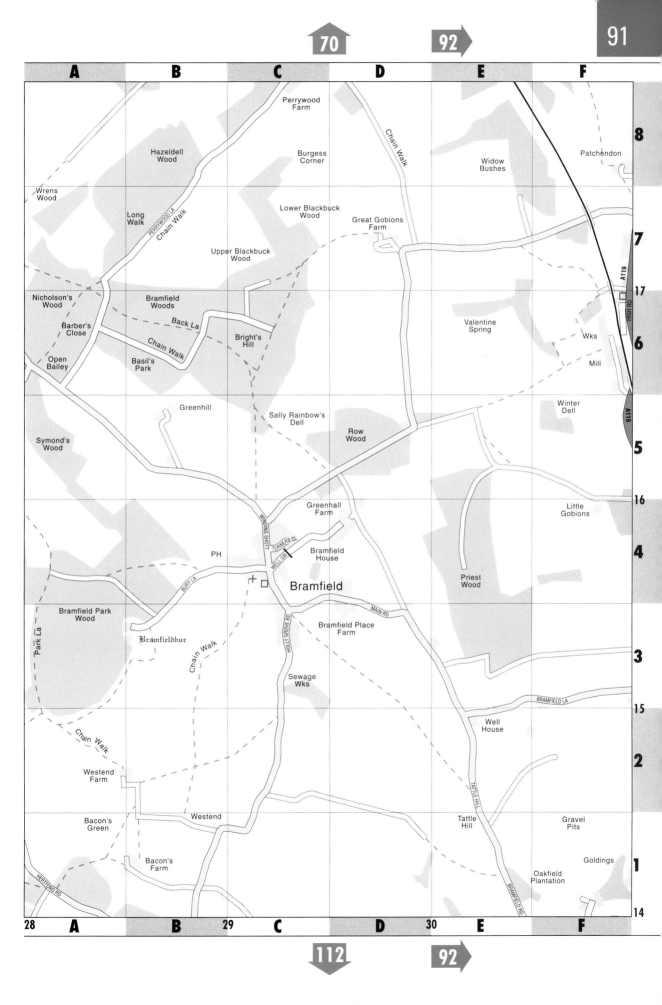

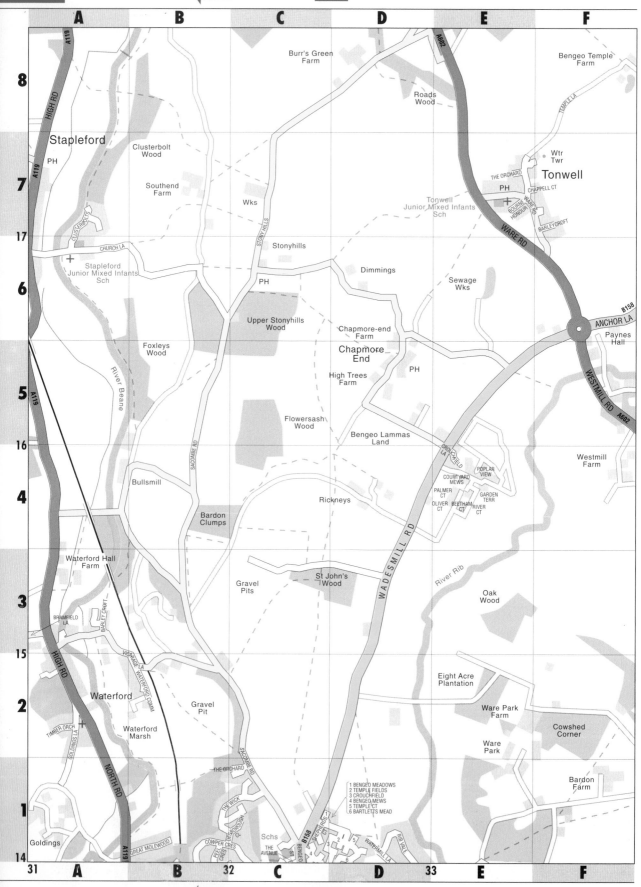

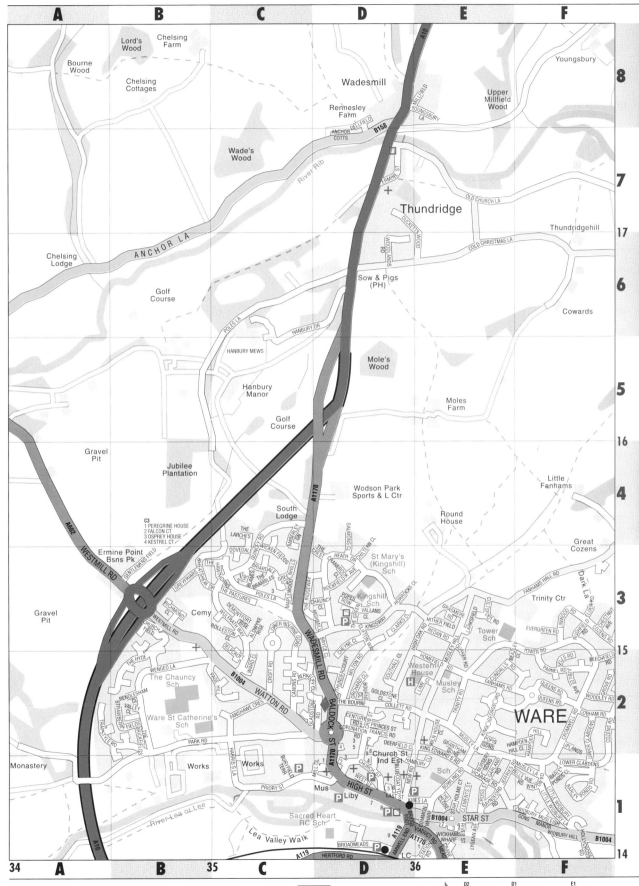

D2
1 THUNDER HALL
2 THE BAKERY
3 ROKEWOOD MEWS
4 WAGGONERS YD
5 ST EVROUL CT
6 HARTFIELD CT
7 MONKS ROW
8 CAMERON CT
9 THE ALBION

D1
1 BLACK SWAN CT
2 CHURCH ROW MEWS
3 ST MARY'S CTYD
4 OMEGA CT
5 LEASIDE WLK
6 DOLPHIN YD
7 RIVERSIDE MEWS
8 WELLS YD
9 BECKETS WLK

E1
1 MILLACRES
2 OMEGA MALTINGS
3 ALBANY MEWS

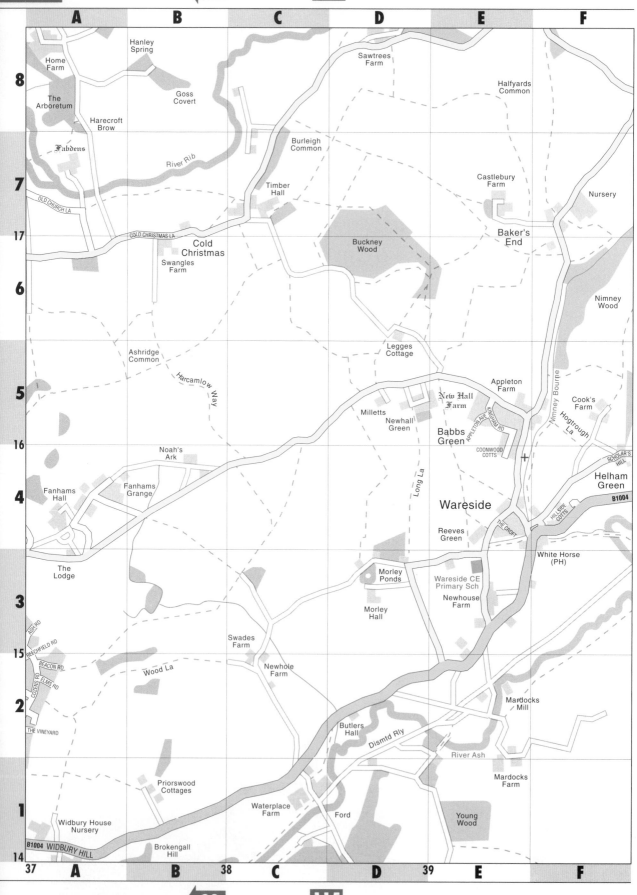

A B C D E F

8

Home Farm
Hanley Spring
The Arboretum
Goss Covert
Harecroft Brow
Fabdens
River Rib
Sawtrees Farm
Halfyards Common

7

OLD CHURCH LA
COLD CHRISTMAS LA
Timber Hall
Burleigh Common
Castlebury Farm
Nursery

17

Cold Christmas
Swangles Farm
Buckney Wood
Baker's End

6

Nimney Wood

5

Ashridge Common
Harcamlow Way
Legges Cottage
New Hall Farm
Appleton Farm
Nimney Bourne
Cook's Farm
Hogtrough La
Milletts
Newhall Green
Babbs Green
KINGHAM RD
APPLETON AVE

16

Noah's Ark
COONWOOD COTTS
SCHOLAR'S HILL
Helham Green

4

Fanhams Hall
Fanhams Grange
Long La
Wareside
HILL SIDE COTTS
B1004
Reeves Green
THE CROFT
White Horse (PH)

3

The Lodge
Morley Ponds
Wareside CE Primary Sch
Newhouse Farm
Morley Hall

15

ASH RD
BEECHFIELD RD
BEACON RD
COZENS RD
ELMS RD
Swades Farm
Newhole Farm
Mardocks Mill

2

THE VINEYARD
Wood La
Butlers Hall
Dismtd Rly
River Ash
Mardocks Farm

1

Priorswood Cottages
Widbury House Nursery
Waterplace Farm
Ford
Young Wood

14

B1004 WIDBURY HILL
Brokengall Hill

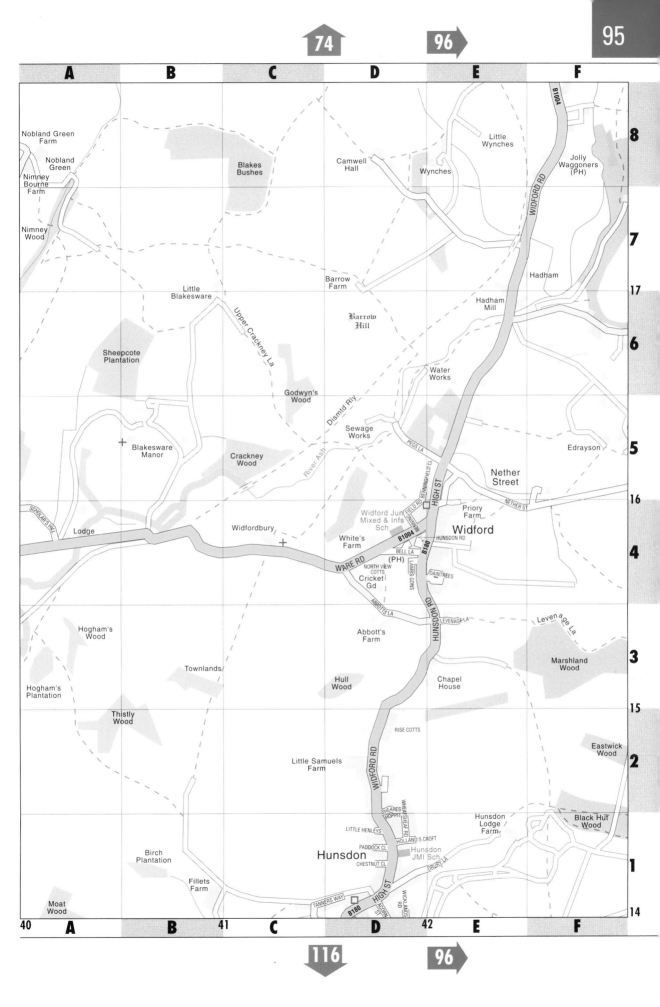

A   B   C   D   E   F

8

Nobland Green Farm

Nobland Green

Little Wynches

Blakes Bushes

Camwell Hall

Wynches

Jolly Waggoners (PH)

B1004

WIDFORD RD

Nimney Bourne Farm

7

Nimney Wood

Hadham

Little Blakesware

Barrow Farm

17

Hadham Mill

Sheepcote Plantation

Upper Crackney La

Barrow Hill

6

Godwyn's Wood

Water Works

Dismtd Rly

Edrayson

5

Blakesware Manor

Crackney Wood

River Ash

Sewage Works

PEGS LA

Nether Street

NETHER ST

SCHOLAR'S WK

Lodge

Widfordbury

Widford Jun Mixed & Infs Sch

FIELD RD

BENNINGFIELD CL

HIGH ST

Priory Farm

Widford

16

White's Farm

B1004

B180

HUNSDON RD

4

WARE RD

BELL LA (PH)

NORTH VIEW COTTS

LAMBS GDNS

DAINTREES

Cricket Gd

ABBOTT'S LA

HUNSDON RD

LEVENAGE LA

Levenage La

Hogham's Wood

Abbott's Farm

Marshland Wood

3

Townlands

Hull Wood

Chapel House

15

Hogham's Plantation

Eastwick Wood

Thistly Wood

RISE COTTS

2

WIDFORD RD

Little Samuels Farm

Hunsdon Lodge Farm

Black Hut Wood

Birch Plantation

SHEARES RD

WHEATSHEAF RD

SHOPPIT

LITTLE HENLEYS

HOLLAND'S CROFT

Hunsdon

Hunsdon JMI Sch.

1

PADDOCK CL

Fillets Farm

CHESTNUT CL

DRURY LA

Moat Wood

TANNERS WAY

B180

HIGH ST

ACORN

WICKLANDS RD

14

40   A   B   41   C   D   42   E   F

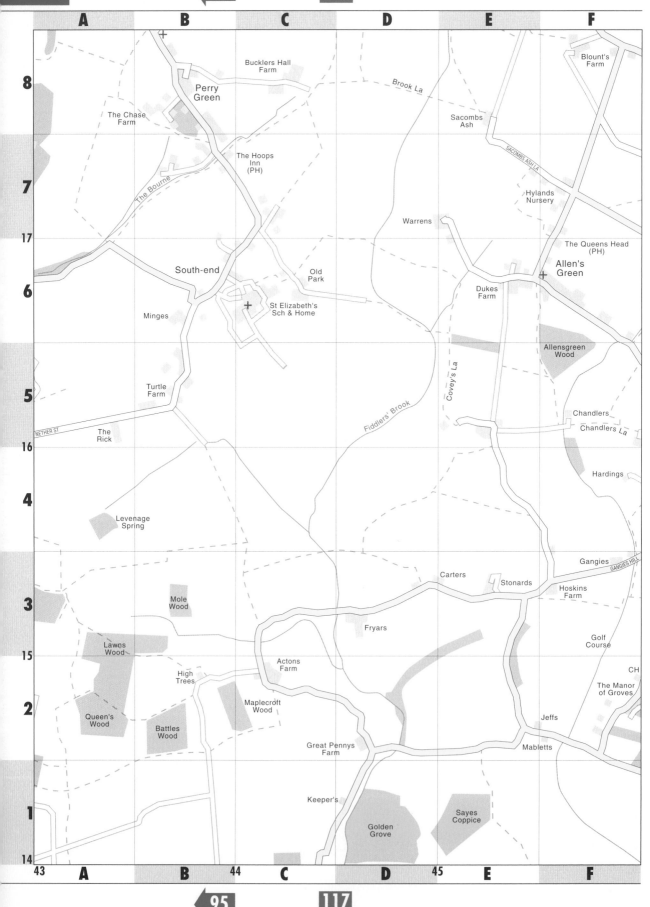

95
75

A B C D E F

Blount's
Farm

8

Bucklers Hall
Farm

Brook La

Perry
Green

Sacombs
Ash

The Chase
Farm

SACOMBS ASH LA

7

The Hoops
Inn
(PH)

The Bourne

Hylands
Nursery

Warrens

17

The Queens Head
(PH)

South-end

Old
Park

Allen's
Green

6

St Elizabeth's
Sch & Home

Dukes
Farm

Minges

Allensgreen
Wood

Turtle
Farm

Covey's La

5

Chandlers

Fiddlers' Brook

Chandlers La

NETHER ST

The
Rick

16

Hardings

4

Levenage
Spring

Gangies

GANGIES HILL

Carters

Stonards

Hoskins
Farm

Mole
Wood

3

Fryars

Golf
Course

15

Lawns
Wood

Actons
Farm

CH

High
Trees

The Manor
of Groves

Maplecroft
Wood

2

Queen's
Wood

Jeffs

Battles
Wood

Mabletts

Great Pennys
Farm

Keeper's

1

Sayes
Coppice

Golden
Grove

14

43 A 44 B C 44 D 45 E F

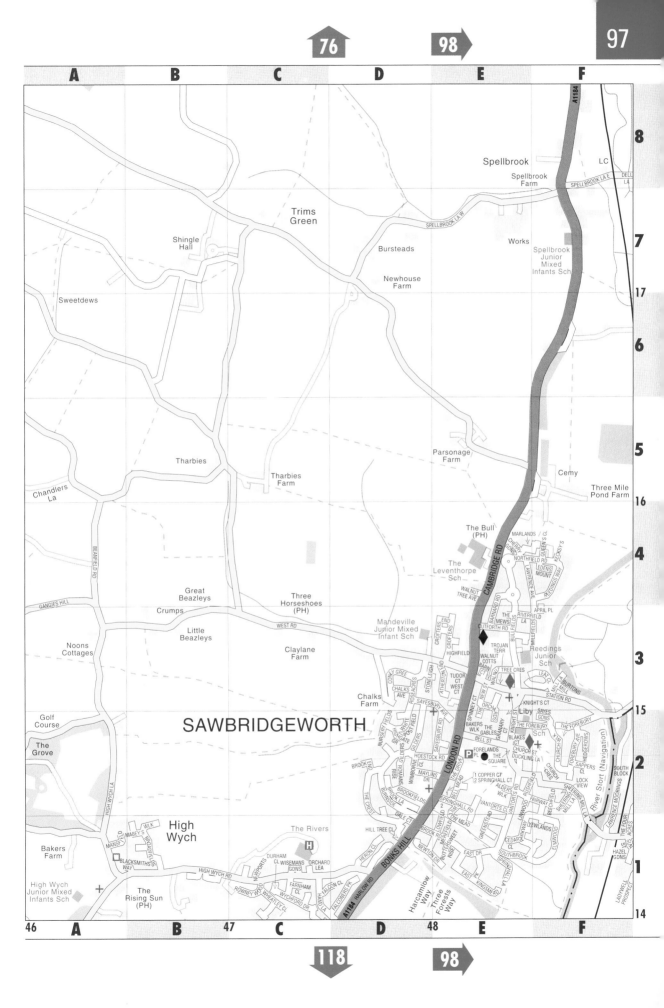

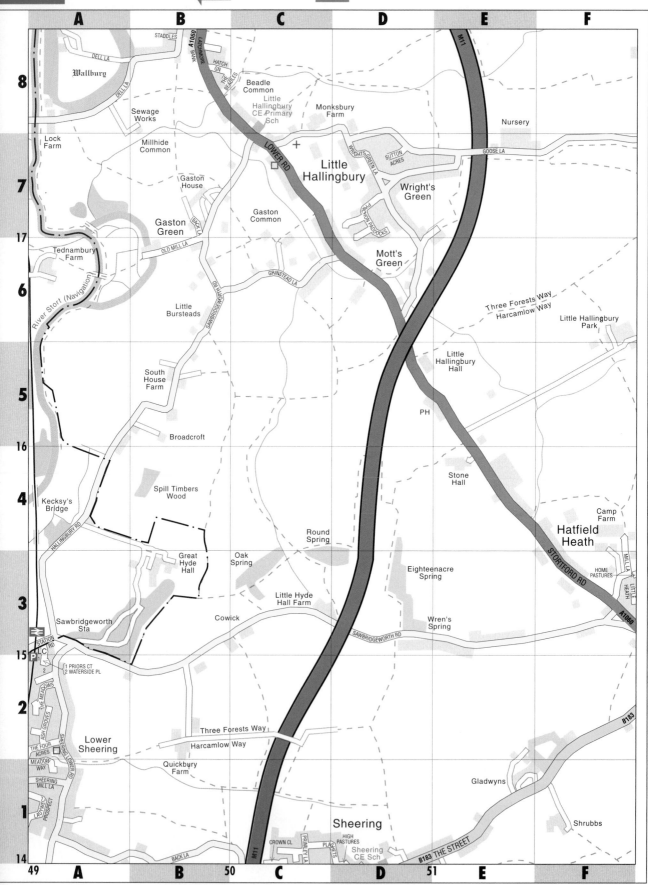

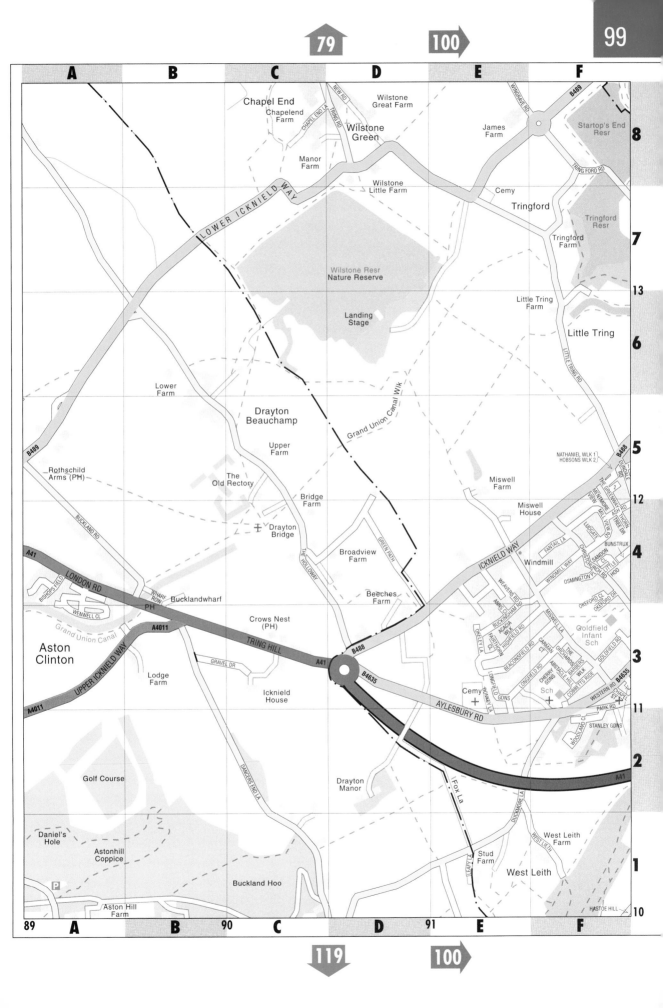

99
80

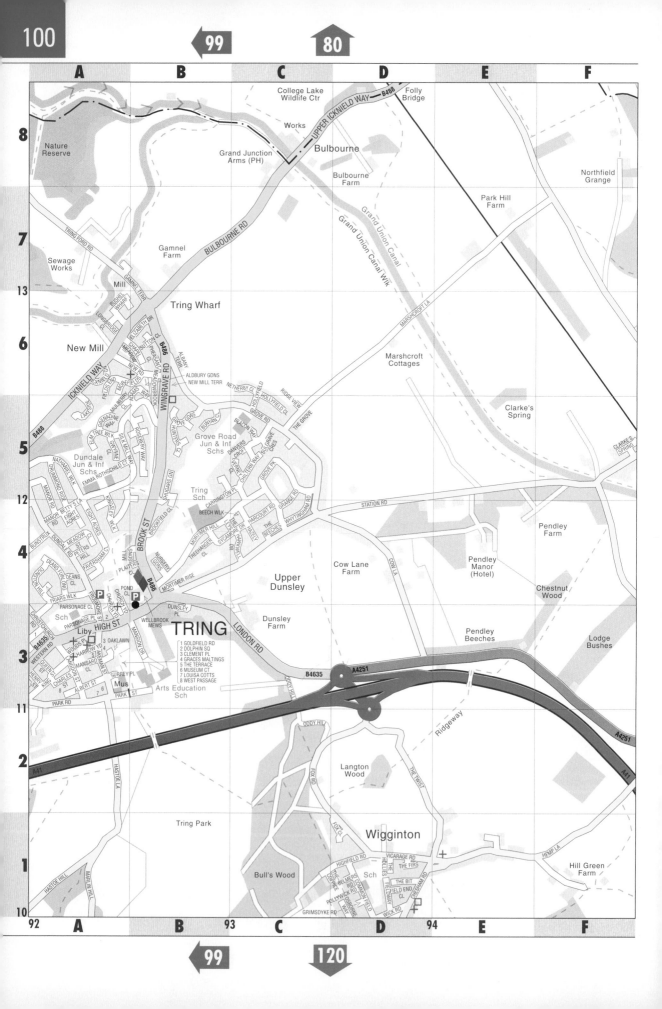

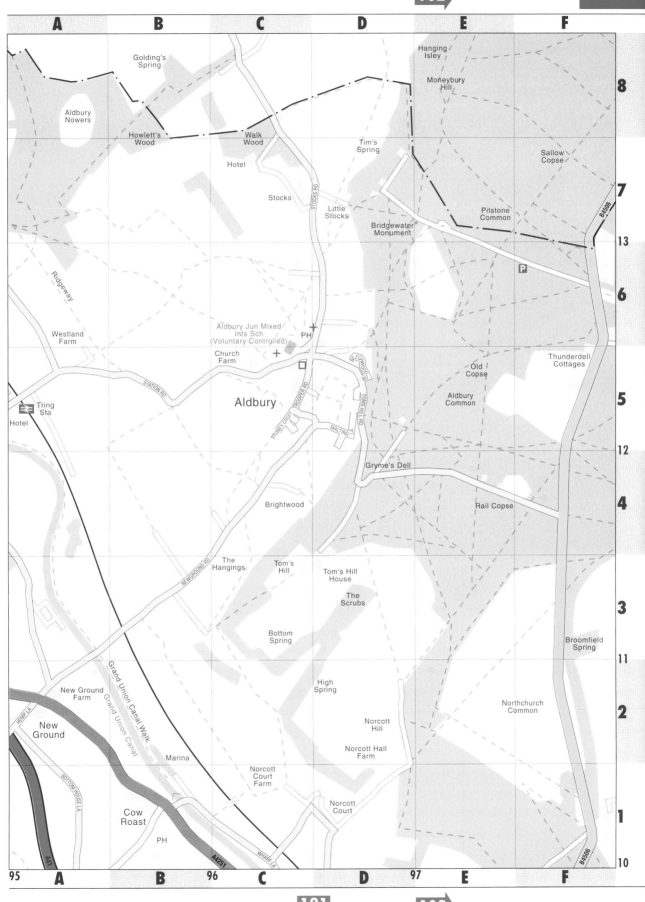

101
81

A B C D E F

8

Badger Wood

Church Farm

B4506

ALDERTON DR

Bridgewater CT

Bridgewater Arms (PH)

RUSSHALL DR

GATESDENE CL

BEDE CT

CHURCH RD

Little Gaddesden C of E Sch

Hudnall Common Plantation

7

Pitstone Park Copse

B4506

Little Gaddesden

Hudnall LA

Hudnall Common

Hudnall

13

Ashridge

CH

Hudnall Farm

6

Old Park Lodge

Golf Course

Ashridge Park

Golden Valley

CHAPEL CL

Robin Hood Farm

Little Brownlow Farm

Prince's Riding

The Rookery

Little Gaddesden House

5

Thunderdell Wood

Home Farm

Lady Grove

12

Ashridge Management Coll

Cromer Wood

CROMER CL

CROMER CL

NETTLEDEN RD

4

Woodyard Cottage

Harding's Rookery

Berkhamstead Common

Pulridge Wood

3

Little Coldharbour Farm

Coldharbour Spring

Coldharbour Farm

Golden Valley Farm

11

Furzefield Wood

Nettleden Lodge

2

Ashridge

Webb's Copse

Bluebell Spring

Brickkiln Cottage

Frithsden Beeches

Frithsden Gardens

1

Golf Course

10

98 A 99 B C 00 D E F

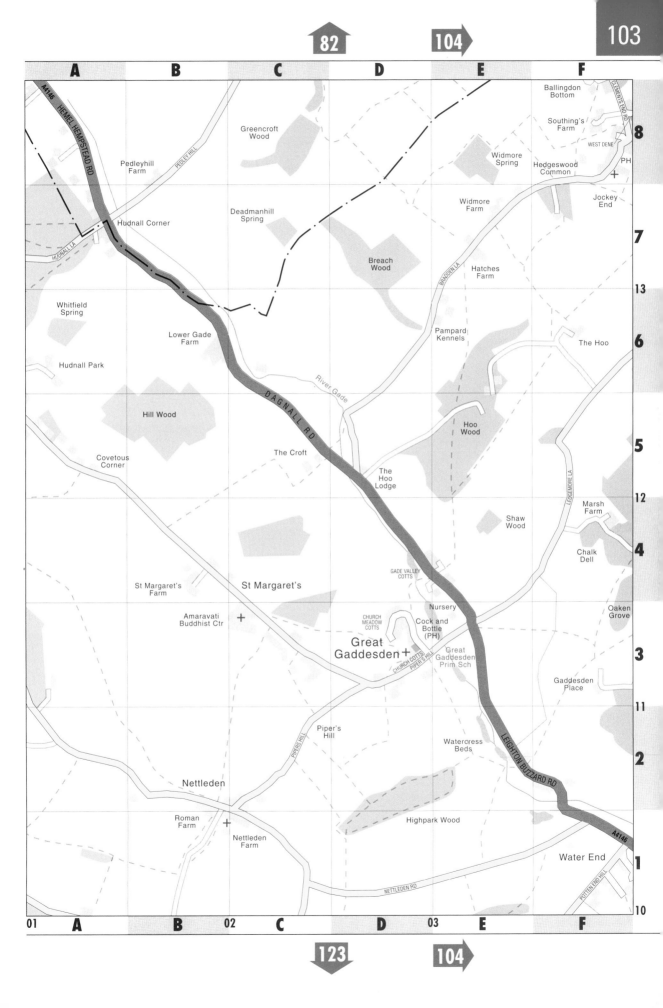

A B C D E F

A4146

HEMEL HEMPSTEAD RD

Ballingdon
Bottom

CLEMENTS END RD

Southing's
Farm

WEST DENE

Greencroft
Wood

Widmore
Spring

Hedgeswood
Common

PH

Pedleyhill
Farm

PEDLEY HILL

Jockey
End

Deadmanhill
Spring

Widmore
Farm

Hudnall Corner

HUDNALL LA

BRADDEN LA

Hatches
Farm

Breach
Wood

Whitfield
Spring

Pampard
Kennels

The Hoo

Lower Gade
Farm

River Gade

Hudnall Park

DAGNALL RD

Hoo
Wood

Hill Wood

LEDGEMORE LA

The Croft

Marsh
Farm

Covetous
Corner

The
Hoo
Lodge

Shaw
Wood

Chalk
Dell

GADE VALLEY
COTTS

St Margaret's
Farm

St Margaret's

Nursery

Oaken
Grove

Amaravati
Buddhist Ctr

CHURCH
MEADOW
COTTS

Cock and
Bottle
(PH)

Great
Gaddesden

CHURCH COTTS

Great
Gaddesden
Prim Sch

Gaddesden
Place

PIPER'S HILL

Piper's
Hill

PIPERS HILL

Watercress
Beds

LEIGHTON BUZZARD RD

Nettleden

Highpark Wood

Roman
Farm

Water End

Nettleden
Farm

A4146

NETTLEDEN RD

POTTEN END HILL

103
83

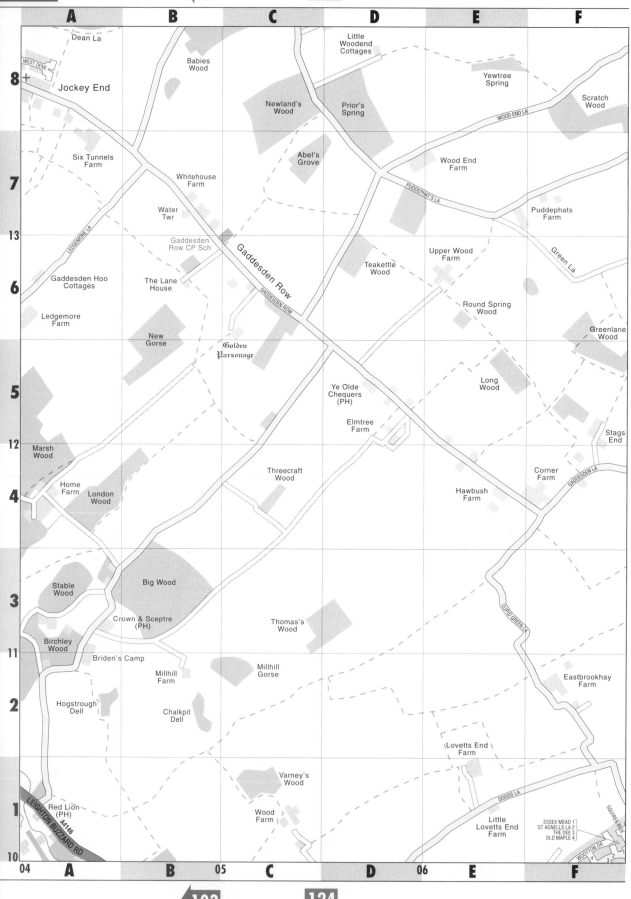

103
124

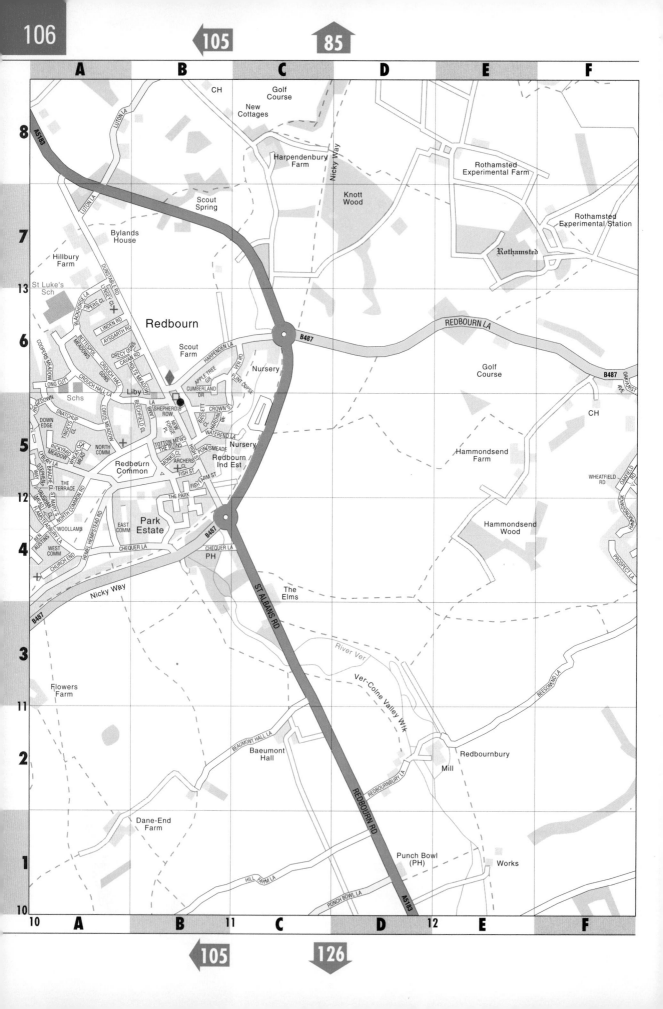

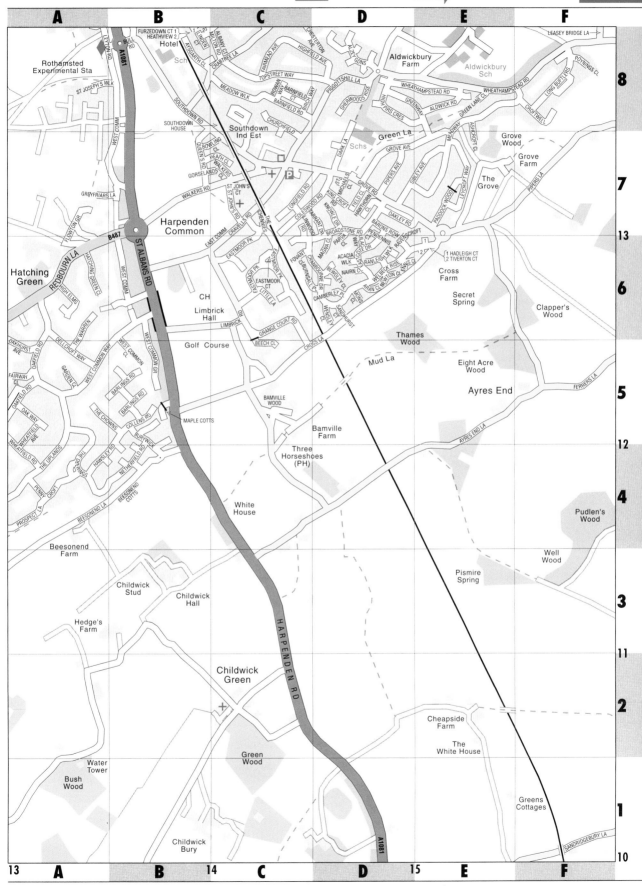

86
108
127
108

Map labels

Rothamsted Experimental Sta
St Joseph's Wlk
Greyfriars La
Hatching Green
High Elms
Redbourn La
Hatching Green Cl
Flowton Gr
West Comm
West Common
B487
St Albans Rd
A1081
Leyton Rd
Bull Rd
Furzedown Ct 1
Heathview 2
Hotel
Sch
Linden Cl
Aysgarth Cl
Crabtree La
Milton Rd
Albany Ct
Southdown Rd
Southdown House
Meadow Wlk
Topstreet Way
Fairmead Rd
Chesterton Rd
Highfield Ave
Alley Gdns
Aldwickbury Farm
Aldwickbury Sch
Leasey Bridge La
Poynings Cl
Long Butlers
Croftwell
Wheatfield Rd
Wheatfield Ave
Oak Way
Oakfield Rd
Fairway Cl
Oakhurst Ave
Dellcroft Way
The Warren
Gardenia Cl
West Common Way
West Common Cl
Barlings Rd
Barlings Rd
Collens Rd
Burtwick
Netherfield Rd
Hansler Rd
The Chowns
The Crescent
The Uplands
Penny Croft
Skys Wood Rd
Prospect La
Beesonend La
Beesonend Cotts
Maple Cotts
Bamville Wood
Bamville Farm
Three Horseshoes (PH)
White House
Beesonend Farm
Childwick Stud
Childwick Hall
Hedge's Farm
Childwick Green
Childwick Bury
Green Wood
Water Tower
Bush Wood
Southdown Ind Est
Barnfield Cl
Barnfield Rd
Churchfield
Piggottshill La
High Firs Cres
Sherwoods Rise
Green La
Wheathampstead Rd
Greenway
Green Lane Cl
Aldwick Rd
Ashcroft Cl
Wheathampstead Rd
Grove Wood
Grove Farm
The Grove
Pipers Rd
Grove Ave
Dark La
Schs
Pipers Ave
Sibley Ave
Meadway
Green La
Letchworth Way
Harpenden Common
East Comm
Gravels Rd
Eastmoor Pk
Eastmoor Rd
Eastmoor Ct
Little La
St John's Ct
Walkers Rd
Queen's Rd
Heath Cl
Gorselands
Gorsevale Cl
Bowling Cl
Walkers Cl
The Chennies
Longfield Rd
Coleswood Rd
Colwyn Cl
St Michael's St
King Croft Rd
Hawthorn Cl
Knowle Dr
Field Cl
Grove Rd
Oakley Rd
Tennant Rd
Paddock Rd
Barons Row
Broadstone Rd
Pendennis
Ravenscroft
Cross Farm
1 Hadleigh Ct
2 Tiverton Ct
Secret Spring
Clapper's Wood
Fovant
Crabtree La
Framingham Dr
Burnsall Cl
Bewley Cl
Nairn Cl
Magna Cl
Parva Cl
Acacia Wlk
Ranleigh Wlk
Webcock Rise
Alban Cl
Newton's Cl
Cleaves Cl
Camberley Pl
Wensley Cl
Sandhurst
CH
Limbrick Hall
Limbrick Rd
Golf Course
Grange Court Rd
Beech Cl
Cross La
Mud La
Thames Wood
Eight Acre Wood
Ayres End
Ferrers La
Ayres End La
Pismire Spring
Well Wood
Pudlen's Wood
Childwick Green
Harpenden Rd
Cheapside Farm
The White House
Greens Cottages
Sandridgebury La
A1081

Grid references

A B C D E F
8 7 13 6 5 12 4 3 11 2 1 10
13 14 15

107
87

A B C D E F

8

Wheathampstead Rd

Down Green House

Lea Valley Wlk

BURY GN
CHURCH ST
ST THOMAS'S
GRANARY CL
BROCKET VIEW
Marford Farm
The Nelson (PH)
B653
CORY-WRIGHT WAY

HARPENDEN RD
HIGH MEAD
BREWHOUSE HILL
ASH GR 1
OLD RECTORY GDNS 2
TOWN FARM 3
WALNUT CT 4
Sch
PARKINSON CL
Liby
NECTON RD
SHEEPCOTE LA

Poultry Farm

LATTIMORE RD
BARTON RD
WICK AVE
THE HILL
B651 HIGH ST
ST HELEN'S CL
FOUR LIMES
OFFAS WAY
GARRARD WAY
MARFORD RD
TUDOR RD
BATTLEVIEW

7

Pipers
PIPERS LA
AMWELL LA
HIGH ASH RD
BUTTERFIELD RD

Amwell

Wheathampstead Sch

Wheathampstead

CONQUERORS HILL
CAESARS RD
SAXON RD
NURSERIES RD
HEWITT CL
CEC CL
WRIGHT CL
HILL DYKE RD
VALE CT
DAVYS CL
HOUSDEN CL
SMALLWOOD CL
LAMB CT
Sch
BEECH CRES

Belgic Oppidum

13

Stocking Wood

Little Piggotts Wood

The Elephant & Castle (PH)
DOWN GREEN LA

Beech Hyde Farm
DYKE LA
BEECH HYDE LA

6

West Farm
BULL LA

Glen Nurseries

PH

Nomansland

Wicked Lady (PH)

Pearman's Spring

PH

5

P
FERRERS LA
P

Nomansland Common

Darblay

Coleman Green

12

Round Wood

Nomansland Farm

4

Hillend Farm

COLEMAN GREEN LA

Hammond's Farm Cottages

TOWER HILL LA

3

Hammond's Farm

HAMMONDS LA

11

Langley Wood

2

SANDRIDGEBURY LA
POUND CL
HIGH ST
SPENCER PL
LANGLEY GR
SHOTFIELD
Sandridge Junior Mixed Infant Sch
Fairshot Court

Harlowdell Spring

1

Sandridgebury

Sandridgebury Farm

The Green Man (PH)
HOPKINS CRES
CHURCH END
LYNDON MEAD
ST LEONARD'S CT
GILES CL
ANSON CL
Cemy
ST LEONARDS CRES
HOUSE LA
Harefield
WOODCOCK HILL
Mast

Fairfolds

10

B651
ST ALBANS RD
HIGHFIELD RD
NORTHSIDE
REYNOLDS CRES
JERSEY LA
GIBBONS CL

Sandridge

Wireless Station

Fairfold's Farm

16 A B 17 C D 18 E F

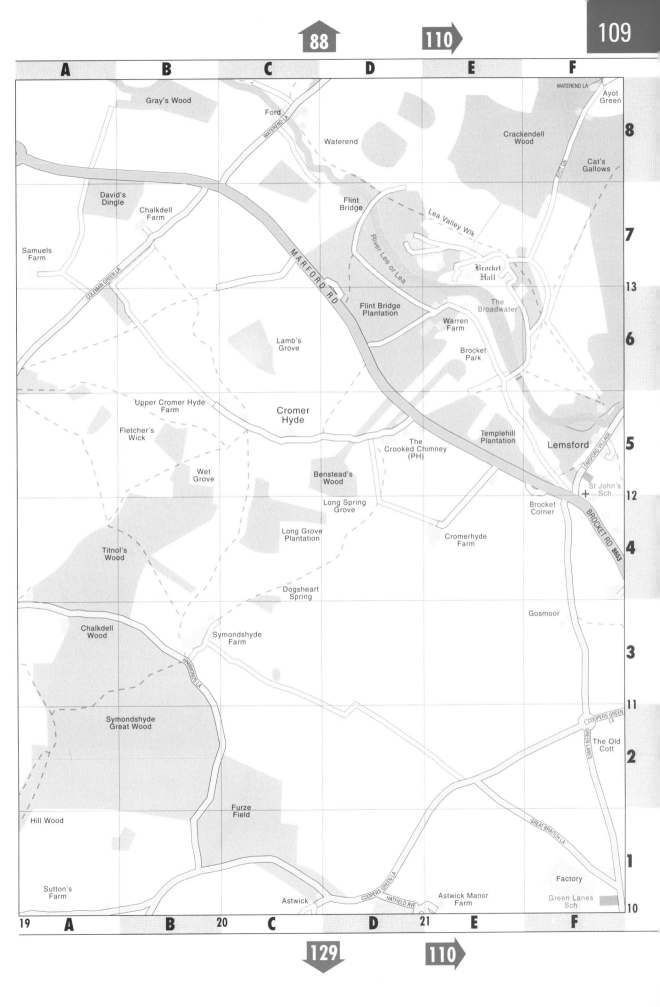

109
89

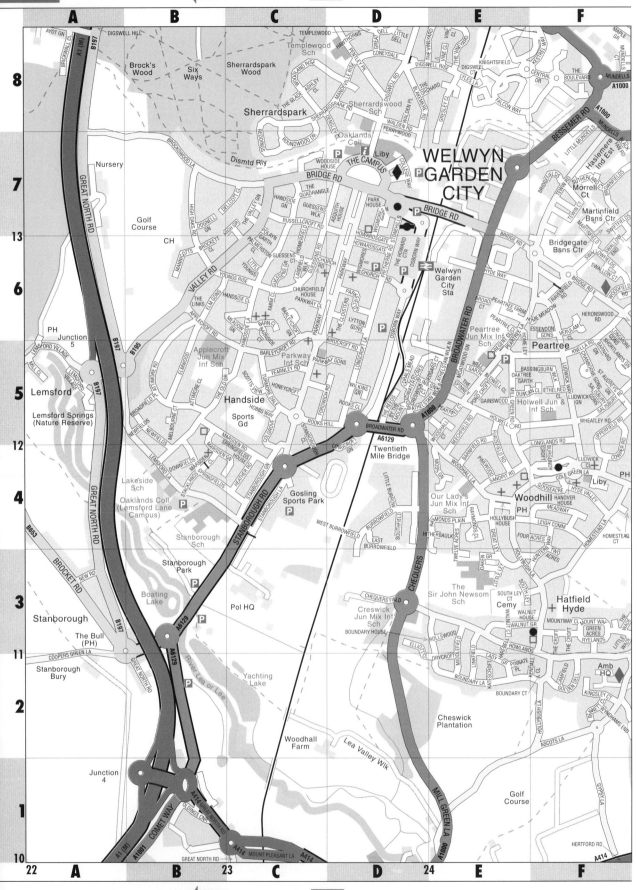

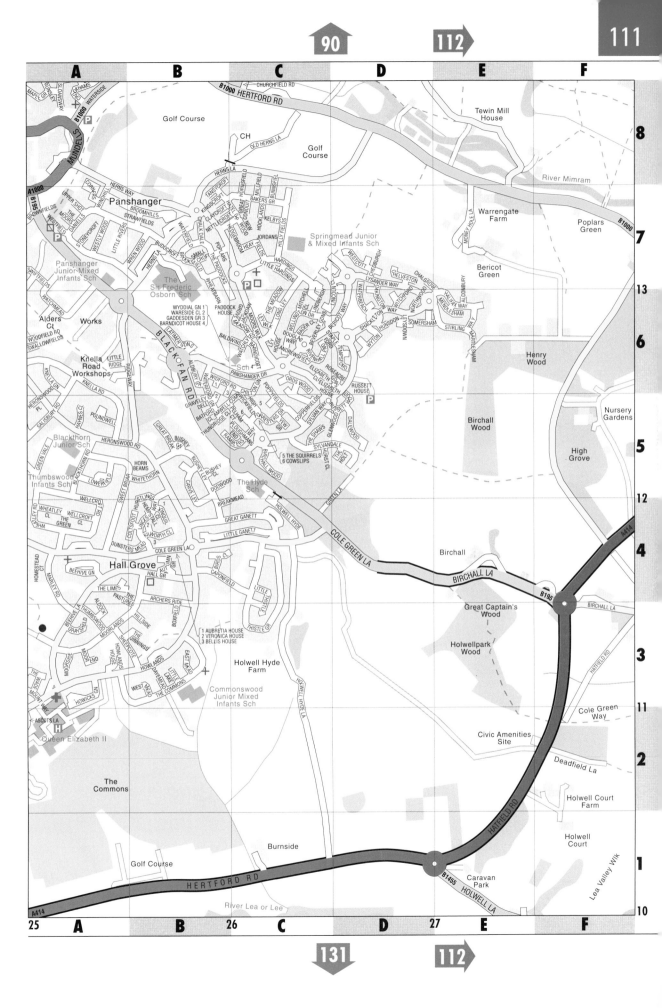

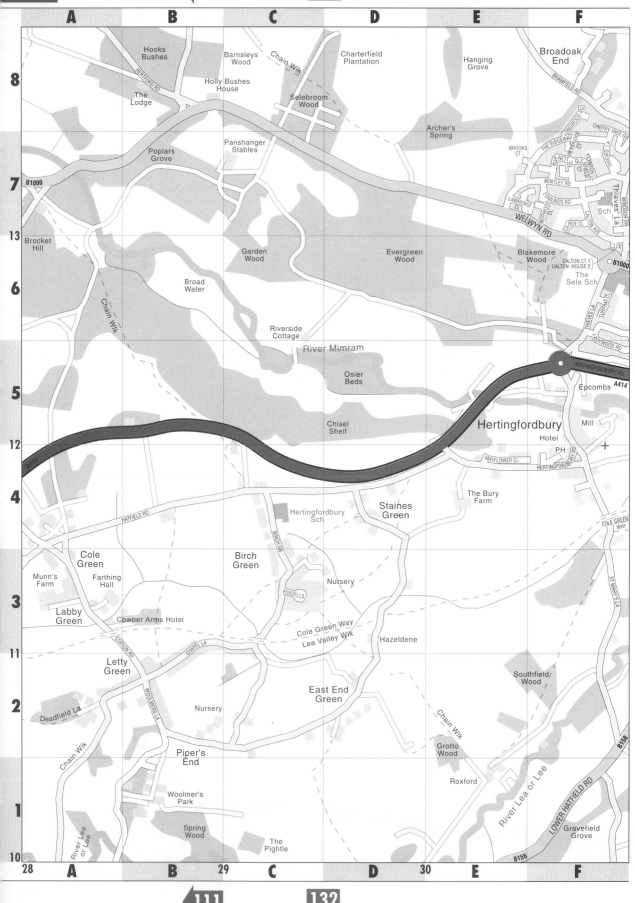

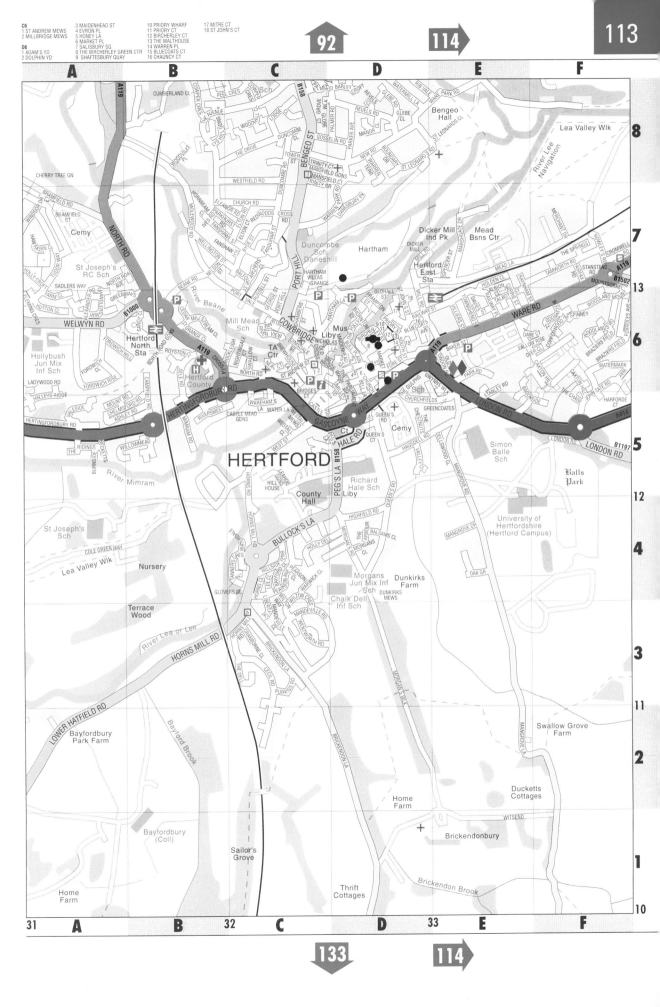

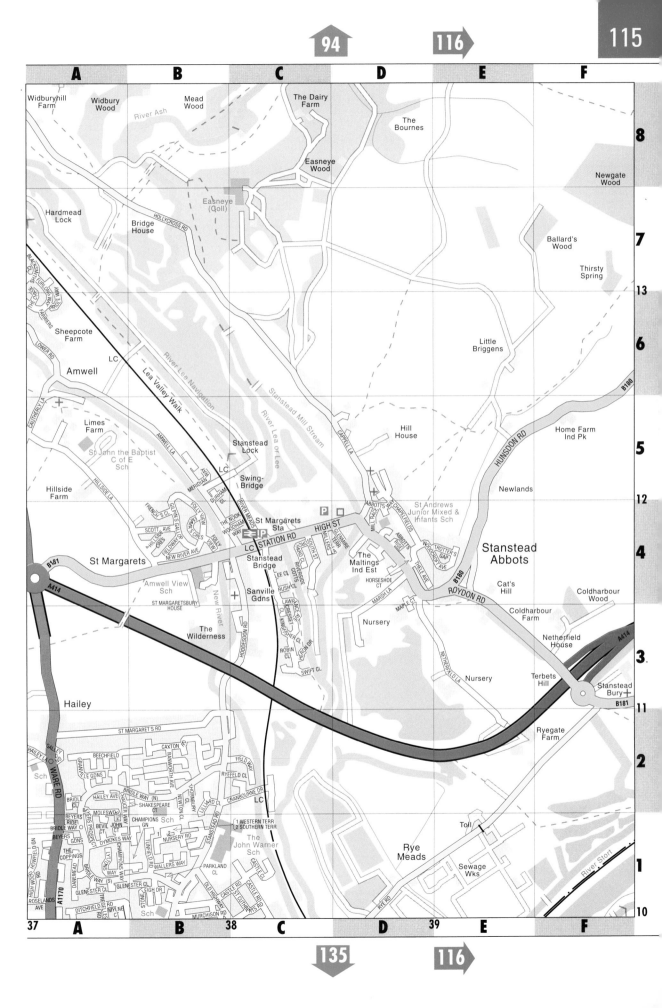

A B C D E F

8
7
13
6
12
5
4
3
11
2
1
10

40 A B 41 C D 42 E F

Moat Wood
Newgate Wood
Newgate Plantation
The Wilderness
Little Spellers
Spellers
Nine Ashes Farm
Tuck's Spring
Black Bushes
Bonningtons
Hunsdonbury
Copthall
Eastwick Hall Farm
Halfway House
HUNSDON RD
B180
Olives Farm
Bury Plantation
Hunsdon House
Square Spring
Hunsdon Brook
Cemy
Long Spring
Harcamlow Way
Lord's Wood
Brickhouse Farm
Pogden's Wood
A414
Briggens Home Farm
Hunsdon Mill House
Mead Lodge
A414
The Grove
Briggens Park
Eastwick Mead
Stanstead Bury Farm
Stanstead Lodge
Briggens House Hotel
Hunsdon Mead
B181
Golf Course
River Stort
Roydon Sta
LC
Three Forests Way
River Stort (Navigation)
Roydon Mead
Roydon Lea
LC
THE GRANARY
DICKETS MEAD
Roydon Lodge Chalet Est
Golf Course
Roydon Mill Leisure Pk (Caravan & Camping Pk)
Temple Farm
HIGH ST
FARM CL
Roydon
CHURCH MEAD
B181
TEMPLE MEAD
HARLOW RD
Mount Pleasant
East End Farm
Eastend
Barrows Farm
ROYDON RD
A1169
ELIZABETH WAY

TANNERS WAY
ST DUNSTAN'S RD
HIGH ST
TUDOR CL
WICKLANDS RD
RECTORY CL
B180
ACORN ST

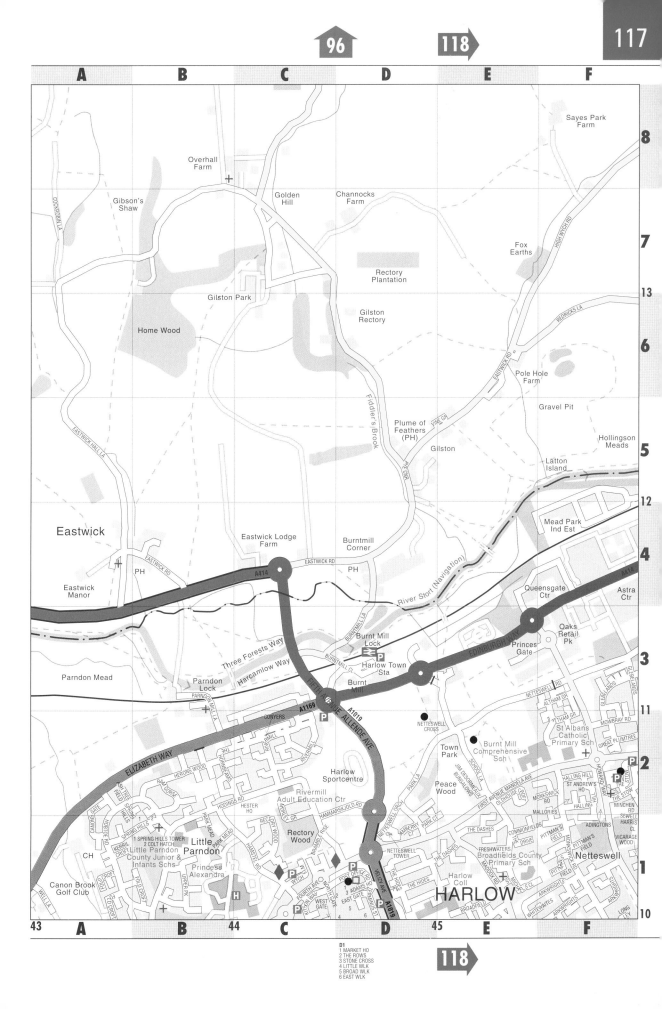

D1
1 MARKET HO
2 THE ROWS
3 STONE CROSS
4 LITTLE WLK
5 BROAD WLK
6 EAST WLK

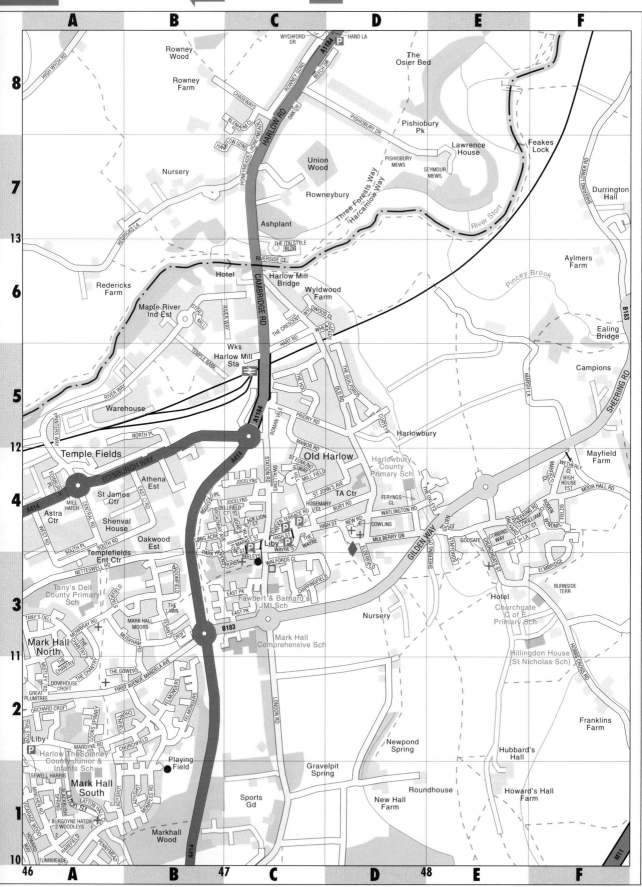

99
120

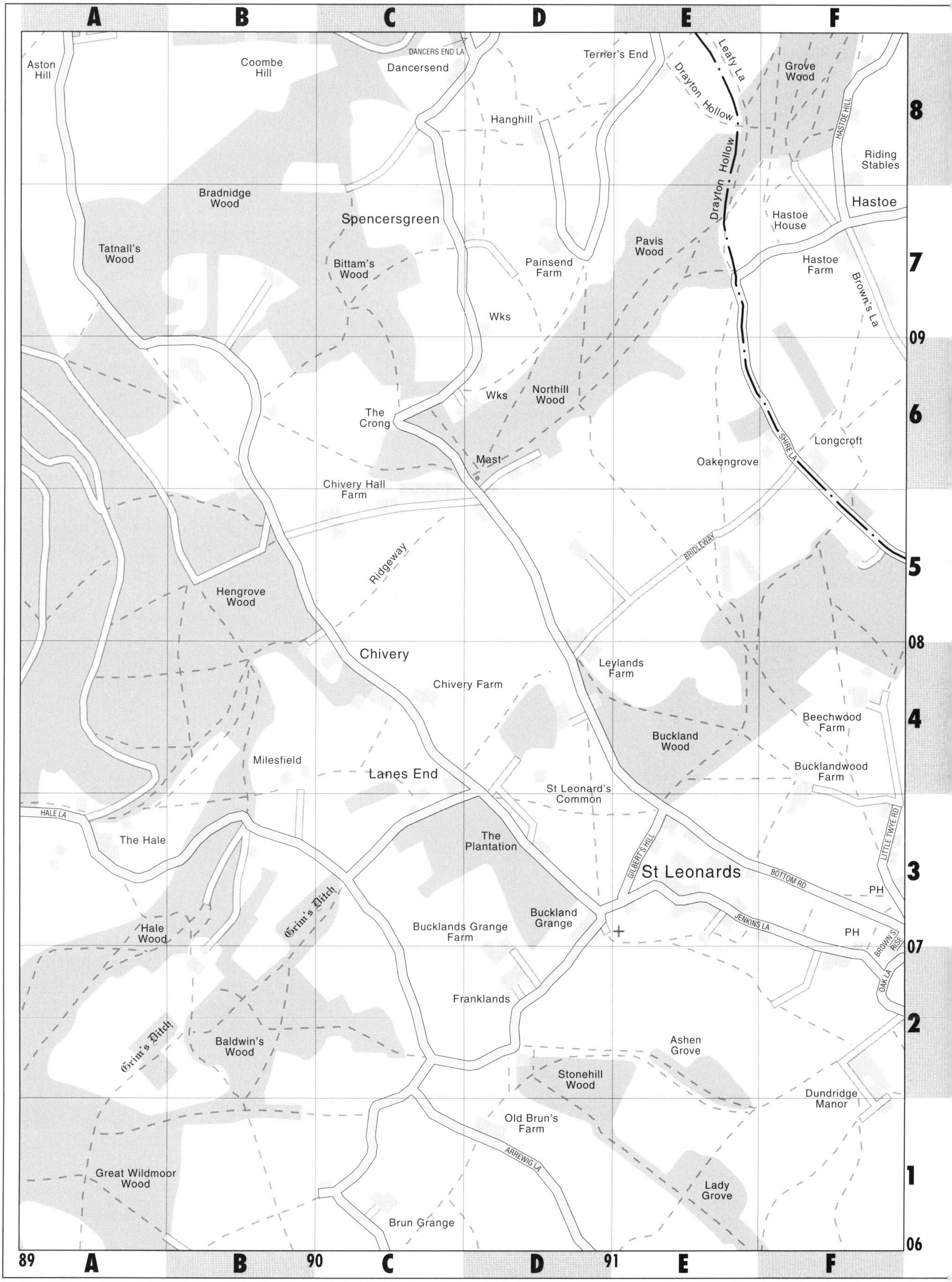
A
B
C
D
E
F
Aston Hill
Coombe Hill
DANCERS END LA
Dancersend
Terrier's End
Leafy La
Drayton Hollow
Grove Wood
HASTOE HILL
Hanghill
Riding Stables
Bradnidge Wood
Spencersgreen
Drayton Hollow
Hastoe
Hastoe House
Tatnall's Wood
Bittam's Wood
Painsend Farm
Pavis Wood
Hastoe Farm
Brown's La
Wks
Northill Wood
Wks
The Crong
Mast
Longcroft
SHIRE LA
Oakengrove
Chivery Hall Farm
Ridgeway
BRIDLEWAY
Hengrove Wood
Chivery
Leylands Farm
Chivery Farm
Beechwood Farm
Buckland Wood
Milesfield
Lanes End
Bucklandwood Farm
St Leonard's Common
HALE LA
LITTLE TWYE RD
The Hale
The Plantation
GILBERT'S HILL
St Leonards
BOTTOM RD
PH
Grim's Ditch
Buckland Grange
JENKINS LA
Hale Wood
Bucklands Grange Farm
PH
BROWN'S RISE
OAK LA
Franklands
Grim's Ditch
Baldwin's Wood
Ashen Grove
Stonehill Wood
Dundridge Manor
Old Brun's Farm
ARREWIG LA
Great Wildmoor Wood
Lady Grove
Brun Grange
8
7
09
6
5
08
4
3
07
2
1
06
89
90
91

120

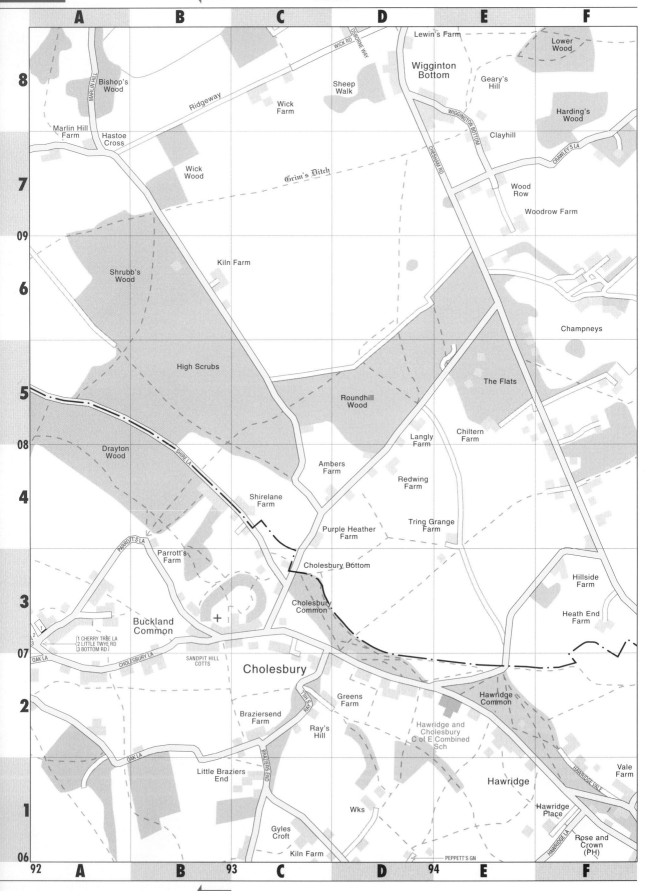

A B C D E F

8

Bishop's Wood

Marlin Hill

Ridgeway

Wick Farm

Sheep Walk

Wick Rd

Osborne Way

Lewin's Farm

Wigginton Bottom

Geary's Hill

Lower Wood

Harding's Wood

Marlin Hill Farm

Hastoe Cross

7

Wick Wood

Grim's Ditch

Chesham Rd

Wigginton Bottom

Clayhill

Crawley's La

Wood Row

Woodrow Farm

09

6

Shrubb's Wood

Kiln Farm

Champneys

High Scrubs

The Flats

5

Drayton Wood

Roundhill Wood

Langly Farm

Chiltern Farm

08

Shire La

Ambers Farm

Redwing Farm

4

Shirelane Farm

Purple Heather Farm

Tring Grange Farm

Parrott's La

Parrott's Farm

Cholesbury Bottom

Hillside Farm

3

Oak La

Buckland Common

1 CHERRY TREE LA
2 LITTLE TWYE RD
3 BOTTOM RD

Cholesbury Common

Cholesbury Common

Heath End Farm

07

Cholesbury La

SANDPIT HILL COTTS

Cholesbury

2

Braziersend Farm

Ray's Hill

Greens Farm

RAY'S HILL

Hawridge Common

Hawridge and Cholesbury C of E Combined Sch

Oak La

Braziers End

Little Braziers End

Wks

Hawridge

Hawridge Vale

Vale Farm

1

Gyles Croft

Hawridge Place

Hawridge La

Rose and Crown (PH)

06

Kiln Farm

PEPPETT'S GN

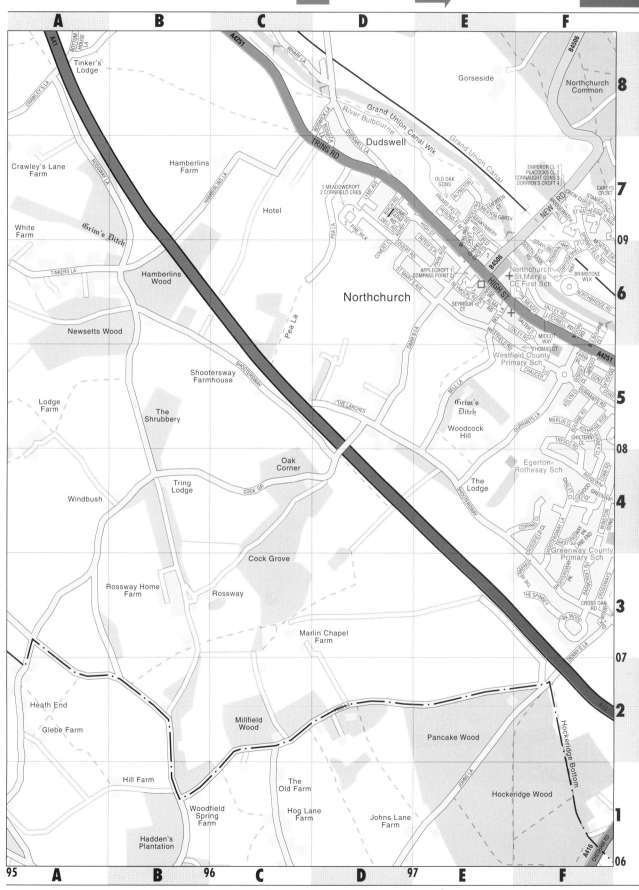

121 102

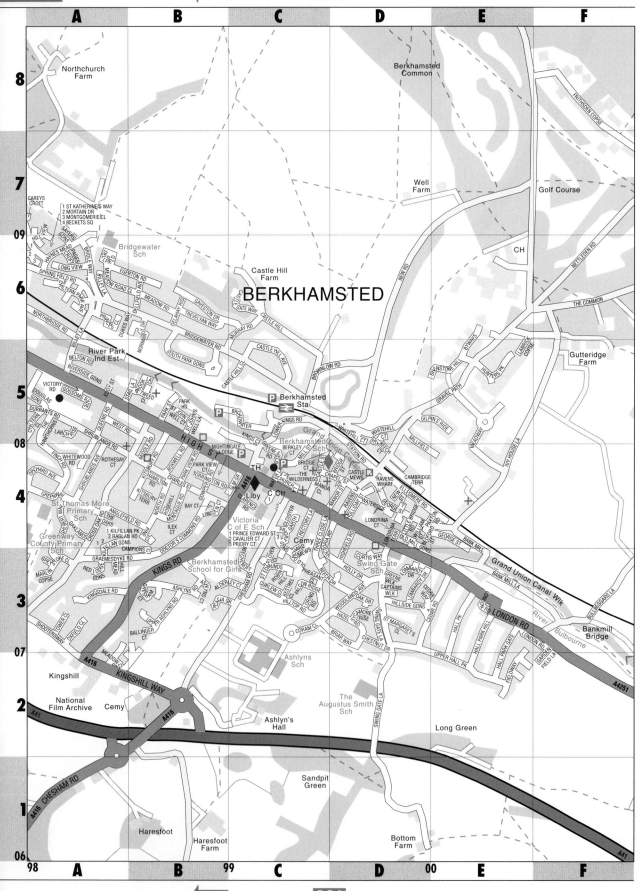

BERKHAMSTED

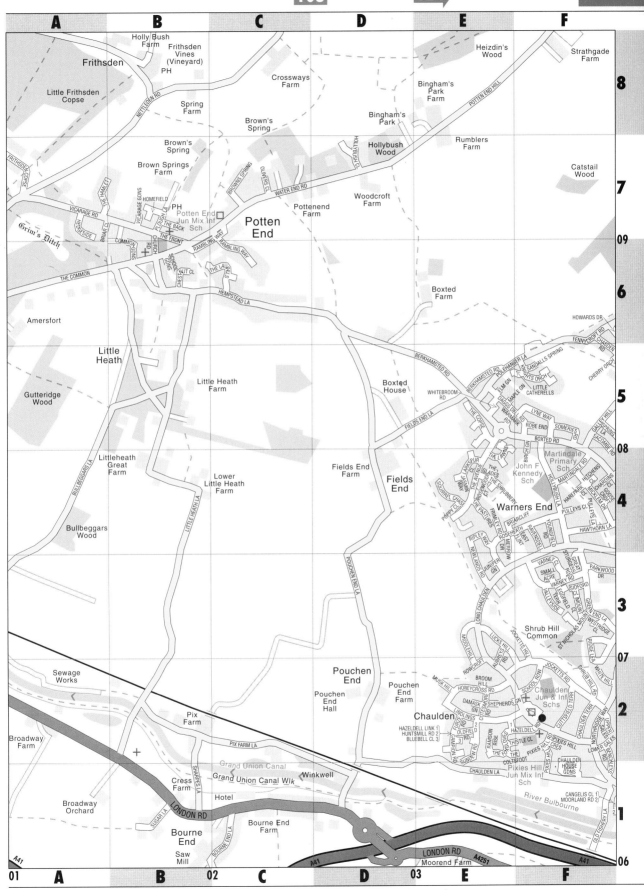

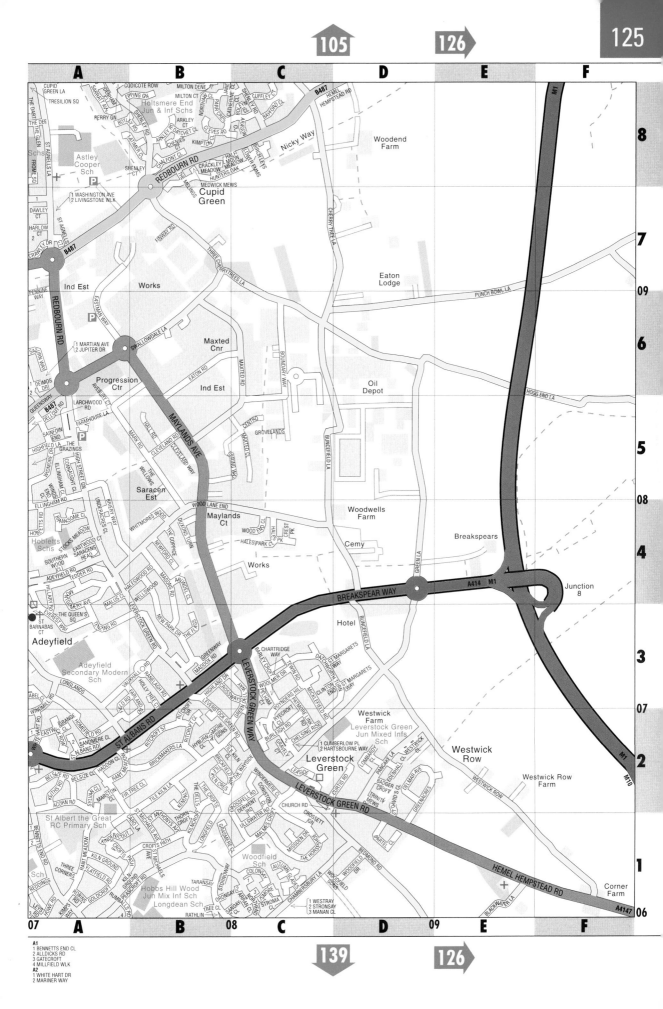

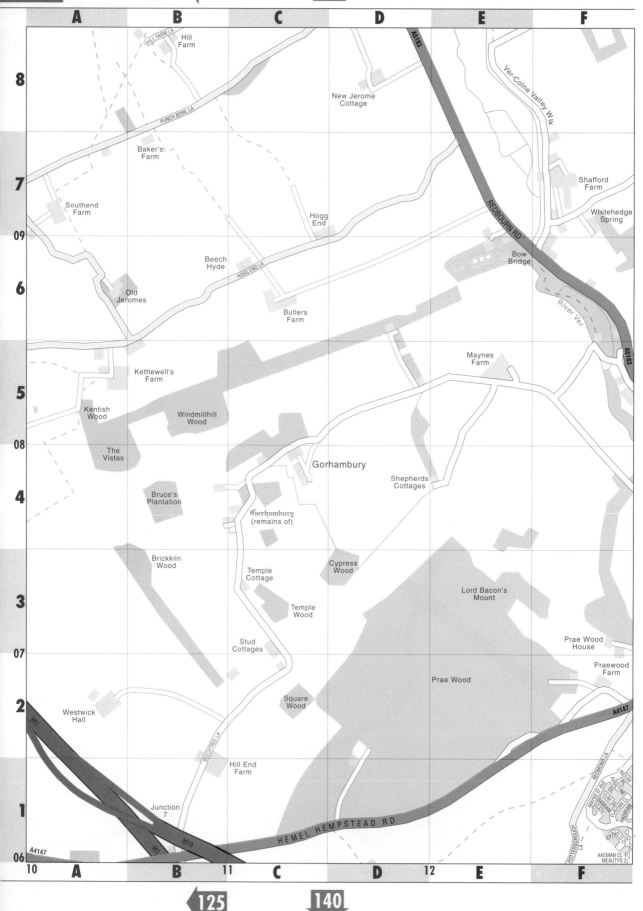

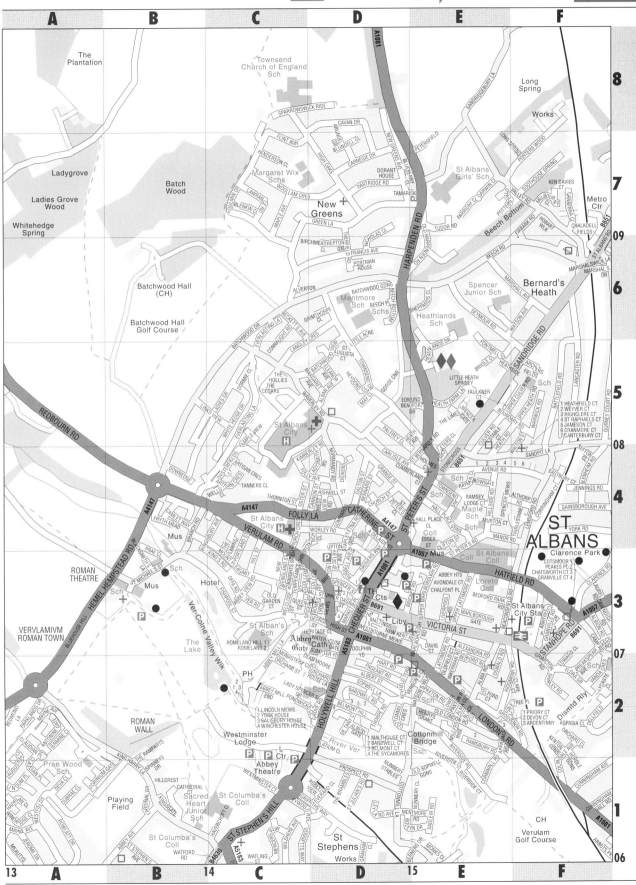

D3
1 WADDINGTON RD
2 CROSS ST
3 CHRISTOPHER PL
4 FRENCH ROW
5 HALF MOON MEWS

127 108

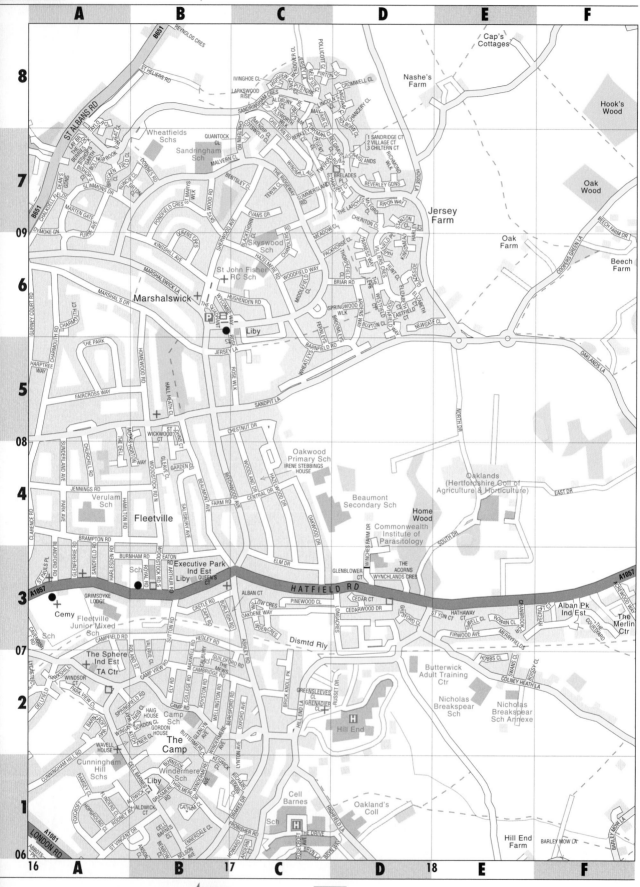

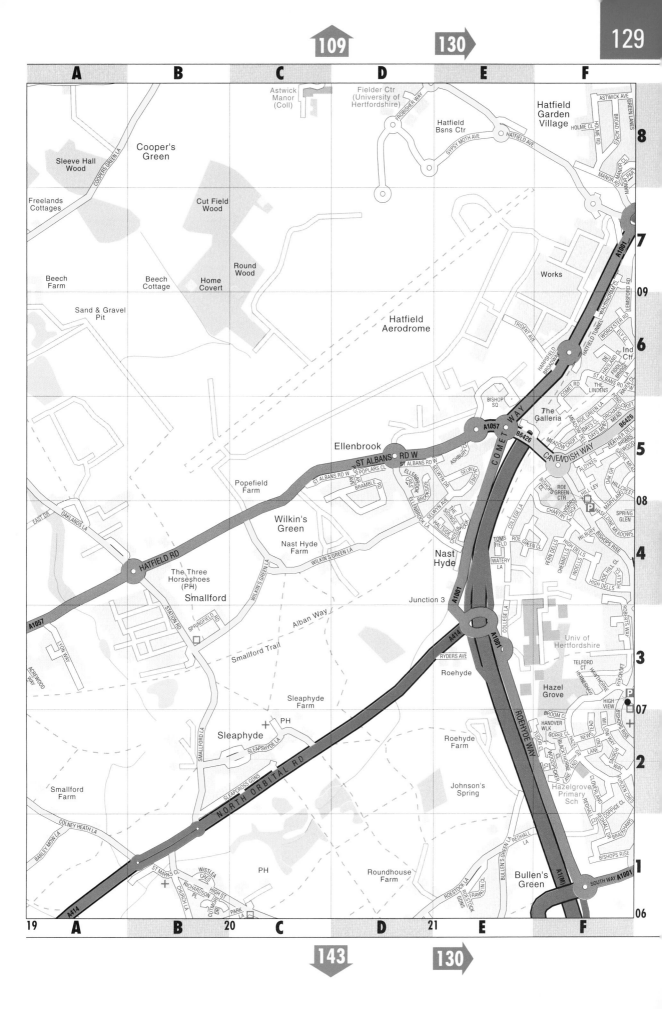

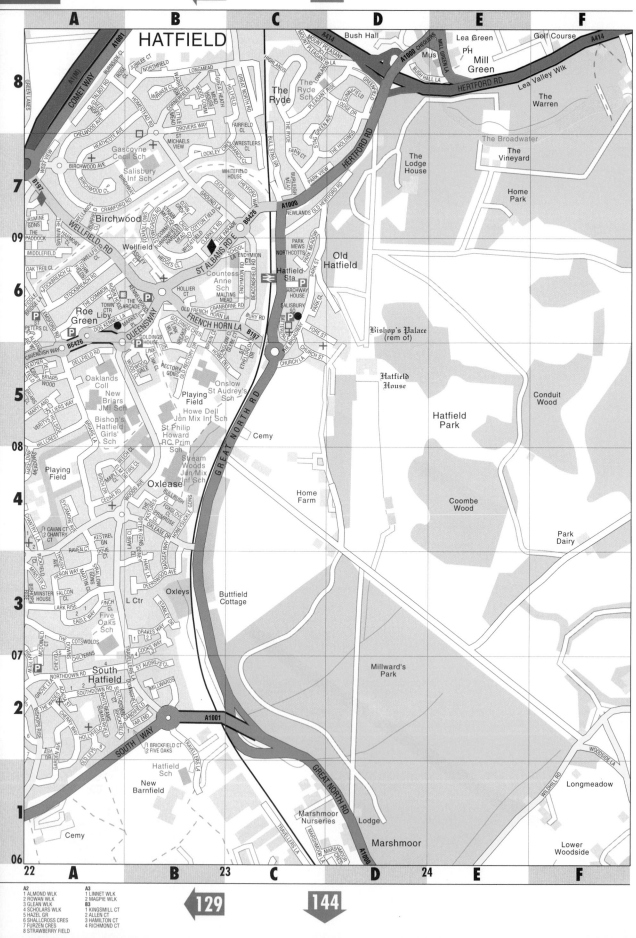

HATFIELD

A2
1 ALMOND WLK
2 ROWAN WLK
3 GLEAN WLK
4 SCHOLARS WLK
5 HAZEL GR
6 SHALLCROSS CRES
7 FURZEN CRES
8 STRAWBERRY FIELD

A3
1 LINNET WLK
2 MAGPIE WLK
B3
1 KINGSMILL CT
2 ALLEN CT
3 HAMILTON CT
4 RICHMOND CT

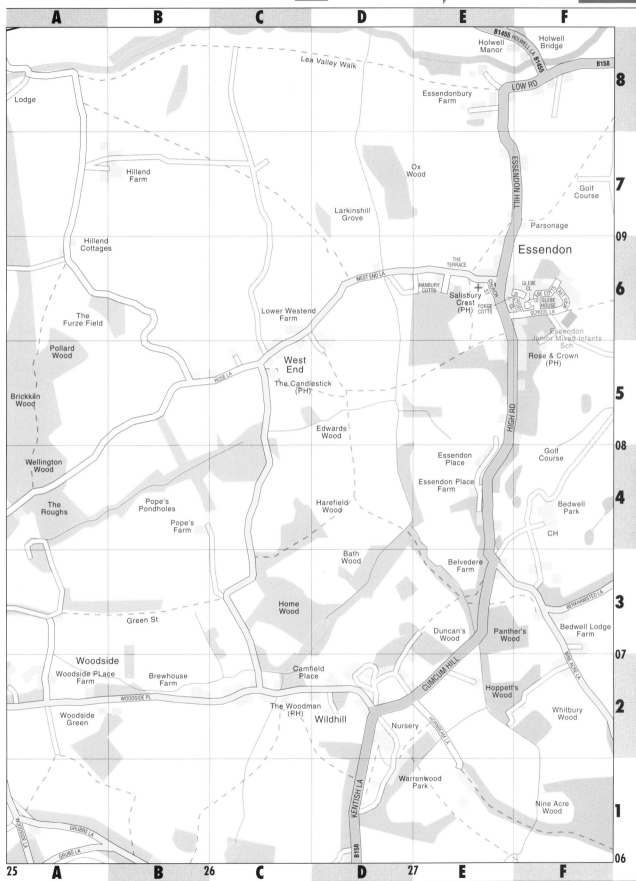

131
112

131
146

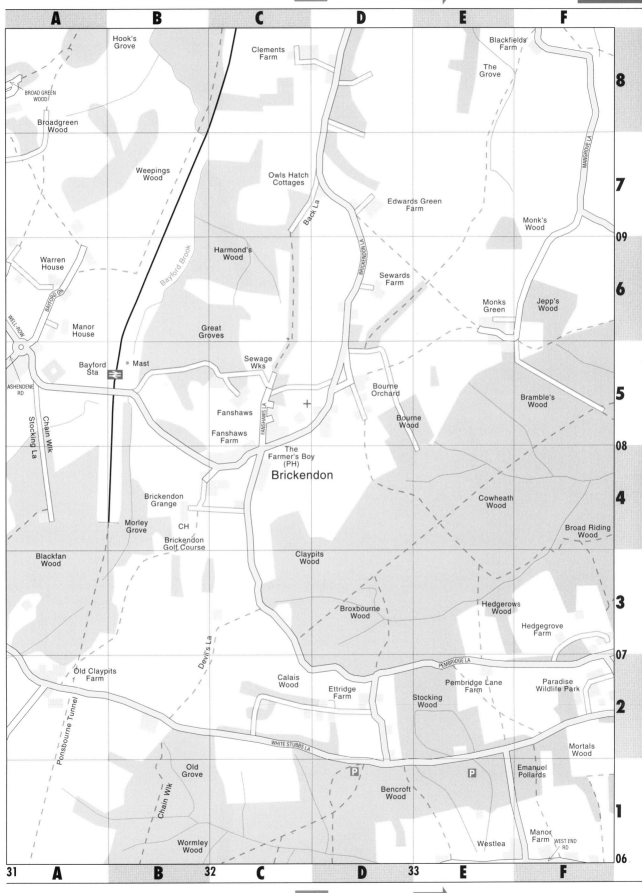

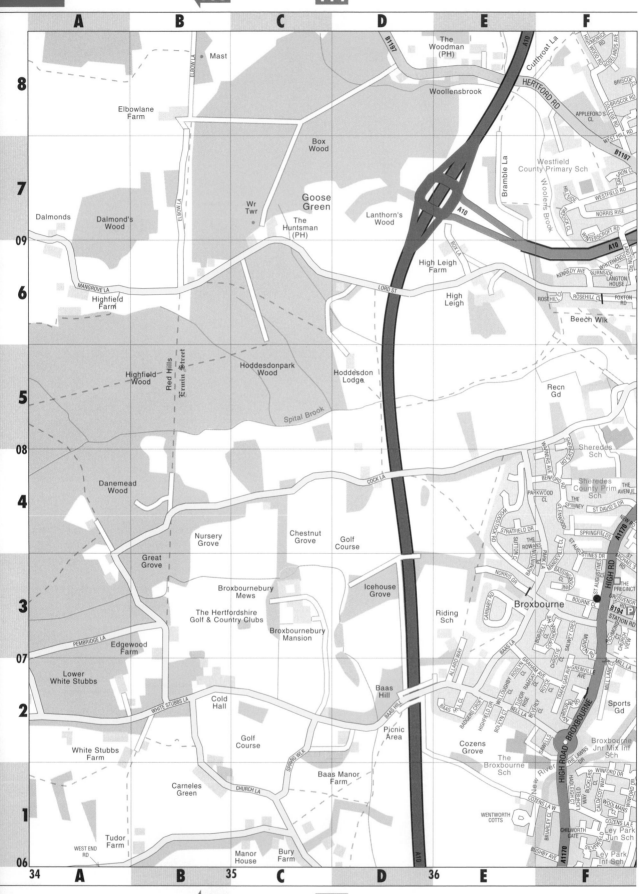

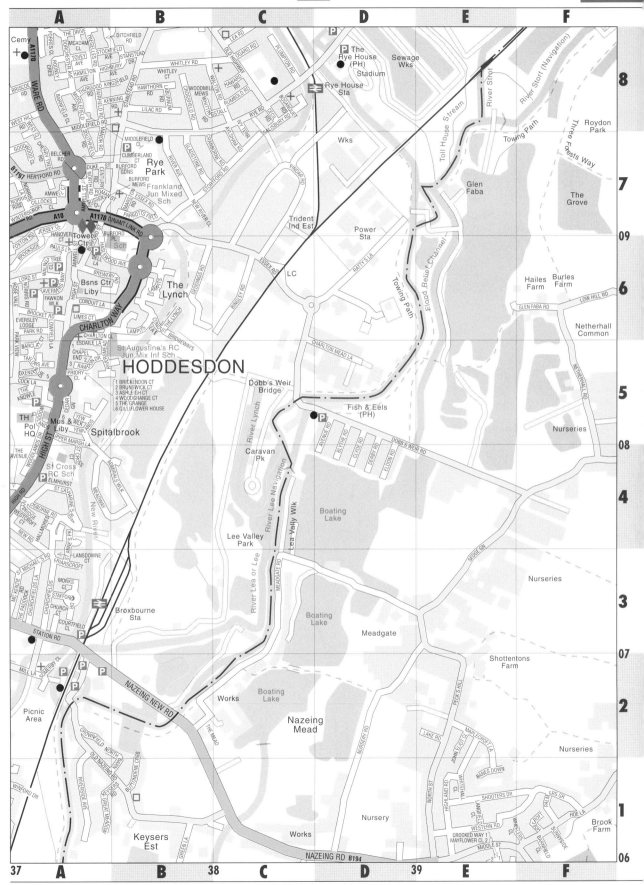

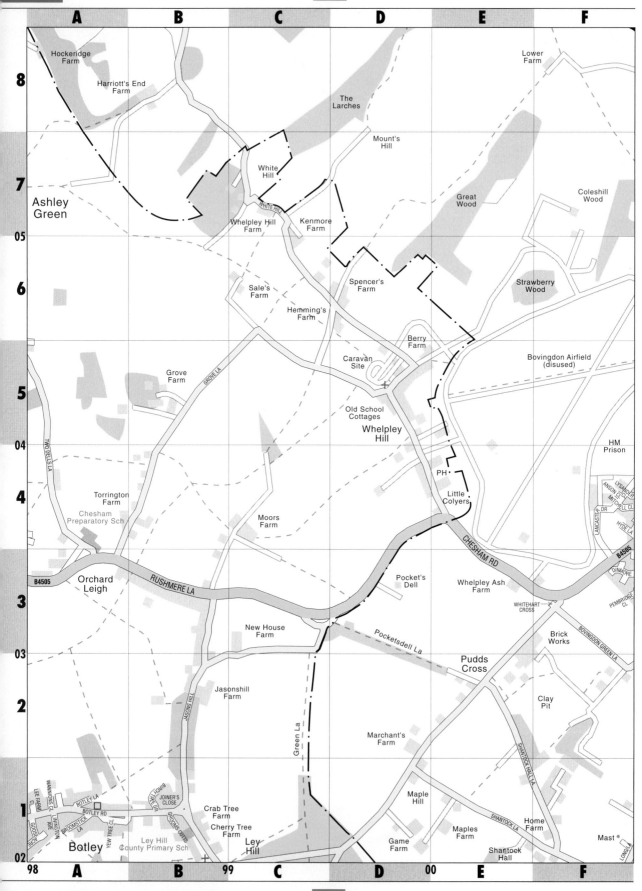

8

Hockeridge
Farm

Harriott's End
Farm

Lower
Farm

The
Larches

Mount's
Hill

White
Hill

7

Ashley
Green

Coleshill
Wood

Great
Wood

Whelpley Hill
Farm

Kenmore
Farm

WHITE HILL

05

Sale's
Farm

Spencer's
Farm

Strawberry
Wood

6

Hemming's
Farm

Grove
Farm

Berry
Farm

GROVE LA

Bovingdon Airfield
(disused)

Caravan
Site

5

Old School
Cottages

Whelpley
Hill

04

HM
Prison

4

Torrington
Farm

Chesham
Preparatory Sch

Moors
Farm

PH

Little
Colyers

LYSANDER CL
ANSON CL
MITCHELL CL
LANCASTER DR
HYDE LA

TWO DELLS LA

CHESHAM RD

B4505

DINMORE

Orchard
Leigh

RUSHMERE LA

Pocket's
Dell

Whelpley Ash
Farm

Brick
Works

PEMBRIDGE CL

3

B4505

WHITEHART
CROSS

BOVINGDON GREEN LA

03

New House
Farm

Pocketsdell La

Pudds
Cross

JASONS HILL

Jasonshill
Farm

Clay
Pit

2

Green La

Marchant's
Farm

SHANTOCK HALL LA

WANNIONS CL
LEE FARM CL
LIVINGTON AVE
ABBEY GOSE
BROOMSTICK LA

BOTLEY LA

BIRCH GR
JOINER'S
CLOSE

Crab Tree
Farm

Maple
Hill

Maples
Farm

Home
Farm

1

BOTLEY RD

GROOMS DITCH

Cherry Tree
Farm

SHANTOCK LA

Mast

LONG LA

Botley

Ley Hill
County Primary Sch

Ley
Hill

Game
Farm

Shantock
Hall

02

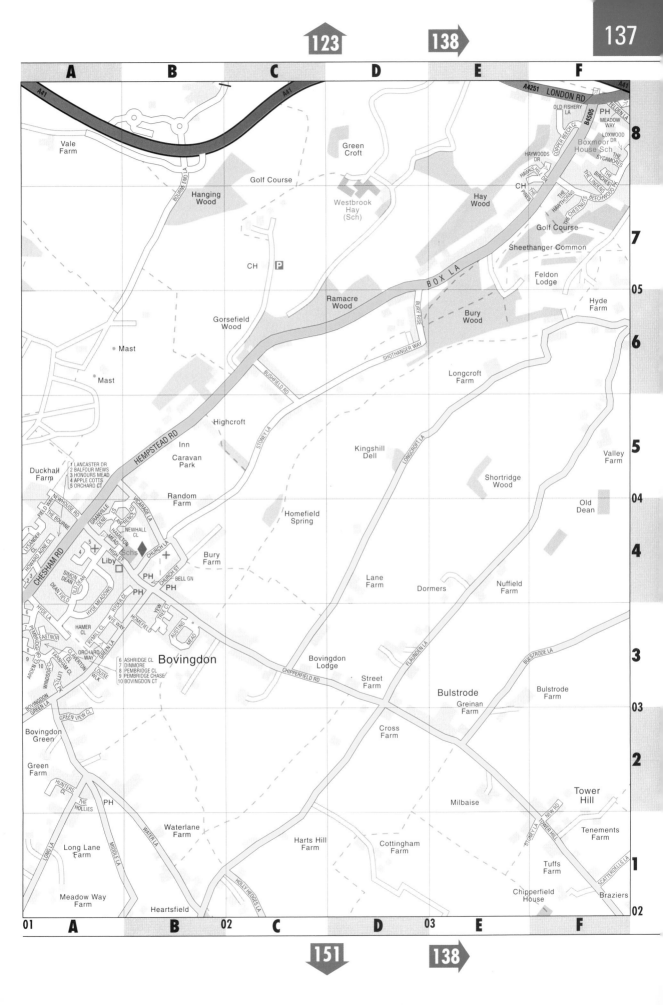

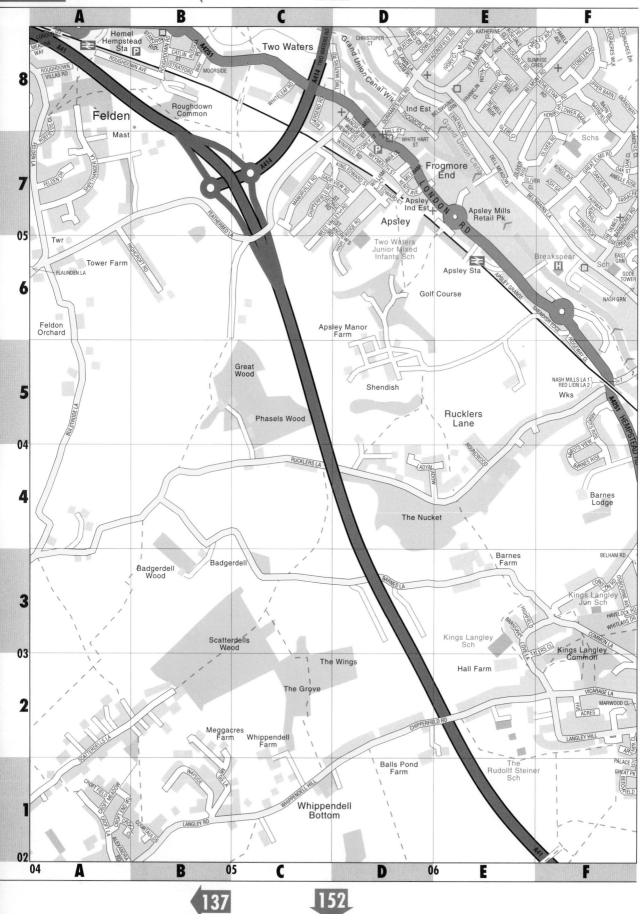

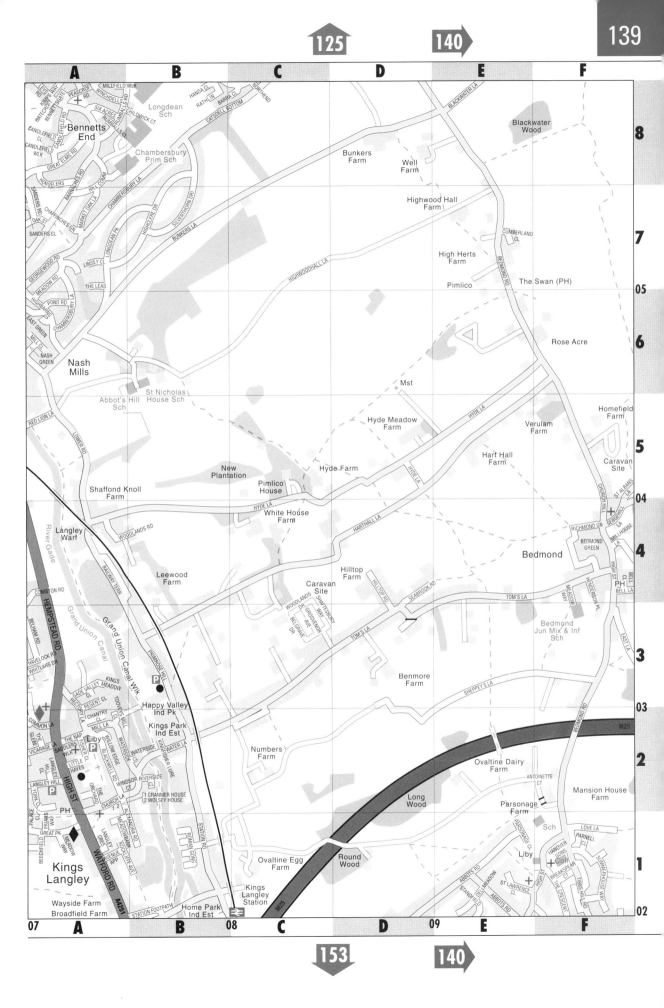

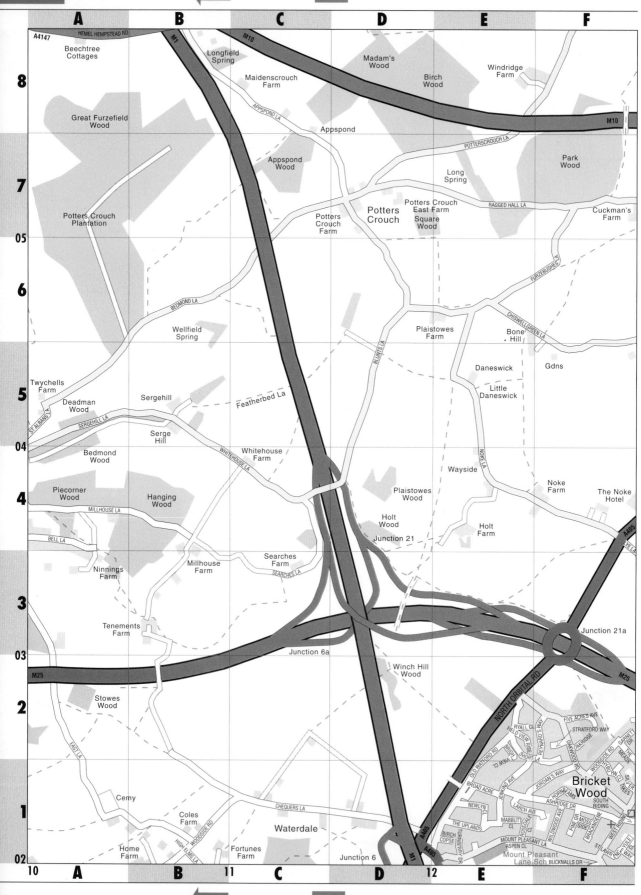

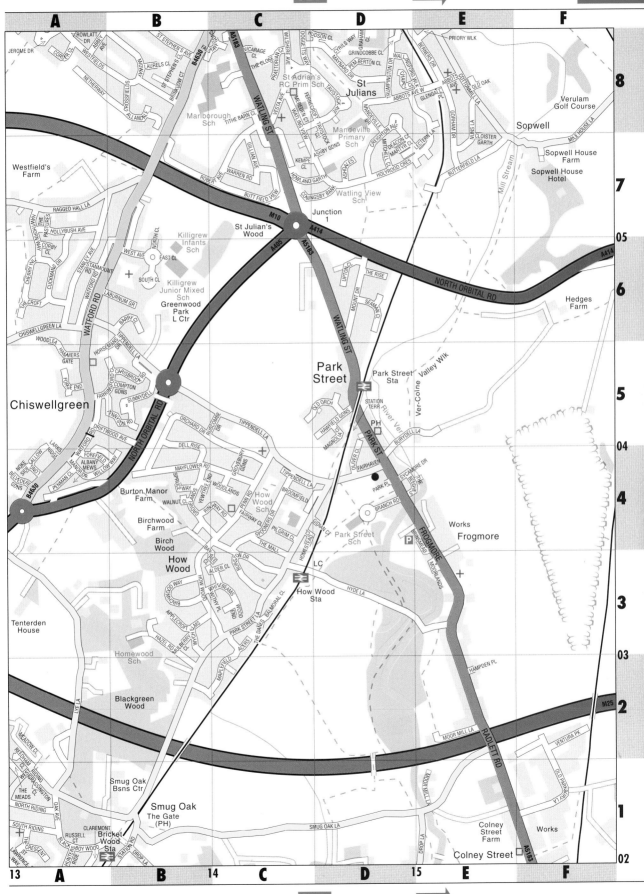

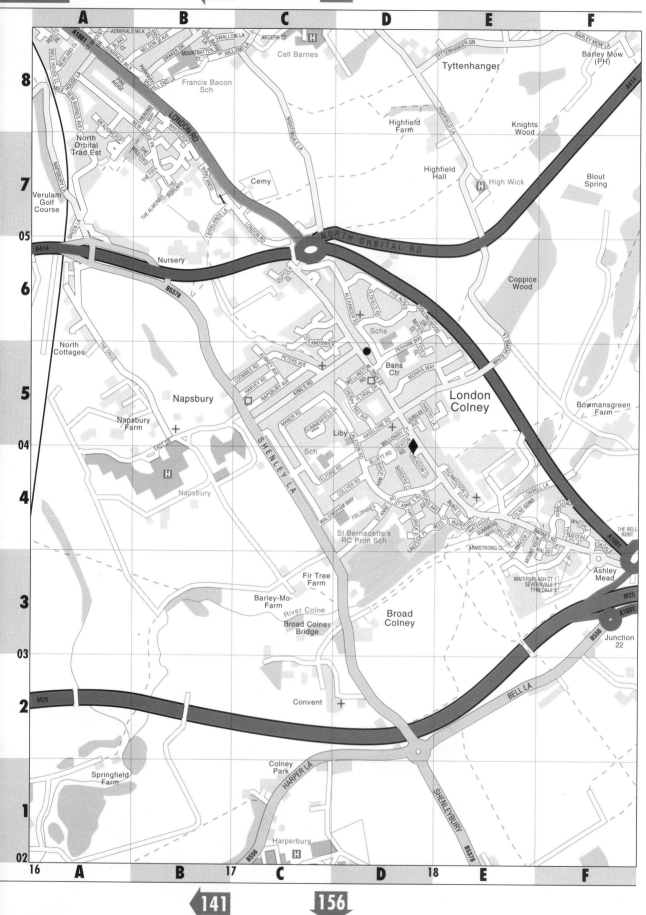

129
144
157
144

A B C D E F

8
7
05
6
5
04
4
3
03
2
1
02

Park Corner

Colney Heath

Roestock

Junction 2

HEATH SIDE
PARK LA
CHURCH LA
SCHOLARS CT
HIGH ST
ROESTOCK LA
MEADWAY
HALL GDNS
PENNETTS CL
ADMIRAL'S CL
FELLOWES CL
BILLEN'S GREEN LA
DELLSOME LA
DELLSOME LA
A1 (M)
A1 (M)

River Colne

Water Works

PH
Colney Heath Farm

Tollgate Wood

Windmill

Warren Farm

Tollgate Farm

TOLLGATE RD

Park Cottage

Frederick's Wood

The Osierbeds

Tyttenhanger Farm

Garden Wood

The New Plantation

North Mymms Park

Tyttenhanger Park

COURSERS RD

Coursers Farm

Red Lodge

Walsingham Wood

North Mymms Park

Lodge Plantation

The Bell (PH)

Cangsley Grove

A1081

Cobs Ash

B556

Round Wood

Potwells

Junction 22

Hawkshead Wood

Salisbury Hall Farm

Salisbury Hall

Mus

Redwell Wood Farm

Oak Lodge

Redwell Wood

Ridgehill Stud

Shenley Lodge Cottage

Manor Lodge Sch

RECTORY LA

Ridgehill

PACKHORSE LA

BLACKHORSE LA

ST ALBANS RD

B556

M25

Woodhill Farm

Shenley Lodge Farm

NORTH ORBITAL RD
A414

19 A B 20 C D 21 E F

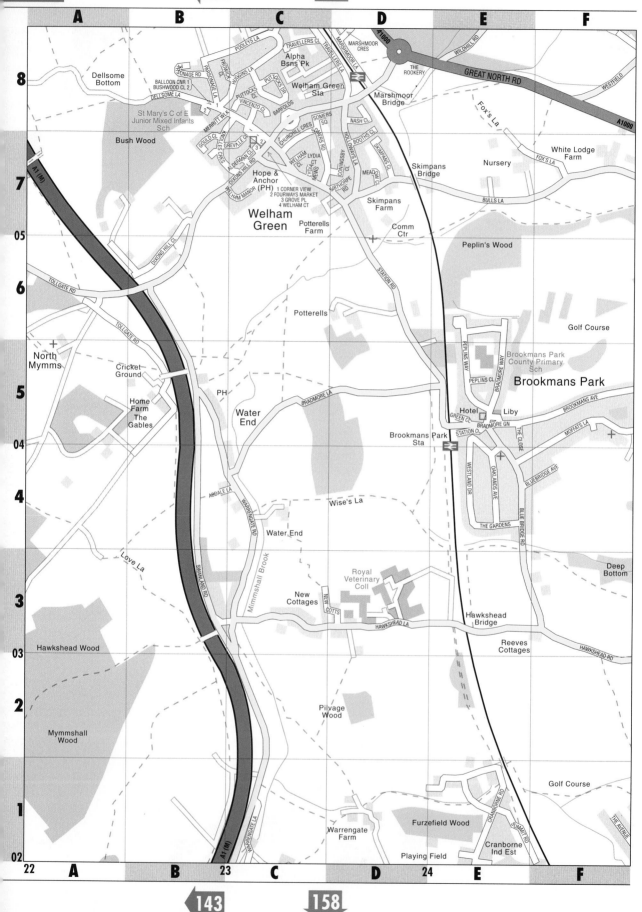

143
130
143
158

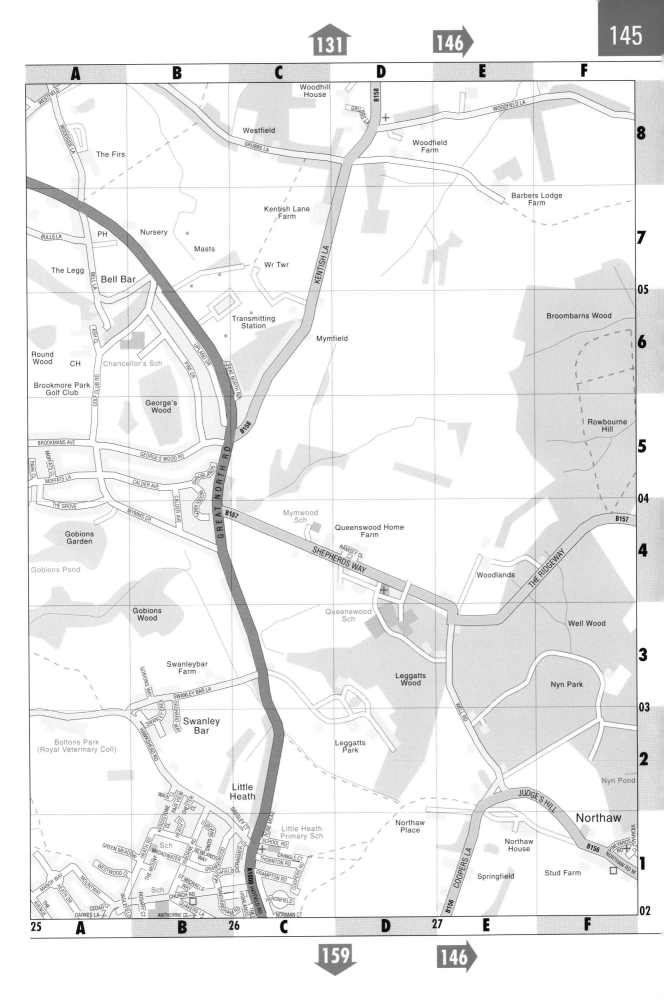

A B C D E F

8 Nine Acre La
Birchwood Cottages
Tylers Cswy
Woodfield La
Ponsfall Farm
The Warren
Chain Wlk
Ponsbourne Park Cotts
Home Farm

Coldharbour Farm
Ponsbourne House

7 Hell Wood
Newgate St
Ponsbourne Park
Ponsbourne St Mary's JMI Sch
Newgate Street

New Park Rd
05 New Park Farm
Home Farm
Newgate Street Village
PH
Tolmers Park Farm
Tolmers Mews
Newgate Street Bridge
Darnicle Hill

Coldharbour Plantation

6 Chain Wlk

Justice Hill
Postern Gate
Carbone Hill
Postern Bridge
Tolmers

5 Great Wood Country Park
Grimes Bottom
County School Camp
Tolmers Rd

04 P The Cottage
Grimes Brook
Home Wood
Brookside Cres
Homewood Avenue
Brookside
Cuffley Brook

B157
THE RIDGEWAY
Homewood La
Carbone Bottom
Bradgate
Farm Cl
High Ridge

4 THE RIDGEWAY
Calton Cl
Bradgate Cl
Warwick Ave
Warwick Cl
Wood View
Hanyards End
Highfields
Robins Way
Hill Leys
Tolmers Rd
Hill La

Nyn Manor Farm
Hanyards La
Hill Rise
Orchard Cl
Tolmers Rd
Thrush La
Starling La

3 Splitts
Leepe Way
Woodland Ave
Tolmers Ave
Cuffley
Kingsms
Sutherland Way
The Driveway
Kingsmead
Oak La
The Meadway

Thornton's Farm
High Willows
EAST RIDGEWAY
Plough Hill
Bacons Dr
Tolmers Gdns
Maynard Pl
P Cuffley Sta
B156

03 Vineyards Rd
Cranefield Cres
B157
Liby
STATION RD
Cuffley Hill
Sopers Rd

Vineyard Bridge
Cuffley Hills Farm
Church Cl
Lambs Cl
James Ave
Northaw Rd E
Theobald's Rd
Theobalds

2 The Vineyard
Northaw C of E JMI Sch
Hemps Hill
Kingswell Ride
Burleigh Way
Kingsway
Colesdale
South Hr
Cuffley JMI Sch

Chain Wlk
Greenfields

1 Church La
Vicarage Cl
Waterworks Cottages
Wells Farm

B156
Northaw Rd W
Park Rd
Hook La

02
28 A B 29 C 30 D E F

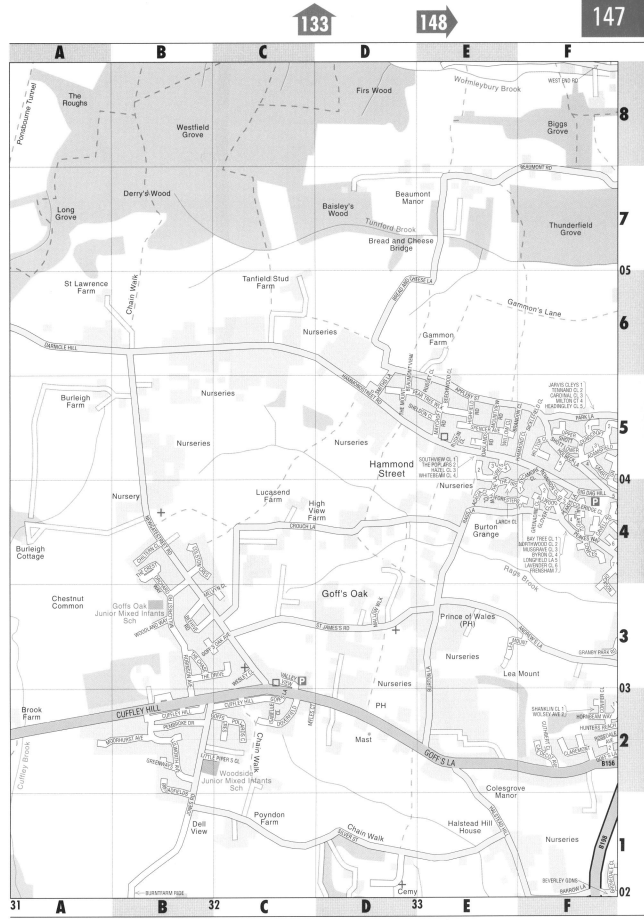

A B C D E F

8 7 05 6 5 04 4 3 03 2 1 02

31 32 33

Ponsbourne Tunnel
The Roughs
Firs Wood
Wormleybury Brook
WEST END RD
Biggs Grove
Westfield Grove
Derry's Wood
Beaumont Manor
BEAUMONT RD
Baisley's Wood
Thunderfield Grove
Long Grove
Tunrford Brook
Bread and Cheese Bridge
St Lawrence Farm
Chain Walk
Tanfield Stud Farm
BREAD AND CHEESE LA
Gammon's Lane
DARNICLE HILL
Nurseries
Gammon Farm
Burleigh Farm
Nurseries
HAMMONDSTREET RD
SMITHS LA
THE MOUNT
BEAUMONT VIEW
RUSSET CL
BEECHWOOD CL
APPLEBY ST
PEAR TREE WALK
HIGHFIELD RD
MOUNTVIEW RD
BRAMDON CL
SICKLEFIELD CL
SHELDON CL
SPENCER AVE
WILLOW CL
HAMMOND CL
HILLTOP CL
PARK LA
JARVIS CLEYS 1
TENNAND CL 2
CARDINAL CL 3
MILTON CT 4
HEADINGLEY CL 5
UPPER SHOTT
LOWER SHOTT
ROUGHCROFT
ADAMSFIELD
Nurseries
Nurseries
Nurseries
MAYCROF RD
RISKIN CL
OAKLANDS RD
Hammond Street
SOUTHVIEW CL 1
THE POPLARS 2
HAZEL CL 3
WHITEBEAM CL 4
HOLBECK LA
SMARTS
Nursery
Lucasend Farm
High View Farm
Nurseries
Nurseries
RAGS LA
THE ALDERS
THE FIRS
FORESTERS
ACACIA CL
GRENADINE CL
ALLWOOD
GLOVER CL
SYCAMORE CL
PENNISON CL
RAGS RD
COLERIDGE CL
DIG DAG HILL
CAHILL RD
Burleigh Cottage
CROUCH LA
Burton Grange
LARCH CL
BAY TREE CL 1
NORTHWOOD CL 2
MUSGRAVE CL 3
BYRON CL 4
LONGFIELD CL 5
LAVENDER CL 6
FRENSHAM 7
PEAKES WAY
ALLARD
COLES
SOLCROFT
Rags Brook
Chestnut Common
Goff's Oak
Prince of Wales (PH)
ANDREW'S LA
GRANBY PARK RD
CHILTERN CL
THE CREST
ORCHARD WAY
COLSTON CRES
MELVYN CL
MALLOW WALK
Nurseries
LEA MOUNT
Lea Mount
Goffs Oak Junior Mixed Infants Sch
WOODLAND WAY
MILLCREST RD
BEENLEY RD
GOFF'S OAK AVE
ST JAMES'S RD
BURTON LA
Nurseries
PH
SHANKLIN CL 1
WOLSEY AVE 2
CONIFER CL
HORNBEAM WAY
HUNTERS REACH
Brook Farm
ROBINSON AVE
THE CHASE
THE DRIVE
WESLEY CL
VALLEY VIEW
P
Mast
CUTHBERT CL
ROSEDALE AVE
CLAREMONT
CUFFLEY HILL
CUFFLEY HILL
GOFFS CRES
POLLARDS CL
ISABELLE RIDE
DOVERFIELD
MYLES CT
GOFF'S LA
CAT DECOY AVE
CAT DECOY AVE
GOFF'S LA
B156
Cuffley Brook
PEMBROKE DR
MOORHURST AVE
GREENWAYS
ULLWORTH AVE
Chain Walk
LITTLE PIPER'S CL
Woodside Junior Mixed Infants Sch
Colesgrove Manor
BROADFIELDS
JONES RD
Dell View
Poyndon Farm
SILVER ST
Chain Walk
HALSTEAD HILL
Halstead Hill House
Nurseries
B198
GROVEDALE CL
BURNTFARM RIDE
Cemy
BEVERLEY GDNS
BARROW LA

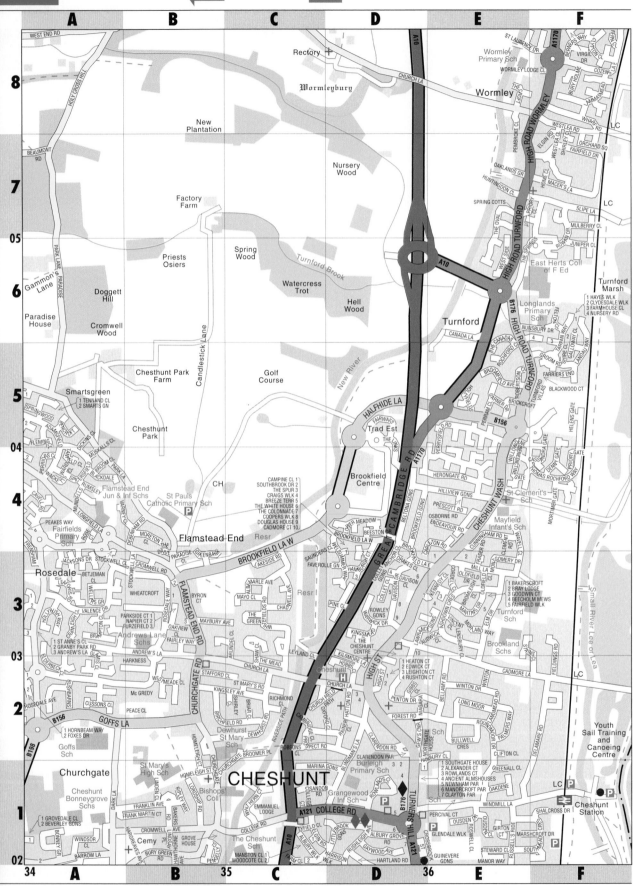

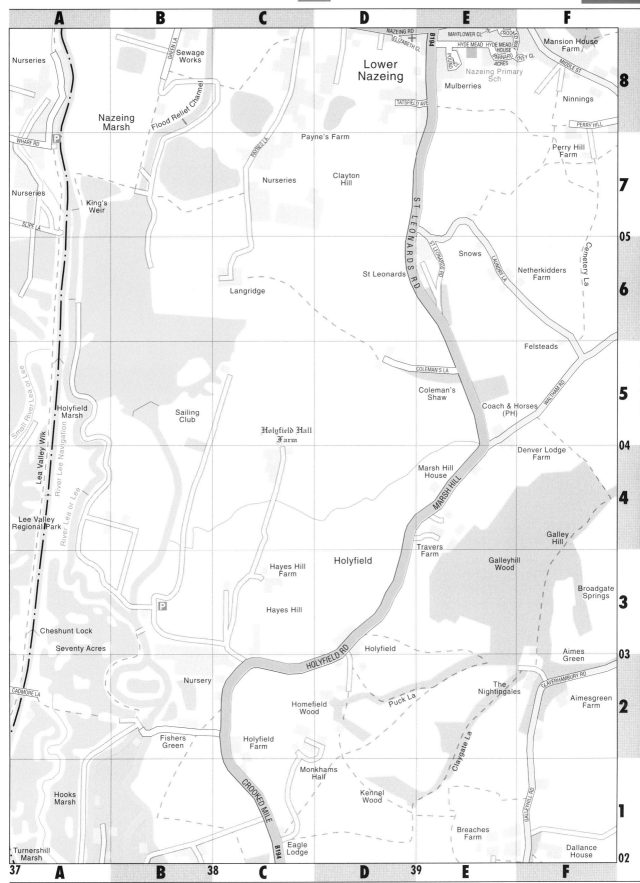

A   **B**   **C**   **D**   **E**   **F**

Nurseries

Sewage Works

GREEN LA

Nazeing Marsh

Flood Relief Channel

NAZEING RD

ELIZABETH CL

MAYFLOWER CL

B194

HYDE MEAD HYDE MEAD

HOUSE

BARNARD

ACRES

CROOK

COVEY CL

MIDDLE ST

Mansion House Farm

8

Lower Nazeing

Nazeing Primary Sch

Mulberries

Ninnings

PERRY HILL

WHARF RD

P

Payne's Farm

TATSFIELD AVE

Perry Hill Farm

PAYNES LA

Nurseries

Clayton Hill

7

Nurseries

King's Weir

05

SLIPE LA

Langridge

ST LEONARDS RD

St Leonards

ST LEONARDS RD

Snows

LAUNDRY LA

Netherkidders Farm

Cemetery La

6

Small River Lea or Lee

COLEMAN'S LA

Felsteads

Sailing Club

Coleman's Shaw

Coach & Horses (PH)

WALTHAM RD

5

Holyfield Marsh

River Lee Navigation

Holyfield Hall Farm

Denver Lodge Farm

04

Lea Valley Wlk

Marsh Hill House

MARSH HILL

4

River Lea or Lee

Lee Valley Regional Park

Galley Hill

Travers Farm

Galleyhill Wood

Broadgate Springs

3

P

Hayes Hill Farm

Holyfield

CADMORE LA

Cheshunt Lock

Hayes Hill

HOLYFIELD RD

Holyfield

Aimes Green

03

Seventy Acres

Nursery

Holyfield

Puck La

CLAVERHAMBURY RD

The Nightingales

Aimesgreen Farm

2

Homefield Wood

CLAYGATE LA

Fishers Green

Holyfield Farm

Monkhams Hall

GALLEYHILL RD

Hooks Marsh

CROOKED MILE

Kennel Wood

1

Turnershill Marsh

B194

Eagle Lodge

Breaches Farm

Dallance House

02

37   **A**   **B**   **38**   **C**   **D**   **39**   **E**   **F**

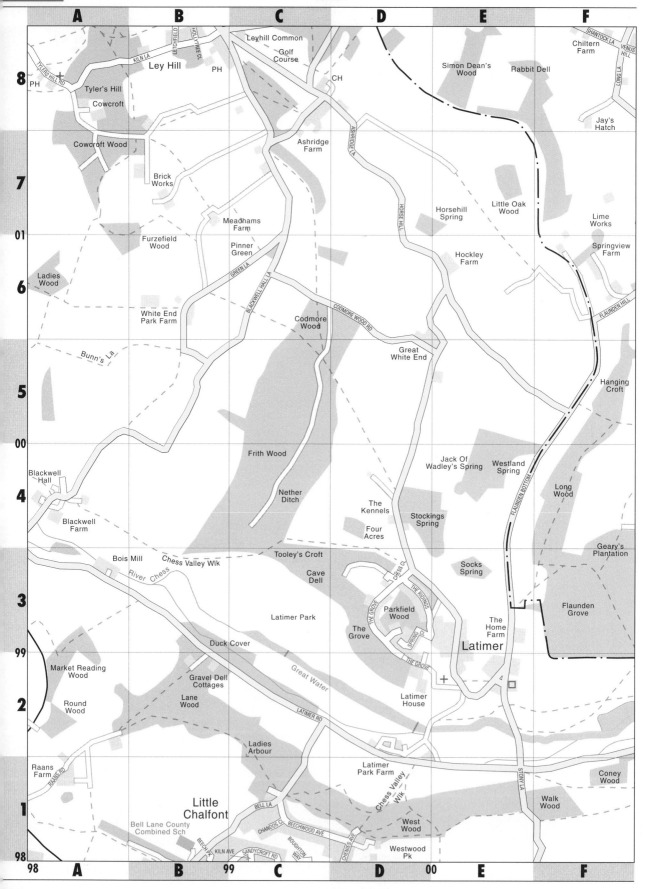

A B C D E F

8

7

01

6

5

00

4

3

99

2

1

98

98 A B 99 C D 00 E F

PH
TYLERS HILL RD
KILN LA
Ley Hill
LETCHFIELD
HOLLYTREE CL
PH
PH
Tyler's Hill
Cowcroft
Cowcroft Wood
Brick Works
Furzefield Wood
Meadhams Farm
Pinner Green
GREEN LA
BLACKWELL HALL LA
Ladies Wood
White End Park Farm
Bunn's La
Leyhill Common
Golf Course
CH
Ashridge Farm
ASHRIDGE LA
Codmore Wood
CODMORE WOOD RD
HORSE HILL
Simon Dean's Wood
Rabbit Dell
Horsehill Spring
Little Oak Wood
Hockley Farm
Great White End
Chiltern Farm
SHANTOCK LA
VENUS HILL
LONG LA
Jay's Hatch
Lime Works
Springview Farm
FLAUNDEN HILL
Hanging Croft
Frith Wood
Nether Ditch
Blackwell Hall
Blackwell Farm
Bois Mill
Chess Valley Wlk
River Chess
Tooley's Croft
Cave Dell
Latimer Park
Duck Cover
Great Water
LATIMER RD
The Kennels
Four Acres
Jack Of Wadley's Spring
Westland Spring
Stockings Spring
Socks Spring
CHESS CL
THE RIDINGS
THE GROVE
Parkfield Wood
The Grove
SPRING CL
THE GROVE
Latimer House
Latimer
The Home Farm
Long Wood
FLAUNDEN BOTTOM
Geary's Plantation
Flaunden Grove
Market Reading Wood
Round Wood
Gravel Dell Cottages
Lane Wood
Ladies Arbour
Raans Farm
RAANS RD
Little Chalfont
Bell Lane County Combined Sch
BELL LA
BEECH PK
CHANDOS CL
KILN AVE
SANDYCROFT RD
BEECHWOOD AVE
BOUGHTON WAY
CHENIES AVE
Latimer Park Farm
Chess Valley Wlk
West Wood
Westwood Pk
STONY LA
Walk Wood
Coney Wood

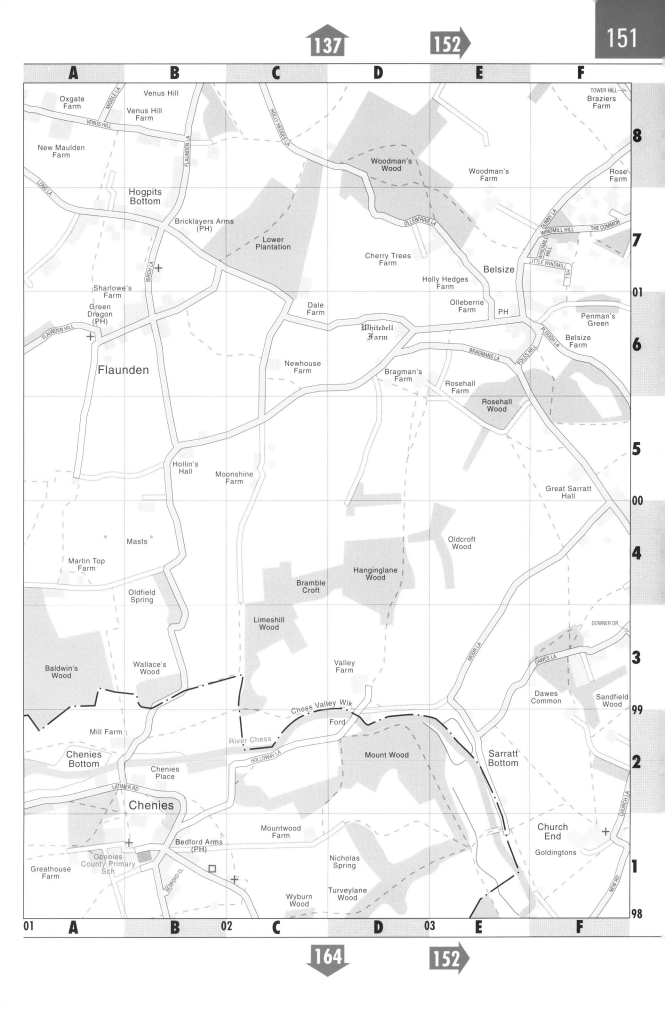

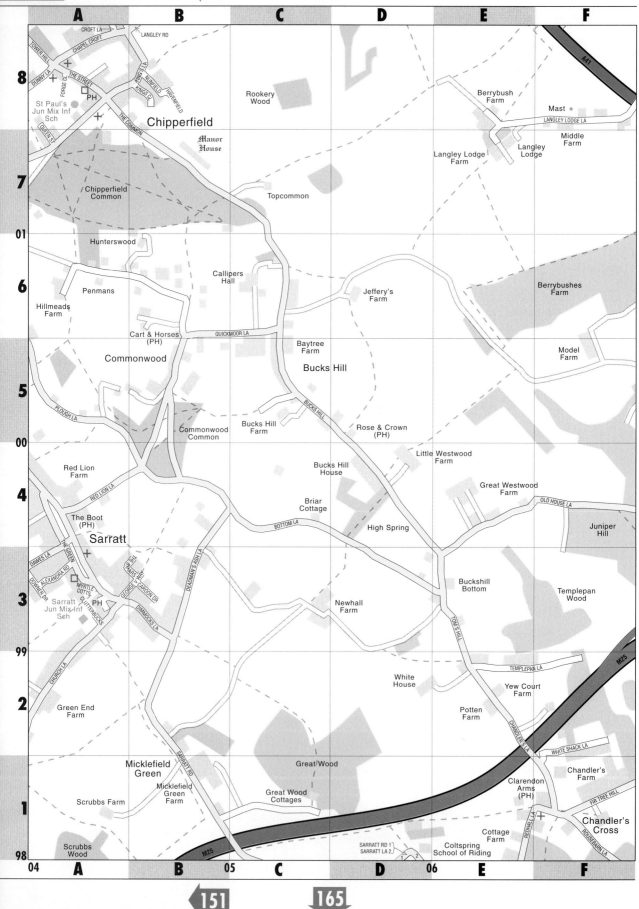

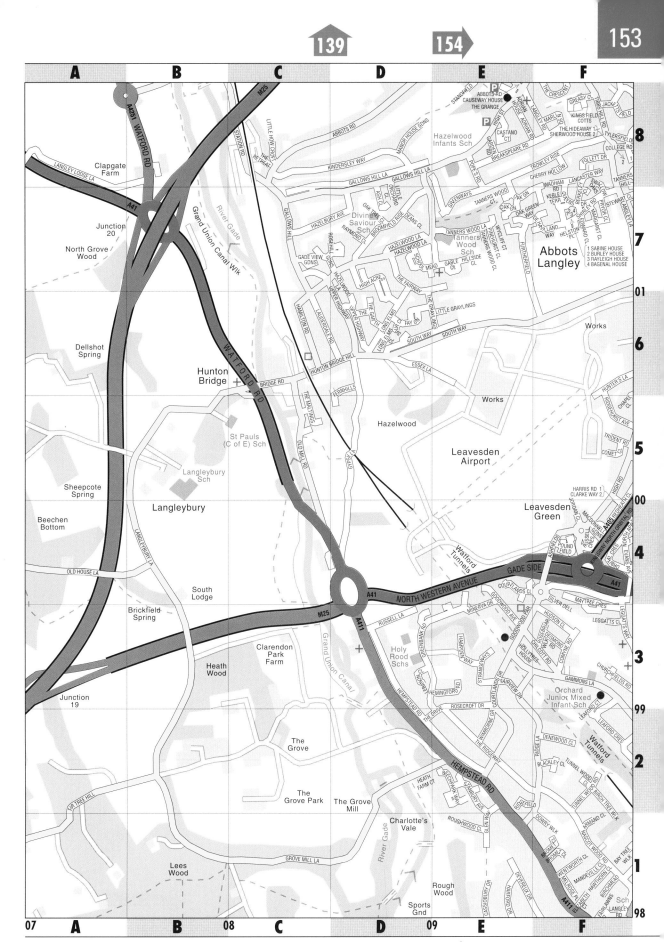

153 140

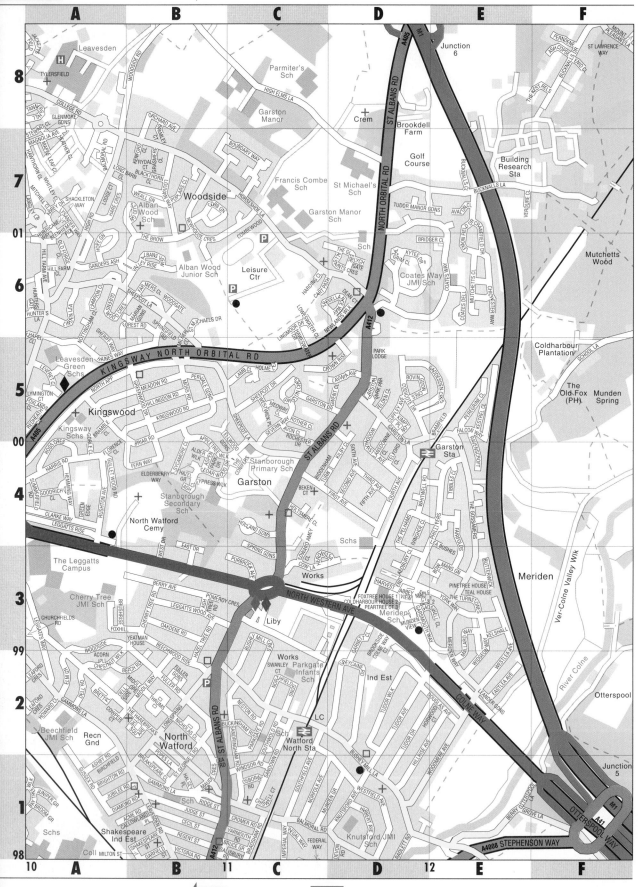

153 167

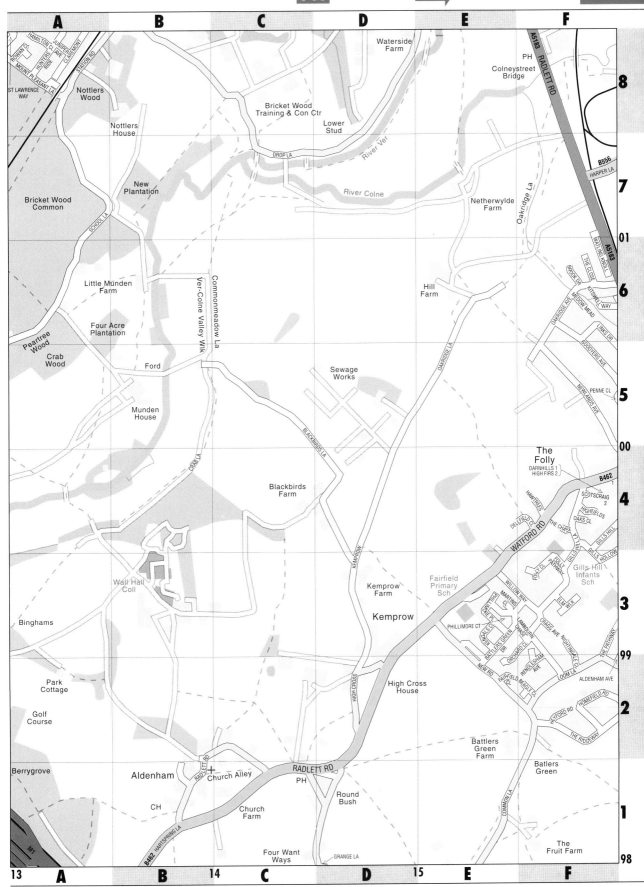

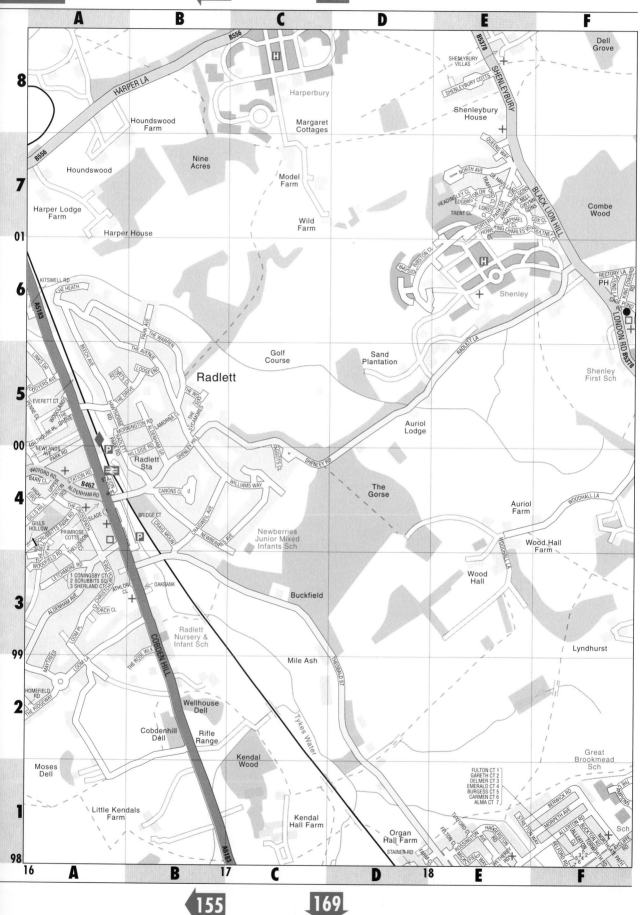

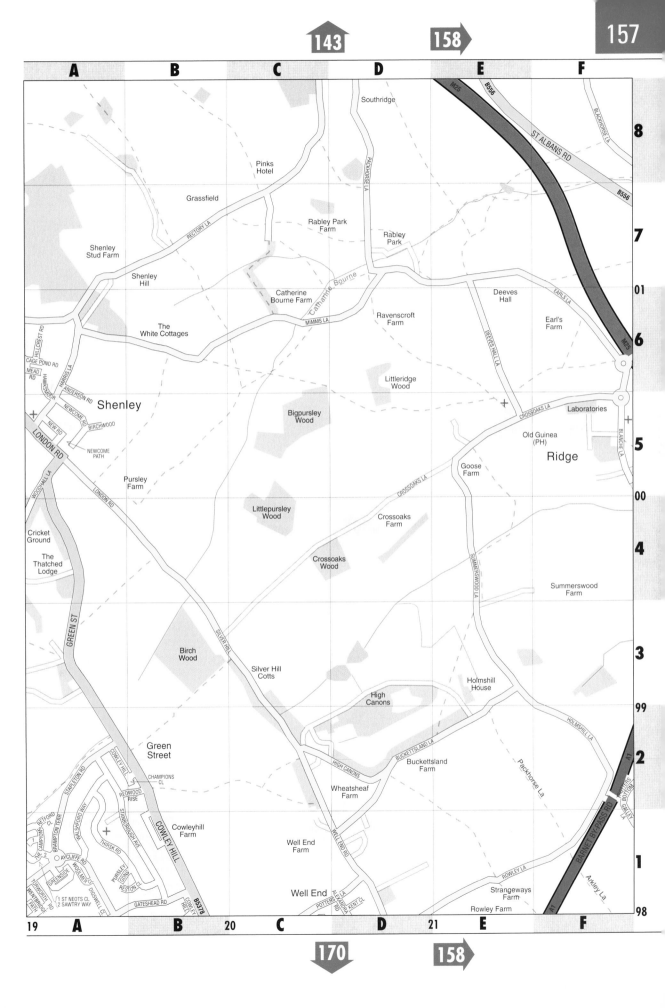

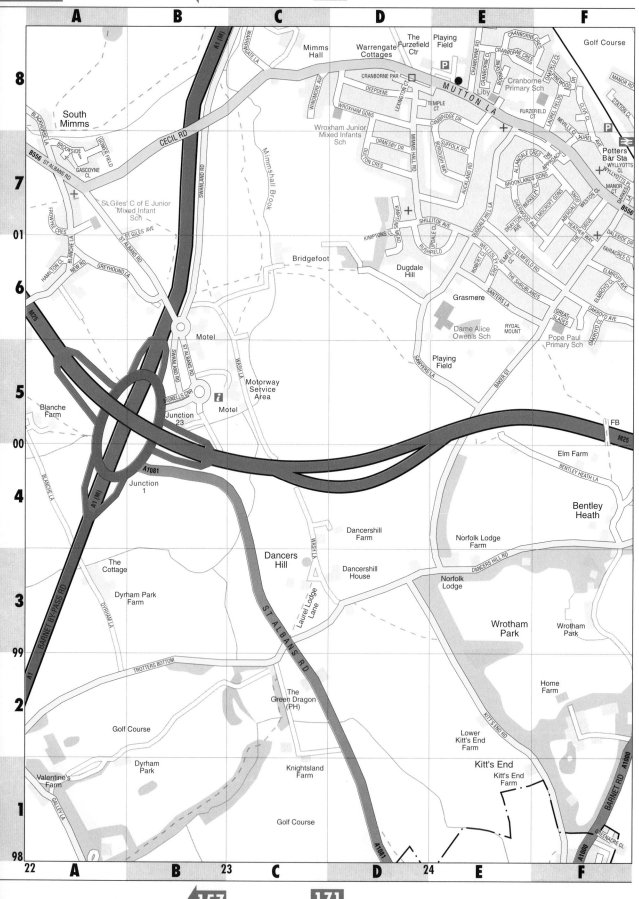

157
144
157
171

Map labels:

South Mimms

Mimms Hall

Warrengate Cottages

The Furzefield Ctr

Playing Field

Golf Course

Cranborne Cres

Cranborne Rd

Cranborne Cl

Cranfield Cl

Pinewood Dr

MANOR RD

Cranborne Par

MUTTON LA

Liby

Cranborne Primary Sch

STATION CL

Deepdene

Lexington Ct

Temple Ct

Furzefield Ct

Laurel Fields

Neville Ct

Laurel Ave

Potters Bar Sta

Wyllyotts La

Wyllyotts Pl

B556

MANOR CT

CLIVE CT

Wroxham Gdns

Cambridge Dr

Windmore Ave

Wroxham Junior Mixed Infants Sch

Ormesby Dr

Oulton Cres

Mimms Hall Rd

Suffolk Rd

Borough Way

Auckland Rd

The Approach

Brooklands Gdns

Berkely Ct

Sherwoods Rd

Elmscroft Gdns

Aberdale Ct

Snug

Weston Ct

Manor Ct

B556

CECIL RD

ST ALBANS RD

Blackhorse La

Brookside

Gower Field

Gascoyne Cl

B556

St Albans Rd

Frowyke Cres

Blanche La

St Albans Rd

St Giles' Ave

Hamilton Cl

New Rd

Greyhound La

St Giles' C of E Junior Mixed Infant Sch

Mimmshall Brook

SWANLAND RD

Kimptons Cl

Kimptons Mead

Shillitoe Ave

Lupdale Rd

Rushfield

Welleys Ct

Robert Cl

Elmfield Rd

Drayton Gdns

Ave

Elmfield Rd

The Shrublands

Dugdale Hill La

Heather Way

Drive

Dalewood Dr

Fairacres Cl

Elmroyd Ave

Bridgefoot

Dugdale Hill

Grasmere

Dame Alice Owen's Sch

Santers La

Great Slades

Oakroyd Ave

Oakroyd Ct

Pope Paul Primary Sch

Rydal Mount

M25

Motel

ST ALBANS RD

SWANLAND RD

WASH LA

Bignells Cnr

Junction 23

Motel

Playing Field

Baker St

Motorway Service Area

FB

M25

Elm Farm

Bentley Heath La

Blanche Farm

A7081

Junction 1

A1 (M)

Barnet By-Pass Rd

A1

Bentley Heath

Blanche La

The Cottage

Dyrham Park Farm

Dyrham La

Dancershill Farm

Dancers Hill

WASH LA

Dancershill House

Norfolk Lodge Farm

Dancers Hill Rd

Norfolk Lodge

Wrotham Park

Wrotham Park

Laurel Lodge Lane

ST ALBANS RD

Trotters Bottom

The Green Dragon (PH)

Home Farm

Golf Course

Dyrham Park

Knightsland Farm

Kitt's End Rd

Lower Kitt's End Farm

Kitt's End

Kitt's End Farm

Valentine's Farm

Galley La

Golf Course

A7081

Barnet Rd

A1000

Greenacre Cl

A1000

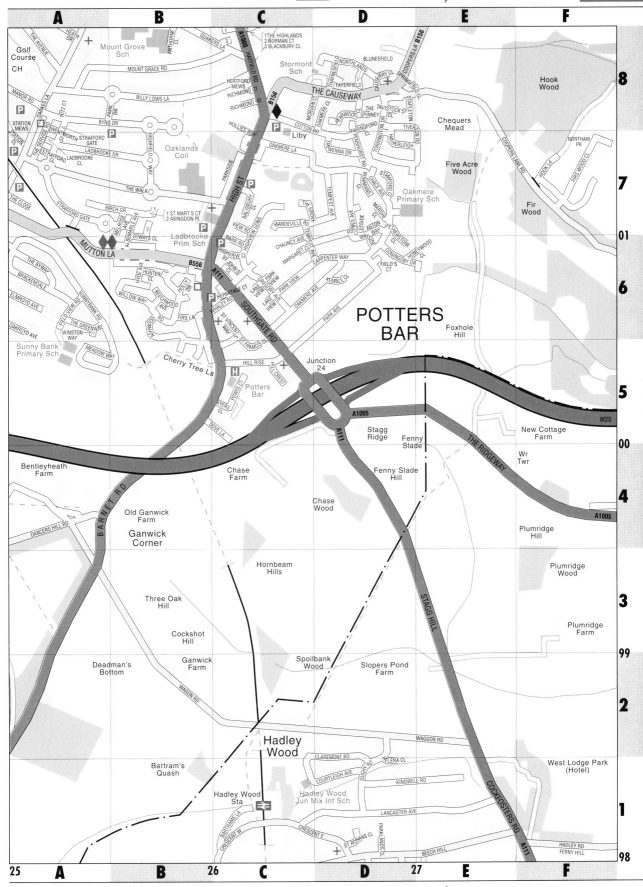

POTTERS
BAR

A B C D E F

8
01
7
6
5
00
4
99
3
2
1
98

28 A B 29 C D 30 E F

Park Farm
Coles Hill
Colesdale Farm
NORTHAW RD W
B156
NORTHAW RD E B156
Chain Wlk
Northaw Brook
Cattlegate Cottages
Nursery PLantation
Northaw Brook
Barvin Park
Cattlegate Wood
Cattlegate Farm
Abbotswood
COOPERS LANE RD
Barvin Hill
Woodhurst Farm Cottages
CATTLEGATE HILL
CATTLEGATE RD
Hooke Hill
Woodhurst Farm
M25
Owls Hall
Turkey Brook
Crews Hill Sta
Crews Hill CH
M25
Holly Hill Farm
South Hill
CREWS HILL
Crews Hill
North Lodge Farm
St Nicholas House
Golf Course
Chain Wlk
South Barvin Farm
A1005
Holyhill Brook
EAST LODGE LA
Vault Hill
Parting Hill
Botany Bay
East Lodge
Robin Hood (PH)
Little Beechhill Wood
THE RIDGEWAY
Bay Farm
Vault Hill Wood
Roundhedge Hill
Rectory Farm
Salmon's Brook
Duncan's Wood
Cuckolds Hill
Ash Wood
WILLIAM COVELL CL
Park Farm
Parkside Farm
Hotel
ROUNDHEDGE WAY
FERNY HILL
Obelisk
Moat Wood
HADLEY RD
Ride Wood
OAK AVE
MOAT VIEW
HIGH OAKS
A1005
Ferny HIll Farm

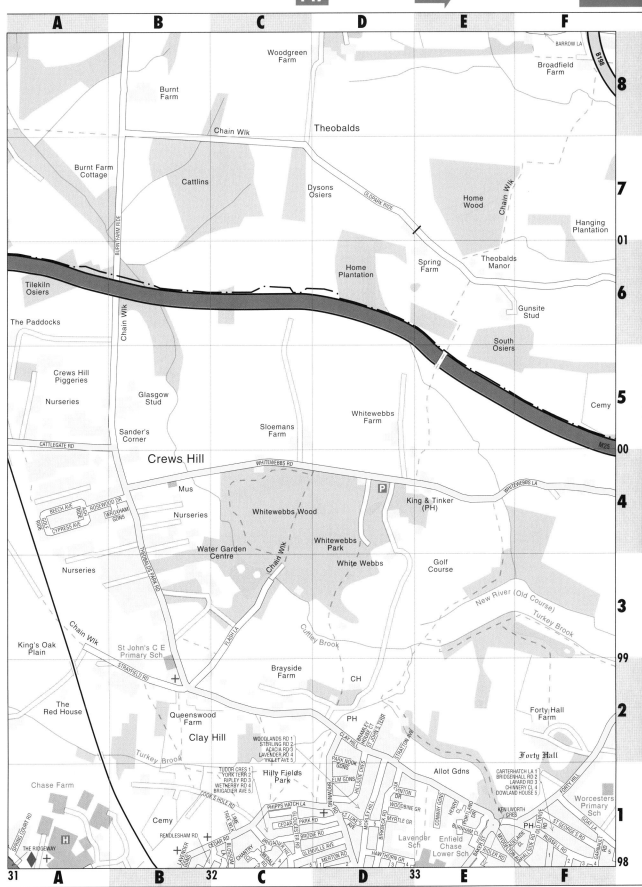

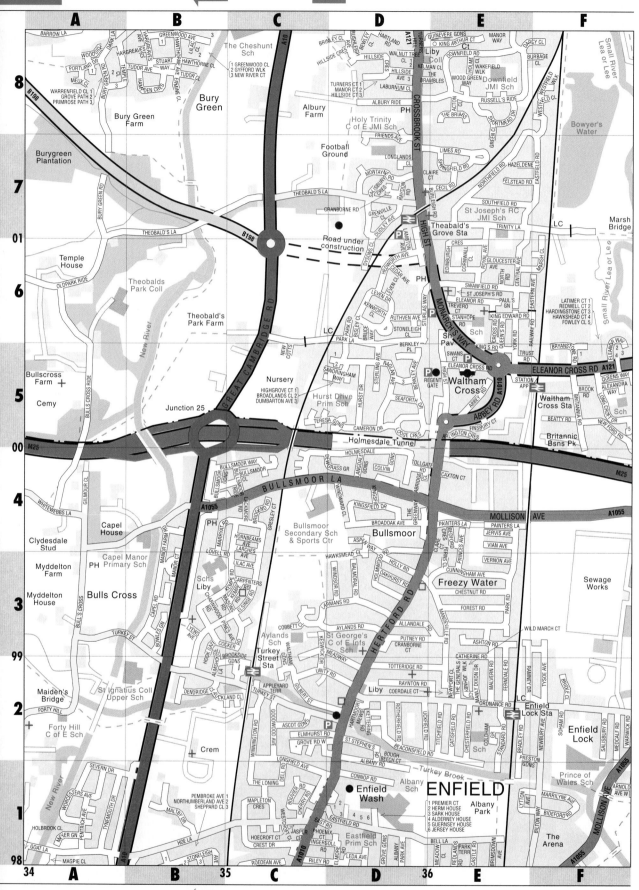

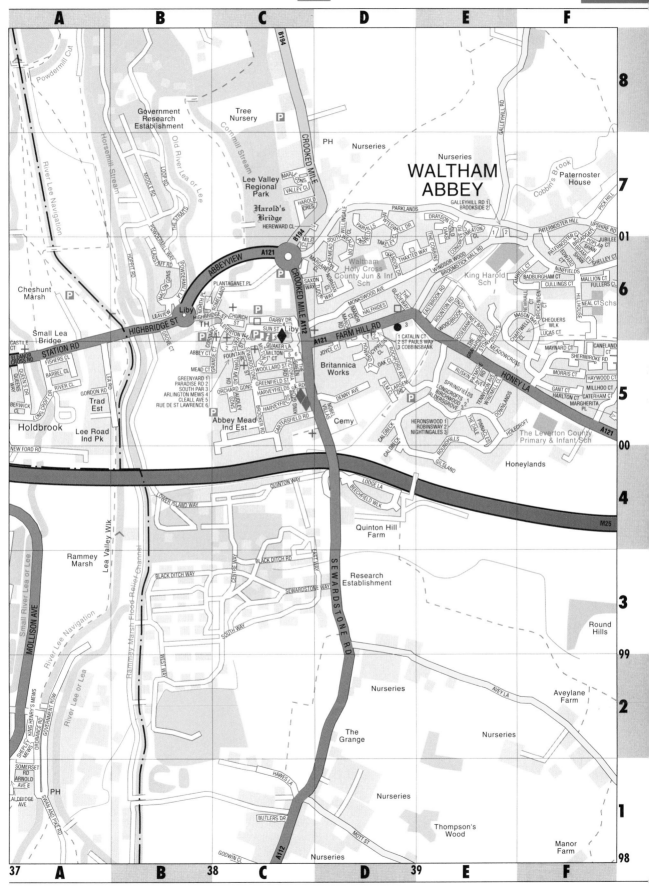

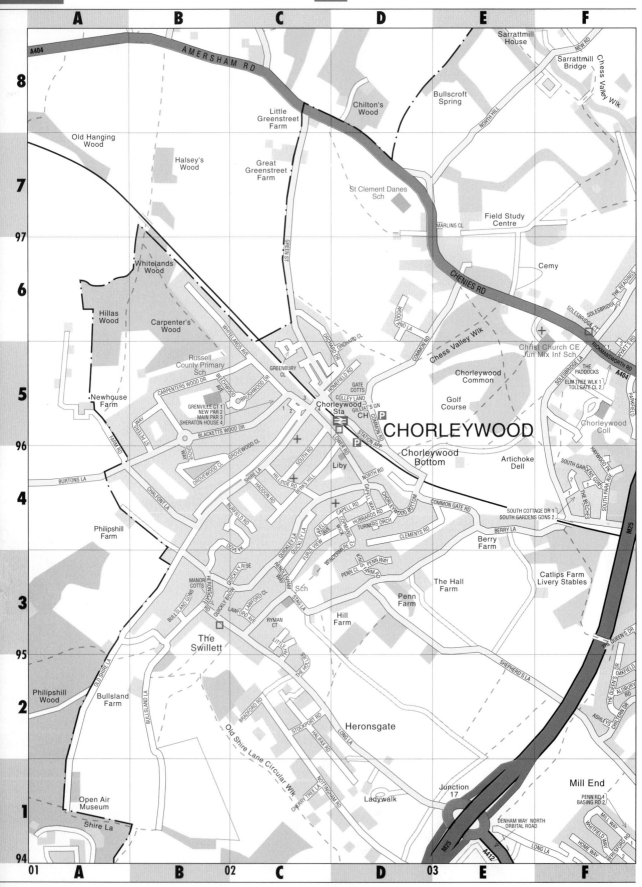

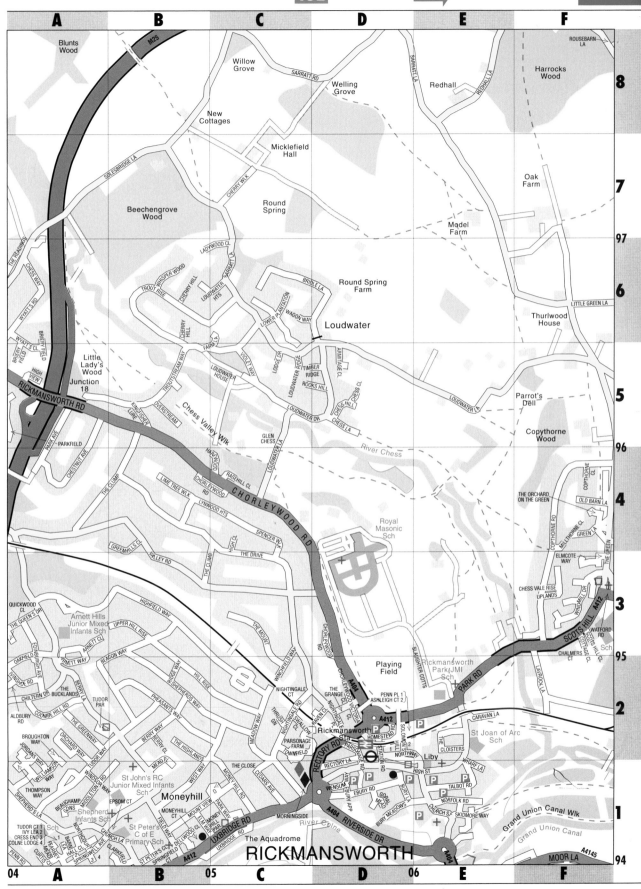

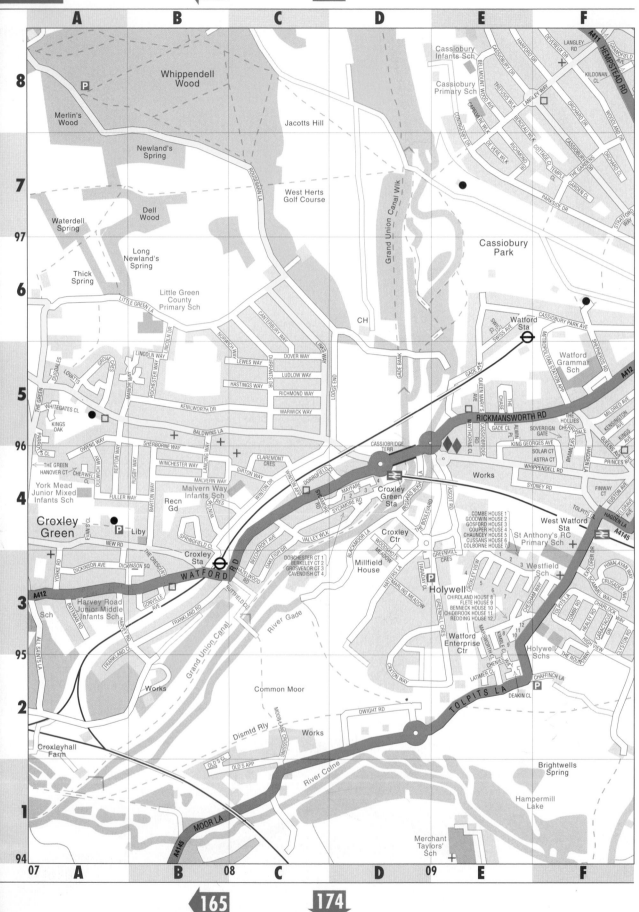

A B C D E F

8

Whippendell
Wood

Merlin's
Wood

Jacotts Hill

Cassiobury Infants Sch

Cassiobury
Primary Sch

HEMPSTEAD RD

Newland's
Spring

7

West Herts
Golf Course

Grand Union Canal Wlk

Cassiobury
Park

Waterdell
Spring

97

Dell
Wood

Thick
Spring

Long
Newland's
Spring

Little Green
County
Primary Sch

6

Watford
Sta

CASSIOBURY PARK AVE

Watford
Grammar
Sch

CH

A412

5

RICKMANSWORTH RD

The Green

Kings
Oak

Cassiobridge
Terr

Works

96

York Mead
Junior Mixed
Infants Sch

Malvern Way
Infants Sch

Recn
Gd

Croxley
Green
Sta

Croxley
Ctr

COMBE HOUSE 1
GOODWIN HOUSE 2
GOSFORD HOUSE 3
COUPER HOUSE 4
CHAUNCEY HOUSE 5
CUSSANS HOUSE 6
COLBORNE HOUSE 7

St Anthony's RC
Primary Sch

West Watford
Sta

A4145

4

Croxley
Green

Liby

Croxley
Sta

WATFORD RD

Millfield
House

Holywell

CHIRDLAND HOUSE 8
FLETE HOUSE 9
BENNECK HOUSE 10
CHIDBROOK HOUSE 11
REDDING HOUSE 12

Westfield
Sch

3

A412

Sch

Harvey Road
Junior Middle
Infants Sch

Grand Union Canal

River Gade

Watford
Enterprise
Ctr

Holywell
Schs

95

TOLPITS LA

2

Works

Common Moor

DWIGHT RD

Works

Brightwells
Spring

Croxleyhall
Farm

Dismtd Rly

River Colne

Hampermill
Lake

1

MOOR LA

A4145

Merchant
Taylors'
Sch

94

07 A B 08 C D 09 E F

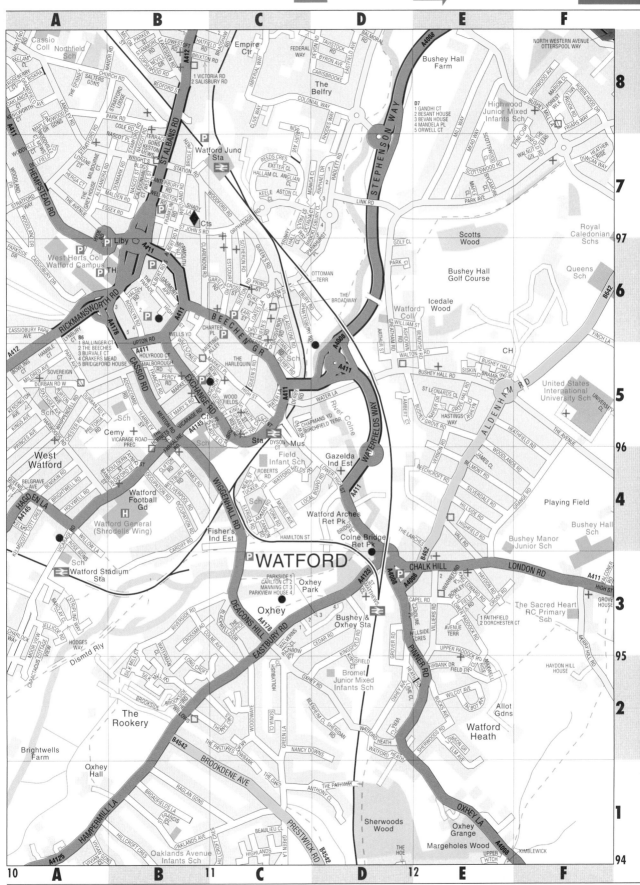

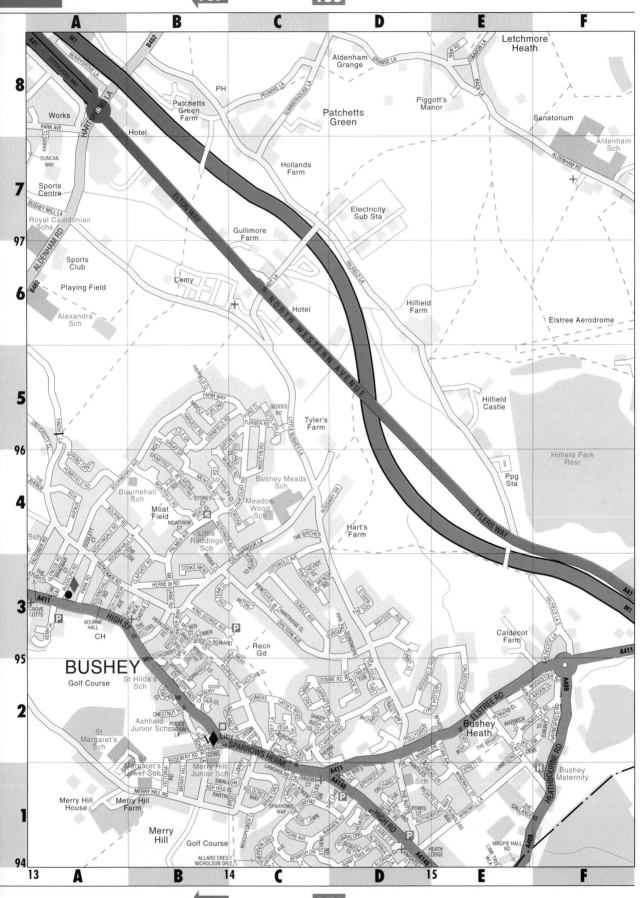

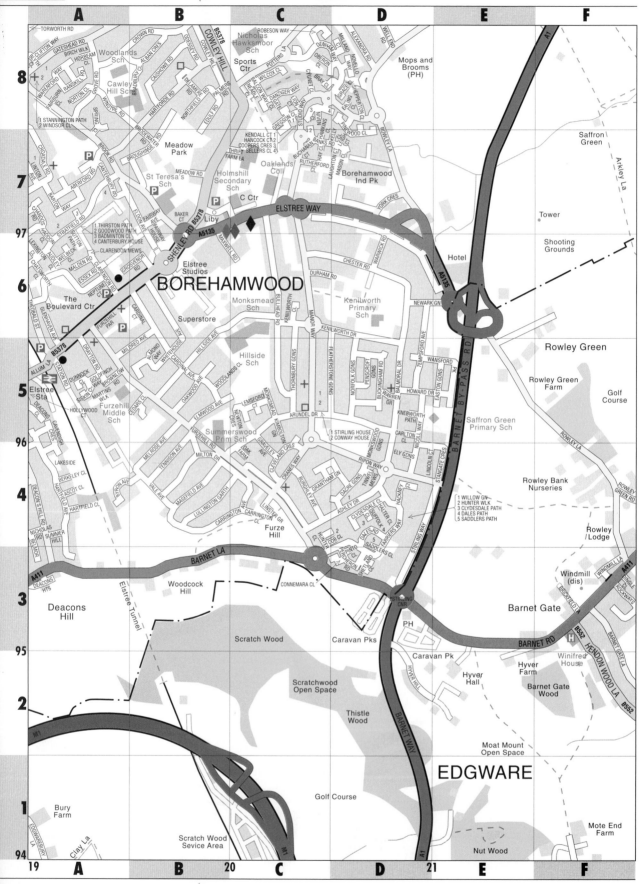

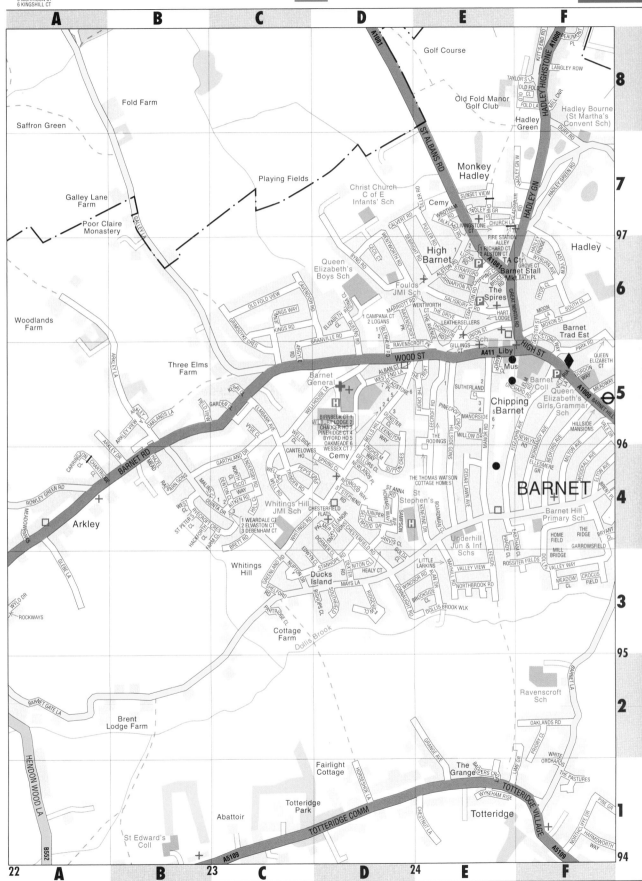

164

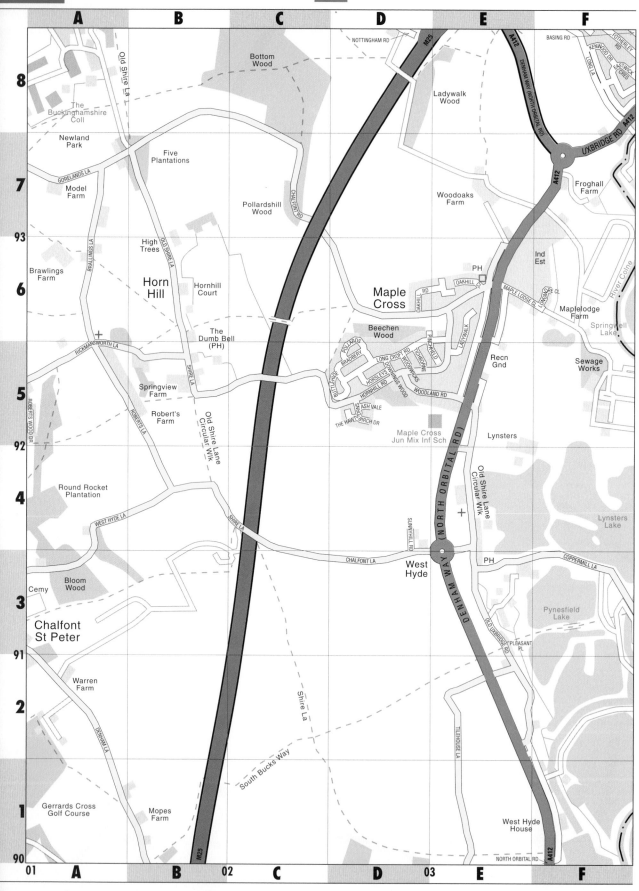

A B C D E F

8

7

93

6

5

92

4

3

91

2

1

90

BASING RD
FOTHERLEY
KENWOOD DR
LONG LA
EASTWICK CRES

UXBRIDGE RD

NOTTINGHAM RD

Bottom Wood

Ladywalk Wood

A412
DENHAM WAY (NORTH ORBITAL RD)

Froghall Farm

Woodoaks Farm

Ind Est

River Cone

The Buckinghamshire Coll

Newland Park

GORELANDS LA

Model Farm

Five Plantations

CHALFONT RD

OLD SHIRE LA

Pollardshill Wood

PH

OAKHILL RD
OAKHILL CL

Maple Cross

Maple Lodge Cl

LONGMORE CL

Maplelodge Farm

Springwell Lake

High Trees

BRALLINGS LA

Horn Hill

Hornhill Court

Beechen Wood

POLLARDS
BRADBERY
BUTTLEHIDE
LONG CROFT RD
WOODWICKS
PINCHFIELD
ICKBERNE

LADYWALK

Recn Gnd

Sewage Works

Brawlings Farm

RICKMANSWORTH LA

SHIRE LA

The Dumb Bell (PH)

HORSLEYS
DOWNINGS WOOD
WOODLAND RD
SNASH VALE
ASH VALE

Springview Farm

ROBERTS LA

Robert's Farm

Old Shire Lane Circular Wlk

THE HAWS
BIRCH DR

Maple Cross Jun Mix Inf Sch

Lynsters

ROBERTS WOOD DR

Round Rocket Plantation

WEST HYDE LA

SHIRE LA

Old Shire Lane Circular Wlk

Lynsters Lake

Cemy

Bloom Wood

CHALFONT LA

SUNNYHILL RD

West Hyde

PH

COPPERMILL LA

DENHAM WAY (NORTH ORBITAL RD)

OLD UXBRIDGE RD

PLEASANT PL

Pynesfield Lake

Chalfont St Peter

Warren Farm

DENHAM LA

Shire La

TILEHOUSE LA

Gerrards Cross Golf Course

Mopes Farm

South Bucks Way

M25

West Hyde House

A412

NORTH ORBITAL RD

01 A B 02 C D 03 E F

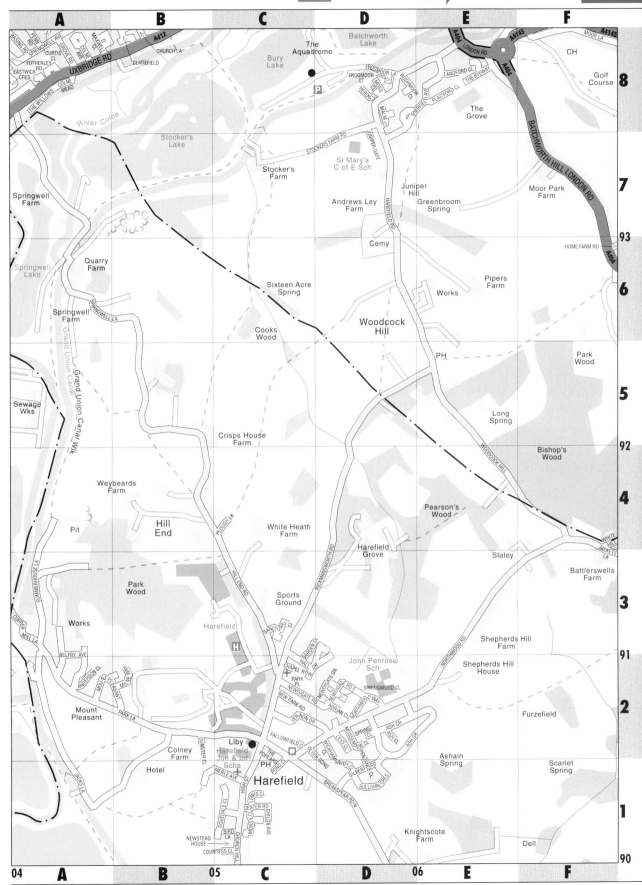

A B C D E F

8
7
93
6
5
92
4
3
91
2
1
90

UXBRIDGE RD
A412
CHURCH LA
CLARKFIELD
PENN PL
SPRINGWELL GDNS
MAXWELL CL
COLNE AVE
GROVE RD
FOTHERLEY RD
CURTIS RD
BASING RD
EASTWICK CRES
COLNE MEAD
THE WILLOWS

River Colne
Stocker's Lake
Springwell Farm
Springwell Lake
Quarry Farm
Springwell Farm
Springwell La
Grand Union Canal
Grand Union Canal Wlk
Sewage Wks
Summerhouse La
Pit
Park Wood
Copper Mill La
Works
Belfry Ave
Anderson Cl
Moll Ave
Ash Mill Ave
Mount Pleasant
Park La
Dunster Cl
Jacks La
Colney Farm
Hotel
Merle Ave
Newstead House
Dovedale Cl
Bird La
Lewis Cl
Mors Cl
Dexter Rd
Childs Ave
Church Hill
Countess Cl

The Aquadrome
Bury Lake
Batchworth Lake
Stocker's Farm
Stockers Farm Rd
P
Frogmoor La
Frogmoor Ct
Moss Cl
Heron Cl
Malm Cl
Juniper Gate
Rushmoor Cl
Sherfield Ave
Plaitford Cl
Landford Cl
The Byeway
London Rd
A404
A4145
Moor La
A4145
CH
Golf Course
The Grove
Batchworth Hill London Rd
A404
Moor Park Farm
Home Farm Rd
A404
St Mary's C of E Sch
Andrews Ley Farm
Juniper Hill
Greenbroom Spring
Cemy
Harefield Rd
Sixteen Acre Spring
Cooks Wood
Woodcock Hill
Works
Pipers Farm
Park Wood
Long Spring
Bishop's Wood
PH
Woodcock Hill
Pearson's Wood
White Hill
Jackets La
Crisps House Farm
Weybeards Farm
Hill End
Plough La
Hill End Rd
White Heath Farm
Harefield Grove
Slaley
Battlerswells Farm
Rickmansworth Rd
Sports Ground
Harefield
H
Sanctuary Cl
Barden Cl
Hall Dr
Chapel Row
Park Pl
Newgate Cl
Newgate Gn
Springwood Cl
John Penrose Sch
Northwood Rd
Northwood Way
Shepherds Hill Farm
Shepherds Hill House
91
Furzefield
New Park Rd
Newdigate Rd
Vernon Dr
Adrian Rd
Mossendew Cl
Keys Cl
Spring Cl
Ash Gr
Ash Cl
Ash Gr
Liby
The Poplars
Fallowfield Cl
Olivia Gdns
Pond Cl
PH
Harefield Jun & Inf Schs
Wickham Cl
Savoy Cl
Gilbert Rd
Pinchfield
Sullivan Cres
Breakspear Rd
Breakspear Rd N
Ashain Spring
Scarlet Spring
Harefield
Knightscote Farm
Dell

173
166

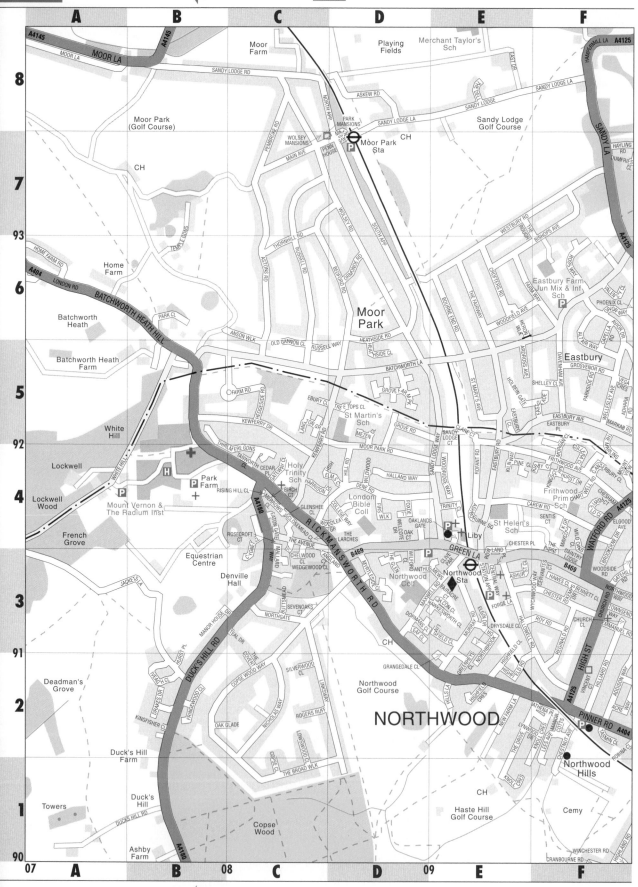

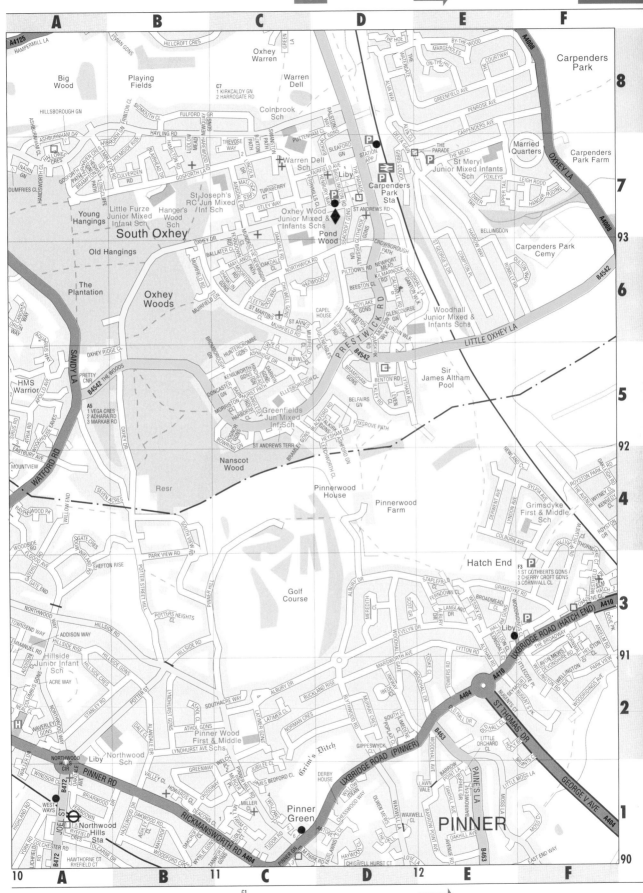

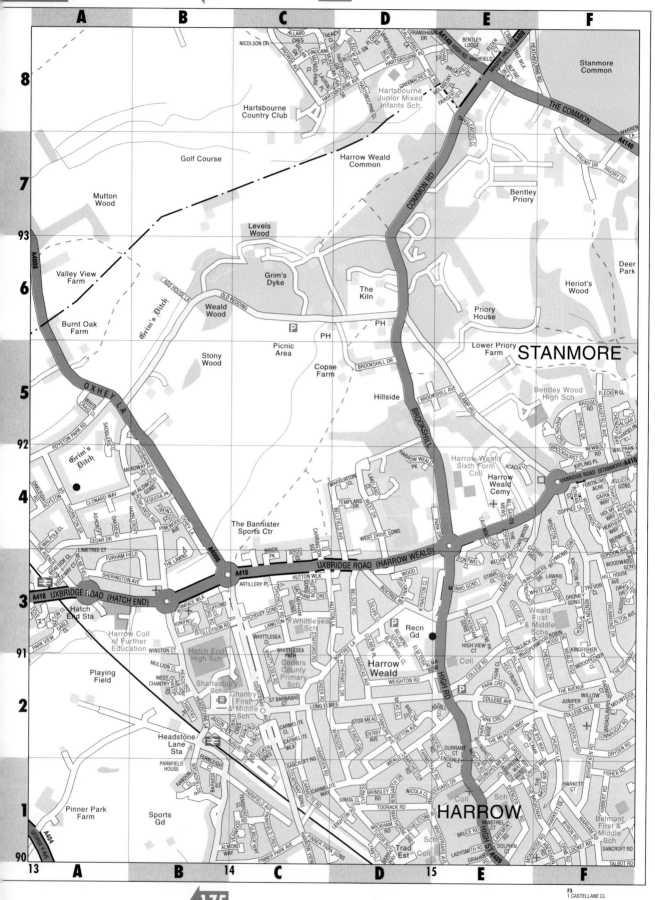

EXPLANATION OF THE STREET INDEX REFERENCE SYSTEM

Street names are listed alphabetically and show the locality, the Post Office Postcode District, the page number and a reference to the square in which the name falls on the map page.

Example: Peterlee Ct. Heml H HP2....................................124 F7 2

Peterlee Ct	This is the full street name, which may have been abbreviated on the map.
Heml H	This is the abbreviation for the town, village or locality in which the street falls.
HP2	This is the Post Office Postcode District for the street name.
124	This is the page number of the map on which the street name appears.
F7	The letter and figure indicate the square on the map in which the centre of the street falls. The square can be found at the junction of the vertical column carrying the appropriate letter and the horizontal row carrying the appropriate figure.
2	In congested areas numbers may have been used to indicate the location of a street. In certain circumstances, the number used to represent a street will follow the reference in the gazetteer entry.

ABBREVIATIONS USED IN THE INDEX
Road Names

Approach	App	Corner	Cnr	Grove	Gr
Arcade	Arc	Cottages	Cotts	Heights	Hts
Avenue	Ave	Court	Ct	Industrial Estate	Ind Est
Boulevard	Bvd	Courtyard	Ctyd	Interchange	Intc
Buildings	Bldgs	Crescent	Cres	Junction	Junc
Business Park	Bsns Pk	Drive	Dr	Lane	La
Business Centre	Bsns Ctr	Drove	Dro	North	N
Bungalows	Bglws	East	E	Orchard	Orch
Causeway	Cswy	Embankment	Emb	Parade	Par
Centre	Ctr	Esplanade	Espl	Park	Pk
Circle	Circ	Estate	Est	Passage	Pas
Circus	Cir	Gardens	Gdns	Place	Pl
Close	Cl	Green	Gn	Precinct	Prec
Common	Comm				

Promenade	Prom
Retail Park	Ret Pk
Road	Rd
Roundabout	Rdbt
South	S
Square	Sq
Stairs	Strs
Steps	Stps
Street,Saint	St
Terrace	Terr
Trading Estate	Trad Est
Walk	Wlk
West	W
Yard	Yd

Key to abbreviations of Town, Village and Rural locality names used in the index of street names.

Name	Abbr	Page	Sq	Name	Abbr	Page	Sq
Abbots Langley	Abb L	153	F7	Kensworth Common	Ken Co	82	E8
Albury	Alb	57	A6	Kimpton	Kim	66	C1
Aldbury	Ald	101	C5	Kings Langley	Kin L	139	A1
Anstey	Ans	29	B6	Kings Walden	Kin Wd	48	A3
Ardeley	Ard	38	F3	Knebworth	Kneb	69	A5
Arlesey	Arl	11	B5	Kneesworth	Knee	2	A5
Ashley Green	Ash Gr	136	A7	Langley	Lan	49	F1
Ashwell	Ashw	4	D3	Langley (Essex)	Lang	18	F2
Aspenden	Asp	40	D5	Latimer	Lat	150	E3
Aston	Ast	51	E2	Letchworth	Letw	22	F7
Aston Clinton	Ast Cl	99	A3	Lilley	Lily	32	D2
Ayot St Lawrence	A St L	88	B6	Little Berkhamsted	L Berk	132	C4
Ayot St Peter	A St P	88	F3	Little Chalfont	L Chal	150	B1
Baldock	Bal	23	E8	Little Gaddesden	L Gad	102	D7
Barkway	Bark	17	D4	Little Hadham	L Had	57	D2
Barley	Bar	8	F1	Little Hallingbury	L Hal	98	D7
Barnet	Barn	171	F4	Little Wymondley	L Wym	35	E3
Bassingbourn	Bas	6	F8	London Colney	Lon C	142	E5
Bayford	Bay	132	F6	Long Marston	Lon M	79	B3
Benington	Ben	52	E4	Lower Nazeing	Lo Naz	149	D8
Berden	Berd	43	F7	Lower Stondon	L Ston	10	A3
Berkhamsted	Berk	122	C6	Luton	Luton	45	C3
Birchanger	Birhr	59	E2	Maple Cross	Map Cr	172	D6
Bishop's Stortford	Bis St	76	D7	Markyate	Mark	83	F5
Borehamwood	Bor	170	B6	Marsworth	Mars	80	A1
Botley	Bot	136	A1	Meesden	Mee	29	F6
Bovingdon	Bov	137	B3	Melbourn	Melb	2	F5
Bramfield	Bram	91	C4	Mentmore	Men	61	D4
Braughing	Brag	8	F1	Moor Park	Mo Pk	174	D6
Breachwood Green	Bre Gr	47	E1	Much Hadham	Muc H	74	F3
Brent Pelham	Bre P	30	A2	New Mill End	Nwml E	64	D1
Brickendon	Bric	133	C4	Newgate Street	New St	146	C7
Bricket Wood	Bri Wd	140	F1	Newnham	Newn	12	F7
Brookmans Park	Bro Pk	144	F5	Northaw	Nort	145	F1
Buckland	Buck	27	D8	Northchurch	Nthch	121	D6
Buntingford	Bun	40	F7	Northwood	Norwd	174	E2
Bushey	Bus	168	A2	Nuthampstead	Nut	18	B2
Bygrave	Byg	13	C5	Odsey	Odsey	5	C1
Caddington	Cad	62	E4	Park Street	Pk St	141	D5
Chalfont St Peter	C St P	172	A3	Pinner	Pnr	175	E1
Cheddington	Ched	80	A8	Pirton	Pirt	20	C4
Chenies	Chen	151	B2	Pitstone	Pit	80	D4
Cheshunt	Ches	148	C1	Potten End	Pot En	123	C7
Chipperfield	Chipf	152	B8	Potters Bar	Pot B	159	D6
Chiswellgreen	Chis	141	A5	Preston	Pres	48	D6
Cholesbury	Chol	120	C2	Radlett	Radl	156	B5
Chorleywood	Chor	164	E5	Redbourn	Redb	106	B6
Clavering	Clav	30	F5	Reed	Reed	16	F5
Clothall	Clo	24	E4	Rickmansworth	Ric	165	D1
Codicote	Cod	67	E1	Ridge	Ridge	157	F5
Colney Heath	Coln H	143	D8	Roydon	Roy	116	C1
Cottered	Cotrd	39	C7	Royston	Royst	7	C5
Crews Hill	Cre H	161	B4	Rushden	Rus	25	F3
Croxley Green	Cro Gr	166	A4	Sacombe	Sac	71	E3
Cuffley	Cuf	146	E3	Sandon	San	15	B1
Dagnall	Dagn	81	C6	Sandridge	Sand	108	C1
Dane End	Dan En	71	F8	Sarratt	Sar	152	A4
Datchworth	Dat	69	E2	Sawbridgeworth	Saw	97	C2
Dunstable	Dun	44	A2	Sheering	Sheer	98	D1
Dunton	Dunt	1	A5	Shenley	Shen	157	A5
Eastwick	East	117	A4	Shillington	Shill	19	E8
Edgware	Edg	170	E1	South Oxhey	Sth Ox	175	B7
Edworth	Edw	3	A6	St Albans	St Alb	127	F4
Elstree	Elst	169	E3	St Ippolitts	St Ipp	35	B3
Enfield	Enf	162	B1	St Leonards	St Le	119	E3
Essendon	Ess	131	F6	Standon	Stand	55	E1
Farnham	Far	58	D6	Stanmore	Stan	176	F5
Felden	Fel	138	A8	Stanstead Abbotts	Sta Ab	115	F4
Flamstead	Fla	84	B1	Stanstead Mountfitchet	Sta M	59	C7
Flaunden	Flau	151	C4	Stapleford	Stap	92	A7
Furneux Pelham	Fur P	43	A5	Steeple Morden	Ste Mo	5	B8
Goff's Oak	Gofs O	147	D3	Stevenage	Stev	50	D8
Graveley	Gra	36	C4	Stocking Pelham	Sto P	43	E7
Great Amwell	Gt Am	114	F5	Stotfold	Stot	11	E7
Great Chishill	Gt Ch	9	F2	Streatley	Str	31	A5
Great Gaddesden	Gt Gd	103	D3	Studham	Stu	82	C4
Great Hallingbury	Gt Ha	77	E4	Tewin	Tewin	90	E2
Great Hormead	Gt Ho	29	B8	Therfield	Ther	15	F7
Great Munden	Gt Mu	54	C5	Thundridge	Thun	93	E7
Great Offley	Gt Of	33	D2	Tonwell	Ton	92	F7
Great Wymondley	Gt Wy	35	F6	Tring	Tri	100	B3
Guilden Morden	Gu M	1	F5	Walkern	Walk	38	B1
Hadley Wood	Had W	159	C2	Wallington	Wal	25	D8
Hammond Street	Ham St	147	D5	Waltham Abbey	Wa Aby	163	E7
Harefield	Hare	173	C1	Ware	Ware	93	F2
Harlow	Harl	117	E1	Wareside	Wars	94	E4
Harpenden	Harp	86	B2	Watford	Watf	167	C3
Harrow	Har	176	E1	Watton at Stone	Wat St	70	D4
Hatfield	Hat	130	B8	Welham Green	Wel Gr	144	C7
Hatfield Heath	Hat H	98	F4	Welwyn	Welw	89	B4
Hemel Hempstead	Heml H	124	D1	Welwyn Garden City	Wel G C	110	E7
Henlow	Henlw	10	D8	Westmill	West	40	F3
Hertford	Hert	113	C5	Weston	Wes	24	C1
Hertford Heath	Hert H	114	B3	Wheathampstead	Whea	108	C7
Hertingfordbury	Hertng	112	F5	Whipsnade	Whip	82	A8
Hexton	Hex	19	B2	Whitwell	Whit	66	E6
High Wych	H Wy	97	B1	Widford	Widf	95	C4
Hinxworth	Hin	3	D6	Wigginton	Wigg	100	D1
Hitchin	Hit	34	E8	Wilstone	Wils	79	D1
Hoddesdon	Hod	135	B5	Wingrave	Wing	60	C3
Holwell	Hol	21	B7	Wyddial	Wyd	28	B3
Hunsdon	Hun	95	D1				
Ickleford	Ick	21	E4				
Kelshall	Kel	15	D5				

Abbey Ave. St Alb AL3 .... 127 B1
Abbey Ct. Wa Aby EN9 .... 163 B5
Abbey Dr. Abb L WD5 .... 154 A7
Abbey Dr. Luton LU2 .... 46 A1
Abbey Hts. St Alb AL1 .... 127 E3
Abbey Mead Ind Est. Wa Aby 163 C5
Abbey Mill End. St Alb AL3 .... 127 C2
Abbey Mill La. St Alb AL3 .... 127 C2
Abbey Rd. Ches EN8 .... 162 E6
Abbey Sch The. St Alb 127 D2
Abbey Theatre. St Alb 127 D1
Abbey Theatre. St Alb 127 C1
Abbey View Rd. St Alb AL3 .... 127 C3
Abbey View. St Alb AL1 .... 127 D1
Abbey View. Watf WD2 .... 154 D3
Abbeygate Bsns Ctr The. Luton 63 D7
Abbeyview. Wa Aby EN9 .... 163 C6
Abbis Orch. Ick SG5 .... 21 E5
Abbot John Mews. Whea AL4 .... 87 D1
Abbots Ave. St Alb AL1 .... 141 E8
Abbots Ave W. St Alb AL1 .... 141 D8
Abbots Cl. Dat SG3 .... 69 D1
Abbots Cl. Luton LU2 .... 46 A1
Abbots Gr. Stev SG1 .... 50 F5
Abbots Langley Sch. Abb L 139 F1
Abbots Pk. St Alb AL1 .... 128 A1
Abbots Rise. Kin L WD4 .... 139 E1
Abbots Rd. Abb L WD5 .... 139 E1
Abbots View. Kin L WD4 .... 138 F4
Abbotswood Par. Luton LU2 .... 46 A1
Abbotts La. Letw SG6 .... 22 E6
Abbotts Rise. Sta Ab SG12 .... 115 D4
Abbotts Way. Bis St CM23 .... 76 E3
Abbotts Way. Wing HP22 .... 60 A4
Abbotts Wood Rd. Luton LU2 .... 46 A1
Abbotts Yd. Royst SG8 .... 7 B8
Abdale La. Wel G AL9 .... 144 C4
Abel Cl. Heml H HP3 .... 125 A3
Abel Smith Jun Mix Inf Sch.Hert .. 113 C6
Aberdale Gdns. Pot B EN6 .... 158 F7
Aberdeen Rd. Har HA3 .... 176 F1
Aberford Rd. Bor WD6 .... 170 C7
Abigail Cl. Luton LU3 .... 45 D3
Abingdon Pl. Pot B EN6 .... 159 B7
Abingdon Rd. Dun LU4 .... 44 C3
Aboyne Lodge Prim Sch. St Alb 127 D4
Abridge Ct. Enf EN8 .... 162 D4
Abstacle Hill. Tri HP23 .... 99 F3
Acacia Cl. Ham St EN7 .... 147 E4
Acacia Ct. Stan HA7 .... 176 F3
Acacia Gr. Berk HP4 .... 122 B3
Acacia Rd. Enf EN2 .... 161 D1
Acacia St. Hat AL10 .... 130 A4
Acacia Wlk. Harp AL5 .... 107 D6
Acacia Wlk. Tri HP23 .... 99 E3
Acers. Chis AL2 .... 141 C3
Achilles Cl. Heml H HP2 .... 124 F5
Ackroyd Rd. Royst SG8 .... 7 B8
Acme Rd. Watf WD2 .... 154 B1
Acorn Cl. Cuf EN6 .... 146 E2
Acorn Pl. Watf WD2 .... 154 A2
Acorn Rd. Heml H HP3 .... 125 A2
Acorn St. Hun SG12 .... 116 D8
Acorns The. St Alb AL4 .... 128 D3
Acre Piece. Hit SG4 .... 35 A6
Acre Way. Norwd HA6 .... 174 F2
Acre Wood. Heml H HP2 .... 124 F5
Acremore St. L Had SG11 .... 75 C7
Acrewood Way. Coln H AL4 .... 128 F3
Acton Cl. Ches EN8 .... 162 E8
Acworth Cres. Luton LU4 .... 44 A4
Acworth Pl. Luton LU4 .... 44 C5
Adam's Yd. Hert SG14 .... 113 D6
Adams House. Harl CM20 .... 117 D1
Adams Way. Tri HP23 .... 100 B6
Adamsfield. Ham St EN7 .... 148 A5
Adderley Rd. Bis St CM23 .... 76 F7
Adderley Rd. Har HA3 .... 176 F2
Addiscombe Rd. Watf WD1 .... 167 B5
Addiscombe Road Jun Sch. Watf . 167 B5
Addison Cl. Norwd HA6 .... 174 A2
Addison Way. Norwd HA6 .... 174 F2
Adelaide Cl. Enf EN1 .... 161 F1
Adelaide St. Luton LU1 .... 63 D7
Adelaide St. St Alb AL3 .... 127 D4
Adele Ave. Welw AL6 .... 89 F3
Adeyfield Gdns. Heml H HP2 .... 124 F4
Adeyfield Rd. Heml H HP2 .... 124 D4
Adeyfield Sec Mod Sch. Heml H .. 125 A3
Adhara Rd. Mo Pk HA6 .... 175 A5
Adinger Cl. Stev SG1 .... 50 E7
Adingtons. Harl CM20 .... 117 F2
Admiral St. Hert SG13 .... 114 A6
Admiral Way. Nthch HP4 .... 121 E6
Admirals Cl. Col H AL4 .... 143 E8
Admirals Wlk. Hod EN11 .... 135 A4
Admirals Wlk. St Alb AL1 .... 142 A8
Adrian Cl. Hare UB9 .... 173 D2
Adrian House. Abb L WD5 .... 153 E8
Adrian Rd. Abb L WD5 .... 153 E8
Adstone Rd. Cad LU2 .... 62 F3
Ailsworth Rd. Luton LU3 .... 45 A7
Ainsdale Rd. Sth Ox WD1 .... 175 C5
Aintree Rd. Royst SG8 .... 7 F6
Aintree Way. Stev SG1 .... 51 C8
Airedale. Heml H HP2 .... 124 E6
Airport Approach Rd. Luton LU2 .... 64 B4
Airport Executive Pk. Luton 64 D8
Airport Way. Luton LU1,LU2 .... 64 B4
Aitken Rd. Barn EN5 .... 171 C4
Akeman Cl. St Alb AL3 .... 126 F1
Akeman St. Tri HP23 .... 100 A3
Alan Dr. Barn EN5 .... 171 E3
Alandale Dr. Pnr HA5 .... 175 B2
Alban Ave. St Alb AL3 .... 127 D5
Alban Cres. Bor WD6 .... 170 B8
Alban Ct. Barn EN5 .... 171 D5
Alban Ct. St Alb AL1 .... 128 C3
Alban Pk Ind Est. Coln H 128 E2
Alban Rd. Letw SG6 .... 23 C5
Alban Wood Jun Sch. Watf 154 B6
Albans View. Watf WD2 .... 154 B6
Albert Cl. Bus WD2 .... 168 D3
Albany Ct. Harp AL5 .... 107 C8

Albany Mews. Chis AL2 .... 141 A4
Albany Mews. Ware SG12 .... 93 E1 3
Albany Park Ave. Enf EN3 .... 162 D1
Albany Rd. Enf EN3 .... 162 D1
Albany Sch. Enf 162 D1
Albany Terr. Tri 100 B6
Albemarle Ave. Ches EN8 .... 148 C3
Albemarle Ave. Pot B EN6 .... 159 B7
Albert Gate. St Alb AL1 .... 127 D2
Albert Rd. Arl SG15 .... 11 A4
Albert Rd. Luton LU1 .... 63 E6
Albert Rd N. Watf WD1 .... 167 B6
Albert Rd. Watf WD1 .... 167 B6
Albert St. Mark AL3 .... 83 E5
Albert St. St Alb AL1 .... 127 D2
Albert St. Stev SG1 .... 50 D7
Albert St. Tri HP23 .... 100 A3
Albion Cl. Hert SG13 .... 113 E7
Albion Cl. Luton LU2 .... 63 E8 5
Albion Hill. Heml H HP2 .... 124 D2
Albion Rd. Luton LU2 .... 63 E8
Albion Rd. Pit LU7 .... 80 D5
Albion Rd. St Alb AL1 .... 127 F3
Albion The. Ware SG12 .... 93 D2 9
Albury Cl. Luton LU3 .... 31 A1
Albury Dr. Pnr HA5 .... 175 D3
Albury Dr. Pnr HA5 .... 175 D3
Albury Grove Rd. Ches EN8 .... 148 E8
Albury Rd. L Had SG11 .... 57 C2
Albury Ride. Ches EN8 .... 162 D8
Albury Sch. Alb 57 A6
Albury Wlk. Ches EN8 .... 148 C1
Alconbury. Bis St CM23 .... 59 B1
Alconbury. Wel G C AL7 .... 111 E6
Aldbury Cl. St Alb AL4 .... 128 C8
Aldbury Cl. Watf WD2 .... 154 D3
Aldbury Gdns. Tri HP23 .... 100 B6
Aldbury Gr. Wel G C AL7 .... 111 B6
Aldbury Jun Mix Inf Sch
(Voluntary Controlled). Ald .. 101 C6
Aldbury Rd. Ric WD3 .... 164 D3
Aldcock Rd. Stev SG1 .... 50 E7
Aldeburgh Cl. Stev SG1 .... 36 A1
Aldenham Ave. Radl WD7 .... 156 A3
Aldenham Country Pk. Elst 169 B4
Aldenham Radl WD7 .... 156 B5
Aldenham Rd. Bus WD2 .... 168 A6
Aldenham Rd. Elst WD6 .... 169 A6
Aldenham Rd. Radl WD7 .... 156 A4
Aldenham Rd. Radl WD7 .... 169 A6
Aldenham Rd. Watf WD2 .... 167 E5
Aldenham Sch. Radl 168 F7
Alder Cl. Bis St CM23 .... 76 D4
Alder Cl. Chis AL2 .... 141 C3
Alder Cres. Luton LU3 .... 45 A3
Alder Ct. Luton LU3 .... 45 A3
Alder Wlk. Watf WD2 .... 154 B4
Alderbury Rd. Sta M CM24 .... 59 E7
Alderley Ct. Berk HP4 .... 122 C3
Alderman Cl. Wel G AL9 .... 144 C7
Alderney House. Enf EN3 .... 162 D1
Alders Cl. Wel G C 111 A6
Alders End La. Harp AL5 .... 85 F2
Alders Wlk. Saw CM21 .... 97 E2
Aldersgrove. Wa Aby EN9 .... 163 E5
Alderton Cl. Luton LU2 .... 46 D1 4
Alderton Dr. L Gad HP4 .... 102 B8
Aldhous Cl. Luton LU3 .... 45 B5
Aldock. Wel G C AL7 .... 111 A3
Aldridge Ave. Enf EN3 .... 163 A1
Aldwick Ct. St Alb AL1 .... 128 B1
Aldwick Rd. Harp AL5 .... 107 E8
Aldwick. St Alb AL1 .... 128 B1
Aldwickbury Cres. Harp AL5 .... 86 D1
Aldwyck Ct. Heml H HP1 .... 124 C4
Aldwyke Rise. Ware SG12 .... 93 C3
Aldykes. Hat AL10 .... 129 F5
Alesia Rd. Luton LU3 .... 44 F6
Alex Ct. Heml H HP2 .... 124 D4
Alexander Ct. Ches EN8 .... 148 D1
Alexander Gate. Stev SG1 .... 51 C8
Alexander Rd. Hert SG14 .... 113 A6
Alexander Rd. Lon C AL2 .... 142 D6
Alexander Rd. Stot SG5 .... 11 F5
Alexandra Ave. Luton LU3 .... 45 C2
Alexandra Rd. Bor WD6 .... 170 D8
Alexandra Rd. Chipf WD4 .... 138 A1
Alexandra Rd. Heml H HP2 .... 124 D4
Alexandra Rd. Hit SG5 .... 21 F1
Alexandra Rd. Sar WD3 .... 152 A3
Alexandra Rd. St Alb AL1 .... 127 E3
Alexandra Rd. Watf WD1 .... 167 A7
Alexandra Sch. Bus 168 A6
Alexandra Way. Ches EN8 .... 162 E6
Aleyn Way. Bal SG7 .... 13 B1
Alfriston Cl. Luton LU2 .... 46 C3
Algar Cl. Stan HA7 .... 176 F5
Alington La. Letw SG6 .... 22 F3
All Saints C of E Jun Mix Inf Sch.
Bis St 77 B8
All Saints Cl. Bis St CM23 .... 77 A8
All Saints La. Cro Gr WD3 .... 166 A3
All Saints Mews. Stan HA3 .... 176 E4
All Saints Prim Sch. Dat 69 D3
Allandale Cres. Pot B EN6 .... 158 E7
Allandale. Heml H HP2 .... 124 D5
Allandale. Enf EN3 .... 162 B4
Allandale. St Alb AL3 .... 141 B8
Allard Cl. Ham St EN7 .... 147 F4
Allard Cres. Bus WD2 .... 168 C1
Allard Way. Hod EN10 .... 134 E2
Alldicks Rd. Heml H HP3 .... 124 F1
Allen Cl. Whea AL4 .... 108 D7
Allen Ct. Hat AL10 .... 130 B3 2
Allenby Ave. Dun LU5 .... 44 A1
Allendale. Luton LU3 .... 31 A1
Allende Ave. Harl CM20 .... 117 D2
Allerton Cl. Bor WD6 .... 156 F1
Allerton Rd. Bor WD6 .... 156 F1
Alleyns Rd. Stev SG1 .... 50 D7
Allison. Wel G C 110 B5
Allsaints Cres. Watf WD2 .... 154 D6
Allsaints Cl. Ston SG16 .... 10 A4
Allum La. Radl WD6 .... 169 E5
Allwood Rd. Ham St EN7 .... 147 F4
Alma Ct. Bor HA2 .... 156 F1
Alma Cut. St Alb AL1 .... 127 E2

Alma Link. Luton LU1 .... 63 D7
Alma Rd. Nthch HP4 .... 121 E6
Alma Rd. St Alb AL1 .... 127 E2
Alma Row. Har HA3 .... 176 D2
Alma St. Luton LU1 .... 63 D7
Almond Hill Jun Sch. Stev 50 E8
Almond Way. Bor WD6 .... 170 B5
Almond Way. Har HA2 .... 176 C1
Almond Wlk. Hat AL10 .... 130 A2 1
Almonds La. Stev SG1 .... 50 E8
Almonds The. St Alb AL1 .... 142 B7
Alms La. Ashw SG7 .... 4 D4
Almshouse La. Enf EN1 .... 162 B2
Alnwick Dr. Lon M HP23 .... 78 F7
Alpha Bsns Pk. Wel G 144 C8
Alpha Pl. Bis St CM23 .... 76 F8
Alpine Cl. Hit SG4 .... 35 A5
Alpine Way. Luton LU3 .... 44 D8
Alpine Wlk. Stan HA7 .... 176 E8
Alston Ct. Barn EN5 .... 171 E6
Alston Rd. Barn EN5 .... 171 E6
Altair Way. Mo Pk HA6 .... 174 F5
Altham Gr. Harl CM20 .... 117 F2
Althorp Rd. Luton LU3 .... 45 C1
Althorp Rd. St Alb AL1 .... 127 F4
Alton Ave. Har HA3 .... 176 F3
Alton Rd. Luton LU1 .... 63 F5
Altwood. Harp AL5 .... 86 D1
Alva Cl. Sth Ox WD1 .... 175 D8
Alva Way. Sth Ox WD1 .... 175 D8
Alverton. St Alb AL3 .... 127 C6
Alwin Pl. Watf WD1 .... 166 E5
Alwyn Cl. Bor WD6 .... 169 F3
Alwyn Cl. Luton LU2 .... 45 E2
Alyngton. Nthch HP4 .... 121 E7
Alzey Gdns. Harp AL5 .... 107 D8
Amberley Cl. Harp AL5 .... 86 B2
Amberley Gn. Ware SG12 .... 93 C4
Amberry Ct. Harl CM20 .... 117 D1
Ambleside. Luton LU3 .... 44 F5
Ambrose La. Harp AL5 .... 85 F4
Amenbury La. Harp AL5 .... 86 A1
Amersham Rd. Chen HP6,WD3 .. 164 B8
Ames Cl. Luton LU2 .... 44 F8
Amor Way. Letw SG6 .... 23 B6
Amwell Comm. Wel G C AL7 .... 111 C5
Amwell Ct. Wa Aby EN9 .... 163 E6
Amwell End. Ware SG12 .... 93 D1
Amwell Hill. Gt Am SG12 .... 114 F6
Amwell La. Gt Am SG12 .... 115 B5
Amwell La. Whea AL4 .... 108 B7
Amwell Pl. Hert H SG13 .... 114 C4
Amwell St. Hod EN11 .... 135 A6
Amwell View Sch. Gt Am 115 B4
Anchor Cl. Ches EN8 .... 148 D3
Anchor Cotts. Thun SG12 .... 93 D7
Anchor La. Heml H HP1 .... 124 C2
Anchor La. Heml H HP1 .... 124 C2
Anchor La. Ton SG12 .... 93 B6
Anchor Rd. Bal SG7 .... 23 F7
Anchor St. Bis St CM23 .... 77 A6
Ancient Almshouses. Ches EN8 .. 148 D1
Anderson Rd. Hare UB9 .... 173 A2
Anderson Rd. Shen WD7 .... 157 A6
Anderson Rd. Stev SG2 .... 51 D6
Anderson's House. Hit SG5 .... 34 F8 3
Andover Cl. Luton LU4 .... 44 C6
Andrew Cl. Ches EN8 .... 148 B3
Andrew's La. Ches EN8 .... 148 B3
Andrew's La. Gofs O EN7 .... 147 F3
Andrews Cl. Heml H HP2 .... 124 D5
Andrews Lane Jun & Inf Sch.
Ches 148 B3
Andrewsfield. Wel G C AL7 .... 111 C6
Anelle Rise. Heml H HP3 .... 138 F7
Anershall. Wing HP22 .... 60 B3
Angel Cotts. Gt Of SG5 .... 33 D2
Angel Pavement. Royst SG8 .... 7 C6
Angell's Meadow. Ashw SG7 .... 4 D4
Angle Ways. Stev SG2 .... 51 B2
Anglefield Rd. Berk HP4 .... 122 A4
Anglesey Cl. Bis St CM23 .... 76 C7
Anglesey Rd. Sth Ox WD1 .... 175 C5
Anglian Bsns Pk. Royst 7 B7
Anglian Cl. Watf WD1 .... 167 C7
Angotts Mead. Stev SG1 .... 50 B6
Angus Cl. Dun LU4 .... 44 A3
Anmer Gdns. Dun LU4 .... 44 B4
Annables La. Harp AL5 .... 85 A4
Annette Cl. Har HA3 .... 176 E1
Anns Cl. Tri HP23 .... 99 E3
Ansell Ct. Stev SG1 .... 36 B1
Anselm Rd. Pnr HA5 .... 175 F3
Anson Cl. Bal SG7 .... 23 F7
Anson Cl. St Alb AL1 .... 128 B1
Anson Wlk. Mo Pk HA6 .... 174 C6
Anstee Rd. Luton LU4 .... 44 B6
Anstey Sch. Ans 29 A6
Anthony Cl. Watf WD1 .... 167 B1
Anthony Gdns. Luton LU1 .... 63 D6
Anthony Rd. Bor WD6 .... 169 F7
Anthorne Cl. Pot B EN6 .... 159 B8
Anthus Mews. Norwd HA6 .... 174 A3
Antoinette Cl. Abb L WD5 .... 139 F2
Antoneys Cl. Pnr HA5 .... 175 D1
Antonine Gate. St Alb AL3 .... 127 A2
Anvil Cl. St Alb AL3 .... 141 E5
Anvil House. Harp AL5 .... 86 A2
Aplins Cl. Harp AL5 .... 85 F2
Apollo Ave. Mo Pk HA6 .... 175 A5
Apollo Way. Heml H HP2 .... 124 F5
Apple Cotts. Bov HP3 .... 137 A4
Apple Orch The. Heml H HP2 .... 124 F5
Apple Tree Gr. Red AL3 .... 106 B6
Appleby St. Ham St EN7 .... 147 E5
Applecroft Rd. Wel G C AL8 .... 110 B6
Applecroft. St Alb AL3 .... 127 B5
Applecroft Jun Mix Inf Sch.
Wel G C 110 B5
Applecroft. Nthch HP4 .... 121 E6
Applecroft Rd. Luton LU2 .... 46 C4
Appleford's Cl. Hod EN11 .... 134 F8
Appleton Ave. Wars SG8 .... 94 E5

Appleton Fields. Bis St CM23 .... 76 E4
Appletree Wlk. Watf WD2 .... 154 B4
Appletrees. Hit SG5 .... 34 C6
Applewood Cl. Harp AL5 .... 85 E3
Appleyard Terr. Enf EN3 .... 162 C2
Approach Rd. St Alb AL1 .... 127 E2
Approach The. Pot B EN6 .... 158 F7
Appspond La. St Alb AL2 .... 140 C8
April Pl. Saw CM21 .... 97 F3
Apsley Cl. Bis St CM23 .... 76 F4
Apsley End Rd. Shil SG5 .... 19 E4
Apsley Grange. Heml H HP3 .... 138 E6
Apsley Sta. Heml H 138 E6
Apsley Mills Ret Pk. Heml H 138 E7
Apsley Sta. Heml H 138 E6
Apton Cl. Bis St CM23 .... 76 F7
Apton Fields. Bis St CM23 .... 76 F7
Apton Rd. Bis St CM23 .... 76 F7
Aquadrome The. Ric 173 C8
Aquarius Way. Mo Pk HA6 .... 175 A6
Aragon Cl. Heml H HP2 .... 125 C8
Aran Cl. Harp AL5 .... 107 D6
Arbour The. Hert SG13 .... 113 D4
Arbour Cl. Luton LU3 .... 31 A1
Arbroath Gn. Sth Ox WD1 .... 175 B7
Arcade. Hit SG5 .... 34 E7 5
Arcade The. Hat AL10 .... 130 B6
Arcade The. Letw SG6 .... 22 F6
Arcade Wlk. Hit SG5 .... 34 E7 4
Arch Rd. L Wym SG4 .... 35 E4
Archer Cl. Kin L WD4 .... 138 F2
Archer Rd. Stev SG1 .... 51 A7
Archers. Bun SG9 .... 40 F7
Archers Cl. Red AL3 .... 106 B5
Archers Fields. St Alb AL1 .... 127 F5
Archers Ride. Wel G C AL7 .... 111 B4
Archers Way. Letw SG6 .... 23 A7
Arches The. Letw SG6 .... 23 A7
Archfield. Wel G C AL7 .... 89 E1
Archway Rd. Mile HA8 .... 130 C6
Archway Par. Luton LU3 .... 44 E4
Archway Wlk. Luton LU3 .... 44 E4
Ardeley Voluntary Prim Sch. Ard .. 38 F3
Arden Cl. Bov HP3 .... 137 A3
Arden Cl. Bus WD2 .... 168 A3
Arden Gr. Harp AL5 .... 86 B1
Arden Pl. Luton LU2 .... 45 E1
Arden Press Way. Letw SG6 .... 23 B6
Ardens Way. St Alb AL4 .... 128 D6
Ardentinny. St Alb AL1 .... 127 E2
Ardern Ct. St Alb AL1 .... 128 C1
Ardleigh Gn. Luton LU2 .... 46 E1 2
Ardross Ave. Mo Pk HA6 .... 174 C7
Arena Par. Letw SG6 .... 22 F6
Arena The. Enf 162 F1
Argyle Rd. Barn EN5 .... 171 C5
Argyle Way. Stev SG1 .... 50 C5
Argyll Ave. Luton LU3 .... 45 C2
Argyll Rd. Heml H HP2 .... 124 E8
Arkley Ct. Heml H HP2 .... 125 B8
Arkley Dr. Barn EN5 .... 171 B4
Arkley La. Barn EN5 .... 171 B5
Arkley Pk. Bor NW7 .... 170 D3
Arkley Rd. Heml H HP2 .... 125 B8
Arkley View. Barn EN5 .... 171 B5
Arkwrights. Harl CM20 .... 117 F1
Arlesey New Rd. Arl SG15 .... 22 A7
Arlesey Rd. Arl SG15 .... 22 A7
Arlesey Rd. Arl SG16 .... 11 A8
Arlesey Rd. Henlw SG16 .... 10 D8
Arlesey Rd. Henlw SG16 .... 10 E8
Arlesey Rd. Ick SG5 .... 21 F5
Arlesey Rd. Stot SG5 .... 11 E6
Arlesey Sta. Arl 11 A8
Arlington Cres. Ches EN8 .... 162 E5
Arlington Mews. Wa Aby EN9 .... 163 C6
Armand Cl. Watf WD1 .... 153 F1
Armitage Cl. Ric WD3 .... 165 D5
Armitage Gdns. Luton LU4 .... 44 D1
Armour Rise. Hit SG4 .... 22 D1
Armstrong Cl. Lon C AL2 .... 142 E4
Armstrong Gdns. Shen WD7 .... 156 E7
Armstrong Pl. Heml H HP1 .... 124 D4 1
Arncliffe Cres. Luton LU2 .... 45 E1
Arnett Cl. Ric WD3 .... 165 B5
Arnett Hills Jun Mix Inf Sch. Ric .. 165 A3
Arnett Way. Ric WD3 .... 165 A2
Arnold Ave E. Enf EN3 .... 163 A1
Arnold Ave W. Enf EN3 .... 162 F1
Arnold Cl. St Alb AL1 .... 35 B8
Arnold Cl. Luton LU2 .... 46 A3
Arnold Cl. Stev SG1 .... 36 D2
Arnolds La. Hin SG7 .... 3 D6
Arran Cl. Heml H HP3 .... 125 C1
Arran Ct. Luton LU1 .... 63 D7
Arretine Cl. St Alb AL3 .... 126 F1
Arrewwig La. St Le HP5 .... 119 D1
Arrow Cl. Luton LU3 .... 44 E6
Arthur Gibbens Ct. Stev SG1 .... 37 A1
Arthur Rd. St Alb AL1 .... 128 B3
Arthur St. Luton LU1 .... 63 E6
Arthur St. Watf WD2 .... 167 D5
Artillery Pl. Har HA3 .... 176 C3
Artisan Cres. St Alb AL3 .... 127 C4
Arts Education Sch. Tri 100 B3
Arundel Cl. Ast SG2 .... 51 E3
Arundel Cl. Ches EN8 .... 148 E3
Arundel Cl. Heml H HP2 .... 125 B4
Arundel Dr. Bor WD6 .... 170 C5
Arundel Gr. St Alb AL3 .... 127 D7
Arundel Rd. Luton LU4 .... 44 F2
Ascot Cl. Bis St CM23 .... 77 C8
Ascot Cl. Bor WD6 .... 170 A4
Ascot Cres. Stev SG1 .... 37 B1
Ascot Gdns. Enf EN3 .... 162 C2
Ascot End Est. Letw 23 B7
Ascot Rd. Luton LU3 .... 45 B2
Ascot Rd. Royst SG8 .... 7 F6
Ascot Rd. Watf WD1 .... 166 E4
Ascots La. Wel G C AL7 .... 110 F2
Ash Cl. Abb L WD5 .... 153 D7
Ash Cl. Bro Pk AL9 .... 145 A6
Ash Cl. Hare UB9 .... 173 D2
Ash Copse. Bri Wd AL2 .... 154 F8
Ash Dr. Hat AL10 .... 130 A2
Ash Dr. Hit SG4 .... 35 A4
Ash Gr. Hare UB9 .... 173 D2

Ash Gr. Heml H HP3 .... 138 F7
Ash Gr. Whea AL4 .... 87 C1
Ash Groves. Sheer CM21 .... 98 A2
Ash Hill Cl. Bus WD2 .... 168 B1
Ash Meadow. Muc H SG10 .... 74 F2
Ash Mill. Bark SG8 .... 17 C3
Ash Rd. Luton LU4 .... 63 B8
Ash Rd. Tri HP23 .... 99 F4
Ash Rd. Ware SG12 .... 94 A3
Ash Ride. Cre H EN2 .... 161 A4
Ash Tree Field. Harl CM20 .... 117 A2
Ash Tree Rd. Watf WD2 .... 154 B3
Ash Vale. Map Cr WD3 .... 172 D5
Ash Way. Royst SG8 .... 7 F6
Ashanger La. Clo SG7 .... 24 D4
Ashbourne Sq. Norwd HA6 .... 174 E4
Ashbourne Cl. Letw SG6 .... 23 B3
Ashbourne Rd. Hod EN10 .... 134 F2
Ashbrook La. St Ipp SG4 .... 35 C3
Ashburnam Wlk. Stev SG2 .... 50 F1
Ashburnham Cl. Sth Ox WD1 .... 175 A7
Ashburnham Dr. Sth Ox WD1 .... 175 A7
Ashburnham Rd. Luton LU1 .... 63 C7
Ashbury Cl. Hat AL10 .... 129 E5
Ashby Gdns. St Alb AL1 .... 141 D7
Ashby Rd. Nthch HP4 .... 121 D7
Ashby Rd. Watf WD2 .... 154 A1
Ashby Rise. Bis St CM23 .... 59 B1
Ashcombe. Wel G C AL8 .... 89 E2
Ashcroft Cl. Harp AL5 .... 107 E8
Ashcroft High Sch. Luton 46 C2
Ashcroft. Pnr HA5 .... 176 A4
Ashcroft Rd. Luton LU2 .... 46 B3
Ashdale. Bis St CM23 .... 76 D4
Ashdale Gdns. Luton LU3 .... 31 A1
Ashdale Gr. Har HA7 .... 176 F4
Ashdales. St Alb AL1 .... 141 D7
Ashdown Cres. Ches EN8 .... 148 E3
Ashdown Dr. Bor WD6 .... 169 F7
Ashdown. Letw SG6 .... 11 F1
Ashdown Rd. Stev SG2 .... 69 B8
Ashdown Rd. Watf WD2 .... 167 B6
Ashendene Rd. Bay SG13 .... 132 F4
Ashfield Ave. Bus WD2 .... 168 C2
Ashfield Jun Sch. Bus 168 B2
Ashfield Way. Luton LU3 .... 45 A6
Ashfields. Watf WD2 .... 153 F4
Ashford Gn. Sth Ox WD1 .... 175 D5
Ashleigh Ct. Hod EN10 .... 135 A5
Ashleigh Ct. Ric WD3 .... 165 D2
Ashleigh. Stev SG2 .... 51 B4
Ashley Cl. Ched LU7 .... 80 A8
Ashley Cl. Heml H HP3 .... 124 F1
Ashley Cl. Pnr HA5 .... 175 B1
Ashley Cl. Wel G C AL8 .... 110 C8
Ashley Cl. Hat AL10 .... 130 B6
Ashley Dr. Bor WD6 .... 170 D4
Ashley Gdns. Harp AL5 .... 85 D3
Ashley Rd. Hert SG14 .... 113 B5
Ashley Rd. St Alb AL1 .... 128 C2
Ashleys. Ric WD3 .... 164 F2
Ashlyn Cl. Watf WD2 .... 167 E5
Ashlyns Rd. Berk HP4 .... 122 B3
Ashlyns Rd. Berk HP4 .... 122 B3
Ashlyns Sch. Berk 122 C4
Ashmore Gdns. Heml H HP3 .... 125 B2
Ashridge Cl. Bov HP3 .... 137 A3
Ashridge Dr. Bri Wd AL2 .... 140 F1
Ashridge Dr. Sth Ox WD1 .... 175 C5
Ashridge Est. Bal HP3 .... 150 D7
Ashridge Management Coll.
L Gad 102 C3
Ashridge Rise. Berk HP4 .... 121 F5
Ashton Rd. Enf EN3 .... 162 E3
Ashton Rd. Luton LU1 .... 63 E5
Ashton's La. Bal SG7 .... 23 F6
Ashtree Ct. St Alb AL1 .... 127 F3
Ashtree Prim Sch. Stev 51 C4
Ashtree Way. Heml H HP1 .... 124 A2
Ashurst Cl. Norwd HA6 .... 174 E3
Ashville Way. Bal SG7 .... 13 A1
Ashwell Ave. Luton LU3 .... 44 C8
Ashwell Cl. Gra SG4 .... 36 B4
Ashwell Comm. Gra SG4 .... 36 B4
Ashwell Jun Mix Inf Sch. Ashw 4 E4
Ashwell & Morden Sta. Odsey 5 D2
Ashwell Par. Luton LU3 .... 44 C8
Ashwell Pk. Harp AL5 .... 86 D1
Ashwell Byg SG7 .... 13 C4
Ashwell Rd. Gu M SG8 .... 1 F2
Ashwell Rd. Hin SG7 .... 3 E5
Ashwell Rd. Newn SG7 .... 12 E8
Ashwell Rd. Ste Mo SG8 .... 5 A8
Ashwell Rd. St Alb AL3 .... 127 D4
Ashwell. Stev SG1 .... 36 C2
Ashwood Rd. Pot B EN6 .... 159 B6
Askew Rd. Mo Pk HA6 .... 174 D8
Aspasia Cl. St Alb AL1 .... 127 F3
Aspen Cl. Bri Wd AL2 .... 140 E1
Aspen Cl. Stev SG2 .... 69 B7
Aspen Park Dr. Watf WD2 .... 154 B4
Aspen Way. Enf EN3 .... 162 D4
Aspenden Rd. Bun SG9 .... 40 E6
Aspens The. Bis St CM23 .... 59 B3
Aspens The. Hit SG4 .... 35 A6
Aspfield Row. Heml H HP1 .... 124 B5
Asquith Cl. Stev SG2 .... 69 C7
Asquith House. Wel G C AL8 .... 110 D7
Ass House La. Stan HA3 .... 176 A6
Astall Cl. Har HA3 .... 176 E2
Aster Cl. Bis St CM23 .... 76 D6
Astley Cooper Sch. Heml H 125 A8
Astley Cl. Luton LU2 .... 46 D2
Astley Rd. Heml H HP1 .... 124 C4
Aston Cl. Bus WD2 .... 168 C2
Aston Cl. Stev SG2 .... 36 C2
Aston Cl. Watf WD1 .... 167 D2
Aston End Rd. Ast SG2 .... 51 E3
Aston La. Ast SG2 .... 69 E8
Aston Rd. Stand SG11 .... 55 D2
Aston Rise. Hit SG4 .... 35 B6
Aston View. Heml H HP2 .... 105 A1
Aston Way. Pot B EN6 .... 159 D7
Astonia House. Bal 23 F7
Astons Rd. Mo Pk HA6 .... 174 C6
Astra Cl. Luton LU2 .... 45 F2
Astra Ct. Watf WD1 .... 166 F4
Astra Ctr. Harl 117 F4

Astral Cl. Henlw SG16 .... 10 B3
Astrope La. Lon M HP23 .... 79 B3
Astwick Ave. Hat AL10 .... 129 F8
Astwick Rd. Stot SG5 .... 3 A2
Astwick Rd. Stot SG5 .... 11 F8
Athelstan Rd. Heml H HP3 .... 138 F8
Athelstan Wlk N. Wel G C AL7 .... 110 E5
Athelstan Wlk S. Wel G C AL7 .... 110 D5
Athelstone Rd. Har HA3 .... 176 D1
Athena Est. Harl 118 B4
Athena Pl. Norwd HA6 .... 174 F2
Atherstone Ave. Luton LU4 .... 44 D1
Atherton End. Saw CM21 .... 97 E3
Athlone Cl. Radl WD7 .... 156 B3
Athol Cl. Pnr HA5 .... 175 B2
Athol Gdns. Pnr HA5 .... 175 B2
Atholl Cl. Luton LU3 .... 44 D8
Atria Rd. Luton LU3 .... 44 D8
Attimore Cl. Wel G C AL8 .... 110 B5
Attimore Rd. Wel G C AL8 .... 110 B5
Aubretia House. Wel G C AL7 ..... 111 B4
Aubrey Ave. Lon C AL2 .... 142 C5
Aubrey Gdns. Luton LU4 .... 44 B6
Aubrey La. Red AL3 .... 105 E2
Aubreys. Letw SG6 .... 23 A2
Aubreys Rd. Heml H HP1 .... 123 E3
Aubries. Walk SG2 .... 38 B1
Auckland Cl. Enf EN1 .... 162 B2
Auckland Rd. Pot B EN6 .... 158 E7
Audley Cl. Bor WD6 .... 170 A6
Audley Ct. Pnr HA5 .... 175 C1
Audley Gdns. Wa Aby EN9 .... 163 C5
Audrey Gdns. Bis St CM23 .... 76 F4
Audwick Cl. Ches EN8 .... 148 E3
Augustine Rd. Har HA3 .... 176 C2
Augustus Cl. St Alb AL3 .... 127 A1
Augustus Gate. Stev SG2 .... 51 D8
Augustus Smith Sch The. Berk ... 122 D2
Austen Paths. Stev SG2 .... 51 C6
Austins Mead. Bov HP3 .... 137 B3
Austins Pl. Heml H HP2 .... 124 D4
Autumn Glades. Heml H HP3 ..... 125 C1
Autumn Gr. Wel G C AL7 .... 111 B4
Avalon Cl. Watf WD2 .... 154 E7
Avebury Ave. Luton LU2 .... 45 D4
Avebury Ct. Heml H HP2 .... 125 A5
Avenue App. Kin L WD4 .... 139 A1
Avenue One. Letw SG6 .... 23 C6
Avenue Rd. Bis St CM23 .... 77 B6
Avenue Rd. Lo Naz EN11 .... 135 D5
Avenue Rd. Pnr HA5 .... 175 E1
Avenue Rd. St Alb AL1 .... 127 E4
Avenue Rise. Bus WD2 .... 168 A4
Avenue Terr. Watf WD1 .... 167 E3
Avenue The. Barn EN5 .... 171 E6
Avenue The. Bus WD2 .... 167 F5
Avenue The. Heml H HP1 .... 123 E4
Avenue The. Hit SG4 .... 35 A7
Avenue The. Hod EN11 .... 135 A4
Avenue The. Luton LU4 .... 44 D5
Avenue The. Norwd HA6 .... 174 C4
Avenue The. Pot B EN6 .... 145 A1
Avenue The. Radl WD7 .... 156 B5
Avenue The. Stev SG1 .... 50 D8
Avenue The. Stot SG5 .... 11 F6
Avenue The. Watf WD1 .... 167 A4
Avenue The. Watf WD2 .... 167 F5
Avenue The. Welw AL6 .... 89 D7
Avey La. Wa Aby EN9 .... 163 E2
Avia Cl. Heml H HP3 .... 138 D7
Avior Dr. Mo Pk HA6 .... 174 F6
Avocet. Letw SG6 .... 11 E1
Avon Chase. Henlw SG16 .... 10 C4
Avon Cl. Watf WD2 .... 154 C5
Avon Ct. Harp AL5 .... 86 B1 9
Avon Mews. Pnr HA5 .... 175 F2
Avon Rd. Henlw SG16 .... 10 C4
Avon Sq. Heml H HP2 .... 124 F8
Avondale Ct. St Alb AL1 .... 127 E3
Avondale Rd. Luton LU1 .... 63 C8
Axe Cl. Luton LU4 .... 44 E6
Aycliffe Dr. Heml H HP2 .... 124 E7
Aycliffe Drive Jun Mix Inf Sch.
  Heml H 124 E7
Aycliffe Rd. Bor WD6 .... 156 F1
Aydon Rd. Luton LU3 .... 45 B6
Aylands Rd. Enf EN3 .... 162 D3
Aylands Sch. Enf 162 C3
Aylesbury Rd. Tri HP23 .... 99 E3
Ayllots The. Wat St SG14 .... 70 D4
Ayllotts Cl. Bun SG9 .... 40 D8
Aylsham Rd. Hod EN11 .... 135 C7
Aylward Dr. Stev SG2 .... 51 B4
Aynho St. Watf WD1 .... 167 B4
Aynswoth Ave. Bis St CM23 ..... 59 B2
Ayot Gn. A St P AL6 .... 89 A1
Ayot Gn. Hat AL6 .... 89 F8
Ayot Little Green La. A St P AL6 .. 88 F1
Ayot St Peter Rd. A St P AL6 .... 88 E1
Ayr Cl. Stev SG1 .... 51 C8
Ayres End La. Whea AL3,AL5 .... 107 E5
Aysgarth Cl. Harp AL5 .... 107 A8
Aysgarth Rd. Red AL3 .... 106 A6

Baas Hill Cl. Hod EN10 .... 134 E2
Baas Hill. Hod EN10 .... 134 D2
Baas La. Hod EN10 .... 134 E3
Babbage Rd. Stev SG1 .... 50 B5
Back La. Buck SG9 .... 27 D8
Back La. L Hal CM22 .... 98 B2
Back La. Pres SG4 .... 48 D6
Back La. Radl WD2 .... 168 G3
Back La. Sheer CM22 .... 98 B1
Back La. Whew SG6 .... 90 F2
Back St. Ashw SG7 .... 4 C3
Back St. Luton LU1 .... 63 E8
Back The. Pot En HP4 .... 123 B7
Bacon's Yd. Ashw SG7 .... 4 C3
Bacons Dr. Cuf EN6 .... 146 E2
Badburgham Ct. Wa Aby EN9 ... 163 F6
Baddeley Cl. Stev SG2 .... 51 B2
Bader Cl. Stev SG1 .... 36 F1
Bader Cl. Wel G C AL7 .... 111 C6
Badger Cl. Kneb SG3 .... 69 A6
Badger Croft. Heml H HP2 .... 125 C3
Badger Way. Hat AL10 .... 130 B3
Badgers. Bis St CM23 .... 76 E5
Badgers Cl. Bor WD6 .... 169 F7

Badgers Cl. Hert SG13 .... 114 B6
Badgers Cl. Stev SG1 .... 50 E4
Badgers Croft. Barn NP6 .... 171 E1
Badgers Croft. Enf EN10 .... 134 E2
Badgers Wlk. Tewin AL6 .... 90 C5
Badington Dr. Harp AL5 .... 85 E1
Badminton Cl. Bor WD6 .... 170 A7
Badminton Cl. Stev SG2 .... 69 B7
Badminton Pl. Hod EN10 .... 134 E3
Bagenal House. Abb L WD5 ...... 153 F7
Bagwicks Cl. Luton LU3 .... 44 E7
Bailey Hill Cl. Bor WD6 .... 170 B7
Bailey St. Luton LU1 .... 63 F6
Baines La. Dat SG3 .... 69 C4
Baird Cl. Bus WD2 .... 168 B3
Bairstow Ct. Bor WD6 .... 169 E8
Baker Ct. Bor WD6 .... 170 B7
Baker St. Enf EN1 .... 161 E1
Baker St. Hert SG13 .... 113 E6
Baker St. Luton LU1 .... 63 E5
Baker St. Pot B EN6 .... 158 E5
Baker St. Stev SG1 .... 50 C7 2
Baker's La. Cod SG4 .... 67 F1
Bakers Ct. Bis St CM23 .... 77 A7 4
Bakers Gr. Wel G C AL7 .... 111 C7
Bakers La. Bar SG8 .... 8 F2
Bakers La. Ken Co LU6 .... 82 E8
Bakers Rd. Ches EN7 .... 148 B1
Bakers Wlk. Saw CM21 .... 97 E3
Bakerscroft. Ches EN8 .... 148 E3
Bakery The. Ware SG12 .... 93 D2 2
Bakewell Cl. Dun LU4 .... 44 C1
Balcombe Cl. Luton LU2 .... 46 D1
Balcon Way. Bor WD6 .... 170 C8
Baldock Cl. Letw SG6 .... 23 D4
Baldock Rd. Asp SG9 .... 40 B8
Baldock Rd. Letw SG6 .... 23 B5
Baldock Rd. Stot SG5 .... 12 A5
Baldock Rd. Ther SG8 .... 6 C4
Baldock St. Royst SG8 .... 7 C6
Baldock St. Ware SG12 .... 93 D2
Baldock Sta. Bal 12 F1
Baldock Way. Bor WD6 .... 169 F8
Baldways Cl. Wing HP22 .... 60 C3
Baldwins La. Cro Gr WD3 .... 166 B5
Baldwins. Wel G C AL7 .... 111 C6
Balfour Ct. Harp AL5 .... 86 C3
Balfour Mews. Wat SG14 .... 137 A4
Balfour St. Hert SG14 .... 113 C7
Baliol Rd. Hit SG5 .... 34 F8
Ballater Cl. Sth Ox WD1 .... 175 C6
Ballinger Ct. Berk HP4 .... 122 B3
Ballinger Ct. Watf WD1 .... 167 B6 1
Balloon Cnr. Wel G C AL7 .... 144 B8
Ballslough Hill. Kim SG4 .... 66 D1
Balmoral Cl. Chis AL2 .... 141 D4
Balmoral Cl. Stev SG2 .... 69 C7
Balmoral Ct. Bor WD6 .... 170 D5
Balmoral Rd. Abb L WD5 .... 154 A7
Balmoral Rd. Enf EN3 .... 162 D3
Balmoral Rd. Hit SG5 .... 21 E1
Balmoral Rd. Watf WD2 .... 154 C1
Balmore Wood. Luton LU3 ...... 31 B3
Balsams Cl. Hert SG13 .... 113 D4
Bampton Rd. Dun LU4 .... 44 B2
Bamville Wood. Harp AL5 .... 107 C5
Banbury Cl. Luton LU4 .... 44 A4
Banbury St. Watf WD1 .... 167 B4
Bancroft Gdns. Har HA3 .... 176 C2
Bancroft. Hit SG5 .... 34 F7
Bancroft Rd. Har HA3 .... 176 C1
Bancroft Rd. Luton LU3 .... 45 B5
Bandley Rise. Stev SG2 .... 51 C3
Banes Down. Lo Naz EN9 .... 135 E1
Bank Cl. Luton LU4 .... 44 C4
Bank Mill. Heml H HP1 .... 124 C2
Bank Mill. Berk HP4 .... 122 C3
Bank Mill La. Berk HP4 .... 122 D3
Banks Rd. Bor WD6 .... 170 C7
Bannister Sports Ctr The. Stan ... 176 E2
Barbel Cl. Ches EN8 .... 163 A5
Barberry Rd. Heml H HP1 .... 124 A3
Barbers Wlk. Tri HP23 .... 99 F3
Barchester Rd. Har HA3 .... 176 D1
Barclay Cl. Hert H SG13 .... 114 B4
Barclay Cl. Watf WD1 .... 167 A3
Barclay Cres. Stev SG1 .... 50 E7
Barclay Cl. Hod EN11 .... 135 A5
Barclay Sch The. Stev 50 E7
Barden Cl. Hare UB9 .... 173 C3
Bards Cnr. Heml H HP1 .... 124 B4
Bardwell Cl. St Alb AL1 .... 127 D2
Bardwell Rd. St Alb AL1 .... 127 D2
Barfolds. Wel G AL9 .... 144 C8
Barford Rise. Luton LU2 .... 46 D1
Bargrove Ave. Heml H HP1 ...... 124 A2
Barham Ave. Bor WD6 .... 169 F5
Barham Rd. Stev SG2 .... 51 C5
Barkers Mead. L Hal CM22 ..... 77 B1
Barkham Cl. Ched SG14 .... 79 F7
Barking Cl. Luton LU4 .... 44 B6
Barkway Fst Sch. Bark 17 C4
Barkway Hill. Bark SG8 .... 17 C6
Barkway Rd. Royst SG8 .... 7 E5
Barkway St. Royst SG8 .... 7 D5
Barley Cl. Bus WD2 .... 168 B4
Barley Croft. Heml H HP2 .... 125 C3
Barley Croft. Hert SG13 .... 113 B6
Barley Croft. Stap SG14 .... 92 A3
Barley Hills. Bis St CM23 .... 76 E4
Barley La. Luton LU4 .... 44 C5
Barley Mow La. Coln H AL4 ..... 142 F8
Barley Ponds Cl. Ware SG12 .... 93 F1
Barley Ponds Rd. Ware SG12 ... 93 F1
Barley Rise. Gt Ch SG8 .... 9 A7
Barley Rise. Gt Ch SG8 .... 9 A7
Barley Rise. Melb SG8 .... 9 A7
Barley Rise. Bal SG7 .... 24 B8
Barley Rise. Harp AL5 .... 86 C5
Barley Voluntary Prim Sch. Bar ... 9 x
Barleycorn The. Luton LU3 ..... 63 D8 2
Barleycroft. Bun SG9 .... 40 E6
Barleycroft Gn. Wel G C AL8 .... 110 C5
Barleycroft Rd. Wel G C AL8 .... 110 C5
Barleycroft. Stev SG2 .... 51 D3
Barleyvale. Luton LU3 .... 45 A8
Barlings Rd. Harp AL5 .... 107 B5
Barmor Cl. Har HA2 .... 176 B1
Barn Cl. Heml H HP3 .... 138 F8

Barn Cl. Radl WD7 .... 156 A4
Barn Cl. Wel G C AL8 .... 110 C6
Barn Ct. Saw CM21 .... 97 E3
Barn Lea. Ric WD3 .... 165 A1
Barn Rd. The. Muc H 74 F2
Barnacres Rd. Heml H HP3 ...... 139 A8
Barnard Acres. Lo Naz EN9 ..... 149 E8
Barnard Gn. Wel G C AL7 .... 110 F5
Barnard Rd. Luton LU1 .... 63 A7
Barnard Way. Heml H HP3 ...... 124 E1
Barncroft. Alb SG11 .... 57 C7
Barncroft Jun Mix Inf Sch.
  Heml H 124 D8
Barncroft Rd. Berk HP4 .... 121 F3
Barncroft Way. St Alb AL1 ...... 128 A2
Barndell Cl. Stot SG5 .... 11 F6
Barndicot House. Wel G C AL7 .. 111 C6
Barndicott. Wel G C AL7 .... 111 C6
Barnes Rise. Kin L WD4 .... 138 F4
Barnet By-Pass Rd. Bor EN5 .... 170 E5
Barnet By-Pass Rd. Pot B EN5 .. 158 A3
Barnet Gate La. Edg EN5 .... 170 F3
Barnet General Hospl. Barn 171 D5
Barnet Hill. Barn EN5 .... 171 F4
Barnet Hill Prim Sch. Barn 171 F4
Barnet La. Barn EN5,N20 .... 171 F2
Barnet La. Bor WD6 .... 170 B3
Barnet Mus. Barn 171 E5
Barnet Rd. Barn EN5 .... 171 B4
Barnet Rd. Edg EN5 .... 170 F3
Barnet Rd. Lon C AL2 .... 142 F4
Barnet Rd. Pot B EN6,EN5 ...... 159 A4
Barnet Stall Mkt. Barn 171 E6
Barnet Trad Est. Barn 171 F6
Barnet Way. Edg EN5 .... 170 D2
Barnfield Cl. Hod EN11 .... 135 A8
Barnfield Cl. Lo Naz EN9 .... 135 F1
Barnfield Coll. Luton 63 B5
Barnfield Coll (Luton). Luton 45 D5
Barnfield Cl. Harp AL5 .... 107 C8
Barnfield. Heml H HP3 .... 138 F8
Barnfield Rd. Harp AL5 .... 107 C8
Barnfield Rd. St Alb AL4 .... 128 C5
Barnfield Rd. Wel G C AL7 ...... 110 D5
Barnhurst Path. Sth Ox WD1 ... 175 C5
Barns Dene. Harp AL5 .... 85 E2
Barnsdale Cl. Bor WD6 .... 169 F8
Barnside Ct. Wel G C AL8 .... 110 C6
Barnside Cl. Luton LU2 .... 46 D1
Barnsway. Kin L WD4 .... 138 E3
Barnwell Sch. Stev 51 B2
Barnwell. Stev SG2 .... 51 B2
Baron Ct. Stev SG1 .... 36 B1
Barons Cl. Luton LU2 .... 45 D1 6
Barons Row. Harp AL5 .... 107 D7
Barons The. Bis St CM23 .... 76 D5
Baronsmere Ct. Barn EN5 ...... 171 E5 7
Barr Rd. Pot B EN6 .... 159 C4
Barra Cl. Heml H HP3 .... 139 C8
Barratt Way. Har HA3 .... 176 D1
Barrells Down Rd. Bis St CM23 . 58 E1
Barrett La. Bis St CM23 .... 76 F7
Barrington Rd. Letw SG6 .... 22 F4
Barrow La. Ches EN7 .... 147 F1
Barrow Point Ave. Pnr HA5 .... 175 E1
Barrow Point La. Pnr HA5 ...... 175 E1
Barrowby Cl. Luton LU2 .... 46 D1
Barrowdene Cl. Pnr HA5 .... 175 E1
Barry Cl. Chis AL2 .... 141 B6
Bartel Cl. Heml H HP3 .... 139 D8
Bartholomew Court Sh Pavilion.
  Ches 162 E6
Bartholomew Rd. Bis St CM23 .. 76 F6
Bartletts Mead. Hert SG14 ..... 92 D1
Barton Cl. Harp AL5 .... 86 D1
Barton Rd. Hex SG5 .... 19 A1
Barton Rd. Luton LU3 .... 45 C7
Barton Rd. Str LU3 .... 31 B3
Barton Rd. Whea AL4 .... 108 C8
Barton Way. Bor WD6 .... 170 A4
Barton Way. Cro Gr WD3 ...... 166 B4
Bartons The. Elst WD6 .... 169 D3
Bartrams La. Had W EN4 .... 159 C1
Barwick La. Stand SG11 .... 73 C3
Basbow La. Bis St CM23 .... 76 F7
Basildon Sq. Heml H HP2 .... 124 F7
Basils Rd. Stev SG1 .... 50 D7
Baslow Cl. Har HA3 .... 176 D1
Bassett Cl. Red AL3 .... 106 B5
Bassil Rd. Heml H HP2 .... 124 D5
Bassingbourne Cl. Hod EN10 ... 134 F3
Bassingburn Wlk. Wel G C AL7 .. 110 F5
Batchelors. Stand SG11 .... 55 E2
Batchwood Dr. St Alb AL3 ...... 127 C6
Batchwood Gdns. St Alb AL3 ... 127 D6
Batchwood Hall Golf Course.
  St Alb 127 B6
Batchwood View. St Alb AL3 ... 127 D5
Batchworth Heath Hill. Ric WD3 . 174 A6
Batchworth La. Mo Pk HA6 ..... 174 D5
Batchworth London Rd.
  Ric WD3 .... 173 F7
Bateman Rd. Cro Gr WD3 ...... 166 A4
Bates House. Stev SG1 .... 50 E6 2
Batford Cl. Wel G C AL7 .... 111 B5
Batford Cty Prim Sch. Harp ... 86 D4
Batford Rd. Harp AL5 .... 86 D3
Bath Pl. Barn EN5 .... 171 F6
Bath Rd. Luton LU3 .... 45 C7
Bathurst Rd. Heml H HP2 ...... 124 E6
Batterdale. Hat AL9 .... 130 C6
Battlefield Rd. St Alb AL1 ..... 127 E6
Battlers Green Dr. Radl WD7 ... 155 E3
Battleview. Whea AL4 .... 108 E8
Baud Cl. Alb SG11 .... 57 C8
Baulk The. Cuf LU7 .... 79 F7
Baulk The. Lily LU2 .... 32 C8
Baulk The. Pit LU7 .... 80 F5
Bay Cl. Luton LU4 .... 44 B8
Bay Ct. Berk HP4 .... 122 B4
Bay Tree Cl. Chis AL2 .... 141 C8
Bay Tree Ct. Berk HP4 .... 122 B4
Bay Tree Wlk. Watf WD1 .... 154 A1
Bayford Cl. Heml H HP2 .... 125 C8
Bayford Cl. Hert SG13 .... 133 C7
Bayford Gn. Bay SG13 .... 133 A6

Bayford La. Bay SG13 .... 132 F7
Bayford Prim Sch. Bay 132 F6
Bayford Sta. Bay 133 A6
Bayhurst Dr. Norwd HA6 .... 174 F4
Baylam Dell. Luton LU2 .... 46 E1
Baylie Ct. Heml H HP2 .... 124 E4
Baylie La. Heml H HP2 .... 124 E4
Bayworth. Letw SG6 .... 23 B5
Beacon Ct. Wat SG13 .... 114 C3
Beacon Rd. Dagn HP4 .... 81 A1
Beacon Rd. Ware SG12 .... 94 A2
Beacon Way. Ric WD3 .... 165 A2
Beacon Way. Tri HP23 .... 100 C5
Beaconsfield. Luton LU2 .... 64 B8
Beaconsfield Rd. Enf EN3 .... 162 D2
Beaconsfield Rd. Hat AL10 ..... 130 C6
Beaconsfield Rd. St Alb AL1 .... 127 E3
Beadles The. L Hal CM22 .... 98 B8
Beadlow Rd. Dun LU4 .... 44 A4
Beagle Cl. Radl WD7 .... 155 F2
Beale Cl. Stev SG2 .... 51 C6
Beamish Dr. Bus WD2 .... 168 C1
Beane Ave. Stev SG2 .... 51 D6
Beane Rd. Hert SG14 .... 70 D4
Beane River View. Hert SG14 ... 113 C6
Beane Wlk. Stev SG2 .... 51 D6
Beaneside The. Wat St SG14 ... 70 D4
Beanfield Rd. H Wy CM21 ...... 97 A4
Beanley Cl. Luton LU2 .... 46 E2
Bear La. Ashw SG7 .... 4 D4
Bearton Ave. Hit SG5 .... 34 E8
Bearton Gn. Hit SG5 .... 21 D1
Bearton Rd. Hit SG5 .... 21 E1
Bearwood Cl. Pot B EN6 .... 159 D8
Beatty Rd. Ches EN8 .... 162 F5
Beauchamp Gdns. Ric WD3 .... 165 A1
Beaulieu Cl. Watf WD1 .... 167 C1
Beaumayes Cl. Heml H HP1 .... 124 B2
Beaumont Ave. St Alb AL1 ..... 128 B4
Beaumont Cl. Hit SG5 .... 34 D8 3
Beaumont Cl. Harp AL5 .... 86 B5 5
Beaumont Pl. Barn EN5 .... 171 F8
Beaumont Rd. Ham St EN7 ..... 147 D6
Beaumont Sec Sch. St Alb 128 C4
Beaumont View. Ham St EN7 ... 147 D5
Beazley Ct. Ware SG12 .... 93 D4
Becket Gdns. Welw AL6 .... 89 C4
Beckets Sq. Berk HP4 .... 122 A6
Beckets Wlk. Ware SG12 .... 93 D1 9
Beckett's Ave. St Alb AL3 ...... 127 C4
Becketts. Hert SG14 .... 113 A5
Beckfield La. San SG9 .... 26 D7
Becks Cl. Mark AL3 .... 83 D5
Bedale Rd. Enf EN2 .... 161 C1
Bede Cl. Pnr HA5 .... 175 D2
Bede Ct. L Gad HP4 .... 102 C8
Bedford Cl. Chen WD3 .... 151 B1
Bedford Cres. Enf EN3 .... 162 E4
Bedford Gdns. Luton LU3 ...... 63 D8 5
Bedford Park Rd. St Alb AL1 ... 127 E3
Bedford Rd. Henlw SG16 ...... 10 B3
Bedford Rd. Chen WD3 .... 34 E7
Bedford Rd. Ick SG5 .... 21 D4
Bedford Rd. Letw SG6 .... 22 D7
Bedford Rd. Mo Pk HA6 .... 174 D6
Bedford Rd. St Alb AL1 .... 127 E2
Bedford Rd. Berk HP4 .... 122 A4
Bedford Rd. Watf WD2 .... 167 B8
Bedmond Gn. Abb L WD5 ..... 139 E7
Bedmond La. Bri Wd AL2 ...... 140 B6
Bedmond La. St Alb AL3 ...... 126 F1
Bedmond Rd. Abb L WD5 ..... 139 F7
Bedmond Rd. Abb L WD5 ..... 139 E7
Bedmond Rd. Heml H HP3 .... 125 D1
Bedwell Ave. L Berk AL9 ...... 132 A7
Bedwell Cl. Wel G C AL7 ...... 110 E5
Bedwell Cres. Stev SG1 .... 50 F5
Bedwell Jun Mix Inf Sch. Stev .. 51 A5
Bedwell Rise. Stev SG1 .... 50 F5
Bedwell The. Stev 51 A6
Beech Ave. Cre H EN2 .... 161 A4
Beech Ave. Radl WD7 .... 156 A5
Beech Bottom. St Alb AL3 .... 127 D6
Beech Cl. Harp AL5 .... 107 C5
Beech Cl. Hat AL10 .... 130 A4
Beech Cres. Whea AL4 .... 108 D7
Beech Dr. Berk HP4 .... 122 B5
Beech Dr. Bor WD6 .... 169 F7
Beech Dr. Saw CM21 .... 118 C8
Beech Dr. Stev SG2 .... 51 B3
Beech Farm Dr. Hat AL4 ..... 128 C8
Beech Hill. Had W EN4 .... 159 E1
Beech Hill High Sch. Luton ... 45 B1
Beech Hill. Letw SG6 .... 22 D7
Beech Hill. Lily LU2 .... 46 D8
Beech Hyde Jun Mix Inf Sch.
  Whea 108 D7
Beech Hyde La. Whea AL4 .... 108 F6
Beech Mews. Ware SG12 ..... 114 C8
Beech Pk. L Chal HP6 .... 150 B1
Beech Pl. St Alb AL3 .... 127 D6
Beech Rd. Luton LU1 .... 63 C8
Beech Rd. St Alb AL3 .... 127 C6
Beech Rd. Watf WD2 .... 154 B2
Beech Ridge. Bal AL5 .... 23 F6
Beech Way. Kim AL4 .... 87 B6
Beech Wlk. Hit HP23 .... 100 C4
Beechcroft Ave. Cro Gr WD3 . 166 C4
Beechcroft. Berk HP4 .... 122 C4
Beechcroft. Dat SG3 .... 69 D3
Beechcroft Rd. Watf WD2 ... 167 C6
Beechen Gr. Watf HA5 .... 167 C5
Beeches The. Chor WD3 ..... 164 F4
Beeches The. Hit SG4 .... 35 A6
Beeches The. Pk St AL2 ..... 141 D4
Beeches The. Royst SG8 .... 7 D6
Beeches The. Tri HP23 ...... 100 C4
Beeches The. Watf WD1 .... 167 B6 2
Beeches The. Welw AL6 .... 89 C4
Beechfield Cl. Red AL3 ..... 106 A5
Beechfield. Hod EN11 ...... 115 A2

Beechfield Jun Mix Inf Sch. Watf . 154 A2
Beechfield. Kin L WD4 .... 138 F1
Beechfield Rd. Heml H HP1 .... 124 B8
Beechfield Rd. Ware SG12 ..... 93 F2
Beechfield Rd. Wel G C AL7 ... 110 C5
Beechfield. Saw CM21 .... 97 F2
Beechfield Wlk. Wa Aby EN9 .. 163 D4
Beeching Cl. Harp AL5 .... 86 B4
Beechlands. Bis St CM23 ..... 76 F5
Beecholm Mews. Ches EN8 ... 148 E4
Beechpark Way. Watf WD1 ... 153 E2
Beechtree La. St Alb AL3 ..... 126 B2
Beechwood Ave. Chor WD3 .. 164 B5
Beechwood Ave. L Chal HP6 . 150 C1
Beechwood Ave. Pot B EN6 .. 159 B6
Beechwood Ave. St Alb AL1 .. 128 C4
Beechwood Cl. Bal SG7 .... 23 F5
Beechwood Cl. Ham St EN7 .. 147 E6
Beechwood Cl. Hit SG5 .... 21 D2
Beechwood Cl. Ald HP23 ..... 101 C5
Beechwood Inf Sch. Luton 44 E4
Beechwood Jun Sch. Luton ... 44 E4
Beechwood Park (Sch). Fla 83 B1
Beechwood Pk. Heml H HP3 .. 137 F7
Beechwood Rd. Luton LU4 ... 44 E3
Beechwood Rise. Watf WD2 .. 154 B2
Beecroft La. Walk SG2 .... 38 C2
Beehive Cl. Elst WD6 .... 169 D3
Beehive Gn. Wel G C AL7 ..... 111 A3
Beehive La. Wel G C AL7 ..... 111 A3
Beehive Rd. Gofs O EN7 ..... 147 B5
Beesonend Cotts. Harp AL5 .. 107 B4
Beesonend La. Harp AL5 ..... 106 C3
Beeston Cl. Sth Ox WD1 ..... 175 D6
Beeston Dr. Ches EN8 .... 148 E4
Beetham Ct. Sac SG14 .... 92 E4
Beethoven Rd. Elst WD6 ..... 169 D3
Beeton Cl. Pnr HA5 .... 176 A3
Beggarman's La. Dan En SG11 . 72 D8
Beggars Bush La. Watf WD1 .. 166 C3
Beken Ct. Watf WD2 .... 154 C4
Belcher Rd. Hod EN11 .... 135 A7
Beldam Ave. Royst SG8 ...... 7 E5
Beldams La. Bis St CM23 .... 77 B5
Belfairs. Sth Ox WD1 .... 175 D5
Belford Rd. Bor WD6 .... 156 F1
Belfry Ave. Hare UB9 .... 173 A2
Belfry The. Luton LU2 .... 45 E6
Belfry The. Watf 167 D8
Belgrave Ave. Watf WD1 .... 166 F4
Belgrave Cl. St Alb AL4 ..... 128 C2
Belgrave Rd. Abb L WD5 .... 139 C3
Belgrave Rd. Luton LU4 .... 44 D5
Belham Rd. Kin L WD4 ..... 139 A3
Bell Acre. Barn EN5 .... 171 D5
Bell Acre. Letw SG6 .... 23 B4
Bell Cl. Abb L WD5 .... 139 F4
Bell Cl. Hit SG4 .... 35 B6
Bell Cl. Kneb SG3 .... 69 A5
Bell Cl. Pnr HA5 .... 175 C1 3
Bell Gn. Bov HP3 .... 137 B4
Bell La. Abb L WD5 .... 140 A4
Bell La. Bro Pk AL9 .... 145 A7
Bell La. Enf EN3 .... 162 E1
Bell La. Hert SG14 .... 113 D6
Bell La. Hod EN11 .... 135 A6
Bell La. L Chal HP6 .... 150 C1
Bell La. Nthch HP4 .... 121 E5
Bell La. Shen AL2 .... 142 E2
Bell La. Stev SG1 .... 50 C7
Bell Lane City Combd Sch. L Chal . 150 B1
Bell Leys. Wing HP22 ..... 60 B3
Bell Mead. Saw CM21 .... 97 E3
Bell Rdbt The. Lon C AL2 . 142 F4
Bell St. Saw CM21 .... 97 E3
Bell Wlk. Wing HP22 .... 60 B3
Bellamy Cl. Watf WD1 ... 167 A8
Bellamy Rd. Ches EN8 .. 148 E2
Belle Vue La. Bus WD2 . 168 D1
Belle Vue Rd. Ware SG12 . 93 F1
Bellerby Rise. Luton LU4 . 44 B6
Bellfield Ave. Stan HA3 .. 176 D4
Bellgate. Heml H HP2 .... 124 E5
Bellgate Inf Sch. Heml H . 124 E5
Bellgate Jun Sch. Heml H . 124 E5
Bellingdon. Sth Ox WD1 . 175 C4
Bellis House. Wel G C AL7 . 111 B4
Bellmount Wood Ave. Watf WD1 . 166 B3
Bells Hill. Barn EN5 ..... 171 D5
Bells Hill. Bis St CM23 .. 76 E7
Belmers Rd. Wigg HP23 . 100 C3
Belmont Ct. St Alb AL1 .. 127 D2
Belmont Fst & Mid Sch. Har . 176 F1
Belmont La. St Alb AL1 .. 127 D2
Belmont Lodge. Har HA3 . 176 D3
Belmont Rd. Heml H HP3 . 138 A8
Belmont Rd. Luton LU1 .. 63 C7
Belmont Rd. Watf WD2 .. 167 E4
Belmor. Bor WD6 .... 170 A3
Belper Rd. Luton LU4 ... 44 D2
Belsham Pl. Luton LU3 .. 46 E2 3
Belsize Cl. Heml H HP3 . 125 A2
Belsize Cl. St Alb AL4 .. 128 C8
Belsize Rd. Har HA3 .... 176 D3
Belsize Rd. Heml H HP3 . 125 A2
Belswains Jun Mix Sch. Heml H . 138 B1
Belswains La. Heml H HP3 . 138 F7
Belswains Prim Sch. Heml H . 138 F7
Belton Rd. Berk HP4 .... 122 A5
Beltona Gdns. Ches EN8 . 148 D4
Belvedere Gdns. Chis AL2 . 141 A4
Belvedere Rd. Luton LU3 . 45 C4
Bembridge Gdns. Luton LU3 . 44 F7
Ben Austins. Red AL3 ... 106 A4
Benbow Cl. St Alb AL1 .. 128 B1
Benchley Hill. Hit SG4 .. 35 C5
Benchleys Rd. Heml H HP1 . 123 F2
Bencroft. Ham St EN7 .. 148 A5
Bencroft Rd. Heml H HP2 . 124 F5
Bendish La. Whit SG4 ... 66 F2
Bendysh Rd. Watf WD2 .. 167 E6
Benedictine Gate. Ches EN8 . 148 E4
Benford Rd. Hod EN11 .. 134 F4

Bengarth Dr. Har HA3 .... 176 D1
Bengeo Inf Sch. Hert 92 C1
Bengeo Jun Sch. Hert 92 C1
Bengeo Mews. Hert SG14 ...... 92 C1
Bengeo St. Hert SG14 .... 113 C8
Benhooks Ave. Bis St CM23 .... 76 E5
Benhooks Pl. Bis St CM23 ..... 76 E5
Benington Cl. Luton LU2 .... 45 C5
Benington Jun Mix Inf Sch. Ben .. 52 D2
Benington Rd. Ast SG2 .... 51 F2
Benington Rd. Ben SG2 .... 52 A7
Bennett Cl. Norwd HA6 .... 174 F3
Bennett Cl. Wel G C AL7 .... 110 F2
Bennett. Letw 23 A5
Bennetts Cl. Col H AL4 .... 143 D8
Bennetts End Cswy. Sta M CM24 . 59 D7
Bennetts End Hospl. Heml H 124 F1
Bennetts End Rd. Heml H HP3 .. 125 A1
Bennettsgate. Heml H HP3 ..... 139 A8
Bennick House. Watf WD1 ..... 166 E3
Benningfield Rd. Widf SG12 .... 95 D4
Benningfield. Widf SG12 .... 95 D5
Benskin Rd. Watf WD1 .... 167 A4
Benslow La. Hit SG4 .... 35 A7
Benslow Rise. Hit SG4 .... 35 A8
Benson Cl. Luton LU3 .... 44 F7
Bensted. Stev SG2 .... 69 C8
Bentfield Cty Prim Sch. Sta M .. 59 C8
Bentfield End Cswy. Sta M CM24 . 59 D7
Bentfield Gdns. Sta M CM24 ... 59 D7
Bentfield Green. Sta M CM24 .. 59 D8
Bentfield Rd. Sta M CM24 ...... 59 D7
Bentick Way. Cod SG4 .... 67 F2
Bentley Cl. Bis St CM23 .... 76 F5
Bentley Ct. Luton LU4 .... 63 C8
Bentley Heath La. Pot B EN5 ... 158 F4
Bentley Lodge. Bus WD2 .... 176 E8
Bentley Rd. Hert SG14 .... 112 F7
Bentley Wood High Sch. Stan .. 176 F5
Benton Rd. Sth Ox WD1 .... 175 D5
Bentsley Cl. St Alb AL4 .... 128 C7
Berceau Wlk. Watf WD1 .... 166 E8
Berefield. Heml H HP2 .... 124 D5
Beresford Rd. Luton LU4 .... 45 A1
Beresford Rd. Ric WD3 .... 164 F1
Beresford Rd. St Alb AL1 ...... 128 C2
Bericot Way. Wel G C AL7 ..... 111 D6
Berkeley Cl. Abb L WD5 .... 153 F8
Berkeley Cl. Bor WD6 .... 170 A4
Berkeley Cl. Hit SG5 .... 34 D8 6
Berkeley Cl. Pot B EN6 .... 158 F7
Berkeley Ct. Stev SG2 .... 69 A8
Berkeley Ct. Ware SG12 .... 93 C2
Berkeley Ct. Cro Gr WD3 ...... 166 D4
Berkeley Ct. Harp AL5 .... 86 A2
Berkeley. Letw SG6 .... 23 A4
Berkeley Path. Luton LU2 ...... 63 C8 3
Berkeley Sq. Heml H HP2 ...... 105 C1
Berkhamsted La. L Berk AL9 .. 132 B3
Berkhamsted Rd. Heml H HP1 .. 123 E5
Berkhamsted Sch. Berk 122 A4
Berkhamsted Sch for Girls. Berk . 122 B3
Berkhamsted Sta. Berk 122 C5
Berkley Ave. Ches EN8 .... 162 E5
Berkley Cl. St Alb AL4 .... 128 C7
Berkley Ct. Berk HP4 .... 122 C4
Berkley Pl. Ches EN8 .... 162 D5
Berks Hill. Chor WD3 .... 164 C4
Bernard St. St Alb AL3 .... 127 D4
Bernard's Heath Inf Sch. St Alb . 127 F5
Berners Dr. St Alb AL1 .... 141 E8
Berners Way. Hod EN10 .... 148 F8
Bernhardt Cres. Stev SG2 .... 51 C6
Berries The. St Alb AL4 .... 128 A4
Berrow Cl. Luton LU2 .... 46 B3
Berry Ave. Watf WD2 .... 154 B3
Berry Cl. Ric WD3 .... 165 B2
Berry Grove La. Bus WD2 ...... 154 E1
Berry La. Ric WD3 .... 165 A2
Berry Leys. Luton LU3 .... 44 E7
Berry Way. Ric WD3 .... 165 B2
Berryfield. Ched LU7 .... 79 F7
Berrygrove La. Bus WD2 .... 168 A8
Berrymead. Heml H HP2 .... 124 F5
Bertram House. Stev SG1 .... 50 E6 4
Berwick Cl. Ches EN8 .... 163 A6
Berwick Cl. Har HA2 .... 176 F4
Berwick Cl. Bor WD6 .... 156 F1
Besant House. Watf WD2 ...... 167 D7 2
Besford Cl. Luton LU2 .... 46 F2
Bessemer Cl. Hit SG5 .... 21 E2
Bessemer Dr. Stev SG1 .... 50 B4
Bessemer Rd. Wel G C AL7,AL8 . 89 E2
Bethune Cl. Luton LU1 .... 63 B6
Bethune Ct. Luton LU1 .... 63 B6
Betjeman Cl. Ches EN7 .... 148 A3
Betjeman Way. Heml H HP1 ... 124 B4
Betony Vale. Royst SG8 .... 7 E5
Bettespol Meadows. Red AL3 .. 106 A4
Betty's La. Tri HP23 .... 100 A4
Bevan Cl. Heml H HP2 .... 124 E1
Bevan House. Watf WD2 .... 167 D7 3
Beverley Cl. Royst SG8 .... 7 B8
Beverley Gdns. Ches EN7 ...... 148 A4
Beverley Gdns. St Alb AL4 ..... 128 D7
Beverley Gdns. Wel G C AL7 .. 111 C6
Beverley Rd. Luton LU4 .... 44 F1
Beverley Rd. Luton LU4 .... 45 A1
Beverley Rd. Stev SG1 .... 37 B2
Beverly Cl. Hod EN11 .... 134 E2
Bevil Ct. Hod EN11 .... 115 A1
Bewdley Cl. Harp AL5 .... 107 D6
Bewley Cl. Ches EN8 .... 162 D8
Bexhill Rd. Luton LU2 .... 46 D2
Beyers Gdns. Hod EN11 .... 115 A1
Beyers Prospect. Hod EN11 .... 115 A1
Beyers Ride. Hod EN11 .... 115 A1
Bibbs Hall La. Kim SG4 .... 87 E6
Biddenham Turn. Watf WD2 ... 154 C4
Bideford Gdns. Luton LU3 ...... 45 D4
Bideford Rd. Enf EN3 .... 162 F1
Bidwell Cl. Letw SG6 .... 23 C5
Biggin Hill. Wyd SG9 .... 28 D7
Biggin La. Hit SG5 .... 34 F7
Bignells Cnr. Pot B EN6 .... 158 B5
Billet La. Berk HP4 .... 122 A6

Billy Lows La. Pot B EN6 .... 159 B8
Bilton Rd. Hit SG4 .... 21 F2
Bilton Way. Enf EN3 .... 162 F1
Bingen Rd. Hit SG4 .... 21 C1
Bingley Rd. Hod EN11 .... 135 C6
Binham Cl. Luton LU2 .... 45 D7
Binyon Cres. Stan HA7 .... 176 F5
Birch Copse. Bri Wd AL2 .... 140 E1
Birch Ct. Norwd HA6 .... 174 C4
Birch Dr. Hat AL10 .... 130 A4
Birch Dr. Map Cr WD3 .... 172 D5
Birch Gn. Heml H HP1 .... 123 F5
Birch Gn. Hertng SG14 .... 112 C4
Birch Gr. Pot B EN6 .... 159 B7
Birch Gr. Welw AL6 .... 89 E8
Birch La. Flau HP3 .... 151 B7
Birch Leys. Heml H HP2 .... 125 C8
Birch Link. Luton LU4 .... 45 C1
Birch Pk. Stan HA3 .... 176 C3
Birch Rd. Welw SG3 .... 69 B1
Birch Tree Gr. Bot HP5 .... 136 B1
Birch Tree Wlk. Watf WD1 ..... 153 F2
Birch Way. Harp AL5 .... 107 C8
Birch Way. Lon C AL2 .... 142 D4
Birch Wlk. Bor WD6 .... 170 A8
Birchall La. Wel G C AL7 .... 111 C5
Birchall Wood. Wel G C AL7 ... 111 C5
Birchalls. Sta M CM24 .... 59 D8
Birchanger C of E Prim Sch. Birhr . 59 D2
Birchanger Green
  Motorway Service Area. Gt Ha .. 77 E7
Birchanger Ind Est. Bis St 59 B2
Birchanger La. Birhr CM23 .... 59 D2
Birchen Gr. Luton LU2 .... 45 F3
Bircherley Ct. Hert SG14 .... 113 D6 12
Bircherley Green Ctr The. Hert . 113 C6 8
Bircherley St. Hert SG14 .... 113 D6
Birches The. Bus WD2 .... 168 C4
Birches The. Cod SG4 .... 89 A8
Birches The. Heml H HP3 ...... 137 B4
Birches The. Letw SG6 .... 22 E8
Birchfield Rd. Ches EN8 .... 148 C2
Birchfield Terr. Watf WD1 ...... 167 C5
Birchfield. Watf WD1 .... 154 A1
Birchmead Cl. St Alb AL3 ...... 127 D6
Birchmead. Watf WD1 .... 153 F1
Birchway. Hat AL10 .... 130 B7
Birchwood Ave. Hat AL10 ...... 130 A7
Birchwood Cl. Birhr CM23 ..... 59 E2
Birchwood Cl. Hat AL10 .... 130 A7
Birchwood High Sch. Bis St 77 C8
Birchwood. Shen WD7 .... 157 A5
Birchwood. Wa Aby EN9 .... 163 A6
Birchwood Way. Chis AL2 ...... 141 B3
Bird La. Hare UB9 .... 173 C1
Birdcroft Rd. Wel G C AL8 .... 110 D5
Birdie Way. Hert SG13 .... 114 B2
Birds Cl. Wel G C AL7 .... 111 A4
Birds Hill. Letw SG6 .... 23 A6
Birdsfoot La. Luton LU3 .... 45 B6
Birkbeck Rd. Enf EN2 .... 161 D1
Birkdale Gdns. Sth Ox WD1 ... 175 D4
Birklands La. St Alb AL1 .... 142 B7
Birklands. St Alb AL1 .... 142 B7
Birling Dr. Luton LU2 .... 46 C4
Birstall Gn. Sth Ox WD1 .... 175 D6
Birtley Croft. Luton LU2 .... 46 E1
Biscot Rd. Luton LU1 .... 45 C2
Bishop Ken Rd. Har HA3 .... 176 F2
Bishop Sq. Hat AL10 .... 129 E5
Bishop Wood Jun Sch. Tri 100 A3
Bishop's Cl. Bis St CM23 .... 76 F3
Bishop's Cl. St Alb AL4 .... 128 A7
Bishop's Garth. St Alb AL4 ..... 128 A7
Bishop's Hatfield Girls' Sch. Hat . 130 A4
Bishop's Stortford Bsns Ctr. Bis St . 77 A6
Bishop's Stortford Coll. Bis St . 76 E7
Bishop's Stortford Golf Course.
  Bis St 77 D6
Bishop's Stortford High Sch The.
  Bis St 76 F4
Bishop's Stortford High Sch The. Bis St . 77 A6
Bishops Ave. Bor WD6 .... 169 F4
Bishops Ave. Mo Pk HA6 .... 174 F7
Bishops Cl. Barn EN5 .... 171 D3
Bishops Cl. Hat AL10 .... 129 F5
Bishops' Coll. Ches 148 B1
Bishops Field. Ast Cl HP22 .... 99 A4
Bishops Mead. Heml H HP1 ... 124 B1
Bishops Park Way. Bis St CM23 . 76 B7
Bishops Rd. Tewin AL6 .... 90 E6
Bishops Rise. Hat AL10 .... 129 F4
Bishops Rise. Hat AL10 .... 129 F4
Bishopscote Rd. Luton LU3 .... 45 B3
Biskra. Watf WD1 .... 167 A8
Bisley Cl. Ches EN8 .... 162 D6
Bit The. Wigg HP23 .... 100 D1
Bittern Cl. Stev SG2 .... 51 D2
Bittern Way. Letw SG6 .... 11 C1
Black Boy Wood. Bri Wd AL2 . 141 A1
Black Cut. St Alb AL1 .... 127 E2
Black Ditch Rd. Wa Aby EN9 .. 163 D3
Black Ditch Way. Wa Aby EN9 . 163 B3
Black Fan Rd. Wel G C AL7 .... 110 F7
Black Fan Rd. Wel G C AL7 .... 111 A6
Black Lion Cl. Harl CM17 ...... 118 C4
Black Lion Hill. Shen WD7 ..... 156 F7
Black Swan Cl. Ware SG12 ..... 93 D1 1
Black Swan La. Luton LU3 ...... 45 A5
Blackberry Mead. Stev SG2 .... 51 D3
Blackbury Ct. Pot B EN6 .... 159 D8
Blackbirds La. Radl WD2 .... 155 C5
Blackbushe. Bis St CM23 .... 59 C1
Blackdale. Sta M EN7 .... 148 A4
Blacketts Wood Dr. Chor WD3 . 164 B5
Blackford Rd. Sth Ox WD1 ..... 175 D5
Blackhorse Cl. Hit SG4 .... 35 A5
Blackhorse La. Hit SG4 .... 35 A5
Blackhorse La. Radl WD2 .... 106 A6
Blackhorse La. Ridge AL2 ...... 157 F8
Blackhorse La. Welw SG6 .... 23 C8
Blackley Cl. Watf WD1 .... 153 F2
Blackmoor La. Watf WD1 .... 166 D4
Blackmore. Letw SG6 .... 23 B3
Blackmore Way. Kim AL4 .... 87 B6
Blackmore's La. Reed SG8 ...... 16 C5
Blacksmith's La. St Alb AL3 .... 127 B3

Blacksmiths Cl. Gt Am SG12 ... 115 A7
Blacksmiths Hill. Ben SG2 ...... 52 E4
Blacksmiths Row. Mark AL3 ... 85 D8
Blacksmiths. H Wy CM21 .... 97 B1
Blackthorn Cl. St Alb AL4 ...... 128 B7
Blackthorn Dr. Luton LU2 ...... 46 C4
Blackthorn Rd. Wel G C AL7 ... 111 A4
Blackthorne Cl. Hat AL10 ...... 129 F2
Blackthorn Jun Sch. Wel G C .. 111 A5
Blackwater La. Heml H HP3 ... 125 E1
Blackwell Cl. Har HA3 .... 176 D3
Blackwell Dr. Watf WD1 .... 167 C3
Blackwell Hall La. Lat HP5 ..... 150 C5
Blackwell Rd. Kin L WD4 .... 139 A2
Blackwood. Ham St 148 A4
Bladon Dr. Lu Wym SG4 .... 35 D3
Blair Cl. Heml H HP2 .... 105 B1
Blair Cl. Stev SG2 .... 50 F1
Blairhead Dr. Sth Ox WD1 ...... 175 D4
Blake Cl. St Alb AL1 .... 142 A8
Blakemere Rd. Wel G C AL8 ... 110 D8
Blakemore End Rd. L Wym SG4 . 35 D3
Blakeney Cl. Luton LU2 .... 46 A7
Blakeney Ho. Stev SG1 .... 50 A7
Blakeney Rd. Stev SG1 .... 50 A7
Blakes Ct. Saw CM21 .... 97 E2
Blakes Way. Welw AL6 .... 89 C6
Blanche La. Ridge WD6 .... 157 F5
Blandford Ave. Luton LU2 ...... 45 F1
Blandford Rd. St Alb AL1 .... 128 A3
Blanes The. Ware SG12 .... 93 C3
Blaydon Rd. Luton LU2 .... 64 A8
Blenheim Cl. Saw CM21 .... 118 C8
Blenheim Cl. Watf WD1 .... 167 D2
Blenheim Cres. Luton LU3 ...... 45 C4
Blenheim Ct. Bis St CM23 ...... 76 C7
Blenheim Rd. Barn EN5 .... 171 D5
Blenheim Rd. St Alb AL1 .... 127 F4
Blenheim Way. Stev SG2 .... 50 D7
Blenheim Way. Abb L WD5 .... 154 A7
Blenkin Cl. St Alb AL3 .... 127 C7
Blind La. Ard SG2 .... 38 F5
Blindman's La. Ches EN8 .... 148 D2
Bloomfield Ave. Luton LU2 ..... 46 A1
Bloomfield House. Stev SG1 .... 50 E6 6
Bloomfield Rd. Harp AL5 .... 85 F3
Blossom La. Enf EN2 .... 161 C1
Blue Bridge Rd. Bro Pk AL9 ... 144 A4
Bluebell Cl. Heml H HP1 .... 123 E2
Bluebell Cl. Hert SG13 .... 114 A6
Bluebells. Welw AL6 .... 89 D7
Bluebridge Ave. Bro Pk AL9 ... 144 A4
Bluecoat Yd. Ware SG12 .... 93 D1
Bluecoats Ave. Hert SG14 ..... 113 D6
Bluecoats Ct. Hert SG14 .... 113 D6 15
Bluehouse Hill. St Alb AL3 ..... 127 A3
Bluett Rd. Lon C AL2 .... 142 D4
Blundell Cl. St Alb AL3 .... 127 D7
Blundell Rd. Luton LU3 .... 45 A4
Blunesfield. Pot B EN6 .... 159 D8
Blunts La. Bri Wd AL2 .... 140 E3
Blyth Cl. Bor WD6 .... 170 A8
Blyth Ct. Stev SG1 .... 50 A7
Blyth Pl. Luton LU1 .... 63 D8
Blythe Rd. Lo Naz EN11 .... 135 D5
Blythway House. Wel G C AL7 . 89 F1
Blythway. Wel G C AL7 .... 89 F1
Blythwood Gdns. Sta M CM24 . 59 D8
Blythwood Rd. Pnr HA5 .... 175 D2
Boardman Cl. Barn EN5 .... 171 E4
Bockings. Walk SG2 .... 38 C1
Bodmin Rd. Luton LU4 .... 44 F3
Bodwell Cl. Heml H HP1 .... 124 A4
Bogmoor Rd. Bar SG8 .... 18 A4
Bognor Gdns. Sth Ox WD1 .... 175 C5
Bohemia. Heml H HP2 .... 124 E5
Boissy Cl. Coln H AL4 .... 128 E2
Boleyn Cl. Heml H HP2 .... 124 F3
Boleyn Dr. St Alb AL1 .... 127 D1
Bolingbroke Rd. Luton LU1 .... 63 A8
Bolingbrook. St Alb AL4 .... 128 A7
Bolney Gn. Luton LU2 .... 46 A1
Bolton Rd. Luton LU1 .... 63 F7
Boltons Park
  (Royal Veterinary Coll). Pot B . 145 A2
Bond Cl. Harp AL5 .... 85 F3 4
Bondley Hill Jun Mix Inf Sch. Stev . 51 C2
Boniface Gdns. Har HA3 .... 176 B3
Boniface Wlk. Har HA3 .... 176 B3
Bonks Hill. Saw CM21 .... 97 D1
Bonney Gr. Ches EN7 .... 148 A1
Bonnick Cl. Luton LU1 .... 63 C6
Booths Cl. Wel G C AL9 .... 144 D7
Boreham Holt. Bor WD6 .... 169 F5
Borehamwood Ind Pk. Bor 170 D7
Bornedene. Pot B EN6 .... 158 E8
Borodale. Harp AL5 .... 86 A1
Borough Way. Pot B EN6 ...... 158 E7
Borrell Cl. Hod EN10 .... 134 F3
Borrowdale Ct. Heml H HP2 ... 124 E6 4
Borton Ave. Henlw SG16 .... 10 B4
Bosanquet Rd. Hod EN11 ...... 135 C8
Bosmore Rd. Luton LU3 .... 44 F5
Boswell Dr. Ick SG5 .... 21 E4
Boswell Gdns. Stev SG1 .... 36 A5
Boswick La. Dag HP1 .... 101 D8
Botley La. Bot HP5 .... 136 A1
Botley Rd. Bot HP5 .... 136 A1
Botley Rd. Heml H HP2 .... 125 B8
Bottom La. Sar WD3 .... 152 C4
Bottom St. Le HP23 .... 119 F3
Bough Beech Ct. Enf EN3 ...... 162 D2
Boughton Way. L Chal HP6 .... 150 C7
Boulevard Ctr The. Bor 170 A6
Boulevard The. Watf WD1 ...... 166 D6
Boulevard The. Wel G C AL7 .. 110 F8
Boulton Rd. Stev SG2 .... 51 D2
Bounce The. Heml H HP2 ...... 124 D5
Boundary Dr. Hert SG14 .... 113 D8
Boundary House. Wel G C AL7 . 110 F8
Boundary La. Wel G C AL7 ..... 110 E2
Boundary Rd. Bis St CM23 ..... 77 A5
Boundary Rd. St Alb AL1 .... 127 E5
Boundary Way. Heml H HP2 ... 105 A1
Boundary Way. Watf WD2 ..... 154 C7
Bounds Field. L Had SG11 ..... 75 F8

Bourne Cl. Hod EN10 .... 134 F3
Bourne Cl. Ware SG12 .... 93 D2
Bourne End Rd. Mo Pk HA6 ... 174 E6
Bourne Hall. Bus WD2 .... 168 A4
Bourne Honour. Ton SG12 ..... 92 E7
Bourne Rd. Berk HP4 .... 121 F5
Bourne Rd. Bus WD2 .... 168 A4
Bourne The. Bov HP3 .... 137 A4
Bourne The. Ware SG12 .... 93 D2
Bournehall Ave. Bus WD2 ...... 168 A4
Bournehall La. Bus WD2 .... 168 A4
Bournehall Rd. Bus WD2 .... 168 A3
Bournehall Sch. Bus 168 A4
Bournemouth Rd. Stev SG1 .... 50 B8 3
Bouvier Rd. Enf EN3 .... 162 C1
Bovingdon Cres. Watf WD2 .... 154 D5
Bovingdon Ct. Bov HP3 .... 137 A3
Bovingdon Green La. Bov HP3 . 136 F3
Bovingdon Inf Sch. Bov 137 B4
Bovingdon Jun Mix Sch. Bov ... 137 A3
Bowbrook Vale. Luton LU2 ..... 46 F1
Bowcock Wlk. Stev SG1 .... 50 B8
Bower Heath La. Whea AL5 .... 86 C6
Bower's Par. Harp AL5 .... 86 B1
Bowers Way. Harp AL5 .... 86 A1
Bowershott. Letw SG6 .... 23 A4
Bowes Lyon Mews. St Alb AL3 . 127 D3
Bowgate. St Alb AL1 .... 127 D4
Bowlers Mead. Bun SG9 .... 40 D7
Bowles Gn. Enf EN1 .... 162 B3
Bowling Cl. Bis St CM23 .... 76 F6
Bowling Cl. Harp AL5 .... 107 C2
Bowling Cl. Watf WD1 .... 167 A5
Bowling Gn. Stev SG1 .... 50 D8
Bowling Green La. Bun SG9 .... 40 D8
Bowling Green La. Luton LU2 .. 45 E7
Bowling Gn. Ware SG12 .... 93 E1
Bowman Trad Est. Stev 50 B5
Bowmans Ave. Hit SG4 .... 35 B6
Bowmans Cl. Pot B EN6 .... 159 D7
Bowmans Ct. Heml H HP2 ..... 124 E5
Bowmans Cl. Welw AL6 .... 89 C6
Bowmans Gn. Watf WD2 .... 154 E2
Bowmansgreen Prim Sch.
  (Jun Mix & Inf). Lon C 142 C4
Bowring Gn. Sth Ox WD1 ...... 175 C5
Bowyer's Cl. Hit SG5 .... 21 D1
Bowyers. Heml H HP2 .... 124 D5 6
Box La. Heml H HP3 .... 137 E7
Box La. Heml H HP3 .... 137 F7
Boxberry Cl. Stev SG1 .... 50 E6
Boxfield. Wel G C AL7 .... 111 B3
Boxfield Gn. Stev SG2 .... 51 D8
Boxgrove Cl. Luton LU2 .... 46 C5
Boxhill. Heml H HP2 .... 124 E5
Boxmoor House Sch. Heml H .. 137 F8
Boxmoor Jun Mix Inf Sch. Heml H . 124 A1
Boxted Cl. Luton LU4 .... 44 C5
Boxted Rd. Heml H HP1 .... 123 E5
Boxtree Cl. Har HA3 .... 176 D3
Boxtree Rd. Har HA3 .... 176 D3
Boxwell Rd. Berk HP4 .... 122 B4
Boyce Cl. Bor WD6 .... 169 E8
Boyd Cl. Bis St CM23 .... 77 A8
Boyle Cl. Luton LU2 .... 63 E8
Braceby Cl. Luton LU3 .... 44 F6
Brache Cl. Red AL3 .... 106 A5
Brache Ct. Luton LU1 .... 63 D7
Bracken La. Welw AL6 .... 89 F7
Brackendale Gr. Harp AL5 ..... 85 B5
Brackendale. Pot B EN6 .... 159 A6
Brackens The. Heml H HP2 .... 124 D4
Bracklesham Gdns. Luton LU2 . 46 D8
Brackndene. Bri Wd AL2 .... 140 F1
Bracknell Pl. Heml H HP2 ..... 124 E5
Bradbery. Map Cr WD3 .... 172 D5
Bradbury Cl. Bor WD6 .... 170 B8
Bradden La. Gt Gd HP2 .... 103 E7
Bradford Rd. Chor WD3 .... 164 C2
Bradford St. Hit SG5 .... 34 D7
Bradgate Cl. Cuf EN6 .... 146 D4
Bradgate. Cuf EN6 .... 146 D4
Bradgers Hill Rd. Luton LU2 ... 45 E4
Bradley Comm. Birhr CM23 .... 59 E2
Bradley End. Enf EN3 .... 162 E2
Bradley Rd. Luton LU4 .... 44 D1
Bradleys Cnr. Hit SG4 .... 35 C8
Bradman Way. Stev SG1 .... 37 A1
Bradmore Gn. Bro Pk AL9 ..... 144 A5
Bradmore La. Bro Pk AL9 ..... 144 A5
Bradmore Way. Bro Pk AL9 ... 144 A5
Bradshaw Rd. Watf WD2 ...... 154 C1
Bradshaws. Hat AL10 .... 130 A7
Bradway. Whit SG4 .... 66 E6
Braemar Cl. Stev SG2 .... 69 D7
Braemar Dr. Bus WD2 .... 168 A3
Braeside Cl. Pnr HA5 .... 176 A3
Bragbury Cl. Stev SG2 .... 69 D7
Bragbury La. Dat SG3 .... 69 D6
Bragmans La. Sar HP5 .... 151 E6
Braham Ct. Hit SG5 .... 34 E7 2
Brain Cl. Hat AL10 .... 130 B6
Braithwaite Ct. Luton LU3 ..... 45 D1 1
Braknybery. Nthch HP4 .... 121 D7
Brallings La. C St P SL9 .... 172 A6
Bramble Cl. Harp AL5 .... 85 F3
Bramble Cl. Luton LU4 .... 44 C4
Bramble Cl. Watf WD2 .... 154 A5
Bramble Rd. Hat AL10 .... 129 D5
Bramble Rise. Harl CM20 ...... 117 C1
Brambles The. Bis St CM23 .... 76 D7
Brambles The. Ches EN8 ...... 162 D8
Brambles The. Royst SG8 .... 7 E5
Brambles The. St Alb AL1 ..... 127 D1
Brambles The. Stev SG2 .... 36 D2
Brambles The. Ware SG12 ..... 93 C3
Brambles The. Welw AL6 ...... 89 A5
Brambling Cl. Watf WD2 .... 167 E5
Brambling Rise. Heml H HP2 .. 124 D5
Bramfield. Hert SG14 .... 113 A7
Bramfield La. Stap SG14 .... 91 F3
Bramfield Pl. Heml H HP2 ..... 105 A1
Bramfield Rd. Dat SG3 .... 90 E8
Bramfield Rd. Hert SG14 .... 112 F4

Bramfield. Watf WD2 .... 154 E5
Bramhanger Acre. Luton LU3 .. 44 D7
Bramingham Bsns Pk. Luton ... 45 B8
Bramingham Prim Sch. Luton .. 45 B8
Bramingham Rd. Luton LU3 .... 44 F7
Bramleas. Watf WD1 .... 166 F5
Bramley Cl. Bal SG7 .... 12 F1
Bramley Ct. Watf WD2 .... 154 B8
Bramley Gdns. Sth Ox WD1 ... 175 C5
Bramley House Ct. Enf EN2 .... 161 D2
Bramley Shaw. Wa Aby EN9 ... 163 F6
Brampton Cl. Ches EN7 .... 148 A3
Brampton Cl. Harp AL5 .... 86 D5
Brampton Park Rd. Hit SG5 .... 21 E1
Brampton Rd. St Alb AL1 ...... 128 A4
Brampton Rd. Sth Ox WD1 .... 175 A7
Brampton Terr. Bor WD6 ...... 157 A7
Bramshaw Gdns. Sth Ox WD1 . 175 D5
Bramshott Cl. Hit SG4 .... 34 F5
Branch Cl. Hat AL10 .... 130 C7
Branch Rd. Pk St AL2 .... 141 D4
Branch Rd. St Alb AL3 .... 127 B4
Brand St. Hit SG5 .... 34 E7
Brandles Close Sch. Bal 23 E7
Brandles Rd. Letw SG6 .... 23 A3
Brandon Cl. Ham St EN7 .... 147 F5
Branksome Cl. Heml H HP2 .... 125 A4
Branton Cl. Luton LU2 .... 46 E2
Brantwood Rd. Luton LU1 ...... 63 C7
Bray Cl. Bor WD6 .... 170 C8
Bray Lodge. Ches EN8 .... 148 E3
Brayes Manor. Stot SG5 .... 11 F6
Brays Ct. Luton LU2 .... 46 B3
Brays Rd. Luton LU2 .... 46 B3
Braziers End. Chol HP5 .... 120 C1
Braziers Field. Hert SG13 ...... 113 F6
Braziers Quay. Bis St CM23 ... 77 A6
Breachwood Green Cty Prim Sch.
  Bre Gr 87 E1
Bread & Cheese La. Ham St EN7 . 147 E6
Breadcroft La. Harp AL5 .... 86 B1
Breakmead. Wel G C AL7 ...... 111 B4
Breaks Rd. Hat AL10 .... 130 B6
Breakspear Ave. St Alb AL1 ... 127 F2
Breakspear Coll. Abb L 139 F1
Breakspear Ct. Abb L WD5 .... 139 F1
Breakspear Hospl. Heml H 138 F6
Breakspear Rd N. Hare UB9 ... 173 D1
Breakspear. Stev SG2 .... 51 C3
Breakspeare Cl. Watf WD2 .... 154 B1
Breakspeare Rd. Abb L WD5 .. 153 F8
Brecken Cl. St Alb AL4 .... 128 A7
Brecon Cl. Luton LU3 .... 63 D6
Breeze Terr. Ches EN8 .... 148 D3
Brent Cl. Stev SG1 .... 50 E5
Brent Pl. Barn EN5 .... 171 F4
Brett Pl. Watf WD2 .... 154 A2
Brett Rd. Barn EN5 .... 171 C4
Bretts Mead. Luton LU1 .... 63 C6
Brewery La. Bal SG7 .... 23 E8
Brewery La. Sta M CM24 ...... 59 E7
Brewery Rd. Hod EN11 .... 135 A8
Brewhouse Hill. Whea AL4 .... 108 C8
Brewhouse La. Hert SG14 ..... 113 C6
Briants Cl. Pnr HA5 .... 175 F1
Briar Cl. Ches EN8 .... 148 C2
Briar Cl. Luton LU2 .... 46 C4
Briar Ct. Pot En HP4 .... 123 A7
Briar Patch La. Letw SG6 ...... 22 D3
Briar Rd. St Alb AL4 .... 128 D6
Briar Rd. Watf WD2 .... 154 B4
Briar Way. Berk HP4 .... 122 D3
Briarcliff. Heml H HP1 .... 123 E4
Briardale. Stev SG1 .... 50 E4
Briardale. Ware SG12 .... 93 C3
Briarley Cl. Hod EN10 .... 134 F1
Briars Cl. Hat AL10 .... 130 A5
Briars La. Hat AL10 .... 130 A5
Briars The. Bus WD2 .... 168 E2
Briars The. Ches EN8 .... 162 E8
Briars The. Hert SG13 .... 114 A6
Briars Wood. Hat AL10 .... 130 A5
Briarwood Dr. Pnr HA6 .... 175 A1
Briary La. Royst SG8 .... 7 C5
Briary Wood End. Welw AL6 ... 89 F8
Briary Wood La. Welw AL6 .... 89 F8
Brick Kiln La. Hit SG4 .... 34 F5
Brick Knoll Pk. St Alb AL1 ..... 128 C2
Brickcroft. Ches EN10 .... 148 E5
Brickenden Ct. Wa Aby EN9 ... 163 F6
Brickenden Cl. Hod EN11 ...... 135 A5
Brickendon Golf Course. Bric .. 133 B4
Brickendon La. Bric SG13 ...... 133 D6
Bricket Rd. St Alb AL1 .... 127 E3
Bricket Wood Sta. Bri Wd 141 A1
Brickfield Ave. Heml H HP3 ... 125 B2
Brickfield. Hat AL10 .... 130 B2
Brickfield. Hat AL10 .... 130 B2
Brickfield La. Edg EN5 .... 170 F3
Brickfields The. Ware SG12 .... 93 B2
Brickkiln Rd. Stev SG1 .... 50 C6
Brickly Rd. Luton LU4 .... 44 C5
Brickmakers La. Heml H HP3 .. 125 B2
Brickwall Cl. A St P AL6 .... 110 A8
Brickyard La. Reed SG8 .... 16 E5
Bride Hall La. A St L AL6 .... 88 C3
Bridewell Cl. Bun SG9 .... 40 E8
Bridge Cl. Berk HP4 .... 122 D4
Bridge Ct. Harp AL5 .... 85 F3 5
Bridge Ct. Radl WD7 .... 156 A4
Bridge End. Bun SG9 .... 40 E8
Bridge Foot. Ware SG12 .... 93 D1
Bridge Pl. Watf WD1 .... 167 B6
Bridge Rd E. Wel G C AL7 ..... 110 E7
Bridge Rd. Letw SG6 .... 22 F6
Bridge Rd. Wel G C AL8 .... 110 C7
Bridge Rd. Welw SG3 .... 69 A2
Bridge St. Berk HP4 .... 122 D4
Bridge St. Bis St CM23 .... 76 F7
Bridge St. Heml H HP1 .... 124 C2
Bridge St. Knee SG8 .... 2 B8
Bridge St. Luton LU1 .... 63 E8
Bridgefields. Wel G C AL8 ..... 110 C7
Bridgefoot. Bun SG9 .... 40 E7

Bridgeford House. Watf WD1 ..... 167 B6 5
Bridgegate Bsns Ctr. Wel G C 110 F7
Bridgend Rd. Enf EN1 .... 162 C4
Bridgenhall Rd. Enf EN1 .... 161 F1
Bridger Cl. Watf WD2 .... 154 E6
Bridges Rd. Stan HA7 .... 176 F5
Bridgewater Ct. L Gad HP4 .... 102 C8
Bridgewater Hill. Nthch HP4 ...... 121 F7
Bridgewater Rd. Berk HP4 .... 122 B5
Bridgewater Sch. Berk 122 A6
Bridgewater Way. Bus WD2 .... 168 B3
Bridgeways. Hod EN11 .... 135 B6
Bridle Cl. Enf EN3 .... 162 F2
Bridle Cl. Hod EN11 .... 115 A2
Bridle Cl. St Alb AL3 .... 127 E5
Bridle La. Ric WD3 .... 165 D6
Bridle Path. Watf WD2 .... 167 B7
Bridle Way. Berk HP4 .... 122 A6
Bridle Way. Gt Am SG12 .... 115 A6
Bridle Way (N). Hod EN11 .... 115 B2
Bridle Way (S). Hod EN11 .... 115 A1
Bridleway. St Le HP23 .... 119 E5
Bridlington Rd. Sth Ox WD1 ...... 175 D7
Brierley Cl. Luton LU2 .... 46 D2
Briery Field. Chor WD3 .... 165 A5
Briery Way. Heml H HP2 .... 125 A4
Brigadier Ave. Enf EN2 .... 161 C1
Brigadier Hill. Enf EN2 .... 161 C1
Brightman Cotts. Luton LU3 ...... 45 A7
Brighton Rd. Watf WD2 .... 154 A1
Brighton Way. Stev SG1 .... 50 A8
Brightview Cl. Bri Wd AL2 .... 140 E2
Brightwell Rd. Watf WD1 .... 167 A4
Brill Cl. Luton LU2 .... 46 D2
Brimfield Cl. Luton LU2 .... 46 D2
Brimsdown Ave. Enf EN3 .... 162 F1
Brimstone Wlk. Berk HP4 .... 121 F6
Brinklow Ct. St Alb AL3 .... 141 B8
Brinley Cl. Ches EN8 .... 162 D8
Brinsley Rd. Har HA3 .... 176 D1
Brinsmead. Pk St AL2 .... 141 E4
Briscoe Cl. Hod EN11 .... 134 F8
Briscoe Rd. Hod EN11 .... 134 F8
Bristol Rd. Luton LU3 .... 45 B4
Britannia Ave. Luton LU3 .... 45 B4
Britannia Rd. Ches EN8 .... 162 F5
Britannia. Stand SG11 .... 55 E2
Britannic Bsns Pk. Ches 162 F5
Britannica Works. Wa Aby 163 D5
Brittain Way. Stev SG2 .... 51 B4
Britten Cl. Elst WD6 .... 169 D3
Britton Ave. St Alb AL3 .... 127 D3
Brixham Cl. Stev SG1 .... 50 B7
Brixton Rd. Watf WD2 .... 167 B8
Broad Acre. Bri Wd AL2 .... 140 E1
Broad Acres. Hat AL10 .... 129 F8
Broad Gn. Bay SG13 .... 132 F8
Broad Green Wood. Bay SG13 ... 133 A8
Broad Mead. Luton LU3 .... 45 A3
Broad Oak Ct. Luton LU2 .... 46 D3 2
Broad Oak Way. Stev SG2 .... 50 F1
Broad St. Heml H HP2 .... 124 D4
Broad Wlk. Harl CM20 .... 117 D1
Broad Wlk. The. Norwd HA6 ..... 174 C1
Broadacres. Luton LU2 .... 45 D6
Broadcroft. Heml H HP2 .... 124 D5 2
Broadcroft. Letw SG6 .... 22 F2
Broadfield. Bis St CM23 .... 58 F2
Broadfield Cl. Muc H SG10 .... 74 E1
Broadfield Ct. Bus WD2 .... 176 E8
Broadfield. Harl CM20 .... 117 E1
Broadfield Inf Sch. Heml H 124 F3
Broadfield Jun Mix Inf Sch. Heml H 124 F3
Broadfield Pl. Wel G C AL8 .... 110 B5
Broadfield Rd. Heml H HP2 .... 124 F3
Broadfield Rd. Welw SG3 .... 69 B1
Broadfield Way. Muc H SG10 .... 74 F1
Broadfields Cty Prim Sch. Harl ... 117 E1
Broadfields. Gofs O EN7 .... 147 B2
Broadfields. H Wyc M21 .... 97 B1
Broadfields. Har HA2 .... 176 B1
Broadfields. Harp AL5 .... 85 F2
Broadfields La. Watf WD1 .... 167 B1
Broadgate. Wa Aby EN9 .... 163 F7
Broadhall Way. Stev SG2 .... 51 B2
Broadlake Cl. Lon C AL2 .... 142 D4
Broadlands Cl. Ches EN8 .... 162 D5
Broadlawns Ct. Har HA3 .... 176 F2
Broadleaf Ave. Bis St CM23 ...... 76 D4
Broadmead Cl. Pnr HA5 .... 175 E3
Broadmead. Hit SG4 .... 35 B5
Broadmead Ind Sch. Luton 63 C8
Broadmeadow Ride. Hit SG4 ..... 35 A4
Broadmeads. Ware SG12 .... 93 D1
Broadoak Ave. Enf EN2 .... 162 D4
Broadstone Rd. Harp AL5 .... 107 D7
Broadview. Stev SG1 .... 50 E6
Broadwater Ave. Letw SG6 ...... 22 E5
Broadwater. Berk HP4 .... 122 C5
Broadwater Cres. Stev SG2 ...... 69 C8
Broadwater Cres. Wel G C AL7 .. 110 D5
Broadwater Dale. Letw SG6 ..... 22 E5
Broadwater La. Ast SG2 .... 51 D1
Broadwater. Pot B EN6 .... 145 B1
Broadwater Rd. Wel G C AL7 .... 110 D6
Broadway Ave. Harl CM17 .... 118 B4
Broadway Cl. Letw SG6 .... 22 E3
Broadway. Letw SG6 .... 22 F5
Broadway. The. Har HA3 .... 176 F1
Broadway The. Hat AL9 .... 130 C6
Broadway The. Kim AL4 .... 87 D5
Broadway The. Pnr HA5 .... 175 F3
Broadway The. Watf WD1 .... 167 C6
Brocket Cl. Luton LU4 .... 44 D5
Brocket Rd. Hat AL8 .... 110 A3
Brocket Rd. Hod EN11 .... 135 A6
Brocket View. Wheat AL4 .... 108 D8
Brockett Cl. Wel G C AL8 .... 110 B6
Brockhurst Cl. Watf WD1 .... 167 A4
Brockley Hill. Stan HA7 .... 169 C1
Brockswood La. Wel G C AL8 .... 110 B7
Brockswood Prim Sch. Heml H .. 105 C1
Brockwell Shott. Watf WD2 ...... 38 B1
Brodewater Rd. Bor WD6 .... 170 B7
Brodie Rd. Enf EN2 .... 161 C1
Bromborough Gn. Sth Ox WD1 .. 175 C5

Bromet Cl. Watf WD1 .... 153 F1
Bromet Jun Mix Inf Sch. Watf ... 167 D2
Bromleigh Cl. Ches EN8 .... 148 E3
Bromley. Lon M HP23 .... 79 A4
Brompton Cl. Luton LU3 .... 44 F8
Bronte Cres. Heml H HP2 .... 105 B1
Bronte Paths. Stev SG2 .... 51 C6
Brook Cotts. Sta M CM24 .... 59 E5
Brook Dr. Radl WD7 .... 155 F6
Brook Dr. Stev SG2 .... 69 B8
Brook End. Saw CM21 .... 97 D2
Brook Field. Ast SG2 .... 51 E2
Brook La. Berk HP4 .... 122 B5
Brook La. Saw CM21 .... 97 D2
Brook Rd. Bor WD6 .... 170 A7
Brook Rd. Saw CM21 .... 97 D1
Brook Rd. Sta M CM24 .... 59 E6
Brook St. Luton LU3 .... 63 D8
Brook St. Stot SG5 .... 11 E6
Brook St. Tri HP23 .... 100 B4
Brook View. Hit SG4 .... 35 C6
Brookbridge La. Dat SG3 .... 69 D2
Brookdene Ave. Watf WD1 .... 167 C1
Brookdene Dr. Norwd HA6 .... 174 F4
Brooke Cl. Bus WD2 .... 168 C2
Brooke Gdns. Bis St CM23 .... 77 C7
Brooke Rd. Royst SG8 .... 7 D8
Brooke Way. Bus WD2 .... 168 C2
Brooker Rd. Wa Aby EN9 .... 163 C5
Brookfield Dr. Ches 148 D4
Brookfield Cl. Tri HP23 .... 100 B4
Brookfield Gdns. Ches EN8 ...... 148 D4
Brookfield La. Ast SG2 .... 51 F3
Brookfield La. Ches EN8 .... 148 B3
Brookfield La E. Ches EN8 .... 148 D3
Brookfield La W. Ches EN8 ...... 148 C4
Brookfields. Saw CM21 .... 97 D2
Brookhill. Stev SG2 .... 68 F8
Brookland Inf Sch. Ches 148 E3
Brookland Jun Sch. Ches 148 E3
Brooklands Cl. Luton LU4 .... 44 C6
Brooklands Gdns. Pot B EN6 .... 158 D7
Brookmans Ave. Bro Pk AL9 .... 144 F5
Brookmans Park Cty Prim Sch.
Bro Pk 144 E5
Brookmans Park. Bro Pk 144 E5
Brookmead Cty Prim Sch. Pit 80 E5
Brookmore Park Golf Club. Bro Pk 145 A7
Brooks Ct. Hert SG14 .... 112 F7
Brooksfield. Wel G C AL7 .... 111 B7
Brookshill Ave. Stan HA3 .... 176 E5
Brookshill Dr. Stan HA3 .... 176 D5
Brookshill. Stan HA3 .... 176 D5
Brookside Cl. Barn EN5 .... 171 E3
Brookside Cres. Cuf EN6 .... 146 E4
Brookside Gdns. Enf EN1 .... 162 C2
Brookside. Hat AL10 .... 129 D5
Brookside. Hert SG13 .... 113 E5
Brookside. Hod EN11 .... 135 A6
Brookside. Letw SG6 .... 22 F5
Brookside. Pot B EN6 .... 158 A7
Brookside Rd. Watf WD1 .... 167 B2
Brookside. Wa Aby EN9 .... 163 E7
Brookside. Watf WD2 .... 154 D3
Brooksside. Wel G C AL7 .... 111 B7
Broom Cl. Ham St EN7 .... 148 A4
Broom Cl. Hat AL10 .... 129 F2
Broom Gr. Kneb SG3 .... 68 F5
Broom Gr. Watf WD1 .... 154 A1
Broom Hill. Heml H HP1 .... 123 E2
Broom Wlk. Stev SG1 .... 50 E5
Broomer Pl. Ches EN8 .... 148 C2
Broomfield Ave. Ches EN10 ..... 148 E5
Broomfield. Chis AL2 .... 141 C4
Broomfield Cl. Welw AL6 .... 89 C4
Broomfield. Harl CM20 .... 118 B3
Broomfield. Welw AL6 .... 89 C4
Broomfield Rise. Abb L WD5 .... 153 D7
Broomhills. Wel G C AL7 .... 111 B7
Broomleys. St Alb AL4 .... 128 D6
Brooms Cl. Wel G C AL8 .... 89 D1
Brooms Rd. Luton LU2 .... 46 B8
Broomstick Hall Rd. Wa Aby EN9 . 163 E6
Broomstick La. Bot HP5 .... 136 A1
Broughinge Rd. Bor WD6 .... 170 B7
Broughton Ave. Luton LU3 .... 45 C5
Broughton Hill. Letw SG6 .... 23 B6
Broughton Way. Ric WD3 .... 165 A2
Brow The. Watf WD2 .... 154 B6
Brown's Cl. Luton LU4 .... 44 D5
Brown's Rise. St Le HP23 .... 119 F3
Brownfield Way. Kim AL4 .... 87 B6
Brownfields. Wel G C AL7 .... 110 F7
Browning Dr. Hit SG4 .... 35 B8
Browning Rd. Dun LU4 .... 44 A2
Browning Rd. Enf EN2 .... 161 D1
Browning Rd. Harp AL5 .... 86 C2
Brownlow La. Ched LU7 .... 80 A7
Brownlow Rd. Berk HP4 .... 122 C5
Brownlow Rd. Bor WD6 .... 170 A5
Browns Spring. Pot En HP4 ...... 123 C7
Brox Dell. Stev SG1 .... 50 E6
Broxbourne Jun Mix Inf Sch. Hod 134 F1
Broxbourne Sch. The. Hod 134 E1
Broxbournebury Sch. Hod 135 A3
Broxbournebury Sch. Hod 134 E3
Broxley Mead. Luton LU4 .... 44 D5
Bruce Gr. Watf WD2 .... 154 C1
Bruce Rd. Barn EN5 .... 171 E6
Bruce Rd. Har HA3 .... 176 E1
Bruce Way. Ches EN8 .... 162 D6
Brunel Rd. Stev SG2 .... 51 B7
Brunswick Ct. Hod EN11 .... 135 A5
Brunswick St. Stev SG1 .... 50 A7
Brunswick St. Luton LU2 .... 63 E8
Brushrise. Watf WD2 .... 154 A3
Brushwood Dr. Chor WD3 .... 164 C5
Brussels Way. Luton LU3 .... 44 D8
Bryan Rd. Bis St CM23 .... 76 F8
Bryanstone Rd. Ches EN8 .... 162 F5
Bryant Cl. Barn EN5 .... 171 F4
Bryce Cl. Harp AL5 .... 86 A3
Bryn La. St Alb AL4 .... 128 C1
Bryn Way. St Alb AL4 .... 128 C1
Bsns Ctr E. Letw 23 C6
Bsns Ctr W. Letw 23 C6

Buchanan Cl. Bor WD6 .... 170 C7
Buchanan Ct. Luton LU2 .... 64 B8
Buchanan Dr. Luton LU2 .... 64 B8
Buckettsland La. Shen WD6 ..... 157 D2
Buckingham Dr. Luton LU2 ...... 46 D2
Buckingham Rd. Watf WD6 ...... 170 D5
Buckingham Rd. Tri HP23 .... 99 E3
Buckingham Rd. Watf WD2 ..... 154 C2
Buckinghamshire Coll The. L Chal 172 A8
Buckland Rd. Ast Cl HP22 .... 99 A4
Buckland Rise. Pnr HA5 .... 175 D2
Bucklands The. Ric WD3 .... 165 A2
Bucklers Cl. Hod EN10 .... 134 F1
Bucklersbury. Hit SG5 .... 34 E6
Buckley Cl. Luton LU3 .... 44 F7
Bucknalls Cl. Watf WD2 .... 154 E7
Bucknalls Dr. Bri Wd AL2 .... 154 F8
Bucknalls La. Bri Wd WD2 .... 154 E7
Bucknalls La. Watf WD2 .... 154 E7
Bucks Alley. L Berk SG13 .... 132 D4
Bucks Ave. Watf WD1 .... 167 E2
Bucks Hill. Sar WD4 .... 152 C5
Buckthorn Ave. Stev SG1 .... 50 E4
Buckton Rd. Bor WD6 .... 156 F1
Buckwood La. Whip LU6 .... 82 C7
Buckwood Rd. Mark AL3 .... 83 C6
Bude Cres. Stev SG1 .... 50 A7
Bulbourne Cl. Berk HP4 .... 121 F6
Bulbourne Cl. Heml H HP1 ...... 124 A2
Bulbourne Rd. Tri HP23 .... 100 B7
Bull La. Buck SG8 .... 27 C8
Bull La. Cotrd SG9 .... 39 C8
Bull La. Whea 108 A6
Bull Plain. Hert SG14 .... 113 D6
Bull Rd. Harp AL5 .... 107 B8
Bull Stag Gn. Hat AL9 .... 130 C7
Bull's Cross. Enf EN2 .... 162 A3
Bullace Cl. Heml H HP1 .... 124 A4
Bullbeggars La. Berk HP4 .... 123 A4
Bullbeggars La. Pot En HP4 ..... 123 A4
Bullen's Green La. Coln H AL4 .. 143 E8
Bullfields. Saw CM21 .... 97 E3
Bullhead Rd. Bor WD6 .... 170 C6
Bullock's Hill. Whit SG4 .... 49 B1
Bullock's La. Hert SG13 .... 113 C4
Bullrush Cl. Hat AL10 .... 130 B4
Bulls Cross Ride. Gofs O EN7 ... 162 A5
Bulls La. Bro Pk AL9 .... 144 E7
Bulls La. Wel G AL9 .... 144 E7
Bullsland Gdns. Chor WD3 ...... 164 B3
Bullsland La. Chor WD3 .... 164 B2
Bullsmoor Cl. Enf EN8 .... 162 C4
Bullsmoor Gdns. Enf EN8 .... 162 B4
Bullsmoor La. Enf EN1,EN3 ..... 162 C4
Bullsmoor Ride. Enf EN8 .... 162 C4
Bullsmoor Sec Sch & Sports Ctr.
Enf 162 C4
Bullsmoor Way. Enf EN8 .... 162 C4
Bullwell Ctes. Ches EN8 .... 148 E2
Bulstrode La. Chipf HP3 .... 137 F3
Bulstrode La. Heml H HP3 .... 138 A5
Bulwer Link. Stev SG1 .... 50 E3
Buncefield La. Heml H HP2 ...... 125 C5
Bungalows The. Harp AL5 .... 86 C3
Bunkers La. Heml H HP3 .... 139 B7
Bunnsfield. Wel G C AL7 .... 111 C7
Bunstrux. Tri HP23 .... 100 A4
Bunting Rd. Dun LU4 .... 44 A4
Buntingford Rd. Stand SG11 .... 55 D4
Bunyan Cl. Pirt SG5 .... 20 D4
Bunyan Cl. Tri HP23 .... 100 B5
Bunyan Rd. Hit SG5 .... 34 F8
Bunyans Cl. Luton LU3 .... 45 A5
Burbage Cl. Ches EN8 .... 162 F8
Burchell Ct. Bus WD2 .... 168 C2
Burfield Cl. Hat AL10 .... 130 A4
Burfield Ct. Luton LU2 .... 46 D3 1
Burfield Rd. Chor WD3 .... 164 C4
Burford Cl. Luton LU3 .... 31 A1
Burford Gdns. Hod EN11 .... 135 B7
Burford Mews. Hod EN11 .... 135 A7
Burford Pl. Hod EN11 .... 135 A7
Burford St. Hod EN11 .... 135 A7
Burford Way. Hit SG5 .... 21 D2
Burge End La. Pirt SG5 .... 20 C5
Burgess Ct. Bor WD6 .... 156 F1
Burghley Ave. Bis St CM23 ...... 76 C7
Burghley Ave. Bor WD6 .... 170 C4
Burghley Cl. Stev SG1 .... 69 A8
Burgoyne Hatch. Harl CM20 .... 118 A1
Burgundy Croft. Wel G C AL7 ... 110 F4
Burhill Gr. Pnr HA5 .... 175 E1
Burleigh Mead. Hat AL9 .... 130 C7
Burleigh Prim Sch. Ches 148 D1
Burleigh Rd. Ches EN8 .... 162 E4
Burleigh Rd. Heml H HP2 .... 125 C2
Burleigh Rd. Hert SG13 .... 114 A7
Burleigh Rd. St Alb AL1 .... 128 B3
Burleigh Way. Cuf EN6 .... 146 E1
Burley Cl. Letw SG6 .... 11 F2
Burley Rd. Bis St CM23 .... 77 A4
Burnell Rise. Letw SG6 .... 22 D5
Burnell Wlk. Letw SG6 .... 22 E5
Burnells Way. Sta M CM24 ...... 59 E7
Burnet Cl. Heml H HP3 .... 124 E2
Burnett Ave. Henlw SG16 .... 10 B4
Burnett Sq. Hert SG14 .... 112 F7
Burnham Cl. Dat AL6 .... 90 C6
Burnham Cl. Enf EN1 .... 161 E1
Burnham Green Rd. Dat AL6,SG3 90 D6
Burnham Rd. Luton LU2 .... 46 B2
Burnham Rd. St Alb AL1 .... 128 B3
Burnley Cl. Sth Ox WD1 .... 175 C5
Burns Cl. Hit SG4 .... 35 B8
Burns Cl. Stev SG1 .... 51 C8
Burns Dr. Heml H HP2 .... 105 B1
Burnsall Pl. Harp AL5 .... 107 C6
Burnside Cl. Hat AL10 .... 130 A4
Burnside. Hert SG13 .... 113 A5
Burnside. Hod EN11 .... 134 F6
Burnside. Saw CM21 .... 97 D2
Burnside. St Alb AL1 .... 128 B1
Burnside Terr. Harl CM17 .... 118 F3
Burnt Cl. Luton LU3 .... 44 F7
Burnt Mill Comp Sch. Harl 117 E2
Burntfarm Ride. Gofs O EN2,EN7 . 161 B7
Burntmill Cl. Harl CM20 .... 117 C3

Burntmill La. Harl CM20 .... 117 D3
Burr Cl. Lon C AL2 .... 142 E4
Burr St. Luton LU2 .... 63 E8
Burr's Pl. Luton LU1 .... 63 E6
Burrowfield. Wel G C AL7 .... 110 D4
Burrs La. Bark SG8 .... 17 C3
Bursland. Letw SG6 .... 22 D6
Burston Dr. Chis AL2 .... 141 C3
Burton Ave. Watf WD1 .... 167 A4
Burton Cl. Kim AL4 .... 87 C5
Burton La. Gofs O EN7 .... 147 E3
Burtons La. L Chal WD3 .... 164 A4
Burtons Mill. Saw CM21 .... 97 F3
Burvale Cl. Watf WD1 .... 167 B6 3
Burwell Rd. Stev SG2 .... 51 C4
Bury Cotts. Fla AL3 .... 105 E5
Bury End. Pirt SG5 .... 20 D4
Bury Gn. Heml H HP1 .... 124 C4
Bury Gn. Whea AL4 .... 108 C8
Bury Green Rd. Ches EN7 .... 162 A7
Bury Green Rd. Ches EN7 .... 162 A8
Bury Hill Cl. Heml H HP1 .... 124 C4
Bury Hill. Heml H HP1 .... 124 C4
Bury Holme. Hod EN10 .... 148 F8
Bury La. Bram SG14 .... 91 B4
Bury La. Cod SG4 .... 67 F2
Bury La. Dat SG3 .... 69 D3
Bury La. Ric WD3 .... 165 D1
Bury La. Str LU3 .... 31 A5
Bury Mead. Arl SG15 .... 11 A7
Bury Mead Rd. Hit SG5 .... 21 F1
Bury Meadows. Ric WD3 .... 165 D1
Bury Park Rd. Luton LU1 .... 63 C8
Bury Rd. Harl CM17 .... 118 D4
Bury Rd. Hat AL10 .... 130 C6
Bury Rd. Heml H HP1 .... 124 C3
Bury Rise. Heml H HP3 .... 137 D6
Bury The. Cod SG4 .... 67 F2
Burycroft. Wel G C AL8 .... 89 E1
Burydale Jun Sch. Stev 51 B1
Burydell La. Pk St AL2 .... 141 D5
Buryfield Terr. Ware SG12 ...... 93 C1
Burymead. Stev SG1 .... 36 C1
Burywick. Harp AL5 .... 107 B5
Bush Hall La. Hat AL9 .... 130 D8
Bush Spring. Bal SG7 .... 13 A1
Bushbarns. Ches EN7 .... 148 A2
Bushby Ave. Hod EN10 .... 134 F1
Bushel Wharf. Tri HP23 .... 100 A6
Bushell Gn. Bus WD2 .... 176 D8
Bushey Cl. Wel G C AL7 .... 111 B5
Bushey Gn. Wel G C AL7 .... 111 B5
Bushey Grove Rd. Watf WD2 ... 167 E5
Bushey Hall Dr. Watf WD2 ...... 167 E8
Bushey Hall Rd. Watf WD2 ...... 167 D7
Bushey Hall Sch. Bus 167 F4
Bushey Heath
Jun Mix Inf Prim Sch. Bus ... 168 D1
Bushey Ley. Wel G C AL7 .... 111 B5
Bushey Manor Jun Sch. Watf ... 167 E4
Bushey Maternity Hospl. Stan ... 168 F1
Bushey Meads Sch. Bus 168 C4
Bushey Mill Cres. Watf WD2 .... 154 C3
Bushey Mill La. Bus WD2 .... 167 E8
Bushey Mill La. Watf WD2 ...... 154 D1
Bushey & Oxhey Sta. Watf 167 D3
Bushfield Rd. Bor WD6 .... 137 C6
Bushmead Prim Sch. Luton 45 E5
Bushmead Rd. Luton LU2 .... 45 E5
Bushwood Cl. Wel G AL9 .... 144 B8
Bute Sq. Luton LU1 .... 63 E7
Bute St. Luton LU1 .... 63 E7
Butely Rd. Luton LU4 .... 44 B5
Butler's Hall La. H Wyc CM23 ... 76 A3
Butlers Dr. Wa Aby EN9 .... 163 C1
Butlin Rd. Luton LU1 .... 63 B7
Butt Field View. St Alb AL1 ..... 141 C7
Butterfield Green Rd. Str LU2 ... 46 A6
Butterfield La. St Alb AL1 .... 141 E7
Butterfield Rd. Whea AL4 .... 108 C7
Butterfly La. Radl WD6 .... 169 B7
Buttermere Cl. St Alb AL1 .... 128 B2
Buttersweet Rise. Saw CM21 ... 97 E1
Butterwick Adult Training Ctr.
St Alb 128 D2
Butterwick. Watf WD2 .... 154 E3
Butterworth Path. Luton LU2 ... 63 E8 2
Buttlehide. Map Cr WD3 .... 172 D5
Buttondene Cres. Lo Naz EN10 . 135 B1
Butts End. Heml H HP1 .... 124 A5
Buttsmead. Norwd HA6 .... 174 C4
Buxton Cl. St Alb AL4 .... 128 D6
Buxton Path. Sth Ox WD1 ...... 175 D7
Buxton Rd. Luton LU1 .... 63 D7
Buxtons La. Gu M SG8 .... 1 F5
Buzzard Rd. Dun LU4 .... 44 A4
By The Mount. Wel G C AL7 .... 110 D5
By-The-Wood. Sth Ox WD1 ..... 175 D7
Byde St. Hert SG14 .... 113 C7
Bye Way The. Har HA3 .... 176 F2
Byers Cl. Pot B EN6 .... 159 C5
Byeway. The. Ric WD3 .... 173 E8
Byfield Cl. Dun LU4 .... 44 B1
Byfield. Wel G C AL8 .... 89 E1
Byford House. Barn EN5 .... 171 E5
Bygrave Rd. Bal SG7 .... 12 F1
Bygrave. Stev SG1 .... 36 C2
Bylands Cl. Bis St CM23 .... 76 D6
Byng Dr. Pot B EN6 .... 159 A8
Byng Rd. Barn EN5 .... 171 D6
Byrd Wlk. Bal SG7 .... 23 F7
Byron Ave. Bor WD6 .... 170 A4
Byron Ave. Watf WD1 .... 167 B6
Byron Ct. Ham St EN7 .... 147 F4
Byron Cl. Hit SG4 .... 35 B8
Byron Cl. Stev SG2 .... 51 C7
Byron Ct. Ches EN2 .... 148 B3
Byron Pl. Heml H HP2 .... 105 B1
Byron Rd. Dun LU4 .... 44 B1
Byron Rd. Har HA3 .... 176 F1
Byron Rd. Harp AL5 .... 86 A2
Byron Rd. Royst SG8 .... 7 E8
Byslips Rd. Stu LU6 .... 82 D5
Byslips Rd. Whip LU6 .... 82 D5
Byway The. Pot B EN6 .... 159 A6
Byways. Berk HP4 .... 122 E5

Caddington Comm. Mark AL3 ... 83 E8
Caddis Cl. Har HA7 .... 176 F3
Cade Cl. Letw SG6 .... 12 C1
Cades Cl. Luton LU1 .... 63 A6
Cades La. Luton LU1 .... 63 A6
Cadia Cl. Cad LU1 .... 62 E4
Cadmore Cl. Heml H HP2 .... 124 D3
Cadmore La. Ches EN8 .... 148 E2
Cadwell Ct. Hit SG4 .... 22 A2
Cadwell La. Hit SG4 .... 22 A2
Caernarvon Cl. Heml H HP2 .... 124 D3
Caernarvon Cl. Stev SG2 .... 69 B7
Caernarvon Ct. Heml H HP2 .... 124 D3
Caesars Rd. Whea AL4 .... 108 E8
Cage Pond Rd. Shen WD7 ...... 156 F6
Cairn Way. Har HA7 .... 176 F4
Caishowe Rd. Bor WD6 .... 170 A8
Caister Cl. Stev SG1 .... 36 A1
Calbury Cl. St Alb AL1 .... 128 B2
Caldbeck. Wa Aby EN9 .... 163 D5
Caldecot Ave. Gofs O EN7 ...... 147 F2
Caldecot Way. Hod EN10 .... 134 F1
Caldecote Gdns. Bus WD2 ...... 168 F3
Caldecote La. Bus WD2 .... 168 F3
Caldecote Rd. Newn SG7 .... 12 E8
Calder Ave. Bro Pk AL9 .... 145 B5
Caldwell Rd. Sth Ox WD1 ...... 175 D6
Caleb Cl. Luton LU4 .... 44 F2
Caledon Rd. Lon C AL2 .... 142 D5
Caledonian Ct. Watf WD1 ...... 167 B6
California. Bal SG7 .... 12 F1
California La. Bus WD2 .... 168 D1
Callanders The. Bus WD2 .... 168 E1
Callisto Ct. Heml H HP2 .... 124 D6
Callowland Pl. Watf WD2 .... 154 B1
Calnwood Rd. Dun LU4 .... 44 C3
Calton Ave. Hert SG14 .... 112 F7
Calton Ct. Hert SG14 .... 112 F6
Calton House. Hert SG14 .... 112 F6
Calverley Cl. Bis St CM23 ...... 76 E4
Calvert Rd. Barn EN5 .... 171 C7
Calverton Rd. Luton LU3 .... 44 F6
Cam Ctr. Hit SG4 .... 22 A3
Cam Sq. Hit SG4 .... 22 A3
Camberley Pl. Harp AL5 .... 107 D6
Camborne Dr. Heml H HP2 ..... 124 F6
Cambrian Way. Heml H HP2 .... 124 F6
Cambridge Cl. Ches EN8 .... 148 C2
Cambridge Cotts. Thun SG11 .. 72 E2
Cambridge Cres. Knee SG8 ..... 2 A8
Cambridge Dr. Pot B EN6 .... 158 E2
Cambridge Rd. Bar SG8 .... 9 A3
Cambridge Rd. Bar SG8 .... 17 F7
Cambridge Rd. Bark SG8 .... 17 D5
Cambridge Rd. Harl CM20 ..... 118 C6
Cambridge Rd. Hit SG4 .... 35 B8
Cambridge Rd. Saw CM21 ..... 97 E3
Cambridge Rd. St Alb AL1 ...... 128 E2
Cambridge Rd. Sta M CM24 ... 59 E8
Cambridge Rd. Stand SG11 .... 55 C2
Cambridge Rd. Watf WD1 ...... 167 C5
Cambridge St. Luton LU1 .... 63 F5
Cambridge Terr. Berk HP4 ...... 122 D4
Cameron Ct. Ware SG12 .... 93 D2 8
Cameron Dr. Ches EN8 .... 162 D5
Camfield. Wel G C AL7 .... 110 F2
Camford Way. Luton LU3 .... 44 B8
Camlet Way. St Alb AL3 .... 127 B4
Camp Jun Mix Inf Sch. St Alb ... 128 B2
Camp Rd. St Alb AL1 .... 128 B2
Camp View Rd. St Alb AL1 ...... 128 B2
Campana Ct. Barn EN5 .... 171 D6
Campania Gr. Luton LU3 .... 45 A8
Campbell Cl. Hit SG4 .... 35 B8
Campers Ave. Letw SG6 .... 22 E5
Campers Rd. Letw SG6 .... 22 E5
Campers Wlk. Letw SG6 .... 22 E5
Campfield Rd. Hert SG14 .... 113 B5
Campfield Rd. St Alb AL1 .... 128 A3
Campfield Way. Letw SG6 ...... 22 E5
Campine Cl. Ches EN8 .... 148 D3
Campion Cl. Watf WD2 .... 154 A6
Campion Ct. Stev SG1 .... 50 C8
Campion Rd. Heml H HP1 .... 123 E4
Campion Way. Royst SG8 .... 7 E8
Campions Cl. Berk HP4 .... 122 B3
Campions Ct. Berk HP4 .... 122 B3
Campions The. Bor WD6 .... 157 A1
Campions The. Sta M CM24 .... 59 E8
Campkin Mead. Stev SG2 ...... 51 B4
Camps End Jun Mix Inf Sch. Stev 51 B6
Campus Five. Letw 23 C7
Campus The. Wel G C AL8 ...... 110 D7
Canada La. Ches EN10 .... 148 E6
Canadas The. Ches EN10 .... 148 E6
Canberra Cl. Knee SG8 .... 2 B5
Canberra Cl. St Alb AL3 .... 127 F7
Canberra Gdns. Luton LU3 ..... 45 B6
Candlefield Cl. Heml H HP3 .... 139 A8
Candlefield Rd. Heml H HP3 .... 139 A8
Candlefield Wlk. Heml H HP3 ... 139 A8
Caneland Ct. Wa Aby EN9 ...... 163 F5
Canfield. Bis St CM23 .... 76 E8
Cangelis Cl. Heml H HP1 .... 124 A4
Canham Cl. Kim SG4 .... 60 D1
Cannix Cl. Stev SG2 .... 51 A2
Cannon House. Hit SG4 .... 34 F6 1
Cannon La. Luton LU2 .... 46 B3
Cannon Rd. Watf WD1 .... 167 C4
Cannon St. St Alb AL3 .... 127 D4
Cannons Cl. Bis St CM23 .... 59 A1
Cannons Cl. Gu M SG8 .... 1 F5
Cannons Cl. Stand SG11 .... 55 D3
Cannons Mead. Sta M CM24 ... 59 D7
Cannons Meadow. Tewin AL6 .. 90 E2
Cannons Mill La. Bis St CM23 .. 59 A1
Canon Brook Golf Club. Harl ... 117 A1
Canons Cl. Radl WD7 .... 156 B4
Canons Field. Welw AL6 .... 89 C7
Canons Field. Welw AL6 .... 87 D1
Canons Gate. Harl CM20 .... 117 A3
Canons Rd. Ware SG12 .... 93 C2
Canonsfield Ct. Welw AL6 ...... 89 C7
Canonsfield Rd. Welw AL6 ..... 89 C7
Canopus Way. Mo Pk HA6 ..... 175 A4
Cantelowes House. Barn EN5 ... 171 D4
Canterbury Cl. Luton LU3 .... 44 F4
Canterbury Cl. Norwd HA6 ..... 174 F4

Canterbury Ct. St Alb AL1 .... 127 F4
Canterbury House. Bor WD6 .... 170 A7
Canterbury Rd. Bor WD6 .... 170 A7
Canterbury Rd. Watf WD1 .... 167 B7
Canterbury Way. Cro Gr WD3 .... 166 C6
Canterbury Way. Stev SG1 .... 36 F2
Cape Rd. St Alb AL1 .... 128 B3
Capel Cl. St Alb SG11 .... 57 E2
Capel House. Sth Ox WD1 .... 175 D6
Capel Manor Prim Sch. Enf 162 B4
Capel Rd. Enf EN1 .... 162 B3
Capel Rd. Watf WD1 .... 167 E3
Capell Ave. Chor WD3 .... 164 C4
Capell Rd. Chor WD3 .... 164 D4
Capell Way. Chor WD3 .... 164 D4
Capella Rd. Mo Pk HA6 .... 174 F6
Capelvere Wlk. Watf WD1 .... 166 E8
Caponfield. Wel G C AL7 .... 111 B4
Cappell La. Sta Ab SG12 .... 115 D5
Capron Rd. Luton LU4 .... 44 E4
Captains Wlk. Berk HP4 .... 122 D3
Caractacus Cottage View.
   Watf WD1 .... 167 A3
Caractacus Gn. Watf WD1 .... 166 F3
Caravan La. Ric WD3 .... 165 E2
Carbone Hill. Cuf EN6,SG13 .... 146 D5
Carde Cl. Hemt H HP4 .... 112 F7
Cardiff Cl. Stev SG2 .... 69 B7
Cardiff Gr. Luton LU1 .... 63 D7
Cardiff Pl. Knee SG8 .... 2 A8
Cardiff Rd. Luton LU1 .... 63 D7
Cardiff Rd. Watf WD1 .... 167 B4
Cardigan Ct. Luton LU1 .... 63 D7
Cardigan St. Luton LU1 .... 63 D7
Cardinal Ave. Bor WD6 .... 170 A5
Cardinal Cl. Ham St EN7 .... 147 F5
Cardinal Cl. Bor WD6 .... 170 B6
Cardinal Gr. St Alb AL3 .... 127 B1
Cardinal Newman Sch. Luton 31 C1
Cardy Rd. Hemt H HP1 .... 124 B3
Carew Rd. Norwd HA6 .... 174 F4
Careys Croft. Berk HP4 .... 122 A7
Carisbrook Rd. Chis AL2 .... 141 B5
Carisbrooke Ave. Watf WD2 .... 167 D8
Carisbrooke Rd. Harp AL5 .... 86 C2
Carisbrooke Rd. Luton LU4 .... 44 E1
Carleton Rd. Ches EN8 .... 148 E4
Carleton Rise. Welw AL6 .... 89 C6
Carlisle Ave. St Alb AL3 .... 127 D4
Carlton Bank. Harp AL5 .... 86 B1
Carlton Cl. Bor WD6 .... 170 C4
Carlton Cl. Luton LU3 .... 45 C2
Carlton Cres. Luton LU3 .... 45 C2
Carlton Ct. Harp AL5 .... 86 B1
Carlton Ct. Watf WD1 .... 167 C4
Carlton Rd. Harp AL5 .... 86 B2
Carman Cr. Tri HP23 .... 99 F3
Carmelite Cl. Har HA3 .... 176 C2
Carmelite Rd. Dun LU4 .... 44 A3
Carmelite Rd. Har HA3 .... 176 C1
Carmelite Way. Har HA3 .... 176 C1
Carmelite Wlk. Har HA3 .... 176 C2
Carmen Cr. Bor WD6 .... 156 F1
Carnaby Rd. Hod EN10 .... 134 E3
Carnarvon Rd. Barn EN5 .... 171 E6
Carnegie Dr. St Alb AL3 .... 127 D7
Carnegie Gdns. Luton LU3 .... 45 A8
Caro La. Hemt H HP3 .... 125 B1
Carol Cl. Luton LU3 .... 45 B4
Caroline Pl. Watf WD1 .... 167 E3
Caroon Dr. Sar WD3 .... 152 B3
Carpenders Ave. Sth Ox WD1 .... 175 E8
Carpenders Cl. Harp AL5 .... 85 D4
Carpenders Park Sta. Sth Ox 175 D7
Carpenter Way. Pot B EN6 .... 159 D6
Carpenters The. Bis St CM23 .... 76 E6
Carpenters Wood Dr. Chor WD3 .... 164 B5
Carrigans. Bis St CM23 .... 76 E8
Carrington Ave. Bor WD6 .... 170 C4
Carrington Cl. Barn EN5 .... 171 A4
Carrington Cl. Bor WD6 .... 170 C4
Carrington Pl. Tri HP23 .... 100 C5
Carrington Sq. Stan HA3 .... 176 C3
Carsdale Cl. Luton LU3 .... 45 A6
Cart Path. Watf WD2 .... 154 C6
Carteret Rd. Luton LU2 .... 46 C1
Carterhatch La. Enf EN1 .... 161 F1
Carters Cl. Arl SG15 .... 11 A7
Carters Cl. Ast SG2 .... 51 D4
Carters La. Hit SG5 .... 34 A6
Carters Leys. Bis St CM23 .... 76 D8
Carters Wlk. Arl SG15 .... 11 A7
Cartersfield Rd. Wa Aby EN9 .... 163 C5
Cartwright Rd. Royst SG8 .... 7 C7
Cartwright Rd. Stev SG1 .... 37 C2
Carve Ley. Wel G C AL7 .... 111 B5
Carvers Croft. Welw SG3 .... 69 B2
Cashio La. Letw SG6 .... 23 A8
Caslon Way. Letw SG6 .... 11 F1
Cassandra Gate. Ches EN8 .... 148 F4
Cassio Coll. Watf 154 A1
Cassio Rd. Watf WD1 .... 167 B5
Cassiobridge Rd. Watf WD1 .... 166 E5
Cassiobury Terr. Cro Gr WD3 .... 166 D4
Cassiobury Dr. Watf WD1 .... 166 F7
Cassiobury Rd. Watf WD1 .... 167 A6
Cassiobury Inf Sch. Watf 166 E6
Cassiobury Park Ave. Watf WD1 .... 166 F6
Cassiobury Prim Sch. Watf 166 E8
Castano Ct. Abb L WD5 .... 153 E8
Castellane Cl. Har HA7 .... 176 F1
Castile Ct. Ches EN8 .... 163 A5
Castle Cl. Bus WD2 .... 168 B3
Castle Cl. Hod EN11 .... 115 C1
Castle Croft Rd. Luton LU1 .... 63 A6
Castle Gate Way. Berk HP4 .... 122 C6
Castle Hill Ave. Berk HP4 .... 122 C5
Castle Hill. Berk HP4 .... 122 C5
Castle Hill. Berk HP4 .... 122 C5
Castle Mead Gdns. Hert SG14 .... 113 C6
Castle Mead. Hemt H HP1 .... 124 B1
Castle Mews. Berk HP4 .... 122 C5
Castle Rd. Enf EN3 .... 162 E1
Castle Rd. Hod EN11 .... 115 C1
Castle Rd. St Alb AL1 .... 128 B3

Castle Rise. Whea AL4 .... 86 F2
Castle St. Berk HP4 .... 122 C4
Castle St. Bis St CM23 .... 76 F6
Castle St. Hert SG14 .... 113 C5
Castle St. Luton LU1 .... 63 E6
Castle St. Wing HP22 .... 60 B3
Castle View. Bis St CM23 .... 77 A7
Castles Cl. Stot SG5 .... 11 F8
Catalin Ct. Wa Aby EN9 .... 163 D6
Caterham Ct. St Alb AL1 .... 128 B1
Catesby Gn. Luton LU3 .... 31 A1
Catham Cl. St Alb AL1 .... 128 B1
Cathedral Ct. St Alb AL3 .... 127 B1
Catherall Rd. Luton LU3 .... 45 B6
Catherine Cl. Hemt H HP2 .... 125 B8
Catherine St. Enf EN3 .... 162 E1
Catherine St. St Alb AL3 .... 127 D4
Catisfield Rd. Enf EN3 .... 162 E2
Catkin Cl. Hemt H HP1 .... 124 B4
Catlin St. Hemt H HP3 .... 138 B8
Catsbrook Rd. Luton LU3 .... 45 B6
Catsey La. Bus WD2 .... 168 C2
Catsey Wood. Bus WD2 .... 168 C2
Catterick Way. Bor WD6 .... 169 F8
Cattlegate Hill. Nort EN6 .... 160 D7
Cattlegate Rd. Cre H EN2 .... 161 A5
Cattlegate Rd. Nort EN6 .... 160 D6
Cattsdell. Hemt H HP2 .... 124 E5
Causeway Cl. Pot B EN6 .... 159 D8
Causeway House. Abb L WD5 .... 153 E8
Causeway The. Bis St CM23 .... 76 F7
Causeway The. Brag SG9 .... 42 D1
Causeway The. Bre P SG9 .... 30 B1
Causeway The. Bun SG9 .... 40 F8
Causeway The. Fur P SG9 .... 43 A4
Causeway The. Knee SG8 .... 2 A5
Causeway The. Pot B EN6 .... 159 D8
Causeway The. Ther SG8 .... 15 F7
Cautherly La. Art Gam SG12 .... 115 A5
Cavalier Cl. Luton LU3 .... 45 A5
Cavalier Ct. Berk HP4 .... 122 C4
Cavalier. Stev SG1 .... 36 B1
Cavan Cl. Hat AL10 .... 130 A4
Cavan Dr. St Alb AL3 .... 127 D8
Cavan Rd. Red AL3 .... 106 A6
Cavell Rd. Ham St EN7 .... 148 A4
Cavell Wlk. Stev SG2 .... 51 C5
Cavendish Cres. Bor WD6 .... 170 A5
Cavendish Ct. Cro Gr WD3 .... 166 E4
Cavendish Rd. Barn EN5 .... 171 C6
Cavendish Rd. Luton LU3 .... 45 B2
Cavendish Rd. Mark AL3 .... 83 D6
Cavendish Rd. St Alb AL1 .... 127 F3
Cavendish Rd. Stev SG1 .... 50 B5
Cavendish Sch The. Hemt H 124 B4
Cavendish Way. Hat AL10 .... 129 F5
Cawkell Cl. Sta M CM24 .... 59 D7
Cawley Wlk Sch. Bor 170 A8
Caxton Cl. Enf EN3 .... 162 E4
Caxton Hill. Hert SG13 .... 113 F6
Caxton Rd. Hod EN11 .... 115 B2
Caxton Way. Mo Pk WD1 .... 166 D2
Caxton Way. Stev SG1 .... 50 B4
Cecil Cl. Bis St CM23 .... 77 D7
Cecil Cres. Hat AL10 .... 130 B7
Cecil Rd. Barn EN5 .... 171 D6
Cecil Rd. Bric SG13 .... 113 C3
Cecil Rd. Ches EN8 .... 162 E7
Cecil Rd. Hod EN11 .... 135 C8
Cecil Rd. Pot B EN6 .... 158 B7
Cecil Rd. St Alb AL1 .... 127 F3
Cecil St. Watf WD1 .... 167 B1
Cedar Ave. Ches EN8 .... 162 D6
Cedar Ave. Ick SG5 .... 21 E4
Cedar Cl. Hert SG14 .... 113 B6
Cedar Cl. Pot B EN6 .... 145 A1
Cedar Cl. Saw CM21 .... 97 E1
Cedar Cl. Ware SG12 .... 114 D8
Cedar Cres. Royst SG8 .... 7 B6
Cedar Cl. Bis St CM23 .... 58 F1
Cedar Ct. St Alb AL4 .... 128 D3
Cedar Dr. Pnr HA5 .... 176 A4
Cedar Gn. Hod EN11 .... 135 A5
Cedar Lawn Ave. Barn EN5 .... 171 E6
Cedar Park Rd. Enf EN2 .... 161 C1
Cedar Pk. Bis St CM23 .... 76 D4
Cedar Pl. Norwd HA6 .... 174 C4
Cedar Rd. Berk HP4 .... 122 E3
Cedar Rd. Enf EN2 .... 161 C1
Cedar Rd. Hat AL10 .... 130 A4
Cedar Rd. Watf WD1 .... 167 D3
Cedar Way. Berk HP4 .... 122 D3
Cedar Wlk. Hemt H HP3 .... 124 D1
Cedar Wood Dr. Watf WD2 .... 154 B4
Cedars Ave. Ric WD3 .... 165 C1
Cedars Cl. Bor WD6 .... 170 B5
Cedars The. Harp AL5 .... 86 B1
Cedars The. St Alb AL3 .... 127 C5
Cedarwood Dr. St Alb AL4 .... 128 D7
Celandine Dr. Luton LU3 .... 45 A8
Cell Barnes Cl. St Alb AL1 .... 128 D7
Cell Barnes Hospl. St Alb 128 C1
Cell Barnes La. St Alb AL1 .... 128 D6
Cemetery Hill. Hemt H HP1 .... 124 C2
Cemetery Rd. Bis St CM23 .... 77 F6
Cemmaes Court Rd. Hemt H HP1 . 124 C3
Cemmaes Meadow. Hemt H HP1 .. 124 C3
Central App. Letw SG6 .... 22 F6
Central Ave. Ches EN8 .... 148 B1
Central Ave. Henlw SG16 .... 10 B3
Central Ave. Whip LU6 .... 81 E8
Central St. St Alb AL4 .... 128 C4
Central Dr. Wel G C AL7 .... 111 F8
Central Dr. Harl CM20 .... 118 A4
Central Way. Wa Aby EN9 .... 163 E3
Centre Way. Wa Aby EN9 .... 163 C1
Centro. Hemt H HP2 .... 124 D4
Century Rd. Hod EN11 .... 135 A7
Century Rd. Ware SG12 .... 93 D2
Cervantes Ct. Norwd HA6 .... 174 F4
Chace Ave. Pot B EN6 .... 159 D4
Chace The. Stev SG2 .... 50 F1
Chad La. Fla AL3 .... 84 C4
Chadwell Ave. Ches EN8 .... 148 B1
Chadwell Cl. Luton LU2 .... 45 F1
Chadwell Rd. Stev SG1 .... 50 B4
Chadwell Rise. Ware SG12 .... 114 C8

Chadwell. Ware SG12 .... 114 C8
Chaffinch La. Watf WD1 .... 166 E5
Chaffinches Gn. Hemt H HP3 .... 139 A7
Chagney Cl. Letw SG6 .... 22 E6
Chalet Cl. Berk HP4 .... 121 F4
Chalfont Cl. Hemt H HP2 .... 125 B8
Chalfont Cl. Stev SG2 .... 69 B7
Chalfont La. Chor WD3 .... 164 B4
Chalfont La. Map Cr WD3 .... 172 D3
Chalfont Pl. St Alb AL1 .... 127 E3
Chalfont Rd. Map Cr WD3 .... 172 C7
Chalfont Way. Luton LU2 .... 46 D2
Chalfont Wlk. Pnr HA5 .... 175 C1
Chalgrove. Wel G C AL7 .... 111 F3
Chalk Dale. Wel G C AL7 .... 111 B7
Chalk Field. Letw 23 C3
Chalk Hill. Gt Of LU2 .... 47 A5
Chalk Hill. Watf WD1 .... 167 C3
Chalk Hills. Bal 23 F5
Chalkdell Fields. St Alb AL4 .... 128 A7
Chalkdell Hill. Hemt H HP2 .... 124 E3
Chalkdell Path. Hit SG5 .... 34 D8
Chalkdown. Luton LU2 .... 45 F6
Chalkdown. Stev SG2 .... 51 D7
Chalks Ave. Saw CM21 .... 97 D3
Challney Cl. Luton LU4 .... 44 E1
Challney High Sch. Luton 44 D2
Chalmers Ct. Cro Gr WD3 .... 165 F3
Chalton Rd. Luton LU4 .... 44 C5
Chamberlaines. Harp AL5 .... 85 A5
Chambers La. Ick SG5 .... 21 E4
Chambers St. Hert SG14 .... 113 C6
Chambersbury La. Hemt H HP3 ... 139 A7
Chambersbury Prim Sch. Hemt H . 139 B8
Champions Cl. Bor WD6 .... 157 B2
Champions Gn. Hod EN11 .... 115 B1
Champions Way. Hod EN11 .... 115 A1
Chancellor's Sch. Bro Pk 145 A6
Chancellors Rd. Stev SG1 .... 36 D1
Chancery Cl. St Alb AL4 .... 128 D8
Chandler's La. Sar WD3 .... 152 E2
Chandlers Rd. St Alb AL4 .... 128 C6
Chandlers Way. Hert SG14 .... 113 A6
Chandos Cl. L Chal HP6 .... 150 C1
Chandos Rd. Bor WD6 .... 170 A7
Chandos Rd. Luton LU4 .... 44 F1
Chantry Cl. Bis St CM23 .... 76 E6
Chantry Cl. Kin L WD4 .... 139 A2
Chantry Cl. Hat AL10 .... 130 A2
Chantry La. Hat AL10 .... 129 F4
Chantry La. Hat AL10 .... 130 A4
Chantry La. L Wy SG4 .... 36 A3
Chantry La. Lon C AL2 .... 142 D5
Chantry Pl. Har HA3 .... 176 B2
Chantry Rd. Bis St CM23 .... 76 E6
Chantry Rd. Har HA3 .... 176 B2
Chantry The. Bis St CM23 .... 76 F8
Chantry The. Harl CM20 .... 118 A2
Chaomans. Letw SG6 .... 22 F3
Chapel Cl. L Gad HP4 .... 102 D6
Chapel Cl. Luton LU2 .... 45 C8
Chapel Cotts. Hemt H HP2 .... 124 A4
Chapel Croft. Chipf WD4 .... 152 A8
Chapel Crofts. Nthch HP4 .... 121 E6
Chapel End. Bun SG9 .... 40 E7
Chapel End La. Wils HP23 .... 99 C8
Chapel Hill. Sta M CM24 .... 59 E6
Chapel La. Hertng SG14 .... 112 B3
Chapel La. L Had SG11 .... 75 A8
Chapel La. Lon M HP23 .... 99 B4
Chapel Meadow. Tri HP23 .... 100 B6
Chapel Pl. Stot SG5 .... 11 F5
Chapel Rd. Bre Gr SG4 .... 65 E8
Chapel Rd. Fla AL3 .... 84 B2
Chapel Row. Hare UB9 .... 173 C2
Chapel Row. Hit SG5 .... 34 F8
Chapel St. Berk HP4 .... 122 B4
Chapel St. Hemt H HP2 .... 124 D4
Chapel St. Hin SG7 .... 3 D6
Chapel St. Luton LU1 .... 63 E6
Chapel St. Tri HP23 .... 99 F3
Chapel Viaduct. Luton LU1 .... 63 E7
Chapelfields. Sta Ab SG12 .... 115 D4
Chapman Rd. Stev SG1 .... 50 C5
Chapmans End. Stand SG11 .... 55 D3
Chapmans Yd. Watf WD1 .... 167 C5
Chappell Cl. Bis St CM23 .... 92 E7
Chapter House Rd. Dun LU4 .... 44 A3
Chard Dr. Luton LU3 .... 31 B1
Chardins Cl. Hemt H HP1 .... 123 F4
Charles St. Berk HP4 .... 122 B4
Charles St. Hemt H HP1 .... 124 C2
Charles St. Luton LU2 .... 63 F8
Charles St. Tri HP23 .... 100 A3
Charlesworth Cl. Hemt H HP3 ...... 124 D1
Charlock Way. Watf WD1 .... 166 F3
Charlton Cl. Hod EN11 .... 135 D5
Charlton Mead La. Hod EN11 .... 135 D4
Charlton Rd. Hit SG5 .... 34 D5
Charlton Way. Hod EN11 .... 135 A6
Charlwood Cl. Har HA3 .... 176 E4
Charlwood Dr. Dun LU4 .... 44 B1
Charmbury Rise. Luton LU2 .... 46 A4
Charmouth Ct. St Alb AL1 .... 128 A6
Charmouth Rd. St Alb AL1 .... 128 A5
Charndon Cl. Luton LU3 .... 31 B1
Charnwood Rd. Enf EN1 .... 162 B3
Charter Pl. Watf WD1 .... 167 C6
Chartley Ave. Har HA7 .... 176 F4
Chartridge Cl. Barn EN5 .... 171 A4
Chartridge Cl. Bus WD2 .... 168 B1
Chartridge Way. Hemt H HP2 .... 125 C3
Chartwell Cl. Wa Aby EN9 .... 163 E6
Chartwell Cl. Barn EN5 .... 171 E5
Chartwell Dr. Luton LU2 .... 45 E3
Chartwell Rd. Norwd HA6 .... 174 F4
Chasden Rd. Hemt H HP1 .... 123 F5
Chase Cl. Arl SG15 .... 11 A8
Chase Farm Hospl. Enf 161 A1
Chase St. Luton LU1 .... 63 E6
Chase The. Bis St CM23 .... 76 F6
Chase The. Gofs O EN7 .... 147 B3
Chase The. Gt Am SG12 .... 115 A6
Chase The. Hemt H HP1 .... 124 E2

Chase The. Hert SG13 .... 113 F6
Chase The. Radl WD7 .... 155 F3
Chase The. Watf WD1 .... 166 E5
Chase The. Welw AL6 .... 89 D7
Chaseside Cl. Chal LU7 .... 80 A7
Chaseways. Saw CM21 .... 118 C8
Chasten Hill. Letw SG6 .... 22 D7
Chater Inf Sch. Watf 167 A5
Chatsworth Cl. Bis St CM23 .... 76 E6
Chatsworth Cl. Bor WD6 .... 170 A6
Chatsworth Ct. St Alb AL1 .... 127 F3
Chatsworth Ct. Stev SG2 .... 50 F1
Chatsworth Rd. Luton LU4 .... 45 B1
Chatteris Cl. Luton LU4 .... 44 A4
Chatton Cl. Luton LU2 .... 46 E2
Chaucer Cl. Berk HP4 .... 121 F5
Chaucer House. Barn EN5 .... 171 D5
Chaucer Rd. Royst SG8 .... 7 C8
Chaucer Way. Hit SG4 .... 35 C7
Chaucer Way. Hod EN11 .... 115 A2
Chaucer Wlk. Hemt H HP2 .... 105 F1
Chaul End La. Luton LU4 .... 44 E1
Chaul End Rd. Cad LU1 .... 62 D6
Chaul End Rd. Dun LU1 .... 44 B1
Chaulden House Gdns.
   Hemt H HP1 .... 123 F1
Chaulden Jun & Inf Schs. Hemt H 123 F1
Chaulden La. Hemt H HP1 .... 123 E1
Chaulden Terr. Hemt H HP1 .... 123 E1
Chauncey House. Watf WD1 .... 166 E3
Chauncy Cl. Ware SG12 .... 93 D3
Chauncy Ct. Hert SG14 .... 113 D6
Chauncy Gdns. Bal SG7 .... 13 B1
Chauncy House. Stev SG1 .... 50 E6
Chauncy Sch The. Ware 93 B2
Chaworth Gn. Luton LU4 .... 44 C5
Cheapside. Luton LU1 .... 63 E7
Cheapside Sq. Luton LU1 .... 63 E7
Chedburgh. Wel G C AL7 .... 111 D6
Cheddington Comb Sch. Ched 80 A7
Cheddington La. Lon M HP23 .... 79 C5
Cheddington La. Pit LU7 .... 80 A8
Cheddington Rd. Pit LU7 .... 80 C5
Cheffins Rd. Hod EN11 .... 114 F1
Chells La. Stev SG2 .... 51 D7
Chells Way. Stev SG2 .... 51 B6
Chelmsford Rd. Hert SG14 .... 113 B5
Chelsing Rise. Hemt H HP2 .... 125 C4
Chelsworth Cl. Luton LU2 .... 46 D1
Chelveston. Wel G C AL7 .... 111 D7
Chelwood Ave. Hat AL10 .... 130 A8
Chelwood Cl. Norwd HA6 .... 174 C3
Chenduit Way. Stan HA7 .... 176 F5
Cheney Rd. Luton LU4 .... 44 C5
Chenies Ave. L Chal HP6 .... 150 D1
Chenies Ct. Hemt H HP2 .... 125 B8
Chenies Gr. Bis St CM23 .... 76 D6
Chenies Rd. Chor WD3 .... 164 E6
Chenies Way. Watf WD1 .... 166 E2
Chennells Cl. Hit SG4 .... 22 D2
Chennells. Hat AL10 .... 129 F4
Chennies The. Harp AL5 .... 107 C7
Chepstow Cl. Stev SG1 .... 51 B8
Chepstow. Harp AL5 .... 85 F2
Chequer Cl. Luton LU1 .... 63 F6
Chequer La. Red AL3 .... 106 B4
Chequer La. Pit LU7 .... 80 C5
Chequer St. St Alb AL1 .... 127 D3
Chequers. Bis St CM23 .... 76 D4
Chequers Bridge Rd. Stev SG1 ...... 50 C6
Chequers Cl. Bun SG9 .... 40 D8
Chequers Cl. Pit LU7 .... 80 C4
Chequers Cl. Stand SG11 .... 55 D8
Chequers Cl. Stot SG5 .... 12 A6
Chequers Cotts. Pres SG4 .... 48 D7
Chequers Field. Wel G C AL7 .... 110 D3
Chequers. Hat AL9 .... 130 D8
Chequers Hill. Fla AL3 .... 84 C2
Chequers La. Abb L WD5 .... 140 C1
Chequers La. Pit LU7 .... 80 C5
Chequers La. Pres SG4 .... 48 D7
Chequers. Wel G C AL7 .... 110 D3
Chequers Wlk. Wa Aby EN9 .... 163 F6
Cheriton Cl. St Alb AL4 .... 128 D7
Cherry Bank. Hemt H HP2 .... 124 D5
Cherry Cl. Kneb SG3 .... 68 F4
Cherry Croft Gdns. Pnr HA5 .... 175 F3
Cherry Croft. Wel G C AL8 .... 89 D2
Cherry Dr. Royst SG8 .... 7 E7
Cherry Gdns. Bis St CM23 .... 77 A8
Cherry Gdns. Saw CM21 .... 97 E4
Cherry Hill. Tri HP23 .... 99 F3
Cherry Hill. Chis AL2 .... 141 A6
Cherry Hill. Har HA3 .... 176 E4
Cherry Hill. Ric WD3 .... 165 B6
Cherry Hollow. Abb L WD5 .... 153 F8
Cherry Orchard. Hemt H HP1 .... 124 A5
Cherry Rd. Enf EN3 .... 162 C1
Cherry Tree Ave. Lon C AL2 .... 142 D5
Cherry Tree Cl. Arl SG15 .... 11 A8
Cherry Tree Cl. Luton LU2 .... 46 A1
Cherry Tree Cl. Watf WD1 .... 167 F7
Cherry Tree Jun Mix Inf Sch.
   Watf 154 A3
Cherry Tree La. Chol HP23 .... 120 A3
Cherry Tree La. Chor WD3 .... 164 E1
Cherry Tree La. Hemt H HP2 .... 125 C7
Cherry Tree La. Whea AL4 .... 87 A2
Cherry Tree La. Hod EN11 .... 135 A7
Cherry Tree Rise. Walk SG2 .... 38 B1
Cherry Trees. L Ston SG16 .... 10 B3
Cherry Wlk. Kin L WD4 .... 138 D2
Cherry Wlk. Ric WD3 .... 165 C7
Cherrydale. Watf WD1 .... 166 F5
Chertsey Cl. Luton LU2 .... 64 D8
Chertsey Rise. Stev SG2 .... 51 C4
Cherwell Cl. Cro Gr WD3 .... 166 A4
Chesfield Cl. Bis St CM23 .... 76 C4
Chesford Rd. Luton LU2 .... 46 C4
Chester Ct. Norwd HA6 .... 174 F4
Chesham Prep Sch. Ash Gr 136 A4
Chesham Rd. Bov HP3 .... 136 E3
Chesham Rd. Wigg HP23 .... 137 E7
Chesham Way. Watf WD1 .... 166 F3

Cheshunt Bonneygrove Inf Sch.
   Ches 148 A1
Cheshunt Bonneygrove Jun Sch.
   Ches 148 A1
Cheshunt Cottage Hospl. Ches 148 D2
Cheshunt Ctr The. Ches EN8 .... 148 D1
Cheshunt Gram Sch. Ches 148 E1
Cheshunt Sch The. Ches 148 E4
Cheshunt Wash. Ches EN8 .... 148 E4
Cheslyn Cl. Luton LU2 .... 46 E2
Chess Cl. Lat HP5 .... 150 D3
Chess Cl. Ric WD3 .... 165 D5
Chess Hill. Ric WD3 .... 165 D5
Chess La. Ric WD3 .... 165 D5
Chess Vale Rise. Cro Gr WD3 .... 165 F3
Chess Way. Chor WD3 .... 165 A6
Chesswood Way. Pnr HA5 .... 175 D7
Chester Ave. Luton LU4 .... 44 E3
Chester Cl. Luton LU4 .... 44 F2
Chester Ct. Pot B EN6 .... 145 B2
Chester Pl. Norwd HA6 .... 174 E3
Chester Rd. Bor WD6 .... 170 D6
Chester Rd. Norwd HA6 .... 174 F3
Chester Rd. Stev SG1 .... 37 A1
Chester Rd. Watf WD1 .... 167 A5
Chesterfield Flats. Barn EN5 .... 171 D4
Chesterfield Rd. Barn EN5 .... 171 D4
Chesterfield Rd. Enf EN3 .... 162 E2
Chesterfield Rd. Enf 162 E2
Chesterton Ave. Harp AL5 .... 86 D1
Chestnut Ave. Henlw SG16 .... 10 C1
Chestnut Ave. Luton LU3 .... 44 C8
Chestnut Ave. Ric WD3 .... 174 F2
Chestnut Ave. Ware SG12 .... 93 F3
Chestnut Cl. Bis St CM23 .... 76 E6
Chestnut Cl. Dagn HP4 .... 81 C5
Chestnut Cl. Hun SG12 .... 95 D1
Chestnut Ct. Pot En HP4 .... 123 B6
Chestnut Cl. Hit SG5 .... 34 D8
Chestnut Dr. Berk HP4 .... 122 D4
Chestnut Dr. Har HA3 .... 176 F2
Chestnut Dr. St Alb AL4 .... 128 C5
Chestnut La. Barn N20 .... 171 E1
Chestnut La. Knee SG8 .... 2 A7
Chestnut Rd. Enf EN3 .... 162 E3
Chestnut Rise. Bus WD2 .... 168 B2
Chestnut Wlk. Royst SG8 .... 7 E6
Chestnut Wlk. Stev SG1 .... 36 D1
Chestnut Wlk. Watf WD2 .... 154 A2
Chestnuts The. Cod SG4 .... 67 F2
Chestnuts The. Hemt H HP3 .... 137 F3
Chestnuts The. Hert SG13 .... 113 D5
Cheverells Cl. Mark AL3 .... 83 D4
Cheviot Cl. Bus WD2 .... 168 C3
Cheviot Cl. Luton LU3 .... 44 C8
Cheviot Rd. Luton LU3 .... 44 D7
Cheviots. Hat AL10 .... 130 A3
Cheviots. Hemt H HP2 .... 124 F6
Cheyne Cl. Ware SG12 .... 93 D3
Cheynes Inf Sch. Luton 44 D8
Chicheley Gdns. Har HA3 .... 176 C3
Chichester Way. Watf WD2 .... 154 E6
Chigwell Hurst Ct. Pnr HA5 .... 175 D1
Chilcott Rd. Watf WD2 .... 153 F3
Chilcourt. Royst SG8 .... 7 C6
Childbrook House. Watf WD1 .... 166 F5
Childs Ave. Hare UB9 .... 173 C1
Childwick Ct. Hemt H HP2 .... 124 E2
Chilham Cl. Hemt H HP2 .... 124 E2
Chiltern Ave. Bus WD2 .... 168 C3
Chiltern Cl. Bor WD6 .... 169 F7
Chiltern Cl. Bus WD2 .... 168 B3
Chiltern Cl. Gofs O EN7 .... 147 B4
Chiltern Cl. St Alb AL4 .... 128 C3
Chiltern Dr. Ric WD3 .... 165 A2
Chiltern Gdns. Luton LU4 .... 44 F3
Chiltern Park Ave. Berk HP4 .... 122 A6
Chiltern Rd. Bal SG7 .... 23 F6
Chiltern Rd. Hit SG4 .... 35 A7
Chiltern Rd. St Alb AL4 .... 128 C2
Chiltern Rd. Wing HP22 .... 60 A3
Chiltern View. Letw SG6 .... 22 D5
Chiltern Way. Tri HP23 .... 100 C5
Chilterns. Hat AL10 .... 130 A2
Chilterns. Hemt H HP2 .... 124 F6
Chilterns The. Hit SG4 .... 35 A6
Chilterns The. Ken Co LU6 .... 82 F8
Chilton Ct. Harp AL5 .... 86 B1
Chilvers Bank. Bal SG7 .... 23 E7
Chilwell Gdns. Sth Ox WD1 .... 175 C6
Chilworth Gate. Hod EN10 .... 134 F1
Chinnery Cl. Enf EN1 .... 161 F1
Chinnery Hill. Bis St CM23 .... 76 F5
Chipperfield Rd. Bov HP3 .... 137 C3
Chipperfield Rd. Hemt H HP3 .... 138 C7
Chipperfield Rd. Kin L WD4 .... 138 D2
Chipping Cl. Barn EN5 .... 171 E6
Chippingfield. Harl CM17 .... 118 C3
Chirdland House. Watf WD1 .... 166 E3
Chishill Rd. Bar SG8 .... 9 A2
Chishill Rd. Gt Ch SG8 .... 9 A3
Chishill Windmill. Gt Ch 9 C2
Chiswell Ct. Watf WD2 .... 154 C1
Chiswellgreen La. Chis AL2 .... 140 E4
Chobham Cl. Luton LU1 .... 63 F6
Chobham St. Luton LU1 .... 63 F6
Chobham Wlk. Luton LU1 .... 63 E6
Cholesbury La. Chol HP23 .... 120 A6
Chorleywood Bottom. Chor WD3 .. 164 D4
Chorleywood Cl. Ric WD3 .... 165 D2
Chorleywood Coll. Chor 164 F5
Chorleywood Cty Prim Sch. Chor . 164 C3
Chorleywood Rd. Ric WD3 .... 165 C4
Chorleywood Sta. Chor 164 D5
Chouler Gdns. Stev SG1 .... 36 C2
Chowns The. Harp AL5 .... 86 B2
Christ Church CE Inf Sch. Barn 171 D7
Christ Church CE Jun Mix Inf Sch.
   Chor 164 F5
Christ Church Jun Mix & Inf Sch.
   Ware 93 E1
Christ Church La. Barn EN5 .... 171 E7
Christchurch Cl. St Alb AL3 .... 127 D4
Christchurch Cres. Radl WD7 .... 156 A3
Christchurch Rd. Hemt H HP2 .... 124 D4

Christchurch Rd. Tri HP23 .... 99 F4
Christie Cl. Hod EN10 .... 134 F3
Christie Rd. Stev SG2 .... 51 D5
Christopher Ct. Heml H HP3 .... 138 D8
Christopher Pl. St Alb AL3 .... 127 D3 3
Christy's Yd. Hin SG7 .... 3 D6
Church Cl. Cod SG4 .... 67 F2
Church Cl. Cuf EN6 .... 146 E2
Church Cl. L Berk SG13 .... 132 C4
Church Cl. Norwd HA6 .... 174 F3
Church Cl. Radl WD7 .... 156 A3
Church Cl. Stu LU6 .... 82 B4
Church Cotts. Gt Gd HP1 .... 103 D3
Church Cres. Saw CM21 .... 97 F2
Church Ct. Hod EN10 .... 135 A3
Church End. Arl SG15 .... 11 A8
Church End. Bar SG8 .... 9 A1
Church End. Brag SG11 .... 55 F7
Church End. Fla AL3 .... 84 C2
Church End. Mark AL3 .... 83 D6
Church End. Red AL3 .... 106 A4
Church End. Sand AL4 .... 108 C2
Church End. Walk SG2 .... 38 C2
Church Field Path. Ches EN8 .... 148 C2
Church Field. Ware SG12 .... 93 B3
Church Gn. Ben SG2 .... 52 C4
Church Gn. Gt Wy SG4 .... 35 E6
Church Gn. Harp AL5 .... 86 A1
Church Green Row. Harp AL5 .... 86 A1
Church Hill. Abb L WD5 .... 139 F4
Church Hill. Ched LU7 .... 80 A8
Church Hill. Hare UB9 .... 173 C1
Church Hill. Hert H SG13 .... 114 C4
Church La. Arl SG15 .... 11 A7
Church La. Ashw SG7 .... 4 D4
Church La. Bark SG8 .... 17 C4
Church La. Berk HP4 .... 122 C4
Church La. Bis St CM22 .... 76 D3
Church La. Bov HP3 .... 137 B4
Church La. Ched LU7 .... 80 A8
Church La. Ches EN8 .... 148 C2
Church La. Col H AL4 .... 143 B8
Church La. Dan En SG12 .... 71 F8
Church La. Gra SG4 .... 36 C4
Church La. Gu M SG8 .... 1 F4
Church La. Gu M SG8 .... 1 C1
Church La. Har HA3 .... 176 F2
Church La. Hat AL9 .... 130 C5
Church La. Hod EN10 .... 134 C1
Church La. Kim SG4 .... 66 D1
Church La. Kin L WD4 .... 139 A2
Church La. Letw SG6 .... 12 C1
Church La. Mars HP23 .... 79 F1
Church La. Muc H SG10 .... 74 F3
Church La. Nort EN6 .... 146 A1
Church La. Pres SG4 .... 48 D6
Church La. Reed SG8 .... 16 E5
Church La. Ric WD3 .... 165 B1
Church La. Royst SG8 .... 7 D6
Church La. Sar WD3 .... 152 A2
Church La. Stap SG14 .... 92 A6
Church La. Stev SG1 .... 50 C7
Church La. Ther SG8 .... 15 F7
Church La. Wes SG4 .... 24 D1
Church Manor. Bis St CM23 .... 77 A4
Church Mead. Roy CM19 .... 116 B1
Church Mead. Stu LU6 .... 82 B4
Church Meadow Cotts. Gt Gd HP1 . 103 D3
Church Path. L Wym SG4 .... 35 F3
Church Rd. Cad LU1 .... 63 C2
Church Rd. Fla AL3 .... 84 C2
Church Rd. Gt Ha CM22 .... 77 D3
Church Rd. Heml H HP3 .... 125 C2
Church Rd. Kin Wd SG4 .... 47 F3
Church Rd. L Berk SG13 .... 132 C4
Church Rd. L Gad HP4 .... 102 D8
Church Rd. Norwd HA6 .... 174 F3
Church Rd. Pit LU7 .... 80 E3
Church Rd. Pit LU7 .... 80 F5
Church Rd. Pot B EN6 .... 145 B1
Church Rd. Pot En HP4 .... 123 B6
Church Rd. Stot SG5 .... 11 F6
Church Rd. Str LU3 .... 31 A6
Church Rd. Stu LU6 .... 82 B4
Church Rd. Watf WD1 .... 167 B8
Church Rd. Wel G C AL8 .... 110 D6
Church Row Mews. Ware SG12 .... 93 D1 2
Church St. Bal SG7 .... 12 E1
Church St. Bis St CM23 .... 76 F7
Church St. Bov HP3 .... 137 B4
Church St. Bun SG9 .... 40 E8
Church St. Ess AL9 .... 131 E6
Church St. Gu M SG8 .... 1 F4
Church St. Har HA1 .... 130 C5
Church St. Heml H HP2 .... 124 D5
Church St. Hert SG14 .... 113 D6
Church St. Luton LU1 .... 63 F8
Church St. Ric WD3 .... 165 E1
Church St. Saw CM21 .... 97 E2
Church St. Shil SG5 .... 19 F8
Church St. St Alb AL3 .... 127 D4
Church St. Wa Aby EN9 .... 163 C6
Church St. Ware SG12 .... 93 D1
Church St. Watf WD1 .... 167 C5
Church St. Welw AL6 .... 89 C5
Church St. Whea AL4 .... 108 D8
Church St. Wing HP22 .... 60 B2
Church Street Ind Est. Ware 93 D1
Church View. Hod EN10 .... 134 F3
Church View. Lon M HP23 .... 79 A4
Church Wlk. Bus WD2 .... 168 A3
Church Wlk. Saw CM21 .... 97 F2
Church Yd. Hit SG5 .... 34 E7
Church Yd. Tri HP23 .... 100 A3
Churchfield. Bar SG8 .... 9 A1
Churchfield. Harl CM20 .... 118 C8
Churchfield. Harp AL5 .... 107 C8
Churchfield House. Wel G C AL8 .. 110 C6
Churchfield Rd. Tewin AL6 .... 90 F7
Churchfields. Hert SG13 .... 113 D5
Churchfields. Hod EN10 .... 135 A3
Churchfields La. Hod EN10 .... 135 A3
Churchfields Rd. Watf WD2 .... 153 F3
Churchfields. Sta M CM24 .... 59 F6
Churchfields. Stand SG11 .... 55 E2
Churchgate C of E Prim Sch. Harl . 118 F3
Churchgate. Ches EN8 .... 148 E3
Churchgate. Hit SG5 .... 34 E7 7

Churchgate Rd. Ches EN8 .... 148 B2
Churchgate. Harl CM17 .... 118 E3
Churchill Cres. Wel G AL9 .... 144 C8
Churchill Rd. Luton LU4 .... 45 A1
Churchill Rd. St Alb AL1 .... 128 A4
Churchyard Wlk. Hit SG5 .... 34 E7
Cicero Dr. Luton LU3 .... 45 A8
Cillocks Cl. Hod EN11 .... 135 A7
Claggy Rd. Kim SG4 .... 66 B2
Claire Ct. Bus WD2 .... 168 D1
Claire Ct. Ches EN8 .... 162 D7
Clamp Hill. Stan HA7 .... 176 E5
Clapgate Rd. Bus WD2 .... 168 B3
Clare Cl. Bor WD6 .... 169 F3
Clare Cres. Bal SG7 .... 23 E6
Clare Ct. Enf EN3 .... 162 E4
Clare Ct. Norwd HA6 .... 174 E5
Clare Ct. St Alb AL1 .... 127 F2
Claremont. Bri Wd AL2 .... 155 A8
Claremont Cres. Cro Gr WD3 .... 166 C4
Claremont. Gofs O EN7 .... 147 D2
Claremont Rd. Had W EN4 .... 159 D2
Claremont Rd. Har HA3 .... 176 E1
Claremont Rd. Luton LU4 .... 45 B1
Clarence Cl. Bus WD2 .... 168 D2
Clarence Rd. Berk HP4 .... 122 C4
Clarence Rd. Harp AL5 .... 86 A3
Clarence Rd. Sta M CM24 .... 59 E7
Clarence Rd. St Alb AL1 .... 128 A4
Clarendon Cl. Heml H HP2 .... 124 E4 1
Clarendon Ct. Harp AL5 .... 86 B3 2
Clarendon Mews. Bor WD6 .... 170 A6
Clarendon Par. Ches EN8 .... 148 D2
Clarendon Rd. Bor WD6 .... 170 A6
Clarendon Rd. Ches EN8 .... 148 D2
Clarendon Rd. Harp AL5 .... 86 B3
Clarendon Rd. Luton LU2 .... 45 E1
Clarendon Rd. Watf WD1 .... 167 B6
Clarion Cl. Gt Of SG5 .... 33 C2
Clarion House. Gt Of SG5 .... 33 C2
Clark Rd. Royst SG8 .... 7 D7
Clarke Way. Watf WD2 .... 154 A4
Clarke's Rd. Hal LU2 .... 130 B7
Clarke's Spring. Ald HP23 .... 100 F5
Clarkfield. Ric WD3 .... 165 B1
Clarks Cl. Ware SG12 .... 93 D3
Clarks Mead. Bus WD2 .... 168 D2
Claudian Pl. St Alb AL3 .... 127 A1
Claverhambury Rd. Lo Naz EN9 .... 149 F7
Claverley Gn. Luton LU2 .... 46 E2
Claverton Cl. Bov HP3 .... 137 A3
Clay Hall Rd. Ken Co LU6 .... 82 F7
Clay Hill. Enf EN2 .... 161 D2
Clay La. Bus WD2 .... 168 B2
Claybury. Bus WD2 .... 168 B2
Claybush Rd. Ashw SG7 .... 4 D3
Claycroft. Wel G C AL7 .... 111 B7
Claydown Way. Cad LU1 .... 63 B1
Claygate Ave. Harp AL5 .... 85 E2
Claymore Dr. Ick SG5 .... 21 F5
Claymore. Heml H HP2 .... 124 E7
Claymores. Stev SG1 .... 50 E6
Clayponds. Bis St CM23 .... 77 B7
Clayton Par. Ches EN8 .... 148 D1
Cleall Ave. Wa Aby EN9 .... 163 C5
Cleave The. Harp AL5 .... 86 D1
Clement Pl. Tri HP23 .... 100 A3
Clement Rd. Ches EN8 .... 148 E4
Clements End Rd. Fla LU6 .... 82 E2
Clements End Rd. Ga LU6 .... 82 E2
Clements End Rd. Stu LU6 .... 82 E2
Clements Rd. Chor WD3 .... 164 D4
Clements St. Ware SG12 .... 93 E1
Clevedon Rd. Luton LU2 .... 46 B2
Cleveland Cres. Bor WD6 .... 170 C4
Cleveland Rd. Heml H HP2 .... 125 B5
Cleveland Rd. Mark AL3 .... 83 E5
Cleveland Way. Heml H HP2 .... 125 B5
Cleves Rd. Heml H HP2 .... 125 B8
Cleviscroft. Stev SG1 .... 50 E4
Clewer Cres. Har HA3 .... 176 D2
Clifford Cl. Luton LU4 .... 44 D5
Clifford Ct. Bis St CM23 .... 77 A7 6
Clifton Cl. Ches EN8 .... 148 E4
Clifton Rd. Luton LU1 .... 63 B8
Clifton Rd. Watf WD1 .... 167 B4
Clifton Rd. St Alb AL1 .... 127 E4
Clifton Way. Bor WD6 .... 170 A8
Clifton Way. Ware SG12 .... 93 D3
Climb The. Ric WD3 .... 165 B3
Clinton Ave. Luton LU2 .... 45 F3
Clinton End. Heml H HP2 .... 125 C3
Clitheroe Gdns. Sth Ox WD1 ...... 175 D7
Clive Cl. Pot B EN6 .... 158 F4
Clive Ct. Luton LU2 .... 45 E1
Clive Par. Norwd HA6 .... 174 E3
Clive Way. Watf WD2 .... 167 C8
Cloister Garth. Berk HP4 .... 122 C4
Cloister Garth. St Alb AL1 .... 141 E7
Cloister Lawns. Letw SG6 .... 22 F4
Cloisters The. Dun LU4 .... 44 B3
Cloisters The. Bus WD2 .... 168 B3
Cloisters The. Ric WD3 .... 165 E2
Cloisters The. Wel G C AL8 .... 110 D6
Clonard Way. Pnr HA5 .... 176 A4
Close The. Bar SG8 .... 23 E7
Close The. Bro Pk AL9 .... 144 E5
Close The. Bus WD2 .... 168 A4
Close The. Cod SG4 .... 67 F1
Close The. Harp AL5 .... 85 D4
Close The. Hin SG7 .... 3 D6
Close The. Luton LU3 .... 45 A5
Close The. Mark AL3 .... 83 E5
Close The. Pot B EN6 .... 159 A4
Close The. Radl WD7 .... 155 F6
Close The. Ric WD3 .... 165 B1
Close The. Royst SG8 .... 7 F7
Close The. St Alb AL1 .... 141 C8
Close The. Wal SG9 .... 25 E6
Close The. Ware SG12 .... 93 E1
Closemead Cl. Norwd HA6 .... 174 C4
Clothall Rd. Bal SG7 .... 23 F8
Clothall Rd. Clo SG7 .... 24 C1
Clovelly Way. Stev SG1 .... 50 A7
Clover Ave. Bis St CM23 .... 76 B6
Clover Cl. Dun LU4 .... 44 A3
Clover Way. Heml H HP1 .... 124 A4
Cloverfield. Wel G C AL7 .... 89 F1
Cloverland. Hat AL10 .... 129 F2
Clump The. Ric WD3 .... 165 A4

Clusterbolts. Stap SG14 .... 92 A7
Clutterbucks. Sar WD3 .... 152 A3
Clyde Rd. Bor WD6 .... 170 C4
Clyde Sq. Heml H HP2 .... 124 F8
Clyde St. Hert SG13 .... 114 A6
Clydesdale Cl. Bor WD6 .... 170 C4
Clydesdale Ct. Dun LU4 .... 44 A3
Clydesdale Path. Bor WD6 .... 170 C4
Clydesdale Rd. Dun LU4 .... 44 A3
Clydesdale Wlk. Ches EN10 .... 148 F6
Clyfton Cl. Hod EN10 .... 148 F8
Clyston Rd. Watf WD1 .... 166 F3
Coach Dr. Hit SG4 .... 34 F5
Coachman's La. Bal SG7 .... 23 D8
Coates Dell. Watf WD2 .... 154 E6
Coates Rd. Elst WD6 .... 169 D2
Coates Way Jun Mix Inf Sch.
  Watf 154 E6
Coates Way. Watf WD2 .... 154 E6
Cob Cl. Bor WD6 .... 170 C4
Cobb Gn. Watf WD2 .... 154 B7
Cobb Rd. Berk HP4 .... 121 F4
Cobbett Cl. Enf EN3 .... 162 C3
Cobbetts Ride. Tri HP23 .... 99 F3
Cobbins The. Wa Aby EN9 .... 163 E6
Cobbins Way. Harl CM17 .... 118 E4
Cobbinsbank. Wa Aby EN9 .... 163 D6
Cobblers Wick. Wing HP22 .... 60 B3
Cobden St. Luton LU2 .... 45 F1
Cobham Rd. Ware SG12 .... 93 F2
Cobmead. Hat AL10 .... 130 B7
Cock Gr. Nthch HP23 .... 121 C4
Cock La. Clav CM11 .... 30 F3
Cockbush Ave. Hert SG13 .... 114 B7
Cocker Rd. Enf EN1 .... 162 C3
Cockfosters Rd. Had W EN4 .... 159 E1
Cockrobin La. East CM20 .... 117 A7
Codicote Dr. Watf WD2 .... 154 D5
Codicote Heights. Cod SG4 .... 68 B1
Codicote House. Stev SG1 .... 36 C1
Codicote Jun & Mix Inf Sch. Cod 67 E1
Codicote Rd. A St L AL6 .... 88 C3
Codicote Rd. Welw AL6 .... 89 B7
Codicote Rd. Whea AL4 .... 87 D1
Codicote Rd. Whit SG4 .... 66 F6
Codicote Row. Heml H HP2 .... 105 B1
Codmore Wood Rd. Lat HP5 .... 150 D6
Coerdale Ct. Enf EN3 .... 162 E2
Colborne House. Watf WD1 .... 166 E3
Colburn Ave. Pnr HA5 .... 175 E4
Colchester Rd. Norwd HA6 .... 175 A1
Cold Christmas La. Thun SG12 .... 93 E6
Coldham Gr. Enf EN3 .... 162 E2
Coldharbour La. Bus WD2 .... 168 C4
Coldharbour La. Harp AL5 .... 86 C3
Cole Green La. Hertng AL7 .... 111 D4
Cole Green La. Wel G C AL7 .... 111 B4
Cole Green Way. Hertng SG14 ...... 113 A4
Cole Rd. Watf WD1 .... 167 B8
Colebrook Ave. Luton LU4 .... 44 C7
Coleman Green La. Sand AL4 .... 108 A4
Coleman Green La. Whea AL4 .... 109 A7
Coleman's La. Lo Naz EN9 .... 149 E5
Colemans Rd. Bre Gr SG4 .... 47 D1
Coleridge Cl. Ham St EN7 .... 147 C4
Coleridge Cl. Hit SG4 .... 35 B8
Coleridge Cres. Heml H HP2 .... 105 B1
Coleridge Ct. Harp AL5 .... 86 B1 4
Coles Gn. Bus WD2 .... 168 C1
Coles Hill. Heml H HP1 .... 124 A5
Colesdale. Cuf EN6 .... 146 E1
Colestrete Cl. Stev SG1 .... 51 A5
Colestrete. Stev SG1 .... 50 F5
Coleswood Rd. Harp AL5 .... 107 C2
Colgrove. Wel G C AL8 .... 110 C5
Colin Rd. Luton LU2 .... 45 F2
Colindale Ave. St Alb AL1 .... 127 F1
College Ave. Har HA3 .... 176 E2
College Cl. Bis St CM23 .... 76 D7
College Cl. Fla AL3 .... 84 B1
College Cl. Har HA3 .... 176 E3
College Cl. Ware SG12 .... 114 D8
College Ct. Ches EN8 .... 148 C1
College Hill Rd. Har HA3 .... 176 E3
College La. Hat AL10 .... 129 F2
College Lake Wildlife Ctr. Mars 100 C8
College Pl. St Alb AL1 .... 127 C3
College Rd. Abb L WD5 .... 154 A8
College Rd. Ast Cl HP22 .... 78 C1
College Rd. Ches EN8 .... 148 D1
College Rd. Har HA3 .... 176 E2
College Rd. Hod EN11 .... 134 F8
College Rd. St Alb AL3 .... 127 D3
College Way. Norwd HA6 .... 174 D4
College Way. Wel G C AL8 .... 110 D7
Collens Rd. Harp AL5 .... 107 B5
Collenswood Rd. Stev SG2 .... 51 B4
Collenswood Sch. Stev 51 C4
Collet Cl. Ches EN8 .... 148 D3
Collet Gdns. Ches EN8 .... 148 D3
Collett Rd. Heml H HP1 .... 124 C3
Collett Rd. Ware SG12 .... 93 D2
Collett Sch The. Heml H 124 B4
Colley Land. Chor WD3 .... 164 D5
Collingdon Cl. Luton LU1 .... 63 D8
Collingdon St. Luton LU1 .... 63 D8
Collings Wells Cl. Cad LU1 .... 62 E4
Collingtree. Luton LU2 .... 46 B4
Collingwood Ct. Royst SG8 .... 7 D7
Collingwood Dr. Lon C AL2 .... 142 D6
Collins Cross. Bis St CM23 .... 59 B1
Collison Cl. Hit SG4 .... 22 C2
Collyer Rd. Lon C AL2 .... 142 D4
Colmer Pl. Har HA3 .... 176 D3
Colnbrook Cl. Lon C AL2 .... 142 E4
Colnbrook Sch. Sth Ox 175 C7
Colne Ave. Watf WD1 .... 167 B5
Colne Ave. Watf WD1 .... 167 D5
Colne Bridge Ret Pk. Watf 167 D4
Colne Gdns. Lon C AL2 .... 142 E4
Colne Lodge. Ric WD3 .... 165 A1
Colne Mead. Ric WD3 .... 173 A8
Colne Way Ct. Watf WD2 .... 154 D3
Colne Way. Heml H HP2 .... 124 F4

Colne Way. Watf WD2 .... 154 E2
Colney Heath La. Coln H AL4 .... 128 C3
Colonial Way. Watf WD2 .... 167 D8
Colonnade The. Ches EN8 .... 148 C3
Colonsay. Heml H HP3 .... 125 C1
Colston Cres. Gofs O EN7 .... 147 B4
Colt Hatch. Harl CM20 .... 117 B1
Colts Cnr. Stev SG2 .... 51 B4
Colts Croft. Gt Ch SG8 .... 9 E2
Colts The. Bis St CM23 .... 76 E4
Coltsfield. Sta M CM24 .... 59 E8
Coltsfoot. St Alb AL3 .... 127 F8
Coltsfoot Gn. Dun LU4 .... 44 A5
Coltsfoot Rd. Ware SG12 .... 93 E3
Coltsfoot The. Heml H HP1 .... 123 E2
Coltsfoot. Wel G C AL7 .... 111 B4
Columbus Ct. Stev SG2 .... 51 A7
Columbus Gdns. Norwd HA6 .... 175 A2
Colvin Gdns. Enf EN8 .... 162 D4
Colwell Rd. Stev SG2 .... 51 C3
Colwell Rise. Luton LU2 .... 46 E2
Colwyn Cl. Stev SG1 .... 50 B7
Colyer Cl. Welw AL6 .... 89 F3
Combe House. Watf WD1 .... 166 E3
Combe Rd. Watf WD1 .... 166 E3
Combe St. Heml H HP1 .... 124 C3
Combewood. Watf WD2 .... 154 C7
Comet Cl. Watf WD2 .... 153 F3
Comet Rd. Hat AL10 .... 129 F6
Comet Way. Hat AL10,AL9 .... 129 E5
Commerce Way. Letw SG6 .... 22 F6
Common Field. Wigg HP23 .... 100 D1
Common Gate Rd. Chor WD3 .... 164 A4
Common Gdns. Pot En HP4 .... 123 B6
Common La. Ashw SG7 .... 4 B5
Common La. Kim SG4 .... 66 B1
Common La. Kin L WD4 .... 138 D3
Common La. Radl WD7,WD2 .... 155 E1
Common La. Whea AL5 .... 86 D5
Common Rd. Chor WD3 .... 164 C5
Common Rd. Ken Co LU6 .... 82 F8
Common Rd. Stan HA7 .... 176 D7
Common Rd. Stot SG5 .... 11 F7
Common Rd. Stu LU6 .... 82 B3
Common Rise. Hit SG4 .... 22 A1
Common The. Chif WD4 .... 152 B8
Common The. Harp AL5 .... 85 C4
Common The. Hat AL10 .... 130 A6
Common The. Pot En HP4 .... 123 A6
Common View. Letw SG6 .... 23 B8
Common View Sg. Letw SG6 .... 23 A8
Common Wharf. Ware SG12 .... 93 E1
Commonfields. Harl CM20 .... 117 C1
Commons La. Heml H HP2 .... 124 E4
Commons The. Wel G C AL7 .... 111 B3
Commonswood Jun Mix Inf Sch.
  Wel G C 111 B3
Commonwealth Institute of
  Parasitology. St Alb 128 D3
Compass Point. Nthch HP4 .... 121 E6
Compton Ave. Luton LU4 .... 44 B5
Compton Gdns. Chis AL2 .... 141 B5
Compton Pl. Sth Ox WD1 .... 175 E6
Comyne Rd. Watf WD1 .... 153 F3
Comyns The. Bus WD2 .... 168 C1
Concorde Dr. Heml H HP2 .... 124 D3
Concorde St. Luton LU2 .... 63 F8
Conduit La E. Hod EN11 .... 135 B6
Conduit La. Gt Ho SG9 .... 29 B1
Conduit La. Hod EN11 .... 135 A6
Coney Cl. Hat AL10 .... 130 B3
Coney Gree. Saw CM21 .... 97 D3
Coneydale. Wel G C AL8 .... 110 D8
Congreve Rd. Wa Aby EN9 .... 163 E6
Conifer Cl. Gofs O EN7 .... 147 F2
Conifer Cl. Stev SG2 .... 51 D7
Conifer Cl. Bis St CM23 .... 76 F8
Conifer Wlk. Stev SG2 .... 51 C7
Conifers The. Watf WD2 .... 154 C4
Coningsby Dr. Watf WD1 .... 166 E2
Coningsby Bank. St Alb AL1 .... 141 D7
Coningsby Cl. Wel G AL9 .... 144 D7
Coningsby Cl. Radl WD7 .... 156 A3
Coningsby Dr. Pot B EN6 .... 159 D6
Coniston Cl. Heml H HP3 .... 125 C2
Coniston Cl. Abb L WD5 .... 139 A4
Coniston Rd. Kin L WD4 .... 138 F3
Coniston Rd. Luton LU3 .... 44 F5
Connaught Cl. Heml H HP2 .... 125 A5
Connaught Gdns. Berk HP4 .... 121 F7
Connaught Rd. Barn EN5 .... 171 D3
Connaught Rd. Har HA3 .... 176 F2
Connaught Rd. Harp AL5 .... 86 B2
Connaught Rd. Luton LU4 .... 44 F1
Connaught Rd. St Alb AL3 .... 127 C6
Connemara Cl. Bor WD6 .... 170 D3
Connop Rd. Enf EN3 .... 162 D1
Conquerors Hill. Whea AL4 .... 108 E8
Conquest Cl. Hit SG4 .... 34 F5
Constable Cl. Luton LU4 .... 45 A1
Constantine Cl. Stev SG1 .... 36 F1
Constantine Pl. Bal SG7 .... 13 B1
Convent Cl. Hit SG5 .... 34 F8
Conway Gdns. Enf EN1 .... 161 E1
Conway House. Bor WD6 .... 170 C5
Conway Rd. Luton LU4 .... 45 B1
Conyers. Harl CM20 .... 117 C2
Cook Rd. Stev SG2 .... 51 B7
Cook's Hole Rd. Enf EN2 .... 161 C1
Cooks Mead. Bus WD2 .... 168 B3
Cooks Spinney. Harl CM20 .... 118 A2
Cooks Vennel. Heml H HP1 .... 124 B5
Cooks Way. Hat AL10 .... 130 B3
Coombe Gdns. Berk HP4 .... 121 F5
Coombe Hill Rd. Ric WD3 .... 165 A4
Coombe Rd. Bus WD2 .... 168 D2
Coombe Rd. Kel SG8 .... 6 A1
Coombelands Rd. Royst SG8 .... 2 F2
Coombes Rd. Lon C AL2 .... 142 C5
Coonwood Cotts. Wars SG12 .... 94 A4
Cooper's Cl. Kim SG4 .... 66 B1
Cooper's Hill. Kim SG4 .... 87 B8
Coopers Cl. Ast SG2 .... 51 B6
Coopers Cres. Bor WD6 .... 170 C8
Coopers Green La.
  Hat AL4,AL8,AL10 .... 109 D7
Coopers La. Nort EN6 .... 145 E1
Coopers Lane Rd. Nort EN6 .... 160 B6

Coopers Meadow. Red AL3 .... 106 A6
Coopers Rd. Pot B EN6 .... 145 C1
Coopers Wlk. Ches EN8 .... 148 C1
Cooters End La. Harp AL5 .... 85 F5
Copenhagen Cl. Luton LU3 .... 44 D8
Copmans Wick. Chor WD3 .... 164 D4
Coppens The. Stot SG5 .... 12 A5
Copper Beech Cl. Heml H HP3 ...... 137 F8
Copper Beeches. Harp AL5 .... 86 B5
Copper Beeches. Welw AL6 .... 89 D7
Copper Ct. Saw CM21 .... 97 C3
Copperfields. Royst SG8 .... 7 C6
Copperfields. Wel G C AL7 .... 111 C5
Coppermill La. Map Cr WD3,UB9 . 172 F3
Copperwood. Hert SG13 .... 113 F6
Coppice Cl. Har HA7 .... 176 F4
Coppice Cl. Hat AL10 .... 129 F1
Coppice Mead. Stot SG5 .... 11 E5
Coppice The. Heml H HP2 .... 125 B4
Coppice The. Watf WD1 .... 167 C3
Coppice The. Wigg HP23 .... 100 C1
Coppings The. Hod EN11 .... 115 A4
Coppins Cl. Berk HP4 .... 121 F4
Coppins The. Har HA3 .... 176 E4
Coppins The. Mark AL3 .... 83 D5
Copse Cl. Norwd HA6 .... 174 C1
Copse Hill. Welw AL6 .... 90 A8
Copse The. Bis St CM23 .... 77 C8
Copse The. Heml H HP1 .... 123 E5
Copse The. Hert SG13 .... 114 A6
Copse Way. Luton LU3 .... 44 D8
Copse Wood Way. Norwd HA6 ...... 174 C1
Copsewood Rd. Watf WD2 .... 167 B8
Copthall Cl. Gt Ha CM22 .... 77 F4
Copthorne Ave. Hod EN10 .... 134 F3
Copthorne Cl. Cro Gr WD3 .... 165 F4
Copthorne. Luton LU2 .... 46 D3
Copthorne Rd. Cro Gr WD3 .... 165 F4
Coral Gdns. Heml H HP2 .... 124 F3
Corals Mead. Wel G C AL7 .... 110 D5
Coram Cl. Berk HP4 .... 122 C3
Corbridge Dr. Luton LU2 .... 46 E2
Corby Cl. Chis AL2 .... 141 B4
Cordell Cl. Ches EN8 .... 148 E3
Corder Cl. St Alb AL3 .... 141 A4
Coreys Mill La. Stev SG1 .... 36 C1
Corinium Gate. St Alb AL3 .... 127 A1
Corinium Gdns. Luton LU3 .... 45 A8
Corn Mead. Wel G C AL8 .... 89 C1
Corncastle Rd. Luton LU1 .... 63 D6
Corncrane Cl. Luton LU2 .... 46 C5
Corncroft. Hat AL10 .... 130 B7
Cornel Cl. Luton LU1 .... 63 D6
Cornel Ct. Luton LU1 .... 63 A7
Corner Cl. Letw SG6 .... 23 E6
Corner Hall Ave. Heml H HP3 ...... 124 D1
Corner Hall. Heml H HP3 .... 124 D1
Corner View. Wel G AL9 .... 144 C7
Corner Wood. Mark AL3 .... 83 D5
Cornerfield. Hat AL10 .... 130 B8
Corners. Wel G C AL7 .... 111 A7
Cornfield Cres. Nthch HP4 .... 121 D7
Cornfield Rd. Bus WD2 .... 168 B5
Cornfields. Heml H HP1 .... 124 B2
Cornmill. Wa Aby EN9 .... 163 C6
Cornwall Cl. Ches EN8 .... 162 C6
Cornwall Cl. Pnr HA5 .... 175 F3
Cornwall House. Bis St CM23 ...... 76 E4
Cornwall Rd. Harp AL5 .... 86 B2
Cornwall Rd. Pnr HA5 .... 175 F3
Cornwall Rd. St Alb AL1 .... 127 E1
Coronation Ave. Heml H HP3 ...... 124 C1
Coronation Rd. Bis St CM23 .... 76 E5
Coronation Rd. Ware SG12 .... 93 D2
Corringham Ct. St Alb AL1 .... 127 F4
Corton Cl. Stev SG1 .... 50 B8
Cory-Wright Way. Whea AL4 .... 87 C1
Cosgrove Way. Luton LU1 .... 44 D1
Cotefield. Dun LU4 .... 44 C3
Cotesmore Rd. Heml H HP1 .... 123 E2
Cotlandswick. Lon C AL2 .... 142 C5
Cotney Croft. Stev SG2 .... 51 D3
Cotsmoor. St Alb AL1 .... 127 F3
Cotswold Ave. Bus WD2 .... 168 C3
Cotswold Bsns Pk. Cad LU1 .... 62 D2
Cotswold Cl. St Alb AL4 .... 128 C8
Cotswold Gdns. Luton LU3 .... 44 C7
Cotswold. Heml H HP2 .... 124 E6
Cotswolds. Hat AL10 .... 130 A3
Cottage Cl. Cro Gr WD3 .... 165 F3
Cottage Cl. Watf WD1 .... 166 E3
Cottered Rd. Cotrd SG9 .... 26 F1
Cotterells. Heml H HP1 .... 124 C2
Cotterells Hill. Heml H HP1 .... 124 C3
Cotton Dr. Hert SG13 .... 114 B7
Cotton Field. Hat AL10 .... 130 B7
Cotton Rd. Pot B EN6 .... 159 C8
Cottonmill Cres. St Alb AL1 .... 127 D2
Coulser Cl. Heml H HP1 .... 124 A6
Coulson Ct. Luton LU1 .... 62 F8
Coulter Cl. Cuf EN6 .... 146 D4
Council Rd. Bis St CM23 .... 77 B7
Counters. Heml H HP1 .... 124 A3
Countess Anne Prim Sch. Hat 130 C7
Countess Cl. Hare UB9 .... 173 C1
Couper House. Watf WD1 .... 166 E3
Coursers Rd. Col H WD2,AL4 .... 143 C6
Courtaulds. Chipf WD4 .... 138 B1
Courtenay Ave. Har HA3 .... 176 C2
Courtenay Gdns. Har HA3 .... 176 C1
Courtfield Cl. Hod EN10 .... 135 A3
Courtlands Cl. Watf WD2 .... 153 E4
Courtlands Dr. Watf WD2 .... 153 E3
Courtleigh Ave. Had W EN4 .... 159 D1
Courtway The. Sth Ox WD1 .... 175 E8
Courtyard Mews. Sac SG2 .... 92 E4
Courtyard The. Coln H AL4 .... 128 C2
Covent Garden Cl. Luton LU4 ...... 44 F3
Coventry Cl. Stev SG1 .... 37 C3
Coverdale. Heml H HP2 .... 124 E6
Coverdale. Luton LU4 .... 44 B6
Covert Cl. Nthch HP4 .... 121 D6
Covert Rd. Nthch HP4 .... 121 D6
Covert The. Norwd HA6 .... 174 C2
Cow La. Bus WD2 .... 168 A3
Cow La. Tri HP23 .... 100 D4

Cow La. Watf WD2 .... 154 C3
Cowards La. Cod SG4 .... 88 F8
Cowbridge. Hert SG14 .... 113 C6
Cowdray Cl. Luton LU2 .... 46 C3
Cowles. Ham St EN7 .... 147 F4
Cowley Hill. Bor WD6 .... 157 B1
Cowlins. Harl CM17 .... 118 D4
Cowper Cres. Hert SG14 .... 92 B1
Cowper Ct. Watf WD2 .... 154 A2
Cowper Endowed Prim Sch. Tewin . 90 E2
Cowper Rd. Berk HP4 .... 122 B4
Cowper Rd. Harp AL5 .... 86 C1
Cowper Rd. Heml H HP1 .... 124 B2
Cowper Rd. Mark AL3 .... 83 D5
Cowper Rd. Wel G C AL7 .... 110 F4
Cowper Rise. Mark AL3 .... 83 D5
Cowper. Luton LU1 .... 63 E5
Cowpers Way. Tewin AL6 .... 90 D5
Cowridge Cres. Luton LU2 .... 64 A8
Cowslip Cl. Royst SG8 .... 7 F5
Cowslip Hill. Letw SG6 .... 22 E7
Cowslips. Wel G C AL7 .... 111 C5
Cox Cl. Shen WD7 .... 156 F7
Cox's Way. Arl SG15 .... 11 A4
Coxfield Cl. Heml H HP2 .... 124 E2
Coyney Gn. Luton LU3 .... 45 C1
Cozens La E. Hod EN10 .... 134 F1
Cozens La W. Hod EN10 .... 134 F1
Cozens Rd. Ware SG12 .... 94 A2
Crab La. Radl WD2 .... 155 B4
Crab Tree La. Pirt SG5 .... 20 D4
Crab Tree Rd. Kneb SG3 .... 68 F4
Crabb's La. Sto P SG9 .... 43 F6
Crabbes Cl. Hit SG5 .... 34 E7
Crabtree Cl. Bus WD2 .... 168 B4
Crabtree Cl. Heml H HP3 .... 124 D1
Crabtree Cl. Heml H HP3 .... 124 E1 1
Crabtree Dell. Letw SG6 .... 23 B8
Crabtree Inf Sch. Harp 86 C1
Crabtree La. Harp AL5 .... 86 C8
Crabtree La. Heml H HP3 .... 124 D1
Crabtree Prim Sch. Harp 86 C1
Crackley Meadow. Heml H HP2 ... 125 B8
Cradock Rd. Dun LU4 .... 44 B1
Cragg Ave. Radl WD7 .... 155 F3
Cragside. Stev SG2 .... 69 C7
Craig Mount. Radl WD7 .... 156 B4
Craigavon Rd. Heml H HP2 .... 124 F7
Craiglands. St Alb AL4 .... 128 D7
Craigs Wlk. Ches EN8 .... 148 D3
Craigweil Ave. Radl WD7 .... 156 B4
Crakers Mead. Watf WD1 .... 167 B6 4
Cranborne Ave. Hit SG5 .... 34 D6
Cranborne Cl. Bric SG13 .... 113 C3
Cranborne Cl. Pot B EN6 .... 158 E8
Cranborne Cres. Pot B EN6 .... 158 E8
Cranborne Ct. Enf EN3 .... 162 D3
Cranborne Gdns. Wel G C AL7 ... 110 F5
Cranborne Ind Est. Pot B 144 E1
Cranborne Par. Pot B EN6 .... 158 E8
Cranborne Prim Sch. Pot B 158 F8
Cranborne Rd. Ches EN8 .... 162 D7
Cranborne Rd. Hat AL10 .... 130 B6
Cranborne Rd. Hod EN11 .... 135 C7
Cranborne Rd. Pot B EN6 .... 144 E1
Cranbourne Dr. Harp AL5 .... 107 D6
Cranbourne Rd. Hod EN11 .... 115 C2
Cranbourne Prim Sch. Hod ... 115 B2
Cranbourne Rd. Norwd HA6 ... 174 F1
Cranbourne. Stev SG1 .... 36 B1
Cranbrook Cl. Ware SG12 .... 93 D3
Cranbrook Dr. Coln H AL4 .... 128 E3
Cranbrook Dr. Luton LU3 .... 44 D8
Crane Mead. Ware SG12 .... 114 E8
Cranefield Dr. Watf WD2 .... 154 E6
Cranes Way. Bor WD6 .... 170 C4
Cranfield Cres. Cuf SG9 .... 146 E2
Cranford Cl. Harp AL5 .... 86 C1
Cranleigh Cl. Ches EN7 .... 148 A3
Cranleigh Gdns. Luton LU3 .... 45 D3
Cranmer Cl. Pot B EN6 .... 145 C1
Cranmer House. Kin L WD4 .... 139 A2
Cranmore Ct. St Keith AL1 .... 127 C4
Cranwell Gdns. Bis St CM23 .... 59 C1
Cravells Rd. Harp AL5 .... 107 C2
Crawford Rd. Hat AL10 .... 130 A7
Crawley Cl. Cad LU1 .... 63 C1
Crawley Dr. Heml H HP2 .... 124 F7
Crawley Gn. Luton LU2 .... 46 B1
Crawley Green Rd. Luton LU1,LU2 . 46 B1
Crawley Rd. Luton LU1 .... 63 D8
Crawley's La. Wigg HP23 .... 120 F7
Creamery Ct. Letw SG6 .... 23 C3
Crecy Gdns. Red AL3 .... 106 A6
Creighton Ave. St Alb AL1 .... 141 D8
Crescent E. Had W EN4 .... 159 C1
Crescent Rd. Bis St CM23 .... 77 A6
Crescent Rd. Heml H HP2 .... 124 D8
Crescent Rd. Luton LU2 .... 63 F8
Crescent Rise. Luton LU2 .... 63 F8
Crescent The. Abb L WD5 .... 139 F1
Crescent The. Ard SG2 .... 38 F2
Crescent The. Bri Wd AL2 .... 141 A1
Crescent The. Cad LU1 .... 62 E3
Crescent The. Cro Gr WD3 .... 166 B8
Crescent The. Harl CM17 .... 118 C6
Crescent The. Henlw SG16 .... 10 C1
Crescent The. Hit SG5 .... 21 D1
Crescent The. Letw SG6 .... 23 A5
Crescent The. Mars HP23 .... 80 A1
Crescent The. Pit LU7 .... 80 C4
Crescent The. St Ipp SG4 .... 35 A3
Crescent The. Watf WD1 .... 167 C5
Crescent The. Welw AL6 .... 89 C4
Crescent W. Had W EN4 .... 159 C1
Cress End. Ric WD3 .... 165 A1
Cresset Cl. Gt Am SG12 .... 115 C3
Cresswick. Whit SG4 .... 66 E7
Crest Dr. Enf EN3 .... 162 C1
Crest Pk. Heml H HP2 .... 125 C4
Crest The. Gofs O EN7 .... 147 B4
Crest The. Luton LU3 .... 45 B7
Crest The. Saw CM21 .... 97 D3
Crest The. Ware SG12 .... 93 D3
Crest The. Welw AL6 .... 89 D8

Cresta Cl. Dun LU5 .... 44 A2
Creswick Cl. Wel G C AL7 .... 110 D5
Creswick Hill Sta. Cer H 160 F5
 Wel G C 110 D3
Creswick Hill Sta. Cer H 160 F5
 Crews Hill Sta. Cer H 160 F5
Crew Curve. Berk HP4 .... 121 F7
Crews Hill. En H EN2 .... 160 F5
Crib St. Ware SG12 .... 93 D2
Cricketer's Rd. Arl SG15 .... 11 A4
Cricketers Ct. St Alb AL3 .... 127 E4
Cricketfield La. Bis St CM23 .... 76 E8
Cringle Ct. Pot B EN6 .... 145 C1
Crispin Field. Pit LU7 .... 80 C4
Croasdaile Rd. Sta M CM24 .... 59 E8
Croasdale Cl. Sta M CM24 .... 59 E8
Crocus Field. Barn EN5 .... 171 E3
Croft Cl. Chipf WD4 .... 138 A1
Croft Cl. Hit SG5 .... 34 E7
Croft End Rd. Chipf WD4 .... 138 A1
Croft Field. Chipf WD4 .... 138 A1
Croft Field. Hat AL10 .... 130 A5
Croft La. Chipf WD4 .... 138 A1
Croft La. Letw SG6 .... 12 B1
Croft Meadow. Chipf WD4 .... 138 A1
Croft Meadows. Ched LU7 .... 80 A7
Croft Rd. Luton LU2 .... 46 B3
Croft Rd. Ware SG12 .... 93 C2
Croft The. Barn EN5 .... 171 E5
Croft The. Chis AL2 .... 141 A6
Croft The. Hod EN10 .... 148 E8
Croft The. Luton LU3 .... 44 D8
Croft The. Wars SG12 .... 94 A8
Croft The. Wel G C AL7 .... 110 F3
Crofters End. Saw CM21 .... 97 E3
Crofters Rd. Mo Pk HA6 .... 174 E6
Crofters. Saw CM21 .... 97 E3
Crofts Path. Heml H HP3 .... 125 B2
Crofts The. Heml H HP3 .... 125 B2
Crofts The. Stot SG5 .... 11 F6
Croftwell. Harp AL5 .... 107 F8
Cromer Cl. L Gad HP4 .... 102 E5
Cromer Cl. L Gad HP4 .... 102 E5
Cromer Rd. Watf WD2 .... 154 C1
Crompton Rd. Stev SG1 .... 50 A6
Cromwell Ave. Ches EN7 .... 148 B1
Cromwell Cl. Bis St CM23 .... 76 F6
Cromwell Cl. St Alb AL4 .... 128 D8
Cromwell Gn. Letw SG6 .... 23 B8
Cromwell Hill. Luton LU2 .... 45 D1
Cromwell Rd. Bor WD6 .... 169 E8
Cromwell Rd. Ches EN7 .... 148 B3
Cromwell Rd. Hert SG13 .... 114 A7
Cromwell Rd. Letw SG6 .... 23 B8
Cromwell Rd. Stev SG2 .... 51 C5
Cromwell Way. Ware SG12 .... 93 F2
Cromwell Way. Pirt SG5 .... 20 D4
Crooked Mile. Wa Aby EN9 .... 163 C3
Crookhams. Wel G C AL7 .... 90 A1
Crop Comm. Hat AL10 .... 130 B7
Crosby Cl. Luton LU4 .... 45 A2
Cross La. Harp AL5 .... 107 D5
Cross La. Hert SG14 .... 113 B6
Cross Oak Rd. Berk HP4 .... 122 A4
Cross Rd. Ches EN8 .... 162 E6
Cross Rd. Hert SG14 .... 113 C7
Cross Rd. Watf WD1 .... 167 E3
Cross St. Letw SG6 .... 22 F7
Cross St. Luton LU2 .... 63 E8
Cross St. St Alb AL3 .... 127 D3 2
Cross St. Ware SG12 .... 93 E1
Cross St. Watf WD1 .... 167 C6
Cross Way. Harp AL5 .... 86 C3
Cross Way. The. Har HA3 .... 176 E1
Cross Way The. Luton LU1 .... 63 E3
Crossbrook. Hat AL10 .... 129 E4
Crossbrook St. Ches EN8 .... 148 D1
Crossbrook St. Ches EN8 .... 162 D8
Crossett Gn. Heml H HP3 .... 125 C1
Crossfell Rd. Heml H HP3 .... 125 C2
Crossfield Cl. Berk HP4 .... 121 F4
Crossfield Rd. Hod EN11 .... 135 B8
Crossfields. St Alb AL3 .... 141 B8
Crossgates. Stev SG1 .... 50 E5
Crosslands. Cad LU1 .... 62 E3
Crossleys. Letw SG6 .... 11 F2
Crossmead. Watf WD1 .... 167 B3
Crossoaks La. Ridge WD6 .... 157 F5
Crossoaks La. Shen WD6 .... 157 D5
Crosspath The. Radl WD7 .... 156 A4
Crosspaths. Harp AL5 .... 85 C4
Crossway. Pnr HA5 .... 175 B1
Crossway. Wel G C AL8 .... 89 C2
Crossways. Bar SG8 .... 8 F1
Crossways. Berk HP4 .... 121 F3
Crossways. Heml H HP1 .... 123 F3
Crouch Hall Gdns. Red AL3 .... 106 A6
Crouch Hall La. Red AL3 .... 106 A6
Crouch La. Gofs O EN7 .... 147 C4
Crouchfield. Heml H HP1 .... 124 B2
Crouchfield. Hert SG14 .... 92 C1
Crouchfield La. Hert SG14 .... 92 E4
Crow Furlong. Hit SG5 .... 34 D7
Crowborough Path. Sth Ox WD1 . 175 D6
Crowland Rd. Luton LU2 .... 46 C5
Crown Cl. Sheer CM22 .... 98 C1
Crown La. Reed SG8 .... 16 F5
Crown Lodge. Arl SG15 .... 11 A4
Crown Rd. Bor WD6 .... 170 B8
Crown Rise. Watf WD2 .... 154 D5
Crown St. Red AL3 .... 106 B5
Crown Terr. Bis St CM23 .... 77 A7
Crownfield. Lo Naz EN10 .... 135 A2
Croxdale Rd. Bor WD6 .... 170 A7
Croxley Ctr. Watf 166 D1
Croxley Green Sta. Cro Gr 166 D4
Croxley Sta. Cro Gr 166 B3
Croxley View. Watf WD1 .... 166 E3
Croxton Cl. Luton LU3 .... 45 A7
Crozier Ave. Bis St CM23 .... 76 C8
Crusader Way. Watf WD1 .... 166 F3
Cubbington Cl. Luton LU3 .... 45 A7
Cubitts Cl. Welw AL6 .... 89 F7
Cublands. Hert SG13 .... 114 B6
Cuckmans Dr. Chis AL2 .... 141 A6
Cuckoo's Nest. Luton LU2 .... 46 A6
Cuffley Ave. Watf WD2 .... 154 D5
Cuffley Cl. Luton LU3 .... 44 F4
Cuffley Ct. Heml H HP2 .... 125 C8

Cuffley Hill. Gofs O EN7 .... 147 B2
Cuffley Jun Mix Inf Sch. Cuf ... 146 F1
Cuffley Sta. 146 F2
Cullera Cl. Norwd HA6 .... 174 F4
Cullings Ct. Wa Aby EN9 .... 163 F6
Culver Rd. St Alb AL1 .... 127 E5
Culverden Rd. Sth Ox WD1 .... 175 B7
Culverhouse Rd. Luton LU3 .... 45 C3
Culworth Cl. Cad LU1 .... 62 E3
Cumberland Cl. Abb L WD5 .... 139 E6
Cumberland Cl. Hert SG14 .... 113 C8
Cumberland Ct. Hod EN11 .... 135 A7
Cumberland Ct. St Alb AL3 .... 127 E4
Cumberland Dr. Red AL3 .... 106 B6
Cumberland St. Luton LU1 .... 63 E6
Cumberlow Pl. Heml H HP2 .... 125 C7
Cumcum Hill. Ess AL9 .... 131 E2
Cundalls Rd. Ware SG12 .... 93 E2
Cunningham Ave. Enf EN3 .... 162 E3
Cunningham Ave. St Alb AL1 ... 127 F1
Cunningham Hill Inf Sch. St Alb ... 128 A1
Cunningham Hill Jun Sch. St Alb ... 128 A1
Cunningham Hill Rd. St Alb AL1 ... 128 A1
Cunningham Rd. Ches EN8 ... 148 C2
Cupid Green Ind Est. Heml H HP2 104 E3
Cupid Green La. Gt Gd HP2 .... 104 E3
Cupid Green La. Heml H HP2 ... 105 A1
Curlew Cl. Berk HP4 .... 122 C3
Curlew Cl. Letw SG6 .... 22 E5
Curlew Rd. Luton LU2 .... 46 C5
Currie St. Hert SG13 .... 113 E6
Curteys. Harl CM17 .... 118 D5
Curtis Cl. Ric WD3 .... 165 A1
Curtis Rd. Heml H HP3 .... 125 D2
Curtis Way. Berk HP4 .... 122 D3
Curzon Rd. Luton LU3 .... 45 D3
Cussans House. Watf WD1 .... 166 E3
Cussons Cl. Ches EN7 .... 148 A2
Cut Throat Ave. Whip LU6 .... 81 E7
Cutenhoe Rd. Luton LU1 .... 63 E4
Cutforth Rd. Saw CM21 .... 97 E3
Cuthbert Cl. Gofs O EN7 .... 147 F2
Cutlers Gn. Luton LU2 .... 46 F2
Cutmore Dr. Coln H AL4 .... 129 B3
Cutts La. Kim SG4 .... 66 D1
Cuttsfield Terr. Heml H HP1 ... 123 F2
Cuttys La. Stev SG1 .... 50 E5
Cwmbran Ct. Heml H HP2 .... 124 F7
Cygnet Cl. Bor WD6 .... 170 C8
Cygnet Cl. Norwd HA6 .... 174 C4
Cygnet Ct. Bis St CM23 .... 76 F6
Cylers Thicket. Welw AL6 .... 89 F8
Cypress Ave. Cre H EN2 .... 161 A4
Cypress Cl. Wa Aby EN9 .... 163 D5
Cypress Rd. Har HA3 .... 176 D1
Cypress Wlk. Watf WD2 .... 154 B4
Cyrils Way. St Alb AL1 .... 141 D8

Dacorum Coll of F Ed. Heml H ... 124 C4
Dacorum Way. Heml H HP1 .... 124 C3
Dacre Cres. Kim SG4 .... 66 C1
Dacre Gdns. Bor WD6 .... 170 D4
Dacre Gn. Royst SG8 .... 7 F6
Dacre Rd. Hit SG5 .... 35 A8
Dagger La. Elst WD6 .... 169 B4
Daggs Dell Rd. Heml H HP1 .... 123 E5
Dagnall Cty Fst Sch. Dagn 81 C5
Dagnall Rd. Gt Gd HP1 .... 103 C5
Dagnall Rd. Whip LU6 .... 81 D8
Dagnalls. Letw SG6 .... 22 F2
Daintrees. Widf SG12 .... 95 E4
Daintry Lodge. Norwd HA6 .... 174 F3
Daisy Cl. Letw CM1 .... 23 A8
Dalby Cl. Dun LU4 .... 44 B3
Dalton St. St Alb AL3 .... 127 D4
Dalton Way. Whit SG4 .... 66 E7
Daltry Cl. Stev SG1 .... 36 C2
Daltry Rd. Stev SG1 .... 36 C2
Damask Cl. Wes SG4 .... 37 B8
Damask Gn. Heml H HP1 .... 123 E2
Damask Green Rd. Wes SG4 .... 37 B8
Dame Alice Owen's Sch. Pot B ... 158 E6
Dammersey End La. Ast Cl HP23 ... 99 C2
Dancers Hill Rd. Pot B EN5 .... 158 E3
Dancote. Kneb SG3 .... 68 F5
Dane Acres. Bis St CM23 .... 76 D8
Dane Cl. Harp AL5 .... 86 C4
Dane Cl. Stot SG5 .... 11 F8
Dane Ct. Hert SG13 .... 113 E6
Dane End House. Stev SG1 .... 36 C1
Dane End La. Wes SG4 .... 37 E5
Dane End Rd. Thun SG11 .... 72 A3
Dane House. Bis St CM23 .... 76 D8
Dane O'Coys Rd. Bis St CM23 ... 58 E1
Dane Pk. Bis St CM23 .... 76 D8
Dane Rd. Luton LU3 .... 45 C2
Dane St. Bis St CM23 .... 77 A7
Danebridge Rd. Muc H SG10 .... 75 B2
Danefield Rd. Pirt SG5 .... 20 C4
Danemead. Hod EN11 .... 115 A1
Danes The. Hit SG4 .... 141 C3
Danesbury Hospl. Welw 89 C7
Danesbury La. Welw AL6 .... 89 D8
Danesbury Park Caravan Site.
 Welw 89 D8
Danesbury Pk. Hert SG14 .... 113 D7
Danesgate. Stev SG1 .... 50 D5
Danestrete. Stev SG1 .... 50 D5
Daniells. Wel G C AL7 .... 111 A7
Danvers Croft. Tri HP23 .... 100 C5

Danvers Dr. Luton LU3 .... 31 C1
Danziger Way. Bor WD6 .... 170 C8
Darby Dr. Wa Aby EN9 .... 163 C6
Darby Dr. Welw AL6 .... 68 C3
Darcy Cl. Ches EN8 .... 162 E8
Dark La. Ches EN7 .... 148 A1
Dark La. Harp AL5 .... 107 D7
Dark La. San SG9 .... 15 B1
Dark La. Wing HP22 .... 60 C3
Darkes La. Pot B EN6 .... 159 A8
Darley Rd. Bre Gr SG4 .... 47 C2
Darnicle Hill. Ham St EN7 .... 147 A6
Darr's La. Nthch HP4 .... 121 D6
Darrington Rd. Bor WD6 .... 169 E8
Darwin Cl. Heml H HP2 .... 105 B1
Darwin Cl. St Alb AL3 .... 127 E7
Darwin Gdns. Sth Ox WD1 .... 175 C5
Darwin Rd. Stev SG2 .... 51 B6
Dashes The. Harl CM20 .... 117 F4
Datchet Cl. Heml H HP2 .... 125 C7
Datchworth Turn. Heml H HP2 ... 125 C3
Davenham Ave. Mo Pk HA6 .... 174 F5
Daventer Dr. Har HA7 .... 176 F3
Davies St. Hert SG13 .... 113 E6
Davis Cres. Pirt SG5 .... 20 D4
Davis Ct. St Alb AL1 .... 127 E3
Davis' Row. Arl SG15 .... 11 A4
Davison Cl. Ches EN8 .... 148 D3
Davison Dr. Ches EN8 .... 148 D3
Davys Cl. Whea AL4 .... 108 E7
Dawes La. Sar WD3 .... 151 F3
Dawley Ct. Heml H HP2 .... 125 A7
Dawley. Wel G C AL7 .... 89 F1
Dawlish Cl. Stev SG2 .... 69 C7
Dawlish Rd. Luton LU4 .... 44 F3
Dawson Cl. Henlw SG16 .... 10 C5
Day's Cl. Royst SG8 .... 7 C5
Dayemead. Wel G C AL7 .... 111 B3
Days Cl. Hat AL10 .... 129 F5
Days Mead. Hat AL10 .... 129 F5
De Havilland Cl. Hat AL10 .... 129 F6
De Havilland Ct. Shen WD7 .... 156 E7
De Havilland Way. Abb L WD5 ... 153 F7
De Tany Ct. St Alb AL1 .... 127 D2
De Vere Wlk. Watf WD1 .... 166 E7
Deacon Cl. St Alb AL1 .... 141 D7
Deacons Cl. Bor WD6 .... 170 A5
Deacons Cl. Pnr HA5 .... 175 B1
Deacons Ct. Luton LU3 .... 63 D8 8
Deacon's Hill Rd. Bor WD6 .... 170 A4
Deacons Hill. Watf WD1 .... 167 C4
Deacons Hts. Bor WD6 .... 170 A3
Deacons Way. Hit SG5 .... 21 D1
Deaconsfield Rd. Heml H HP3 ... 138 E7
Dead Woman's La. Pres SG4 .... 48 C7
Deadman's Ash La. Sar WD3 .... 152 B3
Deakin Cl. Watf WD1 .... 166 E2
Dean Ct. Watf WD2 .... 154 D6
Dean Field. Bov HP3 .... 137 A4
Dean Moore Ct. St Alb AL1 .... 127 D2
Dean The. Wing HP22 .... 60 B3
Dean's Gdns. St Alb AL4 .... 128 A4
Deans Cl. Abb L WD5 .... 153 D7
Deans Cl. Tri HP23 .... 100 A4
Deans Furlong. Tri HP23 .... 100 A4
Deans Meadow. Dagn HP4 .... 81 C5
Deanscroft. Kneb SG3 .... 68 F5
Deansway. Heml H HP3 .... 138 F8
Deard's End La. Kneb SG3 .... 68 F6
Deards Wood. Kneb SG3 .... 68 F5
Debenham Cl. Barn EN5 .... 171 C4
Debenham Rd. Ham St EN7 .... 148 B4
Dee The. Heml H HP2 .... 124 F8
Deep Denes. Luton LU2 .... 46 C2
Deepdene. Pot B EN6 .... 158 D8
Deeping Cl. Kneb SG3 .... 68 F4
Deer Cl. Hert SG13 .... 113 F6
Deerfield Cl. Ware SG12 .... 93 D2
Deerings The. Harp AL5 .... 107 A4
Deerswood Ave. Hat AL10 .... 130 B3
Deeves Hall La. Ridge WD6 .... 157 A6
Deimos Dr. Heml H HP2 .... 125 A6
Delahay Rise. Berk HP4 .... 122 B6
Delamare Rd. Ches EN8 .... 148 F2
Delamere Rd. Bor WD6 .... 170 B8
Delcroft. Ware SG12 .... 93 C2
Delfield Cl. Cad LU1 .... 62 E4
Delius Cl. Elst WD6 .... 169 C3
Dell Cl. Harp AL5 .... 86 B3
Dell Cl. L Hal CM22 .... 98 A8
Dell La. Saw CM22 .... 98 A8
Dell Meadow. Heml H HP3 .... 138 E7
Dell Rd. Enf EN3 .... 162 C1
Dell Rd. Nthch HP4 .... 121 D7
Dell Rd. Watf WD2 .... 154 A2
Dell Rise. Chis AL2 .... 141 B5
Dell Side. Watf WD2 .... 154 A2
Dell Springs. Bun SG9 .... 40 E8
Dell The. Bal 23 E6
Dell The. Bric SG13 .... 113 C3
Dell The. Cad LU1 .... 62 E3
Dell The. Luton LU2 .... 46 F1
Dell The. Mark AL3 .... 83 D5
Dell The. Mo Pk HA6 .... 174 E8
Dell The. Pnr HA5 .... 175 D1
Dell The. Radl WD7 .... 156 A4
Dell The. St Alb AL1 .... 128 A4
Dell The. Stev SG1 .... 50 E5
Dell The. Welw AL6 .... 90 A4
Dellcot Cl. Luton LU2 .... 46 B4
Dellcott Cl. Wel G C AL8 .... 110 C2
Dellcroft Way. Harp AL5 .... 107 A5
Dellcut Rd. Heml H HP2 .... 125 A5
Dellfield Ave. Berk HP4 .... 122 A6
Dellfield. Berk HP4 .... 122 A6
Dellfield Cl. Radl WD7 .... 155 F4
Dellfield Cl. Harl CM17 .... 118 C4
Dellfield. St Alb AL1 .... 127 E2
Dellfield Rd. Hat AL10 .... 130 A5
Dellfield. St Alb AL1 .... 127 F2
Dellfield. Tri HP23 .... 93 D8
Dellmeadow. Abb L WD5 .... 139 E1
Dellors Cl. Barn EN5 .... 171 D4
Dells The. Bis St CM23 .... 76 D7 4
Dells The. Heml H HP3 .... 125 B2
Delsome La. Col H AL9 .... 143 F8
Delsome La. Wel G AL9 .... 144 B8
Dellswood Cl. Hert SG13 .... 113 E5

Dellwood Cl. Ric WD3 .... 165 B1
Delmar Ave. Heml H HP2 .... 125 D2
Delmer Ct. Bor WD6 .... 156 F1
Delmerend La. Fla AL3 .... 84 C1
Delphine Cl. Luton LU1 .... 63 A6
Delta Gain. Sth Ox WD1 .... 175 D7
Demontfort Rise. Ware SG12 .... 93 C3
Denbigh High Sch. Luton 45 B2
Denbigh High Sch. Luton 45 C2
Denbigh Rd. Luton LU3 .... 45 B2
Denby. Letw SG6 .... 23 B4
Dencora Way. Luton LU3 .... 44 B8
Dendridge Cl. Enf EN1 .... 162 B2
Dene La. Ast SG2 .... 51 E2
Dene Rd. Norwd HA6 .... 174 D4
Denes The. Heml H HP3 .... 138 F7
Denewood Cl. Watf WD1 .... 153 F2
Denham Cl. Heml H HP2 .... 125 A8
Denham Cl. Luton LU3 .... 44 E8
Denham La. Ch St P SL9 .... 172 A2
Denham Way (North Orbital Rd).
 Bor WD6 .... 170 C8
Denham Way (North Orbital Rd).
 Map Cr WD3 .... 172 E4
Denham Way (North Orbital Rd).
 Ric WD3 .... 164 E1
Denmark Cl. Luton LU3 .... 44 E8
Denmark Rd. Watf WD1 .... 167 B7
Denny Ave. Wa Aby EN9 .... 163 D5
Denny Ct. Bis St CM23 .... 59 B2
Denny Gate. Ches EN8 .... 148 F4
Denny's La. Berk HP4 .... 121 F3
Densley Cl. Wel G C AL8 .... 110 D8
Denton Cl. Barn EN5 .... 171 C4
Denton Cl. Dun LU4 .... 44 B4
Denton Rd. Stev SG1 .... 50 E4
Dents Cl. Letw SG6 .... 23 C3
Derby Ave. Har HA3 .... 176 D2
Derby House. Pnr HA5 .... 175 D1
Derby Rd. Dun LU4 .... 44 C2
Derby Rd. Lo Naz EN11 .... 135 D4
Derby Rd. Watf WD1 .... 167 C5
Derby Way. Stev SG1 .... 51 B8
Derwent Ave. Luton LU3 .... 45 B7
Derwent Ave. Pnr HA5 .... 175 E4
Derwent Lower Sch. Henlw 10 C4
Derwent Rd. Harp AL5 .... 85 C4
Derwent Rd. Heml H HP3 .... 125 C2
Derwent Rd. Henlw SG16 .... 10 B4
Derwent Rd. Luton LU2 .... 64 A8
Desborough Rd. Hert SG14 .... 92 C1
Desborough Dr. Tewin AL6 .... 90 D5
Desborough Rd. Wel G 35 C8
Desmond Rd. Watf WD2 .... 153 F3
Deva Cl. St Alb AL3 .... 127 A1
Devereux Dr. Watf WD1 .... 153 E1
Devoils La. Bis St CM23 .... 76 F7
Devon Cl. St Alb AL1 .... 127 E2
Devon Rd. Luton LU2 .... 64 B8
Devon Rd. Watf WD1 .... 167 D8
Devonshire Cl. Stev SG2 .... 69 A8
Devonshire Rd. Harp AL5 .... 86 B1
Devonshire Rd. Pnr HA5 .... 175 F2
Dewars Cl. Welw AL6 .... 89 C6
Dewes Green Rd. Clav CM23 .... 30 F1
Dewgrass Gr. Enf EN8 .... 162 D4
Dewhurst Rd. Ches EN8 .... 148 C2
Dewhurst St Mary Jun Mix Inf Sch.
 Ches 148 C2
Dewpond Cl. Stev SG1 .... 50 C8
Dewsbury Rd. Luton LU3 .... 45 C6
Dexter Cl. Luton LU3 .... 31 B1
Dexter Rd. Barn EN5 .... 171 D3
Dexter Rd. Hare UB9 .... 173 C1
Diamond Rd. Watf WD2 .... 154 A1
Dickens Cl. St Alb AL3 .... 127 D4
Dickens Ct. Heml H HP2 .... 105 B1
Dicker Mill. Hert SG13 .... 113 D7
Dicker Mill Ind Pk. Hert 113 E7
Dicket Mead. Welw AL6 .... 89 C5
Dickins Cl. Ham St EN7 .... 148 A5
Dickinson Ave. Cro Gr WD3 .... 166 A3
Dickinson Sq. Cro Gr WD3 .... 166 A3
Dickson. Ham St EN7 .... 147 F4
Dig Dag Hill. Ham St EN7 .... 147 F4
Digswell Cl. Bor WD6 .... 157 A1
Digswell La. Welw AL6 .... 89 B2
Digswell House Mews.
 Wel G C AL8 .... 89 D2
Digswell La. Wel G C AL7 .... 89 F2
Digswell Park Rd. Wel G C AL8 ... 89 D3
Digswell Park Rd. Wel G C AL8 ... 89 E1
Digswell Rd. Wel G C AL8 .... 89 E1
Digswell Rise. Wel G C AL8 .... 110 E8
Dimmocks La. Sar WD3 .... 152 B3
Dimsdale Cres. Bis St CM23 .... 77 B6
Dimsdale St. Hert SG13 .... 113 C6
Dinant Link Rd. Hod EN11 .... 135 A7
Dingle Cl. Edg EN5 .... 170 F3
Dinmore. Bov HP3 .... 136 F3
Ditchfield Rd. Hod EN11 .... 115 A1
Ditchling Cl. Luton LU2 .... 46 C3
Ditchmore La. Stev SG1 .... 50 D6
Ditton Gn. Gt Of LU2 .... 46 E3
Divine Saviour RC Jun Mix Inf Sch.
 Abb L 153 D7
Divot Pl. Hert SG13 .... 114 B7
Dixies Cl. Ashw SG7 .... 4 D3
Dixon Pl. Bun SG9 .... 40 E7
Dixons Hill Cl. Wel G AL9 .... 144 B6
Dixons Hill Rd. Wel G AL9 .... 144 C7
Dobb's Weir Rd.
 Lo Naz EN11,CM19 .... 135 D4
Docklands. Pirt SG5 .... 20 D4
Doctor's Commons Rd. Berk HP4 . 122 B4
Dodds La. Fla HP2 .... 104 E1
Dodwood. Wel G C AL7 .... 111 B5
Dog Kennel La. Hat AL10 .... 130 A6
Dog Kennel La. Royst SG8 .... 7 D6
Doggetts Way. St Alb AL1 .... 127 C1
Dognell Gn. Wel G C AL8 .... 110 B7
Dolesbury Dr. Welw AL6 .... 89 E8
Dollis Brook Wlk. Barn EN5 .... 171 E3
Dollis Valley Way. Barn EN5 .... 171 F3
Dolphin Dr. Har HA3 .... 176 F3
Dolphin Sq. St Alb AL1 .... 100 A3
Dolphin Way. Bis St CM23 .... 77 A8
Dolphin Yd. Hert SG14 .... 113 D6 2
Dolphin Yd. St Alb AL1 .... 127 D3
Dolphin Yd. Ware SG12 .... 93 D1 6
Doncaster Cl. Stev SG1 .... 51 C8

Doncaster Gn. Sth Ox WD1 .... 175 C5
Donkey La. Tri HP23 .... 99 E2
Donne Cl. Royst SG8 .... 7 C8
Dorant House. St Alb AL3 .... 127 D7
Dorchester Ave. Hod EN11 .... 135 A8
Dorchester Ct. Cro Gr WD3 .... 166 D4
Dorchester Ct. Watf WD1 .... 167 E3
Dordans Rd. Luton LU4 .... 44 F4
Dorel Cl. Luton LU2 .... 45 F2
Dormans Cl. Norwd HA6 .... 174 D3
Dormer Cl. Barn EN5 .... 171 D4
Dormie Cl. St Alb AL3 .... 127 C5
Dorrien's Croft. Berk HP4 .... 121 F7
Dorrington Cl. Luton LU3 .... 45 C1
Dorrofield Cl. Cro Gr WD3 .... 166 D4
Dorset Cl. Berk HP4 .... 121 F5
Dorset Ct. Luton LU1 .... 63 F6
Douglas Ave. Watf WD2 .... 154 E2
Douglas Dr. Stev SG1 .... 51 A8
Douglas House. Ches EN8 .... 148 D3
Douglas Rd. Harp AL5 .... 85 F2
Douglas Rd. Luton LU4 .... 45 A2
Douglas Way. Wel G C AL7 .... 111 C6
Dove Cl. Bis St CM23 .... 76 E3
Dove Cl. Sta M CM24 .... 59 E8
Dove Ct. Hat AL10 .... 130 A3
Dove House La. Ken Co LU6 .... 82 D8
Dove La. Pot B EN6 .... 159 C5
Dove Pk. Chor WD3 .... 164 C4
Dove Pk. Pnr HA5 .... 176 A3
Dovedale Cl. Hare UB9 .... 173 C1
Dovedale. Luton LU2 .... 45 E6
Dovedale. Stev SG2 .... 51 B4
Dovedale. Ware SG12 .... 93 C3
Dovehouse Croft. Harl CM20 .... 118 A2
Dovehouse Hill. Luton LU2 .... 46 B1
Dover Cl. Luton LU3 .... 45 A3
Dover Way. Cro Gr WD3 .... 166 A5
Doverfield. Gofs O EN7 .... 147 C2
Dower Ct. Hit SG4 .... 34 F5 1
Dowland House. Enf EN1 .... 161 F1
Dowling Ct. Heml H HP3 .... 138 D8
Down Edge. Red AL3 .... 105 F5
Down Green La. Whea AL4 .... 108 B7
Downalong. Bus WD2 .... 168 D1
Downedge. St Alb AL3 .... 127 B4
Downer Dr. Sar WD3 .... 152 A3
Downes Rd. St Alb AL4 .... 128 B7
Downfield Cl. Hert H SG13 .... 114 C4
Downfield Jun Mix Inf Sch. Ches .. 162 E8
Downfield Rd. Ches EN8 .... 162 E8
Downfield Rd. Hert H SG13 .... 114 C5
Downfields. Wel G C AL8 .... 110 B4
Downhall Ley. Bun SG9 .... 40 E7
Downings Wood. Map Cr WD3 .... 172 D5
Downlands. Bal SG7 .... 13 A1
Downlands. Luton LU3 .... 44 C7
Downlands. Royst SG8 .... 7 C6
Downlands. Stev SG2 .... 51 D7
Downlands. Wa Aby EN9 .... 163 E5
Downs Rd. Luton LU1 .... 63 C7
Downs The. Hat AL10 .... 130 A3
Downs View. Luton LU4 .... 44 D4
Downsfield. Hat AL10 .... 130 B2
Downside. Heml H HP2 .... 124 E4
Downside Inf Sch. Luton 44 E1
Downside Jun Sch. Luton 44 E1
Downsway Ct. Royst SG8 .... 7 C6
Downton Ct. Luton LU3 .... 63 D8 3
Downview. Dun LU4 .... 44 B2
Dowry Wlk. Watf WD1 .... 153 F1
Drakes Cl. Ches EN8 .... 148 D3
Drakes Dr. Norwd HA6 .... 174 B2
Drakes Dr. St Alb AL1 .... 128 C1
Drakes Dr. St Alb AL1 .... 142 B8
Drakes Dr. Stev SG2 .... 51 B7
Drakes Way. Hat AL10 .... 130 B3
Drapers Mews. Luton LU3 .... 45 C1
Drapers Way. Stev SG1 .... 50 C7
Drayson Cl. Wa Aby EN9 .... 163 E7
Drayton Ave. Pot B EN6 .... 158 E7
Drayton Rd. Bor WD6 .... 170 A5
Drayton Rd. Dun LU4 .... 44 A3
Driftway. Reed SG8 .... 16 E4
Driftway The. Heml H HP2 .... 124 F3
Driftwood Ave. Chis AL2 .... 141 B5
Drive The. Barn EN5 .... 171 E6
Drive The. Gofs O EN7 .... 147 B3
Drive The. Ham St EN8 .... 148 B3
Drive The. Harl CM20 .... 117 E1
Drive The. Harp AL5 .... 86 A1
Drive The. Hert SG14 .... 113 C8
Drive The. Hod EN11 .... 135 A8
Drive The. Kim AL4 .... 87 B7
Drive The. Lon C AL2 .... 142 A5
Drive The. Norwd HA6 .... 174 E2
Drive The. Pot B EN6 .... 158 F7
Drive The. Radl WD7 .... 156 A5
Drive The. Ric WD3 .... 165 C3
Drive The. Saw CM21 .... 97 E2
Drive The. St Alb AL4 .... 128 C1
Drive The. Watf WD1 .... 153 E2
Drive The. Welw AL6 .... 69 A1
Driver's End La. Cod SG4 .... 68 A4
Driveway The. Cuf EN6 .... 146 E3
Driveway The. Heml H HP1 .... 124 B1
Dromey Gdns. Har HA3 .... 176 F3
Drop La. Bri Wd AL2 .... 155 C7
Drovers Way. Bis St CM23 .... 76 C5
Drovers Way. Hat AL10 .... 130 B8
Drovers Way. St Alb AL3 .... 127 D3
Drovewood Cl. Chor WD3 .... 164 B4
Drummond Dr. Har HA7 .... 176 F3
Drummond Ride. Tri HP23 .... 100 A5
Drummonds The. Dun LU4 .... 44 C2
Drury La. Hun SG12 .... 95 E1
Drycroft. Wel G C AL7 .... 110 E2
Dryden Cres. Stev SG2 .... 51 C8
Dryden Rd. Har HA3 .... 176 F2
Drysdale Cl. Norwd HA6 .... 174 E3
Dubbs Knoll Rd. Gu M SG8 .... 1 F5
Dubrae Cl. St Alb AL3 .... 127 A1
Duchess Cl. Bis St CM23 .... 76 C7
Duchy Rd. Had W EN4 .... 159 D1
Duck La. Ben SG2 .... 52 E4
Duck's Hill Rd. Norwd HA6 .... 174 B2
Ducketts La. Muc H SG10 .... 75 D1
Ducketts Mead. Roy CM19 .... 116 B1
Ducketts Wood. Thun SG12 .... 93 E7
Duckling La. Saw CM21 .... 97 E2
Duckmore La. Tri HP23 .... 99 E2
Dudley Ave. Ches EN8 .... 162 D7
Dudley Hill Cl. Welw AL6 .... 89 E8
Dudley St. Luton LU2 .... 63 E8
Dudswell La. Nthch HP4 .... 121 D7
Dugdale Ct. Hit SG5 .... 21 C1
Dugdale Hill La. Pot B EN6 .... 158 E7
Dugdales. Cro Gr WD3 .... 166 A5
Duke St. Hod EN11 .... 135 A7
Duke St. Luton LU2 .... 63 E8
Duke St. Watf WD1 .... 167 C6
Duke's La. Hit SG5 .... 34 F8
Dukes Ave. Whip LU6 .... 81 E8
Dukes Ride. Bis St CM23 .... 76 C8
Dukes Way. Berk HP4 .... 122 A6
Dulwich Way. Cro Gr WD3 .... 166 A4
Dumbarton Ave. Ches EN8 .... 162 D5
Dumfries Cl. Sth Ox WD1 .... 175 A7
Dumfries St. Luton LU1 .... 63 D6
Duncan Cl. Wel G C AL7 .... 110 E5
Duncan Way. Bus WD2 .... 167 F7
Duncombe Cl. Hert SG14 .... 113 C8
Duncombe Cl. Luton LU3 .... 45 C6
Duncombe Rd. Hert SG14 .... 113 C8
Duncombe Rd. Nthch HP4 .... 121 E6
Duncombe Sch Daneshill. Hert 113 C7
Dundale Inf Sch. Tri 100 A5
Dundale Jun Sch. Tri 100 A5
Dundale Rd. Tri HP23 .... 100 A4
Dunhams La. Letw SG6 .... 23 C6
Dunkirks Mews. Hert SG13 .... 113 D4
Dunlin. Letw SG6 .... 11 E1
Dunlin Rd. Heml H HP2 .... 124 E8
Dunmow Ct. Luton LU3 .... 45 D2
Dunmow Rd. Bis St CM23 .... 77 C7
Dunmow Rd. Gt Ha CM22 .... 77 F7
Dunn Cl. Stev SG1 .... 50 E3
Dunnock Cl. Bor WD6 .... 170 A5
Dunny La. Chipf WD4 .... 151 F7
Dunsby Rd. Luton LU3 .... 45 A6
Dunsley Pl. Tri HP23 .... 100 B3
Dunsmore Cl. Bus WD2 .... 168 D3
Dunsmore Rd. Luton LU1 .... 63 C6
Dunsmore Way. Bus WD2 .... 168 D3
Dunstable Cl. Luton LU4 .... 45 A1
Dunstable Ct. Luton LU4 .... 44 F2
Dunstable Pl. Luton LU1 .... 63 D7
Dunstable Rd. Cad LU1 .... 62 C3
Dunstable Rd. Dagn HP4 .... 81 C7
Dunstable Rd. Dun LU4 .... 44 B2
Dunstable Rd. Luton LU4 .... 45 B1
Dunstable Rd. Red AL3 .... 106 A7
Dunstable Rd. Stu LU6 .... 82 B6
Dunstable Rd. Whip LU6 .... 81 C7
Dunstable Rd. Whip LU6 .... 82 B6
Dunstable Road Jun Inf Sch. Luton 63 C8
Dunster Cl. Barn EN5 .... 171 D5
Dunster Cl. Hare UB9 .... 173 B2
Dunster Rd. Heml H HP2 .... 105 B1
Dunsters Mead. Wel G C AL7 .... 111 B4
Dunston Hill. Tri HP23 .... 100 A4
Durban Rd E. Watf WD1 .... 167 A5
Durban Rd W. Watf WD1 .... 167 A5
Durbar Rd. Luton LU4 .... 45 B1
Durham Cl. Gt Am SG12 .... 115 B5
Durham Cl. Saw CM21 .... 97 C1
Durham Rd. Bor WD6 .... 170 D6
Durham Rd. Luton LU2 .... 64 A7
Durham Rd. Stev SG1 .... 37 A1
Durler Gdns. Luton LU1 .... 63 D5
Durrant Ct. Har HA3 .... 176 E2
Durrants Dr. Cro Gr WD3 .... 166 C5
Durrants Hill Rd. Heml H HP3 .... 138 D8
Durrants La. Berk HP4 .... 121 F5
Durrants Rd. Berk HP4 .... 121 F5
Dury Rd. Barn EN5 .... 171 F7
Duxford Cl. Luton LU3 .... 45 B7
Duxons Turn. Heml H HP2 .... 125 B4
Dwight Rd. Mo Pk WD1 .... 166 D2
Dyes La. Lan SG1 .... 49 F3
Dyke La. Whea AL4 .... 108 E7
Dylan Cl. Elst WD6 .... 169 D2
Dymoke Gn. St Alb AL4 .... 128 A7
Dymokes Way. Hod EN11 .... 115 A1
Dyrham La. Pot B EN5 .... 158 A3
Dyson Ct. Watf WD1 .... 167 C5
Dysons Cl. Ches EN8 .... 162 D6

Eagle Cl. Dun LU4 .... 44 A4
Eagle Ct. Bal SG13 .... 12 E1
Eagle Ct. Hert SG13 .... 114 B7
Eagle Way. Hat AL10 .... 130 A3
Ealing Cl. Bor WD6 .... 170 D8
Earl St. Watf WD1 .... 167 C6
Earls Cl. Bis St CM23 .... 76 D6
Earls Hill Gdns. Royst SG8 .... 7 C6
Earls La. Ridge WD6 .... 157 F6
Earls Meade. Luton LU2 .... 45 D1
Earlsmead. Letw SG6 .... 22 F3
Easington Rd. Dan En SG12 .... 71 E7
Easingwold Gdns. Luton LU1 .... 62 F8
Easneye (Coll). Sta Ab 115 C7
East Burrowfield. Wel G C AL7 .... 110 D4
East Cl. Chis AL2 .... 141 B6
East Cl. Hit SG4 .... 22 B1
East Cl. Stev SG1 .... 50 F5
East Comm. Harp AL5 .... 107 C7
East Comm. Red AL3 .... 106 A4
East Dr. Coln H AL4 .... 128 F4
East Dr. Lon C AL2 .... 142 B5
East Dr. Mo Pk WD1 .... 174 E8
East Dr. Saw CM21 .... 97 E1
East Dr. Watf WD2 .... 154 B3
East End Way. Pnr HA5 .... 175 F1
East Flint. Heml H HP1 .... 123 F4
East Gate. Harl CM20 .... 117 D1
East Gn. Heml H HP3 .... 139 A6
East Herts Coll of F Ed Annexe. Ches 162 D8
East Herts Coll of F Ed. Ches 148 F6
East Herts Hospl. Hert 114 A7
East Hill. Luton LU3 .... 45 B6
East La. Abb L WD5 .... 140 A2
East La. Whea AL4 .... 87 D1
East Lodge La. Had W EN2 .... 160 E4
East Mead. Wel G C AL7 .... 111 B3
East Mimms. Heml H HP2 .... 124 E4 4
East Mount. Whea AL4 .... 87 D1
East Pk. Harl CM17 .... 118 C3
East Pk. Saw CM21 .... 97 E1
East Rd. Bis St CM23 .... 77 B7
East Rd. Enf EN3 .... 162 C1
East Rd. Harl CM20 .... 118 B4
East Reach. Stev SG2 .... 51 A2
East Ridgeway. Cuf EN6 .... 146 E3
East Riding. Tewin AL6 .... 90 D5
East St. Heml H HP2 .... 124 D3
East St. Lily LU2 .... 32 D2
East St. Ware SG12 .... 93 D1
East View. Barn EN5 .... 171 F6
East View. Ess AL9 .... 131 F6
East View. St Ipp SG4 .... 35 C2
East Way. Wa Aby EN9 .... 163 D3
East Wlk. Harl CM20 .... 117 D1
Eastbourne Ave. Stev SG1 .... 50 A6
Eastbrook Inf Sch. Heml H 125 A8
Eastbrook Mix Inf Sch. Heml H 125 A8
Eastbrook Rd. Wa Aby EN9 .... 163 E6
Eastbrook Way. Heml H HP2 .... 124 E3
Eastbury Ave. Mo Pk HA6 .... 174 F5
Eastbury Cl. Mo Pk HA6 .... 174 E5
Eastbury Ct. St Alb AL1 .... 127 F4
Eastbury Farm Jun Mix & Inf Sch. Mo Pk 174 F6
Eastbury Pl. Mo Pk HA6 .... 174 F5
Eastbury Rd. Norwd HA6 .... 174 E4
Eastbury Rd. Watf WD1 .... 167 C3
Eastcheap. Letw SG6 .... 22 F6
Eastcote Dr. Harp AL5 .... 107 D6
Eastcott Cl. Luton LU2 .... 46 D1
Eastern Ave. Ches EN8 .... 162 F6
Eastern Ave. Henlw SG16 .... 10 C3
Eastern Way. Letw SG6 .... 12 A1
Eastfield Ave. Watf WD2 .... 167 D8
Eastfield Cl. Luton LU2 .... 46 C4
Eastfield Ct. St Alb AL4 .... 128 D6
Eastfield Prim Sch. Enf 162 D1
Eastfield Rd. Ches EN8 .... 162 F7
Eastfield Rd. Enf EN3 .... 162 D1
Eastfield Rd. Royst SG8 .... 7 E6
Eastgate. Stev SG1 .... 50 D5
Eastglade. Mo Pk HA6 .... 174 F5
Easthall House. Stev SG1 .... 36 C1
Eastham Cl. Barn EN5 .... 171 F4
Eastholm Gn. Letw SG6 .... 23 A8
Eastholm. Letw SG6 .... 23 A8
Eastlea Ave. Watf WD2 .... 154 E2
Eastman Way. Heml H HP2 .... 125 A6
Eastmoor Ct. Harp AL5 .... 107 C6
Eastmoor Pk. Harp AL5 .... 107 C6
Eastnor. Bov HP3 .... 137 A3
Easton Gdns. Bor WD6 .... 170 E5
Eastor. Wel G C AL7 .... 90 A1
Eastwick Cres. Ric WD3 .... 172 F8
Eastwick Hall La. East CM20 .... 117 A5
Eastwick Rd. East CM20 .... 117 B4
Eastwick Rd. East CM20 .... 117 C4
Eastwick Rd. East CM20 .... 117 E6
Eastwick Row. Heml H HP2 .... 125 A2
Eastwood Ct. Heml H HP2 .... 125 A4
Eaton Gate. Norwd HA6 .... 174 C4
Eaton Green Ct. Luton LU2 .... 64 C8
Eaton Green Rd. Luton LU2 .... 64 C8
Eaton Pl. Luton LU2 .... 46 D1
Eaton Rd. Heml H HP2 .... 125 B6
Eaton Rd. St Alb AL1 .... 128 B3
Eaton Valley Rd. Luton LU2 .... 64 B8
Ebberns Rd. Heml H HP3 .... 138 E8
Ebenezer St. Luton LU1 .... 63 D6
Ebury App. Ric WD3 .... 165 D1
Ebury Cl. Norwd HA6 .... 174 C5
Ebury Rd. Ric WD3 .... 165 D1
Ebury Rd. Watf WD1 .... 167 C6
Echo Hill. Royst SG8 .... 7 C5
Eddy St. Berk HP4 .... 122 A5
Edenhall Cl. Heml H HP2 .... 125 D2
Edens Cl. Bis St CM23 .... 77 B7
Edens Mount. Saw CM21 .... 97 F4
Edgars Ct. Wel G C AL7 .... 110 E5
Edgbaston Dr. Shen WD7 .... 156 E7
Edgcott Cl. Luton LU3 .... 31 B1
Edgecote Cl. Cad LU1 .... 62 E3
Edgehill Gdns. Luton LU3 .... 44 C8
Edgewood Dr. Luton LU2 .... 46 C6
Edgeworth Cl. Stev SG2 .... 51 C1
Edgware Way. Stan HA8 .... 169 D1
Edgwarebury La. Stan WD6,HA8 .. 169 F1
Edinburgh Ave. Ric WD3 .... 165 A2
Edinburgh Cres. Ches EN8 .... 162 E6
Edinburgh Pl. Harl CM20 .... 118 A4
Edinburgh Way. Harl CM20 .... 117 E3
Edison Rd. Stev SG2 .... 51 B6
Edkins Cl. Luton LU2 .... 45 E5
Edlyn Cl. Berk HP4 .... 121 F5
Edmonds Dr. Ast SG2 .... 51 D4
Edmund Beaufort Dr. St Alb AL3 ... 127 E5
Edmunds Rd. Hert SG14 .... 112 F7
Edna Daniels Sch The. St Alb 128 C1
Edridge Cl. Bus WD2 .... 168 C4
Edulf Rd. Bor WD6 .... 170 B8
Edward Amey Cl. Watf WD2 .... 154 C3
Edward Cl. Abb L WD5 .... 153 F7
Edward Cl. St Alb AL1 .... 127 F2
Edward Ct. Heml H HP3 .... 138 D7
Edward Ct. Wa Aby EN9 .... 163 F6
Edward St. Luton LU2 .... 45 F1
Edwards House. Stev SG1 .... 50 E6 5
Edwick Ct. Ches EN8 .... 148 D2
Edwin Ware Ct. Pnr HA5 .... 175 C1 2
Edwinstree Sch. Bun 40 D8
Edwyn Cl. Barn EN5 .... 171 D3
Egdon Dr. Luton LU2 .... 45 D6
Egerton Rd. Berk HP4 .... 122 B6
Egerton-Rothesay Sch. Berk 121 E4
Eight Acres. Tri HP23 .... 100 A4
Eighth Ave. Luton LU3 .... 44 D7
Eisenberg Cl. Bal SG7 .... 13 B1
Elaine Gdns. Cad LU1 .... 63 A1
Elbow La. Hert H SG13 .... 134 B7
Elbow La. Stev SG2 .... 51 B1
Eldefield. Letw SG6 .... 22 D7
Elder Ct. Bus WD2 .... 176 E8
Elder Rd. Ware SG12 .... 93 F3
Elder Way. Stev SG1 .... 50 E3
Elderbeck Cl. Ches EN7 .... 148 A2
Elderberry Cl. Luton LU2 .... 46 B4
Elderberry Dr. Hit SG4 .... 35 A4
Elderberry Way. Watf WD2 .... 154 B4
Elderfield. Harl CM17 .... 118 D3
Eldon Ave. Bor WD6 .... 170 B7
Eldon Rd. Dun LU4 .... 44 C1
Eldon Rd. Lo Naz EN11 .... 135 D4
Eleanor Ave. St Alb AL3 .... 127 D5
Eleanor Cross Rd. Ches EN8 .... 162 F5
Eleanor Gdns. Barn EN5 .... 171 D4
Eleanor Rd. Ches EN8 .... 162 E6
Eleanor Rd. Hert SG14 .... 113 C7
Eleanor Way. Ches EN8 .... 162 F5
Elfrida Rd. Watf WD1 .... 167 C4
Elgar Cl. Elst WD6 .... 169 D2
Elgar Path. Luton LU2 .... 63 E8 1
Elgin Dr. Norwd HA6 .... 174 E3
Elgin House. Hit SG4 .... 35 A6
Elgin Rd. Ches EN8 .... 148 C1
Elgin Rd. Hod EN10 .... 148 F8
Elgood Ave. Norwd HA6 .... 175 A3
Eliot Rd. Royst SG8 .... 7 D8
Eliot Rd. Stev SG2 .... 51 C6
Elizabeth Cl. Barn EN5 .... 171 D6
Elizabeth Cl. Lo Naz EN9 .... 149 D8
Elizabeth Cl. Wel G C AL7 .... 111 C6
Elizabeth Ct. St Alb AL4 .... 128 D6
Elizabeth Ct. Watf WD1 .... 153 F1
Elizabeth Dr. Tri HP23 .... 100 B6
Elizabeth House. Wel G C AL7 .... 111 C6
Elizabeth Rd. Bis St CM23 .... 76 E5
Elizabeth St. Luton LU1 .... 63 D6
Elizabeth Way. Harl CM19, CM20 . 117 B2
Ella Ct. Luton LU2 .... 45 F1
Ellen Cl. Heml H HP2 .... 124 F4
Ellenborough Cl. Bis St CM23 .... 76 D5
Ellenbrook Cres. Hat AL10 .... 129 D5
Ellenbrook La. Hat AL10 .... 129 D4
Ellenhall Cl. Luton LU3 .... 45 C1
Ellerdine Cl. Luton LU3 .... 45 B4
Ellesborough Cl. Sth Ox WD1 .... 175 C5
Ellesfield. Welw AL6 .... 89 B5
Ellesmere Gr. Barn EN5 .... 171 F4
Ellesmere Rd. Berk HP4 .... 122 D4
Ellice. Letw SG6 .... 23 B4
Ellingham Cl. Heml H HP2 .... 125 A5
Ellingham Rd. Heml H HP2 .... 124 F4
Elliott Cl. Wel G C AL7 .... 110 D3
Ellis Ave. Stev SG1 .... 50 E8
Elliswick Rd. Harp AL5 .... 86 B2
Ellwood Gdns. Watf WD2 .... 154 C5
Elm Ave. Cad LU1 .... 62 E3
Elm Ave. Watf WD1 .... 167 E2
Elm Cl. Wa Aby EN9 .... 163 D5
Elm Dr. Ches EN8 .... 148 E3
Elm Dr. Hat AL10 .... 130 A4
Elm Dr. St Alb AL4 .... 128 C3
Elm Gdns. Enf EN2 .... 161 D1
Elm Gdns. Wel G C AL8 .... 110 B6
Elm Gn. Heml H HP1 .... 123 E5
Elm Gr. Berk HP4 .... 122 C4
Elm Gr. Bis St CM23 .... 77 B7
Elm Gr. Watf WD2 .... 154 A2
Elm Hatch. Pnr HA5 .... 175 F3
Elm Park Rd. Pnr HA5 .... 175 D1
Elm Pk. Bal SG7 .... 23 F8
Elm Rd. Barn EN5 .... 171 F5
Elm Rd. Bis St CM23 .... 76 F8
Elm Terr. Har HA3 .... 176 D2
Elm Tree Wlk. Chor WD3 .... 164 F5
Elm Tree Wlk. Tri HP23 .... 100 A5
Elm Way. Ric WD3 .... 165 B1
Elm Wlk. Radl WD7 .... 155 F3
Elm Wlk. Royst SG8 .... 7 F7
Elm Wlk. Stev SG2 .... 51 B3
Elmbank Ave. Barn EN5 .... 171 C5
Elmbridge. Harl CM17 .... 118 F3
Elmbrook Dr. Bis St CM23 .... 76 E3
Elmcote Way. Cro Gr WD3 .... 165 F3
Elmfield Cl. Pot B EN6 .... 158 E6
Elmfield Ct. Luton LU2 .... 46 A1
Elmfield Rd. Pot B EN6 .... 158 E6
Elmhurst Cl. Bis St CM23 .... 76 E7
Elmhurst. Hod EN10 .... 135 A4
Elmhurst Rd. Enf EN3 .... 162 C2
Elmoor Ave. Welw AL6 .... 89 B5
Elmoor Cl. Welw AL6 .... 89 B4
Elmore Rd. Enf EN3 .... 162 D1
Elmore Rd. Luton LU2 .... 46 A1
Elmroyd Ave. Pot B EN6 .... 158 F6
Elmroyd Cl. Pot B EN6 .... 158 F6
Elms Cl. L Wym SG4 .... 35 E3
Elms Rd. Har HA3 .... 176 E3
Elms Rd. Ware SG12 .... 94 A2
Elms The. Cod SG4 .... 67 F2
Elms The. Hert SG13 .... 114 A6
Elmscroft Gdns. Pot B EN6 .... 158 F7
Elmside. Ken Co LU6 .... 82 E8
Elmside Wlk. Hit SG5 .... 34 E7
Elmtree Ave. Gt Of LU2 .... 46 E3
Elmwood Ave. Bal SG7 .... 23 F7
Elmwood Ave. Bor WD6 .... 170 B5
Elmwood Cres. Luton LU2 .... 45 E3
Elmwood Ct. Bal SG7 .... 23 F8
Elmwood. Saw CM21 .... 97 F1
Elmwood. Wel G C AL8 .... 110 B5
Elsinge Rd. Enf EN1 .... 162 C3
Elstree Hill N. Elst WD6 .... 169 D4
Elstree Hill S. Elst WD6 .... 169 D2
Elstree Pk. Bor WD6 .... 170 D3
Elstree Rd. Bus WD2 .... 168 E2
Elstree Rd. Elst WD6 .... 169 A3
Elstree Rd. Heml H HP2 .... 105 A1
Elstree Sta. Bor 170 A5
Elstree Way. Bor WD6 .... 170 C7
Elstree Way. Bor WD6 .... 170 E6
Elton Ave. Barn EN5 .... 171 F4
Elton Ct. Hert SG14 .... 113 C7
Elton Rd. Hert SG14 .... 113 C7
Elton Way. Bus WD2 .... 168 B7
Elvaston Ct. Barn EN5 .... 171 C4
Elveden Cl. Luton LU2 .... 45 E6
Elvington Gdns. Luton LU3 .... 31 B1
Ely Cl. Hat AL10 .... 129 F6
Ely Cl. Stev SG1 .... 37 B2
Ely Gdns. Bor WD6 .... 170 D4
Ely Rd. St Alb AL1 .... 128 B2
Ely Way. Luton LU4 .... 44 D4
Embleton Rd. Sth Ox WD1 .... 175 A7
Emerald Ct. Bor WD6 .... 156 F1
Emerald Rd. Dun LU4 .... 44 A2
Emerton Ct. Nthch HP4 .... 121 E7
Emerton Garth. Nthch HP4 .... 121 E7
Emma Rothschild Ct. Tri HP23 .... 100 A5
Emma's Cres. Gt Am SG12 .... 115 B4
Emmanuel Lodge. Ches EN8 .... 148 C1
Emmanuel Rd. Norwd HA6 .... 174 F3
Emmer Gn. Luton LU2 .... 46 F2
Emperor Cl. Nthch HP4 .... 121 F7
Emperors Gate. Stev SG2 .... 51 D8
Empire Ctr. Watf 167 C8
Empress Rd. Luton LU3 .... 44 E4
Endeavour Rd. Ches EN8 .... 148 E4
Enderby Rd. Luton LU3 .... 45 C6
Enderley Cl. Har HA3 .... 176 E2
Enderley Rd. Har HA3 .... 176 E2
Endersby Rd. Barn EN5 .... 171 C4
Endymion Ct. Hat AL10 .... 130 C6
Endymion Rd. Hat AL10 .... 130 C6
Enfield Chase Lower Sch. Enf 161 E1
Enfield Lock Sta. Enf 162 E2
Englefield. Luton LU2 .... 45 F3
Englehurst. Harp AL5 .... 86 D1
Enid Cl. Bri Wd AL2 .... 154 F8
Enjakes Cl. Stev SG2 .... 69 B7
Ennerdale Cl. St Alb AL1 .... 128 B1
Ennis Cl. Harp AL5 .... 107 D6
Ennismore Cl. Letw SG6 .... 23 C3
Ennismore Gn. Luton LU2 .... 46 F1
Enslow Cl. Cad LU1 .... 62 E3
Enterprise Ctr. Luton 63 F8
Enterprise Ctr The. Stev 50 B8
Enterprise Way. Luton LU3 .... 45 B8
Epping Gn. Heml H HP2 .... 125 B8
Epping House Sch. L Berk 132 C2
Epping Way. Luton LU3 .... 44 C8
Epsom Ct. Ric WD3 .... 165 B1
Ereswell Rd. Luton LU3 .... 45 A7
Erin Cl. Luton LU4 .... 45 A2
Erin Ct. Luton LU4 .... 45 A2
Ermine Cl. Ches EN7 .... 162 B8
Ermine Cl. Royst SG8 .... 7 D8
Ermine Cl. St Alb AL3 .... 127 A2
Ermine Ct. Bun SG9 .... 40 E8
Ermine Point Bsns Pk. Ware 93 B3
Ermine St. Thun SG12 .... 93 D7
Escarpment Ave. Whip LU6 .... 81 D8
Escot Way. Barn EN5 .... 171 C4
Esdaile La. Hod EN11 .... 135 A5
Eskdale Ct. Heml H HP2 .... 124 E6 3
Eskdale. Lon C AL2 .... 142 F4
Eskdale. Luton LU4 .... 44 C5
Essendon Gdns. Wel G C AL7 .... 110 F6
Essendon Hill. Ess AL9 .... 131 E6
Essendon Jun Mix Inf Sch. 131 F6
Essex Cl. Luton LU1 .... 63 F6
Essex Ct. Luton LU1 .... 63 E6 4
Essex La. Abb L WD4 .... 153 D6
Essex Mead. Heml H HP2 .... 105 A1
Essex Rd. Bor WD6 .... 170 A6
Essex Rd. Hod EN11 .... 135 B7
Essex Rd. Hod EN11 .... 135 C6
Essex Rd. Stev SG1 .... 50 B8
Essex Rd. Watf WD1 .... 167 B7
Essex St. St Alb AL1 .... 127 E4
Estcourt Rd. Watf WD1 .... 167 C6
Ethelred Cl. Wel G C AL7 .... 110 F5
Etna Rd. St Alb AL3 .... 127 D4
Etonbury Sch. Arl 11 C7
Europa Rd. Heml H HP2 .... 124 F6
Euston Ave. Watf WD1 .... 166 F4
Evan's Cl. Cro Gr WD3 .... 166 A4
Evans Ave. Watf WD2 .... 153 F4
Evans Gr. St Alb AL4 .... 128 C7
Evedon Cl. Luton LU3 .... 44 F6
Evelyn Dr. Pnr HA5 .... 175 D3
Evelyn Rd. Dun LU5 .... 44 A2
Everard Cl. St Alb AL1 .... 127 D1
Everest Cl. Arl SG15 .... 11 B5
Everest Way. Heml H HP2 .... 125 A3
Everett Cl. Bus WD2 .... 168 E1
Everett Ct. Radl WD7 .... 156 A5
Evergreen Cl. Welw SG3 .... 69 A2
Evergreen Rd. Ware SG12 .... 93 F3
Evergreen Way. Luton LU3 .... 45 A8
Everlasting La. St Alb AL3 .... 127 C5
Eversley Lodge. Hod EN11 .... 135 A6
Evron Pl. Hert SG14 .... 113 D6 4
Exchange Rd. Stev SG1 .... 50 F5
Exchange Rd. Watf WD1 .... 167 B5
Executive Park Ind Est. St Alb 128 B3
Exeter Cl. Stev SG1 .... 37 B2
Exeter Cl. Watf WD1 .... 167 C7
Explorer Dr. Watf WD1 .... 166 F3
Exton Ave. Luton LU2 .... 46 A1
Eynsford Ct. Hit SG4 .... 34 F6
Eywood Rd. St Alb AL1 .... 127 C1

Faggots Cl. Radl WD7 .... 156 C4
Fair Cl. Bus WD2 .... 168 B2
Fair Oak Dr. Luton LU2 .... 45 F3
Fair View. Pot B EN6 .... 145 B2
Fairacre Ct. Norwd HA6 .... 174 E3
Fairacre. Heml H HP3 .... 138 F7
Fairacres Cl. Pot B EN6 .... 158 F6
Fairburn Cl. Bor WD6 .... 170 A8
Faircross Way. St Alb AL1 .... 128 A5
Fairfax Ave. Luton LU3 .... 44 D7
Fairfax Rd. Hert SG13 .... 113 F7
Fairfield Ave. Sth Ox WD1 .... 175 D7
Fairfield. Bun SG9 .... 40 F6
Fairfield Cl. Harp AL5 .... 86 D1
Fairfield Cl. Hat AL10 .... 130 C8
Fairfield Cl. Radl WD7 .... 155 E2
Fairfield Dr. Ches EN10 .... 148 F7
Fairfield Hospl. Stot 11 C3
Fairfield Prim Sch. Radl 155 E3
Fairfield Rd. Hod EN11 .... 135 A8
Fairfield Way. Hit SG4 .... 35 D8
Fairfield Wlk. Ches EN8 .... 148 E3
Fairfields Prim Sch. Ham St 148 A4
Fairfolds. Watf WD2 .... 154 E4
Fairford Ave. Luton LU2 .... 45 E4
Fairgreen Rd. Cad LU1 .... 62 F3
Fairhaven Cres. Sth Ox WD1 .... 175 A7
Fairhaven. Pk St AL2 .... 141 D4
Fairhill. Heml H HP3 .... 138 F7
Fairlands Inf Sch. Stev 50 D6
Fairlands Jun Sch. Stev 50 D6
Fairlands Way. Stev SG1 .... 51 A7
Fairlawns. Pnr WD1 .... 175 D1
Fairlawns. Watf WD1 .... 153 F1

Fairley Way. Ches EN7 148 B3
Fairmead Ave. Harp AL5 107 C8
Fairseat Cl. Bus WD2 176 E8
Fairthorn Cl. Tri HP23 99 E3
Fairview Dr. Watf WD1 153 E3
Fairview Rd. Stev SG1 50 B7
Fairway Ave. Bor WD6 170 B7
Fairway. Bis St CM23 77 C6
Fairway Cl. Chis AL2 141 C4
Fairway Cl. Harp AL5 107 A5
Fairway. Heml H HP3 138 F7
Fairway House. Bor WD6 170 B6
Fairway. Saw CM21 97 F2
Fairway The. Abb L WD5 153 D7
Fairway The. Mo Pk HA6 174 E6
Fairway. Ware SG12 114 C8
Fairways. Ches EN8 148 D5
Faithfield. Watf WD2 167 E3
Falcon Cl. Hat AL10 130 A3
Falcon Cl. Norwd HA6 174 E3
Falcon Cl. Saw CM21 97 C1
Falcon Cl. Stev SG2 51 D2
Falcon Ct. Ware SG12 93 C3 2
Falcon Ridge. Berk HP4 122 C3
Falcon Way. Watf WD2 154 E5
Falcon Way. Wel G C AL7 110 E8
Falconer Rd. Bus WD2 168 A3
Falconer St. Bis St CM23 76 C5
Falconers Field. Harp AL5 85 E3
Falconers Pk. Saw CM21 97 D1
Falconers Rd. Luton LU2 64 C1
Falkirk Gdns. Sth Ox WD1 175 D5
Falkland Rd. Barn EN5 171 E7
Fallow Rise. Hert SG13 113 F6
Fallowfield Cl. Hare UB9 173 C2
Fallowfield. Luton LU3 45 C4
Fallowfield. Stev SG2 51 C3
Fallowfield. Wel G C AL7 89 F1
Fallowfield Wlk. Heml H HP1 124 A6
Fallows Gn. Harp AL5 86 B3
Falstaff Gdns. St Alb AL1 141 C8
Falstone Gn. Luton LU2 46 E1
Fanhams Hall Rd. Ware SG12 93 F3
Fanhams Rd. Ware SG12 93 E2
Fanshaw Ct. Hert SG14 113 C7
Fanshawe Cres. Ware SG12 93 C2
Fanshawe St. Hert SG14 113 B7
Fanshaws La. Bric SG13 133 C5
Fantail La. Tri HP23 99 F4
Far End. Hat AL10 130 B2
Faraday Cl. Watf WD1 166 D3
Faraday Rd. Stev SG2 51 B6
Faringdon Rd. Dun LU4 44 C3
Faringford Cl. Pot B EN6 159 D8
Farland Rd. Heml H HP2 125 B3
Farley Ct. Luton LU1 63 C5
Farley Farm Rd. Luton LU1 63 B5
Farley Hill. Luton LU1 63 C5
Farley Jun Sch. Luton 63 C6
Farley Lodge. Luton LU1 63 D5
Farm Ave. Harp AL5 85 D4
Farm Cl. Barn EN5 171 C4
Farm Cl. Bor WD6 156 E1
Farm Cl. Ches EN8 148 C1
Farm Cl. Cuf EN6 146 E4
Farm Cl. Hert SG14 113 A6
Farm Cl. Letw SG6 12 A1
Farm Cl. Roy CM19 116 B1
Farm Cl. Stev SG1 50 E4
Farm Cl. Wel G C AL8 110 C6
Farm Gn. Luton LU1 63 C5
Farm Hill Rd. Wa Aby EN9 163 D6
Farm La. Ric WD3 165 C6
Farm La. Stand SG11 73 A8
Farm Pl. Berk HP4 121 F5
Farm Rd. L Chal WD3 164 A5
Farm Rd. Norwd HA6 174 C5
Farm Rd. Nwml E LU1 85 B7
Farm Rd. St Alb AL1 128 B4
Farm Way. Bus WD2 168 B5
Farm Way. Mo Pk HA6 174 F6
Farmbrook. Luton LU2 45 D7
Farmers Cl. Watf WD2 154 B6
Farmhouse Cl. Ches EN10 148 F6
Farmhouse La. Heml H HP2 125 A5
Farmstead Rd. Har HA3 176 D1
Farnham C of E Prim Sch. Far 58 D6
Farnham Cl. Bov HP3 137 A3
Farnham Cl. Saw CM21 97 C1
Farnham Rd. Bis St CM23 58 F3
Farquhar St. Hert SG14 113 C7
Farr's La. Nwml E LU2 65 A1
Farraline Rd. Watf WD1 167 B5
Farrant Way. Bor WD6 169 E8
Farrer Top. Mark AL3 83 E5
Farriday Cl. St Alb AL3 127 E7
Farriers Cl. Bal SG7 12 E1
Farriers Cl. Cod SG4 67 F1
Farriers End. Ches EN10 148 F5
Farriers. Gt Am SG12 115 A6
Farriers Way. Bor WD6 170 D4
Farringford Cl. Chis AL2 141 B5
Farrow Cl. Luton LU3 31 C1
Farthing Dr. Letw SG6 23 C3
Farthings The. Heml H HP1 124 B3
Faulkner Ct. St Alb AL1 127 E5
Faverolle Gn. Ches EN8 148 D3
Faversham Cl. Tri HP23 100 A4
Fawbert & Barnard's Jun Mix & Inf Sch. Harl 118 C3
Fawbert & Bernard Inf Sch The. Saw 97 E2
Fawcett Rd. Stev SG2 51 B7
Fawkon Wlk. Hod EN11 135 A6
Fawn Ct. Hat AL9 130 C7
Fay Gn. Abb L WD5 153 D6
Fayerfield. Pot B EN6 159 D8
Fayland Cotts. Gt Ho SG9 41 E7
Feacey Down. Heml H HP1 124 B5
Fearney Mead. Ric WD3 165 A1
Fearnhill Sch. Letw 22 C5
Fearnley Rd. Wel G C AL8 110 C5
Fearnley St. Watf WD1 167 B5
Feather Dell. Hat AL10 130 A5
Featherbed La. Heml H HP3 138 B7
Featherston Rd. Stev SG2 51 C3
Featherstone Gdns. Bor WD6 170 C5
Federal Way. Watf WD2 167 C8
Felbrigg Cl. Luton LU2 46 F2
Felden Cl. Watf WD2 154 D5
Felden Dr. Heml H HP3 138 A7
Felden La. Heml H HP3 138 A7
Feldon Cl. Pnr HA5 175 E3
Felix Ave. Luton LU2 46 A2
Fellowes La. Col H AL4 143 E8
Fellowes Way. Stev SG2 51 A2
Fells Cl. Hit SG5 34 F8
Felmersham Ct. Luton LU1 63 B7
Felmersham Rd. Luton LU1 63 A7
Felmongers. Harl CM20 118 B2
Felstead Cl. Luton LU2 45 F3
Felstead Rd. Ches EN8 162 E7
Felstead Way. Luton LU2 45 F3
Felton Cl. Bor WD6 156 E1
Felton Cl. Ches EN10 148 F6
Felton Cl. Luton LU2 46 D1
Fen End. Stot SG5 11 F8
Fennycroft Rd. Heml H HP1 124 A6
Fensom's Alley. Heml H HP2 124 D4
Fensom's Cl. Heml H HP2 124 D4
Fenwick Cl. Luton LU3 45 B5
Fermor Cres. Luton LU2 46 C1
Fern Cl. Hod EN10 148 F8
Fern Dells. Hat AL10 129 F4
Fern Dr. Heml H HP3 124 E2
Fern Gr. Wel G C AL8 89 D2
Fern Way. Watf WD2 154 B4
Ferndale. Muc H SG10 74 F2
Ferndale Rd. Enf EN3 162 E2
Ferndale Rd. Luton LU1 63 B7
Ferndene. Bri Wd AL2 154 F8
Ferndown Cl. Pnr HA5 175 E3
Ferndown. Pnr HA6 175 A1
Ferndown Rd. Sth Ox WD1 175 C6
Fernecroft. St Alb AL1 141 D8
Fernheath. Luton LU3 31 A1
Fernhills. Abb L WD4 153 D6
Fernleigh Ct. Har HA2 176 B1
Fernleys. St Alb AL4 128 C5
Ferns Cl. Enf EN3 162 E3
Fernville La. Heml H HP2 124 D3
Ferny Hill. Had W EN4 159 F1
Ferrars Cl. Dun LU4 44 B1
Ferrars Inf Sch. Dun 44 B3
Ferrars Jun Sch. Dun 44 B3
Ferrers La. Whea 108 B5
Ferrier Rd. Stev SG2 51 C6
Ferryhills Cl. Sth Ox WD1 175 C7
Feryngs Cl. Harl CM17 118 D4
Fesants Croft. Harl CM20 118 B3
Fetherstone Cl. Pot B EN6 159 D7
Fiddle Bridge La. Hat AL10 129 F6
Fiddlebridge Ind Ctr. Hat 129 F6
Fidler Pl. Bus WD2 168 B3
Field Cl. Harp AL5 107 D7
Field Cl. St Alb AL4 128 A7
Field Cres. Royst SG8 7 F7
Field End Cl. Luton LU2 46 C4
Field End Cl. Watf WD1 167 E2
Field End Cl. Wigg HP23 100 D1
Field Fare Gn. Dun LU4 44 A5
Field House Ct. Harp AL5 86 A2
Field Inf Sch. Watf 167 C4
Field La. Letw SG6 22 F4
Field Rd. Heml H HP2 125 A3
Field Rd. Watf WD1 167 E3
Field View. Barn EN5 171 B5
Field View Rd. Pot B EN6 159 A6
Field View Rise. Bri Wd AL2 140 E2
Field Way. Bov HP3 137 A4
Field Way. Hod EN11 115 C2
Field Way. Ric WD3 165 B1
Field's Ct. Pot B EN6 159 D6
Fielder Ctr (Univ of Herts). Hat 129 D8
Fieldfare. Letw SG6 11 E1
Fieldfare. Stev SG2 51 D3
Fieldfares. Lon C AL2 142 D4
Fieldgate House. Stev SG1 50 F5
Fieldgate Rd. Luton LU4 44 D2
Fieldings Rd. Ches EN8 148 F3
Fields End La. Heml H HP1 123 E5
Fields End. Tri HP23 100 A6
Fieldway. Berk HP4 122 E2
Fieldway. Gt Am SG12 115 B4
Fieldway. Wigg HP23 100 D1
Fifth Ave. Letw SG6 23 C6
Fifth Ave. Watf WD2 154 D4
Fifth Ave. Harl CM20 117 D2
Figtree Hill. Heml H HP2 124 D4
Filey Cl. Stev SG1 50 A7
Filmer Rd. Luton LU4 44 E4
Finch Cl. Dun LU4 44 A4
Finch Cl. Hat AL10 130 A3
Finch La. Bus WD2 168 A5
Finch Rd. Berk HP4 122 A4
Finchdale. Heml H HP1 124 A3
Finche's End. Walk SG2 52 B8
Finches The. Hert SG13 114 B6
Finches The. Hit SG4 35 A7
Finley Rd. Harp AL5 86 D3
Finsbury Ct. Ches EN8 162 E5
Finsbury Rd. Luton LU4 44 D5
Finucane Rise. Bus WD2 176 C8
Finway Ct. Watf WD1 166 F4
Finway. Luton LU1 63 A8
Finway Rd. Heml H HP2 125 B7
Fir Cl. Stev SG2 50 F1
Fir Tree Cl. Heml H HP3 125 B2
Fir Tree Ct. Bor WD6 169 F5
Fir Tree Hill. Sar WD3 153 A2
Firbank Dr. Watf WD1 167 E2
Firbank Rd. St Alb AL3 127 F7
Firbank Trad Est. Luton 63 A8
Fire Station Alley. Barn EN5 171 E7
Firecrest. Letw SG6 11 E1
Firlands. Bis St CM23 76 E6
Firlands House. Bis St CM23 76 E6
Firs Cl. Hat AL10 130 B4
Firs Cl. Hit SG5 34 D8
Firs Dr. Kim AL4 87 C5
Firs Jun Sch The. Bis St 76 E6
Firs La. Pot B EN6 159 B6
Firs The. Ham St EN7 147 E4
Firs The. Harp AL5 86 D2
Firs The. St Alb AL1 142 B7
Firs The. Wel G C AL8 89 C2
Firs The. Wigg HP23 100 D1
Firs Wlk. Norwd HA6 174 D4
Firs Wlk. Tewin AL6 90 E5
Firs Wood Cl. Nort EN6 159 F7
First Ave. Watf WD2 154 D4
First Ave. Harl CM20 117 E2
Firway Cl. Welw AL6 89 F7
Firway. Welw AL6 89 F7
Firwood Ave. Coln H AL4 128 E3
Fish Farm St. Red AL3 106 B5
Fish Hill. Royst SG8 7 D6
Fish St. Red AL3 106 B5
Fisher Cl. Kin L WD4 139 A2
Fisher Rd. Har HA3 176 F1
Fisher's Green Rd. Stev SG1 50 B8
Fisher's Ind Est. Watf 167 C4
Fishers Cl. Ches EN8 163 A5
Fishers Cl. Stand SG11 55 D3
Fishers Gn. Stev SG1 36 A1
Fishers Mead. Stand SG11 55 D3
Fishery Cotts. Heml H HP1 124 A1
Fishery Rd. Heml H HP1 124 A1
Fishponds Rd. Hit SG5 34 E8
Fishpool St. St Alb AL3 127 C3
Fitzjohn Ave. Barn EN5 171 F5
Fitzroy Ave. Luton LU3 45 B3
Fitzwarin Cl. Luton LU3 44 E8
Fitzwilliam Ct. Harl CM17 118 E4
Five Acres Ave. Bri Wd AL2 140 F2
Five Acres. Kin L WD4 138 F2
Five Acres. Lon C AL2 142 D6
Five Acres. Sta M CM24 59 E8
Five Oaks. Cad LU1 62 F4
Five Oaks. Hat AL10 130 B2
Five Oaks Sch. Cad 62 F3
Five Oaks Sch. Hat 130 A3
Five Springs Ct. Luton LU3 44 E6
Five Springs. Luton LU3 44 E6
Five Springs Sch. Luton 44 F7
Flags The. Heml H HP2 125 B3
Flagstaff Rd. Wa Aby EN9 163 B6
Flamstead End Inf Sch. Ham St 148 A4
Flamstead End Jun Sch. Ham St 148 A4
Flamstead End Rd. Ches EN8 148 B3
Flamstead Jun Mix Inf Sch. Fla 84 B1
Flamsteadbury La. Red AL3 106 A4
Flash La. Cre H EN2 161 C3
Flatfield Rd. Heml H HP3 125 A1
Flaunden Bottom. Flau HP5 150 E4
Flaunden Bottom. Lat HP5 150 E4
Flaunden Hill. Flau HP3 151 A6
Flaunden La. Bov HP3 137 D3
Flavian Cl. St Alb AL3 126 F1
Flax Mews. Mark AL3 83 E5
Flecker Cl. Stan HA7 176 F5
Fleet The. Royst SG8 7 C6
Fleetville Inf Sch. St Alb 128 B3
Fleetville Jun Mix Sch. St Alb 128 A3
Fleetwood Cres. Stev SG1 50 B7
Fleetwood. Letw SG6 23 B4
Fleetwood Way. Sth Ox WD1 175 C6
Fleming Cl. Ham St EN7 148 A5
Fleming Cres. Hert SG14 113 A6
Fletcher Way. Heml H HP2 124 D6
Flete House. Watf WD1 166 E3
Flexley Wood. Wel G C AL7 90 A1
Flinders Cl. St Alb AL1 128 A1
Flinders Cl. Stev SG2 51 D5
Flint Cl. Luton LU3 44 E7
Flint Copse. Red AL3 106 C6
Flint Rd. Letw SG6 23 C8
Flint Way. St Alb AL3 127 C7
Flora Gr. St Alb AL1 127 F2
Floral Dr. Lon C AL2 142 D5
Florence Ave. Luton LU3 44 D6
Florence Cl. Watf WD2 154 A4
Florence St. Hit SG5 34 F8
Florence Wlk. Bis St CM23 76 F8
Flowers Ind Est. Luton 63 E6 6
Flowers Way. Luton LU1 63 E7
Flowton Gr. Harp AL5 107 A7
Fold Croft. Harl CM20 117 A1
Foldingshott. Dat SG3 69 D3
Follett Dr. Abb L WD5 153 F8
Folly Ave. St Alb AL3 127 D4
Folly Cl. Hit SG4 35 A5
Folly Cl. Radl WD7 155 F3
Folly Fields. Whea AL4 87 B2
Folly La. Cad LU1 62 E4
Folly La. St Alb AL3 127 C4
Folly Pathway. Radl WD7 155 F3
Folly The. Bun SG9 40 D7
Folly The. Hert SG14 113 D6
Folly View. Gt Am SG12 115 B4
Fontmell Cl. St Alb AL3 127 E5
Fontwell Cl. Har HA3 176 E3
Football Cl. Bal SG7 12 E1
Forbes Ave. Pot B EN6 159 D7
Ford Cl. Bus WD2 168 C5
Ford Hill. L Had SG11 75 B8
Ford St. Brag SG11 55 E6
Fordham Cl. Ashw SG7 4 D4
Fordham Rd. Royst SG8 7 E5
Fordwich Cl. Hert SG14 113 A6
Fordwich Hill. Hert SG14 113 A6
Fordwich Rd. Wel G C AL8 110 C5
Fordwich Rise. Hert SG14 113 A6
Fore St. Harl CM17 118 C4
Fore St. Hat AL9 130 C6
Fore St. Hert SG14 113 D6
Fore St. Wes SG4 24 B1
Forebury Ave. Saw CM21 97 F2
Forebury Cres. Saw CM21 97 F2
Forebury The. Saw CM21 97 F2
Forefield. Chis AL2 141 A4
Forelands Pl. Saw CM21 97 E2
Forest Ave. Heml H HP3 124 D1 5
Forest Rd. Ches EN8 148 D2
Forest Rd. Enf EN3 162 E3
Forest Rd. Watf WD2 154 B6
Forest Row. Stev SG2 50 F1
Forest Wlk. Bus WD2 167 F8
Foresters Cl. Ham St EN7 147 E4
Foresthall Rd. Sta M CM24 59 E4
Forge Cl. Chipf WD4 152 A8
Forge Cl. Hit SG5 34 F8 5
Forge Cotts. Ess AL9 131 E6
Forge End. Chis AL2 141 A5
Forge La. Norwd HA6 174 E3
Forge La. Welw AL6 89 C5
Forres Cl. Hod EN11 135 A8
Forres Jun Mix & Inf Sch. Hod 115 B1
Forrest Cres. Luton LU2 46 A3
Forresters Dr. Wel G C AL7 111 C5
Fortnums Acre. Har HA7 176 F4
Fortuna Cl. Stev SG1 51 C8
Fortune La. Elst WD6 169 D3
Forty Hill C of E Sch. Enf 162 A2
Forty Hill. Enf EN2 161 F1
Fosman Cl. Hit SG5 34 D8 7
Foster Cl. Stev SG1 36 D1
Foster Dr. Hit SG4 35 A5
Foster Rd. Heml H HP1 124 B1
Foston Cl. Luton LU3 44 F6
Fotherley Rd. Ric WD3 172 F8
Foulds Jun Mix Inf Sch. Barn 171 D6
Founceley Ave. Dan En SG12 71 F8
Fountain Pl. Wa Aby EN9 163 C5
Fountains Rd. Luton LU3 45 D3
Four Acres. Stev SG1 50 D7
Four Acres. Wel G C AL7 110 F4
Four Acres The. Sheer CM21 98 A2
Four Limes. Whea AL4 108 D8
Four Swannes Jun Mix Inf Sch. Ches 162 E6
Four Tubs The. Bus WD2 168 D2
Fouracres. Letw SG6 23 A3
Fouracres Dr. Heml H HP3 124 F1
Fouracres Wlk. Heml H HP3 124 F1
Fourth Ave. Harl CM20 117 C1
Fourth Ave. Letw SG6 23 C7
Fourth Ave. Luton LU3 44 D7
Fourth Ave. Watf WD2 154 D4
Fourways Market. Wel G AL9 144 C7
Fovant Cl. Harp AL5 107 C6
Fovant. Stev SG1 36 B1
Fowley Cl. Ches EN8 162 F5
Fowlmere Rd. Gt Ch SG8 9 F8
Fox Cl. Bus WD2 168 B5
Fox Cl. Elst WD6 169 D3
Fox Cl. Wigg HP23 100 D1
Fox Cnr. Gu M SG8 1 F5
Fox La. Ther SG8 15 F7
Fox Rd. Stev SG1 50 E4
Fox Rd. Wigg HP23 100 C2
Fox's La. Bro Pk AL9 144 F7
Foxbury Cl. Luton LU2 45 D6
Foxcroft. St Alb AL1 128 A1
Foxdell Inf Sch. Luton 63 A8
Foxdell Jun Sch. Luton 62 E8
Foxdell. Norwd HA6 174 D4
Foxdells. Hertng SG14 112 C3
Foxdells La. Bis St CM23 58 F2
Foxes Cl. Hert SG13 114 B6
Foxes Dr. Ches EN7 148 A2
Foxfield Cl. Norwd HA6 174 F4
Foxfield. Stev SG2 51 C3
Foxglove Bank. Royst SG8 7 F5
Foxglove Cl. Bis St CM23 76 C6
Foxglove Cl. Hat AL10 130 B4
Foxglove Way. Welw AL6 89 E8
Foxgloves The. Heml H HP1 123 E2
Foxgrove Path. Sth Ox WD1 175 D5
Foxhill. Gu M SG8 1 F5
Foxhill. Luton LU2 45 E5
Foxhill Rd. Gu M SG8 1 F5
Foxhill. Watf WD2 154 A3
Foxholes Ave. Hert SG13 113 F6
Foxhollows. Hat AL10 130 B7
Foxlands Cl. Watf WD2 154 A5
Foxley Dr. Bis St CM23 77 B8
Foxley Gr. Welw AL6 89 F4
Foxleys. Sth Ox WD1 175 E7
Foxton Rd. Hod EN11 135 A6
Foxtree House. Watf WD2 154 E3
Frampton Rd. Pot B EN6 145 C1
Frampton St. Hert SG14 113 D6
Francis Ave. St Alb AL3 127 D6
Francis Bacon Sch. St Alb 142 B8
Francis Cl. Hit SG4 35 A5
Francis Cl. Stot SG5 11 E6
Francis Combe Sch. Watf 154 C7
Francis Rd. Hin SG7 3 C6
Francis Rd. Ware SG12 93 D2
Francis Rd. Watf WD1 167 B5
Francis St. Luton LU1 63 D8
Frank Martin Ct. Ches EN7 148 B1
Frankland Cl. Cro Gr WD3 166 A2
Frankland Rd. Cro Gr WD3 166 B3
Franklin Ave. Ches EN7 148 B1
Franklin Cl. Coln H AL4 129 E1
Franklin Cl. Heml H HP3 138 E8
Franklin Cl. Pirt SG5 20 D4
Franklin Gdns. Hit SG4 22 B1
Franklin Rd. Watf WD1 167 B7
Franklin's Rd. Stev SG1 50 C8
Franks Cl. Henlw SG16 10 B5
Franshams Dr. Bus WD2 176 D8
Fraser Rd. Ches EN8 148 E3
Fred Millard Ct. Stev SG1 50 E5
Frederick St. Luton LU2 45 E1
Frederick St Pas. Luton LU2 45 E1
Freeman Ave. Luton LU3 45 B8
Freemans Cl. Hit SG5 21 D1
Freewaters Cl. Ick SG5 21 E4
Freman Dr. Bun SG9 40 D8
French Horn La. Hat AL10 130 B6
French Row. St Alb AL3 127 D3 4
French's Cl. Gt Am SG12 115 B4
Frensham Dr. Hit SG4 22 C2
Frensham. Ham St EN7 148 A4
Freshwater Cl. Luton LU3 44 F7
Freshwaters. Harl CM20 117 E1
Fretherne Rd. Wel G C AL8 110 D6
Friars Cl. Luton LU1 63 B5
Friars Field. Nthch HP4 121 F7
Friars Rd. Brag SG11 56 A7
Friars Rd. Wes SG4 24 B1
Friars Way. Bus WD2 167 F8
Friars Way. Kin L WD4 139 A1
Friars Way. Luton LU1 63 B5
Friars Wlk. Tri HP23 100 A4
Friars Wood. Bis St CM23 77 C8
Friarscroft. Hod EN10 135 A3
Friday Furlong. Hit SG5 34 C8
Friedberg Ave. Bis St CM23 76 D4
Friendless La. Fla AL3 83 E3
Friends Ave. Ches EN8 162 D7
Friesian Cl. Dun LU4 44 A3
Frimley Rd. Heml H HP1 123 E4
Fringewood Cl. Norwd HA6 174 B2
Frinton Cl. Sth Ox WD1 175 B8
Friston Gn. Luton LU2 46 D1
Frithsden Copse. Pot En HP4 122 F8
Frithwood Ave. Norwd HA6 174 F4
Frithwood Prim Sch. Norwd 174 F4
Frobisher Dr. Stev SG2 51 B7
Frobisher Rd. St Alb AL1 128 C1
Frobisher Way. Hat AL10 129 D8
Froghall La. Walk SG2 38 B1
Frogmoor Ct. Ric WD3 173 D8
Frogmoor La. Ric WD3 173 D8
Frogmore Hill. Ast SG14 70 B7
Frogmore House. Stev SG1 36 C1
Frogmore. Pk St AL2 141 E4
Frogmore Rd. Heml H HP3 138 D8
Frogmore St. Tri HP23 100 A3
Frogs Hall La. Dan En SG11 53 F3
Frome Cl. Luton LU4 44 E4
Frome Sq. Heml H HP2 125 A8
Front St. Cad LU1 63 C1
Front The. Pot En HP4 123 B7
Frowick Cl. Wel G AL9 144 B8
Frowyke Cres. Ridge EN6 158 A7
Fry Rd. Stev SG2 51 C5
Fryth Mead. St Alb AL3 127 B4
Fulbeck Way. Har HA2 176 C1
Fulbourne Cl. Luton LU4 44 E2
Fulford Gr. Sth Ox WD1 175 B8
Fuller Ct. Bis St CM23 77 A7 1
Fuller Gdns. Watf WD2 154 B2
Fuller Rd. Watf WD2 154 B2
Fuller Way. Cro Gr WD3 166 A4
Fullers Ct. Letw SG6 22 E7
Fulling Mill La. Welw AL6 89 B6
Fulmar Cres. Heml H HP1 124 A3
Fulmore Cl. Harp AL5 86 D4
Fulton Cl. Stev SG1 50 C5
Fulton Cres. Bis St CM23 77 C8
Fulton Ct. Bor WD6 156 F1
Furham Field. Pnr HA5 176 A3
Furlay Cl. Letw SG6 22 D7
Furlong Way. Gt Am SG12 115 A7
Furlongs. Heml H HP1 124 A4
Furneux Pelham Jun Mix Inf Sch. Fur P 43 A4
Furrowfield. Hat AL10 130 B7
Furrows The. Luton LU3 45 B7
Furse Ave. St Alb AL4 128 A7
Furtherfield. Abb L WD5 153 E7
Furtherground. Heml H HP2 124 E2 1
Furze Cl. Luton LU2 45 D7
Furze Cl. Sth Ox WD1 175 C5
Furze Gr. Royst SG8 7 E5
Furze Rd. Heml H HP1 123 E2
Furze View. Chor WD3 164 C4
Furzebushes La. Chis AL2 140 F6
Furzedown Ct. Harp AL5 86 B1 10
Furzedown. Stev SG2 51 B4
Furzefield. Ches EN8 148 B3
Furzefield Ct. Pot B EN6 158 E8
Furzefield Ctr The. Pot B 158 D8
Furzefield Rd. Wel G C AL7 110 E4
Furzehill Mid Sch. Bor 170 A5
Furzehill Par. Bor WD6 170 A6
Furzehill Rd. Bor WD6 170 B5
Furzen Cres. Hat AL10 129 F2

Gable Cl. Abb L WD5 153 E7
Gable Cl. Pnr HA5 176 A3
Gables Ave. Bor WD6 169 F6
Gables The. Saw CM21 97 E2
Gaddesden Cres. Watf WD2 154 E5
Gaddesden Gr. Wel G C AL7 111 B6
Gaddesden La. Gt Gd AL3 105 C4
Gaddesden Row CP Sch. Gt Gd 104 B6
Gaddesden Row. Gt Gd HP2 104 C6
Gade Ave. Watf WD1 166 E5
Gade Bank. Cro Gr WD1 166 D5
Gade Cl. Heml H HP1 124 B6
Gade Cl. Watf WD1 166 E5
Gade Side. Watf WD1 153 E4
Gade Valley Cl. Kin L WD4 139 A3
Gade Valley Cotts. Gt Gd HP1 103 D4
Gade Valley Jun Mix Inf Sch. Heml H 124 B4
Gade View Gdns. Abb L WD4 153 C7
Gade View Rd. Heml H HP3 138 D7
Gadebridge Ct. Heml H HP1 124 C4
Gadebridge La. Heml H HP1 124 B5
Gadebridge La. Heml H HP1 124 C5
Gadebridge Rd. Heml H HP1 124 B4
Gadeview. Heml H HP1 124 C3
Gadswell Cl. Watf WD2 154 E3
Gage Cl. Royst SG8 7 D7
Gainsborough Ave. St Alb AL1 127 F4
Gainsford Cres. Hit SG4 22 C2
Gainswood. Wel G C AL7 110 E5
Gall End La. Sta M CM24 59 F7
Galleria The. Hat 129 F5
Galley Gn. Hod SG13 115 A2
Galley Hill. Heml H HP1 124 B6
Galley La. Barn EN5 171 B7
Galley La. Bor EN5 171 B7
Galleyhill Rd. Wa Aby EN9 163 E8
Galliard Cl. Luton LU3 45 B4
Galloway Cl. Bis St CM23 76 F8
Galloway Cl. Ches EN10 148 F5
Galloway Rd. Bis St CM23 58 F1
Gallows Hill. Abb L WD4 153 C7
Gallows Hill La. Abb L WD5 153 D8
Galston Rd. Luton LU3 44 D8
Gammons La. Watf WD1,WD2 154 A2
Gamnel Terr. Tri HP23 100 B7
Ganders Ash. Watf WD2 154 A6
Gandhi Ct. Watf WD2 167 D7 1
Gangies Hill. H Wy CM21 97 A4
Gant Ct. Wa Aby EN9 163 F5
Ganton Wlk. Sth Ox WD1 175 E6
Ganymede Pl. Heml H HP2 124 F6
Gaping La. Hit SG5 34 D7
Garden Ave. Hat AL10 130 A2
Garden Cl. Barn EN5 171 C5
Garden Cl. Harp AL5 107 A5
Garden Cl. Royst SG8 7 E7
Garden Cl. St Alb AL1 128 B4
Garden Cl. Watf WD1 166 F7
Garden Cl. Welw SG3 69 B2
Garden Ct. Whea AL4 87 D1
Garden Field. Ast SG2 51 E2
Garden Field La. Berk HP4 122 F2

Garden Fields Jun Mix Inf Sch.
St Alb 127 D6
Garden La. Royst SG8 .... 7 D5
Garden Rd. Abb L WD5 .... 153 E8
Garden Rd. Bun SG9 .... 40 E8
Garden Rd. Welw SG3 .... 69 B2
Garden Row. Hit SG5 .... 34 F8 6
Garden Terr. Sac SG12 .... 92 E4
Garden Terrace Rd. Harl CM17 ..... 118 C4
Garden Wlk. Royst SG8 .... 7 E7
Garden Wlk. Stev SG1 .... 50 E5
Gardenia Ave. Luton LU3 .... 45 A4
Gardens The. Bal SG7 .... 23 E8
Gardens The. Bro Pk AL9 .... 144 E4
Gardens The. Henlw SG16 .... 10 D8
Gardens The. Stot SG5 .... 11 E6
Gardens The. Watf WD1 .... 166 F7
Gardiners La. Ashw SG7 .... 4 D4
Gareth Ct. Bor WD6 .... 156 F1
Garfield Ct. Luton LU2 .... 46 D3 3
Garfield St. Watf WD2 .... 154 B1
Garland Cl. Heml H HP2 .... 124 D4
Garland Rd. Ware SG12 .... 93 E1
Garnault Rd. Enf EN1 .... 161 F1
Garner Dr. Ches EN10 .... 148 E5
Garnett Cl. Watf WD2 .... 154 D3
Garnett Dr. Bri Wd AL2 .... 140 F2
Garrard Way. Whea AL4 .... 108 D8
Garratts Rd. Bus WD2 .... 168 C2
Garratts Mead. Luton LU2 .... 46 B3
Garrison Ct. Hit SG4 .... 34 F7 2
Garrowsfield. Barn EN5 .... 171 F4
Garsmouth Way. Watf WD2 .... 154 D3
Garston Cres. Watf WD2 .... 154 C5
Garston Dr. Watf WD2 .... 154 C5
Garston La. Watf. Watf 154 D4
Garston La. Watf WD2 .... 154 D5
Garston Manor Medical
Rehabilitation Ctr. Abb L 154 C8
Garston Manor Sch. Watf 154 C7
Garston Park Par. Watf WD2 .... 154 D5
Garston Sta. Watf 154 D4
Garth Rd. Letw SG6 .... 22 E3
Garth The. Abb L WD5 .... 153 D6
Garthland Dr. Barn EN5 .... 171 C4
Gartlet Rd. Watf WD1 .... 167 C6
Gas La. Bark SG8 .... 17 C3
Gascoyne Cecil Prim Sch. Hat 130 A7
Gascoyne Cl. Pot B EN6 .... 158 A7
Gascoyne Way. Hert SG13,SG14 ... 113 D5
Gate Cl. Bor WD6 .... 170 C8
Gate Cotts. Chor WD3 .... 164 D5
Gate End. Norwd HA6 .... 175 A3
Gatecroft. Heml H HP3 .... 124 F1 1
Gatecroft. Heml H HP3 .... 139 A8
Gatehill Gdns. Luton LU3 .... 31 B1
Gatehill Rd. Norwd HA6 .... 175 A3
Gates Way. Stev SG1 .... 50 C6
Gatesbury Way. Stand SG11 .... 55 D3
Gatesdene Cl. L Gad HP4 .... 102 C8
Gateshead Rd. Bor WD6 .... 170 A8
Gateway Cl. Norwd HA6 .... 174 C4
Gatwick Cl. Bis St CM23 .... 59 B1
Gauldie Way. Stand SG11 .... 55 D2
Gaumont App. Watf WD1 .... 167 B6
Gaunts Way. Letw SG6 .... 12 A2
Gaveston Dr. Berk HP4 .... 122 B6
Gayland Ave. Luton LU2 .... 64 B8
Gayton Cl. Luton LU3 .... 45 B4
Gaywood Ave. Ches EN8 .... 148 D1
Gazelda Ind Est. Watf 167 D4
Geddes Rd. Bus WD2 .... 168 C5
Geddings Rd. Hod EN11 .... 135 B6
Generals Wlk The. Enf EN3 .... 162 E2
Gentle Ct. Bal SG7 .... 23 E8
Gentlemens Field. Ware SG12 .... 93 B3
George Gn. L Hal CM22 .... 77 B1
George La. Royst SG8 .... 7 D6
George Leighton Ct. Stev SG2 ...... 51 B4
George St. Berk HP4 .... 122 D4
George St. Heml H HP2 .... 124 C6
George St. Hert SG14 .... 113 C6
George St. Luton LU1 .... 63 E7
George St. Mark AL3 .... 83 E5
George St. St Alb AL3 .... 127 D3
George St W. Luton LU1 .... 63 E7
George St. Watf WD1 .... 167 C5
George Street Sch. Heml H 124 D4
George V Ave. Pnr HA5 .... 175 F1
George V Way. Sar WD3 .... 152 B3
George's Wood Rd. Bro Pk AL9 ... 145 B5
Georges Mead. Elst WD6 .... 169 E3
Georgewood Rd. Heml H HP3 ...... 139 A1
Georgina Ct. Arl SG15 .... 11 A3
Gerard Ave. Bis St CM23 .... 76 A4
Gernon Rd. Letw SG6 .... 22 F5
Gernon Wlk. Letw SG6 .... 22 F5
Gew's Cnr. Ches EN7 .... 148 D2
Gew's Corner Prim Sch. Ches 148 E2
Ghibert Way. Berk HP4 .... 122 A4
Giant Tree Hill. Bus WD2 .... 168 D1
Gibbons Cl. Bor WD6 .... 169 E8
Gibbons Cl. Sand AL4 .... 108 C1
Gibbons Way. Kneb SG3 .... 68 F5
Gibbs Cl. Ches EN8 .... 148 D2
Gibbs Couch. Sth Ox WD1 .... 175 D7
Gibbs Field. Bis St CM23 .... 76 D5
Gibraltar Lodge. Harp AL5 .... 86 D3
Gibson Cl. Hit SG4 .... 35 B7
Gidian Ct. Pk St AL2 .... 141 D4
Gifford's La. Dan E SG11 .... 54 A2
Gilbert Rd. Hare UB9 .... 173 D1
Gilbert St. Enf EN3 .... 162 C2
Gilbert's Hill. St Le HP23 .... 119 E3
Gilbey Ave. Bis St CM23 .... 77 B6
Gilbey Cres. Sta M CM24 .... 59 E8
Gilden Way. Harl CM17 .... 118 E4
Gilden Way. Harl CM17 .... 118 E4
Gilder Cl. Luton LU3 .... 45 A8
Gilderdale. Luton LU4 .... 44 D6
Gilders. Saw CM21 .... 97 D2
Giles Cl. Sand AL4 .... 108 C1
Giles Inf Sch The. Stev 37 A1
Giles Jun Sch The. Stev 37 A1
Gillam St. Luton 63 E8
Gillan Gn. Bus WD2 1
Gillian Ave. St Alb AL1 .... 141 C7
Gilliat's Gn. Chor WD3 .... 164 D5
Gilliflower House. Hod EN11 ...... 135 A1
Gillings Ct. Barn EN5 .... 171 E5

Gillison Cl. Letw SG6 .... 23 B5
Gills Hill. Radl WD7 .... 155 F4
Gills Hill Inf Sch. Radl 155 F4
Gills Hill La. Radl WD7 .... 155 F3
Gills Hollow. Radl WD7 .... 155 F3
Gilmour Cl. Enf EN2 .... 162 A4
Gilpin Cl. Royst SG8 .... 86 C1
Gilpin Gallop. Gt Am SG12 .... 115 B4
Gilpin's Rd. Ware SG12 .... 114 E8
Gilpin's Ride. Berk HP4 .... 122 E5
Gilsland. Wa Aby EN9 .... 163 E4
Ginns Rd. Sto P SG9 .... 43 D6
Gippeswyck Cl. Pnr HA5 .... 175 D2
Gipsy La. Bis St CM23 .... 59 C4
Gipsy La. Kneb SG3 .... 68 E4
Gipsy La. Luton LU1 .... 64 A6
Gipsy La. Sta M CM23 .... 59 C4
Girdle Rd. Hit SG4 .... 22 A2
Girons Cl. Hit SG4 .... 35 B7
Girtin Rd. Bus WD2 .... 168 C5
Girton Way. Cro Gr WD3 .... 166 C4
Glade The. Bal SG7 .... 23 E7
Glade The. Letw SG6 .... 22 F3
Glades The. Heml H HP1 .... 123 E4
Gladeside. St Alb AL4 .... 128 D6
Gladeway The. Wa Aby EN9 ...... 163 D6
Gladsmuir Rd. Luton LU1 .... 63 C7
Gladstone Ct. Stev SG2 .... 69 A8
Gladstone Pl. Barn EN5 .... 171 D5
Gladstone Rd. Dan En SG12 .... 71 F8
Gladstone Rd. Hod EN11 .... 135 B7
Gladstone Rd. Ware SG12 .... 93 C2
Gladstone Rd. Watf WD1 .... 167 C6
Glamis Cl. Ches EN7 .... 148 A2
Glamis Cl. Heml H HP2 .... 105 B1
Glean Wlk. Hat AL10 .... 130 A2 3
Gleave Cl. St Alb AL1 .... 128 B4
Glebe Ave. Arl SG15 .... 11 A7
Glebe Cl. Ess AL9 .... 131 F6
Glebe Cl. Heml H HP3 .... 138 E7
Glebe Cl. Hert SG14 .... 113 D8
Glebe Cl. Pit LU7 .... 80 D5
Glebe Cl. Wat St SG14 .... 70 D3
Glebe Cotts. Ess AL9 .... 131 F6
Glebe Cl. Bis St CM23 .... 77 B8
Glebe Cl. Hat AL10 .... 130 C6
Glebe Cl. Wat St SG14 .... 70 E3
Glebe House. Ess Al9 .... 131 F6
Glebe La. Barn EN5 .... 171 A3
Glebe Rd. Hert SG14 .... 113 D8
Glebe Rd. Letw SG6 .... 23 B8
Glebe Rd. Welw AL6 .... 89 B5
Glebe The. Kin L WD4 .... 139 A2
Glebe The. Stev SG2 .... 51 B6
Glebe The. Watf WD2 .... 154 D6
Glebelands. Harl CM20 .... 117 F3
Gleed Ave. Bus WD2 .... 176 D8
Glemsford Cl. Luton LU4 .... 44 B6
Glemsford Dr. Harp AL5 .... 86 D2
Glen Chess. Ric 165 C6
Glen Faba Rd. Lo Naz CM19 ...... 135 F6
Glen The. Cad LU1 .... 62 E3
Glen The. Heml H HP2 .... 124 F8
Glen The. Heml H HP2 .... 125 A8
Glen The. Norwd HA6 .... 174 D3
Glen Way. Watf WD1 .... 153 E1
Glenblower Ct. St Alb AL4 .... 128 D3
Glencoe Rd. Bus WD2 .... 168 A3
Glencourse Gn. Sth Ox WD1 ...... 175 D6
Glendale. Heml H HP1 .... 124 B3
Glendale Wlk. Ches EN8 .... 148 E1
Gleneagles Cl. Sth Ox WD1 .... 175 D6
Gleneagles Dr. Luton LU2 .... 45 E6
Glenester Cl. Hod EN11 .... 115 B1
Glenferrie Rd. St Alb AL1 .... 128 A3
Glenfield Cl. Hert SG14 .... 112 F7
Glenfield Rd. Luton LU3 .... 45 C6
Glengall Pl. St Alb AL1 .... 141 E4
Glenhaven Ave. Bor WD6 .... 170 A6
Glenlyn Ave. St Alb AL1 .... 128 B2
Glenmire Terr. Sta M SG12 .... 115 D4
Glenmore Gdns. Abb L WD5 ...... 154 A7
Glenshee Cl. Norwd HA6 .... 174 C4
Glenview Gdns. Heml H HP1 ...... 124 B3
Glenview Rd. Heml H HP1 .... 124 B3
Glenville Ave. Enf EN2 .... 161 D1
Glenwood Cl. Stev SG2 .... 51 C2
Glenwood. Hod EN10 .... 134 F4
Glenwood. Wel G C AL7 .... 111 D5
Glevum Cl. St Alb AL3 .... 126 F1
Globe Cl. Harp AL5 .... 86 B1
Globe Cres. Far CM23 .... 58 D6
Globe Cl. Hert SG14 .... 113 C8
Gloucester Ave. Ches EN8 .... 162 E6
Gloucester Cl. Stev SG1 .... 36 D1
Gloucester Rd. Enf EN2 .... 161 C1
Gloucester Rd. Luton LU1 .... 63 F6
Glover Cl. Ham St EN7 .... 147 F4
Glovers Cl. Hert SG13 .... 113 C4
Glynde The. Stev SG2 .... 69 B8
Goat La. Enf EN1 .... 161 F1
Gobions Way. Bro Pk En6 .... 145 B3
Goblins Gn. Wel G C AL7 .... 110 D5
Goddard End. Stev SG2 .... 51 B3
Goddards Cl. L Berk SG13 .... 132 C4
Gode Tower. Heml H HP3 .... 138 F6
Godfrey Cl. Stev SG2 .... 51 B3
Godfreys Rd. Luton LU1 .... 63 B6
Godfries Cl. Luton LU1 .... 63 B6
Godfries Ct. Tewin AL6 .... 90 E3
Godsafe. Harl CM17 .... 118 E4
Godwin Ch. Wa Aby EN9 .... 163 C1
Goff's La. Gofs O EN7 .... 147 E2
Goff's Oak Ave. Gofs O EN7 ...... 147 C3
Goffs Cres. Gofs O EN7 .... 147 C2
Goffs La. Ches EN7 .... 148 C1
Goffs Oak Jun Mix Inf Sch. Gofs O 147 B2
Goffs Sch. Ches 148 B2
Gold Crest Cl. Dun LU4 .... 44 A5
Golda Cl. Barn EN5 .... 171 D3
Goldcrest Way. Bus WD2 .... 168 C1
Goldcroft. Heml H HP3 .... 125 A1
Golden Dell. Wel G C AL7 .... 110 F2
Goldfield Inf Sch. Tri 99 F3
Goldfield Rd. Tri HP23 .... 99 F3
Goldfinch Way. Bor WD6 .... 170 A5
Goldings. Bis St CM23 .... 77 B8

Goldings Cres. Hat AL10 .... 130 B6
Goldings House. Hat AL10 .... 130 B6
Goldings La. Stap SG14 .... 92 A2
Goldington Cl. Hod EN11 .... 114 F1
Goldon. Letw SG6 .... 23 C4
Goldstone Cl. Ware SG12 .... 93 D2
Golf Cl. Bus WD2 .... 167 D6
Golf Club Rd. Bro Pk AL9 .... 145 A6
Golf Ride. Cre H EN2 .... 161 A4
Gombards. St Alb AL3 .... 127 D4
Gomer Cl. God SG4 .... 67 E2
Gonville Ave. Cro Gr WD3 .... 166 B3
Gonville Cres. Stev SG2 .... 51 C2
Goodey Meade. Ben SG2 .... 52 F2
Goodliffe Pk. Bis St C 59 B2
Goodrich Cl. Watf WD2 .... 154 A4
Goodwin Ct. Ches EN8 .... 148 E3
Goodwin House. Watf WD1 ...... 166 E3
Goodwin Stile. Bis St CM23 .... 76 D5
Goodwins Mead. Ched LU7 .... 80 A7
Goodwood Ave. Enf EN3 .... 162 C2
Goodwood Ave. Watf WD2 .... 153 E3
Goodwood Cl. Hod EN11 .... 135 A7
Goodwood Par. Watf WD1 .... 153 E3
Goodwood Path. Bor WD6 .... 170 A7
Goodwood Rd. Royst SG8 .... 7 F6
Goodyers Ave. Radl WD7 .... 155 F5
Goose Acre. Bot HP5 .... 136 A1
Goose Acre. Ched LU7 .... 80 A7
Goose La. Hat AL7 CM22 .... 98 E7
Gooseacre. Wel G C AL7 .... 110 F4
Gooseberry Hill. Luton LU3 .... 45 B7
Goosecroft. Heml H HP1 .... 123 F4
Goral Mead. Ric WD3 .... 165 D1
Gordian Way. Stev SG2 .... 37 C1
Gordon Ave. Har HA7 .... 176 F4
Gordon Cl. St Alb AL1 .... 128 B2
Gordon House. St Alb AL1 .... 128 B2
Gordon Rd. Ches EN8 .... 163 A5
Gordon St. Luton LU1 .... 63 D7
Gordon Way. Barn EN5 .... 171 F6
Gore La. Stand SG11 .... 73 D3
Gorelands La. C St P HP8 .... 172 A7
Gorham Dr. St Alb AL1 .... 141 E6
Gorle Cl. Watf WD2 .... 154 A4
Gorleston Cl. Stev SG1 .... 36 A1
Gorse Cl. Harl CM20 .... 129 F2
Gorse Cnr. St Alb AL3 .... 127 D5
Gorselands. Harp AL5 .... 107 C7
Gorst Cl. Letw SG6 .... 22 E5
Gosford House. Watf WD1 .... 166 E3
Gosforth Path. Sth Ox WD1 ...... 175 B7
Gosforth Path. Sth Ox WD1 ...... 175 A7
Goshawk Cl. Dun LU4 .... 44 A4
Goslett Cl. Bus WD2 .... 168 A4
Gosling Ave. Gt Of SG5 .... 33 C2
Gosling Sports Pk. Wel G C 110 C4
Gosmore Cl. Hit SG4 .... 34 F3
Gosmore Rd. Hit SG4 .... 34 F5
Gosmore. Stev SG1 .... 36 C2
Gossamers The. Watf WD2 .... 154 E4
Gosselin Rd. Hert SG14 .... 113 C8
Gossoms Ryde. Berk HP4 .... 122 A5
Gothic Mede Lower Sch. Arl 11 A5
Gothic Way. Arl SG15 .... 11 B5
Gould Cl. Wel G AL9 .... 144 B7
Government Row. Enf EN3 .... 163 A2
Gower Field. Pot B EN6 .... 158 A7
Gower Rd. Royst SG8 .... 7 C7
Gowers The. Harl CM20 .... 118 B2
Grace Cl. Bor WD6 .... 170 D8
Grace Gdns. Bis St CM23 .... 76 F4
Grace Way. Stev SG1 .... 50 E7
Graces Maltings. Tri HP23 .... 100 A3
Graemesdyke Rd. Berk HP4 ...... 122 A3
Graham Ave. Hod EN10 .... 134 E2
Graham Cl. St Alb AL1 .... 127 D1
Graham Gdns. Luton LU3 .... 45 C4
Graham Rd. Har HA3 .... 176 E1
Grailands. Bis St CM23 .... 59 A2
Grammar School Wlk. Hit SG5 ..... 34 E7
Grampian Way. Luton LU3 .... 44 C8
Granaries The. Wa Aby EN9 ...... 163 E5
Granary Cl. Whea AL4 .... 108 D8
Granary Ct. Saw CM21 .... 97 E2
Granary La. Harp AL5 .... 86 C1
Granary The. Roy CM19 .... 116 B1
Granby Ave. Harp AL5 .... 86 D2
Granby Rd. Luton LU4 .... 44 E2
Granby Rd. Stev SG1 .... 36 C2
Grandfield Ave. Watf WD1 .... 167 A8
Grange Ave. Barn N20 .... 171 E2
Grange Ave. Luton LU4 .... 44 D5
Grange Bottom. Royst SG8 .... 7 D5
Grange Cl. Heml H HP2 .... 125 A2
Grange Cl. Hert SG14 .... 113 B6
Grange Cl. Hit SG4 .... 35 A4
Grange Cl. Mark AL3 .... 83 D6
Grange Court Rd. Harp AL5 ...... 107 C2
Grange Ct. Hert SG14 .... 113 C7
Grange Ct. Wa Aby EN9 .... 163 D5
Grange Dr. Stot SG5 .... 11 F5
Grange Gdns. Ware SG12 .... 114 E8
Grange Hill. Welw AL6 .... 89 C6
Grange Jun Mix Sch The. Letw 12 A2
Grange La. Radl WD7 .... 168 D8
Grange Pk. Bis St CM23 .... 58 F1
Grange Rd. Bis St CM23 .... 77 A7
Grange Rd. Bor WD6 .... 169 F4
Grange Rd. Letw SG6 .... 22 F8
Grange Rd. Pit LU7 .... 80 D5
Grange Rd. Watf WD2 .... 167 F4
Grange Rd. Wils HP23 .... 79 D1
Grange Rise. God SG4 .... 67 F1
Grange The. Abb L WD5 .... 153 E8
Grange The. Bis St CM23 .... 58 F1
Grange The. Hod EN11 .... 135 A5
Grange The. Ric WD3 .... 165 D2
Grange Wlk. Bis St CM23 .... 77 A7
Grangedale Cl. Norwd HA6 .... 174 E2
Grangeside. Bis St CM23 .... 59 A2
Grangewood. Pot B EN6 .... 145 B1
Gransden Cl. Luton LU3 .... 45 A1
Grant Gdns. Harp AL5 .... 86 B2
Grantham Cl. Royst SG8 .... 7 F6
Grantham Gdns. Ware SG12 .... 93 E2
Grantham Gn. Bor WD6 .... 170 C4

Grantham Rd. Luton LU4 .... 45 B1
Granville Ct. St Alb AL1 .... 127 F3
Granville Dene. Bov HP3 .... 137 A4
Granville Rd. Hod EN11 .... 115 A2
Granville Rd. Hit SG4 .... 22 C1
Granville Rd. Luton LU1 .... 63 B8
Granville Rd. St Alb AL1 .... 127 F3
Granville Rd. Watf WD1 .... 167 C5
Grasmere Ave. Harp AL5 .... 86 C5
Grasmere Ave. Luton LU3 .... 45 B7
Grasmere Cl. Heml H HP3 .... 125 B1
Grasmere Cl. Watf WD2 .... 154 B7
Grasmere Cl. Luton LU3 .... 45 C7
Grasmere Rd. St Alb AL1 .... 128 B3
Grasmere Rd. Ware SG12 .... 93 E3
Grass Meadows. Stev SG2 .... 51 D7
Grass Warren. Tewin AL6 .... 90 E1
Grassington Cl. Bri Wd AL2 .... 141 A1
Grassy Cl. Heml H HP1 .... 124 A4
Gravel Dr. Ast Cl HP23 .... 99 B3
Gravel La. Heml H HP1 .... 124 A3
Gravel Path. Berk HP4 .... 122 E5
Gravel Path. Heml H HP1 .... 124 A3
Graveley Ave. Bor WD6 .... 170 C4
Graveley Cl. Stev SG1 .... 36 C2
Graveley Dell. Wel G C AL7 ...... 111 B5
Graveley La. Gt Wy SG4 .... 36 B5
Graveley Rd. Gra SG4 .... 36 B3
Graveley Rd. Gt Wy SG4 .... 35 F6
Gravelhill Terr. Heml H HP1 ...... 124 A3
Gravelly La. Brag SG11 .... 55 F8
Gravely Ct. Heml H HP2 .... 125 C2
Gray's La. Hit SG5 .... 34 D7
Grayling Cl. Nthch HP4 .... 121 F7
Graylings The. Abb L WD5 .... 153 D6
Grays Cl. Royst SG8 .... 7 C8
Grays Ct. Bis St CM23 .... 76 E8
Graysfield. Wel G C AL7 .... 111 A3
Grazings The. Heml H HP2 .... 124 F5
Greasy Cl. Abb L WD5 .... 153 F8
Great Braitch La. Hat AL10 .... 109 F1
Great Break. Wel G C AL7 .... 111 B5
Great Brookmead Sch. Bor 156 F1
Great Cambridge Rd. Ches EN8 .. 148 D4
Great Cambridge Rd. Enf EN1 ... 162 C6
Great Conduit. Wel G C AL7 ...... 111 C7
Great Dell. Wel G C AL8 .... 89 D1
Great Elms Rd. Heml H HP3 ...... 138 F7
Great Gaddesden Prim Sch.
Gt Gd 103 D3
Great Ganett. Wel G C AL7 .... 111 C4
Great Gn. Pirt SG5 .... 20 D4
Great Gr. Bus WD2 .... 168 B5
Great Graham Golf Club. Muc H .. 75 D4
Great Hadham Rd. Bis St CM23 ... 76 C6
Great Heart. Heml H HP2 .... 124 E5
Great Heath. Hat AL10 .... 130 B8
Great Innings N. Wat St SG14 ..... 70 D4
Great Innings S. Wat St SG14 ..... 70 D3
Great Lawne. Dat SG3 .... 69 D2
Great Ley. Wel G C AL7 .... 110 E4
Great Meadow. Lo Naz EN10 ..... 135 A1
Great Molewood. Hert SG14 ...... 92 B1
Great North Rd. Barn EN5 .... 171 E5
Great North Rd. Bro Pk AL9,EN6 145 B5
Great North Rd. Hat AL8 .... 110 A4
Great North Rd. Hat AL9 .... 130 C5
Great North Rd. Newn SG7 .... 12 D4
Great North Rd. Stot SG5 .... 3 A2
Great North Rd. Wel G C AL8 .... 110 A7
Great North Rd. Welw AL6 .... 89 E7
Great Palmers. Heml H HP2 ...... 124 F8
Great Pk. Kin L WD4 .... 139 A1
Great Plumtree. Harl CM20 .... 118 B2
Great Rd. Heml H HP2 .... 124 F4
Great Slades. Pot B EN6 .... 158 F6
Great Sturgess Rd. Heml H HP1 . 123 F3
Great Whites Rd. Heml H HP3 ... 124 F1
Great Wood City Pk. Cuf 146 B5
Greatfield Cl. Harp AL5 .... 85 C4
Greatham Rd. Watf WD2 .... 167 D6
Green Acres. Lily LU2 .... 32 D2
Green Acres. Stev SG2 .... 51 C1
Green Acres. Wel G C AL7 .... 110 F3
Green Bushes. Luton LU4 .... 44 D6
Green Cl. Bro Pk AL9 .... 144 E5
Green Cl. Ches EN8 .... 162 E8
Green Cl. Luton LU4 .... 44 C5
Green Cl. Stev SG2 .... 50 F2
Green Croft. Hat AL10 .... 130 A8
Green Cl. Luton LU4 .... 44 B5
Green Dell Way. Heml H HP3 .... 125 C3
Green Drift. Royst SG8 .... 7 C7
Green Edge. Watf WD2 .... 154 A4
Green End Gdns. Heml H HP1 .... 124 A2
Green End La. Heml H HP1 .... 123 F2
Green End Rd. Heml H HP1 .... 124 A2
Green End. Welw AL6 .... 89 B4
Green Hill. Brag SG11 .... 55 F7
Green La. Ashw SG7 .... 4 E5
Green La. Bov HP3 .... 137 A3
Green La. Brag SG11 .... 55 F7
Green La. Cro Gr WD3 .... 165 F6
Green La. Heml H HP2 .... 125 D4
Green La. Hit SG4 .... 22 B1
Green La. Ken Co LU6 .... 82 E8
Green La. Lat HP5 .... 150 C6
Green La. Letw SG6 .... 23 C8
Green La. Lo Naz EN10 .... 149 B8
Green La. Luton LU2 .... 46 C7
Green La. Mark AL3 .... 83 F5
Green La. Norwd HA6 .... 174 A3
Green La. Pit LU7 .... 80 D5
Green La. St Alb AL1 .... 142 A7
Green La. St Alb AL1 .... 127 D7
Green La. Watf WD1 .... 167 C2
Green La. Wel G C AL7 .... 111 D5
Green Lane Cl. Harp AL5 .... 107 E8
Green Lanes. Hat AL10 .... 109 F2
Green Lanes Sch. Hat 109 F1
Green Leys Cotts. Stand SG11 ..... 55 F7
Green Meadow. Pot B EN6 .... 145 A1
Green Oaks. Luton LU2 .... 45 F3
Green Path. Ast Cl HP22 .... 99 D4
Green St. Chor WD3 .... 164 C6
Green St. Royst SG8 .... 7 D8
Green St. Shen WD7 .... 157 A3

Green St. Stev SG1 .... 50 C7
Green The. Bis St CM23 .... 76 A4
Green The. Ched LU7 .... 80 A7
Green The. Ches EN8 .... 148 C3
Green The. Cod SG4 .... 67 F1
Green The. Kim SG4 .... 65 C3
Green The. Kim SG4 .... 66 D1
Green The. Kneb SG3 .... 68 C5
Green The. Luton LU4 .... 44 C5
Green The. Newn SG7 .... 12 E7
Green The. Pit LU7 .... 80 D4
Green The. Royst SG8 .... 7 D6
Green The. Sar WD3 .... 152 A3
Green The. Stot SG5 .... 11 F7
Green The. Ware SG12 .... 93 D3
Green The. Wel G C AL7 .... 111 A4
Green The. Welw AL6 .... 89 B7
Green Vale. Wel G C AL7 .... 111 A5
Green View Cl. Bov HP3 .... 137 A3
Green Way Gdns. Har HA3 .... 176 E1
Green Way The. Har HA3 .... 176 E2
Greenacre Cl. Barn EN5 .... 158 F1
Greenacres. Bus WD2 .... 176 D8
Greenacres. Heml H HP2 .... 125 D2
Greenacres. Pit LU7 .... 80 C4
Greenall Cl. Ches EN8 .... 148 E1
Greenbank. Ches EN8 .... 148 B3
Greenbank Rd. Watf WD1 .... 153 D3
Greenbury Cl. Bar SG8 .... 8 F1
Greenbury Cl. Chor WD3 .... 164 C5
Greencoates. Hert SG13 .... 113 E5
Greene Field Rd. Berk HP4 .... 122 C4
Greene Wlk. Berk HP4 .... 122 D3
Greenfield Ave. Sth Ox WD1 ..... 175 E8
Greenfield. Hat AL10 .... 130 D6
Greenfield La. Ick SG5 .... 21 E4
Greenfield Rd. Stev SG1 .... 50 E7
Greenfield. Royst SG8 .... 7 B7
Greenfield St. Wa Aby EN9 ...... 163 C1
Greenfield. Wel G C AL8 .... 89 D1
Greenfields. Cuf EN6 .... 146 E1
Greenfields Jun Mix Inf Sch.
Sth Ox 175 C5
Greenfields. Sta M CM24 .... 59 E7
Greengate. Luton LU3 .... 44 C8
Greenheys Cl. Norwd HA6 .... 174 E2
Greenhill Ave. Luton LU2 .... 45 E3
Greenhill Cres. Watf WD1 .... 166 E3
Greenhill Ct. Heml H HP1 .... 124 B2
Greenhill Pk. Bis St CM23 .... 76 D5
Greenhills Cl. Ric WD3 .... 165 B4
Greenland Rd. Barn EN5 .... 171 C3
Greenlands. Bor NW7 .... 170 D3
Greenline Ind Est. Letw 23 C7
Greenriggs. Luton LU2 .... 46 F2
Greenside. Bor WD6 .... 157 A1
Greenside Sch. Stev 51 B2
Greensleeves Cl. St Alb AL4 ...... 128 C2
Greenstead. Saw CM21 .... 97 E1
Greensward. Bus WD2 .... 168 B3
Greenway. Berk HP4 .... 122 A5
Greenway City Prim Sch. Berk ... 121 F4
Greenway. Harp AL5 .... 107 E8
Greenway. Heml H HP2 .... 125 B3
Greenway. Letw SG6 .... 23 A2
Greenway. Pnr HA5 .... 175 B1
Greenway The. Enf EN3 .... 162 A4
Greenway The. Pot B EN6 .... 159 A6
Greenway The. Ric WD3 .... 165 A2
Greenway The. Tri HP23 .... 99 F5
Greenway. Walk SG2 .... 52 B8
Greenways. Abb L WD5 .... 153 E7
Greenways. Bun SG9 .... 40 D3
Greenways. Gofs O EN7 .... 147 B2
Greenways. Hert SG14 .... 113 B6
Greenways. Luton LU2 .... 46 B5
Greenways. Stev SG1 .... 50 E6
Greenwood Ave. Ches EN7 .... 162 B8
Greenwood Cl. Ches EN7 .... 162 A4
Greenwood Dr. Watf WD2 .... 154 B5
Greenwood Park L Ctr. Chis 141 B6
Greenyard. Wa Aby EN9 .... 163 C6
Greer Rd. Har HA3 .... 176 C4
Gregories Cl. Luton LU3 .... 45 D1
Gregory Ave. Pot B EN6 .... 159 C6
Gregson Cl. Bor WD6 .... 170 C8
Grenadier Cl. St Alb AL4 .... 128 C4
Grenadine Cl. Ham St EN7 .... 147 F4
Grenadine Way. Tri HP23 .... 100 A5
Greneway Sch The. Royst 7 E7
Grenville Ave. Hod EN10 .... 134 F2
Grenville Cl. Ches EN8 .... 162 D7
Grenville Cl. Chor WD3 .... 164 C5
Gresford Cl. St Alb AL4 .... 128 C3
Gresham Cl. Luton LU2 .... 64 D8
Gresham Cl. Berk HP4 .... 122 B3
Gresley Cl. Wel G C AL8 .... 110 E8
Gresley Ct. Enf EN1 .... 162 C4
Gresley Ct. Pot B EN6 .... 145 C1
Gresley Way. Stev SG1 .... 51 D5
Greville Cl. Wel G AL9 .... 144 C7
Grey House The. Watf WD1 ...... 167 A7
Greycaine Rd. Watf WD2 .... 154 D2
Greydells Rd. Stev SG1 .... 50 E6
Greyfriars La. Harp AL5 .... 107 A7
Greyfriars. Ware SG12 .... 93 B3
Greyhound La. Pot B EN6 .... 158 A6
Greystoke Cl. Berk HP4 .... 122 A4
Griffiths Way. St Alb AL1 .... 127 C1
Grimaldi Ave. Luton LU3 .... 45 A3
Grimsdyke Cres. Barn EN5 .... 171 C6
Grimsdyke Fst & Mid Sch. Pnr ... 175 F4
Grimsdyke Lodge. St Alb AL1 .... 128 A3
Grimsdyke Rd. Pnr HA5 .... 175 E3
Grimsdyke Rd. Wigg HP23 .... 100 A3
Grimston Rd. St Alb AL1 .... 127 F2
Grimstone Rd. L Wym SG4 .... 35 C5
Grimthorpe Cl. St Alb AL3 .... 127 D6
Grindcobbe Cl. St Alb AL1 .... 141 D8
Grinstead La. Harl CM22 .... 98 C6
Groom Rd. Ches EN10 .... 148 F5
Grooms Cotts. Bot HP5 .... 136 B1
Groomsby Dr. Pit LU7 .... 80 E5
Grosvenor Ave. Abb L WD4 ...... 139 C3

Grosvenor Cl. Bis St CM23 .... 76 D4
Grosvenor Ct. Cro Gr WD3 .... 166 D4
Grosvenor House. Bis St CM23 .... 77 B8
Grosvenor Rd. Bal SG7 .... 12 F1
Grosvenor Rd. Bor WD6 .... 170 B6
Grosvenor Rd. Hod EN10 .... 134 F3
Grosvenor Rd. Luton LU3 .... 45 B5
Grosvenor Rd. Mo Pk HA6 .... 174 F5
Grosvenor Rd W. Bal SG7 .... 12 F1
Grosvenor Rd. St Alb AL1 .... 127 E2
Grosvenor Rd W. Bal SG7 .... 12 F1
Grosvenor Rd. Watf WD1 .... 167 C6
Grosvenor Terr. Heml H HP1 .... 124 A2
Grotto Rd. Ware SG12 .... 114 D8
Ground La. Hat AL10 .... 130 B7
Grove Ave. Harp AL5 .... 107 C7
Grove Cotts. Bus WD2 .... 168 A3
Grove Cres. Cro Gr WD3 .... 166 A5
Grove Ct. Barn EN5 .... 171 F6
Grove Ct. Wa Aby EN9 .... 163 B6
Grove End. Luton LU1 .... 63 B5
Grove Farm Pk. Mo Pk HA6 .... 174 D5
Grove Gdns. Enf EN3 .... 162 D1
Grove Gdns. Tri HP23 .... 100 B5
Grove Hall Rd. Watf WD2 .... 167 E5
Grove Hill. Sta M CM24 .... 59 E2
Grove House. Bus WD2 .... 167 F3
Grove House. Ches EN7 .... 148 B1
Grove La. Ash Gr HP5 .... 136 B5
Grove Lea. Hat AL10 .... 130 A2
Grove Mead. Hat AL10 .... 129 F5
Grove Meadow. Wel G C AL7 .... 111 C6
Grove Mill La. Sar WD1 .... 153 C1
Grove Park Rd. Cad LU1 .... 63 B3
Grove Path. Ches EN7 .... 162 A8
Grove Pk. Tri HP23 .... 100 C5
Grove Pl. Bis St CM23 .... 76 F7
Grove Pl. Wel G AL9 .... 144 C7
Grove Rd. Bor WD6 .... 170 A4
Grove Rd. Cad LU1 .... 63 B2
Grove Rd. Harp AL5 .... 107 D7
Grove Rd. Heml H HP1 .... 124 A1
Grove Rd. Hit SG4,SG5 .... 21 F1
Grove Rd. Luton LU1 .... 63 D7
Grove Rd. Norwd HA6 .... 174 D5
Grove Rd. Ric WD3 .... 173 A8
Grove Rd. St Alb AL1 .... 127 D2
Grove Rd. Stev SG1 .... 50 D7
Grove Rd. Tri HP23 .... 100 C5
Grove Rd W. Enf EN3 .... 162 C2
Grove Rd. Ware SG12 .... 93 F2
Grove Road Inf Sch. Tri 100 C5
Grove Road Jun Sch. Tri 100 C5
Grove The. Bro Pk AL9 .... 145 A4
Grove The. Gt Ha CM22 .... 77 F4
Grove The. L Had SG11 .... 75 E7
Grove The. Lat HP5 .... 150 D3
Grove The. Luton LU1 .... 63 B5
Grove The. Pot B EN6 .... 159 C7
Grove The. Radl WD7 .... 156 A5
Grove The. Tri HP23 .... 100 C5
Grove Way. Chor WD3 .... 164 B4
Grove Wlk. Hert SG14 .... 113 C8
Grovebury Gdns. Chis AL2 .... 141 C4
Grovedale Cl. Ches EN7 .... 147 F1
Groveland Way. Stot SG5 .... 12 A5
Grovelands Ave. Hit SG4 .... 22 C2
Grovelands. Chis AL2 .... 141 B4
Grovelands. Heml H HL2 .... 125 C5
Grover Cl. Heml H HP2 .... 124 D4
Grover Rd. Watf WD1 .... 167 D3
Grovewood Cl. Chor WD3 .... 164 C4
Grubbs Cl. Hat AL9 .... 145 C8
Grubs La. Hat AL9 .... 131 A1
Guardian Ind Est. Luton 63 C8
Guernsey Cl. Dun LU4 .... 44 A3
Guernsey House. Enf EN3 .... 162 D1
Guessens Ct. Wel G C AL8 .... 110 C6
Guessens Gr. Wel G C AL8 .... 110 C6
Guessens Rd. Wel G C AL8 .... 110 C6
Guessens Wlk. Wel G C AL8 .... 110 C7
Guilden Morden Sch. Gu M 1 F5
Guildford Rd. St Alb AL1 .... 128 B2
Guildford St. Luton LU1 .... 63 E7
Guilfords The. Harl CM17 .... 118 D5
Guinevere Gdns. Ches EN8 .... 148 E8
Gulland Cl. Bus WD2 .... 168 C4
Gullbrook. Heml H HP1 .... 124 A3
Gullet Wood Rd. Watf WD2 .... 154 A4
Gulphs The. Hert SG13 .... 113 D5
Gun La. Kneb SG3 .... 68 F4
Gun Meadow Ave. Kneb SG3 .... 69 A4
Gun Rd. Kneb SG3 .... 69 A4
Gun Road Gdns. Kneb SG3 .... 68 F4
Gunnels Wood Ind Est. Stev 50 D3
Gunnels Wood Rd. Stev SG1 .... 50 B5
Gurney Court Rd. St Alb AL1 .... 127 F5
Gurney's La. Hol SG5 .... 21 F3
Gwent Cl. Watf WD2 .... 154 D5
Gwynfa Cl. Welw AL6 .... 89 D7
Gwynne Cl. Tri HP23 .... 100 A5
Gwynns Wlk. Hert SG13 .... 113 E6
Gyfford Wlk. Ches EN7 .... 162 B8
Gypsy La. Gt Am SG12 .... 114 F4
Gypsy La. Abb L WD4 .... 153 D5
Gypsy La. St Alb AL1 .... 128 E7
Gypsy La. Hat AL7 .... 110 F1

Haberdashers' Aske's Sch The.
  Radl 169 B6
Hackford Cl. Barn EN5 .... 171 B4
Hackney Cl. Bor WD6 .... 170 D4
Haddon Cl. Bor WD6 .... 170 A4
Haddon Cl. Heml H HP3 .... 125 A2
Haddon Cl. Stev SG2 .... 69 C7
Haddon Ct. Harp AL5 .... 86 B1
Haddon Cl. Chor WD3 .... 164 C4
Haddon Rd. Luton LU2 .... 63 F8
Hadham Cl. Bis St CM23 .... 76 D8
Hadham Rd. L Had SG11 .... 57 F1
Hadham Rd. Stand SG11 .... 55 F1
Hadleigh Ct. Hod EN10 .... 134 F1
Hadleigh Cl. Whea AL5 .... 107 F6
Hadleigh. Letw SG6 .... 23 B4
Hadley Bourne (St Martha's
  Convent Sch). Barn 171 F8
Hadley Cl. Bor WD6 .... 169 F3
Hadley Ct. Luton LU3 .... 45 D1

Hadley Gn. Barn EN5 .... 171 F7
Hadley Gn W. Barn EN5 .... 171 F7
Hadley Gr. Barn EN5 .... 171 E7
Hadley Green Rd. Barn EN5 .... 171 F7
Hadley Highstone. Barn EN5 .... 171 F8
Hadley Rd. Had W EN2,EN4 .... 160 D1
Hadley Ridge. Barn EN5 .... 171 F6
Hadley Wood Jun Mix Inf Sch.
  Had W 159 C1
Hadlow Down Cl. Luton LU3 .... 45 A5
Hadrain Cl. St Alb AL3 .... 127 A1
Hadrian Way. Letw SG7 .... 23 D7
Hadrians Wlk. Stev SG1 .... 51 C8
Hadwell Cl. Stev SG2 .... 51 A3
Hagdell Rd. Luton LU1 .... 63 C5
Hagden La. Watf WD1 .... 167 A4
Haggerston Rd. Bor WD6 .... 156 E1
Hagsdell Rd. Hert SG13 .... 113 D5
Haig Cl. St Alb AL1 .... 128 B3
Haig House. St Alb AL1 .... 128 B2
Hailey Ave. Hod EN11 .... 115 A2
Hailey Hall Sch. Hol 114 F2
Hailey La. Hert H SG13 .... 114 A3
Hailey La. Hod SG13 .... 114 C2
Haileybury Coll. Hert H 114 D2
Haines Way. Watf WD2 .... 154 A5
Haldens House. Wel G C 3 AL7 .... 89 F1
Haldens. Wel G C AL7 .... 89 F1
Hale La. St Le HP22 .... 119 A3
Hale Rd. Hert SG13 .... 113 D5
Hales Meadow. Harp AL5 .... 86 A2
Hales Park Cl. Heml H HP2 .... 125 C4
Hales Pk. Heml H HP2 .... 125 C4
Haleswood Rd. Heml H HP2 .... 125 B4
Half Acres. Bis St CM23 .... 76 F8
Half Moon La. Cad LU1 .... 63 C1
Half Moon Meadow. Heml H HP2 ..... 125 C4
Half Moon Mews. St Alb AL1 .... 127 D3
Halfacre La. Ches EN8 .... 29 A1
Halfhide La. Ches EN8 .... 148 D5
Halfhides. Wa Aby EN9 .... 163 D6
Halfway Ave. Luton LU4 .... 44 D1
Halifax Rd. Chor WD3 .... 164 C6
Halifax Way. Wel G C AL7 .... 111 C6
Hall Cl. Ric WD3 .... 165 A1
Hall Cotts. Gt Ho SG9 .... 29 A1
Hall Dr. Hare UB9 .... 173 C2
Hall Gdns. Col H AL4 .... 143 D8
Hall Gr. Wel G C AL7 .... 111 B4
Hall Heath Cl. St Alb AL1 .... 128 B5
Hall La. Gt Ho SG9 .... 29 A1
Hall La. Gt Ho SG8 .... 9 F7
Hall La. Kim SG4 .... 87 C8
Hall La. Welw SG3 .... 69 A2
Hall Mead. Letw SG6 .... 22 B6
Hall Park Gate. Berk HP4 .... 122 E3
Hall Park Hill. Berk HP4 .... 122 E3
Hall Pk. Berk HP4 .... 122 E3
Hall Place Cl. St Alb AL1 .... 127 E4
Hall Place Gdns. St Alb AL1 .... 127 E4
Hall Rd. Heml H HP2 .... 125 B5
Hallam Cl. Watf WD1 .... 167 C7
Hallam Gdns. Pnr HA5 .... 175 E3
Halland Way. Norwd HA6 .... 174 D4
Halleys Ridge. Hert SG14 .... 113 A5
Halling Hall. Harl CM20 .... 117 F2
Hallingbury Cl. L Hal CM22 .... 77 B1
Hallingbury Rd. Bis St CM23 .... 77 B4
Hallingbury Rd. Gt Ha CM22 .... 77 B4
Hallingbury Rd. L Hal CM21 .... 98 A4
Hallmores. Hod EN10 .... 135 A4
Hallowell Rd. Norwd HA6 .... 174 D3
Hallowes Cres. Sth Ox WD1 .... 175 A7
Halls Cl. Welw AL6 .... 89 C4
Hallside Rd. Enf EN1 .... 161 F1
Hallwicks Rd. Luton LU2 .... 46 B3
Hallworth Dr. Stot SG5 .... 11 E6
Hallworth House. Stot SG5 .... 11 E6
Halsey Dr. Hit SG4 .... 35 B7
Halsey Pk. Lon C AL2 .... 142 F4
Halsey Pl. Watf WD2 .... 154 B1
Halsey Rd. Watf WD1 .... 167 B6
Halstead Hill. Gofs O EN7 .... 147 E1
Halter Cl. Bor WD6 .... 170 D4
Haltside. Hat AL10 .... 129 E4
Halwick Cl. Heml H HP1 .... 124 B1
Halyard Cl. Luton LU3 .... 45 B6
Halyard High Sch. Dun 44 A3
Hamberlins La. Nthch HP4 .... 121 C7
Hamble Cl. Watf WD1 .... 167 A5
Hambridge Way. Pirt SG5 .... 20 D4
Hambro Cl. Nwml E LU2 .... 85 F7
Hamburgh Cres. Chess EN8 .... 148 D3
Hamels Dr. Hert SG13 .... 114 B7
Hamer Cl. Bov HP3 .... 137 A3
Hamilton Ave. Hod EN11 .... 135 A8
Hamilton Cl. Bri Wd AL2 .... 140 F8
Hamilton Cl. Ridge EN6 .... 158 A6
Hamilton Ct. Hal AL1 .... 130 B3
Hamilton Mead. Bov HP3 .... 137 A4
Hamilton Rd. Abb L WD4 .... 153 C6
Hamilton Rd. Berk HP4 .... 122 B4
Hamilton Rd. St Alb AL1 .... 128 C6
Hamilton Rd. Sth Ox WD1 .... 175 B7
Hamilton St. Watf WD1 .... 167 C4
Hamlet The. Pot En HP4 .... 138 A4
Hammarskjold Rd. Harl CM20 .... 117 D2
Hammer La. Heml H HP2 .... 124 F4
Hammers Gate. Chis AL2 .... 141 A5
Hammond Cl. Ham St EN7 .... 147 F5
Hammond Cl. Stev SG1 .... 50 D6
Hammond Ct. Cad LU1 .... 63 C1
Hammond Jun Mix Inf Sch The.
  Heml H 124 F6
Hammonds La. Sand AL4 .... 109 B3
Hammondstreet Rd. Ham St EN7 ..... 147 F6
Hammondswick. Harp AL5 .... 106 F4
Hamonte. Letw SG6 .... 23 C4
Hampden La. Letw SG6 .... 23 B8
Hampden Cres. Ches EN7 .... 148 B1
Hampden Hill Cl. Ware SG12 .... 93 F2
Hampden Hill. Ware SG12 .... 93 F2
Hampden. Kim SG4 .... 66 C1
Hampden Pl. Lon C AL2 .... 141 E2
Hampden Rd. Har HA3 .... 176 C1
Hampden Rd. Hit SG4 .... 22 C1
Hampden Way. Watf WD1 .... 153 E3
Hampermill La. Watf WD1 .... 167 A1
Hampton Cl. Stev SG2 .... 69 C7
Hampton Gdns. Saw CM21 .... 118 C7

Hampton Rd. Luton LU4 .... 63 B8
Hamstel Rd. Harl CM20 .... 117 C1
Hanaper Dr. Bar SG8 .... 8 F2
Hanbury Cl. Ches EN8 .... 148 D2
Hanbury Cl. Ware SG12 .... 93 D1
Hanbury Cotts. Ess AL9 .... 131 A5
Hanbury Dr. Thun SG12 .... 93 C6
Hanbury Mews. Thun SG12 .... 93 C6
Hancock Cl. Bor WD6 .... 170 C8
Hancock Dr. Luton LU2 .... 45 E1
Hancroft Rd. Heml H HP3 .... 124 F1
Hand La. Saw CM21 .... 97 C1
Handa Cl. Heml H HP3 .... 139 B8
Handcross Rd. Luton LU2 .... 46 D2
Handside Cl. Wel G C AL8 .... 110 C6
Handside Gn. Wel G C AL8 .... 110 C7
Handside La. Wel G C AL8 .... 110 C6
Handsworth Cl. Sth Ox WD1 .... 175 A7
Hangar Ruding. Sth Ox WD1 .... 175 F7
Hanger Cl. Heml H HP1 .... 123 F4
Hanger's Wood Sch. Sth Ox 175 B7
Hangmans Cl. Stew AL6 .... 89 D7
Hanover Cl. Stev SG2 .... 50 F1
Hanover Ct. Cro Gr WD3 .... 166 A3
Hanover Ct. Luton LU4 .... 44 D5
Hanover Gdns. Abb L WD5 .... 139 F1
Hanover Gn. Heml H HP1 .... 124 A1
Hanover Wlk. Hat AL10 .... 130 A3
Hanscombe End Rd. Shil SG5 .... 19 D7
Hanselin Cl. Stan HA7 .... 176 F5
Hanswick Cl. Luton LU2 .... 46 B2
Hanworth Cl. Luton LU2 .... 45 D7
Hanyards End. Cuf EN6 .... 146 A3
Hanyards La. Cuf EN6 .... 146 D3
Happy Valley Ind Pk. Kin L 139 B2
Harbell Cl. Hert SG13 .... 114 B6
Harborne Cl. Sth Ox WD1 .... 175 C5
Harbury Dell. Luton LU3 .... 45 B7
Harcourt Rd. Bus WD2 .... 168 C4
Harcourt St. Luton LU1 .... 44 E7
Harding Cl. Red AL3 .... 106 A5
Harding Cl. Watf WD2 .... 154 C6
Harding Par. Harp AL5 .... 86 B1
Hardings. Wel G C AL7 .... 111 C7
Hardingstone Ct. Ches EN8 .... 162 F5
Hardwick Cl. Stev SG2 .... 69 C7
Hardwick Gn. Luton LU3 .... 45 A5
Hardwick Pl. Lon C AL2 .... 142 D4
Hardy Cl. Barn EN5 .... 171 E4
Hardy Cl. Hit SG4 .... 35 C7
Hardy Dr. Royst SG8 .... 7 D8
Hardy Rd. Heml H HP2 .... 124 F4
Hare Cres. Watf WD2 .... 154 A7
Hare St. Hat AL10 .... 130 B3
Hareball. Wel G C AL7 .... 110 E3
Harebreaks The. Watf WD2 .... 154 A2
Harefield Ct. Luton LU1 .... 62 F8
Harefield. Harl CM20 .... 118 A1
Harefield Inf Sch. Hare 173 C2
Harefield Jun Sch. Hare 173 C2
Harefield Pl. St Alb AL4 .... 128 D6
Harefield Rd. Luton LU1 .... 62 F8
Harefield Rd. Ric WD3 .... 173 D7
Harefield. Stev SG2 .... 51 C3
Harepark Cl. Heml H HP1 .... 123 F4
Harewood Rd. Sth Ox WD1 .... 175 B7
Harewood. Ric WD3 .... 165 C4
Harford Dr. Watf WD1 .... 166 E3
Hargrave Cl. Har HA3 .... 176 C1
Hargrave Ave. Ches EN7 .... 162 B8
Hargreaves Cl. Ches EN7 .... 162 B8
Hargreaves Rd. Royst SG8 .... 7 D5
Harkett Cl. Har HA3 .... 176 F1
Harkness. Ches EN8 .... 148 B2
Harkness Ct. Hit SG4 .... 22 B1
Harkness Way. Hit SG4 .... 22 C2
Harlequin The. Watf WD1 .... 167 C5
Harlesden Rd. St Alb AL1 .... 128 A3
Harlestone Cl. Luton LU3 .... 31 A1
Harley Ct. St Alb AL4 .... 128 D7
Harlings The. Hert SG13 .... 114 C2
Harlow Coll. Harl 117 C1
Harlow Ct. Heml H HP2 .... 125 A7
Harlow Mill Sta. Harl 118 C5
Harlow Rd. Roy CM19 .... 116 C1
Harlow Rd. Saw CM21 .... 118 C8
Harlow Sport Ctr. Harl 117 D2
Harlow The Spinney
Cty Jun & Inf Sch. Harl 118 A1
Harlow Town Sta. Harl 118 A4
Harlowbury Cty Prim Sch. Harl ... 118 D4
Harlton Cl. Wa Aby EN9 .... 163 F5
Harmer Dell. Welw AL6 .... 89 F4
Harmer Green La. Welw AL6 .... 90 B5
Harmony Cl. Hat AL10 .... 130 A7
Harmsworth Way. Barn N20 .... 171 F1
Harness Way. St Alb AL4 .... 128 C6
Harold Cres. Wa Aby EN9 .... 163 C7
Harpenden Central Sta. Harp 86 B1
Harpenden Hospl. Harp 86 A4
Harpenden La. Red AL3 .... 106 B6
Harpenden Memorial Hospl. Harp . 86 A4
Harpenden Rd. Whea AL4 .... 108 B8
Harpenden Rise. Harp AL5 .... 85 F3
Harper Ct. Stev SG1 .... 50 F5
Harper La. Lon C WD7,AL2 .... 156 B8
Harperbury Hospl. Lon C 156 C8
Harps Hill. Mark AL3 .... 83 E5
Harpsfield Broadway. Hat AL10 .... 129 F6
Harptree Way. St Alb AL1 .... 128 A5
Harrington Cl. Bis St CM23 .... 77 A7
Harrington Ct. Hert H SG13 .... 114 C3
Harris La. Gt Of SG5 .... 33 D2
Harris La. Shen WD7 .... 157 A6
Harris Rd. Watf WD2 .... 154 A4
Harris's La. Ware SG12 .... 93 C1
Harrison Cl. Hit SG4 .... 34 F7
Harrison Cl. Norwd HA6 .... 174 D4
Harrisons. Birhr CM23 .... 59 D1
Harrogate Rd. Sth Ox WD1 .... 175 C7
Harrow Coll of F Ed. Pnr 176 A3
Harrow Cl. Stev SG1 .... 50 E5
Harrow View. Har HA2 .... 176 C1

Harrow Way. Sth Ox WD1 .... 175 E6
Harrow Weald Pk. Stan HA3 .... 176 D4
Harrow Weald Sixth Form Coll.
  Stan 176 E4
Harrow Yd. Tri HP23 .... 100 A3
Harrowden Rd. Luton LU2 .... 64 C8
Harrowden Rd. Luton LU2 .... 64 C8
Harrowdene. Stev SG2 .... 51 C4
Harry Scott Ct. Luton LU4 .... 44 C6
Hart Hill Dr. Luton LU2 .... 46 A1
Hart Hill Jun & Inf Sch. Luton .. 63 F8
Hart Hill La. Luton LU2 .... 46 A1
Hart Lodge. Barn EN5 .... 171 A6
Hart Rd. Harl CM17 .... 118 C6
Hart Rd. St Alb AL1 .... 127 D2
Hart Wlk. Luton LU2 .... 46 A1
Hartfield Cl. Bor WD6 .... 170 A4
Hartfield Ct. Ware SG12 .... 93 D2
Hartforde Rd. Bor WD6 .... 170 B8
Harthall La. Abb L WD4,WD5 .... 139 F4
Hartham La. Hert SG14 .... 113 D6
Hartland Rd. Ches EN8 .... 148 C5
Hartley Rd. Luton LU2 .... 63 F8
Hartmoor Mews. Enf EN3 .... 162 D2
Harts Cl. Bus WD2 .... 168 A8
Hartsbourne Cl. Bus WD2 .... 176 D8
Hartsbourne Country Club. Bus 176 D8
Hartsbourne Jun Mix Inf Sch. Bus 176 D8
Hartsbourne Rd. Bus WD2 .... 176 D8
Hartsbourne Way. Heml H HP2 ...... 125 C2
Hartsfield Jun Mix Inf Sch. Bal ... 12 F1
Hartsfield Rd. Luton LU2 .... 46 B2
Hartspring La. Bus WD2 .... 168 A8
Hartswood Gn. Bus WD2 .... 176 D8
Hartwell Gdns. Harp AL5 .... 85 E1
Hartwood. Luton LU2 .... 63 F8
Harvest Cl. Dun LU4 .... 44 A3
Harvest Ct. St Alb AL4 .... 128 D2
Harvest End. Watf WD2 .... 154 D3
Harvest Mead. Hat AL10 .... 130 B7
Harvest Rd. Bus WD2 .... 168 B5
Harvey Rd. Cro Gr WD3 .... 166 A3
Harvey Rd. Lon C AL2 .... 142 C5
Harvey Rd. Stev SG2 .... 51 B6
*Harvey Road Jun Mid Inf Sch.
  Cro Gr* 166 A3
Harvey's Hill. Luton LU2 .... 45 F5
Harveyfields. Wa Aby EN9 .... 163 C5
Harveys Cotts. L Had SG11 .... 75 F8
Harwood Cl. Tewin AL6 .... 90 E2
Harwood Cl. Wel G C AL8 .... 89 E2
*Harwood Hill Jun Mix Inf Sch.
  Wel G C* 89 E2
Harwood Hill. Wel G C AL8 .... 89 F3
Harwoods Rd. Watf WD1 .... 167 A5
Hasedines Rd. Heml H HP1 .... 124 A3
Haseldine Meadows. Hat AL10 ...... 129 F4
Haseldine Rd. Lon C AL2 .... 142 D5
Haselfoot. Letw SG6 .... 22 E6
Hasketon Dr. Luton LU4 .... 44 B6
Haslemere. Bis St CM23 .... 77 A4
Haslemere Ind Est. Wel G C 110 F7
Haslewood Jun Sch. Hod 135 A6
Haslingden Cl. Harp AL5 .... 85 D3
Hassobury Waterside Sch. Far 58 F7
Haste Hill Golf Course. Norwd 174 E1
Hastings Cl. Stev SG1 .... 50 A8
Hastings Cl. Luton LU1 .... 63 D6
Hastings Way. Cro Gr WD3 .... 166 C5
Hastings Way. Watf WD2 .... 167 E5
Hastoe La. Tri HP23 .... 100 A4
Hatch End High Sch. Har 176 B2
Hatch End Sta. Pnr 176 A3
Hatch Gn. L Hal CM22 .... 98 B8
Hatch La. Wes SG4 .... 24 A3
Hatching Green Cl. Harp AL5 ...... 107 A4
Hatfield Aerodrome. Hat 129 D6
Hatfield Ave. Hat AL10 .... 129 E8
Hatfield Bsns Ctr. Hat 129 E8
Hatfield Cres. Heml H HP2 .... 124 F4
Hatfield Rd. Coln H AL4 .... 128 C3
Hatfield Rd. Ess SG14 .... 111 E1
Hatfield Rd. Hertng SG14 .... 112 B4
Hatfield Rd. Pot B EN6 .... 159 C8
Hatfield Rd. St Alb AL1,AL4 .... 128 C3
Hatfield Rd. Watf WD2 .... 167 B8
Hatfield Sch. Wel Gr 130 B1
Hatfield Sta. Hat 130 C6
Hatfield Tunnel. Hat AL10 .... 129 F6
Hathaway Cl. Dun LU4 .... 44 B2
Hathaway Ct. Coln H AL4 .... 128 E3
Hatherleigh Gdns. Pot B EN6 ...... 159 B7
Hatters La. Watf WD1 .... 166 F3
Hatters Way. Luton LU1,LU4 .... 63 B8
Hatton Rd. Ches EN8 .... 148 D2
Havelock Cl. Kin L WD4 .... 138 F3
Havelock Rd. Luton LU2 .... 45 E1
Havelock Rise. Luton LU2 .... 45 E1
Haven Cl. Hat AL10 .... 129 F6
Havencroft Cl. St Alb AL3 .... 127 C1
Haverdale. Luton LU4 .... 44 C4
Havers La. Bis St CM23 .... 76 F5
Havers Par. Bis St CM23 .... 76 F5
Haward Rd. Hod EN11 .... 135 C8
Hawbush Cl. Welw AL6 .... 89 B4
Hawbush Rise. Welw AL6 .... 89 B5
Hawes Cl. Norwd HA6 .... 174 F3
Hawes La. Wa Aby EN9 .... 163 C1
Haweswater Dr. Watf WD2 .... 154 C6
Hawfield Gdns. Pk St AL2 .... 141 D5
Hawkesworth Cl. Norwd HA6 .... 174 E3
Hawkfield. Letw SG6 .... 22 E8
Hawkfields. Luton LU2 .... 45 E6
Hawkins Cl. Bor WD6 .... 170 C7
Hawkins Hall La. Dat SG3 .... 69 E2
Hawkshead Cl. Ches EN8 .... 162 F5
Hawkshead La. Bro Pk AL9 .... 144 D3
Hawkshead Rd. Pot B EN6 .... 159 B8
Hawkshill Dr. Heml H HP3 .... 137 F8
Hawksmead Cl. Enf EN3 .... 162 D3
Hawksmoor. Shen WD7 .... 157 A6
Hawkwell Dr. Tri HP23 .... 100 C4

Hawridge & Cholesbury C of E
  Combined Sch. Chol 120 E2
Hawridge La. Chol HP5 .... 120 F1
Hawridge Vale. Chol HP5 .... 120 F1
Hawsley Rd. Harp AL5 .... 107 A4
Hawthorn Ave. Luton LU2 .... 46 A8
Hawthorn Cl. Abb L WD5 .... 154 A7
Hawthorn Cl. Harp AL5 .... 107 D7
Hawthorn Cl. Hert SG14 .... 113 C5
Hawthorn Cl. Hit SG5 .... 34 E6
Hawthorn Cl. Royst SG8 .... 7 F7
Hawthorn Cl. Watf WD1 .... 153 F1
Hawthorn Cres. Cad LU1 .... 62 E3
Hawthorn Gr. Enf EN2 .... 161 D5
Hawthorn Hill. Letw SG6 .... 22 F7
Hawthorn Rd. Hod EN11 .... 135 B8
Hawthorn Rd. Radl WD7 .... 156 A5
Hawthornes. Hat AL10 .... 129 F3
Hawthorns The. Berk HP4 .... 122 C3
Hawthorns The. Heml H HP3 .... 137 F7
Hawthorns The. Map Cr WD3 .... 172 D5
Hawthorns The. Stev SG1 .... 51 A4
Hawthorns The. Ware SG12 .... 93 C3
Hawthorns. Wel G C AL8 .... 110 D8
Hawtrees. Radl WD7 .... 155 F4
Hay Cl. Bor WD6 .... 170 C7
Hay La. Harp AL5 .... 86 A1
Haybourn Mead. Heml H HP1 .... 124 B2
Haycroft. Bis St CM23 .... 77 C7
Haycroft Rd. Stev SG1 .... 50 E7
Haydock Rd. Royst SG8 .... 7 F6
Haydon Hill House. Bus WD2 .... 167 F2
Haydon Rd. Watf WD1 .... 167 E3
Hayes Cl. Luton LU2 .... 46 C5
Hayes Wlk. Ches EN10 .... 148 F6
Hayfield Cl. Bus WD2 .... 168 B5
Hayfield. Stev SG2 .... 51 D7
Haygarth. Kneb SG3 .... 69 A4
Hayhurst Dr. Dun LU4 .... 44 B1
Hayley Bell Gdns. Bis St CM23 .... 76 F4
Hayley Comm. Stev SG2 .... 51 C3
Hayling Dr. Luton LU2 .... 46 D3
Hayling Rd. Sth Ox WD1 .... 175 B8
Haymeads La. Bis St CM23 .... 77 C6
Haymeads. Wel G C AL7 .... 89 E1
Haymoor. Letw SG6 .... 22 E7
Haynes Cl. Wel G C AL7 .... 111 A5
Haynes Mead. Berk HP4 .... 122 A6
Haysman Cl. Letw SG6 .... 23 B7
Hayton Cl. Luton LU3 .... 31 B2
Haywood Cl. Pnr HA5 .... 175 D1
Haywood Cl. Wa Aby EN9 .... 163 F5
Haywood La. Ther SG8 .... 16 A6
Haywood Rd. Chor WD3 .... 164 F4
Haywoods Dr. Heml H HP3 .... 137 F8
Haywoods La. Royst SG8 .... 7 E7
Hazel Cl. Ham St EN7 .... 147 E5
Hazel Cl. Welw AL6 .... 89 E3
Hazel Ct. Hat AL4 .... 35 A7
Hazel Gdns. Sheer CM21 .... 97 F1
Hazel Gr. Hat AL10 .... 129 F2
Hazel Gr. Stot SG5 .... 11 E5
Hazel Gr. Watf WD2 .... 154 B4
Hazel Gr. Wel G C AL7 .... 111 C7
Hazel Mead. Barn EN5 .... 171 B4
Hazel Rd. Berk HP4 .... 122 D3
Hazel Rd. Chis AL2 .... 141 B3
Hazel Tree Rd. Watf WD2 .... 154 B3
Hazelbury Ave. Abb L WD5 .... 153 C7
Hazelbury Cres. Luton LU1 .... 63 C8
Hazelcroft. Pnr HA5 .... 176 B4
Hazeldell Link. Heml H HP1 .... 123 E2
Hazeldell Rd. Heml H HP1 .... 123 F2
Hazeldell. Watf St SG14 .... 70 D3
Hazeldene. Ches EN8 .... 162 E7
Hazelend Rd. Bis St CM23 .... 59 B4
Hazelgrove Prim Sch. Hat 129 F2
Hazelmere Rd. St Alb AL4 .... 128 C6
Hazelmere Rd. Stev SG2 .... 69 A8
Hazels The. Tewin AL6 .... 90 E2
Hazelwood Cl. Hit SG5 .... 34 F8
Hazelwood Cl. Luton LU2 .... 46 B4
Hazelwood Dr. Pnr HA5 .... 175 B1
Hazelwood Ct. St Alb AL4 .... 128 C4
Hazelwood Inf Sch. Abb L 153 E8
Hazelwood La. Abb L WD5 .... 153 D7
Hazelwood Rd. Cro Gr WD3 .... 166 C3
Hazely. Tri HP23 .... 100 C4
Heacham Cl. Dun LU4 .... 44 B4
Headingley Cl. Ham St EN7 .... 147 F5
Headingley Cl. Shen WD7 .... 156 F7
Headingley Cl. Stev SG1 .... 50 B8
Headstone La. Har HA2,HA3 .... 176 B2
Headstone Lane Sta. Har 176 B2
Healey Rd. Watf WD1 .... 166 F3
Health Farm La. St Alb AL3 .... 127 E5
Healy Ct. Barn EN5 .... 171 D3
Heath Ave. Royst SG8 .... 7 C6
Heath Ave. St Alb AL3 .... 127 D5
Heath Brow. Heml H HP1 .... 124 A1
Heath Cl. Harp AL5 .... 107 C7
Heath Cl. Heml H HP1 .... 124 C2
Heath Cl. Luton LU1 .... 63 B6
Heath Dr. Pot B EN6 .... 145 B1
Heath Dr. Ware SG12 .... 93 D3
Heath Farm Ct. Sar WD1 .... 153 C2
Heath Hall. Bal 23 F7
Heath Hill. Cod SG4 .... 67 E1
Heath La. Cod SG4 .... 67 E1
Heath La. Heml H HP1 .... 124 C2
Heath La. Hert H SG13 .... 114 C2
Heath Lodge. Bus WD2 .... 168 D1
Heath Mount Sch. Wat St 71 B7
Heath Rd. Bre Gr SG4 .... 47 D1
Heath Rd. St Alb AL1 .... 127 E5
Heath Rd. Watf WD1 .... 167 C2
Heath Rd. Welw AL6 .... 68 F1
Heath Row. Bis St CM23 .... 59 B1
Heath The. Bre Gr SG4 .... 47 D2
Heath The. Radl WD7 .... 156 A6
Heathbourne Rd. Stan WD2,HA7 .. 168 F1

Heathbrow Rd. Welw AL6 .... 89 F8
Heathcote Ave. Hat AL10 .... 130 A7
Heathcote Sch. Stev 51 A2
Heather Cl. Abb L WD5 .... 154 A7
Heather Cl. Bis St CM23 .... 76 D6
Heather Rd. Wel G C AL8 .... 110 C4
Heather Rise. Bus WD2 .... 167 F7
Heather Way. Har HA7 .... 176 F4
Heather Way. Heml H HP2 .... 124 D4
Heather Way. Pot B EN6 .... 158 F7
Heathermere. Letw SG6 .... 11 F1
Heathfield Cl. Cad LU1 .... 62 F4
Heathfield Cl. Pot B EN6 .... 145 B1
Heathfield Cl. St Alb AL1 .... 127 E4
Heathfield Lower Sch. Cad 62 E4
Heathfield Rd. Hit SG5 .... 21 F1
Heathfield Rd. Luton LU3 .... 45 C4
Heathfield. Watf WD2 .... 167 F5
Heathfield. Royst SG8 .... 7 B6
Heathgate. Hert H SG13 .... 114 B2
Heathlands Dr. St Alb AL3 .... 127 C5
Heathlands St. Alb 127 E6
Heathlands. Welw AL6 .... 68 F1
Heathside Cl. Mo Pk HA6 .... 174 D5
Heathside Rd. Mo Pk HA6 .... 174 D6
Heathside. St Alb AL3 .... 127 C5
Heathview. Harp AL5 .... 107 B8
Heaton Ct. St Alb AL1 .... E1
Heaton Dell. Luton LU2 .... 46 E1
Heay Fields. Wel G C AL7 .... 111 C7
Hebden Cl. Dun LU4 .... 44 B4
Hedge Row. Heml H HP1 .... 124 A5
Hedgebrooms. Wel G C AL7 .... 111 C7
Hedgerows. Saw CM21 .... 97 F2
Hedgerows The. Stev SG2 .... 51 D8
Hedges Cl. Hat AL10 .... 130 B6
Hedgeside. Pot En HP4 .... 123 A7
Hedgeside Rd. Norwd HA6 .... 174 C5
Hedley Rd. St Alb AL1 .... 128 B3
Hedley Rise. Luton LU2 .... 46 F2
Hedworth Ave. Ches EN8 .... 162 D6
Heights The. Heml H HP2 .... 124 F6
Heights The. Luton LU3 .... 44 E5
Helena Cl. Had W EN4 .... 159 D1
Helena Pl. Heml H HP2 .... 124 D5   5
Helens Gate. Ches EN8 .... 148 F5
Hellards Rd. Stev SG1 .... 50 D7
Hellebore Ct. Stev SG1 .... 51 B8
Helmsley Ct. Luton LU4 .... 44 C5
Helston Cl. Pnr HA5 .... 175 F3
Helston Gr. Heml H HP2 .... 124 D8
Helston Pl. Abb L WD5 .... 153 F7
Hemel Hempstead General Hospl.
  Heml H 124 D3
Hemel Hempstead Rd.
  Heml H HP3 .... 125 E1
Hemel Hempstead Rd. Red AL3 .... 105 E2
Hemel Hempstead Rd. St Alb AL3 .... 126 D1
Hemel Hempstead Rd. Stu HP4 .... 81 E1
Hemel Hempstead Sta. Heml H 123 E1
Hemel Hempstead Sta. Heml H 138 A8
Hemingford Dr. Luton LU2 .... 45 D6
Hemingford Rd. Watf WD1 .... 153 E3
Hemming Way. Watf WD2 .... 154 A4
Hemmings The. Berk HP4 .... 121 F3
Hemp La. Wigg HP23 .... 100 F1
Hempstall. Wel G C AL7 .... 111 B4
Hempstead Rd. Pot En HP4 .... 123 C6
Hempstead Rd. Abb L WD4 .... 139 A3
Hempstead Rd. Bov HP3 .... 137 B5
Hempstead Rd. Watf WD1 .... 153 E2
Henbury Way. Sth Ox WD1 .... 175 D7
Henderson Cl. St Alb AL3 .... 127 C7
Henderson Pl. Abb L WD5 .... 139 F4
Hendon Wood La. Edge NW1 .... 171 A1
Henge Way. Luton LU3 .... 44 E7
Henry Cl. Enf EN2 .... 161 E1
Henry St. Heml H HP3 .... 138 D7
Henry St. Tri HP23 .... 100 A3
Henrys Grant. St Alb AL1 .... 127 E2
Hensley Cl. Hit SG4 .... 35 B6
Hensley St. Welw AL6 .... 89 C6
Henstead Pl. Luton LU2 .... 46 D1   1
Herald Cl. Bis St CM23 .... 76 E3
Herbert St. Heml H HP2 .... 124 D4
Hereford Rd. Dun LU4 .... 44 A3
Hereward Cl. Wa Aby EN9 .... 163 C7
Herga Ct. Watf WD1 .... 167 A7
Heritage Cl. St Alb AL3 .... 127 D3
Herkomer Cl. Bus WD2 .... 168 B3
Herkomer Rd. Bus WD2 .... 168 A3
Herm House. Enf EN3 .... 162 D1
Hermitage Ct. St Alb AL3 .... 127 C7
Hermitage Rd. Hit SG5 .... 34 F7
Herne Ct. Bus WD2 .... 168 C2
Herne Rd. Bus WD2 .... 168 B3
Herne Rd. Stev SG1 .... 36 B1
Herneshaw. Hat AL10 .... 129 F3
Herns La. Wel G C AL7 .... 111 B8
Herns Way. Wel G C AL7 .... 111 B8
Heron Cl. Ric WD3 .... 173 D8
Heron Cl. Saw CM21 .... 97 D1
Heron Ct. Bis St CM23 .... 77 A7
Heron Dr. St Gm SG12 .... 115 C3
Heron Dr. Luton LU2 .... 45 E6
Heron Trad Est. Luton 44 C7
Heron Rd. Hat AL10 .... 130 A3
Heron Wlk. Mo Pk HA6 .... 174 E6
Heronfield. Pot B EN6 .... 145 C1
Herongate Rd. Ches EN8 .... 148 E4
Herons Elm. Nthch HP4 .... 121 E7
Herons Way. St Alb AL1 .... 142 B8
Herons Wood. Harl CM20 .... 117 B2
Heronsgate Rd. Chor WD3 .... 164 B3
Heronslea. Watf WD2 .... 154 B5
Heronswood Pl. Wel G C AL7 .... 111 A5
Heronswood. Wa Aby EN9 .... 163 E5
Hertford Cmplx Hospl. Hert 113 D4
Hertford East Sta. Hert 113 D6
Hertford Heath Cty Prim Sch.
  Hert H 114 C4
Hertford Mews. Pot B EN6 .... 158 F7
Hertford North Sta. Hert 113 B6
Hertford Rd. Enf EN3 .... 162 D3
Hertford Rd. Ess AL9 .... 111 B1
Hertford Rd. Gt Am SG12 .... 114 F4
Hertford Rd. Hat AL9 .... 111 B3
Hertford Rd. Hat AL9 .... 130 E8

Hertford Rd. Hod EN11 .... 134 E8
Hertford Rd. Stev SG2 .... 68 F8
Hertford Rd. Stev SG2 .... 69 B7
Hertford Rd. Tewin AL6 .... 90 F2
Hertford Rd. Welw AL6 .... 89 D3
Hertfordshire Bsns Ctr. Lon C 142 D5
Hertfordshire Coll of Building.
  St Alb 127 E3
Hertfordshire & Essex High Sch.
  Bis St 77 B7
Hertfordshire Golf &
  Country Clubs The. Hod 134 C3
Hertingfordbury Rd. Hert SG14 .... 113 B5
Hertingfordbury Rd. Hertng SG14 .... 112 F4
Hertingfordbury Rd. Hertng 112 C4
Hertswood Ct. Barn EN5 .... 171 E5   1
Hester House. Harl CM20 .... 117 C2
Heswall Cl. Luton LU1 .... 63 F6
Heswall Gn. Sth Ox WD1 .... 175 A7
Hetchleys. Heml H HP1 .... 124 A6
Hewitt Cl. Whea AL4 .... 108 D7
Hewlett Rd. Luton LU3 .... 44 E5
Hexton Jun Mix Inf Sch. Hex 19 A1
Hexton Rd. Gt Of SG5 .... 33 B8
Hexton Rd. Lily LU2 .... 32 C4
Heybridge Ct. Hert SG14 .... 112 F7
Heydon Rd. Gt Ch SG8 .... 9 E3
Heydons Cl. St Alb AL3 .... 127 D5
Heyford Rd. Radl WD7 .... 155 F3
Heyford Way. Hat AL10 .... 130 C7
Heysham Dr. Sth Ox WD1 .... 175 D5
Heywood Dr. Luton LU2 .... 45 F2
Hibbert Ave. Watf WD2 .... 154 D1
Hibbert Rd. Har HA3 .... 176 F1
Hibbert St. Luton LU1 .... 63 E6
Hickling Cl. Luton LU2 .... 46 D1
Hickling Way. Harp AL5 .... 86 C3
Hickman Ct. Luton LU3 .... 44 D8
Hicks Rd. Mark AL3 .... 83 F6
Hidalgo Ct. Heml H HP2 .... 124 F6
Hideaway The. Abb L WD5 .... 153 F8
Hides The. Harl CM20 .... 117 D1
High Acres. Abb L WD5 .... 153 D7
High Ash Rd. Whea AL4 .... 108 C7
High Ave. Letw SG6 .... 22 E4
High Beech Rd. Luton LU3 .... 44 D7
High Beeches. Harp 86 D1
High Canons. Shen WD6 .... 157 D2
High Cl. Ric WD3 .... 165 C4
High Cross. Radl WD7 .... 155 D2
High Dane. Hit SG4 .... 22 A2
High Dells. Hat AL10 .... 129 F4
High Elms Cl. Norwd HA6 .... 174 D4
High Elms. Harp AL5 .... 107 A6
High Elms La. Abb L WD2,WD5 .... 154 F8
High Elms La. Ben SG14 .... 70 E8
High Elms La. Ben SG2 .... 52 F1
High Firs Cres. Harp AL5 .... 107 D8
High Firs. Radl WD7 .... 156 A4
High Gr. Wel G C AL8 .... 110 C7
High House Est. Harl CM17 .... 118 F4
High La. Sta M CM24 .... 59 F8
High Mead. Luton LU3 .... 45 A3
High Meads. Whea AL4 .... 108 C8
High Oak Rd. Ware SG12 .... 93 E3
High Oaks. Enf EN2 .... 160 F1
High Oaks Rd. Wel G C AL8 .... 110 B7
High Oaks. St Alb AL3 .... 127 D7
High Pastures. Sheer CM22 .... 98 D1
High Plash. Stev SG1 .... 50 E5
High Point. Luton LU1 .... 63 D6
High Rd. Bus WD2 .... 168 D1
High Rd. Ess AL9 .... 131 E5
High Rd. Har HA3 .... 176 E3
High Rd. Hod EN10 .... 134 F4
High Rd. Shil SG5 .... 19 E8
High Rd. Stap SG14 .... 92 A2
High Rd. Watf WD2 .... 153 F5
High Rd. Watf WD2 .... 154 A7
High Ridge. Cuf EN6 .... 146 E4
High Ridge. Harp AL5 .... 85 E3
High Ridge. Luton LU2 .... 46 C1
High Ridge Rd. Heml H HP3 .... 138 D7
High Road Broxbourne. Hod EN10 .... 134 F3
High Road Turnford. Ches EN8 .... 148 E6
High Road Wormley. Ches EN8 .... 148 F8
High Road Wormley. Hod EN8 .... 148 F8
High St. Abb L WD5 .... 139 F1
High St. Abb L WD5 .... 139 F4
High St. Arl SG15 .... 11 A5
High St. Ashw SG7 .... 4 D4
High St. Bal SG7 .... 23 F8
High St. Bar SG8 .... 8 F2
High St. Bark SG8 .... 17 C3
High St. Barn EN5 .... 171 F5
High St. Berk HP4 .... 122 B4
High St. Bis St CM23 .... 76 F7
High St. Bov HP3 .... 137 A4
High St. Bun SG9 .... 40 E8
High St. Bus WD2 .... 168 A3
High St. Ched LU7 .... 80 A7
High St. Ches EN8 .... 148 D2
High St. Ches EN8 .... 162 D4
High St. Ches EN8 .... 162 E5
High St. Cod SG4 .... 67 D4
High St. Coln H AL4 .... 129 B1
High St. Elst WD6 .... 169 D3
High St. Fla AL3 .... 84 B2
High St. Gra SG4 .... 36 C4
High St. Gt Am SG12 .... 115 C4
High St. Gt Of SG5 .... 33 C3
High St. Gu M SG8 .... 1 F4
High St. Har HA3 .... 176 E1
High St. Hare UB9 .... 173 C1
High St. Harl CM17 .... 118 D4
High St. Harp AL5 .... 86 A1
High St. Heml H HP1,HP3 .... 124 D4
High St. Hin SG7 .... 3 D8
High St. Hit SG4 .... 34 F3
High St. Hit SG5 .... 34 F5
High St. Hod EN11 .... 135 A5
High St. Hun SG12 .... 95 D1
High St. Kim SG4 .... 66 C1
High St. Kin L WD4 .... 139 A2
High St. Lon C AL2 .... 142 D5
High St. Luton LU4 .... 44 D1
High St. Mark AL3 .... 83 E5
High St. Muc H SG10 .... 74 F3
High St. Norwd HA6 .... 174 F3
High St. Nthch HP4 .... 121 E6

High St. Nthch HP4 .... 121 E7
High St. Pirt SG5 .... 20 D4
High St. Pit LU7 .... 80 E5
High St. Pot B EN6 .... 159 C7
High St. Red AL3 .... 106 B5
High St. Reed SG8 .... 16 E5
High St. Ric WD3 .... 165 E1
High St. Roy CM19 .... 116 B1
High St. Royst SG8 .... 7 D6
High St. Sand AL4 .... 108 C2
High St. St Alb AL3 .... 127 D3
High St. Stand SG11 .... 55 D3
High St. Stand SG11 .... 55 F1
High St. Stev SG1 .... 50 C7
High St. Stot SG5 .... 11 F6
High St. Tri HP23 .... 100 A3
High St. Walk SG2 .... 38 B1
High St. Ware SG12 .... 93 D1
High St. Wat St SG14 .... 70 E3
High St. Watf WD1 .... 167 B6
High St. Watf WD1 .... 167 C5
High St. Welw AL6 .... 89 C5
High St. Whea AL4 .... 87 D1
High St. Whit SG4 .... 66 E6
High St. Widf SG12 .... 95 E5
High Street Gn. Heml H HP2 .... 125 A5
High Town Rd. Luton LU2 .... 45 F1
High View. Birhr CM23 .... 59 D3
High View. Chor WD3 .... 165 A5
High View Ct. Har HA3 .... 176 E3
High View. Hat AL10 .... 130 A2
High View. Hit SG5 .... 34 D7
High View. Mark AL3 .... 83 E4
High View. Watf WD1 .... 166 F3
High Wickfield. Wel G C AL7 .... 111 C5
High Wood Cl. Luton LU1 .... 63 A7
High Wood Rd. Hod EN11 .... 114 F1
High Wych Jun Mix Inf Sch. H Wy 97 A1
High Wych La. H Wy CM21 .... 97 A2
High Wych Rd. H Wy CM21 .... 117 F7
High Wych Rd. Saw CM21 .... 97 B1
High Wych Way. Heml H HP2 .... 105 A1
Higham Dr. Luton LU2 .... 46 D1
Highbanks Rd. Pnr HA5 .... 176 B4
Highbarns. Heml H HP3 .... 139 A6
Highbridge St. Wa Aby EN9 .... 163 B6
Highbury Ave. Hod EN11 .... 135 B8
Highbury Inf Sch. Hit 34 F6
Highbury Rd. Hit SG4 .... 35 A7
Highbury Rd. Luton LU3 .... 45 C1
Highbush Rd. Stot SG5 .... 11 E5
Highclere Ct. St Alb AL1 .... 127 E4
Highclere Dr. Heml H HP3 .... 139 B7
Highcroft Rd. Heml H HP3 .... 138 F6
Highcroft. Stev SG2 .... 50 F1   2
Highfield Ave. Bis St CM23 .... 77 C8
Highfield Ave. Harp AL5 .... 107 D8
Highfield. Bus WD2 .... 176 F8
Highfield Cl. Norwd HA6 .... 174 E2
Highfield Cres. Norwd HA6 .... 174 E2
Highfield Ct. Stev SG1 .... 50 F7
Highfield Dr. Hod EN10 .... 134 E2
Highfield. Kin L WD4 .... 138 E3
Highfield La. Coln H AL1 .... 142 E8
Highfield La. Heml H HP2 .... 124 F5
Highfield. Letw SG6 .... 22 E4
Highfield Oval. Harp AL5 .... 86 A4
Highfield Rd. Berk HP4 .... 122 D4
Highfield Rd. Ham St EN7 .... 147 E5
Highfield Rd. Hert SG13 .... 113 D4
Highfield Rd. Luton LU4 .... 45 B1
Highfield Rd. Norwd HA6 .... 174 E2
Highfield Rd. Sand AL4 .... 108 B1
Highfield Rd. Tri HP23 .... 99 E3
Highfield Rd. Watf WD2 .... 167 E4
Highfield Rd. Wigg HP23 .... 100 D1
Highfield. Saw CM21 .... 97 E3
Highfield Sch The. Letw 22 D3
Highfield Way. Ric WD3 .... 165 B3
Highfields. Cl. Dun LU5 .... 44 A2
Highfields. Cuf EN6 .... 146 E3
Highfields. Radl WD7 .... 155 F4
Highfield Way. Pot B EN6 .... 159 B7
Highgate Gr. Saw CM21 .... 97 D2
Highgrove Ct. Ches EN8 .... 162 D5
Highland Dr. Bus WD2 .... 168 C2
Highland Dr. Heml H HP3 .... 125 B3
Highland Rd. Bis St CM23 .... 76 F3
Highland Rd. Lo Naz EN9 .... 135 E1
Highland Rd. Norwd HA6 .... 175 A1
Highlands. Hat AL9 .... 130 C8
Highlands. Royst SG8 .... 7 D5
Highlands The. Pot B EN6 .... 145 C1
Highlands. The. Ric WD3 .... 165 B2
Highlands. Watf WD1 .... 167 C1
Highmead. Sta M CM24 .... 59 E8
Highmill. Ware SG12 .... 93 D3
Highmoor. Harp AL5 .... 86 A4
Highover Cl. Luton LU2 .... 46 B1
Highover Prim Sch. Hit 22 B1
Highover Rd. Letw SG6 .... 22 B5
Highover Way. Hit SG4 .... 22 B1
Highview Cl. Pot B EN6 .... 159 C6
Highview Gdns. Pot B EN6 .... 159 C6
Highview Gdns. St Alb AL4 .... 128 C8
Highway The. Har HA7 .... 176 F2
Highwick Sch. Stev 50 F7
Highwood Ave. Bus WD2 .... 167 F8
Highwood Jun Mix Inf Sch. Bus 167 E8
Highwoodhall La.
  Heml H WD4,WD5 .... 139 C7
Hilbury. Hat AL10 .... 129 F4
Hilfield La. Radl WD2 .... 168 F3
Hilfield La. S Bus WD2 .... 168 F3
Hill Cl. Barn EN5 .... 171 C4
Hill Cl. Harp AL5 .... 86 C4
Hill Cl. Luton LU3 .... 45 C7
Hill Comm. Heml H HP3 .... 139 A8
Hill Crest. Pot B EN6 .... 159 C5
Hill Crest. Whit SG4 .... 66 C6
Hill Croft. Luton LU4 .... 44 C6
Hill Ct. Berk HP4 .... 122 B5
Hill Dyke Rd. Whea AL4 .... 108 C4
Hill End Hospl. St Alb 141 D1
Hill End La. St Alb AL4,AL1 .... 128 C2
Hill End Rd. Hare UB9 .... 173 C4
Hill Farm Ave. Abb L WD2 .... 154 A6
Hill Farm Cl. Abb L WD2 .... 154 A6

Hill Farm La. A St L AL6 .... 88 C5
Hills La. Red AL3 .... 106 C1
Hill House La. Har HA7 .... 176 D3
Hill House. Hert SG13 .... 113 C5
Hill Ley. Hat AL10 .... 129 F5
Hill Leys. Cuf EN6 .... 146 E3
Hill Mead. Berk HP4 .... 122 A3
Hill Rd. Cod SG4 .... 67 C1
Hill Rd. Norwd HA6 .... 174 D4
Hill Rise. Cuf EN6 .... 146 E3
Hill Rise. Pot B EN6 .... 159 C5
Hill Rise. Ric WD3 .... 165 B2
Hill Side. Ched LU7 .... 79 F7
Hill St. St Alb AL3 .... 127 C3
Hill The. Harl CM17 .... 118 C4
Hill The. Whea AL4 .... 108 D8
Hill Top. Bal 23 E7
Hill Tree Cl. Saw CM21 .... 97 D1
Hill View. Berk HP4 .... 122 A6
Hill View. Buck SG9 .... 27 D8
Hill View. Whit SG4 .... 66 E6
Hillary Cl. Luton LU3 .... 44 D7
Hillary Cres. Luton LU1 .... 63 C6
Hillary Rd. Heml H HP2 .... 125 A4
Hillary Rise. Arl SG15 .... 11 B5
Hillborough Rd. Luton LU1 .... 63 D6
Hillbrow. Letw SG6 .... 22 D5
Hillcrest Ave. Luton LU2 .... 45 C8
Hillcrest. Bal SG7 .... 23 F7
Hillcrest. Hat AL10 .... 130 A5
Hillcrest Rd. Shen WD7 .... 157 A6
Hillcrest. St Alb AL3 .... 127 B1
Hillcrest. Stev SG1 .... 50 F5
Hillcroft. Swd WD1 .... 175 B8
Hilldown Rd. Heml H HP1 .... 124 A5
Hillfield Ave. Hit SG4 .... 22 A2
Hillfield Ct. Heml H HP2 .... 124 F5
Hillfield. Hat AL10 .... 130 C8
Hillfield Rd. Heml H HP2 .... 124 D3
Hillgate. Hit SG4 .... 22 A3
Hillhouse. Wa Aby EN9 .... 163 F6
Hilliard Rd. Norwd HA6 .... 174 F2
Hillingdon House (St Nicholas Sch).
  Harl 118 F3
Hillingdon Rd. Watf WD2 .... 154 B5
Hillmead Jun Mix Inf Sch. Bis St 59 C1
Hillmead. Stev SG1 .... 51 A6
Hillrise Ave. Watf WD2 .... 154 D2
Hills La. Norwd HA6 .... 174 E2
Hillsborough Gn. Sth Ox WD1 .... 175 A7
Hillshott. Letw SG6 .... 23 A6
Hillshott Sch. Letw 23 A6
Hillside Ave. Bis St CM23 .... 77 A7
Hillside Ave. Bor WD6 .... 170 B5
Hillside Ave. Ches EN8 .... 162 D8
Hillside Cl. Abb L WD5 .... 153 E7
Hillside Cl. Barn EN5 .... 171 E5
Hillside Cotts. Wars SG12 .... 94 F4
Hillside Cotts. Ches EN8 .... 162 D8
Hillside Cres. Enf EN2 .... 161 D1
Hillside Cres. Gt Am SG12 .... 115 B4
Hillside Cres. Norwd HA6 .... 175 A2
Hillside Cres. Watf WD2 .... 167 D3
Hillside Ct. Ches EN8 .... 162 D8
Hillside Gdns. Barn EN5 .... 171 E5
Hillside Gdns. Berk HP4 .... 122 D3
Hillside Gdns. Norwd HA6 .... 175 B2
Hillside. Hat AL10 .... 130 A5
Hillside. Hod EN11 .... 134 F7
Hillside House. Stev SG1 .... 50 F5
Hillside Jun Inf Sch. Norwd 175 A3
Hillside La. Gt Am SG12 .... 115 A5
Hillside Mansions. Barn EN5 .... 171 E5
Hillside Rd. Chor WD3 .... 164 C4
Hillside Rd. Harp AL5 .... 85 F3
Hillside Rd. Luton LU3 .... 45 D1   4
Hillside Rd. Norwd HA6,HA5 .... 175 B3
Hillside Rd. Radl WD7 .... 156 B4
Hillside Rd. St Alb AL1 .... 127 E4
Hillside Rd. Watf WD2 .... 167 D3
Hillside Rise. Norwd HA6 .... 175 A3
Hillside. Royst SG8 .... 7 D5
Hillside. Bor 170 C5
Hillside. Stev SG1 .... 50 F5
Hillside Terr. Hert SG13 .... 113 C4
Hillside. Ware SG12 .... 114 D8
Hillside Way. Welw AL6 .... 90 A8
Hillside. Wel G C AL7 .... 111 B3
Hilltop Cl. Ham St EN7 .... 147 F5
Hilltop Cl. St Alb AL4 .... 128 C8
Hilltop Ct. Luton LU1 .... 63 C7
Hilltop Rd. Abb L WD4 .... 139 C4
Hilltop Rd. Berk HP4 .... 122 C4
Hilltop. Red AL3 .... 105 F6
Hilltop. Stev 50 F7
Hillview Cl. Pnr HA5 .... 175 F1
Hillview Cres. Luton LU2 .... 45 C8
Hillview Gdns. Ches EN8 .... 148 E4
Hillview Rd. Pnr HA5 .... 175 F4
Hilly Fields. Wel G C AL7 .... 111 C7
Hilmay Dr. Heml H HP1 .... 124 C2
Hilton Cl. Stev SG1 .... 50 B7
Himalayan Way. Watf WD1 .... 166 F3
Hindhead Gn. Sth Ox WD1 .... 175 C5
Hine Way. Hit SG5 .... 21 C1
Hinxworth Rd. Ashw SG7 .... 4 C3
Hinxworth Rd. Hin SG2 .... 3 C3
Hipkins. Bis St CM23 .... 76 E4
Hitchens Cl. Heml H HP1 .... 123 F4
Hitchin Boys' Sch. Hit 34 F4
Hitchin Girls' Sch. Hit 34 F7
Hitchin Hill. Hit SG4 .... 34 F5
Hitchin Hospl. Hit 34 D8
Hitchin Rd Ind Est. Luton 45 F1
Hitchin Rd. Arl SG15 .... 11 A2
Hitchin Rd. Gt Wy SG4 .... 35 D6
Hitchin Rd. Henlw SG16 .... 10 C6
Hitchin Rd. Letw SG6 .... 34 F3
Hitchin Rd. Kim SG4 .... 66 D3
Hitchin Rd. Letw SG6 .... 22 E3
Hitchin Rd. Luton LU2 .... 46 A4
Hitchin Rd. Luton LU2 .... 46 A4
Hitchin Rd. Pirt SG5 .... 20 D5
Hitchin Rd. Shil SG5 .... 19 E1
Hitchin Rd. Stev SG1 .... 36 B1
Hitchin Rd. Stot SG5 .... 11 D4
Hitchin Rd. Wes SG4 .... 24 D3
Hitchin St. Bal SG7 .... 23 E8

Hitchin Sta. Hit 35 B8
Hither Field. Ware SG12 .... 93 F3
Hitherbaulk. Wel G C AL7 .... 110 C4
Hitherfield La. Harp AL5 .... 86 A2
Hitherway. Wel G C AL8 .... 89 D2
Hitherwell Dr. Har HA3 .... 176 D3
Hive Rd. Bus WD2 .... 176 E8
Hobart Wlk. St Alb AL3 .... 127 F7
Hobbs Cl. Ches EN8 .... 148 D2
Hobbs Cl. Coln H AL4 .... 128 C2
Hobbs Cross. Harl CM17 .... 118 F2
Hobbs Cross. Stev SG1 .... 51 A8
Hobbs Hill Rd. Heml H HP3 .... 138 F8
Hobbs Hill Wood Jun Mix Inf Sch.
  Heml H 125 B1
Hobbs Way. Wel G C AL8 .... 110 C5
Hobletts Inf Sch. Heml H 125 A4
Hobletts Rd. Heml H HP2 .... 124 F4
Hobsons Cl. Hod EN11 .... 114 F1
Hobsons Wlk. Tri HP23 .... 99 F5
Hobtoe Rd. Harl CM20 .... 117 A1
Hockerill Ct. Bis St CM23 .... 77 A7   5
Hockerill Sch. Bis St 77 B7
Hockerill St. Bis St CM23 .... 77 A7
Hockerill. Wat St SG14 .... 70 E3
Hocklands. Wel G C AL7 .... 111 C5
Hockwell Ring. Luton LU4 .... 44 C4
Hoddesdon Bsns Ctr. Hod 135 A6
Hoddesdon Rd. St Am SG12 .... 115 C3
Hodges Way. Watf WD1 .... 167 A3
Hodings Rd. Harl CM20 .... 117 B2
Hodwell. Ashw SG7 .... 4 D4
Hoe La. Enf EN1,EN3 .... 162 B1
Hoe La. Lo Naz EN9 .... 135 F1
Hoe La. Ware SG12 .... 114 D7
Hoe The. Sth Ox WD1 .... 175 D8
Hoecroft Ct. Enf EN3 .... 162 C1
Hoecroft. Lo Naz EN9 .... 135 F1
Hoestock Rd. Saw CM21 .... 97 D2
Hog Hall La. Dagn HP4 .... 81 A5
Hog La. Chol HP5 .... 121 D2
Hogarth Ct. Bus WD2 .... 168 B2
Hogg End La. St Alb AL3 .... 126 C3
Hogg La. Elst WD6 .... 169 A5
Hogsdell La. Hert H SG13 .... 114 B4
Holbeck La. Ham St EN7 .... 147 F5
Holbein Gate. Mo Pk HA6 .... 174 C5
Holborn Cl. St Alb AL4 .... 128 D8
Holbrook Cl. Enf EN1 .... 162 A1
Holcroft Rd. Harp AL5 .... 86 D3
Holdbrook. Hit SG4 .... 35 B7
Holdbrook Sch. Ches 162 F5
Holden Cl. Hert SG13 .... 113 E1
Holders La. Ast SG2 .... 51 E5
Holdings The. Hat AL9 .... 130 D7
Holecroft. Wa Aby EN9 .... 163 E5
Holford Way. Luton LU3 .... 31 B1
Holgate Dr. Dun LU4 .... 44 B3
Holkham Cl. Dun LU4 .... 44 A4
Holland Cl. Luton LU3 .... 45 C2
Holland Gdns. Watf WD2 .... 154 C4
Holland Rd. Luton LU3 .... 45 B2
Holland's Croft. Hun SG12 .... 95 D1
Holliday St. Berk HP4 .... 122 D4
Hollier Ct. Hat AL10 .... 130 B6
Holliers Way. Hat AL10 .... 130 A5
Hollies Cl. Royst SG8 .... 7 E6
Hollies The. Bov HP3 .... 137 A2
Hollies The. Chor WD3 .... 164 C2
Hollies The. St Alb AL3 .... 127 C5
Hollies The. Watf WD1 .... 166 F5
Hollies The. Wigg HP23 .... 100 D1
Hollies Way. Pot B EN6 .... 159 C8
Hollow La. Hit SG4 .... 34 F7
Holloway La. Chen WD3 .... 151 C2
Holloway The. Ast Cl HP22 .... 99 C4
Holloways La. Wel G AL9 .... 144 D7
Holly Cl. Hat AL10 .... 129 F4
Holly Copse. Stev SG1 .... 50 F4
Holly Croft. Hert SG14 .... 113 A7
Holly Dell. Hert SG13 .... 113 C4
Holly Dr. Berk HP4 .... 122 D3
Holly Dr. Pot B EN6 .... 159 B6
Holly Farm Cl. Cad LU1 .... 62 E3
Holly Gr. Pnr HA5 .... 175 F2
Holly Grove Rd. Bram SG14 .... 91 C3
Holly Hedges La. Bov HP3 .... 151 C8
Holly La. Whea AL5 .... 86 C6
Holly Leys. Stev SG2 .... 69 C8
Holly Rd. Enf EN3 .... 162 D3
Holly Rd. Welw SG3 .... 69 B1
Holly Shaws. Stev SG2 .... 51 B1
Holly St. Luton LU1 .... 63 E6
Holly Street Trad Est. Luton 63 E6   7
Holly Tree Ct. Heml H HP2 .... 125 D3
Holly Wlk. Harp AL5 .... 86 D1
Holly Wlk. Wel G C AL8 .... 89 C2
Hollybush Ave. Chis AL2 .... 141 A7
Hollybush Cl. Har HA3 .... 176 E3
Hollybush Cl. Pot En HP4 .... 123 D7
Hollybush Cl. Watf WD1 .... 167 C2
Hollybush Cl. Welw AL6 .... 89 E8
Hollybush Hill. Gt Of LU2 .... 32 F1
Hollybush House. Wel G C AL7 .... 110 F4
Hollybush Jun Mix Inf Sch. Hert 113 A6
Hollybush La. Dag SG3 .... 69 C3
Hollybush La. Fla AL3 .... 84 B3
Hollybush La. Harp AL5 .... 86 A1
Hollybush La. Harp AL5 .... 123 F4
Hollybush Rd. Luton LU4 .... 110 D3
Hollybush Rd. Whit SG4 .... 66 B8
Hollybush Rd. Luton LU2 .... 46 C1
Hollybush Way. Ches EN7 .... 148 A3
Hollycross Rd. Sta Ab SG12 .... 115 B7
Hollyfield Cl. Tri HP23 .... 100 C5
Hollyfield. Hat AL10 .... 130 A2
Hollyfield. Tri HP23 .... 100 C5
Hollyfields. Ches EN10 .... 148 E5
Hollygrove. Bus WD2 .... 168 D2
Hollytree Cl. Bot HP5 .... 150 B8
Hollytree House. Watf WD1 .... 153 E3
Hollywood Rd. Bor WD6 .... 170 A5
Holmbrook Ave. Luton LU3 .... 45 C5
Holmbury Cl. Bus WD2 .... 176 E8
Holmdale Cl. Bor WD6 .... 169 F7
Holmdale. Letw SG6 .... 23 B5

Holme Cl. Ches EN8 .... 162 E8
Holme Cl. Hat AL10 .... 129 F8
Holme Lea. Watf WD2 .... 154 C5
Holme Pk. Bor WD6 .... 169 F7
Holme Way. Har HA7 .... 176 A4
Holmes Ct. St Alb AL3 .... 127 E4
Holmesdale. Enf EN8 .... 162 D4
Holmfield Cl. Luton LU1 .... 63 D5
Holmscroft Rd. Luton LU3 .... 44 F6
Holmshill La. Ridge WD6 .... 157 F2
Holmshill Sec Sch. Bor 170 C7
Holmside Rise. Sth Ox WD1 .... 175 B7
Holmwood Rd. Enf EN3 .... 162 D3
Holroyd Cres. Bal SG7 .... 23 F7
Holt Cl. Bor WD6 .... 169 F5
Holt The. Heml H HP2 .... 124 E2
Holt The. Wel G C AL7 .... 111 D5
Holts Meadow. Red AL3 .... 106 B6
Holtsmere Cl. Luton LU2 .... 46 D1
Holtsmere Cl. Watf WD2 .... 154 C4
Holtsmere End Inf Sch. Heml H 125 B8
Holtsmere End Jun Mix Inf Sch.
     Heml H 125 B8
Holwell Hyde La. Wel G C AL7 .... 111 C3
Holwell Hyde. Wel G C AL7 .... 111 C3
Holwell Jun & Inf Sch. Wel G C ... 110 F5
Holwell La. Ess AL9 .... 131 E8
Holwell Rd. Hol SG5 .... 21 B7
Holwell Rd. Pirt SG5 .... 20 E6
Holwell Rd. Wel G C AL7 .... 110 E5
Holwell. Stev SG1 .... 36 C2
Holy Cross Hill. Bric EN7 .... 148 A8
Holy Family RC Prim Sch The.
     Wel G C 90 A1
Holy Rood RC Inf Sch. Watf 153 D3
Holy Rood RC Jun Mix Sch. Watf . 153 D3
Holy Trinity C of E Jun Mix Inf Sch.
     Ches 162 D7
Holy Trinity C of E Prim Sch.
     .... 174 C4
Holyfield Rd. Wa Aby EN9 .... 149 D2
Holyrood Cres. St Alb AL1 .... 141 D7
Holyrood Dr. Watf WD1 .... 167 B5
Holywell Cl. Whip LU6 .... 82 C6
Holywell Cl. Luton LU3 .... 45 B4
Holywell Cty Inf Sch. Watf 166 F3
Holywell Hill. St Alb AL1 .... 127 D2
Holywell Jun Sch. Watf 166 F3
Holywell Rd. Watf WD1 .... 167 A4
Holywell Rd. Whip LU6 .... 82 B7
Home Cl. Ches EN10 .... 148 F7
Home Cl. Luton LU4 .... 44 C4
Home Cl. Stot SG5 .... 11 F6
Home Cl. Wat4 LU4 .... 44 C4
Home Farm Ind Pk. Sta Ab 115 F5
Home Farm Rd. Nthch HP4 .... 121 D7
Home Farm Rd. Ric WD3 .... 174 A6
Home Field. Barn EN5 .... 171 F4
Home Ley. Wel G C AL7 .... 110 E6
Home Meadow. Wel G C AL7 .... 110 F6
Home Park Ind Est. Kin L 139 B1
Home Pastures. Sheer CM22 .... 98 F3
Home Way. Ric WD3 .... 164 F1
Homedale Dr. Luton LU4 .... 44 D2
Homedell House. Harp AL5 .... 85 E3
Homefield. Bov HP3 .... 137 B3
Homefield. Hin SG7 .... 3 D6
Homefield La. Lan SG4 .... 49 F2
Homefield. Pot En HP4 .... 123 B7
Homefield Rd. Bus WD2 .... 168 A4
Homefield Rd. Chor WD3 .... 164 D5
Homefield Rd. Heml H HP2 .... 125 A2
Homefield Rd. Radl WD7 .... 155 F2
Homefield Rd. Ware SG12 .... 93 E2
Homeleigh Ct. Ches EN8 .... 148 B1
Homeleigh St. Ches EN8 .... 148 B1
Homerfield. Wel G C AL8 .... 110 C7
Homerswood Jun & Inf Sch.
     Wel G C 89 D2
Homerswood La. Welw AL6 .... 89 A2
Homerton Rd. Luton LU3 .... 45 A6
Homestead Cl. Chis AL2 .... 141 C4
Homestead Ct. Wel G C AL7 .... 110 F4
Homestead La. Wel G C AL7 .... 110 F4
Homestead Moat. Stev SG1 .... 50 E4
Homestead Rd. Hat AL10 .... 130 B8
Homestead Rd. Ric WD3 .... 165 D2
Homestead Way. Luton LU1 .... 63 C5
Homewood Ave. Cuf EN6 .... 146 E4
Homewood La. Cuf EN6 .... 146 C4
Homewood Rd. St Alb AL1 .... 128 B5
Homewood Sch. Chis 141 B3
Honey Brook. Wa Aby EN9 .... 163 E6
Honey La. Bun SG9 .... 40 E8
Honey La. Clav CM11 .... 30 F3
Honey La. Hert SG14 .... 113 D6
Honey La. Wa Aby EN9 .... 163 E6
Honeybourne. Bis St CM23 .... 76 E4
Honeycraft. Wel G C AL8 .... 110 C5
Honeycross Rd. Heml H HP1 .... 123 E2
Honeygate. Luton LU2 .... 45 E4
Honeymead. Welw AL6 .... 89 F3
Honeymeade. Saw CM21 .... 118 C7
Honeysuckle Cl. Hert SG13 .... 114 A6
Honeysuckle Gdns. Hat AL10 .... 130 B4
Honeyway. Royst SG8 .... 7 E6
Honilands Inf Sch. Enf 162 B3
Honilands Jun Sch. Enf 162 B3
Honours Mead. Bov HP3 .... 137 A4
Hoo Cotts. Gt Of SG5 .... 33 D1
Hoo Farm Cotts. Gt Of SG5 .... 33 D1
Hoo St. Luton LU1 .... 63 E5
Hoo The. Harl CM17 .... 118 C5
Hook Gate. Enf EN1 .... 162 B3
Hook La. Nort EN6 .... 159 F7
Hook La. Nort EN6 .... 160 A8
Hookers Ct. Luton LU4 .... 44 C5
Hoops La. Ther SG8 .... 15 F6
Hope Gn. Watf WD2 .... 154 A6
Hopewell Rd. Bal SG7 .... 23 D8
Hopground Cl. St Alb AL1 .... 128 A1
Hopkins Cres. Sand AL4 .... 108 B1
Hoppit Rd. Wa Aby EN9 .... 163 B6
Hopton Rd. Stev SG1 .... 50 A8
Horace Brightman Cl. Luton LU3 .... 45 A8
Horace Gay Gdns. Letw SG6 .... 22 E6

Horbeam Cl. Bor WD6 .... 170 A8
Hordle Gdns. St Alb AL1 .... 127 F2
Hormead C of E Prim Sch. Gt Ho ... 41 D8
Horn Hill. Whit SG4 .... 66 E6
Hornbeam Cl. Hat SG14 .... 113 A6
Hornbeam Cl. Gt Wy SG4 .... 35 C5
Hornbeam La. Ess AL9 .... 131 E2
Hornbeam Spring. Kneb SG3 .... 68 D3
Hornbeam Way. Luton LU1 .... 147 F2
Hornbeams Ave. Enf EN1 .... 162 C4
Hornbeams. Bri Wd AL2 .... 140 F1
Hornbeams The. Harl CM20 .... 117 B2
Hornbeams The. Stev SG2 .... 51 B4
Hornbeams. Wel G C AL7 .... 111 B5
Hornets The. Watf WD1 .... 167 B5
Hornhill Rd. Map Cr WD3 .... 172 D5
Horns Cl. Hert SG13 .... 113 C4
Horns Mill Rd. Hert SG13 .... 113 C3
Horns Rd. Hert SG13 .... 113 C5
Hornsby Cl. Luton LU2 .... 46 C1
Hornsfield. Wel G C AL7 .... 111 C7
Horrocks Cl. Ware SG12 .... 93 D3
Horse Hill. Bot HP3 .... 150 D7
Horsecroft Rd. Heml H HP1 .... 124 A1
Horselers. Heml H HP3 .... 139 A8
Horsemans Dr. Chis AL2 .... 141 B6
Horseshoe Ct. Sta Ab SG12 .... 115 D4
Horseshoe Hill. Gt Ho SG9 .... 42 A8
Horseshoe La. Barn N20 .... 171 D1
Horseshoe La. Gt Ho SG9 .... 42 A8
Horseshoe La. Watf WD2 .... 154 C7
Horseshoe The. Heml H HP3 .... 125 C1
Horseshoes Cl. Ched LU7 .... 80 A7
Horsham Cl. Luton LU2 .... 46 D2
Horsleys. Map Cr WD3 .... 172 D5
Horton Gdns. Heml H HP2 .... 105 A1
Horwood Ct. Watf WD2 .... 154 E2
Hospital Rd. Arl SG15 .... 11 A4
Housden Cl. Whea AL4 .... 108 F7
House La. Arl SG15 .... 11 A4
House La. Sand AL4 .... 108 C1
House La. St Alb AL4 .... 128 C1
Housewood End. Heml H HP1 ...... 124 B6
Housman Ave. Royst SG8 .... 2 C1
How Field. Harp AL5 .... 85 E3
How Wood. Chis AL2 .... 141 B3
How Wood Jun Mix Inf Sch. Chis . 141 C3
How Wood Sta. Chis 141 C3
Howard Agne Cl. Bov HP3 .... 137 A4
Howard Cl. Bus WD2 .... 168 E2
Howard Cl. Luton LU3 .... 45 A4
Howard Cl. St Alb AL1 .... 128 C1
Howard Cl. Wa Aby EN9 .... 163 D5
Howard Cl. Watf WD2 .... 154 A4
Howard Ct. Letw 23 B4
Howard Ctr The. Wel G C AL8 ..... 110 D6
Howard Dr. Bor WD6 .... 170 D5
Howard. Letw SG6 .... 23 B3
Howard Gate. Letw SG6 .... 23 B4
Howard. Luton LU4 .... 44 B4
Howard Way. Barn EN5 .... 171 D4
Howard Way. Harl CM20 .... 117 F2
Howards Cl. Pnr HA5 .... 175 B1
Howards Dr. Heml H HP1 .... 124 A5
Howards Wood. Letw SG6 .... 23 B3
Howardsgate. Wel G C AL8 .... 110 D6
Howe Cl. Shen WD7 .... 156 E7
Howe Dell. Hat AL10 .... 130 B5
Howe Dell Jun Mix Inf Sch. Hat ... 130 B5
Howe Rd. Heml H HP3 .... 125 A1
Howell Hill Cl. Men LU7 .... 61 D5
Howfield Gn. Hod EN11 .... 115 A1
Howicks Gn. Wel G C AL7 .... 111 A3
Howland Garth. St Alb AL1 .... 141 C7
Howlands House. Wel G C AL7 .... 111 B3
Howlands. Wel G C AL7 .... 111 B3
Howton Pl. Bus WD2 .... 168 D1
Hoylake Cl. Luton LU1 .... 63 D7
Hoylake Gdns. Sth Ox WD1 .... 175 D6
Hubbards Rd. Chor WD3 .... 164 D4
Huckleberry Cl. Luton LU3 .... 45 A8
Hudnall La. L Gad HP4 .... 102 F7
Hudson Cl. St Alb AL1 .... 141 D8
Hudson Cl. Watf WD2 .... 153 F3
Hudson Rd. Stev SG2 .... 51 B7
Huggins La. Wel G AL9 .... 144 C8
Hugh Villas. Bis St CM23 .... 77 A5
Hugh's Tower. Harl CM20 .... 117 D1
Hughenden Rd. St Alb AL4 .... 128 C6
Hull La. Brag SG11 .... 55 E7
Humberstone Cl. Luton LU4 .... 44 E2
Humberstone Rd. Luton LU4 .... 44 E2
Humphrey Talbot Ave. Whip LU6 ... 81 F7
Hunsdon Jun Mix Inf Sch. Hun 95 D1
Hunsdon Rd. Sta Ab SG12 .... 115 D1
Hunsdon Rd. Widf SG12 .... 95 B3
Hunsdon. Wel G C AL7 .... 111 D6
Hunston Cl. Luton LU4 .... 44 B5
Hunt Cl. St Alb AL4 .... 128 D6
Hunter Cl. Bor WD6 .... 170 C4
Hunter Cl. Pot B EN6 .... 159 B6
Hunter Wlk. Bor WD6 .... 170 C4
Hunter's La. Abb L WD2 .... 153 F6
Huntercrombe Gdns. Sth Ox WD1 175 C5
Hunters Cl. Bov HP3 .... 137 A2
Hunters Cl. Stev SG2 .... 51 D7
Hunters Cl. Stot SG5 .... 11 E6
Hunters Cl. Tri HP23 .... 100 B5
Hunters Gate. Watf WD2 .... 154 E6
Hunters Oak. Heml H HP2 .... 125 B8
Hunters Pk. Berk HP4 .... 122 E3
Hunters Reach. Gofs O EN7 .... 147 F2
Hunters Ride. Bri Wd AL2 .... 155 A8
Hunters Way. Royst SG8 .... 7 E6
Hunters Way. Wel G C AL7 .... 110 F8
Hunting Gate. Heml H HP2 .... 124 E7
Hunting Gate. Hit SG4 .... 34 F6
Huntingdon Cl. Ches EN10 .... 148 E7
Huntingdon Rd. Stev SG1 .... 50 B8
Hunton Bridge Hill. Abb L WD4 .. 153 C6
Hunts Cl. Luton LU1 .... 63 C7
Huntsmans Cl. Dagn HP4 .... 81 C5
Huntsmill Rd. Heml H HP1 .... 123 E2
Hurlock Way. Luton LU4 .... 44 D5
Hurricane Way. Abb L WD5 .... 154 A7
Hurst Cl. Bal SG7 .... 13 A1
Hurst Cl. Hat AL10 .... 130 A2
Hurst Dr. Ches EN8 .... 162 D5
Hurst Drive Prim Sch. Ches 162 D5
Hurst Pl. Norwd HA6 .... 174 B2
Hurst Way. Luton LU3 .... 44 F5

Hurstlings. Wel G C AL7 .... 111 B5
Hutton Cl. Hert SG14 .... 113 A6
Hutton La. Har HA3 .... 176 B3
Hutton Wlk. Har HA3 .... 176 C3
Hyatt Inf Sch. Stev 50 A5
Hyburn Cl. Bri Wd AL2 .... 140 F1
Hyburn Cl. Heml H HP3 .... 125 B2
Hyde Ave. Pot B EN6 .... 159 B6
Hyde Cl. Barn EN5 .... 171 F6
Hyde Cl. Harp AL5 .... 86 B4
Hyde Gn E. Stev SG2 .... 51 C4
Hyde Gn N. Stev SG2 .... 51 C4
Hyde Gn S. Stev SG2 .... 51 B4
Hyde La. Abb L WD4,WD5 .... 139 C4
Hyde La. Bov HP3 .... 137 A3
Hyde La. Kim LU2 .... 65 C2
Hyde La. Pk St AL2 .... 141 C1
Hyde Mead House. Lo Naz EN9 ... 149 E8
Hyde Mead. Lo Naz EN9 .... 149 E8
Hyde Meadows. Bov HP3 .... 137 A4
Hyde Rd. Cad LU1 .... 62 F4
Hyde Rd. Watf WD1 .... 167 A4
Hyde The. Stev SG2 .... 51 C5
Hyde The. Ware SG12 .... 93 B2
Hyde Valley. Wel G C AL7 .... 110 F4
Hyde View Rd. Harp AL5 .... 86 B4
Hyde Way. Wel G C AL7 .... 110 F5
Hydean Way. Stev SG2 .... 51 B3
Hyperion Ct. Heml H HP2 .... 124 F6
Hyver Hill. Edg NW7 .... 170 D2
Ibberson Way. Hit SG4 .... 35 A7
Ickleford Bury. Ick SG5 .... 21 E4
Ickleford Jun Mix Inf Sch. Ick 21 E4
Ickleford Rd. Hit SG5 .... 34 F8
Ickley Cl. Luton LU4 .... 44 B5
Icknield Cl. Ick SG5 .... 21 E4
Icknield Gn. Tri HP23 .... 100 A6
Icknield High Sch. Luton 45 C5
Icknield Inf Sch. Letw 22 E6
Icknield Inf Sch. Luton 45 B5
Icknield Jun Sch. Luton 45 B5
Icknield Rd. Luton LU3 .... 44 F4
Icknield Walk Fst Sch. Royst 7 E7
Icknield Way. Bal SG7 .... 12 E1
Icknield Way. Dagn HP4 .... 81 A8
Icknield Way E. Bal SG7 .... 12 F1
Icknield Way. Letw SG6 .... 22 E6
Icknield Way. Luton LU3 .... 45 A6
Icknield Way. Tri HP23 .... 99 E4
Icknield Wlk. Royst SG8 .... 7 D6
Idenbury Ct. Luton LU1 .... 63 C7
Ilex Ct. Heml H HP2 .... 122 B4
Ilford Cl. Luton LU2 .... 46 D3
Ilkley Rd. Sth Ox WD1 .... 175 D5
Imberfield. Dun LU4 .... 44 C3
Imperial Way. Watf WD2 .... 167 C8
Indells. Hat AL10 .... 129 F4
Ingelheim Ct. Stev SG1 .... 50 D7
Ingersoll Rd. Enf EN3 .... 162 C1
Inglefield. Pot B EN6 .... 145 A1
Ingles. Wel G AL8 .... 89 E2
Ingleside Dr. Stev SG1 .... 36 B1
Inkerman Rd. St Alb AL1 .... 127 E2
Inkerman St. Luton LU1 .... 63 D7
Inn's Ct. Stev SG1 .... 50 A1
Innes Ct. Heml H HP3 .... 138 D8
Inskip Cres. Stev SG1 .... 50 D7
Iredale View. Bal SG7 .... 13 A1
Irene Stebbings House. St Alb AL4 128 C4
Iron Dr. Hert SG13 .... 114 B7
Irving Cl. Bis St CM23 .... 76 D4
Irving Cres. Ched LU7 .... 80 A8
Isabelle Cl. Gofs O EN7 .... 147 C2
Isenburg Way. Heml H HP2 .... 124 D8
Isherwood Cl. Royst SG8 .... 7 C8
Islington Way. Stev SG1 .... 36 F2
Italstyle Bldg The. Harl CM17 ..... 118 C4
Iveagh Cl. Norwd HA6 .... 174 B2
Iveagh Ct. Heml H HP2 .... 124 D4
Ivel Ct. Letw SG6 .... 23 C4
Ivel Rd. Stev SG1 .... 50 C7
Ivel Way. Bal SG7 .... 24 A6
Ivel Way. Stot SG5 .... 11 F8
Ives Rd. Hert SG14 .... 113 B7
Ivinghoe Cl. St Alb AL4 .... 128 C8
Ivinghoe Cl. Watf WD2 .... 154 D4
Ivinghoe Rd. Bus WD2 .... 168 D2
Ivinghoe Rd. Ric WD3 .... 165 A2
Ivory Ct. Heml H HP3 .... 138 C8
Ivy House La. Berk HP4 .... 122 E4
Ivy Lea. Ric WD3 .... 165 A1
Ivy Rd. Luton LU1 .... 63 C8
Ivy Terr. Hod EN11 .... 135 C8
Ivybridge. Hod EN10 .... 135 A4
Jackdaw Cl. Stev SG2 .... 51 D4
Jackdaws. Wel G C AL7 .... 111 C6
Jackets La. Norwd HA6 .... 174 B3
Jacketts Field. Abb L WD5 .... 153 F8
Jackman's Pl. Letw SG6 .... 23 B5
Jacks La. Hare UB9 .... 173 A1
Jackson Sq. Bis St CM23 .... 76 F7
Jackson St. Bal SG7 .... 12 E1
Jackson's La. Reed SG8 .... 16 E5
Jacksons Dr. Ches EN7 .... 148 A3
James Bedford Cl. Pnr HA5 .... 175 C1
James Cl. Watf WD2 .... 167 E4
James Ct. Dun LU4 .... 44 B2
James Ct. Luton LU1 .... 63 E6
James Marshall Commercial Ctr.
     Harp 86 A1
James Way. Stev SG1 .... 50 C7
Jameson Rd. Harp AL5 .... 86 B3
Jane Cl. Heml H HP2 .... 125 B8
Jarden. Letw SG6 .... 23 C4
Jarman Cl. Heml H HP3 .... 124 E1
Jarman Way. Heml H HP2 .... 124 F2
Jarman Way. Royst SG8 .... 7 A7
Jarvis Cl. Barn EN5 .... 171 D4
Jarvis Cres. Ham St EN7 .... 147 F5
Jasmin Way. Heml H HP1 .... 124 A1
Jasmine Dr. Hert SG13 .... 114 A6
Jasmine Gdns. Hat AL10 .... 130 A7
Jasons Hill. Bot HP5 .... 136 B2

Jasper Cl. Enf EN3 .... 162 C1
Jay Cl. Letw SG6 .... 22 C8
Jaywood. Luton LU2 .... 46 C6
Jeans Way. Dun LU5 .... 44 A1
Jeffrey Cl. Royst SG8 .... 7 D7
Jeffries Rd. Ware SG12 .... 93 E1
Jellicoe Gdns. Har HA7 .... 176 F4
Jellicoe Rd. Watf WD1 .... 167 A3
Jenkins Ave. Bri Wd AL2 .... 140 E1
Jenkins La. Gt Ha CM22 .... 77 C5
Jenkins La. St H SG23 .... 119 E3
Jenning Wood. Welw AL6 .... 89 F7
Jennings Cl. Stev SG1 .... 50 E3
Jennings Rd. St Alb AL1 .... 128 A4
Jennings Way. Barn EN5 .... 171 C6
Jennings Way. Heml H HP3 .... 124 E1
Jenningsbury Ct. Hert SG13 .... 114 A4
Jepps La. Royst SG8 .... 7 D6
Jerome Dr. St Alb AL3 .... 127 A1
Jersey Cl. Hod EN11 .... 135 A7
Jersey House. Enf EN3 .... 162 D1
Jersey La. St Alb AL4 .... 128 C5
Jersey La. St Alb AL4 .... 128 C8
Jersey Rd. Dun LU4 .... 44 A3
Jervis Ave. Enf EN3 .... 162 E4
Jervis Rd. Bis St CM23 .... 76 F6
Jessop Rd. Stev SG1 .... 37 A1
Jeve Cl. Bal SG7 .... 23 E7
Jillifer Rd. Dun LU4 .... 44 A2
Jim Desormeaux Bglws.
     Harl CM20 .... 117 E2
Jinnings The. Wel G C AL7 .... 111 B3
Jocelyns. Harl CM17 .... 118 C4
Jocketts Hill. Heml H HP1 .... 123 F2
Jocketts Rd. Heml H HP1 .... 123 F2
Joel St. Norwd HA6 .... 175 A1
John Barker Pl. Hit SG5 .... 21 C1
John Ct. Hod EN11 .... 115 A1
John Dyde Training Coll The. Bis St 77 A8
John Eliot Cl. Lo Naz EN9 .... 135 E2
John F Kennedy Sch. Heml H 123 E1
John Henry Newman RC Sch The.
     .... 36 B1
John Lamt Cl. Har HA3 .... 176 E2
John Penrose Sch. Hare 173 D2
John Rand Sch. Hol 21 B7
John St. Luton LU1 .... 63 E7
John St. Royst SG8 .... 7 D6
John Tate Rd. Hert SG13 .... 114 B7
John Warner Sch The. Hod 115 B1
Johnby Cl. Enf EN3 .... 162 E2
Johns La. Chol HP5 .... 121 E1
Johns Rd. Bis St CM23 .... 59 A1
Johnson Ct. Heml H HP3 .... 124 E1
Joiner's Close. Bot HP5 .... 136 A1
Joint The. Reed SG8 .... 16 E6
Jones Rd. Gofs O EN7 .... 147 B1
Jonquil Cl. Wel G C AL7 .... 111 B4
Jordan Cl. Watf WD2 .... 153 F4
Jordan's Way. Bri Wd AL2 .... 140 F1
Jordans Way. Ric WD3 .... 165 A1
Jordans. Wel G C AL7 .... 111 C7
Jowitt House. Stev SG1 .... 50 E6
Joyce Ct. Wa Aby EN9 .... 163 D5
Jubilee Ave. Lon C AL2 .... 142 D5
Jubilee Ave. Ware SG12 .... 93 F2
Jubilee Ct. Pnr HA5 .... 175 C1
Jubilee Cotts. Asp SG9 .... 40 D5
Jubilee Cres. Arl SG15 .... 11 A2
Jubilee Ct. Harp AL5 .... 86 C3
Jubilee Ct. Hat AL10 .... 130 B8
Jubilee Ct. Wa Aby EN9 .... 89 E7
Jubilee Memorial Ave. Stev SG1 ... 50 D8
Jubilee Rd. Letw SG6 .... 23 C4
Jubilee Rd. Stev SG1 .... 50 B8
Jubilee Rd. Watf WD2 .... 154 A1
Jubilee St. Luton LU2 .... 45 F1
Jubilee Trade Ctr. Letw 23 D7
Judge St. Watf WD2 .... 154 B1
Judge's Hill. Nort EN6 .... 145 F2
Julia Gate. Stev SG2 .... 51 C4
Julian's Cl. Stev SG1 .... 50 C8
Julian's Rd. Stev SG1 .... 50 B8
Julius Gdns. Luton LU3 .... 44 F7
Juniper Ave. Bri Wd AL2 .... 155 A8
Juniper Cl. Barn EN5 .... 171 D4
Juniper Cl. Ches EN10 .... 148 F6
Juniper Cl. Luton LU4 .... 44 E2
Juniper Ct. Har HA3 .... 176 F2
Juniper Gate. Ric WD3 .... 173 D8
Juniper Gdns. Welw AL6 .... 89 E7
Juniper Gn. Heml H HP1 .... 123 E3
Juniper Gr. Watf WD1 .... 154 A1
Juniper Dr. Heml H HP2 .... 124 F5
Jupiter Dr. Heml H HP2 .... 124 F5
Jupiter Drive Jun Mix Inf Sch.
     Heml H 124 F5
Juxon Cl. Har HA3 .... 176 B2

Kemps Dr. Norwd HA6 .... 174 F3
Kempsey Cl. Luton LU2 .... 46 D2
Ken Davies Ct. St Alb AL3 .... 127 F7
Kendal Cl. Luton LU3 .... 44 D7
Kendale. Heml H HP3 .... 125 B2
Kendale Rd. Dun LU4 .... 44 B2
Kendale. Stev SG1 .... 36 F6
Kendall Cl. Wel G C AL7 .... 110 C5
Kendall Ct. Bor WD6 .... 170 C5
Kendals Cl. Radl WD7 .... 155 E3
Kenerne Dr. Barn EN5 .... 171 E4
Kenford Cl. Watf WD2 .... 154 B7
Kenilworth Cl. Bor WD6 .... 170 C6
Kenilworth Cl. Heml H HP2 .... 124 A4
Kenilworth Cl. Stev SG2 .... 69 C7
Kenilworth Cres. Enf EN1 .... 161 E1
Kenilworth Ct. Watf WD1 .... 167 A8
Kenilworth Dr. Bor WD6 .... 170 C6
Kenilworth Dr. Cro Gr WD3 .... 166 B5
Kenilworth Gdns. Sth Ox WD1 .... 175 C5
Kenilworth Sch. Bor 170 D6
Kennedy Ave. Hod EN11 .... 134 F6
Kennedy Cl. Ches EN8 .... 148 E3
Kennedy Cl. Pnr HA5 .... 175 F4
Kennedy Rd. Dan En SG12 .... 71 E7
Kennelwood La. Hat AL10 .... 130 B6
Kenneth Rd. Luton LU2 .... 46 A1
Kenning Rd. Hod EN11 .... 135 B8
Kennington Rd. Luton LU3 .... 45 B8
Kensington Ave. Watf WD1 .... 166 F5
Kensworth Rd. Stu LU6 .... 82 D4
Kensworth Voluntary Controlled
     Lower Sch. Ken 82 F8
Kent Cl. Bor WD6 .... 157 D1
Kent Cres. Bis St CM23 .... 76 E4
Kent Pl. Hit SG5 .... 34 D8
Kent Rd. Luton LU1 .... 62 F8
Kent's La. Stand SG11 .... 55 E2
Kentish La. Hat AL9 .... 145 C7
Kenton Gdns. St Alb AL1 .... 127 F2
Kenton La. Har HA3 .... 176 F3
Kents Ave. Heml H HP3 .... 138 D7
Kenwood Dr. Ric WD3 .... 172 F8
Kenworth Cl. Ches EN8 .... 162 D6
Kerdistone Cl. Pot B EN6 .... 145 B1
Kernow Ct. Luton LU2 .... 46 A1
Kerr Cl. Kneb SG3 .... 68 F5
Kerri Cl. Barn EN5 .... 171 C5
Kerril Croft. Harl CM20 .... 117 A1
Kershaw Cl. Luton LU3 .... 45 A8
Kershaw's Hill. Hit SG4 .... 34 F6
Kessingland Ave. Stev SG1 .... 36 A1
Keston Mews. Watf WD1 .... 167 B7
Kestrel Cl. Berk HP4 .... 122 C3
Kestrel Cl. Stev SG2 .... 51 D2
Kestrel Cl. Watf WD2 .... 154 E5
Kestrel Cl. Ware SG12 .... 93 C3
Kestrel Gdns. Bis St CM23 .... 76 C6
Kestrel Gn. Hat AL10 .... 130 A4
Kestrel La. Dun LU4 .... 44 A5
Kestrel Rd. Watf WD2 .... 154 E5
Kestrel Wlk. Letw SG6 .... 23 B3
Kestrels The. Bri Wd AL2 .... 154 F8
Keswick Cl. St Alb AL1 .... 128 B1
Keswick Dr. Enf EN3 .... 162 C3
Kettering Rd. Enf EN3 .... 162 D2
Kettle Green Rd. Muc H SG10 ...... 74 E2
Ketton Cl. Luton LU2 .... 64 A7
Ketton Ct. Luton LU2 .... 64 A7
Kewferry Dr. Norwd HA6 .... 174 C5
Kewferry Rd. Norwd HA6 .... 174 C5
Keyfield Terr. St Alb AL1 .... 127 D2
Keymer Cl. Luton LU2 .... 46 C3
Keynton Cl. Hert SG14 .... 112 F7
Keysers Rd. Lo Naz EN10 .... 135 A1
Kibes La. Ware SG12 .... 93 E1
Kidner Cl. Luton LU2 .... 45 E5
Kilbride Ct. Heml H HP2 .... 124 F7
Kilby Cl. Watf WD2 .... 154 D4
Kildonan Cl. Watf WD1 .... 166 F8
Kilfillan Gdns. Berk HP4 .... 122 A4
Kilfillan Pk. Berk HP4 .... 122 A4
Killigrew Inf Sch. Chis 141 B6
Killigrew Jun Mix Inf Sch. Chis ... 141 B6
Kilmarnock Dr. Luton LU2 .... 45 E5
Kilmarnock Rd. Sth Ox WD1 .... 175 D6
Kiln Ave. L Chal HP6 .... 150 C1
Kiln Ground. Heml H HP3 .... 139 A8
Kiln House Cl. Ware SG12 .... 93 E2
Kiln House Yd. Royst SG8 .... 7 C5
Kiln La. Bot HP5 .... 150 B8
Kiln Way. Norwd HA6 .... 174 E4
Kilncroft. Heml H HP3 .... 125 B1
Kilnfield. Wel G C AL7 .... 89 F1
Kilsmore La. Ches EN8 .... 148 D2
Kilvinton Dr. Enf EN2 .... 161 D1
Kilworth Cl. Wel G C AL7 .... 111 B4
Kimberley Cl. Bis St CM23 .... 77 A5
Kimberley. Letw SG6 .... 11 F2
Kimberley Rd. St Alb AL3 .... 127 D4
Kimble Cl. Watf WD1 .... 166 E2
Kimble Cres. Bus WD2 .... 168 C2
Kimblewick. Sth Ox WD1 .... 167 E1
Kimbolton Cres. Stev SG2 .... 69 A7
Kimbolton Gn. Bor WD6 .... 170 C5
Kimps Way. Heml H HP3 .... 139 A8
Kimpton Bottom. Kim SG4 .... 86 E7
Kimpton Cl. Heml H HP2 .... 125 B8
Kimpton Cty Prim Sch. Kim 66 C1
Kimpton La. Luton LU2 .... 64 D7
Kimpton Pl. Watf WD2 .... 154 D5
Kimpton Rd. A St P AL6 .... 89 A6
Kimpton Rd. Cod SG4 .... 67 B1
Kimpton Rd. Kim AL4 .... 87 C7
Kimpton Rd. Kim SG4 .... 65 C2
Kimpton Rd. Kim SG4 .... 67 B1
Kimptons Cl. Pot B EN6 .... 158 D7
Kimptons Mead. Pot B EN6 .... 158 D7
Kinderscout. Heml H HP3 .... 125 A1
Kindersley Cl. Welw AL6 .... 89 C6
Kindersley Cl. Welw AL6 .... 153 D8
King Arthur Ct. Ches EN8 .... 162 D6
King Charles Rd. Shen WD7 .... 156 F7
King Croft Rd. Harp AL5 .... 107 D7
King Edward Rd. Ches EN8 .... 162 E6
King Edward Rd. Shen WD7 .... 156 F6
King Edward Rd. Watf WD1 .... 167 E3
King Edward St. Heml H HP3 .... 138 D7

5

4

1

9

5

5

King Edward's Rd. Ware SG12 .... 93 E2
King George Ave. Bus WD2 .... 168 B3
King George Cl. Stev SG1 .... 50 E6
King George Rd. Wa Aby EN9 .... 163 C5
King George Rd. Ware SG12 .... 93 E2
King George's Way. Whit SG4 .... 66 E6
King Georges Ave. Watf WD1 .... 166 E8
King Georges Cl. Hit SG5 .... 21 D1
King Harold Sch. Wa Aby 163 E6
King Harry La. St Alb AL3 .... 127 B1
King Harry St. Heml H HP2 .... 124 D2
King Henry's Mews. Enf EN3 .... 163 A2
King James Ave. Cuf EN6 .... 146 E2
King James Way. Royst SG8 .... 7 D6
King St. Bis St CM23 .... 76 F7
King St. Luton LU1 .... 63 E7
King St. Mark AL3 .... 83 E5
King St. Tri HP23 .... 100 A3
King St. Watf WD1 .... 167 C5
King Street Mews. Bis St CM23 .... 76 F7 1
King's Cotts. Bis St CM23 .... 77 A6
King's La. Chipf WD4 .... 152 B8
King's Mews. Heml H HP2 .... 124 D4 3
King's Rd. Ches EN8 .... 162 E5
King's Rd. Hert SG13 .... 114 A7
King's Rd. Hit SG5 .... 34 F8
King's Rd. Lon C AL2 .... 142 C5
King's Rd. St Alb AL3 .... 127 C3
King's Walden Rd. Gt Of SG5 .... 33 D2
King's Wlk. Royst SG8 .... 7 D5
Kingfisher Cl. Gt Am SG12 .... 115 C3
Kingfisher Cl. Har HA3 .... 176 F3
Kingfisher Cl. Norwd HA6 .... 174 B2
Kingfisher Cl. Whea AL4 .... 87 D1
Kingfisher Lure. Kin L WD4 .... 139 B2
Kingfisher Lure. Ric WD3 .... 165 B5
Kingfisher Rise. Stev SG2 .... 51 D2
Kingfisher Way. Bis St CM23 .... 77 A7
Kingham Rd. Wars SG12 .... 94 E5
Kinghamway. Luton LU2 .... 45 E1
Kings Ave. Heml H HP3 .... 138 F7
Kings Ave. Watf WD1 .... 167 A5
Kings Cl. Chipf WD4 .... 152 B8
Kings Cl. Norwd HA6 .... 174 B4
Kings Cl. Watf WD1 .... 167 C5
Kings Ct. Berk HP4 .... 122 C5
Kings Ct. Bis St CM23 .... 77 A8
Kings Farm Rd. Chor WD3 .... 164 D3
Kings Field Cotts. Abb L WD5 .... 153 F8
Kings Hedges. Hit SG5 .... 34 C8
Kings Langley Jun Sch. Kin L 138 F3
Kings Langley Sch. Kin L 138 E3
Kings Langley Sta. Kin L 139 B1
Kings Meadow. Kin L WD4 .... 139 A3
Kings Oak. Cro Gr WD3 .... 166 A5
Kings Park Ind Est. Kin L 139 B2
Kings Rd. Barn EN5 .... 171 C6
Kings Rd. Berk HP4 .... 122 B3
Kings Walden Rise. Stev SG2 .... 51 C8
Kingsbridge Rd. Bis St CM23 .... 77 A8
Kingsbury Ave. St Alb AL3 .... 127 C4
Kingsbury Water Mill Mus. St Alb 127 B4
Kingscroft. Wel G C AL7 .... 111 B7
Kingsdale House. Welwi AL6 .... 89 B3
Kingsdale Rd. Berk HP4 .... 122 A3
Kingsdown Ave. Luton LU2 .... 45 D5
Kingsdown. Hit SG4 .... 35 B6
Kingsfield Cl. Watf WD1 .... 167 D2
Kingsfield Dr. Enf EN3 .... 162 D4
Kingsfield. Hod EN11 .... 135 A8
Kingsfield Rd. Dan En SG12 .... 71 E8
Kingsfield Rd. Watf WD1 .... 167 D3
Kingsfield Way. Enf EN3 .... 162 D4
Kingsgate. St Alb AL3 .... 127 B1
Kingshill Ave. St Alb AL4 .... 128 B6
Kingshill Ct. Barn EN5 .... 171 C5
Kingshill Inf Sch. Ware 93 D3
Kingshill Way. Berk HP4 .... 122 B2
Kingshott Sch. Hit 35 B5
Kingsland Cl. Luton LU1 .... 63 F6
Kingsland Rd. Heml H HP1 .... 124 A1
Kingsland Rd. Luton LU1 .... 63 F6
Kingsland Way. Ashw SG7 .... 4 D2
Kingsley Ave. Bor WD6 .... 169 F7
Kingsley Ave. Ches EN8 .... 148 C2
Kingsley Ct. Wel G C AL7 .... 110 F2
Kingsley Rd. Luton LU3 .... 45 A5
Kingsley Wlk. Tri HP23 .... 100 A4
Kingsmead. Ches EN8 .... 148 D3
Kingsmead. Cuf EN6 .... 146 E3
Kingsmead Nursery Sch. Hert 114 A5
Kingsmead Rd. Bis St CM23 .... 77 A8
Kingsmead. Saw CM21 .... 97 E1
Kingsmead. St Alb AL4 .... 128 D6
Kingsmill Ct. Hat AL10 .... 130 B3 1
Kingston Pl. Har HA3 .... 176 F3
Kingston Rd. Luton LU2 .... 45 F1
Kingston Vale. Royst SG8 .... 7 E5
Kingsway. Cuf EN6 .... 146 E1
Kingsway Bsns. Stot SG5 .... 11 E7
Kingsway Ind Est. Luton 63 A8
Kingsway Inf Sch. Watf 154 A5
Kingsway Jun Sch. Watf 154 A5
Kingsway. Luton LU1,LU4 .... 45 A1
Kingsway North Orbital Rd. Watf WD2 .... 154 B5
Kingsway. Royst SG8 .... 7 C8
Kingsway. Stot SG5 .... 11 F7
Kingsway. Ware SG12 .... 93 D3
Kingswell Ride. Cuf EN6 .... 146 E1
Kingswood Ave. Hit SG4 .... 35 D8
Kingswood Rd. Watf WD2 .... 154 B8
Kingwell Rd. Had W EN4 .... 159 D1
Kinross Cres. Luton LU3 .... 45 A6
Kinsbourne Cl. Harp AL5 .... 85 C4
Kinsbourne Cres. Harp AL5 .... 85 B3
Kinsbourne Green La. Harp AL5 .... 85 B3
Kipling Cl. Hit SG4 .... 35 C7
Kipling Gr. Heml H HP2 .... 105 B1
Kipling Pl. Stan HA7 .... 176 E1
Kipling Rd. Royst SG8 .... 2 E1
Kipling The. Luton LU3 .... 45 B6
Kipling Way. Harp AL5 .... 86 B1
Kirby Cl. Norwd HA6 .... 174 E4
Kirby Cl. Royst SG8 .... 2 E1
Kirkcaldy Gn. Sth Ox WD1 .... 175 C7 1
Kirkdale Ct. Luton LU1 .... 63 E6 3
Kirkdale Rd. Harp AL5 .... 86 A2
Kirklands. Wel G C AL8 .... 89 D2
Kirkwick Ave. Harp AL5 .... 86 A1

Kit's La. Wal SG7 .... 25 C8
Kitchener Cl. St Alb AL1 .... 128 B2
Kitching La. St Ipp SG4 .... 49 F5
Kitching La. Stev SG1 .... 50 A5
Kite Field. Nthch HP4 .... 121 E7
Kite Way. Letw SG6 .... 22 E8
Kitsbury Rd. Berk HP4 .... 122 B4
Kitsbury Terr. Berk HP4 .... 122 B4
Kitson Way. Harl CM20 .... 117 C1
Kitswell Rd. Radl WD7 .... 156 A6
Kitswell Way. Radl WD7 .... 155 F6
Kitt's End Rd. Pot B EN5 .... 158 E2
Knap Cl. Letw SG6 .... 23 D8
Knebworth Ct. Bis St CM23 .... 76 D6
Knebworth Ctry Pk. Kneb 68 C7
Knebworth Jun & Mix Inf Sch. Kneb 69 A5
Knebworth Path. Bor WD6 .... 170 D5
Knebworth Sta. Kneb 68 T1
Kneesworth House Hospl. Knee 2 C1
Kneesworth Rd. Melb SG8 .... 2 F8
Kneesworth St. Royst SG8 .... 7 C6
Knella Road Workshops. Wel G C 111 A6
Knella Rd. Wel G C AL7 .... 111 A6
Knight St. Saw CM21 .... 97 E2
Knight's Ct. Saw CM21 .... 97 E2
Knights Cl. Bis St CM23 .... 76 C8
Knights Cl. Bun SG9 .... 40 E6
Knights Cl. Bus WD2 .... 168 D1
Knights Cl. Stand SG11 .... 55 F1
Knights Field. Luton LU2 .... 45 D1
Knights Orch. Heml H HP1 .... 123 F5
Knights Orch. St Alb AL2 .... 127 C3
Knights Templar Sch. The. Bal 23 E8
Knights Templars Gn. Stev SG2 .... 51 E8
Knightsbridge Way. Heml H HP2 . 124 E4
Knightsfield. Wel G C AL8 .... 89 D2
Knoll Cres. Norwd HA6 .... 174 F2
Knoll Gn. Heml H HP2 .... 124 E5
Knoll Rise. Luton LU2 .... 45 E4
Knoll The. Hert SG13 .... 114 B7
Knolles Cres. Wel G Al9 .... 144 B7
Knolls Cl. Wing HP22 .... 60 B3
Knowl Piece. Hit SG4 .... 22 A3
Knowl Pk. Elst WD6 .... 169 E4
Knowl Way. Bor WD6 .... 169 F4
Knowle Dr. Harp AL5 .... 107 D7
Knowle. Stev SG1 .... 36 B1
Knowle The. Hod EN11 .... 135 A5
Knutsford Ave. Watf WD2 .... 154 D1
Knutsford Jun Mix Inf Sch. Watf . 154 D1
Koh-I-Noor Ave. Bus WD2 .... 168 A3
Kristiansand Way. Letw SG6 .... 23 C8
Kymswell Rd. Stev SG2 .... 51 C3
Kynance Cl. Luton LU2 .... 46 A2
Kynaston Cl. Har HA3 .... 176 D3
Kynaston Wood. Har HA3 .... 176 D3
Kyrkeby. Letw SG6 .... 23 C4
Kytes Dr. Watf WD2 .... 154 D6

Laburnum Cl. Ches EN8 .... 162 D8
Laburnum Cl. Luton LU3 .... 45 C7
Laburnum Gr. Chis AL2 .... 141 B6
Laburnum Gr. Luton LU3 .... 45 B7
Laburnum Rd. Hod EN11 .... 135 B8
Lachbury Cl. Luton LU1 .... 63 A6
Lackmore Rd. Enf EN1 .... 162 C4
Lacre Way. Letw SG6 .... 23 C7
Ladbrooke Cl. Pot B EN6 .... 159 A7
Ladbrooke Dr. Pot B EN6 .... 159 A7
Ladbrooks Prim Sch. Pot B 159 B7
Ladies Gr. St Alb AL3 .... 127 C5
Lady Gr. Wel G C AL7 .... 110 E2
Lady Spencer's Gr. St Alb AL1 ... 127 C2
Lady Zia Wernher Sch The. Luton .. 46 B3
Lady's Cl. Watf WD1 .... 167 A5
Ladyhill. Luton LU4 .... 44 B6
Ladymeadow. Kin L HP3 .... 138 D4
Ladyshot. Harl CM20 .... 118 A1
Ladysmith Rd. Har HA3 .... 176 E1
Ladysmith Rd. Pit LU7 .... 80 E5
Ladysmith Rd. St Alb AL3 .... 127 D4
Ladywalk. Map Cr WD3 .... 172 E6
Ladwell Prospect. Sheer CM21 .... 98 A1
Ladywood Cl. Ric WD3 .... 165 C6
Ladywood Rd. Hert SG14 .... 112 F6
Laidon Sq. Heml H HP2 .... 124 D7
Lake Dr. Bus WD2 .... 176 D8
Lake Rd. Lo Naz EN9 .... 135 E2
Lake The. Bus WD2 .... 168 D1
Lake View. Pot B EN6 .... 159 C6
Lake Villas. Fur P SG9 .... 43 B4
Lakeland Cl. Stan HA3 .... 176 D4
Lakeside. Bor WD6 .... 170 A4
Lakeside Pl. Lon C AL2 .... 142 D4
Lakeside Rd. Ches EN8 .... 148 C3
Lakeside Sch. Wel G C 110 B4
Lakeside. Tri HP23 .... 100 A5
Lalleford Rd. Luton LU2 .... 46 D1
Lamb Cl. Hat AL10 .... 130 B4
Lamb Cl. Watf WD2 .... 154 C5
Lamb Cl. Whea AL4 .... 108 B5
Lamb La. Red AL3 .... 106 B5
Lamb Meadow. Arl SG15 .... 11 A3
Lambert Ct. Watf WD2 .... 167 D5
Lambourn Chase. Radl WD7 .... 155 F3
Lambourn Gdns. Harp AL5 .... 85 F3
Lambs Cl. Cuf EN6 .... 146 F2
Lambs Cl. Dun LU5 .... 44 A1
Lambs Gdns. Widf SG12 .... 95 D4
Lambton Ave. Ches EN8 .... 162 D6
Lamer La. Whea AL4 .... 87 D2
Lamers Rd. Luton LU2 .... 46 D2
Lammas Mead. Hit SG5 .... 21 E2
Lammas Path. Stev SG2 .... 51 A4
Lammas Rd. Ched LU7 .... 80 A7
Lammas Rd. Wat St SG14 .... 70 D4
Lammas Rd. Watf WD1 .... 167 C4
Lammas Way. Letw SG6 .... 22 F8
Lammasmead. Hod EN10 .... 148 F8
Lamorna Cl. Luton LU3 .... 44 F6
Lamorna Cl. Radl WD7 .... 156 B5
Lampits. Hod EN11 .... 135 B6
Lamsey Rd. Heml H HP3 .... 124 F1
Lancaster Ave. Had W EN4 .... 159 D8
Lancaster Ave. Luton LU3 .... 45 C8
Lancaster Ave. Luton LU2 .... 45 C8
Lancaster Dr. Bov HP3 .... 136 F4
Lancaster Rd. Hit SG5 .... 34 E8
Lancaster Rd. St Alb AL1 .... 127 F5

Lancaster Way. Abb L WD5 .... 153 F8
Lancaster Way. Bis St CM23 .... 76 C8
Lancaster Way. Wel G C AL6 .... 89 C3
Lancing Rd. Luton LU2 .... 46 D3
Lancing Way. Cro Gr WD3 .... 166 B4
Landau Way. Ches EN10 .... 148 F5
Landford Cl. Ric WD3 .... 173 E8
Landmead Rd. Ches EN8 .... 148 E2
Lands' End. Elst WD6 .... 169 D3
Lane End. Berk HP4 .... 121 F4
Lane End. Hat AL10 .... 129 F2
Lane Gdns. Bus WD2 .... 168 E2
Lanefield Wlk. Wel G C AL8 .... 110 C6
Lanercost Cl. Welw AL6 .... 90 A7
Langbridge Cl. Hat AL10 .... 35 A4
Langdale Ave. Harp AL5 .... 86 D2
Langdale Ct. Heml H HP2 .... 124 E6 2
Langdale Gdns. Enf EN3 .... 162 D4
Langdon St. Tri HP23 .... 100 A3
Langfield Cl. Lo Naz EN9 .... 135 E1
Langford Dr. Luton LU2 .... 46 A3
Langham Cl. Luton LU2 .... 45 D7
Langham Cl. St Alb AL4 .... 128 D8
Langholme. Bal SG7 .... 168 C1
Langland Ct. Norwd HA6 .... 174 D3
Langland Dr. Pnr HA5 .... 175 E3
Langley Ave. Heml H HP3 .... 138 F8
Langley Cres. Abb L WD5 .... 139 A1
Langley Cres. St Alb AL3 .... 127 C5
Langley Gr. Sand AL4 .... 108 C2
Langley Hill. Kin L WD4 .... 139 A2
Langley Hill. Kin L WD4 .... 138 F2
Langley La. Abb L WD5 .... 153 F7
Langley La. Lan SG4 .... 49 E2
Langley Lodge La. Kin L WD4 ...... 153 A8
Langley Rd. Abb L WD5 .... 153 F8
Langley Rd. Chipf WD4 .... 138 B1
Langley Rd. Watf WD1 .... 167 A8
Langley Row. Barn EN5 .... 171 F8
Langley St. Luton LU1 .... 63 E6
Langley Warf. Abb L 139 A4
Langley Way. Watf WD1 .... 166 F8
Langleybury La. Abb L WD4 .... 153 B4
Langleybury Sch. Abb L 153 B5
Langmead Dr. Bus WD2 .... 168 D1
Langthorne Ave. Stev SG1 .... 50 E6
Langton Gr. Norwd HA6 .... 174 C5
Langton House. Hod EN11 .... 134 F6
Langton Rd. Har HA3 .... 176 C3
Langton Rd. Hod EN11 .... 134 F6
Langwood Gdns. Watf WD1 .... 167 A8
Lankester Rd. Royst SG8 .... 7 C5
Lannock Hill. Wes SG4 .... 23 E1
Lannock Jun Mix Inf Sch. Letw 23 C4
Lannock. Letw SG6 .... 23 D4
Lanrick Copse. Berk HP4 .... 122 E5
Lansdowne Cl. Watf WD2 .... 154 D4
Lansdowne Ct. Hod EN10 .... 135 A3
Lansdowne Rd. Luton LU3 .... 45 D1
Lanterns La. Stev SG2 .... 51 D5
Lanthony Ct. Arl SG15 .... 11 A4
Laporte Way. Luton LU4 .... 44 F1
Laporte Way. Luton LU4 .... 45 A1
Lapwing Cl. Heml H HP2 .... 124 E6
Lapwing Dell. Letw SG6 .... 23 B3
Lapwing Rd. Dun LU4 .... 44 A4
Lapwing Rise. Stev SG2 .... 51 D3
Larch Ave. Bri Wd AL2 .... 140 E1
Larch Ave. Hit SG4 .... 35 A4
Larch Cl. Ham St EN7 .... 147 E4
Larch La. Welw AL6 .... 89 F8
Larch Rise. Berk HP4 .... 122 A5
Larches Ave. Enf EN1 .... 162 C4
Larches The. Luton LU2 .... 45 D1
Larches The. Nthch HP4 .... 121 D5
Larches The. St Alb AL4 .... 128 D7
Larches The. Ware SG12 .... 93 C4
Larches The. Watf WD2 .... 167 E4
Larchwood. Bis St CM23 .... 76 D5
Lark Rise. Hat AL10 .... 130 A3
Larke Way. Luton LU4 .... 44 C5
Larken Cl. Bus WD2 .... 168 C1
Larken Dr. Bus WD2 .... 168 C1
Larkens Cl. Stand SG11 .... 55 D3
Larkins Cl. Bal SG7 .... 12 F1
Larkinson. Stev SG1 .... 50 C7
Larks Ridge. Chis AL2 .... 141 A4
Larksfield. Ware SG12 .... 93 E3
Larkspur Cl. Bis St CM23 .... 76 C8
Larkspur Cl. Heml H HP1 .... 123 E4
Larkspur Gdns. Luton LU4 .... 44 F2
Larksway. Bis St CM23 .... 76 C6
Larkswood Rise. St Alb AL4 .... 128 C8
Larmans Rd. Enf EN3 .... 162 D3
Larsen Dr. Wa Aby EN9 .... 163 D5
Larwood Gr. Stev SG1 .... 51 A8
Latchmore Bank. L Hal CM22 .... 77 B1
Latchmore Cl. Hit SG4 .... 34 F5
Latimer Cl. Heml H HP2 .... 125 B8
Latimer Cl. Pnr HA5 .... 175 C2
Latimer Cl. Watf WD1 .... 166 E2
Latimer Ct. Ches EN8 .... 162 F5
Latimer Gdns. Pnr HA5 .... 175 C2
Latimer Gdns. Wel G C AL7 .... 111 B6
Latimer Rd. L Chal HP6 .... 150 F2
Latimer Rd. Luton LU1 .... 63 E6
Latium Cl. St Alb AL1 .... 127 D2
Lattimore Cl. St Alb AL1 .... 127 D4
Lattimore Rd. Whea AL4 .... 108 C8
Latton Hall Cl. Harl CM20 .... 118 A1
Lauderdale Rd. Abb L WD4 .... 153 C3
Laughton Dr. Bor WD6 .... 170 D7
Laundry La. Lo Naz EN9 .... 149 E6
Launton Cl. Luton LU3 .... 31 B1
Laurance Haines Inf & Jun Sch The. Watf 167 A3
Laureate Way. Heml H HP1 .... 124 B5
Laurel Ave. Pot B EN6 .... 158 F7
Laurel Cl. Heml H HP2 .... 124 F5
Laurel Fields. Pot B EN6 .... 158 F5
Laurel Mews. Bal SG7 .... 12 F1
Laurel Pk. Har HA3 .... 176 F3
Laurel Way. Ick SG5 .... 21 E3
Laureldene. Muc H SG10 .... 74 F1
Laurels Cl. St Alb AL3 .... 141 B8
Laurels The. Ham St EN7 .... 147 E5
Laurels The. Pot En HP4 .... 123 C6
Laurino Pl. Bus WD2 .... 176 D8

Lavender Cl. Ham St EN7 .... 147 E3
Lavender Cl. Luton LU2 .... 45 E7
Lavender Ct. Bal SG7 .... 12 E1
Lavender Gdns. Enf EN2 .... 161 B1
Lavender Gdns. Har HA3 .... 176 E4
Lavender Rd. Enf EN2 .... 161 D1
Lavender Sch. Enf 161 E1
Lavender Way. Hit SG5 .... 34 D7
Lavender Wlk. Heml H HP2 .... 124 A1
Lavinia Ave. Watf WD2 .... 154 D5
Lavrock La. Cro Gr WD3 .... 165 F2
Law Hall La. Whit SG4 .... 66 A8
Lawford Ave. Chor WD3 .... 164 C3
Lawford Cl. Chor WD3 .... 164 C3
Lawford Cl. Luton LU3 .... 63 C7
Lawn Ave. Kim SG4 .... 66 C1
Lawn Gdns. Luton LU3 .... 63 D6
Lawn La. Heml H HP3 .... 138 D8
Lawn The. Harl CM20 .... 118 B3
Lawn Vale. Pnr HA5 .... 175 E1
Lawns Cl. Gt Of SG5 .... 33 C2
Lawns Ct. Royst SG8 .... 7 D5
Lawns Dr The. Hod EN10 .... 134 F3
Lawns The. Har HA5 .... 176 B3
Lawns The. Heml H HP1 .... 123 E4
Lawns The. St Alb AL3 .... 127 C4
Lawns The. Stev SG2 .... 51 D4
Lawns The. Wel G C AL8 .... 89 D1
Lawrance Gdns. Ches EN8 .... 148 D3
Lawrance Rd. St Alb AL3 .... 127 C7
Lawrence Ave. Gt Am SG12 .... 115 C3
Lawrence Ave. Letw SG6 .... 23 A4
Lawrence Ave. Saw CM21 .... 97 E4
Lawrence Ave. Stev SG1 .... 50 E7
Lawrence Cl. Hert SG14 .... 112 E7
Lawrence End Rd. Bre Gr LU2 ...... 84 E6
Lawrence Moorings. Sheer CM21 .. 97 F1
Lawrie Ct. Har HA3 .... 176 F3
Laxton Cl. Luton LU2 .... 46 E1
Laxton Gdns. Bal SG7 .... 24 A7
Lay Brook. St Alb AL4 .... 128 A7
Layard Rd. Enf EN1 .... 161 F1
Layham Dr. Luton LU2 .... 46 D1
Layhill. Heml H HP2 .... 124 D5
Layston Fst Sch. Bun 40 F6
Layston Meadow. Bun SG9 .... 40 F6
Layston Pk. Royst SG8 .... 7 D5
Lea Bank Cl. Luton LU3 .... 44 E5
Lea Bank. Luton LU3 .... 44 E6
Lea Bushes. Watf WD2 .... 154 E5
Lea Cl. Bis St CM23 .... 59 B1
Lea Cl. Bus WD2 .... 168 B4
Lea Farm Jun Mix Sch. Watf 154 D4
Lea Gr. Bis St CM23 .... 59 B1
Lea Manor High Sch. Luton 44 F8
Lea Manor Recn Ctr. Luton 44 F8
Lea Mount. Gofs O EN7 .... 147 E3
Lea Rd. Ches EN8 .... 163 A5
Lea Rd. Harp AL5 .... 86 B3
Lea Rd. Hod EN11 .... 135 C8
Lea Rd. Luton LU1 .... 63 F7
Lea Rd. Watf WD2 .... 154 B1
Lea Wlk. Harp AL5 .... 86 C4
Leacroft. Harp AL5 .... 86 D3
Leaders Cl. Wing HP22 .... 60 B3
Leaf Cl. Norwd HA6 .... 174 B4
Leafield. Luton LU3 .... 44 E5
Leaford Cres. Watf WD2 .... 153 F2
Leaford Ct. Watf WD2 .... 153 F3
Leaforis Rd. Ches EN7 .... 148 A3
Leafy La. Ast Cl HP23 .... 99 E1
Leagrave High St. Dun LU4 .... 44 B3
Leagrave Inf Sch. Luton 44 C4
Leagrave Jun Mix Inf Sch. Luton .. 44 C4
Leagrave Rd. Luton LU3,LU4 .... 45 B2
Leagrave Sta. Luton 44 C5
Leahoe Gdns. Hert SG13 .... 113 C5
Lealands High Sch. Luton 44 A8
Leamington Cl. Luton LU3 .... 45 A7
Leander Gdns. Watf WD2 .... 154 B2
Leas The. Bal SG7 .... 23 E7
Leas The. Bus WD2 .... 167 F7
Leas The. Heml H HP3 .... 139 A7
Leaside Cl. Harp AL5 .... 86 C3
Leaside. Heml H HP2 .... 125 C2
Leaside Wlk. Ware SG12 .... 93 D1 5
Leat Cl. Saw CM21 .... 97 F3
Leathersellers Cl. Barn EN5 .... 171 E6
Leathwaite Cl. Luton LU3 .... 44 F6
Leaves Spring. Stev SG2 .... 51 A2
Leavesden Green Inf Sch. Watf 154 A5
Leavesden Green Jun Mix Inf Sch. Watf 154 A5
Leavesden Hospl. Abb L 154 A8
Leavesden Rd. Watf WD2 .... 154 B1
Leaview. Wa Aby EN9 .... 163 B6
Lebanon Cl. Watf WD1 .... 153 D3
Lectern La. St Alb AL1 .... 141 E7
Leda Ave. Enf EN3 .... 162 D1
Ledgemore La. Gt Gd HP2 .... 103 F5
Ledwell Rd. Cad LU1 .... 62 F3
Lee Cl. Gt Am SG12 .... 115 C4
Lee Cl. Hert SG13 .... 113 C4
Lee Farm Cl. Bot HP5 .... 136 A1
Lee Road Ind Pk. Ches 163 A5
Leechers Way. Ched LU7 .... 80 A7
Leecroft Rd. Barn EN5 .... 171 E5
Leefe Way. Cuf EN6 .... 146 D3
Leeming Rd. Bor WD6 .... 169 F8
Lees Ave. Norwd HA6 .... 174 F2
Leeside. Barn EN5 .... 171 E3
Leeside. Pot B EN6 .... 159 D7
Leete Pl. Royst SG8 .... 7 D7
Leggatts Campus The. Watf 154 A4
Leggatts Cl. Watf WD2 .... 153 F3
Leggatts Rise. Watf WD2 .... 154 A4
Leggatts Way. Watf WD2 .... 153 F3
Leggatts Wood Ave. Watf WD2 .... 154 A3
Leggett Gr. Stev SG1 .... 50 E8
Leggfield Terr. Heml H HP1 .... 123 F3
Leghorn Cres. Dun LU4 .... 44 A3
Legions Way. Bis St CM23 .... 77 A8
Leicester Rd. Luton LU4 .... 44 E1
Leigh Comm. Wel G C AL7 .... 110 F4
Leigh Rodd. Sth Ox WD1 .... 175 F3
Leighton Buzzard Rd. Gt Gd HP1 .. 103 F2
Leighton Buzzard Rd. Heml H HP1 . 124 A4
Leighton Rd. Ches LU6 .... 148 D5
Leighton Rd. Har HA3 .... 176 C3

Leighton Rd. Wing HP22 .... 60 C3
Lemon Field Dr. Watf WD2 .... 154 E6
Lemsford Cl. Bor WD6 .... 170 C5
Lemsford La. Wel G C AL8 .... 110 B8
Lemsford Rd. Hat AL10 .... 130 A6
Lemsford Rd. St Alb AL1 .... 127 F4
Lemsford Springs (Nature Reserve). Hat 110 A5
Lemsford Village. Wel G C AL8 .... 109 F5
Lennon Cl. Luton LU1 .... 63 D7
Lennox Gn. Luton LU2 .... 46 F2
Lensbury Cl. Ches EN8 .... 148 E3
Leonard's Cl. Welw AL6 .... 89 E8
Lesbury Cl. Luton LU2 .... 46 F2
Leslie Cl. Stev SG2 .... 51 C2
Letchfield. Bot HP5 .... 150 B8
Letchmore Rd. Stev SG1 .... 50 E8
Letchmore Rd. Radl WD7 .... 156 A3
Letchmore Bsns & Ret Pk. Letw ... 23 C6
Letchworth Cl. Sth Ox WD1 .... 175 D5
Letchworth Gate. Letw SG6 .... 23 B4
Letchworth La. Letw SG6 .... 22 F3
Letchworth Rd. Bal SG7 .... 23 D7
Letchworth Rd. Letw SG6 .... 23 D7
Letchworth Rd. Luton LU3 .... 45 A6
Letter Box Row. Hit SG4 .... 34 F8
Leven Cl. Ches EN8 .... 162 D6
Leven Cl. Sth Ox WD1 .... 175 D5
Leven Dr. Ches EN8 .... 162 D6
Leven Way. Heml H HP2 .... 124 D7
Levenage La. Widf SG12 .... 95 E3
Leventhorpe Sch The. Saw 97 E4
Leveret Cl. Watf WD2 .... 154 A5
Leverstock Green Jun Mix Inf Sch. Heml 125 D2
Leverstock Green Rd. Heml H HP2,HP3 .... 125 B3
Leverstock Green Rd. Heml H HP2,HP3 .... 125 C2
Leverstock Green Way. Heml H HP2,HP3 .... 125 C3
Leverton Cty Prim & Inf Sch The. Wa Aby 163 F5
Leverton Way. Wa Aby EN9 .... 163 C6
Lewes Way. Cro Gr WD3 .... 166 C5
Lewis Cl. Hare UB9 .... 173 C1
Lewsey Park Ct. Dun LU4 .... 44 A4
Lewsey Rd. Dun LU4 .... 44 A4
Lexington Cl. Bor WD6 .... 169 F6
Lexington Ct. Pot B EN6 .... 158 D8
Lexington Way. Barn EN5 .... 171 C5
Ley House. Wel G C AL7 .... 111 C6
Ley Park Fst Sch. Hod 134 F1
Ley Park Jun Sch. Hod 134 F1
Ley Wlk. Wel G C AL7 .... 111 C6
Leyburne Cl. Men LU7 .... 61 C8
Leyburne Rd. Luton LU3 .... 45 B3
Leycroft Way. Harp AL5 .... 107 E2
Leyden House (Adult Training Ctr). Stev 50 D2
Leyden Rd. Stev SG1 .... 50 D2
Leygreen Cl. Luton LU2 .... 64 A8
Leyhill Dr. Luton LU1 .... 63 B4
Leyland Ave. St Alb AL1 .... 127 D1
Leyland Cl. Ches EN8 .... 148 C2
Leys Ave. Letw SG6 .... 22 F6
Leys Cl. Hare UB9 .... 173 D2
Leys Rd. Heml H HP3 .... 124 F1
Leys The. St Alb AL4 .... 128 D6
Leys The. Tri HP23 .... 100 A4
Leysdown. Wel G C AL7 .... 111 D6
Leyton Gn. Harp AL5 .... 86 A1
Leyton Rd. Harp AL5 .... 86 A1
Library Rd. Luton LU1 .... 63 E7
Lichfield Rd. Norwd HA6 .... 175 A1
Lichfield Way. Hod EN10 .... 134 F1
Liddel Cl. Luton LU3 .... 45 B3
Lidgate Cl. Luton LU4 .... 44 B6
Lighthorne Rise. Luton LU3 .... 45 A7
Lilac Ave. Enf EN1 .... 162 C1
Lilac Cl. Ches EN7 .... 162 B8
Lilac Gr. Luton LU3 .... 44 C8
Lilac Rd. Hod EN11 .... 135 B8
Lilac Way. Harp AL5 .... 107 D6
Lilley Bottom. Bre Gr SG5 .... 47 C5
Lilley Bottom. Gt Of SG4 .... 47 C5
Lilley Bottom Rd. Bre Gr SG4 ...... 48 B1
Lilley Bottom Rd. Whit SG4 .... 48 B1
Lilley CE Jun Mix Inf Sch. Lily 32 D2
Lilleyhoo La. Lily LU2 .... 32 F2
Lilliard Cl. Hod EN11 .... 115 B3
Limberlost The. Welw AL6 .... 89 B7
Limbrick Rd. Harp AL5 .... 107 C6
Limbury Rd. Luton LU3 .... 44 F4
Lime Ave. Dun LU4 .... 44 C3
Lime Ave. Kim AL4 .... 87 B7
Lime Cl. Ast SG2 .... 51 D4
Lime Cl. Ware SG12 .... 93 E2
Lime Cl. Watf WD1 .... 167 D2
Lime Gr. Barn N20 .... 171 F1
Lime Gr. Royst SG8 .... 7 E8
Lime Tree Pl. St Alb AL1 .... 127 E2
Lime Tree Wlk. Bus WD2 .... 176 E8
Lime Tree Wlk. Enf EN2 .... 161 C1
Lime Tree Wlk. Ric WD3 .... 165 B4
Lime Walk Prim Sch. Heml H 124 F1
Lime Wlk. Heml H HP3 .... 124 F1
Limedene Cl. Pnr HA5 .... 175 D2
Limekiln La. Bal SG7 .... 23 F7
Limekiln La. Sta M CM24 .... 59 C5
Limes Cres. Bis St CM23 .... 77 A7
Limes The. Arl SG15 .... 11 A4
Limes The. Hit SG5 .... 34 D6
Limes The. St Alb AL1 .... 127 C5
Limes The. Wel G C AL7 .... 111 A4
Limetree Ave. Nwml E LU1 .... 85 A7
Limetree Ct. Pnr HA5 .... 176 A3
Linacres. Luton LU4 .... 44 C6
Linbridge Way. Luton LU3 .... 45 A6
Linces Way. Wel G C AL7 .... 111 A3
Lincoln Cl. Bis St CM23 .... 76 D5
Lincoln Cl. Wel G C AL7 .... 111 D6
Lincoln Ct. Berk HP4 .... 122 B4

Lincoln Ct. Bor WD6 .... 170 D4
Lincoln Dr. Cro Gr WD3 .... 166 B6
Lincoln Dr. Sth Ox WD1 .... 175 C7
Lincoln Hill. Ans SG9 .... 29 A5
Lincoln Mews. St Alb AL3 .... 127 A6
Lincoln Rd. Luton LU4 .... 45 B1
Lincoln Rd. Stev SG1 .... 37 B2
Lincoln Way. Cro Gr WD3 .... 166 B5
Lincoln's Cl. St Alb AL4 .... 128 D8
Lincot La. Whit SG4 .... 67 C7
Lindbergh. Wel G C AL7 .... 111 C6
Linden Cl. Ches EN7 .... 148 B1
Linden Cres. St Alb AL4 .... 128 C3
Linden Ct. Harp AL5 .... 107 B8
Linden Ct. Luton LU2 .... 63 F8
Linden Glade. Heml H HP1 .... 124 A2
Linden Lea. Watf WD2 .... 154 A6
Linden Rd. Luton LU4 .... 44 E4
Linden Rd. Red AL3 .... 106 A6
Lindencroft. Letw SG6 .... 12 A1
Lindens The. Bis St CM23 .... 76 F6
Lindens The. Hat AL10 .... 129 F6
Lindens The. Heml H HP3 .... 137 F8
Lindens The. Stev SG1 .... 50 E4
Lindley Cl. Harp AL5 .... 86 A4
Lindley Cl. Harp AL5 .... 86 A4
Lindlings. Heml H HP1 .... 123 E2
Lindsay Ave. Hit SG4 .... 35 B5
Lindsay Cl. Royst SG8 .... 2 C1
Lindsay Pl. Ches EN7 .... 148 B1
Lindsey Cl. Bis St CM23 .... 58 F1
Lindsey Cl. Bis St CM23 .... 58 F1
Lindsey Rd. Luton LU2 .... 46 D1
Lindum Pl. St Alb AL3 .... 127 A1
Lingfield Cl. Norwd HA6 .... 174 C3
Lingfield Rd. Royst SG8 .... 7 E6
Lingfield Rd. Stev SG1 .... 37 C1
Lingholm Way. Barn EN5 .... 171 D4
Lingmoor Dr. Watf WD2 .... 154 C6
Linington Ave. Bot HP5 .... 136 A1
Link Cl. Hat AL10 .... 130 B5
Link Rd. Bis St CM23 .... 76 F8
Link Rd. Bus WD2 .... 167 D4
Link Rd. Welw AL6 .... 89 F8
Link The. Letw SG6 .... 12 A1
Link Way. Bis St CM23 .... 76 E6
Link Wlk. Hat AL10 .... 130 B6
Linkfield. Wel G C AL7 .... 110 E2
Links Ave. Hert SG13 .... 114 B7
Links Bsns Ctr The. Bis St 77 C7
Links Dr. Bor WD6 .... 169 F5
Links Dr. Radl WD7 .... 155 F6
Links The. Ches EN8 .... 148 D5
Links View. St Alb AL3 .... 127 C5
Links Way. Cro Gr WD3 .... 166 C5
Links Way. Luton LU2 .... 45 D8
Linksway. Norwd HA6 .... 174 C2
Linkway. Pnr HA5 .... 175 D2
Linkways E. Stev SG1 .... 50 F5
Linkways W. Stev SG1 .... 50 F5
Linnet Cl. Bus WD2 .... 168 C1
Linnet Cl. Dun LU4 .... 44 A4
Linnet Cl. Letw SG6 .... 22 E8
Linnet Wlk. Hat AL10 .... 130 B4
Linsey Cl. Heml H HP3 .... 139 A7
Linster Gr. Bor WD6 .... 170 C7
Linten Cl. Hit SG4 .... 35 C6
Linton Ave. Bor WD6 .... 169 F7
Lintott Cl. Stev SG1 .... 50 D6
Linwood Rd. Harp AL5 .... 107 C6
Linwood Rd. Ware SG12 .... 93 F3
Linwood. Saw CM21 .... 97 E2
Lion Ct. Bor WD6 .... 170 C8
Lion Yd. Kim SG4 .... 66 D1
Liphook Rd. Sth Ox WD1 .... 175 D6
Lippitts Hill. Luton LU2 .... 45 E5
Lismore. Heml H HP3 .... 125 C1
Lismore. Stev SG2 .... 51 C1
Lister Ave. Hit SG4 .... 34 F5
Lister Cl. Stev SG1 .... 36 C2
Lister Hospl. Stev 36 B1
Liston Cl. Luton LU4 .... 44 B5
Little Acre. St Alb AL3 .... 127 D6
Little Acres. Ware SG12 .... 114 D8
Little Berries. Luton LU3 .... 44 E7
Little Bridge Rd. Berk HP4 .... 122 D4
Little Bushey La. Bus WD2 .... 168 C5
Little Catherells. Heml H HP1 ...... 123 F5
Little Chishill Rd. Gt Ch SG8 .... 18 C8
Little Church Rd. Luton LU2 .... 46 B3
Little Dell. Wel G C AL8 .... 110 D8
Little Furze Jun Mix Inf Sch.
   Sth Ox 175 B7
Little Gaddesden C of E Sch.
   L Gad 102 C8
Little Ganett. Wel G C AL7 .... 111 C4
Little Gr. Bus WD2 .... 168 B5
Little Graylings. Abb L WD5 .... 153 E6
Little Green Cty Prim Sch. Cro Gr 166 B6
Little Green La. Cro Gr WD3 .... 166 B6
Little Green La. Sar WD3 .... 166 B6
Little Hadham Cty Prim Sch. L Had . 57 C2
Little Hallingbury CE Prim Sch.
   L Hal 98 C8
Little Hardings. Wel G C AL7 ...... 111 C7
Little Hayes. Kin L WD4 .... 139 A2
Little Heath La. Berk HP4 .... 123 B4
Little Heath La. Pot En HP4 .... 123 B4
Little Heath Prim Sch. Pot B 145 C1
Little Heath. Sheer CM22 .... 98 F3
Little Heath Spinney. St Alb AL3 .. 127 E5
Little Henleys. Hun SG12 .... 95 D1
Little Hill. Chor WD3 .... 164 C3
Little Hoo. Tri HP23 .... 99 F4
Little La. Harp AL5 .... 107 C6
Little La. Pirt SG5 .... 20 D5
Little Lake. Wel G C AL7 .... 111 B3
Little Larkins. Barn EN5 .... 171 E3
Little Martins. Bus WD2 .... 168 B4
Little Mead. Hat AL10 .... 130 B8
Little Mimms. Heml H HP2 .... 124 E4   2

Little Mollards. Wing HP22 .... 60 A3
Little Moss La. Pnr HA5 .... 175 E1
Little Mundells. Wel G C AL7 ...... 110 F8
Little Mundem Jun Mix & Inf Sch.
   Dan 71 E8
Little Orchard Cl. Abb L WD5 ...... 153 D7
Little Orchard Cl. Pnr HA5 .... 175 E1
Little Oxhey La. Sth Ox WD1 ...... 175 E6
Little Parndon Cty Jun & Inf Sch.
   Harl 117 B1
Little Piper's Cl. Gofs O EN7 ...... 147 B2
Little Pk. Bov HP3 .... 137 A3
Little Potters. Bus WD2 .... 168 E2
Little Reddings Sch. Bus 168 B4
Little Ridge. Wel G C AL7 .... 111 A6
Little Rivers. Wel G C AL7 .... 111 A7
Little Thistle. Wel G C AL7 .... 111 C4
Little Tring. Tri HP23 .... 99 F6
Little Twye Rd. Chol HP23 .... 120 A3
Little Twye Rd. St Le HP23 .... 119 F3
Little Wade. Wel G C AL7 .... 110 F3
Little Widbury La. Ware SG12 ..... 93 F1
Little Widbury. Ware SG12 .... 93 F1
Little Windmill Hill. Chipf WD4 ... 151 F3
Little Wlk. Harl CM20 .... 117 D1
Little Wood Croft. Luton LU3 ..... 44 E7
Little Youngs. Wel G C AL8 .... 110 C6
Littlebrook Gdns. Ches EN8 .... 148 D1
Littlecote Pl. Pnr HA5 .... 175 E2
Littlefield Rd. Luton LU2 .... 46 B2
Littlegreen La. Cad LU1 .... 62 E3
Liverpool Rd. Luton LU1 .... 63 D7
Liverpool Rd. St Alb AL1 .... 127 E3
Liverpool Rd. Watf WD1 .... 167 B4
Livingstone Ct. Barn EN5 .... 171 E7
Livingstone Link. Stev SG2 .... 51 B8
Livingstone Wlk. Heml H HP2 ..... 124 F7
Lloyd Way. Kim SG4 .... 66 C1
Loates La. Watf WD1 .... 167 C6
Loates Pasture. Sta M CM24 ...... 59 D8
Local Board Rd. Watf WD1 .... 167 D4
Locarno Ave. Luton LU4 .... 44 C6
Lochinvar House Sch. Pot B 145 B1
Lochnell Rd. Berk HP4 .... 121 F6
Lock View. Saw CM21 .... 97 F2
Lockers Park La. Heml H HP1 ...... 124 B3
Locket Rd. Har HA3 .... 176 F1
Lockley Cres. Hat AL10 .... 130 B7
Lockleys Dr. Welw AL6 .... 89 C5
Lodge Ave. Bor WD6 .... 169 F4
Lodge Cl. Hert SG14 .... 113 C8
Lodge Cres. Ches EN8 .... 162 D5
Lodge Cl. Abb L HA0 .... 154 A7
Lodge Cl. Ick SG5 .... 21 E3
Lodge Dr. Hat AL9 .... 130 D8
Lodge Dr. Ric WD3 .... 165 C5
Lodge End. Cro Gr WD3 .... 166 D5
Lodge End. Radl WD7 .... 156 B5
Lodge Farm Inf & Jun Sch. Stev .. 51 C7
Lodge Field. Wel G C AL7 .... 89 E1
Lodge Gdns. Harp AL5 .... 86 A2
Lodge La. Wa Aby EN9 .... 163 D4
Lodge Way. Stev SG2 .... 51 A1
Loftus Cl. Dun LU4 .... 44 B3
Logans. Barn EN5 .... 171 D6
Lombardy Cl. Heml H HP2 .... 125 D2
Lombardy Dr. Berk HP4 .... 122 D3
Lombardy Way. Bor WD6 .... 169 E7
Lomond Rd. Heml H HP2 .... 124 D7
London Bible Coll. Norwd 174 D4
London Colney Jun Mix Inf Sch.
   Lon C 142 D6
London Colney Jun Mix Inf Sch.
   Lon C 142 D6
London Airport. Luton 64 C7
London Rd. Ast Cl HP22 .... 99 A4
London Rd. Bal SG7 .... 23 F6
London Rd. Bar SG8 .... 8 F1
London Rd. Bark SG8,SG9 .... 17 D1
London Rd. Berk HP4 .... 122 E3
London Rd. Bis St CM23 .... 77 A4
London Rd. Bun SG9 .... 40 F6
London Rd. Bus WD2 .... 167 F3
London Rd. Harl CM17 .... 118 C2
London Rd. Heml H HP1,HP3 ...... 124 A1
London Rd. Hert H SG13 .... 113 E5
London Rd. Hert H SG13 .... 114 B3
London Rd. Hit SG4 .... 34 F5
London Rd. Kneb SG3 .... 69 A3
London Rd. Lan SG4 .... 49 D5
London Rd. Luton LU1 .... 63 E4
London Rd. Mark AL3 .... 83 F5
London Rd. Nwml E LU1 .... 84 F7
London Rd. Ric WD3 .... 173 E8
London Rd. Royst SG8 .... 7 D5
London Rd. Saw CM21 .... 97 E2
London Rd. Shen WD7 .... 157 A5
London Rd. Stev SG1,SG2 .... 50 D3
London Rd. Tri HP23 .... 100 A3
London Rd. Ware SG12 .... 114 E7
London Rd. Welw AL6 .... 69 A3
London Rd. Welw AL6 .... 89 C4
London Row. Arl SG15 .... 11 A3
Londrina Ct. Berk HP4 .... 122 D4
Londrina Terr. Berk HP4 .... 122 D4
Long Acre. Harl CM17 .... 118 D4
Long Arrotts. Heml H HP1 .... 124 B5
Long Barn Cl. Watf WD2 .... 154 A7
Long Buftlers. Harp AL5 .... 107 F8
Long Chaulden. Heml H HP1 ...... 123 E3
Long Cl. Luton LU2 .... 46 C3
Long Croft Dr. Ches EN8 .... 163 A5
Long Croft Rd. Luton LU2 .... 46 C3
Long Croft Rd. Map Cr WD3 .... 172 D5
Long Croft. Sta M CM22 .... 59 D8
Long Croft. Watf WD1 .... 167 B2
Long Cutt. Redl AL3 .... 106 A6
Long Elmes. Har HA3 .... 176 C1
Long Elms Abb L WD5 .... 153 D6
Long Elms. Abb L WD5 .... 153 D6
Long Fallow. Chis AL2 .... 141 A4
Long Hyde. Stev SG2 .... 51 B4
Long John. Heml H HP3 .... 124 F1
Long La. Ast SG2 .... 51 E5
Long La. Bov HP3 .... 150 F8
Long La. Chor WD3 .... 164 D2
Long La. Whit SG4 .... 66 A7
Long Leaves. Stev SG2 .... 51 A2
Long Ley. Ched LU7 .... 80 A7
Long Ley. Harl CM20 .... 117 F1

Long Ley. Wel G C AL7 .... 111 C6
Long Marston Jun Mix Inf Sch.
   Lon M 79 B4
Long Marston Rd. Mars HP23 ..... 79 F2
Long Meadow. Bis St CM23 .... 76 D6
Long Meadow. Mark AL3 .... 83 F5
Long Mimms. Heml H HP2 .... 124 E4   3
Long Moor. Ches EN8 .... 148 E2
Long Ridge. Ast SG2 .... 51 D1
Long Spring. St Alb AL3 .... 127 F7
Long View. Berk HP4 .... 122 A6
Longacres. St Alb AL4 .... 128 D3
Longbridge Cl. Tri HP23 .... 100 A6
Longcliffe Path. Sth Ox WD1 ...... 175 A7
Longcroft Ave. Harp AL5 .... 85 F1
Longcroft Gn. Wel G C AL8 .... 110 D5
Longcroft La. Bov HP3 .... 137 D5
Longcroft La. Wel G C AL8 .... 110 D5
Longcroft Rd. Stev SG1 .... 50 E7
Longcrofts. Wa Aby EN9 .... 163 E5
Longdean Pk. Heml H HP3 .... 139 A7
Longdean Sch. Bus 139 B8
Longfield Ave. Enf EN3 .... 162 C1
Longfield Cl. Letw SG6 .... 22 D7
Longfield Gdns. Tri HP23 .... 99 E3
Longfield. Heml H HP3 .... 125 B1
Longfield La. Ware SG12 .... 148 A4
Longfield Rd. Harp AL5 .... 107 C7
Longfield Rd. Tri HP23 .... 99 F3
Longfield Sch. Stev 50 B8
Longfields. Stev SG2 .... 51 C1
Longlands Cl. Ches EN8 .... 162 D7
Longlands. Heml H HP2 .... 125 A3
Longlands Prim Sch. Ches 148 F6
Longlands Rd. Wel G C AL7 .... 110 F5
Longleigh. Letw SG6 .... 11 F1
Longmans. Brag SG11 .... 55 F7
Longmead. Bun SG9 .... 40 D7
Longmead. Hat AL10 .... 130 B8
Longmead Jun & Inf Sch. Stev 51 B1
Longmead. Letw SG6 .... 22 E7
Longmead. Welw SG3 .... 69 A2
Longmeadow Dr. Ick SG5 .... 21 F5
Longmore Cl. Map Cr WD3 .... 172 F6
Longmore Gdns. Wel G C AL7 .... 110 F6
Longspring. Watf WD2 .... 154 B4
Longwood Rd. Hert SG14 .... 112 F8
Loning The. Enf EN3 .... 162 C1
Lonsdale Cl. Luton LU3 .... 45 B5
Lonsdale Cl. Pnr HA5 .... 175 E2
Lonsdale Cl. Stev SG1 .... 50 F7
Lonsdale. Heml H HP2 .... 124 E6
Lonsdale Rd. Stev SG1 .... 50 F7
Lonsdale Sch. Stev 50 F7
Loom La. Radl WD7 .... 156 A2
Loom Pl. Radl WD7 .... 156 A3
Loop Rd. Wa Aby EN9 .... 163 B7
Lorane Ct. Watf WD1 .... 167 A2
Lord Mead La. A St L AL6 .... 88 C7
Lord St. Hod EN11 .... 134 D6
Lord St. Watf WD1 .... 167 C4
Lords Ave. Bis St CM23 .... 76 F5
Lords Cl. Shen WD7 .... 156 E7
Lords Meadow. Red AL3 .... 106 A5
Lords Wood. Wel G C AL7 .... 111 A5
Lordship Ctr. Letw SG6 .... 23 A3
Lordship Farm Jun Mix Inf Sch.
   Letw 23 A3
Lordship La. Letw SG6 .... 23 B4
Lordship Rd. Ches EN7 .... 148 B1
Loreto Coll. St Alb 127 E3
Loring Rd. Berk HP4 .... 122 C3
Lorne Rd. Har HA3 .... 176 F1
Lorraine Pk. Har HA3 .... 176 F2
Lorrimer Cl. Luton LU2 .... 45 E6
Lothair Rd. Luton LU2 .... 45 E6
Loudwater Dr. Ric WD3 .... 165 C6
Loudwater House. Ric WD3 .... 165 C5
Loudwater Hts. Ric WD3 .... 165 C6
Loudwater La. Ric WD3 .... 165 C4
Loudwater Ridge. Ric WD3 .... 165 C5
Louisa Cotts. Tri HP23 .... 100 A3
Louise Wlk. Bov HP3 .... 137 A3
Louvain Way. Watf WD2 .... 154 B7
Lovatts. Cro Gr WD3 .... 166 A5
Love La. Abb L WD5 .... 139 F1
Love La. Ashw SG7 .... 4 A4
Love La. Kin L WD4 .... 138 E3
Love La. Luton LU2 .... 175 E1
Lovel Cl. Heml H HP1 .... 124 A3
Lovell Rd. Enf EN1 .... 162 B3
Low Hill Rd. Lo Naz CM19 .... 135 F4
Low Rd. Ess AL9 .... 131 F8
Lowbell La. Lon C AL2 .... 142 F2
Lower Adeyfield Rd. Heml H HP2 . 124 D4
Lower Barn. Heml H HP3 .... 138 F8
Lower Bourne Gdns. Ware SG12 .. 93 C3
Lower Dagnall St. St Alb AL3 ...... 127 C3
Lower Emms. Heml H HP2 .... 125 C8
Lower End. Wing HP22 .... 60 B2
Lower Gower Rd. Royst SG8 ...... 7 D8
Lower Harpenden Rd. Luton LU1 .. 64 C3
Lower Harpenden Rd.
   Nwml E LU2 .... 64 C3
Lower Hatfield Rd. Bay SG13 ..... 112 F1
Lower High St. Watf WD1 .... 167 C4
Lower Ickfield Way. Ast Cl HP22 . 99 C7
Lower Icknield Way. Wils HP23 ... 99 C7
Lower Innings. Hit SG5 .... 34 D8
Lower Island Way. Wa Aby EN9 .. 163 B4
Lower King St. Royst SG8 .... 7 D6
Lower Kings Rd. Berk HP4 .... 122 C5
Lower Luton Rd. Harp AL5 .... 86 B3
Lower Luton Rd. Whea AL4 .... 86 C3
Lower Mardley Hill. Welw AL6 .... 89 F8
Lower Meadow. Ches EN8 .... 148 D4
Lower Paxton Rd. St Alb AL1 ...... 127 E2
Lower Plantation. Ric WD3 .... 165 C6
Lower Rd. Bre Gr SG4 .... 47 C5
Lower Rd. Chor WD3 .... 164 D5
Lower Rd. Gt Am SG12 .... 114 F6
Lower Rd. Harl CM20 .... 117 E2
Lower Rd. Heml H HP3 .... 139 A5
Lower Rd. L Hal CM22 .... 98 C7

Lower Sales. Heml H HP1 .... 123 F2
Lower Sean. Stev SG2 .... 51 A3
Lower St. Sta M CM24 .... 59 E7
Lower Tail. Sth Ox WD1 .... 175 E7
Lower Tub. Bus WD2 .... 168 D2
Lower Yott. Heml H HP2 .... 124 F7
Lowerfield. Wel G C AL7 .... 111 A5
Lowestoft Rd. Watf WD2 .... 167 F4
Loweswater Cl. Watf WD2 .... 154 C6
Lowfield La. Hod EN11 .... 135 A4
Lowfield. Saw CM21 .... 97 E1
Lowgate La. Dan En SG12 .... 72 A4
Lowgate La. Thun SG11 .... 72 C5
Lowlands. Hat AL10 .... 130 C8
Lowson Gr. Watf WD1 .... 167 D2
Lowswood Cl. Norwd HA6 .... 174 C2
Lowther Cl. Bor WD6 .... 169 F4
Loxley Rd. Berk HP4 .... 121 F6
Lucan Rd. Barn EN5 .... 171 E6
Lucas Cl. Wa Aby EN9 .... 163 F6
Lucas Gdns. Luton LU3 .... 45 C4
Lucas La. Hit SG5 .... 34 D7
Lucas La. Ashw SG7 .... 4 A4
Lucerne Way. Luton LU3 .... 45 C4
Lucks Hill. Heml H HP1 .... 123 E3
Ludgate. Tri HP23 .... 99 F4
Ludlow Ave. Luton LU1 .... 63 E4
Ludlow Mead. Sth Ox WD1 .... 175 B7
Ludlow Way. Cro Gr WD3 .... 166 C5
Ludwick Cl. Wel G C AL7 .... 110 F4
Ludwick Gn. Wel G C AL7 .... 110 F4
Ludwick Way. Wel G C AL7 .... 110 F5
Lukes Lea. Mars HP23 .... 80 A1
Lullington Cl. Luton LU2 .... 46 C3
Lullington Garth. Bor WD6 .... 170 B4
Lulworth Ave. Gofs O EN7 .... 147 A2
Lumbards. Wel G C AL7 .... 90 A1
Lumen Rd. Royst SG8 .... 7 D7
Lundin Wlk. Sth Ox WD1 .... 175 D7
Luton Coll of Higher Ed. Luton ... 63 F7
Luton Dr. The. Nwml E LU1 .... 64 B3
Luton & Dunstable Hospl. Dun ... 44 C2
Luton & Dunstable Hospl
   (Faringdon Wing). Dun 44 C2
Luton Hoo. Nwml E 64 A2
Luton Ind Coll. Luton 63 E7
Luton La. Red AL3 .... 106 A8
Luton Maternity Hospl. Dun 44 C2
Luton Rd. Cad LU1 .... 63 A4
Luton Rd. Dun LU5 .... 44 A8
Luton Rd. Gt Of LU2 .... 46 E3
Luton Rd. Gt Of SG5 .... 32 E5
Luton Rd. Harp AL5 .... 85 E4
Luton Rd. Kim SG4 .... 66 B2
Luton Rd. Luton LU4 .... 44 A7
Luton Rd. Mark AL3 .... 83 E7
Luton Rd. Stev SG1 .... 31 A6
Luton Regional Sports Ctr. Luton . 46 A4
Luton Sta. Luton 63 C8
Luton Town Football Gnd. Luton . 63 C8
Luton VIth Form Coll. Luton 46 A4
Luton White Hill. Gt Of SG5 .... 33 B2
Luxembourg Cl. Luton LU3 .... 44 D8
Luynes Rise. Bun SG9 .... 40 E6
Lybury La. Red AL3 .... 105 F7
Lycaste Cl. St Alb AL1 .... 128 A2
Lych Gate. Watf WD2 .... 154 E6
Lydia. Wel G C AL9 .... 144 C7
Lydia Mews. Wel G C AL9 .... 144 C7
Lye Hill. Bre Gr SG4 .... 65 D7
Lye La. Bri Wd AL2 .... 141 A2
Lye La. Chis AL2 .... 141 A2
Lyegean Ave. Watf WD2 .... 93 E1
Lygetun Dr. Luton LU3 .... 44 F7
Lygrave. Stev SG2 .... 69 C8
Lyle's Row. Hit SG4 .... 34 F6
Lyles La. Wel G C AL8 .... 110 E8
Lymans Rd. Arl SG15 .... 11 A5
Lyme Ave. Nthch HP4 .... 121 D7
Lymington Ct. Watf WD2 .... 154 A5
Lymington Rd. Stev SG1 .... 50 B8
Lynbury Ct. Watf WD1 .... 167 A6
Lynch Hill. Ken Co LU6 .... 83 A8
Lynch The. Hod EN11 .... 135 B6
Lyndale. Sth Alb 127 E4
Lyndale. Stev SG1 .... 50 E4
Lyndhurst Ave. Pnr HA5 .... 175 B2
Lyndhurst Cl. Harp AL5 .... 86 C2
Lyndhurst Cty Sec Sch. Bor 169 F8
Lyndhurst Dr. Harp AL5 .... 86 C2
Lyndhurst Gdns. Pnr HA5 .... 175 B2
Lyndhurst Rd. Luton LU1 .... 63 C7
Lyndon Ave. Pnr HA5 .... 175 E4
Lyndon Mead. Sand AL4 .... 108 C2
Lyne Way. Heml H HP1 .... 123 F5
Lyneham Rd. Luton LU2 .... 46 C1
Lynn Cl. Har HA3 .... 176 D1
Lynsey Cl. Red AL3 .... 106 A6
Lynton Ave. Arl SG15 .... 11 A5
Lynton Ave. St Alb AL1 .... 128 C2
Lynton Ct. Bis St CM23 .... 76 E4
Lynton Mead. Stev SG2 .... 50 C3
Lynwood Ave. Luton LU2 .... 46 A3
Lynwood Dr. Norwd HA6 .... 174 F2
Lynwood Hts. Ric WD3 .... 165 C4
Lyon Way. Coln H AL4 .... 129 A3
Lyrical Way. Heml H HP1 .... 124 B5
Lys Hill Gdns. Hert SG14 .... 113 B8
Lysander Cl. Bov HP3 .... 137 A4
Lysander Way. Abb L WD5 .... 154 A7
Lysander Way. Wel G C AL7 ...... 111 D7
Lytham Ave. Sth Ox WD1 .... 175 D5
Lytton Ave. Enf EN3 .... 162 E1
Lytton Ave. Letw SG6 .... 22 E7
Lytton Fields. Kneb SG3 .... 68 F5
Lytton Gdns. Wel G C AL8 .... 110 D6
Lytton Rd. Pnr HA5 .... 175 E3
Lytton Way. Stev SG1 .... 50 D6
Lyttons Way. Hod EN11 .... 115 A1

Mabbott Cl. Bri Wd AL2 .... 140 E1
Mabey's Wlk. H Wy CM21 .... 97 B1
Macaulay Rd. Luton LU4 .... 44 A2
Macdonnell Gdns. Watf WD2 ..... 153 F4
Macer's La. Ches EN10 .... 148 F7
Mackenzie Sq. Stev SG2 .... 51 B3
Mackerel Hill. Royst SG8 .... 7 D8
Maddles. Letw SG6 .... 23 D4
Maddox Rd. Harl CM20 .... 117 E1
Maddox Rd. Heml H HP2 .... 125 B3
Made Field. Stev SG1,SG2 .... 50 F5
Madgeways Cl. Gt Am SG12 ...... 114 F5
Madgeways La. Gt Am SG12 ...... 114 F5
Magellan Cl. Stev SG2 .... 51 D5
Magna Cl. Harp AL5 .... 107 D6
Magnaville Rd. Bis St CM23 .... 76 E4
Magnaville Rd. Bus WD2 .... 168 F2
Magnolia Ave. Abb L WD5 .... 147 A7
Magnolia Cl. Hert SG13 .... 114 A6
Magnolia Cl. Pk St AL2 .... 141 D5
Magpie Cl. Enf EN1 .... 162 A1
Magpie Cres. Stev SG2 .... 51 D5
Magpie Hall Rd. Stan WD2 .... 176 E8
Magpie Wlk. Hat AL10 .... 130 A3   2
Magpies. The. Luton LU2 .... 45 E6
Maiden St. Wes SG4 .... 24 C1
Maidenhall CP Jun & Inf Sch. Luton 45 A2
Maidenhall Rd. Luton LU4 .... 45 A3
Maidenhead Rd. St Hert SG14 .... 113 D6   3
Maidenhead Yd. Hert SG14 .... 113 D6
Main Ave. Mo Pk HA6 .... 174 C7
Main Par. Chor WD3 .... 164 C5
Main Rd. Bram SG4 .... 91 D3
Main Rd N. Dagn HP4 .... 81 A4
Main Rd S. Dagn HP4 .... 81 A6
Maitland Rd. Sta M CM24 .... 59 F7
Malborough Rd. Watf WD1 .... 167 B5
Malden Rd. Bor WD6 .... 170 C5
Malden Rd. Watf WD1 .... 167 B7
Maldon Ct. Harp AL5 .... 86 B2
Malham Cl. Luton LU4 .... 44 F2
Malins Cl. Barn EN5 .... 171 C4
Mall The. Chis AL2 .... 141 C4
Mallard Gdns. Luton LU3 .... 45 A5
Mallard Rd. Royst SG8 .... 7 C5
Mallard Rd. Stev SG1 .... 51 D2
Mallard Way. Norwd HA6 .... 174 E3
Mallard Way. Watf WD2 .... 154 E3
Mallion Ct. Wa Aby EN9 .... 163 F6
Mallories. Harl CM20 .... 117 F2
Mallow Wlk. Gofs O 147 D3
Mallow Wlk. Royst SG8 .... 7 E5
Malm Cl. Ric WD3 .... 173 D8
Malmes Croft. Heml H HP3 .... 125 C1
Malmsdale. Wel G C AL8 .... 89 D2
Maltby Dr. Enf EN1 .... 162 B1
Malthouse Ct. St Alb AL1 .... 127 D2
Malthouse Gn. Luton LU2 .... 46 F1
Malthouse La. Stot SG5 .... 12 A7
Malthouse Pl. Radl WD7 .... 156 A5
Malthouse The. Hert SG14 .... 113 D6   13
Malting Cotts. Asp SG9 .... 40 D5
Malting La. Ald HP23 .... 101 D5
Malting La. Brag SG11 .... 55 E7
Malting La. Dagn HP4 .... 81 C5
Malting La. Muc H SG10 .... 74 F2
Malting Mead. Hat AL10 .... 130 C6
Maltings Cl. Bal SG7 .... 13 B1
Maltings Cl. Ware SG12 .... 114 D8
Maltings Dr. Whea AL4 .... 108 C8
Maltings Ind Est The. Sta Ab 115 C8
Maltings La. Gt Ch SG8 .... 9 E2
Maltings The. Abb L WD4 .... 153 C5
Maltings The. Heml H HP2 .... 124 D4
Maltings The. Letw SG6 .... 12 C1
Maltings The. St Alb AL1 .... 127 D3
Maltings The. Walk SG2 .... 52 B8
Malus Cl. Heml H HP2 .... 125 A4
Malvern Cl. St Alb AL4 .... 128 C7
Malvern Rd. Enf EN3 .... 162 E2
Malvern Rd. Luton LU1 .... 63 B7
Malvern Way. Cro Gr WD3 .... 166 B4
Malvern Way. Heml H HP2 .... 124 E8
Malvern Way Inf Sch. Cro Gr 166 C4
Malzeard Ct. Luton LU3 .... 45 D1   2
Malzeard Rd. Luton LU3 .... 45 D1
Manan Cl. Heml H HP3 .... 125 C1
Manchester Cl. Stev SG1 .... 36 F3
Manchester St. Luton LU1 .... 63 E7
Mancroft Rd. Cad LU1 .... 62 E2
Mandela Ave. Harl CM20 .... 117 E2
Mandela Pl. Watf WD2 .... 167 D7   4
Mandelyns. Nthch HP4 .... 121 C6
Mandeville Cl. Hert SG13 .... 113 C3
Mandeville Cl. Hod EN10 .... 134 F3
Mandeville Dr. St Alb AL1 .... 141 D8
Mandeville Jun Mix Inf Sch. Saw . 97 D3
Mandeville Prim Sch. St Alb 141 D8
Mandeville Rd. Enf EN3 .... 162 E3
Mandeville Rd. Hert SG13 .... 113 C3
Mandeville Rd. Pot B EN6 .... 159 C7
Mandeville Rise. Wel G C AL8 .... 110 D8
Mandeville. Stev SG2 .... 69 C8
Mangrove Dr. Hert SG13 .... 113 E4
Mangrove La. Bric SG13 .... 133 F5
Mangrove La. Bric SG13 .... 133 F7
Mangrove Rd. Gt Of LU2 .... 46 E4
Mangrove Rd. Hert SG13 .... 113 E5
Mangrove Rd. Luton LU2 .... 46 C2
Manland Ave. Harp AL5 .... 86 C2
Manland Way. Harp AL5 .... 86 C3
Manley Rd. Heml H HP2 .... 124 E4
Manly Dixon Dr. Enf EN3 .... 162 E2
Mannicotts. Wel G C AL8 .... 110 B6
Manning Ct. Watf WD1 .... 167 D3
Manor Ave. Heml H HP3 .... 138 D8
Manor Cl. Barn EN5 .... 171 E5
Manor Cl. Berk HP4 .... 122 C4
Manor Cl. Hat AL10 .... 129 F8
Manor Cl. Ick SG5 .... 21 E3
Manor Cl. Letw SG6 .... 23 C2
Manor Cl. Cad LU1 .... 62 F4
Manor Cl. Ches EN8 .... 162 D8
Manor Ct. Enf EN1 .... 162 B8
Manor Ct. Pot B EN6 .... 158 F7
Manor Ct. Wa Aby EN9 .... 163 D4
Manor Dr. Chis AL2 .... 141 A4
Manor Farm Cl. Dun LU4 .... 44 C3
Manor Farm La. Men LU7 .... 61 C8
Manor Farm Rd. Enf EN1 .... 162 B4
Manor Fields Jun, Mid & Inf Sch.
   Bis St 76 D5
Manor House Dr. Norwd HA6 ..... 174 B3
Manor House Gdns. Abb L WD5 .. 153 D8

Man - Mil 193

Manor Links. Bis St CM23 ..... 77 C7
Manor Lodge Sch. Shen 143 C1
Manor Par. Hat AL10 ..... 129 F8
Manor Pound Rd. Ched LU7 ..... 80 A7
Manor Rd. Barn EN5 ..... 171 E5
Manor Rd. Bis St CM23 ..... 77 A7
Manor Rd. Cad LU1 ..... 62 E3
Manor Rd. Ched LU7 ..... 79 F7
Manor Rd. Harl CM17 ..... 118 C6
Manor Rd. Hat AL10 ..... 129 F8
Manor Rd. Hod EN11 ..... 135 A7
Manor Rd. Lon C AL2 ..... 142 C5
Manor Rd. Luton LU1 ..... 63 F6
Manor Rd. Pot B EN6 ..... 159 A8
Manor Rd. St Alb AL1 ..... 127 E4
Manor Rd. Sta M CM24 ..... 59 E5
Manor Rd. Tri HP23 ..... 100 A4
Manor Rd. Wa Aby EN9 ..... 163 D6
Manor Rd. Watf WD1 ..... 167 B8
Manor Rd. Whea AL4 ..... 86 F2
Manor St. Berk HP4 ..... 122 D4
Manor View. Stev SG2 ..... 51 B1
Manor Way. Bor WD6 ..... 170 C6
Manor Way. Ches EN8 ..... 148 E1
Manor Way. Cro Gr WD3 ..... 166 B5
Manor Way. Letw SG6 ..... 22 F3
Manor Way. Pot B EN6 ..... 145 A1
Manorcroft Par. Ches EN8 ..... 148 E1
Manorside. Barn EN5 ..... 171 E5
Manorville Rd. Heml H HP3 ..... 138 C7
Mansard Cl. Tri HP23 ..... 100 A3
Manscroft Rd. Heml H HP1 ..... 124 B5
Mansdale Rd. Red AL3 ..... 105 F4
Mansfield Rd. Luton LU3 ..... 113 C8
Mansfield Gdns. Hert SG14 ..... 113 C8
Mansfield. H Wy CM21 ..... 97 A1
Mansfield Rd. Bal SG7 ..... 23 E8
Mansfield Rd. Luton LU4 ..... 45 B1
Mansion Dr. Tri HP23 ..... 100 B3
Manston Cl. Ches EN8 ..... 148 C1
Manston Dr. Bis St CM23 ..... 59 B1
Manton Dr. Luton LU2 ..... 45 D3
Manton Rd. Hit SG4 ..... 35 B6
Manx Cl. Luton LU4 ..... 45 A2
Maple Ave. Bis St CM23 ..... 76 D8
Maple Ave. St Alb AL3 ..... 127 C7
Maple Cl. Bis St CM23 ..... 76 D8
Maple Cl. Bus WD2 ..... 167 E7
Maple Cl. Hat AL10 ..... 130 A4
Maple Cotts. Harp AL5 ..... 107 B5
Maple Cross Jun Mix Inf Sch. 172 E5
Map Cl. Pnr HA5 ..... 175 C1 5
Maple Ct. Sta Ab SG19 ..... 115 D4
Maple Ct. Watf WD2 ..... 154 D3
Maple Flats. Harp AL5 ..... 86 A3
Maple Gn. Heml H HP1 ..... 123 E5
Maple Gr. Bis St CM23 ..... 76 D8
Maple Gr. Watf WD1 ..... 167 A8
Maple Gr. Wel G C AL7 ..... 89 F1
Maple Leaf Cl. Abb L WD5 ..... 154 A7
Maple Lodge Cl. Map Cr WD3 ..... 172 E6
Maple Rd E. Luton LU4 ..... 63 B8
Maple Rd. Harp AL5 ..... 85 F1
Maple Rd W. Luton LU4 ..... 63 B8
Maple River Ind Est. Harl 118 B6
Maple Sch. St Alb 127 E4
Maple Spring. Bis St CM23 ..... 76 D8
Maple Way. Ken Co LU6 ..... 82 D8
Maple Way. Royst SG8 ..... 7 D7
Maplecroft La. Lo Naz EN9 ..... 135 E2
Maplefield. Chis AL2 ..... 141 C2
Maples Ct. Hit SG5 ..... 34 E7 1
Maples The. Hit SG5 ..... 34 F5
Mapleton Cres. Enf EN3 ..... 162 C1
Maplewood. Ware SG12 ..... 93 C3
Maran Ave. Welw AL6 ..... 89 C4
Marbury Pl. Luton LU3 ..... 45 D1
Marchmont Green. Heml H HP2 ..... 124 D5
Marcus Cl. Stev SG1 ..... 51 C8
Mardley Ave. Welw AL6 ..... 90 A8
Mardley Dell. Welw AL6 ..... 68 F1
Mardley Hts. Welw AL6 ..... 68 F1
Mardley Wood. Welw AL6 ..... 68 F1
Mardleybury Rd. Welw SG3 ..... 69 A1
Mardleybury Rd. Welw SG3 ..... 69 B1
Mardyke Rd. Hat AL4 ..... 109 D6
Marford Rd. Hat AL4 ..... 109 D6
Marford Rd. Whea AL4 ..... 108 E8
Margaret Ave. St Alb AL3 ..... 127 D5
Margaret Cl. Abb L WD5 ..... 153 F7
Margaret Cl. Pot B EN6 ..... 159 C6
Margaret Cl. Wa Aby EN9 ..... 163 F5
Margaret Wix Inf Sch. St Alb 127 C7
Margaret Wix Jun Sch. St Alb 127 C7
Margeholes. Sth Ox WD1 ..... 175 E8
Margery Wood. Wel G C AL7 ..... 90 A1
Margherita Pl. Wa Aby EN9 ..... 163 F5
Marian Gdns. Watf WD2 ..... 154 B6
Maricas Ave. Har HA3 ..... 176 D2
Marigold Pl. Harl CM17 ..... 118 B4
Marina Gdns. Ches EN8 ..... 148 C1
Mariner Way. Heml H HP2 ..... 125 A2 2
Marion Cl. Bus WD2 ..... 167 F8
Marion Wlk. Heml H HP2 ..... 124 F8 4
Mark Hall Comp Sch. Harl 118 C3
Mark Hall Moors. Harl CM20 ..... 118 B3
Mark Rd. Heml H HP2 ..... 125 B5
Markab Rd. Mo Pk HA6 ..... 175 A5 3
Markeston Gn. Sth Ox WD1 ..... 175 F6
Market Hill. Bun SG9 ..... 40 E7
Market Hill. Royst SG8 ..... 7 C6
Market House. Harl CM20 ..... 117 D1
Market Oak La. Heml H HP3 ..... 139 C1
Market Pl. Hat AL10 ..... 130 B7
Market Pl. Hert SG14 ..... 113 D6 6
Market Pl. Hit SG5 ..... 34 F7
Market Pl. St Alb AL3 ..... 127 D3
Market Pl. Stev SG1 ..... 50 D5
Market Pl. Watf WD1 ..... 167 C5
Market Sq. Bis St CM23 ..... 76 F7
Market Sq. Luton LU1 ..... 63 E5
Market Sq. Stev SG1 ..... 50 D5
Market St. Bis St CM23 ..... 76 F7
Market St. Harl CM17 ..... 118 C4
Market St. Hert SG14 ..... 113 D6
Market St. Watf WD1 ..... 167 B5
Markfield Cl. Luton LU3 ..... 45 C6
Markham Rd. Luton LU3 ..... 45 C6
Markyate Jun Mix Inf Sch. Mark 83 D6

Markyate Rd. Cad LU1 ..... 63 B1
Marlands. Saw CM21 ..... 97 E4
Marlborough Cl. Bis St CM23 ..... 76 F5
Marlborough Cl. Welw AL6 ..... 89 F8
Marlborough Cl. Wa SG4 ..... 37 B8
Marlborough Gate. St Alb AL1 ..... 127 C8
Marlborough Rd. Luton LU3 ..... 45 D1
Marlborough Rd. St Alb AL1 ..... 127 C8
Marlborough Rd. Stev SG2 ..... 51 C5
Marlborough Rise. Heml H HP2 ..... 124 E6
Marlborough St. St Alb 141 C8
Marle Gdns. Wa Aby EN9 ..... 163 C7
Marley Rd. Wel G C AL7 ..... 111 A4
Marlin Cl. Berk HP4 ..... 121 F5
Marlin Copse. Berk HP4 ..... 122 A3
Marlin Hill. Tri HP23 ..... 120 A8
Marlin Sq. Abb L WD5 ..... 153 F8
Marlins Cl. Chor WD3 ..... 164 E7
Marlins Meadow. Watf WD1 ..... 166 D3
Marlins The. Mo Pk HA6 ..... 174 F5
Marlins Turn. Heml H HP1 ..... 124 B6
Marlowe Cl. Stev SG2 ..... 51 C8
Marlowes. Heml H HP1 ..... 124 D3
Marmet Ave. Letw SG6 ..... 22 E5
Marnham Rise. Heml H HP1 ..... 124 A5
Marquis Cl. Bis St CM23 ..... 76 B7
Marquis Cl. Harp AL5 ..... 86 B2
Marquis La. Harp AL5 ..... 86 D2
Marrilyne Ave. Enf EN3 ..... 162 F1
Marriott Rd. Barn EN5 ..... 171 D6
Marriott Rd. Luton LU3 ..... 45 B6
Marriotts Way. Heml H HP3 ..... 124 D1
Marryat Rd. Enf EN1 ..... 162 B4
Marschefield. Stot SG5 ..... 11 E6
Marsden Cl. Wel G C AL8 ..... 110 B4
Marsden Gn. Wel G C AL8 ..... 110 B4
Marsden Rd. Wel G C AL8 ..... 110 C5
Marsh Cl. Ches EN8 ..... 162 F6
Marsh Hill. Lo Naz EN9 ..... 149 F4
Marsh La. Sta Ab SG12 ..... 115 D4
Marsh La. Ware SG12 ..... 114 E8
Marsh Rd. Luton LU3 ..... 44 F4
Marshal's Dr. St Alb AL1 ..... 128 A6
Marshall Ave. St Alb AL3 ..... 127 F6
Marshall Rd. Luton LU2 ..... 46 C2
Marshall's La. Thun SG11 ..... 72 C2
Marshalls Heath La. Whea AL4 ..... 87 A4
Marshalls Way. Whea AL4 ..... 86 F2
Marshalswick La. St Alb AL1 ..... 128 B6
Marshbarns. Bis St CM23 ..... 76 C8
Marshcroft Dr. Ches EN8 ..... 148 F1
Marshe Cl. Pot B EN6 ..... 159 D7
Marshgate Dr. Hert SG13 ..... 113 F7
Marshgate. Stev SG1 ..... 50 D5
Marshmoor Cres. Hat AL9 ..... 130 D1
Marshmoor La. Wel G AL9 ..... 144 D8
Marsom Gr. Luton LU3 ..... 45 B8
Marston Cl. Heml H HP3 ..... 125 A2
Marston Ct. Lon M HP23 ..... 79 B4
Marston Gdns. Luton LU2 ..... 45 D4
Marston Rd. Hod EN11 ..... 135 B7
Marsworth Ave. Pnr HA5 ..... 175 D2
Marsworth Cl. Watf WD1 ..... 166 E2
Marsworth Rd. Pit LU7 ..... 80 D4
Marten Dr. Hert SG13 ..... 114 B6
Marten Gate. St Alb AL4 ..... 128 A7
Martham Ct. Harp AL5 ..... 86 C3
Marthorne Cres. Har HA3 ..... 176 D1
Martin Cl. Heml H HP2 ..... 124 F6
Martin Cl. Hat AL10 ..... 130 A3
Martindale Prim Sch. Heml H 123 F4
Martindale Rd. Heml H HP1 ..... 123 F4
Martindales The. Luton LU2 ..... 46 E2
Martinfield Bsns Ctr. Wel G C 110 F7
Martinfield. Wel G C AL7 ..... 110 F7
Martingale Rd. Royst SG8 ..... 7 E6
Martins Cl. Radl WD7 ..... 155 F3
Martins Dr. Ches EN8 ..... 148 E3
Martins Way. Stev SG1 ..... 36 E1
Martins Wlk. Bor WD6 ..... 170 A5
Martins Wood Jun Mix Inf Sch. Stev 37 B1
Martlesham. Wel G C AL7 ..... 111 E6
Martyr Cl. St Alb AL1 ..... 141 D7
Marwood Cl. Kin L WD4 ..... 138 F2
Mary Brash Ct. Luton LU7 ..... 80 D8
Mary Exton Jun Mix Inf Sch. Hit 35 C7
Mary McArthur Pl. Sta M CM24 ..... 59 F8
Mary Park Gdns. Bis St CM23 ..... 76 F4
Mary Proud Ct. Welw AL6 ..... 89 C7
Maryland. Hat AL10 ..... 129 F5
Marymead Cl. Stev SG2 ..... 69 A8
Marymead Dr. Stev SG2 ..... 69 A8
Marymead Ind Est. Stev 69 B8
Maryport Rd. Luton LU4 ..... 45 A4
Masefield Ave. Bor WD6 ..... 170 B4
Masefield Ave. Stan HA7 ..... 176 F5
Masefield Ct. Harp AL5 ..... 86 B4
Masefield. Hit SG4 ..... 35 C7
Masefield Rd. Harp AL5 ..... 86 B4
Mason Cl. Bor WD6 ..... 170 D7
Mason Way. Wa Aby EN9 ..... 163 F5
Masons Cl. Bis St CM23 ..... 76 E7
Masons Rd. Enf EN1 ..... 162 C4
Masons Rd. Heml H HP2 ..... 125 B4
Masters Cl. Luton LU3 ..... 63 B5
Matching La. Bis St CM23 ..... 76 D8
Mathams Dr. Bis St CM23 ..... 76 D5
Matlock Cres. Dun LU4 ..... 44 C1
Matlock Cres. Sth Ox WD1 ..... 175 C7
Matthew Gate. Hit SG4 ..... 35 A5
Mattocke Rd. Hit SG5 ..... 21 C1
Maud Jane's Cl. Pit LU7 ..... 80 E5
Maude Cres. Watf WD2 ..... 154 B1
Maulden Cl. Luton LU2 ..... 46 C1
Maxted Cl. Heml H HP2 ..... 125 C5
Maxted Cnr. Heml H 125 B6
Maxted Rd. Heml H HP2 ..... 125 B5
Maxwell Cl. Ric WD3 ..... 173 A8
Maxwell Rd. Bor WD6 ..... 170 B6
Maxwell Rd. Norwd HA6 ..... 174 E3
Maxwell Rd. St Alb AL1 ..... 128 B2
Maxwell Rise. Watf WD1 ..... 167 E2
May Cl. St Alb AL3 ..... 127 D5
May St. Gt Ch SG8 ..... 9 E2
May St. Luton LU1 ..... 63 E5

Maybury Ave. Ches EN8 ..... 148 B3
Maycock Gr. Norwd HA6 ..... 174 F4
Maycroft. Letw SG6 ..... 12 A1
Maycroft. Pnr HA5 ..... 175 B1
Maycroft Rd. Ham St EN7 ..... 147 E5
Maydencroft La. St Ipp SG4 ..... 34 E3
Maydwell Lodge. Bor WD6 ..... 169 F7
Mayes Cl. Bis St CM23 ..... 77 D8
Mayfair Cl. St Alb AL4 ..... 128 C8
Mayfield Cl. Harl CM17 ..... 118 F4
Mayfield Cl. Harp AL5 ..... 85 E3
Mayfield Pk. Bis St CM23 ..... 76 D3
Mayfield Rd. Luton LU2 ..... 46 B4
Mayfield. Wel G C AL8 ..... 89 C2
Mayflower Ave. Heml H HP2 ..... 124 D3
Mayflower Cl. Cod SG4 ..... 67 F1
Mayflower Cl. Hertng SG14 ..... 112 E4
Mayflower Cl. Lo Naz EN9 ..... 135 E1
Mayflower Gdns. Bis St CM23 ..... 76 C6
Mayflower Rd. Chis AL2 ..... 141 B4
Mayhill Rd. Barn EN5 ..... 171 E3
Maylands Ave. Heml H HP2 ..... 125 B5
Maylands Ct. Heml H 125 B4
Maylin Cl. Hit SG4 ..... 35 C8
Maylins Dr. Saw CM21 ..... 97 D2
Maynard Cl. Wa Aby EN9 ..... 163 F5
Maynard Dr. St Alb AL1 ..... 141 D8
Maynard Pl. Cuf EN6 ..... 146 E2
Maynard Rd. Heml H HP2 ..... 124 D2
Mayne Ave. Luton LU4 ..... 44 C4
Mayne Ave. St Alb AL3 ..... 127 A2
Mayo Cl. Ches EN8 ..... 148 C3
Mays La. Barn EN5 ..... 171 D3
Mayshades Cl. Welw SG3 ..... 69 A2
Maythorne Cl. Watf WD1 ..... 166 E5
Maytree Cres. Watf WD2 ..... 153 F3
Maytree La. Har HA7 ..... 176 F3
Maytrees. Hit SG4 ..... 35 A6
Maytrees. Radl WD7 ..... 156 A2
Maze Green Rd. Bis St CM23 ..... 76 D7
Mazoe Cl. Bis St CM23 ..... 76 F5
Mazoe Rd. Bis St CM23 ..... 76 F5
Mc Gredy. Ches EN8 ..... 148 B2
Mc Kenzie Rd. Hod EN10 ..... 135 A3
McAdam Cl. Hod EN11 ..... 135 A8
McDonald Ct. Hat AL10 ..... 130 A3
McKellar Cl. Bus WD2 ..... 176 C8
Mead Business Ctr. Hert 113 E7
Mead Cl. Har HA3 ..... 176 D2
Mead Cl. Stev SG1 ..... 50 F6
Mead Cl. Sta M CM24 ..... 59 D7
Mead Ct. Wa Aby EN9 ..... 163 B5
Mead House. Hat AL10 ..... 130 B8
Mead La. Hert SG13 ..... 113 E7
Mead Park Ind Est. Harl 117 F4
Mead Pl. Ric WD3 ..... 165 B1
Mead Rd. Shen WD7 ..... 157 A6
Mead The. Ches EN8 ..... 148 C2
Mead The. Hit SG5 ..... 21 F2
Mead The. Lo Naz EN9 ..... 135 B2
Mead The. Sth Ox WD1 ..... 175 E7
Mead View. Sto P SG9 ..... 43 E6
Mead Way. Bus WD2 ..... 167 E7
Meadgate Rd. Lo Naz EN9 ..... 135 C3
Meadow Cl. Barn EN5 ..... 171 F3
Meadow Cl. Berk HP4 ..... 122 A2
Meadow Cl. Bri Wd AL2 ..... 141 A2
Meadow Cl. Dat SG3 ..... 69 D1
Meadow Cl. Enf EN3 ..... 162 E1
Meadow Cl. St Alb AL4 ..... 128 C6
Meadow Cl. Tri HP23 ..... 100 A4
Meadow Cl. Wel G AL9 ..... 144 D7
Meadow Croft. Cad LU1 ..... 62 F4
Meadow Croft. Hat AL10 ..... 129 F5
Meadow Dell. Hat AL10 ..... 129 F5
Meadow Gn. Wel G C AL8 ..... 110 C6
Meadow La. Pit LU7 ..... 80 E3
Meadow Rd. Berk HP4 ..... 122 B6
Meadow Rd. Bor WD6 ..... 170 B7
Meadow Rd. Bus WD2 ..... 168 B4
Meadow Rd. Heml H HP3 ..... 139 A7
Meadow Rd. Luton LU3 ..... 45 A4
Meadow Rd. Watf WD2 ..... 154 B5
Meadow Road Cl. Berk HP4 ..... 122 A6
Meadow The. Hert SG13 ..... 114 E2
Meadow The. Wel G C AL7 ..... 111 C6
Meadow View. Bun SG9 ..... 40 D6
Meadow Way. Abb L WD5 ..... 139 F4
Meadow Way. Cad LU1 ..... 62 E4
Meadow Way. Cod SG4 ..... 67 E1
Meadow Way. Gt Of SG5 ..... 33 C3
Meadow Way. Hit SG5 ..... 34 D6
Meadow Way. Kin L WD4 ..... 139 A1
Meadow Way. Letw SG6 ..... 22 F5
Meadow Way. Pot B EN6 ..... 159 A5
Meadow Way. Ric WD3 ..... 165 C2
Meadow Way. Sheer CM21 ..... 98 A1
Meadow Way. Stev SG1 ..... 50 F7
Meadow Way. Stot SG5 ..... 11 F6
Meadow Way The. Har HA3 ..... 176 E2
Meadow Way. Ther SG8 ..... 16 A6
Meadow Wlk. Harp AL5 ..... 107 C8
Meadow Wlk. Stand SG11 ..... 55 E2
Meadow Wood Sch. Bus 168 C4
Meadowbank. Hit SG4 ..... 22 B1
Meadowbank. Kin L WD4 ..... 139 A1
Meadowbank. Watf WD1 ..... 167 A2
Meadowbanks. Barn EN5 ..... 171 A4
Meadowbrook. Tri HP23 ..... 100 B6
Meadowcroft. Bus WD2 ..... 168 B3
Meadowcroft. Nthch HP4 ..... 121 D7
Meadowcroft. St Alb AL1 ..... 142 A8
Meadowcroft. Sta M CM24 ..... 59 E7
Meadowcross. Wa Aby EN9 ..... 163 E5
Meadowlands. Bis St CM23 ..... 59 A2
Meadows The. Bis St CM23 ..... 76 E5
Meadows The. Bre Gr SG4 ..... 47 E1
Meadows The. Sheer CM21 ..... 98 A2
Meadowsweet Cl. Bis St CM23 ..... 76 C6
Meadow Jun Mix & Inf Sch The. Luton 45 A6
Meads La. Whea AL4 ..... 87 D1
Meads The. Berk HP4 ..... 121 D6
Meads The. Bri Wd AL2 ..... 140 F2
Meads The. Letw SG6 ..... 22 E6
Meads The. Luton LU3 ..... 45 A3

Meads The. Sta M CM24 ..... 59 F6
Meadview Rd. Ware SG12 ..... 114 D8
Meadway. Barn EN5 ..... 171 F5
Meadway. Berk HP4 ..... 122 B6
Meadway. Col H AL4 ..... 143 D5
Meadway. Enf EN3 ..... 162 D3
Meadway. Harp AL5 ..... 107 E8
Meadway. Hod EN11 ..... 135 A4
Meadway. Kneb SG3 ..... 68 F4
Meadway. Stev SG2 ..... 50 A6
Meadway The. Cuf EN6 ..... 146 F2
Meadway. Wel G C AL7 ..... 110 F4
Meautys. St Alb AL3 ..... 127 A1
Medalls Link. Stev SG2 ..... 51 A3
Medalls Path. Stev SG2 ..... 51 A3
Medcalf Rd. Enf EN3 ..... 162 F2
Medina Rd. Luton LU4 ..... 45 A1
Medlows. Harp AL5 ..... 85 E2
Medow Mead. Radl WD7 ..... 155 F6
Medway Cl. Watf WD2 ..... 154 C5
Medway Rd. Heml H HP2 ..... 124 F8
Medwick Mews. Heml H HP2 ..... 125 B8
Mees Cl. Luton LU3 ..... 31 A1
Meeting Alley. Watf WD1 ..... 167 C5
Meeting House La. Bal SG7 ..... 12 E1
Megg La. Chipf WD4 ..... 138 B1
Melbourn Cl. Stot SG5 ..... 11 F5
Melbourn St. Royst SG8 ..... 7 D6
Melbourne Cl. St Alb AL3 ..... 127 F7
Melbourne Cl. Wel G C AL8 ..... 110 B5
Melbourne Rd. Bus WD2 ..... 168 B3
Melford Cl. Luton LU2 ..... 46 D1 2
Melings The. Heml H HP2 ..... 125 B8
Melne Rd. Stev SG2 ..... 69 B8
Melrose Ave. Bor WD6 ..... 170 B4
Melrose Ave. Pot B EN6 ..... 159 B7
Melrose Pl. Watf WD1 ..... 153 F1
Melson Sq. Luton LU1 ..... 63 E7
Melson St. Luton LU1 ..... 63 E7
Melsted Rd. Heml H HP1 ..... 124 B3
Melvyn Cl. Gofs O EN7 ..... 147 B3
Memorial Rd. Luton LU3 ..... 44 F4
Mendip Cl. St Alb AL4 ..... 128 C8
Mendip Rd. Bus WD2 ..... 168 C3
Mendip Way. Heml H HP2 ..... 124 E8
Mendip Way. Luton LU3 ..... 44 C8
Mendlesham. Wel G C AL7 ..... 111 E6
Mentley La E. Stand SG11 ..... 55 D4
Mentley La. Gt Mu SG11 ..... 54 E4
Mentley La. Stand SG11 ..... 54 E4
Mentley La W. Stand SG11 ..... 55 C4
Mentmore Park. Men 61 D3
Mentmore Rd. Ched LU7 ..... 79 F8
Mentmore Rd. St Alb AL1 ..... 127 E1
Mentmore Sch. St Alb 127 D6
Mentmore View. Tri HP23 ..... 99 F5
Mepham Cres. Har HA3 ..... 176 C3
Mepham Gdns. Har HA3 ..... 176 C3
Mercer Pl. Pnr HA5 ..... 175 C1
Mercers Ave. Bis St CM23 ..... 76 C4
Mercers. Heml H HP2 ..... 124 E5
Mercers Row. St Alb AL1 ..... 127 C1
Merchant Dr. Hert SG13 ..... 113 F7
Merchant Taylors' Sch. Mo Pk 166 E1
Merchants Wlk. Bal SG7 ..... 13 B1
Mercia Rd. Bal SG7 ..... 24 A8
Mercury Wlk. Heml H HP2 ..... 124 F6 1
Mereden Ct. St Alb AL1 ..... 141 C8
Meredith Cl. Pnr HA5 ..... 175 D3
Meredith Rd. Stev SG1 ..... 51 A8
Merefield. Saw CM21 ..... 97 E1
Meriden Barn EN5 ..... 171 F5 3
Meriden Way. Watf WD2 ..... 154 E2
Meriden Sch The. Royst 7 E7
Meridian Way. Gt Am SG12 ..... 115 B5
Merle Ave. Hare UB9 ..... 173 C1
Merlin Ctr The. Coln H 128 F3
Merling Croft. Nthch HP4 ..... 121 F7
Merritt Wlk. Wel G AL9 ..... 144 B8
Merrow Dr. Heml H HP1 ..... 123 E4
Merrows Cl. Norwd HA6 ..... 174 C4
Merry Hill Jun Sch. Bus 168 B2
Merry Hill Mount. Bus WD2 ..... 168 B1
Merry Hill Rd. Bus WD2 ..... 168 B1
Merryfield Cl. Bor WD6 ..... 169 F7
Merryfields. Coln H AL4 ..... 128 E3
Mersey Rd. Heml H HP2 ..... 124 F8
Mersey Pl. Luton LU1 ..... 63 D7
Merton Rd. Enf EN2 ..... 161 D1
Merton Rd. Watf WD1 ..... 167 B5
Meryfield Sch. Bor 169 F7
Metro Ctr. St Alb ..... (blank)
Metropolitan Station App. Watf WD1 ..... 166 F5
Meux Cl. Ches EN7 ..... 162 A8
Mews The. Harp AL5 ..... 86 B1 2
Mews The. Letw SG6 ..... 12 C1
Mews The. Saw CM21 ..... 97 E3
Mews The. St Alb AL1 ..... 128 B2
Mews The. Sta M CM24 ..... 59 F7
Meyer Gn. Enf EN1 ..... 162 A1
Meyrick Ave. Luton LU1 ..... 63 C6
Mezen Cl. Norwd HA6 ..... 174 D5
Michaels Rd. Bis St CM23 ..... 59 A2
Micklefield Rd. Heml H HP2 ..... 125 C3
Micklefield Way. Bor WD6 ..... 156 F1
Micklem Dr. Heml H HP1 ..... 123 F4
Micklem Sch The. Heml H 124 A4
Midcot Way. Berk HP4 ..... 121 F6
Middle Drift. Royst SG8 ..... 7 C6
Middle Furlong. Bus WD2 ..... 168 B3
Middle La. Bov HP3 ..... 137 A1
Middle Ope. Watf WD2 ..... 154 B2
Middle Rd. Berk HP4 ..... 122 B4
Middle Row. Bis St CM23 ..... 76 F7
Middle Row. Stev SG1 ..... 50 C7 1
Middle St. Lo Naz EN9 ..... 149 F4
Middle Way The. Har HA3 ..... 176 F1
Middle Way. Watf WD2 ..... 154 B2
Middlefield Cl. Hod EN11 ..... 135 A8
Middlefield Cl. St Alb AL4 ..... 128 C6
Middlefield Ct. Letw SG6 ..... 11 F1
Middlefield. Hat AL10 ..... 130 A4
Middlefield Rd. Hod EN11 ..... 135 A8
Middlefield. Wel G C AL7 ..... 110 D5

Middlefields. Letw SG6 ..... 11 F1
Middlehill. Heml H HP1 ..... 123 E8
Middleknights Hill. Heml H HP1 ..... 124 A6
Middlesborough Cl. Stev SG1 ..... 36 F2
Middleton Mid Sch. Ware 114 D7
Middleton Rd. Luton LU2 ..... 46 D4
Middleton Rd. Ric WD3 ..... 165 A1
Midhurst Gdns. Luton LU3 ..... 45 C4
Midhurst. Letw SG6 ..... 22 F8
Midland Cotts. Hit SG5 ..... 22 A1
Midland Rd. Heml H HP2 ..... 124 D3
Midland Rd. Luton LU2 ..... 63 E8
Midway. St Alb AL3 ..... 141 B8
Milbourne Cl. Watf WD1 ..... 167 A2 7
Milburn Cl. Luton LU3 ..... 31 B1
Mildmay Rd. Stev SG1 ..... 37 B1
Mildred Ave. Bor WD6 ..... 170 B5
Mildred Ave. Watf WD1 ..... 167 A5
Mile Cl. Wa Aby EN9 ..... 163 C6
Mile House Cl. St Alb AL1 ..... 142 A8
Mile House La. St Alb AL1 ..... 141 F8
Milestone Cl. Ast SG2 ..... 51 D4
Milestone Rd. Hit SG5 ..... 21 D2
Milestone Rd. Kneb SG3 ..... 69 A5
Milford Cl. St Alb AL4 ..... 128 D7
Milford Hill. Harp AL5 ..... 86 D3
Miksey La. Gra SG4 ..... 36 C5
Mill Bridge. Barn EN5 ..... 171 F3
Mill Bridge. Hert SG14 ..... 113 C6
Mill Cl. Hat AL8 ..... 110 A5
Mill Cl. Heml H HP1 ..... 124 B7
Mill Cl. Heml H HP3 ..... 139 A6
Mill Cl. Stot SG5 ..... 12 A6
Mill Cl. Ware SG12 ..... 93 D1
Mill Cl. Wing HP22 ..... 60 A3
Mill Cnr. Barn EN5 ..... 171 F8
Mill End. Stand SG11 ..... 55 F2
Mill Farm Cl. Pnr HA5 ..... 175 C1
Mill Field. Harl CM17 ..... 118 C4
Mill Gdns. Tri HP23 ..... 100 A4
Mill Green La. Hat AL9 ..... 110 E1
Mill Green Rd. Wel G C AL7 ..... 110 E5
Mill Hatch. Harl CM20 ..... 118 A4
Mill Hill. Far CM23 ..... 58 E5
Mill Hill. Royst SG8 ..... 7 E4
Mill Hill. Sta M CM24 ..... 59 E6
Mill La. Alb SG11 ..... 57 C6
Mill La. Arl SG15 ..... 10 F4
Mill La. Ches EN8 ..... 148 E1
Mill La. Fla AL3 ..... 84 A1
Mill La. Harl CM17 ..... 118 E4
Mill La. Hex SG5 ..... 19 B3
Mill La. Hit SG4 ..... 34 F3
Mill La. Hod EN10 ..... 135 A2
Mill La. Kin L WD4 ..... 139 A2
Mill La. Mee SG9 ..... 30 A5
Mill La. Saw CM21 ..... 97 F3
Mill La. Sheer CM22 ..... 98 F3
Mill La. Stot SG5 ..... 12 A6
Mill La. Ther SG8 ..... 15 F8
Mill La. Wat St SG12,SG14 ..... 71 A4
Mill La. Welw AL6 ..... 89 C5
Mill La. Wes AL4 ..... 24 C1
Mill La. Wing HP22 ..... 60 C2
Mill Lane Cl. Hod EN10 ..... 134 F2
Mill Mead Sch. Hert 113 C6
Millway Race. Sta Ab SG12 ..... 115 D4
Mill Rd. Hert SG14 ..... 113 D6
Mill Rd. Royst SG8 ..... 7 D7
Mill Rd. St Ipp SG4 ..... 35 A3
Mill Side. Sta M CM24 ..... 59 E6
Mill St. Ashw SG7 ..... 4 D4
Mill St. Berk HP4 ..... 122 C4
Mill St. Bis St CM23 ..... 77 A5
Mill St. Heml H HP3 ..... 138 D8
Mill St. Luton LU1 ..... 63 D8
Mill View Rd. Tri HP23 ..... 99 F4
Mill Way. Bus WD2 ..... 167 E8
Mill Way. Ric WD3 ..... 164 F1
Millacres. Ware SG12 ..... 93 E1 1
Milland Ct. Bor WD6 ..... 170 D8
Millard Way. Hit SG4 ..... 22 C1
Millbank. Heml H HP3 ..... 138 D7
Millbridge Mews. Hert SG14 ..... 113 C6 2
Millbrook Rd. Bus WD2 ..... 167 F8
Millcrest Rd. Gofs O EN7 ..... 147 B3
Millcroft. Bis St CM23 ..... 59 A1
Miller Cl. Pnr HA5 ..... 175 C1
Millers La. Sta Ab SG12 ..... 115 C4
Millers Rise. St Alb AL1 ..... 127 E2
Millers View. Muc H SG10 ..... 74 E1
Millers Yd. Hert SG14 ..... 113 D6
Millfield. Berk HP4 ..... 122 D5
Millfield House. Watf 166 D3
Millfield La. Cad LU1 ..... 62 D2
Millfield La. Hit SG4 ..... 34 F4
Millfield La. L Had SG11 ..... 75 D8
Millfield La. Mark LU1 ..... 83 D8
Millfield Rd. Luton LU3 ..... 45 B3
Millfield Sch. Bun 40 D7
Millfield. Thun SG12 ..... 93 E8
Millfield Way. Cad LU1 ..... 62 D3
Millfield. Wel G C AL7 ..... 111 C7
Millfield Wlk. Heml H HP3 ..... 139 A8
Millfields. Saw CM21 ..... 97 F3
Millfields. Sta M CM24 ..... 59 E6
Millhoo Ct. Wa Aby EN9 ..... 163 F5
Millhouse La. Abb L WD5 ..... 140 A4
Milliners Way. Luton LU3 ..... 45 C1
Millside. Bis St 77 A5
Millstream Cl. Hert SG14 ..... 113 D6
Millstream Cl. Hit SG4 ..... 22 A1
Millthorne Cl. Cro Gr WD3 ..... 165 F4
Millwards. Hat AL10 ..... 130 B2
Millway. Bre Gr SG4 ..... 47 D2
Milne Cl. Letw SG6 ..... 23 B3
Milne Field. Pnr HA5 ..... 176 A3
Milner Cl. Watf WD2 ..... 154 B6
Milner Ct. Bus WD2 ..... 168 B3
Milner Cl. Luton LU2 ..... 63 F8
Milneway. Hare UB9 ..... 173 B2
Milton Ave. Barn EN5 ..... 171 F5
Milton Cl. Royst SG8 ..... 7 E6
Milton Ct. Ham St EN7 ..... 147 F5
Milton Ct. Harp AL5 ..... 86 D1 6
Milton Cl. Heml H HP2 ..... 105 B1
Milton Cl. Wa Aby EN9 ..... 163 C5

Milton Dene. Heml H HP2 125 B8
Milton Dr. Bor WD6 170 B4
Milton Rd. Harp AL5 86 B1
Milton Rd. Luton LU1 63 C6
Milton Rd. Ware SG12 93 D2
Milton St. Wa Aby EN9 163 C5
Milton St. Watf WD2 167 B8
Milton View. Hit SG4 35 C7
Milverton Gn. Luton LU3 45 A7
Mimms Hall Rd. Pot B EN6 158 D7
Mimms La. Shen WD7 157 C6
Mimram Cl. Whit SG4 66 E7
Mimram Pl. Welw AL6 89 C5
Mimram Rd. Hert SG14 113 B5
Mimram Rd. Welw AL6 89 C5
Mimram Wlk. Welw AL6 89 C5
Minchen Rd. Harl CM20 118 A1
Minehead Way. Stev SG1 50 A7
Minerva Dr. Watf WD2 153 E3
Minims The. Hat AL10 130 A7
Minorca Way. Dun LU4 44 A3
Minsden Rd. Stev SG2 51 D3
Minster Cl. Hat AL10 130 A3
Minster House. Hat AL10 130 A3
Minster Rd. Royst SG8 7 C8
Minstrel Cl. Heml H HP1 124 B4
Minstrel Ct. Har HA3 176 E1
Miss Joans Ride. Whip LU6 81 E7
Missden Dr. Heml H HP3 125 C1
Mistletoe Hill. Luton LU2 64 C8
Mistley Rd. Harl CM20 118 A2
Miswell La. Tri HP23 99 F3
Mitchell Cl. Abb L WD5 154 A7
Mitchell Cl. Bov HP3 136 F4
Mitchell Cl. St Alb AL1 141 D7
Mitchell Cl. Wel G C AL7 111 C6
Mitre Ct. Hert SG14 113 D6 17
Mitre Gdns. Bis St CM23 77 A4
Mixes Hill Ct. Luton LU2 46 A4
Mixes Hill Rd. Luton LU2 45 F4
Mixies The. Stot SG5 11 E6
Moakes The. Luton LU3 44 E7
Moat Cl. Bus WD2 168 B4
Moat La. Luton LU3 45 B4
Moat La. Wing HP22 60 B2
Moat The. Stand SG11 55 D3
Moatfield Rd. Bus WD2 168 B4
Moatside. Ans SG9 29 B7
Moatview Ct. Bus WD2 168 B4
Moatwood Gn. Wel G C AL7 110 E5
Mobbsbury Way. Stev SG2 51 C7
Mobley Gn. Luton LU2 46 B3
Moffats Cl. Bro Pk AL9 145 A5
Moffats La. Bro Pk AL9 144 F5
Moira Cl. Luton LU3 44 D7
Moles La. Wyd SG9 28 A3
Molescroft. Harp AL5 85 D4
Molesworth. Hod EN11 115 A2
Molewood Rd. Hert SG14 113 B7
Mollison Ave. Enf EN3 163 A3
Molteno Rd. Watf WD1 167 A8
Momples Rd. Harl CM20 118 B1
Monarch's Way. Ches EN8 162 E6
Monastery Cl. St Alb AL3 127 C3
Money Hill Par. Ric WD3 165 C1
Money Hill Rd. Ric WD3 165 C1
Money Hole La. Tewin AL7 111 E7
Moneyhill Ct. Ric WD3 165 B1
Monica Cl. Watf WD2 167 D7
Monklands. Letw SG6 22 D6
Monks Cl. Hod EN10 135 A3
Monks Cl. Letw SG6 22 C6
Monks Cl. Red AL3 106 B5
Monks Cl. St Alb AL1 127 E1
Monks Horton Way. St Alb AL1 128 A4
Monks Rise. Wel G C AL8 89 D2
Monks Row. Ware SG12 93 D2 7
Monks View. Stev SG2 50 F2
Monks Walk Sch. Wel G C 89 C3
Monks Wlk. Bun SG9 40 E7
Monksmead. Bor WD6 170 C5
Monksmead Sch. Bor 170 C6
Monkswick Rd. Harl CM20 117 F1
Monkswood Ave. Wa Aby EN9 163 D6
Monkswood Dr. Bis St CM23 76 D6
Monkswood Gdns. Bor WD6 170 D5
Monkswood Ret Pk. Stev 50 E3
Monkswood Way. Stev SG1 50 E3
Monkswood. Wel G C AL8 89 C2
Monmouth Rd. Watf WD1 167 B6
Monro Gdns. Har HA3 176 E3
Mons Ave. Bal SG7 23 F6
Mons Cl. Harp AL5 107 D6
Monson Rd. Hod EN10 134 F3
Montacute Rd. Bus WD2 168 E2
Montague Ave. Luton LU4 44 C6
Montague Rd. Berk HP4 122 B4
Montayne Rd. Ches EN8 162 D7
Montesole Ct. Pnr HA5 175 C1 6
Montfitchet Wlk. Stev SG2 51 D7
Montgomerie Cl. Berk HP4 122 A6
Montgomery Ave. Heml H HP2 125 A4
Montgomery Dr. Ches EN8 148 E3
Monton Cl. Luton LU3 44 F6
Montrose Ave. Luton LU3 45 C3
Montrose Rd. Har HA3 176 F1
Moon La. Barn EN5 171 F6
Moor End Rd. Heml H HP1 124 C2
Moor Hall Rd. Harl CM17 118 F4
Moor La. Mo Pk WD3 174 A8
Moor La. Sar WD3 151 E3
Moor Lane Crossing. Mo Pk WD1 166 C2
Moor Mill La. Lon C AL2 142 E3
Moor Park (Golf Course). Mo Pk 174 B8
Moor Park Rd. Norwd HA6 174 D4
Moor Park Sta. Mo Pk 174 D7
Moor St. Luton LU1 63 C8
Moor View. Watf WD1 167 A3
Moore Rd. Berk HP4 121 F6
Moorend. Wel G C AL7 111 A3
Moorfields. Gt Ho SG9 41 E8
Moorhead Cl. Hit SG5 34 D6
Moorhurst Ave. Gofs O EN7 147 B2
Moorland Gdns. Luton LU2 63 D8
Moorland Rd. Harp AL5 86 B4
Moorland Rd. Heml H HP1 124 A1
Moorlands. Pk St AL2 141 E3
Moorlands Sch. Dun 44 C3
Moorlands. Wel G C AL7 111 A3
Moormead Hill. Hit SG5 34 D6
Moors Ley. Walk SG2 38 B1
Moors The. Wel G C AL7 111 A7
Moors Wlk. Wel G C AL7 111 C6
Moorside. Heml H HP3 138 B8
Moorside. Wel G C AL7 111 A3
Moortown Rd. Sth Ox WD1 175 C6
Moorymead Cl. Wat St SG14 70 D3
Morecambe Cl. Stev SG1 50 B7
Morefields. Tri HP23 100 A6
Moremead. Wa Aby EN9 163 D6
Moreton Ave. Harp AL5 85 F2
Moreton Cl. Ham St EN7 148 B4
Moreton End Cl. Harp AL5 85 F2
Moreton End La. Harp AL5 85 F2
Moreton Pl. Harp AL5 85 F3
Moreton Rd. Luton LU2 46 A2
Morgan Cl. Norwd HA6 174 F4
Morgan Cl. Stev SG1 36 D1
Morgan's Rd. Hert SG13 113 D4
Morgan's Wlk. Hert SG13 113 D3
Morgans Cl. Hert SG13 113 D4
Morgans Jun Mix Inf Sch. Hert 113 D4
Morland Way. Ches EN8 148 E3
Morley Gr. Harl CM20 117 C2
Morley Hill. Enf EN2 161 D1
Morningside. Ric WD3 165 C1
Mornington Rd. Radl WD7 156 B5
Mornington. Welw AL6 90 A4
Morpeth Ave. Bor WD6 156 F1
Morrell Cl. Luton LU3 45 A7
Morrell Ct. Wel G C 110 F7
Morris Cl. Henlw SG16 10 C5
Morris Cl. Luton LU3 44 E8
Morris Ct. Wa Aby EN9 163 F5
Morris Way. Lon C AL2 142 D5
Morrison Ct. Barn EN5 171 E5 5
Morriston Cl. Sth Ox WD1 175 C5
Morse Cl. Hare UB9 173 C1
Mortain Dr. Berk HP4 121 F6
Mortimer Cl. Bus WD2 168 B3
Mortimer Cl. Luton LU1 62 F7
Mortimer Gate. Ches EN8 148 F4
Mortimer Hill. Tri HP23 100 B4
Mortimer Rd. Royst SG8 7 E7
Mortimer Rise. Tri HP23 100 B4
Morton St. Royst SG8 7 D7
Morven Cl. Pot B EN6 159 C8
Moss Bury Inf & Jun Sch. Stev 51 A7
Moss Cl. Pnr HA5 175 F1
Moss Cl. Ric WD3 173 D8
Moss Gn. Wel G C AL7 110 E4
Moss La. Pnr HA5 175 E1
Moss Rd. Watf WD2 154 B5
Moss Side. Bri Wd AL2 140 F1
Moss Way. Hit SG5 21 C1
Mossbank Ave. Luton LU2 64 C8
Mossendew Cl. Hare UB9 173 D2
Mostyn Rd. Bus WD2 168 C4
Mostyn Rd. Luton LU3 44 E4
Motor Vehicle Works. Luton 64 B7
Mott St. Wa Aby EN9 163 D1
Motts Cl. Wat St SG14 70 D4
Moulton Rise. Luton LU2 63 F8
Mount Cl. Heml H HP1 123 F3
Mount Dr. Pk St AL2 141 D6
Mount Dr. Sta M CM24 59 E5
Mount Garrison. Hit SG4 34 F7
Mount Grace Rd. Luton LU2 46 C6
Mount Grace Rd. Pot B EN6 159 B8
Mount Grove Sch. Pot B 159 B8
Mount Pleasant Cl. Hat AL9 130 D8
Mount Pleasant. Hare UB9 173 A2
Mount Pleasant. Hit SG5 34 D6
Mount Pleasant La. Bri Wd AL2 140 E1
Mount Pleasant La. Hat AL9 130 C8
Mount Pleasant Lane
Jun Mix Inf Sch. Bri Wd 140 E1
Mount Pleasant Rd. Luton LU3 44 E5
Mount Pleasant. St Alb AL3 127 C3
Mount Rd. Hert SG14 113 A5
Mount Rd. Whea AL4 87 D1
Mount The. Bar SG8 8 F1
Mount The. Ham St EN7 147 D5
Mount The. Luton LU3 63 D8 4
Mount The. Pot B EN6 145 B1
Mount The. Ric WD3 165 C3
Mount Vernon & The Radium
Inst Hospl. Norwd 174 B4
Mount View. Enf EN2 160 F1
Mount View. Lon C AL2 142 F4
Mount View. Ric WD3 165 B1
Mount Way. Wel G C AL7 110 F3
Mountbatten Cl. St Alb AL1 142 B8
Mounteagle. Royst SG8 7 D5
Mountfield Rd. Heml H HP2 124 E3
Mountfield Rd. Luton LU2 45 E2
Mountfitchet High Sch The. Sta M 59 F4
Mountfitchet Rd. Sta M CM24 59 E5
Mountjoy. Hit SG4 22 C1
Mountside. Har HA7 176 F2
Mountsorrel. Hert SG13 113 F6
Mountview. Norwd HA6 174 F4
Mountview Rd. Ham St EN7 147 E5
Mountway Cl. Wel G C AL7 110 F3
Mountway. Pot B EN6 145 A1
Mowbray Cres. Stot SG5 11 F7
Mowbray Gdns. Hit SG4 35 A5
Mowbray Rd. Harl CM20 118 A3
Moxes Wood. Luton LU3 44 E7
Moxon St. Barn EN5 171 F6
Mozart Ct. Stev SG1 50 C5
Muddy La. Letw SG6 22 F3
Muirfield Cl. Sth Ox WD1 175 C6
Muirfield Gn. Sth Ox WD1 175 C6
Muirfield. Luton LU2 45 E6
Muirfield Rd. Sth Ox WD1 175 B6
Muirhead Way. Kneb SG3 68 F5
Mulberry Cl. Ches EN10 148 F7
Mulberry Cl. Chis AL2 141 B3
Mulberry Cl. Luton LU1 63 B7
Mulberry Cl. Stot SG5 11 F5
Mulberry Cl. Tri HP23 100 A5
Mulberry Ct. Bis St CM23 77 A5
Mulberry Gn. Harl CM17 118 D4
Mulberry Way. Hit SG5 21 D2
Mullion Cl. Har HA3 176 B2
Mullion Cl. Luton LU2 46 B5
Mullion Wlk. Sth Ox WD1 175 D6
Mullway. Letw SG6 22 C6
Mundells Ct. Wel G C 110 F8
Mundells. Ham St EN7 148 A4
Mundells. Wel G C AL7 111 A8
Munden Gr. Watf WD2 154 D1
Munden Rd. Dan En SG12 71 E7
Munden View. Watf WD2 154 D3
Mundesley Cl. Stev SG1 36 B1
Mundesly Cl. Sth Ox WD1 175 C6
Mungo-Park Cl. Bus WD2 176 C8
Munro Rd. Bus WD2 168 C4
Muntings The. Stev SG2 51 A3
Munts Meadow. Wes SG4 24 C1
Murchison Rd. Hod EN11 115 B1
Muriel Ave. Watf WD1 167 C4
Murray Cres. Pnr HA5 175 D2
Murray Rd. Berk HP4 122 C6
Murray Rd. Norwd HA6 174 E3
Murrell La. Stot SG5 12 A5
Murton Ct. St Alb AL1 127 E4
Museum Ct. Tri HP23 100 A3
Musgrave Cl. Ham St EN7 147 F4
Musk Hill. Heml H HP1 123 E2
Muskalls Cl. Ham St EN7 148 A4
Muskham Rd. Harl CM20 118 B3
Musleigh Manor. Ware SG12 93 F1
Musley Hill. Ware SG12 93 E2
Musley Inf Sch. Ware 93 E2
Musley La. Ware SG12 93 E2
Mussons Path. Luton LU2 45 E1
Muswell Cl. Luton LU3 45 B6
Mutchetts Cl. Watf WD2 154 E6
Mutford Croft. Luton LU2 46 D1 5
Mutton La. Pot B EN6 158 E8
Myddelton Ave. Enf EN1 161 E1
Myddleton Rd. Ware SG12 114 D8
Myles Ct. Gofs O EN7 147 C2
Mylne Ct. Hod EN11 115 A1
Mymms Dr. Bro Pk AL9 145 B4
Mymwood Sch. Bro Pk 145 C4
Myrtle Cotts. Sar WD3 152 A3
Myrtle Gr. Enf EN2 161 D1
Myrtleside Cl. Norwd HA6 174 D3

Nails La. Bis St CM23 76 F7
Nairn Cl. Harp AL5 107 D6
Nairn Gn. Sth Ox WD1 175 A7
Nan Aires. Wing HP22 60 A3
Nancy Downs. Watf WD1 167 C2
Nap The. Kin L WD4 139 A2
Napier Cl. Lon C AL2 142 D6
Napier Ct. Ches EN8 148 B3
Napier Ct. Luton LU1 63 D7
Napier Dr. Watf WD2 167 E5
Napier Rd. Luton LU1 63 D7
Nappsbury Rd. Luton LU4 44 D5
Napsbury Ave. Lon C AL2 142 C5
Napsbury La. St Alb AL1 142 A7
Nascot Pl. Watf WD1 167 B7
Nascot Rd. Watf WD1 167 B7
Nascot St. Watf WD1 167 B7
Nascot Wood Inf Sch. Watf 154 A1
Nascot Wood Jun Sch. Watf 154 A1
Nascot Wood Rd. Watf WD1 153 F1
Naseby Rd. Luton LU1 63 B7
Nash Cl. Bor WD6 169 F5
Nash Cl. Stev SG2 51 B6
Nash Cl. Wel G AL9 144 D8
Nash Gn. Heml H HP3 138 F6
Nash Gn. Heml H HP3 139 A6
Nash Mills C of E Sch. Heml H 138 F6
Nash Mills La. Heml H HP3 138 F5
Nash Rd. Royst SG8 7 D5
Nathaniel Wlk. Tri HP23 100 A5
Nathans Cl. Welw AL6 89 C6
Nayland Cl. Luton LU2 46 E1 1
Nazeing New Rd. Hod EN10 135 B2
Nazeing New Rd. Lo Naz EN10 135 B2
Nazeing Prim Sch. Lo Naz 149 E8
Nazeing Rd. Lo Naz EN9 135 D1
Neal Cl. Norwd HA6 175 A2
Neal Ct. Hert SG14 113 C6
Neal Ct. Wa Aby EN9 163 F6
Neal St. Watf WD1 167 C4
Neaole Cl. Bor WD6 170 C8
Necton Rd. Whea AL4 108 E8
Needham Rd. Luton LU4 44 B6
Nell Gwynn Cl. Shen WD7 156 E7
Nelson Ave. St Alb AL1 142 B8
Nelson Rd. Bis St CM23 77 A5
Nelson Rd. Dagn HP4 81 C5
Nelson St. Hert SG14 113 B7
Nene Rd. Henlw SG16 10 B4
Neptune Ct. Bor WD6 170 A6
Neptune Dr. Heml H HP2 124 E5
Neston Rd. Watf WD2 154 C2
Nether St. Widf SG12 95 E4
Netherby Cl. Tri HP23 100 C6
Nethercott Cl. Luton LU2 46 C1
Netherfield La. Sta Ab SG12 115 E3
Netherfield Rd. Harp AL5 107 B4
Netherhall Rd. Lo Naz CM19 135 F5
Netherstones. Stot SG5 11 F7
Netherway. St Alb AL3 141 A8
Netley Dell. Letw SG6 23 B3
Netteswell Cross. Harl CM20 117 E2
Netteswell Orch. Harl CM20 117 D1
Netteswell Rd. Harl CM20 117 F3
Netteswell Tower. Harl CM20 117 D1
Nettlecroft. Heml H HP1 124 B2
Nettlecroft. Wel G C AL7 111 B7
Nettleden Rd. L Gad HP4 102 E4
Nettleden Rd. Pot En HP1 103 D1
Nettleden Rd. Pot En HP4 123 B8
Nevell's Gn. Letw SG6 22 F6
Nevells Rd. Letw SG6 22 F6
Nevill Gr. Watf WD2 167 B8
Neville Cl. Pot B EN6 158 F8
Neville Rd. Luton LU3 45 A5
Neville's Ct. Letw SG6 23 B7
New Barn La. L Hal CM22 77 D1
New Barnes Ave. St Alb AL1 142 A8
New Barns La. Muc H SG10 74 E4
New Bedford Rd.
Luton LU1,LU2,LU3 45 D3
New Briars Jun Mix Inf Sch. Hat 130 A5
New Cl. Kneb SG3 68 F6
New Cotts. Bro Pk AL9 144 D3
New Cotts. Ches EN8 162 C5
New Cotts. Mark AL3 83 E6
New Ct. Welw SG3 69 A2
New England Cl. Hit SG4 34 F4
New England St. St Alb AL3 127 C3
New Farm La. Norwd HA6 174 E2
New Ford Rd. Ches EN8 162 F5
New Forge Pl. Red AL3 106 B5
New Greens Ave. St Alb AL3 127 D7
New House Pk. St Alb AL1 142 B7
New Inn Rd. Hin SG7 3 D5
New Kent Rd. St Alb AL1 127 D3
New Mill Terr. Tri HP23 100 B6
New Par. Chor WD3 164 C5
New Park Dr. Heml H HP2 125 B3
New Park La. Ast SG2 51 F2
New Park Rd. Hare UB9 173 C2
New Park Rd. New St SG13 146 D7
New Pl. Welw AL6 89 B4
New Rd. Berk HP4 122 D6
New Rd. Chipf WD4 137 F1
New Rd. Cro Gr WD3 166 A4
New Rd. Elst WD6 169 D3
New Rd. Gt Ch SG8 9 D6
New Rd. Harl CM17 118 D4
New Rd. Hat AL8 110 A3
New Rd. Henlw SG16 10 A8
New Rd. Hert SG14 113 D8
New Rd. Hod EN10 135 A4
New Rd. L Had SG11 75 A7
New Rd. Nthch HP4 121 F7
New Rd. Radl WD7 155 E2
New Rd. Radl WD7 168 E8
New Rd. Ridge EN6 158 A6
New Rd. Sar WD3 151 F1
New Rd. Shen WD7 157 A5
New Rd. Tri HP23 100 B6
New Rd. Ware SG12 93 D1
New Rd. Watf WD1 167 C5
New Rd. Welw AL6 89 F3
New Rd. Welw SG3 69 B3
New River Ave. Gt Am SG12 115 B4
New River Cl. Hod EN11 135 B7
New River Ct. Ches EN7 162 B8
New River Trad Est. Ches 148 D5
New St. Berk HP4 122 D4
New St. Cad LU1 63 C1
New St. Ched LU7 79 F7
New St. Luton LU1 63 E6
New St. Saw CM21 97 E3
New St. Watf WD1 167 C5
New Town. Cod SG4 67 F1
New Town Rd. Luton LU1 63 E6
New Town St. Luton LU1 63 E6
New Wood. Wel G C AL7 111 C7
Newark Cl. Royst SG8 7 C8
Newark Gn. Bor WD6 170 D6
Newark Rd. Luton LU4 45 A2
Newberries Ave. Radl WD7 156 B4
Newberries Jun Mix Inf Sch.
Radl 156 C4
Newbiggin Path. Sth Ox WD1 175 C6
Newbold Rd. Luton LU3 45 B7
Newbolt Rd. Stan HA7 176 F5
Newbolt. Royst SG8 7 D8
Newbury Ave. Enf EN3 162 F2
Newbury Cl. Bis St CM23 76 E8
Newbury Cl. Luton LU4 44 E2
Newbury Cl. Stev SG1 36 D1
Newcastle Cl. Stev SG1 36 F2
Newcombe Rd. Luton LU1 63 C7
Newcome Path. Shen WD7 157 A5
Newcome Rd. Shen WD7 157 A5
Newdigate Gn. Hare UB9 173 D2
Newdigate Rd E. Hare UB9 173 D2
Newdigate Rd. Hare UB9 173 C2
Newell La. Ard SG2 38 D7
Newell Rd. Heml H HP3 138 E8
Newell Rise. Heml H HP3 138 E8
Newells Hedge. Pit LU7 80 D5
Newells. Letw SG6 23 D4
Newfield La. Heml H HP2 124 F3
Newfields. Wel G C AL8 110 B5
Newford Cl. Heml H HP2 125 B4
Newgate Cl. St Alb AL4 128 D6
Newgate St. New St SG13 146 D7
Newgate. Stev SG2 51 A4
Newgate Street Village.
New St SG13 146 E6
Newgatestreet Rd. Gofs O EN7 147 B4
Newground Rd. Ald HP23 101 B3
Newhall Cl. Bov HP3 137 A4
Newhall Ct. Wa Aby EN9 163 F6
Newhouse Cres. Watf WD2 154 B6
Newhouse Rd. Bov HP3 137 A4
Newland Cl. Pnr HA5 175 F4
Newland Cl. St Alb AL1 142 A8
Newlands Ave. Radl WD7 155 F5
Newlands Cl E. Hit SG4 34 F4
Newlands Cl W. Hit SG4 34 F4
Newlands. Hat AL9 130 C7
Newlands La. Hit SG4 34 F4
Newlands. Letw SG6 23 A3
Newlands Pl. Barn EN5 171 D4
Newlands Rd. Heml H HP1 123 E3
Newlands Rd. Luton LU1 63 C3
Newlands. Pot B EN6 145 B1
Newlands Wlk. Watf WD2 154 D6
Newlyn Cl. Bri Wd AL2 140 E1
Newlyn Cl. Stev SG1 50 A6
Newlyn Rd. Barn EN5 171 F5
Newman Ave. Royst SG8 7 F6
Newmans Ct. Wat St SG14 70 D3
Newmans Dr. Harp AL5 85 F2
Newmarket Rd. Royst SG8 7 E6
Newnham Cl. Luton LU2 46 D1
Newnham Par. Ches EN8 148 D1
Newnham Rd. Newn SG7 12 E6
Newnham Way. Ashw SG7 4 B2
Newport Cl. Enf EN3 162 E2
Newport Mead. Sth Ox WD1 175 D6
Newports. Saw CM21 97 C1
Newquay Gdns. Sth Ox WD1 175 B8
Newstead. Hat AL10 129 F2
Newstead House. Hare UB9 173 C1
Newteswell Dr. Wa Aby EN9 163 D7
Newton Cl. Harp AL5 107 D6
Newton Cl. Hod EN11 115 B2
Newton Cres. Bor WD6 170 C5
Newton Dr. Saw CM21 97 D1
Newton Rd. Har HA3 176 E1
Newton Rd. Stev SG2 51 B6
Newtondale. Luton LU4 44 C5
Newtons Way. Hit SG4 34 F6
Newtown Rd. Bis St CM23 76 F6
Niagara Cl. Ches EN8 148 D2
Nicholas Breakspear Sch Annexe.
Coln H 128 E2
Nicholas Breakspear Sch. Coln H 128 E2
Nicholas Cl. St Alb AL3 127 D7
Nicholas Cl. Watf WD2 154 B2
Nicholas Hawksmoor Sch. Bor 170 C8
Nicholas La. Hert SG14 113 D6
Nicholas Pl. Stev SG1 36 D1
Nicholas Rd. Bor WD6 169 F4
Nicholas Way. Heml H HP2 124 F5
Nicholas Way. Norwd HA6 174 C2
Nicholls Cl. Red AL3 105 F5
Nichols Cl. Luton LU2 46 C2
Nicola Cl. Har HA3 176 D1
Nicoll Way. Bor WD6 170 D5
Nicolson Dr. Bus WD2 176 C8
Nidderdale. Heml H HP2 124 F6
Nightingale Ave. Knee SG8 2 A5
Nightingale Cl. Luton LU2 46 C6
Nightingale Cl. Radl WD7 155 F3
Nightingale Ct. Hert SG14 113 C6
Nightingale Ct. Hit SG5 35 A8
Nightingale Ct. Luton LU3 63 C8
Nightingale Ct. Ric WD3 165 C2
Nightingale La. St Alb AL1 142 C7
Nightingale Lodge. Berk HP4 122 B4
Nightingale Pl. Ric WD3 165 D2
Nightingale Rd. Bus WD2 168 A4
Nightingale Rd. Hit SG5 34 F8
Nightingale Rd. Ric WD3 165 C2
Nightingale Terr. Arl SG15 11 A3
Nightingale Way. Bal SG7 23 F6
Nightingale Wlk. Heml H HP2 105 C1
Nightingale Wlk. Stev SG2 51 C5
Nightingales. Wa Aby EN9 163 E5
Nimmo Dr. Bus WD2 168 D2
Nine Acre La. Ess AL9 132 A1
Ninefields. Wa Aby EN9 163 F6
Ninesprings Way. Hit SG4 35 B6
Ninian Rd. Heml H HP2 124 E8
Ninning's La. Welw AL6 68 D2
Ninth Ave. Luton LU3 44 D7
Niton Cl. Barn EN5 171 D3
Niven Cl. Bor WD6 170 C8
Nobel Sch. Stev 51 C7
Nobel Villas. Wa Aby EN9 163 D5
Nobles The. Bis St CM23 76 D6
Nodes Dr. Stev SG2 51 A1
Noke La. Bri Wd AL2 140 E4
Noke Shot. Harp AL5 86 C4
Noke Side. Chis AL2 141 A4
Noke The. Stev SG2 69 B8
Nokes The. Heml H HP1 124 A5
Nokeside. Stev SG2 69 B8
Nook The. Gt Am SG12 115 C4
Norbury Ave. Watf WD1 167 C7
Norfolk Ave. Watf WD2 154 C1
Norfolk Ct. Barn EN5 171 E5 4
Norfolk Gdns. Bor WD6 170 D5
Norfolk Rd. Bun SG9 40 E8
Norfolk Rd. Luton LU2 64 A7
Norfolk Rd. Ric WD3 165 E1
Norfolk Way. Bis St CM23 76 F5
Norman Ave. Bis St CM23 76 D6
Norman Cl. Wa Aby EN9 163 D6
Norman Cres. Pnr HA5 175 C2
Norman Ct. Pot B EN6 145 C1
Norman Ct. Sta M CM24 59 E7
Norman Ct. Stev SG1 36 F1
Norman Rd. Luton LU3 45 B2
Norman Rd. Welw AL6 89 B3
Norman's La. Royst SG8 7 D5
Norman's Way. Sta M CM24 59 E7
Normandy Ave. Barn EN5 171 F5
Normandy Dr. Berk HP4 122 B6
Normandy Rd. St Alb AL3 127 D4
Normans Cl. Letw SG6 11 F1
Normans La. Welw AL6 68 E2
Normansfield Cl. Bus WD2 168 B2
Norris Cl. Bis St CM23 77 C7
Norris Gr. Hod EN10 134 E3
Norris La. Hod EN11 135 A7
Norris Rd. Hod EN11 135 A6
Norris Rise. Hod EN11 134 F7
North App. Mo Pk HA6 174 C8
North App. Watf WD2 154 A5
North Ave. Letw SG6 23 B8
North Ave. Shen WD7 156 E7
North Barn. Lo Naz EN10 135 B1
North Cl. Barn EN5 171 C4
North Cl. Chis AL2 141 B6
North Cl. Royst SG8 7 C7
North Comm. Red AL3 106 A5
North Common Rd. Red AL3 106 A4
North Ct. Mark AL3 83 E5
North Dr. St Alb AL5 128 E5
North Dr. Thun SG11 72 E1
North Drift Way. Luton LU1 63 B6
North Gate. Harl CM20 117 C1
North Hertfordshire Coll
(Hitchin Ctr). Hit 35 B8
North Hertfordshire Coll
(Lethchworth Ctr). Letw 22 F6
North Hertfordshire Coll
(Shephalbury Ctr). Stev 51 A1
North Hertfordshire Coll
(Stevenage Ctr). Stev 50 D4
North Hill. Chor WD3 164 E8
North Luton Ind Est. Luton 44 B7
North Orbital Rd. Bri Wd AL2 140 E2
North Orbital Rd. Chis AL2 141 B5
North Orbital Rd. Coln H AL4 129 C2
North Orbital Rd. Lon C 142 D6
North Orbital Rd. Pk St AL2 141 E6
North Orbital Rd. Watf WD2 154 D7
North Orbital Trad Est. St Alb 142 A7
North Pl. Harl CM20 118 B5
North Pl. Hit SG5 21 D1
North Pl. Wa Aby EN9 163 B6
North Rd. Bal SG7 12 E2
North Rd. Berk HP4 122 B4
North Rd. Ches EN8 162 E6
North Rd. Chor WD3 164 D4
North Rd. Hert SG14 113 A7
North Rd. Hert SG14 113 C6

North Rd. Hod EN11 .... 135 A7
North Rd. Stev SG1 .... 36 C2
North Ride. Welw AL6 .... 89 C6
North Riding. Bri Wd AL2 .... 141 A1
North Road Ave. Hert SG14 .... 113 A7
North Road Gdns. Hert SG14 .... 113 B6
North St. Bis St CM23 .... 76 F7
North St. Lo Naz EN9 .... 135 E1
North St. Luton LU2 .... 45 E1
North Terr. Bis St CM23 .... 76 F8
North View Cotts. Widf SG12 .... 95 D4
North Western Ave. Abb L WD2 .... 153 D4
North Western Ave. Stan WD6 .... 169 B2
North Western Ave. Watf WD2 .... 154 C3
Northaw C of E Jun Mix Inf Sch.
  Nort 146 A1
Northaw Cl. Heml H HP2 .... 125 B8
Northaw Pk. Nort EN6 .... 159 F7
Northaw Rd E. Cuf EN6 .... 146 E1
Northaw Rd W. Nort EN6 .... 160 C8
Northbridge. Berk HP4 .... 122 A6
Northbridge Way. Heml H HP1 .... 124 A3
Northbrook Dr. Norwd HA6 .... 174 E3
Northbrook Rd. Barn EN5 .... 171 E3
Northchurch St Mary's CE Fst Sch.
  Nthch 121 E6
Northcliffe Dr. Barn N20 .... 171 F1
Northcote. Pnr HA5 .... 175 C1 1
Northcotts. Hat AL9 .... 130 C6
Northcourt. Ric WD3 .... 165 A1
Northdown Rd. Hat AL10 .... 130 A2
Northend. Heml H HP3 .... 125 C1
Northern Ave. Henlw SG16 .... 10 B3
Northern House. Hit 35 B7
Northfield. Brag SG11 .... 55 F7
Northfield Gdns. Watf WD2 .... 154 C2
Northfield. Hat AL10 .... 130 B8
Northfield Rd. Ashw SG7 .... 1 C3
Northfield Rd. Bor WD6 .... 170 B8
Northfield Rd. Ches EN8 .... 162 E7
Northfield Rd. Harp AL5 .... 86 C4
Northfield Rd. Saw CM21 .... 97 E4
Northfield Sch. Watf 167 A8
Northfield. Stand SG11 .... 55 E2
Northfields Inf Sch. Letw 11 F1
Northfields. Letw SG6 .... 11 F1
Northgate End. Bis St CM23 .... 76 F8
Northgate House. Ches EN8 .... 148 D2
Northgate Jun Mix Inf Sch. Bis St 76 E8
Northgate. Norwd HA6 .... 174 C4
Northgate Path. Bor WD6 .... 169 F8
Northlands. Pot B EN6 .... 159 D8
Northolt Ave. Bis St CM23 .... 59 B1
Northridge Way. Heml H HP1 .... 124 A3
Northside. Sand 108 B1
Northumberland Ave. Enf EN1 .... 162 B1
Northview Rd. Luton LU2 .... 45 F2
Northway. Ric WD3 .... 165 D2
Northway. Wel G C I AL7 .... 89 F1
Northwell Dr. Luton LU3 .... 44 F7
Northwick Rd. Sth Ox WD1 .... 175 C6
Northwood Cl. Ham St EN7 .... 147 F4
Northwood Coll. Norwd 174 D3
Northwood Golf Course. Norwd 174 C2
Northwood Hills Cir. Norwd HA6 .... 175 A2
Northwood Hills Sta. Pnr 175 A1
Northwood, Pinner & District Hospl.
  Norwd 175 A2
Northwood Rd. Hare UB9 .... 173 D2
Northwood Sch. Pnr 175 B2
Northwood Sta. Norwd 174 D3
Northwood Way. Hare UB9 .... 173 D2
Northwood Way. Norwd HA6 .... 175 A3
Northwood. Wel G C AL7 .... 111 D6
Norton Bury La. Letw SG7 .... 12 C2
Norton Cl. Bor WD6 .... 170 A8
Norton Cres. Bal SG7 .... 23 E8
Norton Gn. Stev SG1 .... 50 B3
Norton Green Rd. Stev SG1 .... 50 C4
Norton Mill La. Newn SG7 .... 12 D3
Norton Rd. Bal SG7 .... 12 C2
Norton Rd. Letw SG6 .... 12 A4
Norton Rd. Luton LU3 .... 44 F4
Norton Rd Prim Sch. Luton 44 F4
Norton Rd. Stev SG1 .... 50 D4
Norton Rd. Stot SG5 .... 12 A4
Norton Sch The. Letw 23 A8
Norton Way N. Letw SG6 .... 23 A7
Norton Way S. Letw SG6 .... 23 A5
Nortonstreet La. Whit SG4 .... 67 B7
Norvic Rd. Mars HP23 .... 80 A1
Norwich St. Stev SG1 .... 37 B1
Norwich Way. Cro Gr WD3 .... 166 B5
Norwood Cl. Hert SG14 .... 112 F7
Nottingham Cl. Watf WD2 .... 154 A6
Nottingham Rd. Chor WD3 .... 164 C1
Novello Way. Bor WD6 .... 170 D8
Nugent's Pk. Pnr HA5 .... 175 F2
Nugents Ct. Pnr HA5 .... 175 E2
Nun's Cl. Hit SG5 .... 34 E7
Nunfield. Chipf WD4 .... 152 B8
Nunnery Cl. St Alb AL1 .... 127 E1
Nunnery La. Luton LU3 .... 45 B5
Nunnery Stables. St Alb AL1 .... 127 D1
Nuns La. St Alb AL1 .... 141 E8
Nunsbury Dr. Ches EN10 .... 148 E6
Nup End Cl. Wing HP22 .... 60 B3
Nup End La. Wing HP22 .... 60 B3
Nupton Dr. Barn EN5 .... 171 C3
Nurseries Rd. Whea AL4 .... 108 E7
Nursery Cl. Bis St CM23 .... 76 F6
Nursery Cl. Stev SG2 .... 69 A8
Nursery Cotts. Stev SG1 .... 50 A6
Nursery Fields. Saw CM21 .... 97 D2
Nursery Gdns. Tri HP23 .... 100 B4
Nursery Gdns. Ware SG12 .... 93 E1
Nursery Gdns. Wel G C AL7 .... 89 E1
Nursery Hill. Wel G C AL7 .... 89 E1
Nursery Par. Luton LU3 .... 44 E5
Nursery Rd. Bis St CM23 .... 76 F6
Nursery Rd. Ches EN10 .... 148 F6
Nursery Rd. Hert SG14 .... 113 B1
Nursery Rd. Lo Naz EN9 .... 135 D2
Nursery Rd. Luton LU3 .... 44 F5
Nut Gr. Wel G C AL8 .... 89 D1
Nut Slip. Bun SG9 .... 40 E6
Nutcroft. Dat SG3 .... 69 D2
Nutfield. Wel G C AL7 .... 90 A1

Nutleigh Gr. Hit SG5 .... 21 D1
Nuttfield Cl. Cro Gr WD3 .... 166 B3
Nye Way. Bov HP3 .... 137 A3
Nymans Cl. Luton LU2 .... 46 D3

Oak Ave. Bri Wd AL2 .... 141 A1
Oak Ave. Enf EN2 .... 160 F1
Oak Cl. Heml H HP3 .... 138 F7
Oak Cl. Sth W Aby EN9 .... 163 D5
Oak Ct. Norwd HA6 .... 174 D4
Oak Dr. Berk HP4 .... 122 D3
Oak Dr. Saw CM21 .... 118 C8
Oak End. Bun SG9 .... 40 D7
Oak Farm. Bor WD6 .... 170 C4
Oak Glade. Norwd HA6 .... 174 B2
Oak Gn. Abb L WD5 .... 153 E7
Oak Gr. Hat AL10 .... 129 F5
Oak Gr. Hert SG13 .... 113 E4
Oak Green Way. Abb L WD5 .... 153 E7
Oak La. Chol HP23 .... 120 B2
Oak La. Cuf EN6 .... 146 F3
Oak La. Gra SG4 .... 36 C4
Oak Piece Ct. Welw AL6 .... 89 E7
Oak Piece. Welw AL6 .... 89 E7
Oak Rd. Luton LU4 .... 63 C8
Oak Rd. Welw SG3 .... 89 B1
Oak St. Bis St CM23 .... 76 F6
Oak St. Heml H HP3 .... 138 F7
Oak Tree Cl. Abb L WD5 .... 153 D7
Oak Tree Cl. Hat AL10 .... 130 A6
Oak Tree Cl. Hert H SG13 .... 114 C3
Oak Tree Cl. Elst WD6 .... 169 D3
Oak Tree Cl. Welw AL6 .... 89 E8
Oak Way. Harp AL5 .... 107 A5
Oak Wood. Berk HP4 .... 121 F3
Oakbank. Kim SG4 .... 66 D1
Oakcroft Cl. Pnr HA5 .... 175 B1
Oakdale Ave. Pnr HA5 .... 175 A1
Oakdale Cl. Sth Ox WD1 .... 175 C6
Oakdale. Wel G C AL8 .... 89 D1
Oakdene. Ches EN8 .... 148 E1
Oakdene Cl. Pnr HA5 .... 175 F3
Oakdene Rd. Heml H HP3 .... 138 F7
Oakdene Way. St Alb AL4 .... 128 C3
Oaken Gr. Wel G C AL7 .... 110 E3
Oakenholt. Heml H HP3 .... 125 B1
Oakes Cl. Welw AL6 .... 89 E3
Oakfield Ave. Hit SG4 .... 35 B5
Oakfield Cl. Pot B EN6 .... 158 F8
Oakfield Rd. Harp AL5 .... 107 A5
Oakfield. Ric WD3 .... 165 A2
Oakfields Ave. Kneb SG3 .... 69 A6
Oakfields Cl. Stev SG2 .... 51 C1
Oakfields Rd. Kneb SG3 .... 69 A6
Oakfields. Stev SG2 .... 51 C1
Oakhill Ave. Pnr HA5 .... 175 E1
Oakhill Cl. Map Cr WD3 .... 172 E3
Oakhill Dr. A St P AL6 .... 89 A6
Oakhill. Letw SG6 .... 23 D4
Oakhill Map Cr WD3 .... 172 D6
Oakhurst Ave. Harp AL5 .... 107 A5
Oakhurst Rd. Enf EN3 .... 162 D3
Oakington. Wel G C AL7 .... 111 D6
Oakland's Coll. St Alb 128 D1
Oaklands Ave. Bro Pk AL9 .... 144 E4
Oaklands Ave. Watf WD1 .... 167 B1
Oaklands Avenue Inf Sch. Watf 167 B1
Oaklands. Berk HP4 .... 122 A4
Oaklands Cl. Bis St CM23 .... 59 B2
Oaklands Coll. Bor 170 C7
Oaklands Coll. Hat 130 A5
Oaklands Coll (Lemsford Lane
  Campus). Wel G C 110 B4
Oaklands Coll. Pot B 159 B7
Oaklands Coll. Wel G C 110 D7
Oaklands Ct. Watf WD1 .... 167 A8
Oaklands Dr. Bis St CM23 .... 59 B2
Oaklands Gate. Norwd HA6 .... 174 E4
Oaklands Gr. Ches EN10 .... 148 E7
Oaklands (Herts Coll of Agriculture
  & Horticulture). St Alb 128 D3
Oaklands La. Barn EN5 .... 171 B5
Oaklands La. Coln H AL4 .... 128 F5
Oaklands Pk. Bis St CM23 .... 59 B2
Oaklands Rd. Barn EN7 .... 171 F2
Oaklands Rd. Ham St EN7 .... 147 E5
Oaklands Rise. Welw AL6 .... 89 E7
Oaklands Sch. Welw 89 E7
Oaklawn. Tri HP23 .... 100 A3
Oaklea Cl. Welw AL6 .... 89 E8
Oaklea. Welw AL6 .... 89 E7
Oaklea Wood. Welw AL6 .... 89 E7
Oakleigh Dr. Cro Gr WD3 .... 166 C3
Oakleigh Rd. Pnr HA5 .... 175 F4
Oakley Cl. Luton LU4 .... 44 D7
Oakley Cl. Royst SG8 .... 7 D7
Oakley Rd. Harp AL5 .... 107 D2
Oakley Rd. Luton LU4 .... 44 E3
Oakmeade. Barn EN5 .... 171 D5
Oakmeade. Pnr HA5 .... 176 A4
Oakmere Ave. Pot B EN6 .... 159 C6
Oakmere Cl. Pot B EN6 .... 159 D8
Oakmere La. Pot B EN6 .... 159 C7
Oakridge Ave. Radl WD7 .... 155 F6
Oakridge. Bri Wd AL2 .... 140 F2
Oakridge La. Radl WD2 .... 155 E5
Oakroyd Ave. Pot B EN6 .... 158 F6
Oakroyd Cl. Pot B EN6 .... 158 F6
Oaks Cl. Hit SG4 .... 34 F5
Oaks Cl. Radl WD7 .... 155 F4
Oaks Cross. Stev SG2 .... 51 B1
Oaks Ret Pk. Harl 117 F3
Oaks The. Berk HP4 .... 122 A4
Oaks The. Cad LU1 .... 63 C1
Oaks The. Watf WD1 .... 167 C1
Oaktree Garth. Wel G C AL7 .... 110 E5
Oakview Ct. Ches EN7 .... 148 B3
Oakway. Whip HP6 .... 82 B7
Oakwell Cl. Stev SG2 .... 69 D7
Oakwood Ave. Bor WD6 .... 170 B5
Oakwood Cl. Stev SG2 .... 51 B2
Oakwood Dr. Luton LU3 .... 44 C8
Oakwood Dr. St Alb AL4 .... 128 C4
Oakwood Est. Harl 118 C4
Oakwood Prim Sch
  (Jun Mix & Inf). St Alb 128 C4
Oakwood Rd. Bri Wd AL2 .... 140 F2
Oakwood Rd. Pnr HA5 .... 175 B1
Oberon Cl. Bor WD6 .... 170 D8
Occupation Rd. Watf WD1 .... 167 B4

Octavia Ct. Watf WD2 .... 167 C7
Oddy Hill. Tri HP23 .... 100 C3
Oddy Hill. Wigg HP23 .... 100 C2
Odessey Rd. Bor WD6 .... 170 B8
Odhams Trad Est. Watf WD2 .... 167 C8
Offas Way. Whea AL4 .... 108 D8
Offley Endowed Jun Mix Inf Sch.
  Gt Of 33 C3
Offley Hill. Gt Of SG5 .... 33 C3
Offley Rd. Hit SG5 .... 34 E6
Ogard Rd. Hod EN11 .... 135 C8
Okeford Cl. Tri HP23 .... 99 F4
Okeford Dr. Tri HP23 .... 99 F4
Okeley La. Tri HP23 .... 99 E3
Old Barn La. Cro Gr WD3 .... 165 F4
Old Bedford Rd. Luton LU2 .... 45 D6
Old Bedford Rd. Luton LU2 .... 45 E4
Old Brewery Pl. Kim SG4 .... 66 D1
Old Chantry La. L Wym SG4 .... 35 F2
Old Charlton Rd. Hit SG5 .... 34 E6
Old Church La. Thun SG12 .... 93 B7
Old Common The. Fur P SG9 .... 43 B4
Old Cross. Hert SG14 .... 113 C6
Old Dean. Bov HP3 .... 137 A4
Old Dr The. Wel G C AL8 .... 110 B5
Old Farm. Pit LU7 .... 80 D4
Old Fishery La. Heml H HP1 .... 123 F1
Old Fishery La. Heml H HP1 .... 137 F8
Old Fold Cl. Barn EN5 .... 171 F8
Old Fold La. Barn EN5 .... 171 F8
Old Fold Manor Golf Club. Barn 171 E8
Old Fold View. Barn EN5 .... 171 C6
Old Forge Cl. Abb L WD5 .... 154 A6
Old Forge Cl. Wel G C AL7 .... 89 F2
Old Forge Rd. Enf EN1 .... 161 F1
Old French Horn La. Hat AL10 .... 130 B6
Old Gannon Cl. Mo Pk HA6 .... 174 C5
Old Garden Ct. St Alb AL3 .... 127 C3
Old Hale Way. Hit SG5 .... 21 E2
Old Hall Cl. Pnr HA5 .... 175 E2
Old Hall Dr. Pnr HA5 .... 175 E2
Old Harpenden Rd. St Alb AL3 .... 127 E6
Old Herns La. Wel G C AL7 .... 111 C8
Old Hertford Rd. Hat AL9 .... 130 C7
Old Highway. Hod EN11 .... 135 C8
Old House Ct. Heml H HP2 .... 124 F3
Old House La. Sar WD4 .... 152 F4
Old House Rd. Heml H HP2 .... 124 F3
Old Knebworth La. Kneb SG2 .... 68 D8
Old La. Kneb SG3 .... 69 B3
Old Leys. Hat AL10 .... 130 A2
Old London Rd. Hat SG13 .... 113 E6
Old London Rd. St Alb AL1 .... 127 E2
Old Maltings The. Bis St CM23 .... 77 A7 2
Old Maple. Fla HP2 .... 104 F1
Old Mill Gdns. Berk HP4 .... 122 D4
Old Mill La. L Hal CM22 .... 98 B6
Old Mill Rd. Abb L WD4 .... 153 C5
Old Nazeing Rd. Hod EN11 .... 135 B1
Old Nazeing Rd. Lo Naz EN10 .... 135 B1
Old North Rd. Knee SG8 .... 2 B7
Old North Rd. Royst SG8 .... 7 C8
Old Oak Cl. Arl SG15 .... 11 A8
Old Oak Gdns. Nthch HP4 .... 121 E7
Old Oak. St Alb AL1 .... 141 E8
Old Oaks. Wa Aby EN9 .... 163 E7
Old Orch. Pk St AL2 .... 141 D5
Old Orchard. Luton LU1 .... 63 D5
Old Orchard Mews. Berk HP4 .... 122 C3
Old Park Rd. Hit SG5 .... 34 E7
Old Parkbury La. Lon C AL2 .... 141 F1
Old Rd. Harl CM17 .... 118 D5
Old Rectory Cl. Harp AL5 .... 86 A2
Old Rectory Dr. Hat AL10 .... 130 B5
Old Rectory Gdns. Whea AL4 .... 108 D8
Old Redding. Stan HA3 .... 176 C6
Old School Cl. Cod SG4 .... 67 F1
Old School Gn. Ben SG2 .... 52 E5
Old School Orch. Wat St SG14 .... 70 E3
Old School The. Shil SG5 .... 19 E8
Old School Wlk. Arl SG15 .... 11 A4
Old School Wlk. Cad LU1 .... 63 C1
Old Shire La. C St P WD3 .... 172 B6
Old Shire La. Chor WD3 .... 164 A2
Old Sopwell Gdns. St Alb AL1 .... 127 E1
Old Uxbridge Rd. Map Cr WD3 .... 172 E3
Old Vicarage Gdns. Mark AL3 .... 83 D6
Old Walled Garden The. Stev SG1 .. 36 C1
Old Watford Rd. Bri Wd AL2 .... 140 E2
Old Watling St. Fla AL3 .... 84 B3
Old's App. Mo Pk WD1 .... 166 C1
Old's Cl. Mo Pk WD1 .... 166 B1
Olden Mead. Letw SG6 .... 23 B3
Oldfield Cl. Ches EN8 .... 148 E3
Oldfield Cl. St Alb AL1 .... 127 E3
Oldfield Dr. Ches EN8 .... 148 E3
Oldfield Farm Rd. Henlw SG16 .... 10 C1
Oldfield Rd. Heml H HP1 .... 123 E2
Oldfield Rd. Lon C AL2 .... 142 D6
Oldfield Rise. Whit SG4 .... 66 F5
Oldhall Cl. Whit SG4 .... 66 E7
Oldhall St. Hert SG14 .... 113 D6
Oldhouse Croft. Harl CM20 .... 117 E2
Oldings Cnr. Hat AL10 .... 130 B1
Oldpark Ride. Gofs O EN7 .... 161 D7
Oldwood. Welw AL6 .... 89 D7
Olive Taylor Ct. Heml H HP2 .... 124 F7
Oliver Cl. Heml H HP3 .... 138 E7
Oliver Cl. Pk St AL2 .... 141 D4
Oliver Ct. Sac SG12 .... 92 E4
Oliver Rd. Heml H HP3 .... 138 F7
Oliver Rise. Heml H HP3 .... 138 E7
Oliver's La. Stot SG5 .... 11 F7
Olivers Cl. Pot En HP23 .... 123 C7
Olivia Gdns. Hare UB9 .... 173 C2
Olleberrie La. Sar WD3 .... 151 D7
Olwen Mews. Pnr HA5 .... 175 D1
Olympus Rd. Henlw SG16 .... 10 B4
Omega Ct. Ware SG12 .... 93 D1 4
Omega Maltings. Ware SG12 .... 93 E1 2
On-The-Hill. Sth Ox WD1 .... 175 C6
Onslow Cl. Hat AL10 .... 130 B5
Onslow Rd. Luton LU4 .... 44 D5
Onslow St Audrey's Sch. Hat 130 B5
Open Air Museum. Chor 164 A1
Opening The. Cod SG4 .... 88 F8
Openshaw Way. Letw SG6 .... 23 A6
Oram Pl. Heml H HP3 .... 138 D8
Orbital Cres. Watf WD3 .... 153 F2
Orchard Ave. Berk HP4 .... 122 A4

Orchard Ave. Harp AL5 .... 85 F1
Orchard Ave. Watf WD4 .... 154 B8
Orchard Cl. Bor WD6 .... 169 F6
Orchard Cl. Bus WD2 .... 168 D1
Orchard Cl. Chor WD3 .... 164 D5
Orchard Cl. Cuf EN6 .... 146 E3
Orchard Cl. Heml H HP2 .... 124 F5
Orchard Cl. Knee SG8 .... 2 A5
Orchard Cl. L Berk SG13 .... 131 F4
Orchard Cl. Letw SG6 .... 22 F8
Orchard Cl. Radl WD7 .... 155 E3
Orchard Cl. Sta Ab SG12 .... 115 C4
Orchard Cl. Ware SG12 .... 93 D2
Orchard Cl. Watf WD1 .... 166 F7
Orchard Cl. Wing HP22 .... 60 B3
Orchard Cres. Stev SG1 .... 50 C7
Orchard Croft. Harl CM20 .... 118 A2
Orchard Ct. Bov HP9 .... 137 A4
Orchard Dr. Chis AL2 .... 141 B5
Orchard Dr. Chor WD3 .... 164 D5
Orchard Dr. Watf WD1 .... 166 F8
Orchard Gdns. Wa Aby EN9 .... 163 C5
Orchard House La. St Alb AL1 .... 127 D2
Orchard La. Harl CM17 .... 118 E4
Orchard Lea. Saw CM21 .... 97 C1
Orchard Mead. Hat AL10 .... 129 F5
Orchard On The Green The.
  Cro Gr WD3 .... 165 F4
Orchard Rd. Bal SG7 .... 12 E1
Orchard Rd. Barn EN5 .... 171 F5
Orchard Rd. Bis St CM23 .... 59 B1
Orchard Rd. Hit SG4 .... 22 B1
Orchard Rd. Royst SG8 .... 7 B7
Orchard Rd. Stev SG1 .... 50 C7
Orchard Rd. Tewin AL6 .... 90 C5
Orchard Rd. Welw AL6 .... 89 C5
Orchard Sq. Hod EN10 .... 148 F8
Orchard St. Heml H HP3 .... 138 D8
Orchard St. St Alb AL3 .... 127 C4
Orchard The. Bal SG7 .... 23 F8
Orchard The. Cod SG4 .... 67 F1
Orchard The. Hert SG14 .... 92 C1
Orchard The. Kin L WD4 .... 139 A2
Orchard The. Ton SG12 .... 92 E7
Orchard The. Wel G C AL8 .... 110 B8
Orchard Way. Bov HP3 .... 137 A3
Orchard Way. Bre Gr SG4 .... 47 E1
Orchard Way. Bro Pk EN6 .... 145 B2
Orchard Way. Gofs O EN7 .... 147 B3
Orchard Way. Kneb SG3 .... 68 E5
Orchard Way. L Ston SG16 .... 10 B3
Orchard Way. Luton LU4 .... 44 C4
Orchard Way. Pit LU7 .... 80 E5
Orchard Way. Ric WD3 .... 165 A2
Orchard Way. Royst SG8 .... 7 C8
Orchards The. Saw CM21 .... 97 E3
Orchards The. Tri HP23 .... 99 F3
Ordelmere. Letw SG6 .... 11 F1
Ordnance Rd. Enf EN3 .... 162 E2
Oregon Way. Luton LU3 .... 45 A8
Organ Hall Rd. Bor WD6 .... 169 E8
Oriole Way. Bis St CM23 .... 76 C6
Orion Way. Mo Pk HA6 .... 175 A6
Orlando Cl. Hit SG4 .... 35 A6
Ormesby Dr. Pot B EN6 .... 158 D7
Ormonde Rd. Mo Pk HA6 .... 174 D6
Ormsby Cl. Luton LU1 .... 63 E5
Ormskirk Rd. Sth Ox WD1 .... 175 D5
Oronsay. Heml H HP3 .... 125 B1
Orphanage Rd. Watf WD1 .... 167 C7
Orpington Cl. Dun LU4 .... 44 A3
Orton Cl. St Alb AL4 .... 128 A7
Orwell Cl. Watf WD2 .... 167 D7 5
Orwell View. Bal SG7 .... 13 B1
Osborn Way. Wel G C AL8 .... 110 C6
Osborne Cl. Luton LU1 .... 63 F6
Osborne Gdns. Pot B EN6 .... 145 B1
Osborne Rd. Ches EN8 .... 148 E4
Osborne Rd. Hod EN10 .... 135 A4
Osborne Rd. Luton LU1 .... 63 F6
Osborne Rd. Pot B EN6 .... 145 B1
Osborne Rd. Watf WD2 .... 154 C1
Osbourne Ave. Kin L WD4 .... 138 F3
Osmington Pl. Tri HP23 .... 99 F4
Osprey Gdns. Stev SG2 .... 51 D2
Osprey House. Ware SG12 .... 93 C3 3
Osprey Wlk. Dun LU4 .... 44 A5
Oster St. St Alb AL3 .... 127 C4
Osterley Cl. Stev SG2 .... 69 C7
Oswald Rd. St Alb AL1 .... 127 C2
Otley Way. Sth Ox WD1 .... 175 C7
Otter Gdns. Hat AL10 .... 130 B4
Otterspool La. Watf WD1 .... 154 E1
Otterspool Way. Bus WD2 .... 154 F1
Ottoman Terr. Watf WD1 .... 167 C6
Ottway Wlk. Welw AL6 .... 89 C4
Otways Cl. Pot B EN6 .... 159 B6
Oudle La. Muc H SG10 .... 74 F2
Oughton Cl. Hit SG5 .... 34 C8
Oughton Head Way. Hit SG5 .... 34 B8
Oughtonhead Inf Sch. Hit 21 E1
Oughtonhead Jun Sch. Hit 21 E1
Oughtonhead La. Hit SG5 .... 34 B8
Oulton Cres. Pot B EN6 .... 158 D7
Oulton Rise. Harp AL5 .... 86 C3
Oulton Way. Sth Ox WD1 .... 175 F6
Oundle Ave. Bus WD2 .... 168 C2
Oundle Ct. Stev SG2 .... 69 C8
Oundle Path. Stev SG2 .... 69 C8
Oundle The. Stev SG2 .... 69 C8
Our Lady of Light Independant
  Day Sch. Tri 99 F3
Our Lady's Jun Mix Inf Sch.
  Hit 34 F5
Our Lady's RC Jun Mix Inf Sch. Hit 21 E2
Ousden Cl. Ches EN8 .... 148 E1
Ousden Dr. Ches EN8 .... 148 E1
Oval The. Ches EN10 .... 148 E2
Oval The. Henlw SG16 .... 10 C4
Oval The. Stev SG1 .... 37 A1
Overfield Cl. Luton LU2 .... 46 C1
Overstone Rd. Harp AL5 .... 86 C1
Overstone Rd. Luton LU4 .... 44 D1
Overstream. Ric WD3 .... 165 B5

Overtrees. Harp AL5 .... 85 F3 6
Oving Cl. Luton LU2 .... 46 D2
Owen Jones Cl. Henlw SG16 .... 10 C5
Owens Way. Cro Gr WD3 .... 166 A5
Owles La. Bun SG9 .... 41 A6
Ox La. Harp AL5 .... 86 B3
Oxcroft. Bis St CM23 .... 76 F3
Oxen Rd. Luton LU2 .... 45 F1
Oxendon Dr. Hod EN11 .... 135 A5
Oxfield Cl. Berk HP4 .... 122 A3
Oxford Ave. St Alb AL1 .... 128 C2
Oxford Cl. Ches EN8 .... 148 D2
Oxford Cl. Knee SG8 .... 2 A7
Oxford Ct. Bre Gr SG4 .... 47 E1
Oxford St. Watf WD1 .... 167 B4
Oxhey Ave. St Alb AL1 .... 128 C4
Oxhey Dr. Sth Ox HA6 .... 175 B5
Oxhey Dr. Sth Ox WD1 .... 175 B5
Oxhey La. Pnr HA5 .... 176 A5
Oxhey La. Sth Ox WD1 .... 175 F3
Oxhey La. Watf WD1 .... 167 D2
Oxhey Rdg Watf WD1 .... 167 D2
Oxhey Ridge Cl. Sth Ox HA6 .... 175 B5
Oxhey Wood Jun Mix Inf Schs.
  Sth Ox 175 C7
Oxlease Dr. Hat AL10 .... 130 B4
Oxleys Rd. Stev SG2 .... 51 B3
Oxleys The. Harl CM17 .... 118 E4
Oysterfields. St Alb AL3 .... 127 C4

Pacatian Way. Stev SG1 .... 51 C8
Packhorse Cl. St Alb AL4 .... 128 C6
Packhorse La. Shen WD7,AL2 .... 157 B8
Paddick Cl. Hod EN11 .... 134 F7
Paddock Cl. Hun SG12 .... 95 D1
Paddock Cl. Letw SG6 .... 23 A5
Paddock House. Wel G C AL7 .... 111 B6
Paddock The. Bun SG9 .... 40 E8
Paddock The. Bis St CM23 .... 76 F3
Paddock The. Hat AL10 .... 130 A6
Paddock The. Hit SG4 .... 35 A5
Paddock The. Hod EN10 .... 135 A3
Paddock Wood. Harp AL5 .... 107 E7
Paddocks Cl. Stev SG2 .... 51 B4
Paddocks The. Chor WD3 .... 164 F5
Paddocks The. Cod SG4 .... 68 A1
Paddocks The. Hert H SG13 .... 114 B3
Paddocks The. Kim SG4 .... 87 B6
Paddocks The. Wel G C AL7 .... 111 B6
Page Cl. Bal SG7 .... 23 F6
Page Hill. Ware SG12 .... 93 C2
Page Rd. Hert SG13 .... 114 A6
Pageant Rd. St Alb AL1 .... 127 D2
Pages Cl. Bis St CM23 .... 76 D5
Pages Croft. Berk HP4 .... 122 A6
Paget Cotts. Dan En SG12 .... 71 F7
Paine's La. Pnr HA5 .... 175 E1
Paines Orch. Ched LU7 .... 80 A8
Painters La. Enf EN3 .... 162 E4
Palace Cl. Kin L WD4 .... 139 A1
Palace Gdns. Royst SG8 .... 7 C6
Palfrey Cl. St Alb AL3 .... 127 D5
Pallas Rd. Heml H HP2 .... 124 F5
Palmer Ave. Bus WD2 .... 168 B4
Palmer Cl. Hert SG14 .... 113 C8
Palmer Ct. Sac SG12 .... 92 E4
Palmer Gdns. Barn EN5 .... 171 D4
Palmer Rd. Hert SG14 .... 113 D8
Palmers Gr. Lo Naz EN9 .... 135 F1
Palmers La. Bis St CM23 .... 76 F7
Palmers Rd. Bor WD6 .... 170 B8
Palmers Way. Ches EN8 .... 148 E2
Palmerston Cl. Wel G C AL8 .... 110 C6
Palmerston Ct. Stev SG2 .... 51 C5
Pamela Ave. Heml H HP3 .... 138 F8
Pamela Gdns. Bis St CM23 .... 76 D5
Pamela La. Kim SG4 .... 66 D1
Pancake La. Heml H HP2 .... 125 D2
Pankhurst Cres. Stev SG2 .... 51 C5
Pankhurst Pl. Watf WD2 .... 167 C6
Panshanger Dr. Wel G C AL7 .... 111 C6
Panshanger Jun Mix Inf Sch.
  Wel G C 111 A7
Pantiles The. Bus WD2 .... 168 D1
Panxworth Rd. Heml H HP3 .... 124 D1 1
Paper Mill La. Stand SG11 .... 55 E1
Parade The. Hat AL10 .... 130 C7
Parade The. Luton LU3 .... 44 C7
Parade The. Sth Ox WD1 .... 175 D7
Parade The. Sth Ox WD1 .... 175 D7
Parade The. Watf WD1 .... 167 B6
Paradise Cl. Ham St EN7 .... 148 B3
Paradise. Heml H HP2 .... 124 D5
Paradise Rd. Wa Aby EN9 .... 163 C5
Paradise Wildlife Park. Bric 133 F2
Parishes Mead. Ast SG2 .... 51 D4
Park Ave. Bis St CM23 .... 76 F7
Park Ave. Bus WD2 .... 167 E7
Park Ave. Luton LU3 .... 44 C7
Park Ave N. Harp AL5 .... 85 F1
Park Ave. Pot B EN6 .... 159 D6
Park Ave. Radl WD7 .... 156 B6
Park Ave. Ric WD3 .... 165 A5
Park Ave S. Harp AL5 .... 85 F1
Park Ave. St Alb AL1 .... 128 A4
Park Ave. Watf WD1 .... 167 A5
Park Avenue Trad Est. Luton 23 F7
Park Cl. Bus WD2 .... 167 E7
Park Cl. Bro Pk AL9 .... 145 A5
Park Cl. Bus WD2 .... 167 D6
Park Cl. Har HA3 .... 176 E2
Park Cl. Hat AL9 .... 130 C6
Park Cl. Ric WD3 .... 174 B6
Park Cl. Stev SG2 .... 51 B1
Park Cl. Watf WD1 .... 167 B2
Park Cres. Bor WD6 .... 169 F6
Park Cres. Har HA3 .... 176 E2
Park Cres. Harl CM20 .... 117 D1
Park Ct. Letw SG6 .... 23 E7
Park Dr. Bal SG7 .... 23 F7
Park Dr. Pot B EN6 .... 159 B8
Park Dr. Stan HA3 .... 176 E4
Park Dr. Stand SG11 .... 55 D3
Park Farm Cl. Henlw SG16 .... 10 D8
Park Farm Ind Est. Bun 40 D8

Park Farm La. Nut SG8 18 C2
Park Gate. Hit SG4 34 F6
Park Gdns. Bal SG7 23 E7
Park Hill. Harl CM17 118 B3
Park Hill. Harp AL5 85 F2
Park Hill Rd. Heml H HP1 124 B3
Park House. Berk HP4 122 B5
Park House. Wel G C AL8 110 D7
Park La. Bis St CM23 76 F4
Park La. Ches EN7 162 D6
Park La. Col H AL4 143 C8
Park La. Coln H AL4 129 C1
Park La. Ham St EN7 148 A4
Park La. Hare UB9 173 B2
Park La. Harl CM20 117 D2
Park La. Heml H HP2 124 D2
Park La. Hod EN10 134 F3
Park La. Kim SG4 66 C1
Park La. Kneb SG3 68 D5
Park La. Stand SG11 55 D3
Park Lane Paradise. Ham St EN7 148 A6
Park Lodge. Watf WD2 154 D5
Park Mansions. Mo Pk HA6 174 C7
Park Mead. Harl CM20 117 B1
Park Meadow. Hat AL9 130 C6
Park Mews. Hat AL9 130 C6
Park Mount. Harp AL5 85 F3
Park Nook Gdns. Enf EN2 161 D2
Park Pl. Hare UB9 173 C2
Park Pl. Pk St AL2 141 D4
Park Pl. Stev SG1 50 D5
Park Rd. Barn EN5 171 F5
Park Rd. Bus WD2 168 A3
Park Rd. Ches EN8 162 D6
Park Rd. Enf EN3 162 E3
Park Rd. Heml H HP1 124 C1
Park Rd. Hert SG13 113 E6
Park Rd. Hod EN11 135 A6
Park Rd. Nort EN6 146 A1
Park Rd. Radl WD7 156 A4
Park Rd. Ric WD3 165 E2
Park Rd. Sta M CM24 59 E6
Park Rd. Tri HP23 100 A3
Park Rd. Ware SG12 93 B2
Park Rd. Watf WD1 167 B8
Park Rise Cl. Harp AL5 85 E3
Park Rise. Har HA3 176 E2
Park Rise. Harp AL5 85 E3
Park Rise. Nthch HP4 121 E6
Park Sq. Luton LU1 63 E7
Park St. Bal SG7 23 E8
Park St. Berk HP4 122 B5
Park St. Hat AL9 130 C6
Park St. Hit SG4 34 E6
Park St. Luton LU1 63 F6
Park St. Pk St AL2 141 D5
Park St. Tri HP23 100 A3
Park St W. Luton LU1 63 E7
Park Street La. Chis AL2 141 C3
Park Street Sch. Pk St 141 D4
Park Terr. Enf EN3 162 E1
Park The. Red AL3 106 B5
Park The. St Alb AL1 128 A5
Park Viaduct. Luton LU1 63 E6
Park View Cl. Luton LU3 44 D6
Park View Cl. St Alb AL1 128 A2
Park View Ct. Berk HP4 122 B4
Park View Dr. Mark AL3 83 D6
Park View. Hat AL9 130 C7
Park View. Hod EN11 135 A5
Park View. Pnr HA5 175 F2
Park View. Pot B EN6 159 C6
Park View Rd. Berk HP4 122 B4
Park View Rd. Pnr HA5 175 B3
Park View. Stev SG2 51 B1
Park Way. Hit SG5 34 E6
Park Way. Ric WD3 165 C1
Parker Ave. Hert SG14 113 D8
Parker Cl. Letw SG6 22 E4
Parker St. Watf WD2 167 B8
Parker's Field. Stev SG2 51 C4
Parkfield Ave. Har HA2 176 C1
Parkfield. Chor WD3 164 F5
Parkfield Cres. Har HA2 176 C1
Parkfield Cres. Kim SG4 66 D1
Parkfield House. Har HA2 176 B2
Parkfield. Letw SG6 23 D4
Parkfield Rd. Mark AL3 83 D5
Parkfields. Wel G C AL8 110 D6
Parkgate Inf Sch. Watf 154 C2
Parkgate Jun Sch. Watf 154 C2
Parkgate Rd. Watf WD2 154 C2
Parkhurst Rd. Hert SG14 113 C7
Parkinson Cl. Whea AL4 108 D8
Parkland Cl. Hod EN11 115 B1
Parkland Dr. Luton LU1 63 D5
Parklands Cl. Had W EN4 159 D1
Parklands Dr. St Alb AL3 127 A2
Parklands. Royst SG8 7 E6
Parklands. Wa Aby EN9 163 D7
Parkmead. Luton LU1 63 F6
Parkside Ct. Ches EN7 148 B3
Parkside Dr. Watf WD1 166 F7
Parkside Fst Sch. Bor 156 F1
Parkside. Pot B EN6 159 C7
Parkside Rd. Mo Pk HA6 174 F5
Parkside. Watf WD1 167 C3
Parkside. Welw AL6 89 C5
Parkside. Wyd SG9 27 D2
Parkview House. Watf WD1 167 D3
Parkway Cl. Wel G C AL8 110 C6
Parkway Ct. St Alb AL1 142 B8
Parkway Gdns. Wel G C AL8 110 D5
Parkway Inf Sch. Wel G C 110 C5
Parkway. Saw CM21 97 E1
Parkway. Stev SG2 51 A1
Parkway. Wel G C AL8 110 C6
Parkwood Cl. Hod EN10 134 F4
Parkwood Dr. Heml H HP1 123 F3
Parliament Sq. Hert SG14 113 D5
Parmiter's Sch. Abb L 154 C8
Parndon Mill La. Harl CM20 117 B3
Parnel Rd. Ware SG12 93 F2
Parnell Cl. Abb L HA8 139 F1
Parr Cres. Heml H HP2 125 B8
Parrott's La. Chol HP23 120 A4
Parrotts Cl. Cro Gr WD3 166 A4
Parrotts Field. Hod EN11 135 B7
Parson's Cl. Fla AL3 84 B1
Parsonage Cl. Abb L WD5 139 E1
Parsonage Cl. Tri HP23 100 A4
Parsonage Farm. Ric WD3 165 C2
Parsonage Farm Trad Est. Sta M 59 F3
Parsonage Farm. Wing HP22 60 B3
Parsonage La. Alb SG11 57 A6
Parsonage La. Bis St CM23 77 C8
Parsonage La. Sta M CM24 59 F4
Parsonage La. Wel G AL9 144 B8
Parsonage Pl. Tri HP23 100 A3
Parsonage Rd. Ric WD3 165 D2
Parsonage Rd. Wel G AL9 144 B8
Parsons Green Est. Stev 37 C2
Parthia Cl. Royst SG8 7 E6
Partridge Cl. Barn EN5 171 C3
Partridge Cl. Bus WD2 168 C1
Partridge Cl. Dun LU4 44 A5
Partridge Hill. Ashw SG7 4 C3
Partridge Rd. St Alb AL3 127 D7
Parva Cl. Harp AL5 107 D6
Parvills. Wa Aby EN9 163 D7
Parys Rd. Luton LU3 45 B6
Pascal Way. Letw SG6 23 B8
Pasfield. Wa Aby EN9 163 D6
Passfield Cotts. Thun SG11 72 F1
Passingham Ave. Hit SG4 35 A6
Paston Rd. Heml H HP2 124 E5
Pasture Cl. Bus WD2 168 C2
Pasture La. Bre Gr SG4 65 E8
Pasture Rd. Letw SG6 22 E3
Pastures Ct. Dun LU4 44 A3
Pastures The. Barn N20 171 F1
Pastures The. Chis AL2 141 A7
Pastures The. Hat AL10 130 B4
Pastures The. Heml H HP1 123 E4
Pastures The. Stev SG2 51 D8
Pastures The. Ware SG12 93 C3
Pastures The. Watf WD1 167 C2
Pastures The. Wel G C AL7 111 B4
Pastures Way. Dun LU4 44 A4
Paternoster Cl. Wa Aby EN9 163 F6
Paternoster Hill. Wa Aby EN9 163 F7
Pathway The. Radl WD7 155 F3
Pathway The. Watf WD1 167 D1
Patmore Cl. Bis St CM23 76 C8
Patmore Link Rd. Heml H HP2 125 C2
Patmore Rd. Wa Aby EN9 163 E5
Patricia Gdns. Bis St CM23 76 E5
Paul's Gn. Ches EN8 162 E6
Pauls La. Hod EN11 135 A6
Paxton Rd. Berk HP4 122 D4
Paxton Rd. St Alb AL1 127 E2
Payne End. San SG9 15 B1
Payne's Pk. Hit SG5 34 E7
Paynes Cl. Letw SG6 12 A1
Paynes La. Lo Naz EN9 149 C7
Paynesfield Rd. Bus WD2 168 F2
Pea La. Nthch HP4 121 D7
Peace Cl. Ches EN8 148 B2
Peace Gr. Welw AL6 90 A7
Peach Ct. Luton LU1 63 F6
Peacocks Cl. Berk HP4 121 F6
Peakes La. Ham St EN7 147 F4
Peakes Pl. St Alb AL1 127 F3
Peakes Way. Ham St EN7 147 F4
Pear Tree Cl. L Ston SG16 10 B3
Pear Tree Dell. Letw SG6 23 B3
Pear Tree Wlk. Ham St EN7 147 E5
Pearman Dr. Dan En SG12 71 E7
Pearsall Cl. Letw SG6 23 B5
Pearson Ave. Hert SG13 113 C4
Pearson Cl. Hert SG13 113 C4
Peartree Cl. Heml H HP1 124 A4
Peartree Cl. Wel G C AL7 110 E6
Peartree Ct. Watf WD2 154 D3
Peartree Ct. Wel G C AL7 110 E5
Peartree Farm. Wel G C AL7 110 E6
Peartree Jun Mix Inf Sch.
Wel G C 110 E5
Peartree La. Wel G C AL7 110 E6
Peartree Rd. Heml H HP1 124 A4
Peartree Rd. Luton LU2 46 C4
Peartree Spring Inf Sch. Stev 51 B3
Peartree Spring Jun Sch. Stev 51 B3
Peartree Way. Stev SG2 51 A3
Peascroft Rd. Heml H HP3 125 B1
Peasecroft. Cotrd SG9 39 C7
Peasmead. Bun SG9 40 E6
Peck's Hill. Lo Naz EN9 135 E2
Pedlars La. Ther SG8 15 E7
Pedley Hill. Stu LU6 82 C2
Peel Cres. Hert SG14 113 C8
Peel Pl. Luton LU1 63 D7
Peel St. Luton LU1 63 D7
Peerglow Ctr. Ware 114 E8
Peg's La. Hert SG13 113 D5
Pegmire La. Radl WD2 168 C8
Pegs La. Widf SG12 95 D5
Pegsdon Cl. Luton LU3 45 B7
Pegsdon Way. Shil SG5 19 E1
Pelham Ct. Heml H HP2 125 C3
Pelham Ct. Wel G C AL7 111 C5
Pelham Rd. Brag SG11 55 F7
Pelhams The. Watf WD2 154 D4
Pelican Way. Letw SG6 11 F1
Pemberton Cl. St Alb AL1 141 D8
Pembridge Chase. Bov HP3 137 A3
Pembridge La. Bric EN10 133 E2
Pembridge Rd. Bov HP3 137 A3
Pembroke Ave. Enf EN1 162 B1
Pembroke Ave. Luton LU4 44 F3
Pembroke Cl. Hod EN10 148 E8
Pembroke Dr. Gofs O EN7 147 B2
Pembroke Rd. Bal SG7 23 F8
Pembroke Rd. Mo Pk HA6 174 C7
Pemsel Ct. Heml H HP3 124 E1
Penda Cl. Luton LU3 44 F7
Pendennis Ct. Harp AL5 107 D7
Pengelly Cl. Ches EN7 148 B1
Penhill Ct. Luton LU3 44 E6
Penhill. Luton LU3 44 E6
Penman Cl. Chis AL2 141 A4
Penn Cl. Chor WD3 164 D3
Penn House. Mo Pk HA6 174 C7
Penn Pl. Ric WD3 165 D2
Penn Rd. Chis AL2 141 C4
Penn Rd. Ric WD3 165 A1
Penn Rd. Stev SG1 50 E4
Penn Way. Chor WD3 164 D3
Penn Way. Letw SG6 23 B3
Penne Cl. Radl WD7 156 A5
Pennine Ave. Luton LU3 44 D8
Pennington La. Sta M CM24 59 D8
Penningtons. Bis St CM23 76 D5
Penny Croft. Harp AL5 107 A4
Pennyfathers La. Welw AL6 90 B4
Pennymead. Harl CM20 118 A1
Penrose Ave. Sth Ox WD1 175 E8
Penrose Ct. Heml H HP2 124 E7
Penscroft Gdns. Bor WD6 170 D5
Penshurst Cl. Harp AL5 85 D4
Penshurst. Harl CM17 118 B3
Penshurst Rd. Pot B EN6 159 D7
Pentland. Heml H HP2 124 F6
Pentland Rd. Bus WD2 168 C3
Pentley Cl. Wel G C AL8 89 D1
Penton Dr. Ches EN8 148 D2
Pentrich Ave. Enf EN1 162 A1
Penzance Cl. Hare UB9 173 D1
Peplins Cl. Bro Pk AL9 144 E5
Peplins Way. Bro Pk AL9 144 E5
Pepper Ct. Bal SG7 23 F8
Pepper Hill. Gt Am SG12 114 F4
Peppett's Gn. Chol HP5 120 D1
Pepsal End Rd. Cad LU1 84 C7
Pepsal End Rd. Fla LU1 84 C7
Pepsal End. Stev SG2 69 B8
Pepys Cres. Barn EN5 171 C4
Pepys Way. Bal SG7 23 E8
Percheron Dr. Dun LU4 44 A3
Percheron Rd. Bor WD6 170 D3
Percival Way. Luton LU2 64 C7
Percy Rd. Watf WD1 167 B5
Peregrine Cl. Bis St CM23 76 D6
Peregrine Cl. Watf WD2 154 E5
Peregrine House. Ware SG12 93 C3 1
Peregrine Rd. Dun LU4 44 A4
Perham Way. Lon C AL2 142 D6
Perivale Gdns. Watf WD2 154 B5
Periwinkle Cl. Bark SG8 17 C5
Periwinkle La. Hit SG5 21 F1
Perowne Way. Stand SG11 55 E3
Perram Cl. Ches EN10 148 E5
Perriors Cl. Ham St EN7 148 A4
Perry Dr. Royst SG8 7 E7
Perry Gn. Heml H HP2 105 A1
Perry Hill. Lo Naz EN9 149 F8
Perry Mead. Bus WD2 168 C3
Perrymead. Luton LU2 46 F2
Perrysfield Rd. Ches EN8 148 E5
Perrywood La. Wat St SG14 91 B7
Perrywood. Wel G C AL8 110 D8
Pescot Hill. Heml H HP1 124 B5
Petard Cl. Dun LU4 44 A2
Peter Kirk Sch. Sta M 59 E6
Peter's Pl. Nthch HP4 121 E6
Peterlee Ct. Heml H HP2 124 F7 2
Peters Ave. Lon C AL2 142 C5
Peters Way. Kneb SG3 68 F6
Peters Wood Hill. Ware SG12 114 E7
Petersfield. St Alb AL3 127 E7
Petunia Ct. Luton LU3 45 C1
Petworth Cl. Stev SG2 69 C7
Pevensey Cl. Luton LU2 46 D4
Pheasant Cl. Berk HP4 122 C3
Pheasant Cl. Tri HP23 100 B6
Pheasants Way. Ric WD3 165 B2
Phillimore Pl. Radl WD7 155 E3
Phillipers. Watf WD2 154 E4
Phillips Ave. Royst SG8 7 C8
Phipps Hatch La. Enf EN2 161 C1
Phoenix Cl. Mo Pk HA6 174 F6
Phoenix Ct. Enf EN3 162 C1
Phyllis Courtnage House.
Heml H HP2 124 D5 4
Piccotts End. Heml H HP1 124 C6
Piccotts End La. Heml H HP2 124 D7
Piccotts End Rd. Heml H HP1 124 B7
Pick Hill. Wa Aby EN9 163 F7
Pickets Cl. Bus WD2 168 E1
Picketts. Wel G C AL8 89 D1
Pickford Hill. Harp AL5 86 D4
Pickford Rd. Fla AL3 83 C4
Pickford Rd. Mark AL3 83 C4
Picknage Cnr. Bar SG8 9 A2
Picknage Rd. Bar SG8 9 A2
Pie Cnr. Fla AL3 84 B1
Pie Garden. Fla AL3 84 C1
Pietley Hill. Fla AL3 84 A1
Pig La. Bis St CM22,CM23 77 A3
Pigeonwick. Harp AL5 86 B3
Piggotts La. Luton LU4 44 D4
Piggotts Way. Bis St CM23 76 E5
Piggottshill La. Harp AL5 107 D8
Pightle Cl. Royst SG8 7 D7
Pikes Cl. Luton LU1 63 E7
Pilgrim Cl. Chis AL2 141 C4
Pilgrim Cl. Watf WD2 154 D6
Pilgrims Row. West SG9 40 F3
Pilgrims Way. Stev SG1 37 B2
Piltdown Rd. Sth Ox WD1 175 D6
Pin Green Jun Mix Inf Sch. Stev 50 F6
Pinchfield. Map Cr WD3 172 D5
Pindar Rd. Hod EN11 135 C7
Pine Cl. Berk HP4 122 B4
Pine Cl. Ches EN8 148 D3
Pine Cl. Norwd HA6 174 E4
Pine Crest. Welw AL6 89 E8
Pine Gr. Barn N20 171 F1
Pine Gr. Bis St CM23 77 B6
Pine Gr. Bri Wd AL2 140 F1
Pine Gr. Bro Pk AL9 145 B6
Pine Gr. Bus WD2 167 F8
Pine Ridge. St Alb AL1 142 A8
Pine Tree Cl. Heml H HP2 124 D4
Pine Wlk. Nthch HP4 121 D7
Pinecroft Cres. Barn EN5 171 E5
Pinecroft. Heml H HP3 138 F7
Pinehall Hospl. Hit 35 A7
Pinehurst Cl. Abb L WD5 153 F7
Pinelands. Bis St CM23 58 F1
Pineridge Ct. Barn EN5 171 D5
Pines Ave. Enf EN1 162 B3
Pines Hill. Sta M CM24 59 D5
Pines Jun Mix Inf Sch The. Hert 114 B7
Pines The. Bor WD6 169 F7
Pines The. Heml H HP3 137 F7
Pinetree House. Watf WD2 154 E3
Pinewood Ave. Pnr HA5 176 B4
Pinewood Cl. Bor WD6 170 D7
Pinewood Cl. Pnr HA5 176 B4
Pinewood Cl. St Alb AL4 128 C3
Pinewood Dr. Pot B EN6 158 F8
Pinewood Gdns. Heml H HP1 124 B3
Pinewood Sch. Ware 114 D7
Pinewood. Wel G C AL7 110 E4
Pinewoods. Stev SG2 50 F1 4
Pinfold Rd. Bus WD2 167 F7
Pinford Dell. Luton LU2 46 D1 3
Pinnacles. Wa Aby EN9 163 E5
Pinnate Pl. Wel G C AL7 110 E2
Pinner Gn. Pnr HA5 175 C1
Pinner Hill. Pnr HA5 175 B3
Pinner Hill Rd. Pnr HA5 175 C1
Pinner Park Ave. Har HA2 176 C1
Pinner Park Gdns. Har HA2 176 C1
Pinner Rd. Norwd HA6 175 A1
Pinner Rd. Pnr HA5 175 A1
Pinner Rd. Watf WD1 167 E2
Pinner Wood Fst & Mid Schs. Pnr 175 C2
Pinnocks Cl. Bal SG7 23 F7
Pinnocks La. Bal SG7 23 F8
Pinto Cl. Bor WD6 170 D3
Piper's Hill. Gt Gd HP1 103 D3
Pipers Ave. Harp AL5 107 D7
Pipers Cl. Red AL3 106 A6
Pipers La. Cad LU1 62 F1
Pipers La. Mark AL3 62 F1
Pipers La. Whea AL5 107 F7
Pippens. Wel G C AL8 89 E1
Pirton Cl. Heml H HP2 124 F4
Pirton Cl. Hit SG5 34 D6
Pirton Cl. St Alb AL4 128 C8
Pirton Hill Inf Sch. Luton 44 B6
Pirton Hill Jun Sch. Luton 44 B6
Pirton Jun Mix Inf Sch. Pirt 20 D4
Pirton Rd. Hit SG5 34 C6
Pirton Rd. Hol SG5 21 A7
Pirton Rd. Luton LU4 44 D5
Pishiobury Dr. Saw CM21 118 D8
Pishiobury Mews. Saw CM21 118 D7
Pitsfield. Wel G C AL8 89 D1
Pitstone Cl. St Alb AL4 128 C8
Pitt Ct. Stev SG2 51 B1
Pittman's Field. Harl CM20 117 F1
Pix Farm La. Heml H HP1 123 C2
Pix Rd. Letw SG6 23 A6
Pix Rd. Stot SG5 11 E5
Pixies Hill Cres. Heml H HP1 123 F2
Pixies Hill Jun Mix Inf Sch.
Heml H 123 F2
Pixies Hill Rd. Heml H HP1 123 F2
Pixmore Ave. Letw SG6 23 B6
Pixmore Ind Est. Letw 23 A6
Pixmore Jun Sch. Letw 23 A5
Pixmore Way. Letw SG6 23 A5
Plaistow Way. Gt Ch SG8 9 E2
Plaiters Cl. Tri HP23 100 B4
Plaitford Cl. Ric WD3 173 E8
Plantaganet Pl. Wa Aby EN9 163 B6
Plantation Rd. Luton LU3 44 D7
Plantation Wlk. Heml H HP1 124 A6
Plash Dr. Stev SG1 50 E5
Plashes Cl. Stand SG11 55 D2
Plashets. Sheer CM22 98 D1
Plaw Hatch Cl. Bis St CM23 77 C8
Playford Sq. Luton LU4 44 D5
Pleasance The. Harp AL5 85 D4
Pleasant Mount. Hert H SG13 114 C4
Pleasant Pl. Map Cr WD3 172 E3
Pleasant Rd. Bis St CM23 76 E8
Pleasant Rise. Hat AL9 130 C8
Plewes Cl. Ken Co LU6 82 E8
Plough Hill. Cuf EN6 146 E2
Plough La. Hare UB9 173 C4
Plough La. Kin Wd SG4 48 A5
Plough La. Pot En HP4 123 B7
Plough La. Sar WD3 151 F6
Ploughmans End. Wel G C AL7 111 C5
Plover Cl. Berk HP4 122 C3
Plum Tree Rd. L Ston SG16 10 B2
Plummers La. Kim SG4 65 C2
Plumpton Cl. Luton LU2 46 D3
Plumpton Rd. Hod EN11 135 C8
Pluto Rise. Heml H HP2 124 F5
Plymouth Cl. Luton LU2 46 B1
Poets Cl. Heml H HP1 124 B4
Poets Gn. Dun LU4 44 A2
Polayn Garth. Wel G C AL8 110 C7
Polegate. Luton LU2 46 D2
Polehanger La. Heml H HP1 123 E5
Poles Hill. Sar HP5 151 E6
Poles La. Thun SG12 93 C6
Poles La. Ware SG12 93 C3
Police Row. Ther SG8 15 F7
Police Station La. Bus WD2 168 B2
Pollard Gdns. Stev SG1 50 F8
Pollards Cl. Gofs O EN7 147 C2
Pollards. Map Cr WD3 172 D5
Pollards Way. Pirt SG5 20 C4
Pollicott Cl. St Alb AL4 128 C8
Pollywick Rd. Wigg HP23 100 D1
Polzeath Cl. Luton LU2 64 C8
Pomeroy Cres. Watf WD2 154 B3
Pomeroy Gr. Luton LU2 45 E6
Pomfret Ave. Luton LU2 63 F8
Pond Cl. Hare UB9 173 C1
Pond Cl. Luton LU4 44 B5
Pond Cl. Stev SG1 50 C7
Pond Cl. Tri HP23 100 A4
Pond Croft. Hat AL10 129 F5
Pond Croft. Wel G C AL7 110 E5
Pond Field. Wel G C AL7 90 A1
Pond La. Bal SG7 23 E8
Pond Lodge. Cod SG4 67 F1
Pond Rd. Heml H HP3 139 A6
Pondcroft Rd. Kneb SG3 69 A4
Pondfield Cres. St Alb AL4 128 B7
Pondside. Gra SG4 36 C4
Pondsmeade. Red AL3 106 B5
Pondwick Rd. Harp AL5 85 E2
Pondwicks Cl. St Alb AL1 127 C2
Pondwicks Rd. Luton LU1 63 F7
Ponsbourne Park Cotts.
New St SG13 146 F8
Ponsbourne St Mary's
Jun Mix Inf Sch. New St 146 E7
Pooleys La. Wel G AL9 144 C8
Pope Paul Prim Sch. Pot B 158 F6
Pope's Rd. Abb L WD5 153 E8
Popes La. Watf WD2 154 B1
Popes Row. Ware SG12 93 D3
Popis Gdns. Ware SG12 93 E2
Poplar Ave. Hat AL4 129 D5
Poplar Ave. Luton LU3 45 C8
Poplar Cl. Hit SG4 35 B6
Poplar Cl. Pnr HA5 175 D2
Poplar Cl. Royst SG8 7 E7
Poplar Cl. Thun SG11 72 F2
Poplar Dr. Royst SG8 7 E7
Poplar Rd. Ken Co LU6 82 E8
Poplar Shaw. Wa Aby EN9 163 F6
Poplar View. Sac SG14 92 E4
Poplars Cl. Hat AL10 129 D5
Poplars Cl. Luton LU2 46 B3
Poplars Cl. Watf WD2 154 B7
Poplars The. Arl SG15 11 A8
Poplars The. Gt Ha CM22 77 F4
Poplars The. Ham St EN7 147 E5
Poplars The. Hare UB9 173 C2
Poplars The. Heml H HP1 124 B2
Poplars The. Ick SG5 21 F5
Poplars The. St Alb AL1 142 B7
Poplars. Wel G C AL7 111 B7
Popple Way. Stev SG1 50 E6
Poppy Cl. Heml H HP1 123 E4
Poppy Mead. Stev SG1 50 F4
Poppyfields. Wel G C AL7 111 C5
Porlock Dr. Luton LU2 46 C1
Port Hill. Hert SG14 113 C7
Port La. L Hal CM22 77 B2
Port Vale. Hert SG14 113 C6
Porters Cl. Bun SG9 40 E8
Porters Hill. Harp AL5 86 C4
Porters Park Dr. Shen WD7 156 E7
Porters Wood. St Alb AL3 127 F7
Portland Dr. Ches EN7 162 A8
Portland Dr. Enf EN2 161 E1
Portland Pl. Bis St CM23 76 F7
Portland Pl. Hert H SG13 114 C4
Portland Rd. Bis St CM23 76 F7
Portland Rd. Luton LU4 45 A1
Portland St. St Alb AL3 127 C4
Portman Cl. Hit SG5 21 D2
Portman Cl. St Alb AL4 128 C7
Portman House. St Alb AL3 127 D6
Portmill La. Hit SG5 34 F7
Post Office Rd. Harl CM20 117 D1
Post Office Row. Wes SG4 24 B1
Post Wood Rd. Ware SG12 114 E7
Postfield. Wel G C AL7 90 A1
Postwood Gn. Hert H SG13 114 C3
Potash La. Lon M HP23 79 A5
Potten End Hill. Heml H HP1 123 E8
Potten End Jun Mix Inf Sch.
Pot En 123 B6
Potter St. Bis St CM23 76 F7
Potter St. Pnr HA5 175 B2
Potter Street Hill. Norwd HA5 175 B3
Potters Bar Sta. Pot B 158 F7
Potters Field. St Alb AL3 127 E7
Potters Heights Cl. Pnr HA5 175 B3
Potters La. Bor WD6 170 C8
Potters La. Stev SG1 50 B4
Potters Mews. Elst WD6 169 D3
Potterscrouch La. St Alb AL2 140 E7
Pottersheath Rd. Cod AL6 68 D1
Pottery Cl. Luton LU3 44 F7
Potton Rd. Gu M SG8 1 F6
Pouchen End La. Heml H HP1 123 D3
Poulteney Rd. Sta M CM24 59 E8
Poultney Cl. Shen WD7 156 F7
Pound Ave. Stev SG1 50 D6
Pound Cl. Lo Naz EN9 149 E8
Pound Cl. Sand AL4 108 C2
Pound Field. Watf WD2 153 F4
Pound Gn. Gu M SG8 1 F5
Pound La. Shen WD7 156 F6
Poundwell. Wel G C AL7 111 A5
Powdermill La. Wa Aby EN9 163 B6
Powdermill Way. Wa Aby EN9 163 B6
Power Ct. Luton LU1 63 F7
Powis Ct. Bus WD2 168 D1
Powis Ct. Pot B EN6 159 C5
Poynders Hill. Heml H HP2 125 C3
Poynders Meadow. Cod SG4 88 F8
Poynings Cl. Harp AL5 107 F8
Poynters Rd. Dun LU5 44 A2
Prae Cl. St Alb AL3 127 B3
Prae Wood Sch. St Alb 127 A1
Praetorian Ct. St Alb AL1 141 C8
Prebendal Dr. Cad LU1 63 B2
Precinct The. Hod EN10 134 F3
Premier Ct. Enf EN3 162 D1
Prescott Rd. Ches EN8 148 E4
Presdales Dr. Ware SG12 114 E8
Presdales Sch. Ware 114 D7
President Way. Luton LU2 64 D8
Prestatyn Cl. Stev SG1 50 B8
Preston Gdns. Enf EN3 162 E2
Preston Gdns. Luton LU2 45 F2
Preston Prim Sch. Pres 48 D6
Preston Rd. Pres SG4 48 E7
Preston Rd. St Ipp SG4 34 F1
Prestwick Cl. Luton LU2 45 E5
Prestwick Dr. Bis St CM23 59 B1
Prestwick Rd. Sth Ox WD1 175 D6
Pretoria Rd. Watf WD1 167 A5
Pretty Cnr. Mo Pk HA6 175 A5
Priestleys. Luton LU1 63 A7
Primary Way. Arl SG15 11 A4
Primett Rd. Stev SG1 50 C7
Primley La. Sheer CM22 98 C1
Primrose Cl. Arl SG15 11 A4
Primrose Cl. Hat AL10 130 B4
Primrose Cotts. Radl WD7 156 A4
Primrose Ct. Stev SG1 50 D7
Primrose Dr. Hert SG13 114 B6
Primrose Gdns. Bus WD2 168 B2
Primrose Hill. Abb L WD4 139 B3
Primrose Hill Rd. Stev SG1 50 D7
Primrose La. Arl SG15 11 A4
Primrose Path. Ches EN7 162 A8
Primrose View. Royst SG8 7 F5
Prince Andrew's Cl. Royst SG8 7 D5
Prince Edward St. Berk HP4 122 C4
Prince of Wales Sch. Enf 162 F2
Prince Pk. Heml H HP1 124 A2

Prince St. Watf WD1 167 C6
Prince Way. Luton LU2 64 D8
Prince's St. Stot SG5 11 F7
Princes Ave. Enf EN3 162 E4
Princes Ave. Watf WD1 167 A5
Princes Cl. Berk HP4 122 A6
Princes Cl. Bis St CM23 76 C7
Princes Gate. Bis St CM23 76 C7
Princes Gate. Harl 117 E3
Princes Mews. Royst SG8 7 C6
Princes St. Ware SG12 93 D2
Princess Alexandra Hospl. Harl 117 B1
Princess Helena Coll. Pres 48 E6
Princess St. Luton LU1 63 D7
Printers Way. Harl CM20 118 A5
Priors Cl. Hert H SG13 114 B3
Priors Ct. Sheer CM21 98 A2
Priors Hill. Pirt SG5 20 C4
Priors Wood Rd. Hert H SG13 114 C3
Priory Cl. Barn N20 171 F2
Priory Cl. Ches EN8 148 E7
Priory Cl. Hod EN11 135 A5
Priory Cl. Royst SG8 7 E6
Priory Cl. Stan HA7 176 F7
Priory Ct. Berk HP4 122 C4
Priory Ct. Bis St CM23 76 F7
Priory Ct. Bus WD2 168 C1
Priory Ct. Hert SG14 113 C6 11
Priory Ct. Hit 34 F5
Priory Ct. St Alb AL1 127 E2
Priory Dell. Stev SG1 50 F5
Priory Dr. Sta M CM24 59 E5
Priory Dr. Stan HA7 176 F7
Priory End. Hit SG4 34 F5
Priory Gate. Ches EN8 148 F4
Priory Gdns. Berk HP4 122 C4
Priory Gdns. Luton LU2 45 D4
Priory La. Gt Wy SG4 35 F4
Priory La. Royst SG8 7 D6
Priory Orch. Fla AL3 84 B2
Priory Rd. Harl CM17 118 C5
Priory Sch The. Hit 21 E2
Priory St. Hert SG14 113 D6
Priory St. Ware SG12 93 C1
Priory View. Bus WD2 168 E2
Priory View. L Wym SG4 35 E4
Priory Way. Hit SG4 34 F4
Priory Wharf. Hert SG14 113 C6 10
Priory Wlk. St Alb AL1 141 E8
Proctor Way. Luton LU2 64 C7
Proctors Way. Bis St CM23 77 A4
Progress Way. Luton LU4 44 B7
Progression Ctr. Heml H 125 A6
Prospect La. Harp AL5 107 A4
Prospect Pl. Welw AL6 89 C5
Prospect Rd. Ches EN8 148 C2
Prospect Rd. St Alb AL1 127 D1
Protea Way. Letw SG6 23 B6
Providence Gr. Stev SG1 50 E8
Providence Way. Bal SG7 23 F7
Provost Way. Luton LU2 64 C8
Prowse Ave. Bus WD2 176 C8
Pryor Cl. Abb L WD5 153 F7
Pryor Rd. Bal SG7 23 F6
Pryor Way. Letw SG6 23 D5
Pryors Cl. Bis St CM23 77 A6
Puddephat's La. Fla AL3 104 D7
Pudding La. Bar SG8 9 A1
Pudding La. Heml H HP1 124 A5
Pudgell The. Gt Ch SG8 9 E2
Pullar Memorial Jun Mix & Inf Sch.
Thun 72 E2
Puller Rd. Barn EN5 171 E7
Puller Rd. Heml H HP1 124 A2
Pulleys Cl. Heml H HP1 123 F4
Pulleys La. Heml H HP1 123 F4
Pulter's Way. Hit SG4 35 A6
Pump Hill. Bre P SG9 30 A2
Punch Bowl La. Red AL3 126 B8
Purbrock Ave. Watf WD2 154 C3
Purcell Cl. Dat AL6 90 E6
Purcell Cl. Radl WD6 169 D8
Purcell Ct. Stev SG1 50 C8
Purkiss Rd. Bric SG13 113 C3
Purley Ctr. Luton 44 E7
Purlings Rd. Bus WD2 168 B4
Pursley Gdns. Bor WD6 157 A1
Purway Cl. Luton LU3 44 E8
Purwell La. Hit SG4 35 C8
Purwell Sch (Jun Mix & Inf). Hit 35 D8
Putney Rd. Enf EN3 162 D3
Puttenham Cl. Sth Ox WD1 175 D8
Putteridge High Sch. Luton 46 C5
Putteridge Inf Sch. Luton 46 C5
Putteridge Prim Sch. Luton 46 C5
Putteridge Rd. Luton LU2 46 C5
Putteridge Rec Ctr. Luton 46 C5
Putterills The. Harp AL5 86 A1
Putters Croft. Heml H HP2 124 F8
Puttocks Cl. Wel G AL9 144 C8
Puttocks Dr. Wel G AL9 144 C8
Pye Cnr. East CM20 117 D5
Pyghtle Ct. Luton LU1 63 A7
Pyghtle The. Bun SG9 40 D7
Pyghtle The. Luton LU1 63 A7
Pyms Cl. Letw SG6 23 B8
Pynchbek. Bis St CM23 76 E3
Pynchon Paddocks. L Hal CM22 98 D7
Pytchley Cl. Luton LU2 45 E5

Quadrangle The. Wel G C AL8 110 C7
Quadrant The. Letw SG6 22 F6
Quadrant The. Royst SG8 7 C8
Quadrant The. St Alb AL4 128 B6
Quadrant The. Stev SG1 50 D4
Quaker La. Wa Aby EN9 163 C5
Quaker Rd. Ware SG12 93 E3
Quakers La. Pot B EN6 159 B8
Quantock Cl. Luton LU3 45 B8
Quantock Cl. St Alb AL4 128 C7
Quantock Rise. Luton LU3 31 B1
Quantocks. Heml H HP2 124 F6
Quartermass Cl. Heml H HP1 124 A4
Quartermass Rd. Heml H HP1 124 A4
Queen Anne's Cl. Stot SG5 11 F5
Queen Elizabeth Ct. Barn EN5 171 F5
Queen Elizabeth II Hospl.
Wel G C 111 A2
Queen Elizabeth's Boys Sch.
Barn 171 D6
Queen Elizabeth's Girls Gram Sch.
Barn 171 F5
Queen Hoo La. Tewin AL6 90 D6
Queen Mary's Ave. Watf WD1 166 E5
Queen St. Chipf WD4 152 A7
Queen St. Hit SG4,SG5 34 F7
Queen St. Pit LU7 80 D4
Queen St. St Alb AL3 127 C3
Queen St. Stot SG5 12 A6
Queen St. Tri HP23 100 A3
Queen Victoria Memorial Hospl.
Welw 89 B4
Queen's Cl. Saw CM21 97 F4
Queen's Ct. Asp SG9 40 D5
Queen's Ct. Hert SG13 113 D5
Queen's Ct. St Alb AL1 128 B3
Queen's Dr. Ches EN8 163 A5
Queen's Dr The. Ric WD3 165 A3
Queen's Pl. Watf WD1 167 C6
Queen's Rd. Ches EN8 162 E6
Queen's Rd. Harp AL5 107 B7
Queen's Rd. Hert SG13 113 D5
Queen's Rd. Watf WD1 167 C6
Queen's Sq The. Heml H HP2 124 F4
Queens Ave. Watf WD1 166 F4
Queens Cl. Luton LU1 63 F6
Queens Cl. Sta M CM24 59 E8
Queens Cres. Bis St CM23 76 E5
Queens Cres. St Alb AL4 128 B6
Queens Dr. Abb L WD5 153 F7
Queens Rd. Barn EN5 171 D6
Queens Rd. Berk HP4 122 A5
Queens Rd. Royst SG8 7 D7
Queens Rd. Ware SG12 93 F2
Queens Sch. Bus 167 F6
Queens Way. Ches EN8 162 F5
Queens Way. Shen WD7 156 E7
Queensgate Ctr. Harl 117 F4
Queenside Dr. Hit SG5 34 D8
Queensway. Hat AL10 130 B6
Queensway. Heml H HP1,HP2 124 E4
Queensway. Royst SG8 7 D7
Queensway. Stev SG1 50 D5
Queenswood Cres. Watf WD2 154 A6
Queenswood Dr. Hit SG4 22 C1
Queenswood Sch. Bro Pk 145 D3
Quendell Wlk. Heml H HP2 124 E3
Quendon Dr. Wa Aby EN9 163 D6
Quickbeams. Wel G C AL7 90 A1
Quickley La. Chor WD3 164 C3
Quickley Rise. Chor WD3 164 C3
Quickly Brow. Chor WD3 164 B3
Quickmoor La. Sar WD4 152 C6
Quickswood. Luton LU3 45 A7
Quickwood Cl. Ric WD3 165 A3
Quills. Letw SG6 23 D4
Quilter Cl. Luton LU3 44 F4
Quinces Croft. Heml H HP1 124 A5
Quincey Rd. Ware SG12 93 C4
Quinn Ct. Brag SG11 55 F7
Quinn Way. Letw SG6 23 C5
Quinta Dr. Barn EN5 171 C4
Quinton Way. Wa Aby EN9 163 C4

Raans Rd. L Chal HP6 150 A1
Raban Cl. Stev SG2 51 C1
Rabley Heath Rd. Cod AL6 68 B2
Radburn Sch (Jun Mix & Inf). Letw 23 C5
Radburn Way. Letw SG6 23 C4
Radcliffe Rd. Hit SG5 35 A8
Radlett La. Shen WD7 156 E6
Radlett Nursery & Inf Sch. Radl 156 B3
Radlett Park Rd. Radl WD7 156 A5
Radlett Rd. Lon C AL2 141 E2
Radlett Rd. Radl WD2 155 C1
Radlett Rd. Watf WD1,WD2 167 D7
Radnor Ct. Har HA3 176 F2
Radstone Pl. Luton LU2 46 E1 3
Radwell La. Letw SG7 12 C4
Raebarn Gdns. Barn EN5 171 B4
Raffin Cl. Dat SG3 69 E3
Raffin Green La. Dat SG3 69 F4
Raffin Pk. Dat SG3 69 E3
Ragged Hall La. Chis AL2 140 E7
Raglan Ave. Ches EN8 162 D5
Raglan Gdns. Watf WD1 167 B1
Raglan House. Berk HP4 122 A4
Rags La. Ham St EN7 147 E4
Railway Pl. Hert SG13 113 E6
Railway Rd. Ches EN8 162 F6
Railway St. Hert SG13,SG14 113 D6
Railway Terr. Abb L WD4 139 A4
Rainbow Cl. Red AL3 105 F6
Rainbow Ct. Watf WD1 167 C3
Rainer Cl. Ches EN8 148 D2
Rainsford Rd. Sta M CM24 59 E8
Raleigh Cres. Stev SG2 51 B8
Raleigh Gr. Luton LU4 44 D1
Rally The. Arl SG15 11 A7
Ralph Sadleir Mid Sch. Stand 55 E3
Ralston Way. Sth Ox WD1 175 D8
Ram Gorse. Harl CM20 117 B2
Ramblers Way. Wel G C AL7 111 C5
Rambling Way. Pot En HP4 123 C6
Ramerick Gdns. Arl SG15 11 A2
Ramney Dr. Enf EN3 162 E2
Ramparts The. St Alb AL3 127 B2
Ramridge Jun Sch. Luton 46 B2
Ramridge Rd. Luton LU2 46 A2
Ramsay Cl. Hod EN10 134 E2
Ramsbury Rd. St Alb AL1 127 E2
Ramsdell. Stev SG1 50 F5
Ramsey Cl. Bro Pk AL9 145 D4
Ramsey Cl. St Alb AL1 128 A1
Ramsey Lodge Ct. St Alb AL1 127 E4
Ramson Rise. Heml H HP1 123 E2
Rand's Cl. Hol SG5 21 B7
Rand's Meadow. Hol SG5 21 B7
Randalls Ride. Heml H HP2 124 E5
Randals Hill. Stev SG2 51 C3
Randon Cl. Har HA2 176 B1
Ranelagh Rd. Heml H HP2 125 B3
Ranleigh Wlk. Harp AL5 107 D6
Ranock Cl. Luton LU3 44 D8
Ranskill Rd. Bor WD6 170 A8
Ransom Cl. Hit SG4 34 F4
Rant Meadow. Heml H HP3 125 A1
Rant Meadow. Heml H HP3 125 A2
Ranworth Ave. Hod EN11 115 B2
Ranworth Ave. Stev SG2 69 C7
Ranworth Cl. Heml H HP3 124 D1 2
Raphael Cl. Shen WD7 156 E7
Raphael Dr. Watf WD2 167 D7
Rasehill Cl. Ric WD3 165 C4
Rathlin. Heml H HP3 139 B8
Ratty's La. Hod EN11 135 D6
Raven Cl. Ric WD3 165 D2
Raven Ct. Hat AL10 130 A4
Ravenbank Rd. Luton LU2 46 C5
Ravenfield Rd. Wel G C AL7 110 F6
Ravenhill Way. Dun LU4 44 B4
Ravens La. Berk HP4 122 D4
Ravens Wharf. Berk HP4 122 D4
Ravenscroft. Harp AL5 107 D6
Ravenscroft Pk. Barn EN5 171 D5
Ravenscroft Sch. Barn 171 F2
Ravenscroft. Watf WD2 154 E4
Ravensdell. Heml H HP1 123 F4
Ravensthorpe. Luton LU2 46 B4
Ravenswood Pk. Norwd HA6 175 A4
Rawdon Dr. Hod EN11 135 A5
Ray's Hill. Chol HP5 120 C2
Rayburn Rd. Heml H HP1 124 A5
Raydon Rd. Ches EN8 162 D7
Rayfield. Wel G C AL8 89 D1
Rayleigh House. Abb L WD5 153 F7
Raymer Cl. St Alb AL1 127 E4
Raymond Cl. Abb L WD5 153 D7
Raymonds Cl. Wel G C AL7 110 E4
Raymonds Plain. Wel G C AL7 110 E4
Raynham Cl. Bis St CM23 77 C8
Raynham Rd. Bis St CM23 77 B8
Raynham St. Hert SG13 113 E6
Raynham Way. Luton LU2 46 D1
Raynsford Rd. Ware SG12 93 E1
Raynton Rd. Enf EN3 162 D2
Readings The. Chor WD3 164 F6
Recreation Ground. Sta M CM24 59 E6
Rectory Cl. Bis St CM23 76 D3
Rectory Cl. Ess AL9 131 F6
Rectory Cl. Hun SG12 116 D8
Rectory Gdns. Hat AL10 130 B5
Rectory La. Berk HP4 122 C4
Rectory La. Far CM23 58 D6
Rectory La. Kin L WD4 139 A3
Rectory La. Lily LU2 32 D2
Rectory La. Ric WD3 165 D1
Rectory La. Shen WD7,AL2 157 B7
Rectory La. Stev SG1 36 D1
Rectory La. Wat St SG14 70 D3
Rectory La. Welw SG3 69 C2
Rectory Rd. Ric WD3 165 D2
Rectory Rd. Wel G C AL8 89 B1
Rectory Wood. Harl CM20 117 C1
Red House Cl. Ware SG12 114 E8
Red Lion Cotts. Gt Of SG5 33 D2
Red Lion Ct. Bis St CM23 77 A7
Red Lion La. Heml H HP3 139 A5
Red Lion La. Sar WD3 152 A4
Red Lodge. Bor WD6 169 F6
Red Lodge Gdns. Berk HP4 122 A3
Red Rails. Luton LU1 63 C5
Red Rd. Bor WD6 169 F6
Redan Rd. Ware SG12 93 E3
Redbourn Ind Est. Red 106 B5
Redbourn Inf Sch. Red 106 A6
Redbourn Jun Sch. Red 106 A6
Redbourn La. Harp AL5 106 E6
Redbourn Rd. Heml H HP2 125 A6
Redbourn Rd. Heml H HP2 125 B8
Redbourn Rd. St Alb AL3 126 E7
Redbournbury La. Red AL3 106 D2
Redcar Dr. Stev SG1 50 A6
Redding House. Watf WD1 166 E3
Redding La. Red AL3 105 F8
Reddings Ave. Bus WD2 168 B4
Reddings Cty Prim Sch The.
Heml H 125 A1
Reddings. Heml H HP3 125 A1
Reddings. The. Bor WD6 169 F6
Reddings. Wel G C AL8 110 C7
Redfern Ct. Luton LU1 63 A6
Redferns Cl. Luton LU1 63 A6
Redgrave Gdns. Luton LU3 44 F7
Redhall Cl. Hat AL10 129 F1
Redhall Dr. Hat AL10 129 F1
Redhall La. Coln H AL4 129 E1
Redhall La. Sar WD3 165 E8
Redheath Cl. Watf WD2 153 F4
Redhill Rd. Hit SG5 34 D8
Redhoods Way E. Letw SG6 22 E7
Redhoods Way W. Letw SG6 22 E6
Redlands Rd. Enf EN3 162 E1
Redmire Cl. Luton LU4 44 B6
Redricks La. Saw CM21 118 B7
Redvers Cl. Bis St CM23 59 A2
Redwell Ct. Ches EN8 162 F5
Redwood Cl. Sth Ox WD1 175 D6
Redwood Dr. Heml H HP3 124 E1
Redwood Dr. Luton LU3 44 C8
Redwood Rise. Bor WD6 157 B2
Redwood Way. Barn EN5 171 D4
Redwoods. Hert AL8 113 C7
Redwoods. Wel G C AL8 89 D3
Reed Cl. Lon C AL2 142 E4
Reed Jun Mix Inf Sch. Reed 16 E5
Reed Pl. Harp AL5 85 F3 1
Reedham Cl. Bri Wd AL2 141 A2
Reedings Jun Sch. Saw 97 E3
Reedings Way. Saw CM21 97 F4
Reeds Cres. Watf WD1 167 C7
Reeds The. Wel G C AL7 110 D5
Reedsdale. Luton LU2 46 F2
Reeves Ave. Luton LU3 44 B4
Reeves Pightle. Gt Ch SG8 9 F3
Regal Cl. Stand SG11 55 E2
Regal Ct. Hit SG5 34 F8 4
Regal Way. Watf WD2 154 C1
Regency Cl. Bis St CM23 76 E7
Regency Heights. Heml H HP2 124 D3
Regent Cl. Kin L WD4 139 A3
Regent Cl. St Alb AL4 128 C7
Regent Cl. Wel G C AL7 110 E5
Regent Ct. Stot SG5 11 F7
Regent Gate. Ches EN8 162 E5
Regent St. Luton LU1 63 E7
Regent St. Stot SG5 11 F7
Regent St. Watf WD2 154 B1
Regents Cl. Radl WD7 156 A5
Regina Cl. Barn EN5 171 D6
Reginald Rd. Norwd HA6 174 F3
Reginald St. Luton LU2 45 E1
Rendlesham Ave. Radl WD7 155 F2
Rendlesham Cl. Ware SG12 93 B2
Rendlesham Rd. Enf EN2 161 B1
Rendlesham Way. Chor WD3 164 C3
Rennison Cl. Ham St EN7 147 F4
Renshaw Cl. Luton LU2 46 E2
Repton Cl. Luton LU3 44 F6
Repton Gn. St Alb AL3 127 D6
Repton Way. Cro Gr WD3 166 A4
Reson Way. Heml H HP1 124 B2
Reston Cl. Bor WD6 157 B1
Retford Cl. Bor WD6 157 A1
Retreat The. Abb L WD5 153 C8
Revels Cl. Hert SG14 113 D8
Revels Rd. Hert SG14 113 D8
Reynard Copse. Bis St CM23 58 F1
Reynard Way. Hert SG13 114 B6
Reynard's Way. Bri Wd AL2 140 F2
Reynards Rd. Welw AL6 89 C7
Reynolds Cl. Heml H HP1 124 A4
Reynolds Cres. Sand AL4 128 B8
Reynolds. Letw SG6 11 F1
Rhee Spring. Bal SG7 13 B1
Rhodes Ave. Bis St CM23 76 F5
Rhodes Memorial Mus &
Commonwealth Ctr. Bis St 77 A6
Rhodes Way. Watf WD2 167 D8
Rib Cl. Stand SG11 55 E2
Rib Vale. Hert SG14 92 D1
Ribbledale. Lon C AL2 142 F4
Ribblesdale. Heml H HP2 124 E6
Ribocon Way. Luton LU4 44 B7
Ribston Cl. Shen WD7 156 D6
Rice Cl. Heml H HP2 124 F4
Richard Ct. Barn EN5 171 E6
Richard Hale Sch. Hert 113 D5
Richard Stagg Cl. St Alb AL1 128 C1
Richard Whittington
Jun Mix Inf Sch. Bis St 76 E4
Richards Cl. Bus WD2 168 D2
Richards Cl. Luton LU1 63 B6
Richards Ct. Luton LU1 63 B6
Richardson Cl. Lon C AL2 142 E4
Richardson Pl. Coln H AL4 129 B1
Richfield Rd. Bus WD2 168 C2
Richmond Cl. Bis St CM23 76 C7
Richmond Cl. Ches EN8 148 C2
Richmond Cl. Ware SG12 93 B3
Richmond Ct. Hat AL10 130 B3 4
Richmond Ct. Hod EN10 134 F3
Richmond Ct. Luton LU2 45 F1
Richmond Ct. Pot B EN6 159 C8
Richmond Dr. Watf WD1 166 E7
Richmond Gdns. Har HA3 176 F3
Richmond Gn. Abb L WD5 139 F4
Richmond Hill. Luton LU2 45 F2
Richmond Hill Sch. Luton 45 E2
Richmond Rd. Pot B EN6 159 C8
Richmond Way. Cro Gr WD3 166 C5
Richmond Wlk. St Alb AL4 128 D7
Rickfield Cl. Hat AL10 130 A3
Rickmansworth La. C St P SL9 172 A5
Rickmansworth Park
Jun Mix Inf Sch. Ric 165 E2
Rickmansworth Rd. Chor WD3 164 F5
Rickmansworth Rd. Cro Gr WD1 166 E5
Rickmansworth Rd. Hare UB9 173 D3
Rickmansworth Rd. Norwd HA6 174 D3
Rickmansworth Rd. Pnr HA5 175 C1
Rickmansworth Rd. Watf WD1 166 E5
Rickmansworth Rd. Watf WD1 167 B6
Rickmansworth Sch. Cro Gr 165 F3
Rickmansworth Sta. Ric 165 D2
Rickyard Cl. Luton LU2 46 B3
Rickyard Meadow. Red AL3 106 A5
Rickyard The. Ashw SG7 4 D4
Rickyard The. Letw SG7 12 C1
Riddell Gdns. Bal SG7 23 F8
Riddy Hill Cl. Hit SG4 35 A6
Riddy La. Hit SG4 35 A6
Riddy La. Luton LU3 45 C5
Riddy The. Cod SG4 88 F8
Ridge Ave. Harp AL5 85 E4
Ridge Ave. Letw SG6 23 A6
Ridge Ct. Luton LU2 46 A1
Ridge La. Watf WD1 153 F2
Ridge Lea. Heml H HP1 123 F2
Ridge Rd. Letw SG6 23 A6
Ridge St. Watf WD2 154 B1
Ridge The. Barn EN5 171 F4
Ridge The. Letw SG6 23 A6
Ridge The. Norwd HA6 174 F3
Ridge View. Tri HP23 100 C5
Ridge Way. Ric WD3 165 B2
Ridgedown. Red AL3 106 A5
Ridgefield. Watf WD1 153 E2
Ridgehurst Ave. Watf WD2 153 F5
Ridgeview Cl. Barn EN5 171 D3
Ridgeway. Berk HP4 121 F4
Ridgeway Cl. Heml H HP3 138 F5
Ridgeway Ct. Pnr HA5 176 A3
Ridgeway. Harp AL5 85 E4
Ridgeway. Ken Co LU6 82 E8
Ridgeway. L Had SG11 57 B1
Ridgeway. Stev SG1 50 F5
Ridgeway The. Cod SG4 67 F1
Ridgeway The. Cuf EN6 146 A4
Ridgeway The. Had W EN2,EN4 160 D3
Ridgeway The. Hert SG14 112 F7
Ridgeway The. Hit SG5 34 D6
Ridgeway The. Radl WD7 155 F2
Ridgeway The. St Alb AL4 128 C7
Ridgeway The. Ware SG12 93 C3
Ridgeway The. Watf WD1 153 E2
Ridgeway. Wel G C AL7 111 B6
Ridgewood Dr. Harp AL5 85 E4
Ridgewood Gdns. Harp AL5 85 E4
Ridgmont Rd. St Alb AL1 127 E2
Ridgway Rd. Luton LU2 45 F1
Ridings The. Bis St CM23 76 D4
Ridings The. Hert SG14 113 A5
Ridings The. Lat HP5 150 D3
Ridings The. Luton LU3 45 C1
Ridings The. Mark AL3 83 E6
Ridings The. Stev SG2 51 B3
Ridler Rd. Enf EN1 161 E1
Ridlins End. Stev SG2 51 C2
Rigery La. Stand SG11 72 F6
Riley Rd. Enf EN3 162 C1
Ringshall Dr. L Gad HP4 102 C8
Ringshall Rd. Dagn HP4 81 B3
Ringtale Pl. Bal SG7 13 B1
Ringway Rd. Chis AL2 141 C4
Ringwood Rd. Luton LU2 45 D6
Ripley Rd. Dun LU4 44 C1
Ripley Rd. Enf EN2 161 C1
Ripley Way. Ches EN7 148 B1
Ripley Way. Heml H HP1 123 E4
Ripon Rd. Stev SG1 37 A2
Ripon Way. Bor WD6 170 D4
Ripon Way. St Alb AL4 128 D7
Rise Cotts. Hun SG12 95 D2
Rise The. Bal SG7 23 E7
Rise The. Bor WD6 169 F4
Rise The. Pk St AL2 141 D6
Risedale Cl. Heml H HP3 138 E8
Risedale Hill. Heml H HP3 138 E8
Risedale Rd. Heml H HP3 138 E8
Rising Hill Cl. Norwd HA6 174 C4
Risingholme Cl. Bus WD2 168 B2
Risingholme Cl. Har HA3 176 E2
Risingholme Rd. Har HA3 176 E1
Ritcroft Cl. Heml H HP3 125 B2
Ritcroft Dr. Heml H HP3 125 B2
Ritcroft St. Heml H HP3 125 B2
Ritz Ct. Pot B EN6 159 A8
Rivenhall End. Wel G C AL7 111 C6
River Ave. Hod EN11 135 B7
River Cl. Ches EN8 163 A5
River Ct. Ick SG5 21 F4
River Ct. Sac SG14 92 E4
River Gn. Bun SG9 40 E8
River Hill. Fla AL3 84 B2
River Mead. Hit SG5 21 C2
River Meads. Gt Am SG12 115 C4
River Park Ind Est. Berk 122 A5
River Pk. Heml H HP1 124 A1
River St. Ware SG12 93 E1
River View. Wel G C AL7 89 F2
River Way. Harl CM20 118 A5
River Way. Harl CM20 118 C6
River Way. Luton LU3 44 E5
Riverfield La. Saw CM21 97 E3
Riverford Cl. Harp AL5 86 B4
Rivermill Adult Education Ctr. Harl 117 C2
Rivermill Ct. Royst SG8 7 C7
Rivermill. Harl CM20 117 C2
Rivers Hospl The. Saw 97 C1
Riversend Rd. Heml H HP3 138 C8
Rivershill. Wat St SG14 70 E3
Riverside Ave. Lo Naz EN10 135 A1
Riverside. Bis St CM23 76 F7
Riverside. Bun SG9 40 E7
Riverside Cl. Kin L WD4 139 B2
Riverside Cl. St Alb AL1 127 E1
Riverside Cotts. Gt Am SG12 115 C4
Riverside Ct. Saw CM17 118 C6
Riverside Ct. St Alb AL1 127 E1
Riverside Dr. Ric WD3 165 D1
Riverside Gdns. Berk HP4 122 A5
Riverside Mews. Ware SG12 93 D1 7
Riverside Path. Ches EN8 148 C2
Riverside Rd. Luton LU3 45 A5
Riverside Rd. St Alb AL1 127 E2
Riverside Rd. Watf WD1 167 B3
Riverside. Welw AL6 89 B5
Riverside Wlk. Bis St CM23 76 F7
Riversmead. Hod EN11 135 A5
Riversmeet. Hert SG14 113 B5
Rivett Cl. Bal SG7 13 A1
Roan Wlk. Royst SG8 7 E6
Roaring Meg Ret & Leisure Pk.
Stev 50 D3
Robbery Bottom La. Welw AL6 90 A8
Robbs Cl. Heml H HP1 124 A5
Robe End. Heml H HP1 123 F5
Robert Allen Ct. Luton LU1 63 E6 1
Robert Ave. St Alb AL1 141 C7
Robert Cl. Pot B EN6 158 E6
Robert Humbert House. Letw SG6 23 A5
Robert Saunders Ct. Letw SG6 22 E4
Robert Tebbutt Ct. Hit SG5 34 E6
Robert Wallace Cl. Bis St CM23 58 F1
Roberts La. C St P SL9 172 B5
Roberts Rd. Watf WD1 167 C4
Roberts Way. Hat AL10 129 F3
Roberts Wood Dr. C St P SL9 172 A5
Robertson Cl. Ches EN10 148 E5
Robeson Way. Bor WD6 170 C8
Robin Cl. Gt Am SG12 115 C3
Robin Hill. Berk HP4 122 C3
Robin Hood Dr. Bus WD2 167 F8
Robin Hood Dr. Har HA3 176 F3
Robin Hood La. Hat AL10 130 A6
Robin Hood Meadow. Heml H HP2 124 F8
Robin Mead. Wel G C AL7 90 A1
Robin Way. Cuf EN6 146 E3
Robina Cl. Norwd HA6 174 F2
Robins Nest Hill. L Berk SG13 132 C6
Robins Rd. Heml H HP3 125 A1
Robins Way. Hat AL10 129 F2
Robinsfield. Heml H HP1 124 A3
Robinson Ave. Gofs O EN7 147 B3
Robinson Cl. Bis St CM23 76 F5
Robinson Cres. Bus WD2 168 C1
Robinsway. Wa Aby EN9 163 E5
Robinswood. Luton LU2 45 E5
Robsons Cl. Ches EN8 148 C2
Rochdale Ct. Luton LU1 63 E6 2
Rochester Ave. Luton LU2 46 C4
Rochester Dr. Watf WD2 154 C4
Rochester Way. Cro Gr WD3 166 B5
Rochester Way. Royst SG8 7 D8
Rochford Ave. Wa Aby EN9 163 D5
Rochford Cl. Ches EN10 148 E5
Rochford Dr. Luton LU2 46 E2
Rochford Rd. Bis St CM23 59 C1
Rock Rd. Royst SG8 7 C8
Rockfield Ave. Ware SG12 93 D3
Rockingham Way. Stev SG1 50 E4
Rockleigh. Hert SG14 113 C6
Rockley Rd. Luton LU1 63 A7
Rockliffe Ave. Kin L WD4 139 A1
Rockways. Edg EN5 170 F3
Rodeheath. Luton LU4 44 D3

Roden Cl. Harl CM17 .... 118 F4
Rodgers Cl. Elst WD6 .... 169 D3
Rodings The. Barn EN5 .... 171 E5
Rodney Ave. St Alb AL1 .... 128 A1
Rodney Cres. Hod EN11 .... 135 A8
Roe Cl. Stot SG5 .... 11 E5
Roe End La. Mark AL3 .... 83 B4
Roe Green Cl. Hat AL10 .... 129 F4
Roe Green Ctr. Hat AL10 .... 129 F4
Roe Green La. Hat AL10 .... 129 F5
Roe Hill Cl. Hat AL10 .... 129 F4
Roebuck Cl. Luton LU1 .... 63 B6
Roebuck Ct. Stev SG2 .... 50 F1 1
Roebuck Gate. Stev SG2 .... 50 F1
Roebuck Jun Mix & Inf Sch. Stev .. 50 F2
Roebuck Ret Pk. Stev 50 E2
Roedean Ave. Enf EN3 .... 162 C1
Roedean Cl. Luton LU2 .... 46 D3
Roefields Cl. Heml H HP3 .... 138 A7
Roehyde Way. Hat AL10 .... 129 E2
Roestock Gdns. Coln H AL4 .... 129 E1
Roestock La. Coln H AL4 .... 129 E1
Rofant Rd. Norwd HA6 .... 174 E4
Rogate Rd. Luton LU2 .... 46 C5
Roger de Clare Fst Sch. Stand 55 E2
Rogers Ruff. Norwd HA6 .... 174 C2
Rokewood Mews. Ware SG12 ...... 93 D2 3
Roland St. St Alb AL1 .... 128 B2
Rolleston Cl. Ware SG12 .... 93 C3
Rollswood Rd. Welw AL6 .... 89 B8
Rollswood. Wel G C AL7 .... 110 C3
Rollys La. Ashw SG7 .... 4 D4
Roman Gdns. Abb L WD4 .... 139 B1
Roman La. Bal SG7 .... 24 A8
Roman Rd. Luton LU3,LU4 .... 44 E3
Roman St. Hod EN11 .... 135 A7
Roman Vale. Harl CM17 .... 118 C5
Roman Way Fst Sch. Royst 7 C8
Roman Way. Mark AL3 .... 83 E6
Roman Way. Stand SG11 .... 55 D3
Roman Way. Welw AL6 .... 89 C6
Romans Rise. Saw CM21 .... 97 D2
Romany Cl. Letw SG6 .... 22 C6
Romeland. Elst WD6 .... 169 D3
Romeland Hill. St Alb AL3 .... 127 C3
Romeland. St Alb AL3 .... 127 C3
Romeland. Wa Aby EN9 .... 163 C6
Romilly Dr. Sth Ox WD1 .... 175 F6
Rondini Ave. Luton LU3 .... 45 B3
Rook Tree Cl. Stot SG5 .... 12 A6
Rook Tree La. Stot SG5 .... 12 A6
Rookery Dr. Luton LU2 .... 45 E6
Rookery The. Hat AL9 .... 144 D8
Rookery The. Sta M CM24 .... 59 E8
Rookery The. West SG9 .... 40 F3
Rookery Yd. Stev SG1 .... 50 C7
Rookes Cl. Letw SG6 .... 23 B3
Rooks Cl. Wel G C AL8 .... 110 D5
Rooks Hill. Wel G C AL8 .... 110 C5
Rooks Nest La. Ther SG8 .... 16 A5
Rookwood Dr. Stev SG2 .... 51 B1
Rosary Ct. Pot B EN6 .... 145 B1
Rose Acre. Red AL3 .... 105 F6
Rose Cl. Hat AL10 .... 130 A8
Rose Cotts. Wyd SG9 .... 28 A3
Rose Ct. Ham St LU6 .... 148 A4
Rose Ct. St Alb AL4 .... 128 C5
Rose Gdns. Watf WD1 .... 167 A4
Rose La. Ess AL9 .... 131 C5
Rose La. Whea AL4 .... 87 C2
Rose Lawn. Bus WD2 .... 168 C1
Rose Mead. Pot B EN6 .... 145 C1
Rose Meadow. Gt Ho SG11 ...... 41 E4
Rose Vale. Hod EN11 .... 135 A6
Rose Wlk. Royst SG8 .... 7 C7
Rose Wlk. St Alb AL4 .... 128 C5
Rose Wlk The. Radl WD7 .... 156 B3
Rose Wood Cl. Luton LU2 .... 45 F3
Roseacre Gdns. Wel G C AL7 .... 111 D6
Roseacres. Saw CM21 .... 97 D3
Rosebank. Wa Aby EN9 .... 163 E6
Roseberry Cl. Watf WD1 .... 167 A8
Rosebery Ave. Harp AL5 .... 85 F1
Rosebery. Bis St CM23 .... 77 C6
Rosebery Mews. Men LU7 .... 61 D4
Rosebery Rd. Bus WD2 .... 168 B2
Rosebery Way. Tri HP23 .... 100 B5
Rosebriar Wlk. Watf WD2 .... 153 F3
Rosecroft Ct. St Alb AL4 .... 128 C1
Rosecroft Dr. Norwd HA6 .... 174 C4
Rosecroft Dr. Watf WD1 .... 153 E3
Rosecroft La. Welw AL6 .... 90 A8
Rosecroft Sch. Stot 11 F6
Rosedale Ave. Gofs O EN7 .... 147 F2
Rosedale Cl. Bri Wd AL2 .... 140 E1
Rosedale Cl. Luton LU3 .... 44 C7
Rosedale Way. Ches EN7 .... 148 A3
Rosedale. Wel G C AL7 .... 89 F2
Roseheath. Heml H HP1 .... 123 E4
Rosehill. Berk HP4 .... 122 B4
Rosehill Cl. Hod EN11 .... 134 F6
Rosehill Cl. Heml H HP1 .... 124 A1
Rosehill Gdns. Abb L WD5 .... 153 C7
Rosehill Hospl. Hit 22 D2
Roselands Ave. Hod EN11 .... 114 F1
Roselands Jun Mix Inf Sch. Hod .. 114 F1
Rosemary Cl. Harl CM17 .... 118 C4
Rosemont Cl. Letw SG6 .... 22 E6
Rosewood Cl. Heml H HP1 .... 123 E4
Rosewood Dr. Cre H EN2 .... 161 A4
Roslyn Cl. Hod EN10 .... 134 E2
Ross Cl. Luton LU1 .... 63 B6
Ross Cl. Stan HA3 .... 176 C3
Ross Cres. Watf WD2 .... 154 A4
Ross Ct. Stev SG2 .... 51 B7
Ross Way. Mo Pk HA6 .... 174 F6
Rossfold Rd. Luton LU3 .... 44 D8
Rossgate. Heml H HP1 .... 124 A5
Rossgate Sch. Heml H 124 A5
Rossington Ave. Bor WD6 .... 156 E1
Rossiter Fields. Barn EN5 .... 171 F3
Rosslyn Cres. Luton LU3 .... 45 C5
Rosslyn Rd. Watf WD1 .... 167 B6
Rossway. Gad LU1 .... 63 B1
Rossway Dr. Bus WD2 .... 168 D4
Rossway La. Wigg HP4 .... 121 A7

Roswell Cl. Ches EN8 .... 148 E1
Rothamsted Ave. Harp AL5 ...... 86 A1
Rothamsted Experimental Sta. Harp 107 A8
Rother Cl. Watf WD2 .... 154 C5
Rother Field. Luton LU2 .... 46 D3
Rotheram Ave. Luton LU1 .... 63 B5
Rotherfield Rd. Enf EN3 .... 162 D2
Rothesay Rd. Luton LU1 .... 63 D7
Roughcroft. Ham St EN7 .... 147 F5
Roughdown Ave. Heml H HP3 ... 138 A8
Roughdown Rd. Heml H HP3 .... 138 A8
Roughdown Villas Rd. Heml H HP3 138 A8
Roughwood Cl. Watf WD1 .... 153 E1
Round Diamond Jun Mix Inf Sch. Stev 51 B8
Roundabout La. Welw AL6 .... 89 F8
Roundcroft. Ham St EN7 .... 147 F5
Roundfield Ave. Harp AL5 .... 86 D3
Roundhaye. Stand SG11 .... 55 D3
Roundhedge Way. Enf EN2 ...... 160 F1
Roundhills. Wa Aby EN9 .... 163 E4
Roundings The. Hert H SG13 .... 114 C2
Roundmoor Dr. Ches EN8 .... 148 E2
Roundway The. Watf WD1 .... 166 F2
Roundwood Cl. Hit SG4 .... 22 C2
Roundwood. Wel G C AL8 .... 110 C7
Roundwood Gdns. Harp AL5 .... 85 D3
Roundwood. Kin L HP3 .... 138 E4
Roundwood La. Harp AL5 .... 85 D3
Roundwood Park Sch & Roundwood Jun Mix Inf Sch. Harp 85 E2
Roundwood Pk. Harp AL5 .... 85 E3
Rounton Rd. Wa Aby EN9 .... 163 E6
Rousebarn La. Sar WD3 .... 166 C7
Rowan Cl. Bri Wd AL2 .... 155 A8
Rowan Cl. Coln H AL4 .... 128 E3
Rowan Cl. Har HA7 .... 176 F4
Rowan Cl. Luton LU1 .... 63 A7
Rowan Cl. Wes SG4 .... 37 B8
Rowan Cres. Letw SG6 .... 22 E7
Rowan Cres. Stev SG1 .... 50 E7
Rowan Dr. Ches EN10 .... 148 F6
Rowan Gr. Hit SG4 .... 35 A4
Rowan Way. Harp AL5 .... 107 C8
Rowan Wlk. Hat AL10 .... 130 A2 2
Rowans Jun Mix Inf Sch The. Wel G C 90 A1
Rowans The. Bal SG7 .... 23 E1
Rowans The. Heml H HP1 .... 124 A3
Rowans The. Hod EN10 .... 134 F4
Rowans. Wel G C AL7 .... 90 A1
Rowcroft. Heml H HP1 .... 123 E2
Rowelfield. Luton LU2 .... 46 C1
Rowington Cl. Luton LU2 .... 46 C1
Rowland Pl. Norwd HA6 .... 174 E3
Rowland Rd. Stev SG1 .... 50 F4
Rowland Way. Letw SG6 .... 22 F6
Rowlands Ave. Pnr HA5 .... 176 B4
Rowlands Cl. Ches EN8 .... 148 D1
Rowlands Ct. Ches EN8 .... 148 D1
Rowlatt Dr. St Alb AL3 .... 127 A1
Rowley Cl. Watf WD1 .... 167 E3
Rowley Gdns. Ches EN8 .... 148 D3
Rowley Green Rd. Barn EN5 ..... 171 A4
Rowley La. Bor WD6 .... 170 D7
Rowley La. Edg EN5 .... 170 F5
Rowley's Rd. Hert SG13 .... 113 F7
Rowney Gdns. Saw CM21 .... 118 C8
Rowney La. Dan En SG12 .... 72 B5
Rowney Wood. Saw CM21 ...... 97 C1
Rows The. Harl CM20 .... 117 D1
Roy Rd. Norwd HA6 .... 174 F3
Royal Ave. Ches EN8 .... 162 E6
Royal Caledonian Sch. Bus 168 A7
Royal Oak St. Bis St CM23 ..... 76 F6
Royal Oak La. Pirt SG5 .... 20 D4
Royal Rd. St Alb AL1 .... 128 B3
Royal Veterinary Coll. Bro Pk .. 144 D3
Royce Cl. Hod EN10 .... 134 F2
Roydon Ct. Dun LU4 .... 44 A4
Roydon Ct. Heml H HP2 .... 105 A1
Roydon Lodge Chalet Est. Roy .. 116 C1
Roydon Mill Leisure Pk. Roy 116 A1
Roydon Rd. Roy CM19 .... 116 E1
Roydon Rd. Sta Ab SG12 ...... 115 E4
Royse Gr. Royst SG8 .... 7 D4
Roysia Mid Sch. Royst 7 D8
Royston Cl. Hert SG14 .... 113 B6
Royston Gr. Pnr HA5 .... 176 A4
Royston Hospl. Royst 7 D4
Royston Park Rd. Pnr HA5 ..... 176 A5
Royston Rd. Bal SG7 .... 13 C2
Royston Rd. Bar SG8 .... 8 F3
Royston Rd. Bark SG8 .... 17 C5
Royston Rd. Clo SG7 .... 13 C2
Royston Rd. St Alb AL1 .... 128 B2
Royston Sta. Royst 7 C7
Rucklers La. Kin L WD4 .... 138 C4
Ruckles Cl. Stev SG1 .... 50 E5
Rudd Cl. Stev SG2 .... 51 B3
Rudham Gr. Letw SG6 .... 23 C3
Rudolf Steiner Sch The. Kin L .. 138 E2
Rudolph Rd. Bus WD2 .... 168 A3
Rudyard Cl. Luton LU4 .... 44 D3
Rue de St Lawrence. Wa Aby EN9 163 C5
Rueley Dell Rd. Lily LU2 .... 32 D2
Rugby Way. Cro Gr WD3 .... 166 B4
Ruins The. Red AL3 .... 106 B5
Rumballs Cl. Heml H HP3 ...... 139 A8
Rumballs Rd. Heml H HP3 ..... 139 A8
Rumbold Rd. Hod EN11 .... 135 C8
Rumsley. Ham St EN7 .... 148 A4
Runcie Cl. St Alb AL4 .... 128 C4
Runcorn Cres. Heml H HP2 .... 124 F8
Rundells. Letw SG6 .... 23 D4
Runfold Ave. Luton LU3 .... 45 A5
Runham Rd. Heml H HP3 .... 124 E1
Runley Rd. Luton LU1 .... 62 F7
Runnalow. Letw SG6 .... 22 F1
Runsley. Wel G C AL7 .... 90 A1

Ruscombe Dr. Chis AL2 .... 141 C5
Rush Cl. Gt Am SG12 .... 115 C4
Rushall Gn. Luton LU2 .... 46 E2
Rushby Mead. Letw SG6 .... 23 A5
Rushby Pl. Letw SG6 .... 23 A5
Rushby Wlk. Letw SG6 .... 23 A6
Rushden Rd. San SG9 .... 26 A8
Rushdon Furlong. Pit LU7 ...... 80 E5
Rushes Cl. Bis St CM23 .... 77 A5
Rushfield. Pot B EN6 .... 158 E6
Rushfield Rd. Ware SG12 ...... 93 F3
Rushfield. Saw CM21 .... 97 E2
Rushleigh Ave. Ches EN8 ...... 148 D1
Rushleigh Gn. Bis St CM23 .... 76 D4
Rushmere La. Ash Gr HP5 ..... 136 B3
Rushmoor Cl. Ric WD3 .... 173 D8
Rushmore Cl. Cad LU1 .... 62 E5
Rushton Ave. Watf WD2 .... 154 A4
Rushton Ct. Ches EN8 .... 148 D2
Ruskin Ave. Wa Aby EN9 ...... 163 E5
Ruskin Ct. Ham St EN7 .... 147 E5
Ruskin La. Hit SG4 .... 35 C7
Rusper Gn. Luton LU2 .... 46 D3
Russell Ave. St Alb AL3 .... 127 D3
Russell Cl. Ken Co LU6 .... 82 A8
Russell Cl. Stev SG2 .... 51 B2
Russell Cres. Watf WD2 ...... 153 F4
Russell Ct. Bri Wd AL2 .... 141 A1
Russell Cty Prim Sch. Chor 164 B5
Russell La. Watf WD1 .... 153 D3
Russell Pl. Heml H HP3 .... 138 B8
Russell Rd. Enf EN1 .... 161 F1
Russell Rd. Mo Pk HA6 .... 174 C6
Russell Rise. Luton LU1 .... 63 D6
Russell St. Hert SG14 .... 113 C6
Russell St. Luton LU1 .... 63 D6
Russell Way. Mo Pk HA6 ..... 174 C5
Russell's Ride. Ches EN8 ..... 162 E8
Russellcroft Rd. Wel G C AL8 110 C7
Russet Cl. Ham St EN7 .... 147 E5
Russet Dr. St Alb AL4 .... 128 D2
Russett House. Wel G C AL7 . 111 D6
Russett Wood. Wel G C AL7 . 111 D5
Rutherford Cl. Bor WD6 ...... 170 C7
Rutherford Cl. Stev SG1 ...... 50 B6
Rutherford Way. Bus WD2 ... 168 A1
Ruthin Cl. Luton LU1 .... 63 D5
Ruthven Ave. Ches EN8 ...... 162 D6
Rutland Cres. Luton LU2 ..... 64 A7
Rutland Pl. Bus WD2 .... 168 D1
Rutts The. Bus WD2 .... 168 D1
Ryall Cl. Bri Wd AL2 .... 140 E2
Rydal Ct. Watf WD2 .... 154 C5
Rydal Mount. Pot B EN6 ..... 158 E6
Rydal Way. Luton LU3 .... 44 F5
Ryde The. Hat 130 C8
Ryde The. Hat AL9 .... 130 C8
Ryder Ave. Ick SG5 .... 21 D3
Ryder Cl. Bov HP3 .... 137 A4
Ryder Cl. Bus WD2 .... 168 B3
Ryder Ct. Hert SG13 .... 114 B7
Ryder Way. Ick SG5 .... 21 D3
Ryders Ave. Coln H AL4 ... 129 E3
Rye Cl. Harp AL5 .... 86 B4
Rye Gdns. Bal SG7 .... 13 B1
Rye Hill. Harp AL5 .... 86 B4
Rye House Sta. Hod 135 C8
Rye Rd. Hod EN11 .... 135 C8
Rye Rd. Sta Ab EN11 .... 115 D1
Rye St. Bis St CM23 ..... 58 F1
Ryecroft Cl. Heml H HP2 . 125 C2
Ryecroft Ct. Coln H AL4 . 128 F3
Ryecroft. Hat AL10 ...... 129 F3
Ryecroft. Stev SG1 ...... 50 E7
Ryecroft Way. Luton LU2 46 A4
Ryefeld Cl. Hod EN11 ... 115 B2
Ryefield Cres. Pnr HA6 .. 175 A1
Ryefield. Luton LU3 ..... 31 A1
Ryelands Heath. Luton LU2 46 F2
Ryelands. Wel G C AL7 . 110 F3
Ryley Cl. Henlw SG16 ... 10 B5
Ryman Ct. Chor WD3 ... 164 C3
Rymill Cl. Bov HP3 ...... 137 A3
Ryton Cl. Luton LU1 .... 63 B6

Saberton Cl. Red AL3 .... 105 F4
Sabine House. Abb L WD5 .... 153 F7
Sacombe Gn. Luton LU3 ...... 31 B1
Sacombe Green Rd. Sac SG12 . 71 E4
Sacombe Pound. Sac SG12 ... 71 E3
Sacombe Rd. Heml H HP1 .... 123 F5
Sacombe Rd. Hert SG14 ...... 92 C1
Sacombe Rd. Stap SG14 ...... 92 B4
Sacombs Ash La. H Wy SG10 . 96 E7
Sacred Heart High Sch. Har ... 176 E1
Sacred Heart Inf Sch. Luton .. 46 A3
Sacred Heart Jun Sch. St Alb . 127 B1
Sacred Heart RC Jun Mix Inf Sch. Ware 93 D1
Sacred Heart RC Prim Sch The. Bus 167 F6
Saddlers Cl. Bal SG7 .... 23 E8
Saddlers Cl. Bor WD6 .... 170 D3
Saddlers Ct. Pnr HA5 .... 176 A4
Saddlers Path. Bor WD6 .... 170 D4
Saddlers Pl. Royst SG8 ..... 7 C7
Saddlers Wlk. Kin L WD4 ... 139 A2
Sadleir Rd. St Alb AL1 ..... 127 E1
Sadlers Way. Hert SG14 ... 113 A6
Sadlier Rd. Stand SG11 .... 55 F8
Saffron Cl. Bri Wd AL2 .... 141 A1
Saffron Cl. Hod EN11 ..... 134 F7
Saffron Cl. Luton LU3 ..... 45 A5
Saffron Green Prim Sch. Bor . 170 E6
Saffron Hill. Letw SG6 .... 22 E6
Saffron La. Heml H HP1 ... 124 B4
Saffron Meadow. Stand SG11 55 E2
Saffron St. Royst SG8 .... 7 E5
Sainfoin End. Heml H HP2 . 124 F5
SS Alban & Stephen Jun Mix Sch. St Alb 128 A3
SS Alban & Stephen Sch. St Alb 127 F2
St Adrian's RC Prim Sch. St Alb 141 C8
St Agnells Ct. Heml H HP2 .. 125 A7
St Agnells La. Heml H HP2 .. 125 A8
St Alban's Cath. St Alb 127 D1
St Alban's Sch. St Alb 127 C3

St Albans Catholic Prim Sch. Harl 117 F2
St Albans City Hospl.
  Mid Herts Wing. St Alb 127 C5
St Albans City Hospl. St Alb .. 127 C5
St Albans City Sta. St Alb 127 F3
St Albans Dr. Stev SG1 ...... 36 E1
St Albans Girls' Sch. St Alb .. 127 C4
St Albans High Sch. St Alb ... 127 D4
St Albans Hill. Heml H HP3 .. 124 F1
St Albans La. Abb L WD5 .... 140 A5
St Albans Link. Stev SG1 .... 36 E1
St Albans Music Sch. St Alb .. 127 D6
St Albans Rd. Barn EN5 ..... 171 E7
St Albans Rd. Cod SG4 ...... 88 F7
St Albans Rd E. Hat AL10 ... 130 B6
St Albans Rd. Heml H HP2,HP3 124 E2
St Albans Rd. Pot B EN6 .... 158 C3
St Albans Rd. Red AL3 ...... 106 C3
St Albans Rd. Ridge AL2,WD6 157 F8
St Albans Rd. Sand AL4 ..... 108 B1
St Albans Rd. St Alb AL4 .... 128 A8
St Albans Rd W. Hat AL10 .. 129 D5
St Albans Rd. Watf WD1,WD2 167 B7
St Albans Rd. Watf WD2 .... 154 C5
St Albert the Great RC Prim Sch. Heml H 125 A2
St Alders Ct. Luton LU3 ..... 45 B3
St Andrew St. Hert SG14 ... 113 C6
St Andrew's Ave. Harp AL5 . 85 F1
St Andrew's CE Prim Sch. Hit . 35 A7
St Andrew's Cl. Cad LU1 .... 63 B1
St Andrew's House. Harl CM20 117 F2
St Andrew's Pl. Hit SG4 ..... 34 F6 2
St Andrew's Rd. Heml H HP3 138 D7
St Andrews C of E Jun Mix Inf Sch. Muc H 74 F2
St Andrews Dr. Stev SG1 .... 36 F2
St Andrews Jun Mix & Inf Sch. Sta Ab 115 D4
St Andrews Mews. Hert SG14 113 C6 1
St Andrews Rd. Sth Ox WD1 175 D7
St Andrews Terr. Sth Ox WD1 175 C5
St Andrews Wlk. Cad LU1 ... 63 C1
St Ann's Rd. Luton LU1 ..... 63 F7
St Anna Rd. Barn EN5 ...... 171 D4
St Anne's Cl. Ches EN7 ..... 148 A3
St Anne's Pk. Hod EN10 .... 135 A4
St Anne's Rd. Hit SG5 ...... 34 F8
St Anne's Rd. Lon C AL2 ... 142 D4
St Annes Cl. Sth Ox WD1 .. 175 C6
St Anthony's RC Prim Sch. Watf 166 E4
St Anthonys Ave. Heml H HP3 125 B1
St Audreys Cl. Hat AL10 .... 130 B2
St Audreys Gn. Wel G C AL7 110 F5
St Augusta Ct. St Alb AL3 .. 127 D5
St Augustine Ave. Luton LU3 45 C3
St Augustine Cl. Hit SG5 .... 34 F8 1
St Augustine's RC Jun Mix Inf Sch. Hod 135 B5
St Augustines Cl. Hod EN10 134 F3
St Augustines Dr. Hod EN10 134 F4
St Barnabas Ct. Har HA3 ... 176 C2
St Barnabas Ct. Heml H HP2 125 A3
St Bartholomew's Prim Sch. Wigg 100 D1
St Bernadette's RC Prim Sch. Lon C 142 D4
St Bernard's Cl. Luton LU3 .. 45 C3
St Bernard's Rd. St Alb AL3 . 127 E4
St Brelades Pl. St Alb AL4 .. 128 D7
St Catharine's Rd. Hod EN10 135 A4
St Catherine of Siena RC Jun Mix Inf Sch. Watf 154 D6
St Catherines Ave. Luton LU3 45 B3
St Catherines Ct. Bis St CM23 76 E7
St Christopher Sch. Letw ... 22 F3
St Clement Danes Sch. Chor . 164 D7
St Clement's C of E Jun Mix Sch. Ches 148 E4
St Columba's Coll. St Alb ... 127 C1
St Cross Ct. Hod EN11 ..... 135 A4
St Cross Rd. Hod 135 A4
St Cuthbert Mayne RC Jun Mix Sch. Heml H 124 B4
St Cuthberts Gdns. Pnr HA5 175 F3 1
St Cuthberts Rd. Hod EN11 . 115 C1
St David's Cl. Heml H HP2 .. 125 D2
St David's Dr. Hod EN10 ... 134 F4
St Davids Cl. Stev SG1 ..... 36 F2
St Dominics RC Jun Mix Inf Sch. Harp 107 B8
St Dunstan's Rd. Hun SG12 . 116 D8
St Edmund's Coll. Stand 73 B8
St Edmund's Way. Harl CM17 118 C4
St Edmunds. Berk HP4 ..... 122 C4
St Edward's Cath. Barn 171 B1
St Elizabeth's Sch & Home. Muc H 96 C6
St Elmo Ct. Hit SG4 .... 34 F5
St Ethelbert Ave. Luton LU3 45 C4
St Etheldreda's Dr. Hat AL10 130 C5
St Evroul Ct. Ware SG12 ... 93 D2 5
St Faiths Cl. Hit SG4 ...... 22 B1
St Francis Cl. Pot B EN6 ... 159 C5
St Francis Cl. Watf WD1 ... 167 B1
St Francis' Coll. Letw 22 E4
St Francis Sch. Bun 40 F6
St George's C of E Inf Sch. Enf . 162 D3
St George's Rd. Enf EN1 ... 161 F1
St George's Rd. Heml H HP3 138 D2
St George's Rd. Watf WD2 . 154 B2
St George's Sch. Harp 86 B2
St George's Way. Stev SG1 . 50 D5
St Georges Sq. Luton LU1 .. 63 E7
St Giles' Ave. Pot B EN6 ... 158 B7
St Giles C of E Jun Mix Inf Sch. Pot B 158 A7
St Giles Rd. Cod SG4 ..... 67 D2
St Helen's Cl. Whea AL4 .. 108 D8
St Helens C of E Prim Sch. Whea 108 D8
St Heliers Rd. St Alb AL4 .. 128 C4
St Hilda's Sch. Bus 168 B2
St Ignatius Coll Upper Sch. Enf 162 B2
St Ippolitts CE Sch. St Ipp . 35 B3
St Ives Cl. Luton LU2 ..... 46 E2
St Ives Cl. Welw AL6 ..... 89 F3
St James Ct. Harl 118 A4
St James Rd. Harp AL5 ... 86 B4

St James' Rd. Luton LU3 ...... 45 B3
St James Rd. Watf WD1 ...... 167 B4
St James Way. Bis St CM23 .. 76 B5
St James's Ct. Harp AL5 ..... 86 B3 1
St James's Rd. Gofs O EN7 .. 147 D3
St John Cl. Luton LU1 .... 63 B5
St John Fisher RC Jun Mix Sch. 128 C6
St John the Baptist C of E Sch. Gt Am 115 A5
St John's CE Prim Sch. Cre H 161 B2
St John's Cl. Pot B EN6 ..... 159 C6
St John's Cres. Sta M CM24 . 59 E7
St John's Ct. Harp AL5 ...... 107 C7
St John's Hert SG13 .... 113 D6 18
St John's La. Sta M CM24 ... 59 E7
St John's RC Jun Mix & Inf Sch. Bal 23 C7
St John's RC Jun Mix Inf Sch. Ric 165 B11
St John's Rd. Arl SG15 ..... 11 A4
St John's Rd. Harp AL5 ..... 107 C7
St John's Rd. Heml H HP1 .. 124 B1
St John's Rd. Hit SG4 ...... 34 F6
St John's Rd. Sta M CM24 .. 59 E7
St John's Rd. Watf WD1 .... 167 B4
St John's Sch. Hat 109 F5
St John's St (Jun Mix Inf).
  Wel G C 89 F2
St John's St. Hert SG13 .... 113 D6
St John's Terr. Enf EN2 .... 161 D2
St John's Well Ct. Berk HP4 122 B5
St John's Well La. Berk HP4 122 B5
St Johns Cl. Welw AL6 ..... 89 C6
St Johns Cl. Luton LU1 ..... 63 B5
St Johns Ct. St Alb AL1 .... 128 B5
St Johns. Stand SG11 ...... 55 E3
St Johns Wlk. Harl CM17 .. 118 C4
St Joseph's Cl. Luton LU3 .. 45 A4
St Joseph's Inf Sch. Luton . 45 A4
St Joseph's Jun Mix Inf Sch. Bis St 76 D1
St Joseph's RC Jun Mix & Inf Sch. Ches 162 E7
St Joseph's RC Jun Sch. Sth Ox 175 C7
St Joseph's RC Sch. Hert ... 113 A7
St Joseph's Rd. Ches EN8 .. 162 E6
St Joseph's Rd. Hertng 113 A4
St Julian's Rd. St Alb AL1 .. 127 D1
St Katharines Cl. Ick SG5 .. 21 D3
St Katherine's Way. Berk HP4 121 F7
St Laurence Dr. Hod EN10 . 148 F8
St Lawrence C of E Jun Sch. Wa Aby 163 F6
St Lawrence Cl. Abb L HP3 139 E1
St Lawrence Cl. Bov HP3 .. 137 A4
St Lawrence Way. Bri Wd AL2 140 F1
St Lawrences Ave. Luton LU3 45 C3
St Leonard's Rd. Hert SG14 113 D8
St Leonards Cl. Hert SG14 . 113 E8
St Leonards Cl. Watf WD2 . 167 E5
St Leonards Cres. Sand AL4 108 C1
St Leonards Rd. Lo Naz EN9 149 D6
St Luke's Ave. Enf EN2 .... 161 D1
St Luke's Cl. Luton LU4 .... 44 E2
St Luke's Sch. Red 106 A6
St Margaret Clitheroe RC Prim Sch. Stev 50 F2
St Margaret of Scotland Inf Sch. Luton 63 B5
St Margaret of Scotland Jun Sch. Luton 63 B5
St Margaret's Cl. Berk HP4 122 D3
St Margaret's Lower Sch. Bus 168 B1
St Margaret's Rd. Hod EN11 115 B2
St Margarets Sch. Bus 168 A2
St Margarets Ave. Luton LU3 45 B3
St Margarets Cl. Str LU3 ... 31 A6
St Margarets. Stev SG2 .... 50 F2
St Margarets Way. Heml H HP2 125 D3
St Margaretsbury House.
  Gt Am SG12 .... 115 B4
St Mark's Cl. Hit SG5 ..... 21 D1
St Marks Cl. Coln H AL4 .. 129 E8
St Martha's Convent Sch. Barn 171 E5
St Martin de Parres RC Jun Sch. Dun 44 A4
St Martin de Parres RC Jun Sch. Dun 44 A4
St Martin's Ave. Luton LU2 45 F2
St Martin's Rd. Kneb SG3 . 69 A5
St Martins Cl. Norwd 174 D5
St Martins Cl. Harp AL5 ... 86 C4
St Martins Cl. Sth Ox WD1 175 C6
St Mary's Ave. Mo Pk HA6 174 E5
St Mary's Ave. Nthch UB2 121 D6
St Mary's Ave. Stot SG5 .. 11 E5
St Mary's C of E Jun Mix Inf Sch. Wel G 144 B8
St Mary's C of E Prim Sch. Sta M 59 E7
St Mary's C of E Sch. Ric .. 173 D7
St Mary's Catholic Prim Sch. Royst 7 D7
St Mary's Catholic Sch. Bis St 76 E8
St Mary's Cl. Letw SG6 ... 22 F2
St Mary's Cl. Pirt SG5 .... 20 D4
St Mary's Cl. Red AL3 .... 106 A4
St Mary's Cl. Heml H HP2 124 D4 4
St Mary's Cl. Pot B EN6 .. 159 B7
St Mary's Cl. Welw AL6 .. 89 C5
St Mary's Ctyd. Ware SG12 93 D1 3
St Mary's Dr. Sta M CM24 59 F5
St Mary's High Sch. Ches . 148 B1
St Mary's Inf Sch. Bal ... 23 D8
St Mary's Jun Mix Inf Sch. Ast 51 E2
St Mary's Jun Mix Inf Sch. Welw 89 E6
St Mary's Jun Sch. Bal ... 23 E6
St Mary's (Kingshill) Jun Mix Inf Sch. Ware 93 D3
St Mary's La. Hertng SG14 112 F3
St Mary's Park Convent Sch. Royst 7 D6
St Mary's Rd. Ches EN8 .. 148 C2
St Mary's Rd. Heml H HP2 124 D4
St Mary's Rd. Luton LU1 . 63 F7
St Mary's Rd. Stand SG11 55 D2

St Mary's Rd. Watf WD1 167 B5
St Mary's Rise. Bre Gr SG4 47 D1
St Mary's Way. Bal SG7 23 E6
St Marys Cl. Ast SG2 51 E2
St Marys Rd. Welw AL6 89 C5
St Marys Wlk. St Alb AL4 128 B7
St Matthew's Jun Mix Inf Sch. Sth Ox 175 F8
St Matthews Cl. Luton LU2 63 F8
St Matthews Rd. Watf WD1 167 D3
St Meryl Jun Mix Inf Sch. Sth Ox 175 F7
St Michael's Cl. Harl CM20 117 E1
St Michael's Cres. Luton LU3 45 D3
St Alb 127 B3
St Michael's Mount. Hit SG4 35 A8
St Michael's Prim Sch. Bis St 76 F7
St Michael's Rd. Hod CM7 135 A3
St Michael's St. Watf 154 D7
St Michael's St. St Alb AL3 127 B3
St Michaels Ave. Heml H HP3 125 B1
St Michaels Cl. Harp AL5 107 D7
St Michaels Dr. Watf WD2 154 B6
St Michaels Rd. Hit SG4 35 B6
St Michaels View. Hat AL10 130 B7
St Michaels Way. Pot B EN6 145 B1
St Micheals Ct. Stev SG1 51 B6
St Mildreds Ave. Luton LU3 45 C3
St Monicas Ave. Luton LU3 45 B3
St Neots Cl. Bor WD6 157 A1
St Nicholas Ave. Harp AL5 86 A1
St Nicholas CE Jun Mix Inf Sch.
Letw 12 C1
St Nicholas Cl. Elst WD6 169 D3
St Nicholas Cl. Harp AL5 85 F3 2
St Nicholas House Sch. Heml H 139 B6
St Nicholas Mount. Heml H HP1 123 F3
St Nicholas Prim Sch. Elst 169 D3
St Ninian's Cl. Luton LU2 63 D7
St Olam's Cl. Luton LU3 45 B6
St Olives. Stot SG5 11 E6
St Paul's Jun Mix Inf Sch. Chipf 152 A4
St Paul's Rd. Heml H HP2 124 E4
St Paul's Rd. Luton LU1 63 F8
St Paul's Walden Jun Mix & Inf Sch.
Whit 66 D7
St Pauls (C of E) Sch. Abb L 153 C5
St Pauls Catholic Prim Sch.
Ham AL 148 B4
St Pauls Ct. Stev SG2 50 F1 1
St Pauls Inf Sch. Hod 135 B5
St Pauls Pl. St Alb AL1 128 A3
St Pauls Way. Wa Aby EN9 163 C6
St Pauls Way. Watf WD2 167 C7
St Peter's Ave. Arl SG15 11 A7
St Peter's C of E Prim Sch. Ric 165 B1
St Peter's Cl. Barn EN5 171 D4
St Peter's Cl. Bus WD2 168 D1
St Peter's Cl. Ric WD3 165 B1
St Peter's Cl. St Alb AL1 127 D4
St Peter's Cty Prim Sch. St Alb 127 E2
St Peter's Prim Sch. St Alb 127 E2
St Peter's Rd. St Alb AL1 127 E4
St Peter's St. St Alb AL1 127 D4
St Peters Cl. Hat AL10 130 A6
St Peters Rd. Luton LU1 63 B7
St Peters Way. Chor WD3 164 B5
St Philip Howard RC Prim Sch.
Hat 130 B5
St Raphaels Ct. St Alb AL1 127 E4
St Ronans Ct. Had W EN4 159 D1
St Rose's Inf Sch. Heml H 124 A1
St Saviour's Cres. Luton LU1 63 D6
St Stephen's Ave. St Alb AL3 141 B8
St Stephen's Cl. St Alb AL3 141 B8
St Stephen's Hill. St Alb AL1 127 C1
St Stephen's Hospl. Barn 171 D4
St Stephen's Rd. Enf EN3 162 D2
St Stephens Rd. Barn EN5 171 D4
St Teresa's Sch. Bor 170 B7
St Thomas' Dr. Pnr HA5 175 C8
St Thomas More Prim Sch. Berk 122 A4
St Thomas More Prim Sch. Letw 22 E2
St Thomas of Canterbury RC
Jun Mix Inf Sch. Stand 55 C3
St Thomas Pl. Whea AL4 108 D8
St Thomas's Rd. Luton LU2 46 A4
St Vincent de Paul Jun Mix Inf Sch.
Stev 51 A6
St Vincent Dr. St Alb AL1 128 A1
St Vincent's Way. Pot B EN6 159 C6
St Winifreds Ave. Luton LU3 45 C3
St Yon Ct. Coln H AL4 128 E3
Sale Dr. Bal SG7 13 A1
Salisbury Ave. 85 F1
Salisbury Ave. St Alb AL1 128 B4
Salisbury Cl. Bis St CM23 76 F5
Salisbury Cl. Pot B EN6 159 C7
Salisbury Cres. Ches EN8 162 D7
Salisbury Gdns. Wel G C AL7 110 C5
Salisbury House. St Alb AL3 127 C2
Salisbury Inf Sch. Hat 130 B7
Salisbury Rd. Bal SG7 12 F1
Salisbury Rd. Barn EN5 171 D6
Salisbury Rd. Enf EN3 162 F2
Salisbury Rd. Harp AL5 86 D3
Salisbury Rd. Hod EN11 135 C8
Salisbury Rd. Luton LU1 63 D6
Salisbury Rd. Stev SG1 37 A2
Salisbury Rd. Watf WD1 154 C1
Salisbury Rd. Wel G C AL7 111 A5
Salisbury Sq. Hat AL10 130 C6
Salisbury Sq. Hert SG14 113 D6 7
Sally Deards La. Cod AL6 68 D3
Salmon Cl. Wel G C AL7 90 A1
Salmons Cl. Ware SG12 93 D4
Saltdean Cl. Luton LU2 46 D4
Salter's Cl. Berk HP4 121 F6
Salters Gdns. Watf WD1 167 A8
Saltfield Cres. Luton LU4 44 C4
Salusbury La. El Of SG5 33 C2
Salvatarian RC Coll (Boys Gram).
Har 176 E1
Salwey Cres. Hod EN10 134 F3
Samian Gate. St Alb AL3 126 F1
Sampson Ave. Barn EN5 171 D4
Samuel Lucas Jun Mix Inf Sch. Hit 34 D7
Sancroft Rd. Har HA3 176 A1
Sanctuary Cl. Hare UB9 173 C4
Sandalls Spring. Heml H HP1 123 F5

Sandalwood Cl. Luton LU3 45 B7
Sanday Cl. Heml H HP3 125 D8
Sandbrook La. Wils HP23 79 C1
Sandell Cl. Luton LU2 45 F2
Sanderling Cl. Letw SG6 22 E8
Sanders Cl. Heml H HP3 138 F7
Sanders Cl. Lon C AL2 142 D4
Sanders Rd. Heml H HP3 139 A7
Sandfield Rd. St Alb AL1 128 A3
Sandgate Rd. Luton LU4 44 D2
Sandhurst Ct. Harp AL5 107 D6
Sandifield. Hat AL10 130 B2
Sandle Rd. Bis St CM23 77 A7
Sandmere Cl. Heml H HP2 125 A8
Sandon Cl. Tri HP23 99 F4
Sandon Jun Mix Inf Sch. San 15 C1
Sandon Rd. Ches EN8 148 C1
Sandover Cl. Hit SG4 35 B6
Sandown Rd. Stev SG1 37 C1
Sandown Rd. Watf WD2 154 C1
Sandpit Hill Cotts. Chol HP23 120 B3
Sandpit La. St Alb AL1,AL4 128 C5
Sandpit Rd. Wel G C AL7 110 E4
Sandridge Cl. Heml H HP2 105 A1
Sandridge Ct. St Alb AL4 128 D7
Sandridge Jun Mix Inf Sch. Sand 108 D1
Sandridge Rd. St Alb AL1,AL3 127 F5
Sandridgebury La. Sand AL3 108 A2
Sandridgebury La. St Alb AL3 127 E8
Sandringham Cres. St Alb AL4 128 C8
Sandringham Rd. Pot B EN6 145 B1
Sandringham Rd. Watf WD2 154 C2
Sandringham St. St Alb 128 B7
Sandringham Way. Ches EN8 162 D5
Sandy Cl. Stev SG14 113 B6
Sandy Gr. Hit SG4 34 F6
Sandy La. Bus WD2 168 C6
Sandy La. Mo Pk HA6 175 A5
Sandy Lodge Ct. Norwd HA6 174 E5
Sandy Lodge Golf Course. Mo Pk 174 E8
Sandy Lodge La. Mo Pk HA6 174 E8
Sandy Lodge Rd. Mo Pk HA6 174 E8
Sandy Lodge Rd. Mo Pk WD3 174 C8
Sandy Lodge Way. Norwd HA6 174 E4
Sandycroft Rd. L Chal HP6 150 C1
Sanfoin Rd. Dun LU4 44 A4
Sanfoine Cl. Hit SG4 35 C8
Santers La. Pot B EN6 158 E6
Santingfield N. Luton LU1 63 B6
Santingfield S. Luton LU1 63 B6
Sanville Gdns. Gt Am 115 C4
Sappers Cl. Saw CM21 97 F2
Saracen Est. Heml H 125 B5
Saracens Head. Heml H HP2 125 A4
Sark House. Enf EN3 162 D1
Sarratt Ave. Heml H HP2 125 A8
Sarratt Jun Mix Inf Sch. Sar 152 A3
Sarratt La. Ric WD3 165 C6
Sarratt La. Sar WD3 165 D8
Sarratt Rd. Sar WD3 165 C8
Sarum Pl. Heml H HP2 124 E7
Sarum Rd. Luton LU4 44 F4
Saturn Way. Heml H HP2 124 F6
Sauncey Ave. Harp AL5 86 B3
Sauncey Wood La. Whea AL5 86 A6
Sauncey Wood. Whea AL5 86 A6
Saunders Cl. Ches SG6 148 D4
Saunders Cl. Letw SG6 23 C7
Savoy Cl. Hare UB9 173 D1
Sawbridgeworth Rd. L Hal CM22 98 B7
Sawbridgeworth Rd. Sheer CM22 98 D3
Sawbridgeworth Sta. L Hal 98 A3
Sawells. Hod EN10 134 F2
Sawtry Cl. Luton LU3 45 A6
Sawtry Way. Bor WD6 157 A1
Sawyers La. Pot B EN6 158 D5
Sawyers Way. Heml H HP2 124 F3
Sax House. Letw SG6 11 E1
Saxon Ave. Stot SG5 11 F8
Saxon Cl. Harp AL5 86 C4
Saxon Cl. Letw SG6 11 F1
Saxon Ct. Bor WD6 169 E8
Saxon Rd. Luton LU3 45 C2
Saxon Rd. Welw AL6 89 B3
Saxon Rd. Whea AL4 108 D7
Saxon Way. Bal SG7 13 B1
Saxon Way. Wa Aby EN9 163 C6
Saxtead Cl. Luton LU2 46 D1
Sayer Way. Kneb SG3 68 F4
Sayers Gdns. Berk HP4 122 A6
Sayes Gdns. Saw CM21 97 F2
Sayesbury Ave. Saw CM21 97 E3
Sayesbury Rd. Saw CM21 97 E2
Saywell Rd. Luton LU2 46 B1
Scammel Way. Watf WD1 166 F3
Scarborough Ave. Stev SG1 50 B7
Scatterdells La. Chipf WD4 138 A2
Scholar's Hill. Wars SG12 95 A4
Scholars Ct. Col H AL4 143 C8
Scholars Wlk. Hat AL10 130 A2 4
School Cl. Stev SG2 51 B8
School Gdns. Pot En HP4 123 B6
School La. Ard SG2 38 D7
School La. Ast SG2 51 E2
School La. Bar SG8 9 A1
School La. Bri Wd AL2 155 A4
School La. Bus WD2 168 B4
School La. Ess AL9 131 F6
School La. Gt Of SG5 33 C3
School La. Harl CM20 117 E2
School La. Hat AL10 130 C6
School La. Luton LU4 44 D1
School La. Pres SG4 48 B1
School La. Tewin AL6 90 E2
School La. Wat St SG14 70 E3
School La. Welw AL6 89 B4
School La. Wes SG4 24 C1
School Mead. Abb L WD5 153 D4
School Rd. Pot B EN6 145 C1
School Row. Heml H HP1 123 F2
School Wlk. Letw SG6 23 B6
Schoolfields. Letw SG6 23 C5
Schubert Rd. Elst WD6 169 D3
Scot Gr. Pnr HA5 175 D3
Scotfield Ct. Luton LU2 46 D3 4
Scots Hill Cl. Cro Gr WD3 165 F3
Scots Hill. Cro Gr WD3 165 F3
Scotscraig. Radl WD7 156 A4
Scott Ave. Gt Am SG12 115 B4
Scott Cl. Royst SG8 2 D1

Scott Rd. Bis St CM23 76 E6
Scott Rd. Stev SG1 51 B6
Scott's Rd. Watf WD2 154 D8
Scotts Cl. Ware SG12 114 D8
Scotts View. Wel G C AL8 110 C1
Scottswood Cl. Bus WD2 167 E7
Scottswood Rd. Bus WD2 167 E7
Scriveners Cl. Heml H HP2 124 E3
Scrubbits Sq. Radl WD7 156 A4
Scrubbits Park Rd. Radl WD7 156 A4
Seabrook. Dun LU4 44 B3
Seabrook Rd. Abb L WD5 139 C4
Seacroft Gdns. Sth Ox WD1 175 D7
Seaford Cl. Luton LU2 46 C3
Seaforth Dr. Ches EN8 162 D5
Seaman Cl. Pk St AL2 141 D6
Searches La. Bri Wd WD5 140 C3
Seaton Rd. Heml H HP3 124 E1
Seaton Rd. Lon C AL2 142 D5
Seaton Rd. Luton LU4 44 F3
Sebright Rd. Heml H HP1 124 A1
Sebright Rd. Mark AL3 83 E5
Secker Cres. Har HA3 176 C2
Second Ave. Letw SG6 23 C6
Second Ave. Watf WD2 154 D4
Sedbury Cl. Luton LU3 45 A6
Sedge Gn. Lo Naz EN9 135 E3
Sedgwick Rd. Luton LU4 44 B7
Seebohm Cl. Hit SG5 21 C1
Seeleys. Harl CM17 118 C3
Sefton Ave. Har HA3 176 D2
Sefton Cl. St Alb AL1 127 F4
Selton Rd. Stev SG1 37 B1
Selbourne Rd. Luton LU4 45 A2
Selby Ave. St Alb AL3 127 D3
Selden Hill. Heml H HP2 124 D2
Sele Rd. Hert SG14 113 B6
Sele Sch The. Hert 112 F6
Selina Cl. Luton LU3 44 C7
Sellers Cl. Bor WD6 170 C8
Sells Rd. Ware SG12 93 F2
Sellwood Dr. Barn EN5 171 C4
Selsey Dr. Luton LU2 46 D3
Selwyn Ave. Hat AL10 129 E5
Selwyn Cres. Hat AL10 129 E5
Selwyn Dr. Hat AL10 129 E5
Sempill Rd. Heml H HP3 124 E1
Sentis Ct. Norwd HA6 174 F4
Sequoia Cl. Bus WD2 168 D1
Sequoia Pk. Pnr HA5 176 B4
Serby Ave. Royst SG8 7 D8
Sergehill La. Abb L WD5 140 A5
Service Rd The. Pot B EN6 159 A7
Seven Acres. Mo Pk HA6 175 A4
Sevenoaks Ct. Norwd HA6 174 C3
Severalls The. Luton LU2 46 B3
Severn Dr. Enf EN1 162 A1
Severn Way. Watf WD2 154 C5
Severnmead. Heml H HP2 124 E6
Severnvale. Lon C AL2 142 F4
Sewardstone Rd. Wa Aby EN1 163 D3
Sewardstone St. Wa Aby EN9 163 C5
Sewardstone Way. Wa Aby EN9 163 C3
Sewell Cl. Coln H AL4 128 E3
Sewell Harris Cl. Harl CM20 117 F1
Sewells. Wel G C AL8 89 E7
Seymour Ave. Luton LU1 63 F5
Seymour Cl. Pnr HA5 175 F2
Seymour Cres. Heml H HP2 124 E3
Seymour La. Map Cr WD3 172 A5
Seymour Mews. Saw CM21 118 E7
Seymour Rd. Luton LU1 63 F5
Seymour Rd. Nthch HP4 121 C6
Seymour Rd. St Alb AL3 127 C6
Shackledell. Stev SG2 50 F2
Shacklegate La. Watf SG4 66 E5
Shackleton Spring. Stev SG2 51 A3
Shackleton Way. Abb L WD5 139 C4
Shackleton Way. Wel G C AL7 111 D6
Shady Bush Cl. Bus WD2 168 C2
Shady La. Watf WD1 167 B7
Shaftenhoe End Rd. Bar SG8 9 A1
Shaftesbury Ct. Stev SG1 50 E4
Shaftesbury Ind Est. Watf 154 A1
Shaftesbury Quay. Hert SG14 113 D6 9
Shaftesbury Rd. Luton LU4 45 B1
Shaftesbury Rd. Watf WD1 167 C6
Shaftesbury Sch. Har 176 B2
Shaftesbury Way. Abb L WD4 139 C3
Shaftesbury Way. Royst SG8 7 B5
Shakespeare Ct. Hod EN11 115 B2
Shakespeare Rd. Dun LU4 44 B2
Shakespeare Rd. Harp AL5 86 B1
Shakespeare. Royst SG8 7 D8
Shakespeare St. Watf WD2 154 B1
Shalcross Dr. Ches EN8 148 F1
Shallcross Cres. Hat AL10 130 A2 6
Shangani Rd. Bis St CM23 76 F5
Shanklin Cl. Goffs O EN7 147 F2
Shanklin Cl. Luton LU3 45 A7
Shanklin Gdns. Sth Ox WD1 175 C6
Shantock Hall La. Bov HP3 136 E1
Shantock La. Bov HP3 136 E1
Sharmans Cl. Welw AL6 89 F4
Sharose Ct. Mark AL3 83 E5
Sharpcroft. Heml H HP2 124 D5 1
Sharpenhoe Rd. Str LU3 31 A5
Sharpes La. Heml H HP1 123 B1
Sharples Gn. Luton LU3 45 B8
Shaw Cl. Bus WD2 176 E8
Shaw Cl. Ches EN8 148 C3
Shaws The. Wel G C AL7 111 C5
Sheares Hoppit. Hun SG12 95 B2
Shearwater Cl. Stev SG2 51 B4
Sheepcot Dr. Watf WD2 154 C4
Sheepcot La. Watf WD2 154 B4
Sheepcote. Wel G C AL7 111 C5
Sheepcote La. Whea AL4 87 F1
Sheepcote Rd. Heml H HP2 124 F3
Sheepcote. Wel G C AL7 111 C5
Sheepcroft Hill. Stev SG2 51 B3
Sheephouse Rd. Heml H HP3 124 F1
Sheering CE Sch. Sheer 98 D1
Sheering Dr. Harl CM17 118 E4
Sheering Lower Rd.
Sheer CM21,CM17 118 F7
Sheering Mill La. Saw CM21 97 F2
Sheering Mill La. Sheer CM21 98 A1

Sheering Rd. Harl CM17 118 E4
Sheering Rd. Harl CM17 118 F5
Sheethanger La. Heml H HP3 138 A7
Shefton Rise. Norwd HA6 175 A3
Sheldon Cl. Ham St EN7 147 E5
Shelford Rd. Barn EN5 171 C3
Shelley Cl. Hit SG4 35 C7
Shelley Cl. Mo Pk HA6 174 F5
Shelley Ct. Royst SG8 2 B1 8
Shelley Ct. Harp AL5 86 B1
Shelley Ct. Wa Aby EN9 163 F6
Shelley Rd. Dun LU4 44 B2
Shelton Way. Luton LU2 46 A3
Shendish Edge. Heml H HP3 138 F6
Shenley Ct. Heml H HP2 125 B8
Shenley Fst Sch. Shen 156 F5
Shenley Hill. Radl WD7 156 B4
Shenley Hospl. Shen 156 E6
Shenley La. Lon C AL2 142 C4
Shenley Rd. Bor WD6 170 B6
Shenley Rd. Heml H HP2 105 B1
Shenley Rd. Radl WD7 156 D6
Shenleybury Cotts. Shen WD7 156 E8
Shenleybury. Shen WD7,AL2 156 E8
Shenlybury Villas. Shen AL2 156 E8
Shenstone Hill. Berk HP4 122 E5
Shenval House. Harl 118 A4
Sheperd Jun Mix Inf Sch. Ric 165 A1
Shephall Gn. Stev SG2 51 B2
Shephall View. Stev SG2 51 C3
Shephall Way. Stev SG2 51 C3
Shepherd Cl. Royst SG8 7 B5
Shepherd Inf Sch. Ric 165 A1
Shepherd's La. Chor WD3 164 E2
Shepherd's Row. Red AL3 106 B5
Shepherds Ct. Hert SG14 92 C1
Shepherds Gn. Heml H HP1 123 E2
Shepherds La. Stev SG1 50 A6
Shepherds Mead. Hit SG5 21 C1
Shepherds Rd. Watf WD1 166 F5
Shepherds Way. Bro Pk AL9 145 D4
Shepherds Way. Harp AL5 85 D4
Shepherds Way. Ric WD3 165 D6
Shepherds Wlk. Bus WD2 176 D8
Shepley Mews. Enf EN1 163 A2
Sheppard Ct. Enf EN1 162 B1
Sheppards Cl. St Alb AL3 127 C8
Shepperton Cl. Bor WD6 170 D8
Sheppey's La. Abb L WD5 139 C4
Sheraton Cl. Bor WD6 169 F4
Sheraton House. Chor WD3 164 E4
Sherborne Ave. Luton LU2 45 D6
Sherborne Way. Cro Gr WD3 166 B5
Sherbourne Cl. Heml H HP2 124 E2
Sherd Cl. Luton LU3 44 A7
Sheredes Cty Prim Sch. Hod 134 F4
Sheredes Dr. Hod EN11 134 F4
Sheredes Sch. Hod 134 F5
Sherfield Ave. Ric WD3 173 E8
Sheridan Cl. Heml H HP1 145 D4
Sheridan Cl. Heml H HP1 124 D4
Sheridan Rd. Luton LU3 45 C2
Sheridan Rd. Watf WD1 167 D2
Sheriff Way. Watf WD2 154 A4
Sheringham Ave. Stev SG1 36 B1
Sheringham Cl. Luton LU2 45 C7
Sherington Ave. Pnr HA5 176 A3
Sherland Ct. Radl WD7 156 A4
Shernbroke Rd. Wa Aby EN9 163 F5
Sherrardpark Rd. Wel G C AL8 110 D7
Sherrardswood Sch. Wel G C 110 D8
Sherrardswood. Welw 89 F2
Sherwood Ave. Pot B EN6 158 E7
Sherwood Ave. St Alb AL4 128 B6
Sherwood House. Abb L HA2 153 F8
Sherwood. Letw SG6 22 E8
Sherwood Pl. Heml H HP2 124 F7 1
Sherwood Rd. Luton LU4 45 A2
Sherwoods Rd. Watf WD1 167 F8
Sherwoods Rise. Harp AL5 107 D8
Shetland Cl. Bor WD6 170 D8
Shillington Rd. Pirt SG5 20 B5
Shillitoe Ave. Pot B EN6 158 C4
Shingle Cl. Luton LU3 45 A8
Shire Cl. Luton LU3 148 F5
Shire La. C St P WD3 172 C4
Shire La. Chor WD3 164 C4
Shire La. Map Cr WD3 172 B5
Shire La. Tri HP23 120 B4
Shiremeade. Bor WD6 169 F4
Shires The. Luton LU2 45 D1 5
Shires The. Royst SG8 7 E6
Shirley Cl. Ches EN8 148 C2
Shirley Cl. Hod EN10 148 F8
Shirley Cl. Stev SG2 51 B4
Shirley Ct. Abb L WD5 153 F7
Shirley Rd. Luton LU1 63 C8
Shirley Rd. St Alb AL1 127 C6
Shooters Dr. Lo Naz EN9 135 E1
Shootersway. Berk HP4 121 E4
Shootersway La. Berk HP4 121 C4
Shootersway. Nthch HP23 121 C5
Shootersway Pk. Berk HP4 121 F3
Shoplands. Wel G C AL8 89 E8
Shoreham Cl. Stev SG1 50 A8
Short La. Bal SG7 23 E6
Short La. Bri Wd AL2 140 E2
Shortcroft. Bis St CM23 77 F7
Shortlands Gn. Wel G C AL7 110 F5
Shortlands Pl. Bis St CM23 76 F8
Shortmead Dr. Ches EN8 162 E8
Shothanger Way. Heml H HP3 137 E2
Shott La. Letw SG6 23 A5
Shott Lower. Ham St EN7 147 F8
Shottfield Cl. Sand AL4 108 D2
Shrub Hill Rd. Heml H HP1 123 F2
Shrubbery Gr. Royst SG8 7 D4
Shrubbery The. Heml H HP1 123 E2
Shrublands Ave. Berk HP4 122 A4
Shrublands. Bro Pk AL9 145 D5
Shrublands Rd. Berk HP4 122 A5
Shrublands The. Pot B EN6 158 E6
Shugars Gn. Tri HP23 100 B6
Sibley Ave. Harp AL5 107 D8
Sibthorpe Rd. Wel G AL9 144 D7
Siccut Rd. L Wym SG4 35 A8
Sicklefield Cl. Ham St EN7 147 F5
Siddons Rd. Stev SG2 51 C6
Sidford Cl. Heml H HP1 123 F3

Sidings The. Hat AL10 129 E4
Sidings The. Heml H HP2 124 D3
Sidmouth Cl. Sth Ox WD1 175 B8
Sidney Terr. Bis St CM23 76 F6
Silam Rd. Stev SG1 50 E5
Silecroft Rd. Luton LU2 64 B8
Silk Mill Ct. Watf WD1 167 B2
Silk Mill Rd. Watf WD1 167 B2
Silk Mill Way. Tri HP23 100 A3
Silkin Ct. Stev SG2 51 D3
Silver Cl. Har HA3 176 D3
Silver Dell. Watf WD2 153 F4
Silver Hill. Shen WD6 157 B3
Silver St. Ans SG9 29 A5
Silver St. Ashw SG7 4 D1
Silver St. Gofs O EN7 147 D1
Silver St. Gu M SG8 1 F4
Silver St. Luton LU1 63 E7
Silver St. Sta M CM24 59 D6
Silver St. Wa Aby EN9 163 C6
Silver Trees. Bri Wd AL2 140 F1
Silverbirch Ave. Stot SG5 11 F8
Silverdale Rd. Watf WD2 167 E4
Silverfield. Hod EN10 134 F1
Silverthorn Dr. Heml H HP3 139 B7
Silverwood Cl. Norwd HA6 174 C2
Simmonds Rise. Heml H HP3 138 D1
Simon Balle Sch. Hert 113 E5
Simon Dean. Bov HP3 137 A4
Simpkins Ct. Bal SG7 23 F8
Simpsons Ct. Bal SG7 23 F8
Sinderby Cl. Bor WD6 169 E8
Sinfield Cl. Stev SG1 51 A5
Singlets La. Fla AL3 84 C2
Sir Frederic Osborn Sch The.
Wel G C 111 B7
Sir Herbert Janes Village The.
Luton LU4 44 D4
Sir James Altham Pool. Sth Ox 175 E5
Sir John Lawes Sch. Harp 86 B3
Sir John Newsom Sch The.
Wel G C 110 E3
Sir Peter's Way. Whip LU6 81 E6
Sirita Cl. Har HA3 176 D1
Sirus Rd. Mo Pk HA6 175 A5
Sish Cl. Stev SG1 50 D6
Sish La. Stev SG1 50 D6
Siskin Cl. Bor WD6 170 A5
Siskin Cl. Watf WD25 167 E5
Sisson Cl. Stev SG2 51 C2
Sitwell Gr. Stan HA7 176 F5
Six Acres. Heml H HP3 139 A8
Six Hills Way. Stev SG1,SG2 50 C4
Sixth Ave. Letw SG6 23 C6
Sixth Ave. Watf WD2 154 D4
Skegness Rd. Stev SG1 50 A8
Skegsbury La. Kim SG4 65 F1
Skelton Cl. Luton LU3 31 B1
Skidmore Way. Ric WD3 165 E1
Skimpans Cl. Wel G AL9 144 D7
Skimpot Rd. Dun LU5 44 A1
Skipton Cl. Stev SG2 68 F8
Skua Cl. Dun LU4 44 A5
Skylark Cnr. Stev SG2 51 D3
Skys Wood Rd. St Alb AL4 128 B7
Skyswood Prim Sch (Jun Mix & Inf).
St Alb 128 C6
Slade Cl. Radl WD7 156 A4
Slaughter Cotts. Ric WD3 165 E2
Sleaford Gn. Sth Ox WD1 175 D7
Sleapcross Gdns. Coln H AL4 129 C2
Sleaps Hyde. Stev SG2 51 C1
Sleapshyde La. Coln H AL4 129 C2
Sleddale. Heml H HP2 124 E6
Sleets End. Heml H HP1 124 B5
Slimmons Dr. St Alb AL4 128 A7
Slip End Lower Sch. Cad 63 B1
Slip La. Cod SG3 68 C4
Slipe La. Ches EN10 148 F7
Slipe The. Ched LU7 80 A7
Sloan Ct. Stev SG1 50 F6
Sloansway. Wel G C AL7 90 A1
Slype The. Whea AL4 87 B5
Small Acre. Heml H HP1 123 F3
Smallcroft. Wel G C AL7 111 B7
Smallford La. Coln H AL4 129 B2
Smallwood Cl. Whea AL4 108 E7
Smarts Gn. Ham St EN7 147 F5
Smeaton Cl. Wa Aby EN9 163 E4
Smith St. Watf WD1 167 C5
Smithfield. Heml H HP2 124 D5
Smiths La. Ham St EN7 147 D5
Smiths Lane Mall. Luton LU1 63 E7
Smiths Sq. Luton LU1 63 E7
Smith's End La. Bar SG8 17 F8
Smithy The. L Had SG11 57 B2
Smug Oak Bsns Cntr. Bri Wd 141 B1
Smug Oak La. Bri Wd AL2 141 D1
Snailswell La. Ick SG5 21 E5
Snatchup. Red AL3 106 A5
Snells Mead. Bun SG9 40 F7
Snipe The. Wes SG4 24 B1
Snowford Cl. Luton LU3 45 A7
Snowley Par. Bis St CM23 59 B8
Soham Rd. Enf EN3 162 F2
Solar Ct. Watf WD1 166 F4
Solesbridge Cl. Chor WD3 164 F6
Solesbridge La. Chor WD3 164 F6
Solesbridge La. Sar WD3 165 B7
Sollershott E. Letw SG6 22 F4
Sollershott Hall. Letw SG6 22 F4
Sollershott W. Letw SG6 22 E4
Solomon's Hill. Ric WD3 165 D2
Solway. Heml H HP2 124 E6
Solway Rd N. Luton LU3 45 A4
Solway Rd S. Luton LU3 45 A4
Somerby Cl. Hod EN10 135 A2
Someries Inf Sch. Luton 46 C3
Someries Jun Sch. Luton 46 C3
Someries Rd. Harp AL5 86 C4
Somersby Cl. Luton LU1 63 E6
Somerset Ave. Luton LU2 46 A1

Somerset Rd. Enf EN3 163   A1
Somersham. Wel G C AL7 111   D6
Sonia Cl. Watf WD1 167   C2
Soothouse Spring. St Alb AL3 127   F7
Sopers Rd. Cuf EN6 146   F2
Sopwell Cl. Luton LU3 45   B8
Sorrel Cl. St Alb AL1 127   D2
Sorrel Cl. Royst SG8 7   F5
Sorrel Garth. Hit SG4 35   A6
Sotheron Rd. Watf WD1 167   C6
Souberie Ave. Letw SG6 22   F5
Souldern St. Watf WD1 167   B4
South App. Mo Pk HA6 174   D7
South Bank Rd. Nthch HP4 121   F6
South Block. Sheer CM21 97   F2
South Cl. Bal SG7 23   F7
South Cl. Barn EN5 171   F6
South Cl. Chis AL2 141   B6
South Cl. Pnr HA5 175   D2
South Cl. Royst SG8 7   B7
South Cottage Dr. Chor WD3 164   F4
South Cr. Cuf EN6 146   E1
South Dr. St Alb AL4 128   E4
South Drift Way. Luton LU1 63   B5
South Gardens Gdns. Chor WD3 ... 164   F4
South Hill. Hit SG4 35   A6
South Hill Jun Mix Inf Sch.
   Heml H HP1 124   C2
South Hill Rd. Heml H HP1 124   C3
South Ley Ct. Wel G C AL7 110   E3
South Ley. Wel G C AL7 110   E3
South Par. Wa Aby EN9 163   C6
South Park Ave. Chor WD3 164   F4
South Park Gdns. Berk HP4 122   B5
South Pl. Harl CM20 118   A4
South Pl. Hit SG5 34   D8
South Rd. Bal SG7 24   A7
South Rd. Bis St CM23 77   A5
South Rd. Chor WD3 164   C4
South Rd. Harl CM20 118   A4
South Rd. Luton LU1 63   E6
South Rd. Stand SG11 55   D2
South Riding. Bri Wd AL2 141   A1
South St. Bis St CM23 76   F6
South St. Hert SG14 113   D6
South St. Sta M SG12 115   C4
South Street Commercial Ctr.
   Bis St CM23 76   F6
South View. Letw SG6 22   F5
South View Rd. Pnr HA5 175   B4
South Way. Abb L WD5 153   G6
South Way. Wa Aby EN9 163   C3
South Weald Dr. Wa Aby EN9 163   D6
Southacre Way. Pnr HA5 175   C2
Southall Cl. Ware SG12 93   D2
Southbrook Dr. Ches EN8 148   D3
Southbrook. Saw CM21 97   E1
Southdown Ct. Hat AL10 130   A2
Southdown House. Harp AL5 107   C7
Southdown Ind Est. Harp 107   C8
Southdown Rd. Harp AL5 107   B8
Southdown Rd. Hat AL10 130   A2
Southend Cl. Stev SG1 50   D7
Southern Ave. Henlw SG16 10   C3
Southern Terr. Hod EN11 115   B1
Southern Way. Letw SG6 22   E8
Southern Way. Stu LU6 82   C4
Southernwood Cl. Heml H HP2 125   A4
Southfield Ave. Watf WD2 154   C1
Southfield. Barn EN5 171   D3
Southfield. Brag SG11 55   F7
Southfield Rd. Ches EN8 162   E7
Southfield Rd. Hod EN11 135   A7
Southfield Way. St Alb AL4 128   D6
Southfield. Wel G C AL7 110   D4
Southfields. Letw SG6 11   F1
Southfields. Stand SG11 55   E2
Southgate House. Ches EN8 148   D1
Southgate Rd. Pot B EN6 159   C6
Southgate. Stev SG1 50   D4
Southmead Cres. Ches EN8 148   F1
Southmill Rd. Bis St CM23 77   A5
Southmill Trad Ctr. Bis St 77   A6
Southsea Ave. Watf WD1 167   A5
Southsea Rd. Stev SG1 50   B8
Southside. Wyd SG9 28   A3
Southview Cl. Ham St EN7 147   E5
Southview Rd. Harp AL5 86   D3
Southwark St. Stev SG1 37   B2
Southwold Rd. Watf WD2 154   C2
Sovereign Ct. Watf WD1 167   A5
Sovereign Gate. Watf WD1 166   F5
Sowerby Ave. Luton LU2 46   C3
Sparhawke. Letw SG6 12   A1
Sparrow Cl. Dun LU4 44   A4
Sparrows Herne. Bus WD2 168   C2
Sparrows Way. Bus WD2 168   C1
Sparrowswick Ride. St Alb AL3 ... 127   C8
Spayne Cl. Luton LU3 45   B8
Spear Cl. Luton LU3 44   E6
Speedwell Cl. Luton LU3 45   A8
Speke Cl. Stev SG2 51   D5
Spellbrook Jun Mix Inf Sch. Saw ... 97   F7
Spellbrook La E. Saw CM22 97   F8
Spellbrook La W. Saw CM23 97   E7
Spellbrooke. Hit SG5 34   D8
Spencer Ave. Ham St EN7 147   E5
Spencer Cl. Sta M CM24 59   E6
Spencer Gate. St Alb AL1 127   E6
Spencer Jun Sch. St Alb 127   E6
Spencer Mews. St Alb AL1 127   E4
Spencer Rd. Har HA3 176   E1
Spencer Rd. Luton LU3 45   C2
Spencer St. Hert SG13 113   E7
Spencer St. St Alb AL3 127   D3
Spencer Way. Heml H HP1 124   A6
Spencer Wlk. Ric WD3 165   C4
Spenser Cl. Royst SG8 2   D1
Spenser Rd. Harp AL5 86   C1
Sperberry Hill. St Ipp SG4 35   B2
Sphere Ind Est The. St Alb 127   B6
Spicer St. St Alb AL3 127   C3
Spicersfield. Ham St EN7 148   A4
Spindle Berry Cl. Welw AL6 90   A7

Spinney Ct. Saw CM21 97   E2
Spinney La. Welw AL6 68   E3
Spinney La. Luton LU3 44   D7
Spinney St. Hert SG13 114   A8
Spinney The. Bal SG7 23   E7
Spinney The. Berk HP4 121   F3
Spinney The. Harp AL5 85   E3
Spinney The. Hert SG13 113   F6
Spinney The. Hod EN10 134   F4
Spinney The. Pot B EN6 159   D8
Spinney The. Sta M CM24 59   E6
Spinney The. Stev SG2 51   D7
Spinney The. Watf WD1 167   A8
Spinney The. Wel G C AL7 110   E5
Spinneys Dr. St Alb AL3 127   B1
Spires The. Barn EN5 171   E6
Spittlesea Rd. Luton LU2 64   C6
Spooners Dr. Chis AL2 141   C4
Spratts La. Ken Co LU6 82   F8
Spreckley Cl. Henlw SG16 10   B5
Spring Cl. Barn EN5 171   D4
Spring Cl. Bor WD6 170   A8
Spring Cl. Hare UB9 173   D2
Spring Cl. Lat HP5 150   D3
Spring Cotts. Ches EN10 148   E7
Spring Court Rd. Enf EN2 161   A1
Spring Crofts. Bus WD2 168   A4
Spring Dr. Stev SG2 69   B8
Spring Field Rd. Berk HP4 122   A6
Spring Gdns. Watf WD2 154   C3
Spring Glen. Hat AL10 129   F4
Spring Hills. Harl CM20 117   B1
Spring La. Cotrd SG9 39   C5
Spring La. Heml H HP1 124   A4
Spring Rd. Harp AL5 85   A4
Spring Pl. Luton LU1 63   D6
Spring Way. Heml H HP2 125   C5
Spring Wlk. Hod EN10 134   C2
Springfield. Bus WD2 168   D1
Springfield Cl. Cro Gr WD3 166   B4
Springfield Cl. Nort EN6 159   E8
Springfield Cres. Whea AL5 86   B5
Springfield Ct. Bis St CM23 76   E8
Springfield Ct. Ric WD3 165   B1
Springfield Rd. Ches EN8 162   E7
Springfield Rd. Coln H AL4 129   B3
Springfield Rd. Heml H HP2 124   F4
Springfield Rd. Luton LU3 45   C6
Springfield Rd. St Alb AL1 128   A2
Springfield Rd. Watf WD2 154   B6
Springfields. Hod EN10 148   A6
Springfields. Wa Aby EN9 163   E5
Springfields. Wel G C AL8 110   B4
Springhall Ct. Saw CM21 97   E2
Springhall La. Saw CM21 97   E1
Springhall Rd. Saw CM21 97   E2
Springhead. Ashw SG7 4   D4
Springle La. Hod EN11 114   F2
Springmead Jun & Mix Inf Sch.
   Wel G C AL7 111   C7
Springs The. Ches EN10 148   E6
Springs The. Hert SG13 113   F7
Springshott. Letw SG6 22   E5
Springwell Ave. Ric WD3 173   A8
Springwell La. Hare WD3 173   A6
Springwood Cl. Hare UB9 173   D2
Springwood. Ham St EN7 148   A5
Springwood Wlk. St Alb AL4 128   D6
Spruce Way. Chis AL2 141   B4
Spur Cl. Abb L WD5 153   D6
Spur The. Ches EN8 148   D3
Spur Rd. Stev SG1 50   E4
Spurcroft. Luton LU3 31   C1
Spurrs Cl. Hit SG4 35   B7
Square The. Brag SG11 55   F7
Square The. Buck SG9 27   D5
Square The. Heml H HP1 124   C3
Square The. Muc H SG10 74   F3
Square The. Red AL3 105   F6
Square The. Saw CM21 97   E2
Square The. Watf WD2 154   B2
Squires Cl. Bis St CM23 76   C8
Squires Ride. Ful HP4 104   F1
Squirrel Chase. Heml H HP1 123   E4
Squirrels Cl. Bis St CM23 76   F8
Squirrels The. Bus WD2 168   D3
Squirrels The. Hert SG13 114   B6
Squirrels The. Wel G C AL7 111   C5
Stable Ct. St Alb AL1 127   E5
Stacey Ct. Bis St CM23 76   F6
Stackfield. Harl CM20 118   A3
Stacklands. Wel G C AL8 110   B4
Staddles. L Hal CM22 98   B8
Stafford Cl. Ches EN8 148   B2
Stafford Dr. Hod EN10 135   A3
Stafford Rd. Har HA3 176   C3
Staffords. Harl CM17 118   C4
Stag Green Ave. Hat AL9 130   C7
Stag La. Berk HP4 122   B5
Stag La. Chor WD3 164   C3
Stagg Hill. Had W EN4 159   E3
Stainer Rd. Bor WD6 156   D1
Stainer Rd. Radl WD6 169   D8
Stains Cl. Ches EN8 148   F3
Stake Piece Rd. Royst SG8 7   C5
Stamford Ave. Royst SG8 7   D7
Stamford Cl. Har HA3 176   E3
Stamford Cl. Pot B EN6 159   D7
Stamford Ct. Royst SG8 7   D7
Stamford Rd. Watf WD1 167   B7
Stamford Yd. Royst SG8 7   C6
Stanborough Ave. Bor WD6 157   B1
Stanborough Cl. Wel G C AL8 110   C5
Stanborough Gn. Wel G C AL8 110   C4
Stanborough La. Wel G C AL8 110   C4
Stanborough Prim Sch. Watf 154   C4
Stanborough Rd. Wel G C AL8 110   C4
Stanborough Sch. Wel G C 110   B4
Stanborough Sec Sch. Watf 154   B4
Standard Ave. Enf EN3 162   E2
Standhill Ave. Luton LU2 63   E6
Standhill Cl. Luton LU2 63   E6
Standhill Rd. Hit SG4 34   F6
Standon Ct. Stand SG11 55   F1

Standon Hill. Stand SG11 55   D2
Standon Rd. Brag SG11 56   E3
Standring Rise. Heml H HP3 138   D8
Stane Field. Letw SG6 23   B3
Stane St. Bal SG7 13   A1
Stanelow Cres. Stand SG11 55   D2
Stanford Rd. Luton LU2 46   A1
Stangate Cres. Edg WD6 170   E4
Stanhope Ave. Har HA3 176   D2
Stanhope Rd. Barn EN5 171   D3
Stanhope Rd. Ches EN8 162   E6
Stanhope Rd. St Alb AL1 127   F3
Stanier Rise. Berk HP4 121   F7
Stanley Ave. Chis AL2 141   A6
Stanley Dr. Hat AL10 130   B3
Stanley Gdns. Bor WD6 169   E8
Stanley Gdns. Tri HP23 99   F3
Stanley Rd. Hert SG13 113   E5
Stanley Rd. Norwd HA6 175   A2
Stanley Rd. Stev SG2 51   B7
Stanley Rd. Str LU3 31   A5
Stanley Rd. Watf WD1 167   C5
Stanley St. Luton LU1 63   D6
Stanmore Cres. Luton LU3 44   F4
Stanmore Rd. Stev SG1 50   D7
Stanmore Rd. Watf WD2 167   B8
Stanmount Rd. Chis AL2 141   A6
Stannington Path. Bor WD6 170   A8
Stansted Dr. Hod EN11 135   B8
Stansted Rd. Hert SG13 114   A6
Stansted Rd. Hert H SG13 114   D5
Stansted Rd. Hod EN11 115   B1
Stansted Hill. Muc H SG10 75   A1
Stansted Mountfitchet Sta. Sta M ... 59   E6
Stanton Cl. St Alb AL4 128   D7
Stanton Rd. Dun LU4 44   C1
Staplefield Cl. Pnr HA5 175   E2
Staplefield Rd. Luton LU2 46   C4
Stapleton Cl. Pot B EN6 159   D8
Stapleton Rd. Bor WD6 157   A2
Stapley Rd. St Alb AL3 127   D4
Staplyton Rd. Barn EN5 171   E6
Star Holme Ct. Ware SG12 93   E1
Star St. Ware SG12 93   E1
Starling La. Cuf EN6 146   F3
Startpoint. Luton LU1 63   C7
Statham Ct. Luton LU3 31   B1
Station App. Ches EN8 162   E5
Station App. Chor WD3 164   D5
Station App. Harp AL5 86   B1
Station App. Hit SG4 35   A8
Station App. Kneb SG3 68   F5
Station App. Norwd HA6 174   E3
Station App. Radl WD7 156   A4
Station App. Sth Ox WD1 175   D7
Station Cl. Bro Pk AL9 144   E5
Station Cl. Pot B EN6 158   F8
Station Footpath. Abb L WD4 139   B1
Station Mews. Pot B EN6 159   A8
Station Par. Letw SG6 22   F6
Station Pl. Letw SG6 22   F6
Station Rd. Abb L WD4 139   B1
Station Rd. Ald HP23 101   B5
Station Rd. Arl SG15 11   A4
Station Rd. Ashw SG7 5   B3
Station Rd. Bal SG7 12   F1
Station Rd. Berk HP4 122   D4
Station Rd. Bis St CM23 77   A7
Station Rd. Bor WD6 170   A5
Station Rd. Brag SG11 55   D3
Station Rd. Bri Wd AL2 155   A8
Station Rd. Bro Pk AL9 144   D6
Station Rd. Bun SG9 40   E7
Station Rd. Ched LU7 79   F8
Station Rd. Ches EN8 163   A5
Station Rd. Coln H AL4 129   B3
Station Rd. Cuf EN6 146   F2
Station Rd. Gt Am SG12 115   C4
Station Rd. Harl CM17 118   C4
Station Rd. Harp AL5 86   C2
Station Rd. Heml H HP1 124   C1
Station Rd. Hertng SG14 112   B3
Station Rd. Hod EN10 135   A3
Station Rd. Kneb SG3 68   F5
Station Rd. L Ston SG16 10   A4
Station Rd. Letw SG6 22   F6
Station Rd. Lon M HP23 79   B4
Station Rd. Luton LU1 63   E8
Station Rd. Luton LU4 44   E5
Station Rd. Muc H SG10 74   E1
Station Rd. Odsey SG7 5   B3
Station Rd. Odsey SG7 5   C1
Station Rd. Pit LU7 80   E5
Station Rd. Radl WD7 156   A4
Station Rd. Ric WD3 165   D2
Station Rd. Saw CM21 97   F3
Station Rd. Sta M CM24 59   E6
Station Rd. Stand SG11 55   E2
Station Rd. Ste Mo SG8 5   C5
Station Rd. Tri HP23 100   D4
Station Rd. Ware SG12 93   E1
Station Rd. Wat St SG14 70   D3
Station Rd. Watf WD1 167   B7
Station Rd. Wel G AL9 144   D6
Station Rd. Welw AL6 89   E3
Station Rd. Whea AL4 87   D1
Station Terr. Hit SG4 35   A8
Station Terr. Pk St AL2 141   D5
Station Way. Letw SG6 22   E6
Staveley Rd. Dun LU4 44   C1
Steeplands. Bus WD2 168   B2
Steeple View. Bis St CM23 76   F8
Stephall Green Inf Sch. Stev 51   B2
Stephall Manor Sch. Stev 51   A1
Stephens Cl. Luton LU2 46   A3
Stephens Way. Red AL3 105   F5
Stephenson Cl. Royst SG8 7   B7
Stephenson Way. Bus WD2 167   D7
Stephenson Way. Watf WD2 167   B8
Stepnells. Mars HP23 80   A5
Sterling Ave. Ches EN8 162   D5
Sterling Rd. Enf EN2 161   D1
Stevenage Cres. Bor WD6 169   E7
Stevenage Rd. Hit SG4 34   F5
Stevenage Rd. Kneb SG3 68   F7

Stevenage Rd. L Wym SG4 35   E2
Stevenage Rd. L Wym SG4 35   E3
Stevenage Rd. St Ipp SG4 35   C2
Stevenage Rd. Walk SG2 51   E8
Stevenage Rise. Heml H HP2 124   F7
Stevenage Sta. Stev 50   C5
Stevens Gn. Bus WD2 168   C1
Steward Cl. Ches EN8 148   E1
Stewart Cl. Abb L WD5 154   A7
Stewart Rd. Harp AL5 86   B2
Stewarts The. Bis St CM23 76   E6
Stirling Cl. Stev SG2 69   D7
Stirling Cnr. Bor EN5 170   D3
Stirling House. Bor WD6 170   C5
Stirling Way. Bor WD6 170   D4
Stirling Way. Wel G C AL7 111   A6
Stobarts Cl. Kneb SG3 68   F6
Stock Bank. Bark SG8 8   D7
Stockbreach Cl. Hat AL10 130   A6
Stockbreach Rd. Hat AL10 130   A6
Stockens Dell. Kneb SG3 68   F4
Stockens Gn. Kneb SG3 68   F4
Stockers Farm Rd. Ric WD3 173   D8
Stockfield Ave. Hod EN11 135   B8
Stockholm Way. Luton LU3 44   E8
Stocking Hill. Cotrd SG9 39   B8
Stocking La. Nut SG8 18   C1
Stockings La. L Berk SG13 132   D6
Stockingstone Rd. Luton LU2 45   D2
Stockport Rd. Chor WD3 164   C2
Stocks Meadow. Heml H HP2 125   A4
Stocks Rd. Ald HP23 101   D7
Stockwell Cl. Ches EN7 148   B3
Stockwell La. Ches EN7 148   B3
Stockwood Cres. Luton LU1 63   D6
Stockwood Ct. Luton LU1 63   D6
Stockwood Hospl. Luton 63   F5
Stoffold House. Stot SG5 11   F6
Stone Cross. Harl CM20 117   D1
Stonecroft. Kneb SG3 68   F5
Stonecross Rd. Hat AL10 130   B7
Stonecross. St Alb AL1 127   E4
Stonehill Jun Mix Inf Sch. Letw 11   E1
Stonehills. Wel G C AL8 110   D7
Stonelea Rd. Heml H HP3 138   F8
Stoneleigh Ave. Enf EN1 162   B1
Stoneleigh Cl. Ches EN8 162   D6
Stoneleigh Cl. Luton LU3 45   B7
Stoneleigh Dr. Hod EN11 115   B1
Stoneleigh. Saw CM21 97   D3
Stoneley. Letw SG6 11   F1
Stonemead. Wel G C AL8 89   D3
Stonesdale. Luton LU4 44   C4
Stoneways Cl. Luton LU4 44   C6
Stoney Comm. Sta M CM24 59   E5
Stoney Common Rd. Sta M CM24 ... 59   E5
Stoney Croft. Ald HP23 101   C5
Stoney La. Bov HP3 137   C5
Stoney La. Chipf HP3 137   F1
Stoney Pl. Sta M CM24 59   E5
Stoneycroft. Heml H HP1 124   A3
Stoneycroft. Wel G C AL7 111   A7
Stoneyfield Dr. Sta M CM24 59   E6
Stoneygate Rd. Luton LU4 44   D3
Stonnells Cl. Letw SG6 22   F8
Stony Croft. Stev SG1 50   E6
Stony Hills. Sac SG14 92   C7
Stony La. Chen HP6 150   E1
Stony La. Gt Of SG4 47   C4
Stonyshotts. Wa Aby EN9 163   A6
Stooksdale. Wing HP22 60   A3
Stopsley High Sch &
   Community Coll. Luton 45   F4
Stopsley Inf Sch. Luton 46   A4
Stopsley Way. Luton LU2 46   A3
Storehouse La. Hit SG4 34   F6
Storey Ct. Bus WD2 168   B4
Storey St. Heml H HP3 138   D7
Stormont Rd. Hit SG5 21   F1
Stormont Rd. Pot B 159   D8
Stornaway. Heml H HP3 125   B1
Stort Lodge. Bis St CM23 76   D8
Stort Mill. Harl CM20 118   B6
Stort Rd. Bis St CM23 76   F6
Stort Valley Ind Pk. Bis St 59   B2
Stortford Hall Pk. Bis St CM23 77   B7
Stortford Hall Rd. Bis St CM23 77   B8
Stortford Rd. Hod EN11 135   C7
Stortford Rd. L Had SG11 57   C7
Stortford Rd. Sheer CM22 98   F3
Stortford Rd. Stand SG11 55   F2
Stotfold House. Stot SG5 11   F6
Stotfold Rd. Arl SG15 11   B7
Stotfold Rd. Letw SG6 22   C4
Stotfold Rd. Newn SG7 3   C1
Stow The. Harl CM20 117   F2
Stox Mead. Har HA3 176   D2
Strafford Cl. Pot B EN6 159   A7
Strafford Gate. Pot B EN6 159   A7
Strafford Gate. Pot B EN6 159   A7
Strafford Rd. Barn EN5 171   A6
Straits The. Wa Aby EN9 163   B7
Strangers Way. Luton LU4 44   C4
Strangeways. Watf WD1 153   E3
Stratfield Dr. Hod EN10 134   E4
Stratfield Rd. Bor WD6 170   A7
Stratford Lodge. Watf WD1 167   A8
Stratford Rd. Luton LU4 45   B1
Stratford Rd. Watf WD1 167   A7
Stratford Way. Bri Wd AL2 141   A1
Stratford Way. Heml H HP3 138   B8
Stratford Way. Watf WD1 167   A7
Strathmore Ave. Hit SG5 21   F1
Strathmore Ave. Luton LU1 63   F5
Strathmore Inf & Nursery Sch. Hit .. 21   F2
Strathmore Rd. Whit SG4 66   F6
Strathmore Wlk. Luton LU1 63   F6
Stratton Ave. Enf EN2 161   D2
Stratton Gdns. Luton LU2 45   D4
Straw Plait Way. Arl SG15 11   B7
Strawberry Field. Hat AL10 130   A2
Strawberry Fields. Ware SG12 93   A4
Strawfields. Wel G C AL7 90   F1
Strawmead. Hat AL10 130   B7
Strawplaiters Cl. Welw SG3 69   A2
Strayfield Rd. Cre H EN2 161   D2

Stream Woods Jun Mix Inf Sch.
   Hat 130   B4
Street The. Brag SG11 55   F7
Street The. Chipf WD4 152   A8
Street The. Dan En SG11 53   F7
Street The. Fur P SG9 43   A4
Street The. Sheer CM22 98   E1
Street The. Wal SG7 25   C8
Stretton Way. Bor WD6 156   E1
Stringers La. Ast SG2 51   E2
Stripling Way. Watf WD1 167   A3
Stroma Cl. Heml H HP3 125   C1
Stronsay. Heml H HP3 125   C1
Stuart Ct. Elst WD6 169   D3
Stuart Dr. Royst SG8 7   D8
Stuart Pl. Luton LU1 63   D7
Stuart Rd. Welw AL6 89   B3
Stuart St. Luton LU1 63   D7
Stuart Way. Ches EN7 162   B8
Stuarts Cl. Heml H HP3 124   D1   3
Stud Gn. Watf WD2 154   B7
Studham Cty Prim Sch. Stu 82   B4
Studham La. Dagn HP4 81   D4
Studham La. Whip HP4 82   A7
Studio Way. Bor WD6 170   C4
Studios The. Bor WD6 168   A3
Studlands Rise Fst Sch. Royst 7   E5
Studlands Rise. Royst SG8 7   E6
Studley Rd. Luton LU3 45   D1
Sturgeon's Rd. Hit SG4 22   B2
Sturlas Way. Ches EN8 162   D6
Stylemans La. Bis St CM23 77   B5
Styles Cl. Luton LU2 46   C2
Such Cl. Letw SG6 23   B7
Sudbury Rd. Luton LU4 44   B6
Suffolk Cl. Bor WD6 170   D4
Suffolk Cl. Dun LU4 44   A4
Suffolk Cl. Lon C AL2 142   C6
Suffolk Rd. Pot B EN6 158   F5
Suffolk Rd. Royst SG8 7   C8
Sugar La. Heml H HP1 123   B1
Sulgrave Cres. Tri HP23 100   C5
Sullivan Cres. Hare UB9 173   B5
Sullivan Way. Elst WD6 169   C3
Summer Cl. Heml H HP2 124   D5
Summer Dale. Wel G C AL8 89   D1
Summer Gr. Elst WD6 169   D3
Summer Hill. Bor WD6 170   A4
Summer St. Cad LU1 63   C1
Summer Wlk. Mark AL3 83   E5
Summercroft Inf Sch. Bis St 77   C8
Summercroft Jun Sch. Bis St 77   C8
Summerfield. Lon C AL2 142   C5
Summerfield. Hat AL10 130   A2
Summerfield Rd. Luton LU1 62   F8
Summerfield Rd. Watf WD2 154   A4
Summerhouse La. Hare UB9 173   A3
Summerhouse La. Radl WD2 168   C8
Summerhouse Way. Abb L WD5 139   F1
Summers Rd. Luton LU2 46   C1
Summers Way. Lon C AL2 142   E4
Summersland Rd. St Alb AL4 128   C7
Summerswood La. Ridge WD6 157   E4
Summerswood Prim Sch. Bor 170   B5
Summit Rd. Pot B EN6 144   E1
Sumpter Yd. St Alb AL1 127   D2
Sun Hill. Royst SG8 7   C5
Sun La. Harp AL5 86   A2
Sun Sq. Heml H HP1 124   D4   2
Sun St. Bal SG7 23   E8
Sun St. Hit SG5 34   E6
Sun St. Sheer CM21 97   F1
Sun St. Wa Aby EN9 163   C6
Sunbury Ct. Barn EN5 171   E5   2
Sunderland Ave. St Alb AL1 128   A4
Sundew Rd. Heml H HP1 123   E2
Sundon Park Jun Sch. Luton 44   D3
Sundon Park Rd. Luton LU3 44   C7
Sunmead Rd. Heml H HP2 124   D5
Sunningdale. Bis St CM23 59   E6
Sunningdale. Luton LU2 45   F3
Sunningdale Mews. Wel G C AL7 ... 89   F2
Sunny Bank. Ched LU7 79   F7
Sunny Hill. Bus WD2 168   A4
Sunnybank Rd. Pot B EN6 159   A6
Sunnydell. Chis AL2 141   B5
Sunnyfield. Hat AL9 130   C8
Sunnyhill Rd. Heml H HP1 124   B3
Sunnyhill Rd. Map Cr WD3 172   F8
Sunnyside. Lo Naz EN9 135   F1
Sunnyside Rd. Hit SG4 35   A5
Sunnyside. Sta M CM24 59   E6
Sunridge Ave. Luton LU2 45   E2
Sunrise Cres. Heml H HP3 138   F8
Sunset Dr. Luton LU2 45   F3
Sunset View. Barn EN5 171   E7
Surrey Pl. Tri HP23 100   A3
Surrey St. Luton LU1 63   E6
Surrey Street Prim Sch. Luton 63   E6
Sursham St. Mark AL3 83   E5
Sussex Cl. Hod EN11 135   A7
Sussex Rd. Luton LU2 46   D2
Sussex Rd. Watf WD2 154   A1
Sutcliffe Cl. Bus WD2 168   C5
Sutcliffe Cl. Stev SG1 51   A8
Sutherland Ave. Cuf EN6 146   D3
Sutherland Cl. Barn EN5 171   E5
Sutherland Pl. Wel G C AL7 110   F7
Sutherland Pl. Luton LU1 63   D5
Sutherland Rd. Cuf EN6 146   D3
Sutton Acres. L Hal CM22 98   D7
Sutton Cl. Hod EN10 134   E4
Sutton Cl. Tri HP23 100   B6
Sutton Cres. Barn EN5 171   D4
Sutton Gdns. Luton LU3 44   D6
Sutton Path. Bor WD6 170   A6
Sutton Rd. St Alb AL1 128   B3
Sutton Rd. Watf WD1 167   C6
Swallow Cl. Bus WD2 168   C1
Swallow Cl. Dun LU4 44   A4
Swallow Cl. Ric WD3 165   C2
Swallow Ct. Hert SG14 113   C6
Swallow End. Wel G C AL7 110   F5
Swallow Rd. Wel G C AL7 110   F6
Swallow Gdns. Hat AL10 130   A3
Swallow Oaks. Abb L WD5 153   F7
Swallowdale La. Heml H HP2 125   B6
Swallowfields. Wel G C AL7 110   F6
Swallows. Harl CM17 118   C4

Swallows The. Wel G C AL7 .... 89 F2
Swan And Pike Rd. Enf EN3 .... 163 A1
Swan Ct. Bis St CM23 .... 76 F6
Swan La. Gu M SG8 .... 1 F4
Swan Mead. Dun LU4 .... 44 B4
Swan St. Ashw SG7 .... 4 D4
Swanells Wood. Luton LU6 .... 82 C4
Swanfield Rd. Ches EN8 .... 162 E6
Swangley's La. Kneb SG3 .... 69 B4
Swanhill. Wel G C AL7 .... 90 A1
Swanland Rd. Pot B EN6 .... 144 B3
Swanland Rd. Wel G EN6 .... 144 B3
Swanley Bar La. Bro Pk EN6 .... 145 B3
Swanley Cres. Bro Pk EN6 .... 145 B2
Swanley Ct. Watf WD2 .... 154 C2
Swans Cl. Coln H AL4 .... 128 E2
Swans Ct. Ches EN8 .... 162 E5
Swanstand. Letw SG6 .... 23 D4
Swanston Grange. Dun LU4 .... 44 B2
Swanston Path. Sth Ox WD1 .... 175 C7
Swasedale Rd. Luton LU3 .... 45 A6
Sweet Briar. Wel G C AL7 .... 111 A5
Sweetbriar Cl. Heml H HP1 .... 124 A6
Sweyns Mead. Stev SG2 .... 51 C7
Swift Cl. St Am SG12 .... 115 C3
Swift Cl. Letw SG6 .... 22 E8
Swift Cl. Royst SG8 .... 2 D1
Swiftfields. Wel G C AL7 .... 111 A7
Swifts Green Cl. Luton LU2 .... 46 B5
Swifts Green Rd. Luton LU2 .... 46 B5
Swinburne Ave. Hit SG5 .... 21 C1
Swinburne Cl. Royst SG8 .... 2 D1
Swing Gate La. Berk HP4 .... 122 D2
Swing Gate Sch. Berk 122 D3
Swingate. Stev SG1 .... 50 D5
Swinnell Cl. Knee SG8 .... 2 B5
Swiss Ave. Watf WD1 .... 166 E6
Swiss Cl. Watf WD1 .... 166 E6
Sworders Yd. Bis St CM23 .... 76 F7 2
Sycamore Ave. Hat AL10 .... 130 A4
Sycamore Cl. Bus WD2 .... 167 E4
Sycamore Cl. Ham St EN7 .... 147 F4
Sycamore Cl. Hit SG4 .... 35 A4
Sycamore Cl. Watf WD2 .... 154 B4
Sycamore Dr. Pk St AL2 .... 141 D4
Sycamore Dr. Tri HP23 .... 100 B4
Sycamore Rd. Cro Gr WD3 .... 166 D4
Sycamore Rise. Berk HP4 .... 122 D3
Sycamores The. Bis St CM23 .... 77 B6
Sycamores The. Heml H HP3 .... 137 F8
Sycamores The. Radl WD7 .... 156 B5
Sycamores The. St Alb AL1 .... 127 D2
Sydney Rd. Watf WD1 .... 166 F4
Sylam Cl. Luton LU3 .... 44 E7
Sylvan Cl. Heml H HP3 .... 125 A2
Sylvan Way. Wel G C AL7 .... 111 C5
Sylvandale. Wel G C AL7 .... 111 C5
Sylvia Ave. Pnr HA5 .... 175 F4
Symonds Green La. Stev SG1 .... 50 A6
Symonds Green Rd. Stev SG1 .... 50 A7
Symonds Rd. Hit SG5 .... 34 D8

Tabbs Cl. Letw SG6 .... 23 B7
Tacitus Cl. Stev SG1 .... 51 C8
Takeley Cl. Wa Aby EN9 .... 163 D6
Talbot Ave. Watf WD1 .... 167 E2
Talbot Cl. Heml H HP3 .... 124 D1
Talbot Rd. Har HA3 .... 176 F1
Talbot Rd. Hat AL10 .... 130 A8
Talbot Rd. Luton LU2 .... 45 F2
Talbot Rd. Ric WD3 .... 165 E1
Talbot St. Hert SG13 .... 113 C6
Talbot St. Hit SG5 .... 34 C8
Talbot Way. Letw SG6 .... 12 B1
Tall Trees. Hit SG4 .... 35 A4
Tall Trees. Royst SG8 .... 7 E6
Tallack Cl. Har HA3 .... 176 E3
Tallents Cres. Harp AL5 .... 86 D3
Tallents Farm (Research Farm).
  Kim 86 F8
Tallis Way. Bor WD6 .... 169 E8
Tamar Gn. Heml H HP2 .... 124 F8
Tamarisk Cl. St Alb AL3 .... 127 D7
Tameton Cl. Luton LU2 .... 46 F2
Tamworth Rd. Hert SG13 .... 113 F7
Tancred Rd. Luton LU2 .... 46 A4
Tanfield Cl. Ham St EN7 .... 148 A4
* Tanfield Gn. Luton LU2 .... 46 E1
Tanglewood Cl. Stan HA7 .... 176 E8
Tanglewood. Welw AL6 .... 90 A7
Tanners Cl. St Alb AL3 .... 127 C4
Tanners Cres. Hert SG13 .... 113 C4
Tanners Hill. Abb L WD5 .... 154 A8
Tanners Way. Hun SG12 .... 116 C8
Tanners Wood Cl. Abb L WD5 .... 153 E7
Tanners Wood Ct. Abb L WD5 .... 153 E7
Tanners Wood Jun Mix Inf Sch.
  Abb L 153 E7
Tanners Wood La. Abb L WD5 .... 153 E7
Tannery Cl. Royst SG8 .... 7 C6
Tannery Drift. Royst SG8 .... 7 C6
Tannery Drift Sch. Royst 7 C6
Tannery The. Bun SG9 .... 40 E7
Tannery Yd. Whit SG4 .... 66 F6
Tannsfield Dr. Heml H HP2 .... 124 F5 1
Tannsmore Cl. Heml H HP2 .... 124 F5 2
Tansycroft. Wel G C AL7 .... 111 B7
Tanworth Cl. Norwd HA6 .... 174 C4
Tanworth Gdns. Pnr HA5 .... 175 C1
Tany's Dell Cty Prim Sch. Harl 118 A3
Tany's Dell. Harl CM20 .... 118 A3
Tanyard La. Cod SG4 .... 88 B8
Tapster St. Barn EN5 .... 171 F6
Taransay. Heml H HP3 .... 125 B1
Tarpan Way. Ches CM21 .... 148 F6
Tarrant Dr. Harp AL5 .... 107 D7
Tarrant. Stev SG1 .... 36 B1
Tasmin Cl. Norwd HA6 .... 174 F2
Tassell Hall. Red AL3 .... 105 F6
Tatlers La. Ast SG2 .... 51 E4
Tatsfield Rd. Lo Naz EN9 .... 149 D8
Tattershall Dr. Heml H HP2 .... 105 B1
Tattle Hill. Bram SG14 .... 91 E2
Tattlers Hill. Wing HP22 .... 60 B3
Tauber Rd. Bor WD6 .... 169 F3
Taunton Rd. Luton LU2 .... 46 B1
Taverners. Heml H HP2 .... 124 E5
Taverners Way. Hod EN11 .... 135 A6
Tavistock Ave. St Alb AL1 .... 141 D8
Tavistock Cl. Pot B EN6 .... 159 D4

Tavistock Cl. St Alb AL1 .... 141 D8
Tavistock Cres. Luton LU1 .... 63 E5
Tavistock Rd. Watf WD2 .... 167 D8
Tavistock St. Luton LU1 .... 63 E6
Taylor Cl. St Alb AL4 .... 128 A8
Taylor Cl. Luton LU2 .... 63 F8
Taylor Trad Est. Hert 114 B7
Taylor's Hill. Hit SG4 .... 34 F6
Taylor's La. Kneb SG3 .... 171 F8
Taylor's Rd. Stot SG5 .... 3 A1
Taylor's Rd. Stot SG5 .... 11 F8
Taylors Ave. Hod EN11 .... 135 A5
Taywood Cl. Stev SG2 .... 51 B2
Teal Dr. Norwd HA6 .... 174 C3
Teal House. Watf WD2 .... 154 E3
Teasdale Cl. Royst SG8 .... 2 D1
Teasel Cl. Royst SG8 .... 7 E5
Tedder Ave. Henlw SG16 .... 10 C5
Tedder Rd. Heml H HP2 .... 125 A4
Tee Side. Hert SG13 .... 114 B7
Teesdale. Heml H HP2 .... 124 E6
Teesdale. Luton LU4 .... 44 C5
Telford Cl. Stev SG2 .... 51 B6
Telford Cl. Watf WD2 .... 154 D4
Telford Ct. Hat AL10 .... 129 F3
Telford Ct. St Alb AL1 .... 127 E2
Telford Rd. Lon C AL2 .... 142 C4
Telford Way. Luton LU1 .... 63 D8
Telmere Ind Est. Luton 63 E6 11
Telscombe Way. Luton LU2 .... 46 C3
Temperance St. St Alb AL3 .... 127 C3
Tempest Ave. Pot B EN6 .... 159 D7
Templar Ave. Bal SG7 .... 23 F6
Templars Dr. Stan HA3 .... 176 D4
Templars La. Pres SG4 .... 48 D6
Temple Bank. Harl CM20 .... 118 B5
Temple Cl. Ches EN7 .... 162 A8
Temple Cl. Luton LU2 .... 45 E5
Temple Cl. Pres SG5 .... 34 B4
Temple Cl. Watf WD1 .... 166 F7
Temple Ct. Bal SG7 .... 23 F6
Temple Ct. Hert SG14 .... 92 D1
Temple Ct. Pot B EN6 .... 158 D8
Temple Fields. Hert SG14 .... 92 D1
Temple Gdns. Letw SG6 .... 23 C8
Temple Gdns. Mo Pk WD3 .... 174 B6
Temple La. Ton SG12 .... 92 F8
Temple Mead. Heml H HP2 .... 124 D5
Temple Mead. Roy CM19 .... 116 B1
Temple View. St Alb AL3 .... 127 C5
Templefields Ent Ctr. Harl 118 A3
Templepan La. Sar WD3 .... 152 E2
Templewood Sch. Wel G C 110 D8
Templewood. Wel G C AL8 .... 89 D1
Tempsford Ave. Bor WD6 .... 170 D5
Tempsford. Wel G C AL7 .... 111 D6
Temsford Cl. Har HA2 .... 176 C1
Tenby Dr. Luton LU4 .... 44 F3
Tene The. Bal SG7 .... 23 F8
Tennand Cl. Ham St EN7 .... 147 F5
Tennison Ave. Bor WD6 .... 170 B4
Tennyson Ave. Hit SG4 .... 35 C7
Tennyson Ave. Wa Aby EN9 .... 163 E5
Tennyson Cl. Royst SG8 .... 2 E1
Tennyson Rd. Chis AL2 .... 141 B5
Tennyson Rd. Harp AL5 .... 86 A2
Tennyson Rd. Luton LU1 .... 63 E5
Tennyson Road Prim Sch. Luton 63 E5
Tenterfield House. Welw AL6 .... 89 C4
Tenth Ave. Luton LU3 .... 44 C7
Tenzing Gr. Luton LU1 .... 63 C6
Tenzing Rd. Heml H HP2 .... 125 A3
Teresa Gdns. Ches EN8 .... 162 D5
Terminus St. Harl CM20 .... 117 D1
Terrace Gdns. Watf WD1 .... 167 B7
Terrace The. Ess AL9 .... 131 E6
Terrace The. Red AL3 .... 106 A5
Terrace The. Tri HP23 .... 100 A3
Tethys Rd. Heml H HP2 .... 124 F6
Tewin Cl. St Alb AL4 .... 128 C7
Tewin Cl. Tewin AL6 .... 90 C5
Tewin Cl. Wel G C AL7 .... 110 F7
Tewin Hill. Tewin AL6 .... 90 F5
Tewin Rd. Heml H HP2 .... 125 C3
Tewin Rd. Wel G C AL7 .... 110 F7
Tewin Water Sch. Tewin 90 B2
Thackeray Cl. Royst SG8 .... 2 D1
Thames Ave. Heml H HP2 .... 124 F8
Thames Ct. Luton LU3 .... 45 B3
Thamesdale. Lon C AL2 .... 142 F4
Thatchers Croft. Heml H HP2 .... 124 E7
Thatchers End. Hit SG4 .... 35 D8
Thaxted Cl. Luton LU2 .... 46 F2
Thaxted Way. Wa Aby EN9 .... 163 D6
Thaynesfield. Pot B EN6 .... 159 D8
Theabald's Grove Sta. Ches 162 D7
Thelby Cl. Luton LU3 .... 44 F6
Thele Ave. Sta Ab SG12 .... 115 D4
Thelusson Cl. Radl WD7 .... 156 A3
Theobald Cres. Har HA3 .... 176 C2
Theobald St. Bor WD6 .... 169 F7
Theobald St. Radl WD7 .... 156 D2
Theobald's La. Ches EN8 .... 162 B7
Theobald's La. Ches EN8 .... 162 C7
Theobald's Rd. Cuf EN6 .... 146 F1
Theobalds Cl. Cuf EN6 .... 146 F1
Theobalds Park Coll. Ches 162 A6
Theobalds Park Rd. Cre H EN2 .... 161 B3
Therfield Fst Sch. Ther 15 F7
Therfield Rd. St Alb AL3 .... 127 D6
Thetford Gdns. Luton LU2 .... 45 E6
Thieves' La. Hert SG14 .... 112 F7
Third Ave. Letw SG6 .... 23 C7
Third Ave. Luton LU3 .... 44 D7
Third Ave. Watf WD2 .... 154 D4
Thirlestane. St Alb AL1 .... 127 F4
Thirlestone Rd. Luton LU4 .... 44 D1
Thirlmere Dr. St Alb AL1 .... 128 B1
Thirlmere Gdns. Norwd HA6 .... 174 C4
Thirsk Rd. Bor WD6 .... 157 A1
Thirston Path. Bor WD6 .... 170 A7
Thistle Cl. Heml H HP1 .... 123 E2
Thistle Gr. Wel G C AL7 .... 111 C3
Thistle Rd. Luton LU1 .... 63 F7
Thistlecroft. Heml H HP1 .... 124 B2
Thistles The. Heml H HP1 .... 124 B4
Thistley La. St Ipp SG4 .... 34 F1
Thomas Alleyne Sch The. Stev 50 C8
Thomas Ct. Berk HP4 .... 121 F5
Thomas Heskin Ct. Bis St CM23 .... 77 A7 5

Thomas Rochford Way. Ches EN8 .... 148 F4
Thomas Tallis Cty Inf Sch The.
  Wa Aby 163 F6
Thomas Watson Cottage Homes The.
  Barn EN5 .... 171 F4
Thompson Way. Ric WD3 .... 165 A1
Thompsons Cl. Harp AL5 .... 86 A1
Thorley Ctr The. Bis St 76 D4
Thorley High. Bis St CM23 .... 76 F2
Thorley Hill. Bis St CM23 .... 76 F5
Thorley Hill Prim Sch. Bis St 76 F4
Thorley La. Bis St CM23 .... 76 C4
Thorley Park Rd. Bis St CM23 .... 76 F4
Thorn Ave. Bus WD2 .... 168 C1
Thorn Gr. Bis St CM23 .... 77 B6
Thorn Tree Dr. Tri HP23 .... 99 F4
Thornage Cl. Luton LU2 .... 45 D7
Thornbera Cl. Bis St CM23 .... 76 F4
Thornbera Gdns. Bis St CM23 .... 76 F4
Thornbera Rd. Bis St CM23 .... 76 F4
Thornbury Cl. Heml H HP2 .... 115 B2
Thornbury Cl. Stev SG2 .... 69 A8
Thornbury Gdns. Bor WD6 .... 170 C5
Thornbury. Harp AL5 .... 86 D1
Thorncroft. Heml H HP3 .... 125 B1
Thorndyke Ct. Pnr HA5 .... 175 F3
Thorne Grove Jun Mix Inf Sch.
  Bis St 77 B6
Thornfield Rd. Bis St CM23 .... 76 E8
Thornhill Rd. Luton LU4 .... 44 F2
Thornhill Rd. Mo Pk HA6 .... 174 C6
Thornton Gr. Pnr HA5 .... 176 A4
Thornton Rd. Barn EN5 .... 171 E6
Thornton Rd. Pot B EN6 .... 145 C1
Thornton St. Hert SG14 .... 113 D6
Thornton St. St Alb AL1 .... 127 C4
Thorntondale. Luton LU4 .... 44 C5
Thorpe Cres. Watf WD1 .... 167 C2
Thorpe Rd. St Alb AL1 .... 127 D2
Thorpefield Cl. St Alb AL4 .... 128 D6
Thrales Cl. Luton LU3 .... 44 E7
Three Cherrytrees La.
  Heml H HP2 .... 125 B7
Three Close La. Berk HP4 .... 122 C4
Three Corners. Heml H HP3 .... 125 A1
Three Crosses. Pirt SG5 .... 20 D4
Three Houses La. Kneb SG4 .... 67 D5
Three Stiles. Ben SG2 .... 52 E4
Thremhall Ave. Birhr CM23 .... 77 F8
Thricknells Cl. Luton LU3 .... 44 E7
Thrift Farm La. Bor WD6 .... 170 C7
Thristers Cl. Letw SG6 .... 23 B3
Throcking La. Cotrd SG9 .... 27 C1
Thrums. Watf WD2 .... 154 B2
Thrush Ave. Hat AL10 .... 130 A3
Thrush Gn. Ric WD3 .... 165 C2
Thrush La. Cuf EN6 .... 146 F3
Thumbswood Inf Sch. Wel G C 111 A5
Thumbswood. Wel G C AL7 .... 111 A3
Thumpers. Heml H HP2 .... 124 E5
Thunder Hall. Ware SG12 .... 93 D2 1
Thundercourt. Ware SG12 .... 93 D2
Thundridge Cl. Wel G C AL7 .... 111 B5
Thurgood Rd. Hod EN11 .... 135 A8
Thurlow Cl. Stev SG1 .... 36 D2
Thurnall Ave. Royst SG8 .... 7 D5
Thurnall Cl. Bal SG7 .... 23 F8
Tibbles Cl. Watf WD2 .... 154 E4
Tibbs Hill Rd. Abb L WD5 .... 139 F1
Tiberius Rd. Luton LU3 .... 44 F6
Tichborne. Map Cr WD3 .... 172 D5
Tile Kiln Cl. Heml H HP3 .... 125 B2
Tile Kiln Cres. Heml H HP3 .... 125 B2
Tile Kiln La. Heml H HP3 .... 125 B2
Tilecroft. Wel G C AL8 .... 89 D1
Tilehouse Cl. Bor WD6 .... 169 F6
Tilehouse Cl. Map Cr UB9 .... 172 E2
Tilehouse St. Hit SG5 .... 34 E6
Tilgate. Luton LU2 .... 46 D3
Tillers Link. Stev SG2 .... 51 A2
Tillotson Rd. Har HA3 .... 176 B3
Tilsworth Wlk. St Alb AL4 .... 128 C8
Timber Orch. Stap SG14 .... 92 A2
Timber Ridge. Ric WD3 .... 165 D5
Timbercroft. Wel G C AL7 .... 89 F1
Timbers Ct. Harp AL5 .... 85 F2
Times Cl. Hit SG5 .... 21 D2
Timplings Row. Heml H HP1 .... 124 B5
Timworth Cl. Luton LU2 .... 46 D1
Tingeys Cl. Red AL3 .... 106 A5
Tinkers La. Wigg HP23 .... 121 A6
Tinsley Cl. Luton LU1 .... 63 B5
Tintagel Cl. Heml H HP2 .... 124 D8
Tintagel Cl. Luton LU3 .... 45 B4
Tintern Cl. Harp AL5 .... 85 C4
Tintern Cl. Stev SG2 .... 69 A7
Tinwell Mews. Bor WD6 .... 170 D4
Tippendell La. Chis AL2 .... 141 C5
Tippet Cl. Stev SG1 .... 50 D3
Titan Ct. Luton LU4 .... 44 F1
Titan Rd. Heml H HP2 .... 124 F6
Titchfield Rd. Enf EN3 .... 162 E2
Tithe Barn Cl. St Alb AL1 .... 141 C8
Tithe Cl. Cod SG4 .... 67 F1
Titian Ave. Bus WD2 .... 168 E2
Titmus Cl. Stev SG1 .... 50 E6
Tiverton Cl. Whea AL5 .... 107 E6
Tiverton Ct. Nort EN6 .... 159 E8
Toddington Rd. Luton LU4 .... 44 C1
Toland Cl. Dun LU4 .... 44 C1
Tolcarne Dr. Pnr HA5 .... 175 A1
Tollgate Cl. Chor WD3 .... 164 F5
Tollgate Rd. Col H AL4 .... 143 E7
Tollgate Rd. Enf EN3 .... 162 D4
Tollgate Rd. Wel G AL4 .... 144 A6
Tollpit End. Heml H HP1 .... 124 A6
Tolmers Cl. Cuf EN6 .... 146 F2
Tolmers Gdns. Cuf EN6 .... 146 F2
Tolmers Mews. New St SG13 .... 146 E6
Tolmers Rd. Cuf EN6 .... 146 E3
Tolpits Cl. Watf WD1 .... 166 F2
Tolpits La. Watf WD1 .... 166 E2
Tom's Hill. Sar WD3 .... 152 A3
Tom's La. Abb L WD4,WD5 .... 139 D3
Tomkins Cl. Bor WD6 .... 169 E8
Toms Croft. Heml H HP2 .... 124 F6
Toms Field. Hat AL10 .... 129 F4
Toms Hill Rd. Ald HP23 .... 101 D5
Tonwell Jun Mix Inf Sch. Ton 92 F7
Tooke Cl. Pnr HA5 .... 175 E2

Toorack Rd. Har HA3 .... 176 D1
Tooveys Mill Cl. Kin L WD4 .... 139 A2
Topstreet Way. Harp AL5 .... 107 C8
Torquay Cres. Stev SG1 .... 50 B7
Torquay Dr. Luton LU4 .... 44 D4
Torridge Wlk. Heml H HP2 .... 124 F8 2
Torrington Dr. Pot B EN6 .... 159 D7
Torrington Rd. Berk HP4 .... 122 B4
Tortoiseshell Way. Berk HP4 .... 121 F6
Torwood Cl. Berk HP4 .... 121 F4
Torworth Rd. Bor WD6 .... 157 A1
Tot La. Birhr CM23 .... 59 D4
Totteridge Comm. Barn N20 .... 171 D1
Totteridge Pk. Barn N20 .... 171 C1
Totteridge Rd. Enf EN3 .... 162 D2
Totteridge Village. Barn N20 .... 171 F1
Totton Mews. Red AL3 .... 106 B5
Totts La. Walk SG2 .... 38 C5
Toulmin Dr. St Alb AL3 .... 127 C7
Tovey Ave. Hod EN11 .... 135 A8
Tovey Cl. Lo Naz EN9 .... 149 F8
Tovey Cl. Lon C AL2 .... 142 D5
Tower Cl. Berk HP4 .... 122 A3
Tower Cl. Knee SG8 .... 2 A5
Tower Cl. L Wym SG4 .... 35 F3
Tower Cl. Luton LU2 .... 46 A1 2
Tower Ctr. Hod 135 A7
Tower Hill. Chipf HP3,WD4 .... 137 F1
Tower Hill La. Sand AL4 .... 108 F4
Tower Hill. Muc H SG10 .... 74 F2
Tower Rd. Cod SG4 .... 67 F2
Tower Rd. Luton LU2 .... 64 A8
Tower Rd. Ware SG12 .... 93 F2
Tower Sch. Ware 93 E3
Tower St. Hert SG14 .... 113 D6
Tower Way. Luton LU2 .... 64 A8
Towers Rd. Heml H HP2 .... 124 E4
Towers Rd. Pnr HA5 .... 175 E2
Towers Rd. Stev SG1 .... 50 D4
Towers The. Stev SG1 .... 50 D4
Town Ctr. Hat AL10 .... 130 A6
Town Farm. Ched LU7 .... 80 A7
Town Farm Cres. Stand SG11 .... 55 F2
Town Farm. Whea AL4 .... 108 D4
Town Fields. Hat AL10 .... 130 A6
Town La. Ben SG2 .... 52 E4
Town Mead Rd. Wa Aby EN9 .... 163 C5
Town Sq. Stev SG1 .... 50 D5
Towne Rd. Royst SG8 .... 7 F7
Townfield. Ric WD3 .... 165 C2
Townley. Letw SG6 .... 23 C6
Townsend Ave. St Alb AL1 .... 127 E4
Townsend C of E Sch. St Alb 127 C8
Townsend Cl. Bark SG8 .... 17 C3
Townsend Cl. Harp AL5 .... 85 F1
Townsend Dr. St Alb AL3 .... 127 D5
Townsend. Heml H HP2 .... 124 D5
Townsend La. Harp AL5 .... 85 E1
Townsend Rd. Harp AL5 .... 86 A2
Townsend Way. Norwd HA6 .... 175 A3
Townshend St. Hert SG13 .... 113 E6
Townsley Cl. Luton LU1 .... 63 E6 10
Tracey Ct. Luton LU1 .... 63 E6 10
Trafalgar Ave. Hod EN10 .... 134 F2
Trafford Cl. Shen WD7 .... 156 E7
Trafford Cl. Stev SG1 .... 36 E1
Traherne Cl. Hit SG4 .... 34 F5 2
Trajan Gate. Walk SG2 .... 37 D1
Trapstyle Rd. Hert SG12 .... 93 A2
Travellers Cl. Wel G AL9 .... 144 C8
Travellers La. Hat AL9,AL10 .... 130 B2
Travellers La. Wel Gr AL9 .... 130 C1
Treacle La. Rus SG9 .... 25 F3
Treacy Cl. Bus WD2 .... 176 C8
Trebellan Dr. Heml H HP2 .... 124 F4
Tree Cl. Heml H HP3 .... 125 B1
Tree Ct. Elst WD6 .... 169 D3
Treehanger Cl. Tri HP23 .... 100 B4
Treetops Cl. Norwd HA6 .... 174 D4
Trefoil Cl. Dun LU4 .... 44 A4
Trefusis Wlk. Watf WD1 .... 166 F4
Tregelles Rd. Hod EN11 .... 135 A4
Tremaine Gr. Heml H HP2 .... 124 E7
Trent Cl. Shen WD7 .... 156 E7
Trent Cl. Stev SG1 .... 50 E8
Trent Rd. Luton LU3 .... 45 B4
Tresco Rd. Berk HP4 .... 121 F5
Trescott Cl. Luton LU2 .... 46 E2
Tresilion Sq. Heml H HP2 .... 125 A3
Treslian Sq. Heml H HP2 .... 124 F8 1
Trevalga Way. Heml H HP2 .... 124 E7
Trevellance Way. Watf WD2 .... 154 D6
Trevelyan Way. Berk HP4 .... 122 B6
Trevero Ct. Ches EN8 .... 162 E6
Trevor Cl. Har HA3 .... 176 F3
Trevor Rd. Hit SG4 .... 35 A8
Trevose Way. Sth Ox WD1 .... 175 C7
Trewenna Dr. Pot B EN6 .... 159 D7
Triangle The. Hit SG4 .... 34 F6
Trident Ave. Hat AL10 .... 129 E6
Trident Ind Est. Hod 135 C7
Trident Rd. Watf WD2 .... 153 F5
Triggs Way. Gt Of LU2 .... 46 E3
Trimley Cl. Luton LU4 .... 44 B5
Trinder Rd. Barn EN5 .... 171 C4
Tring Ford Rd. Wils HP23 .... 100 A3
Tring Hill. Ast Cl HP23 .... 99 C3
Tring Rd. Lon M HP23 .... 79 C3
Tring Rd. Nthch HP4 .... 121 D7
Tring Rd. Wing HP22 .... 60 D1
Tring Sch. Tri 100 B4
Tring Sta. Ald 101 A5
Trinity Cl. Bis St CM23 .... 76 F6
Trinity Cl. Norwd HA6 .... 174 E4
Trinity Cl. Hert SG14 .... 113 C8
Trinity Gr. Hert SG14 .... 113 C8
Trinity Hall Cl. Watf WD2 .... 167 C5
Trinity La. Ches EN8 .... 162 E7
Trinity Mews. Heml H HP2 .... 125 A3
Trinity Pl. Stev SG1 .... 50 D6
Trinity Rd. Hert SG13 .... 114 C3
Trinity Rd. Luton LU3 .... 45 B4
Trinity Rd. Stev SG1 .... 50 D6
Trinity Rd. Stot SG5 .... 11 F7
Trinity Rd. Ware SG12 .... 93 F2
Trinity St. Bis St CM23 .... 76 F6
Trinity Way. Bis St CM23 .... 76 F6
Trinity Wlk. Hert St SG13 .... 114 C3
Tristram Rd. Hit SG4 .... 22 B2
Triton Way. Heml H HP2 .... 124 F5

Trojan Terr. Saw CM21 .... 97 E3
Troon Gdns. Luton LU2 .... 45 E6
Trooper Rd. Ald HP23 .... 101 C5
Trotter's Gap. Sta Ab SG12 .... 115 E4
Trotters Bottom. Pot B EN5 .... 158 B2
Trotts Hill Jun & Inf Sch. Stev 36 F1
Trout Rise. Ric WD3 .... 165 B6
Troutstream Way. Ric WD3 .... 165 B5
Trouvere Pk. Heml H HP1 .... 124 B5
Trowbridge Gdns. Luton LU2 .... 45 F3
Trowley Bottom. Fla AL3 .... 105 B8
Trowley Hill Rd. Fla AL3 .... 84 B1
Trowley Rise. Abb L WD5 .... 153 F8
Truemans Rd. Hit SG5 .... 21 D2
Trumper Rd. Stev SG1 .... 36 F1
Trumpington Dr. St Alb AL1 .... 141 D8
Trundlers Way. Bus WD2 .... 168 E1
Truro Gdns. Luton LU3 .... 45 C5
Trust Rd. Ches EN8 .... 162 E5
Tucker St. Watf WD1 .... 167 C4
Tucker's Row. Bis St CM23 .... 76 F6
Tudor Ave. Ches EN7 .... 162 B8
Tudor Ave. Watf WD2 .... 154 D2
Tudor Cl. Ches EN7 .... 162 B8
Tudor Cl. Hat AL10 .... 129 F2
Tudor Cl. Hun SG12 .... 116 D8
Tudor Cl. Stev SG1 .... 36 C1
Tudor Cres. Enf EN2 .... 161 C1
Tudor Ct. Bor WD6 .... 169 E7
Tudor Ct. Hit SG5 .... 34 D6
Tudor Ct. Knee SG8 .... 2 B4
Tudor Ct. Ric WD3 .... 165 A1
Tudor Ct. Saw CM21 .... 97 E3
Tudor Dr. Watf WD2 .... 154 D2
Tudor Jun Mix Inf Sch. Heml H 124 E1
Tudor Manor Gdns. Watf WD2 .... 154 D7
Tudor Par. Ric WD3 .... 165 A2
Tudor Rd. Har HA3 .... 176 D1
Tudor Rd. Luton LU3 .... 45 B2
Tudor Rd. Pnr HA5 .... 175 C1
Tudor Rd. St Alb AL3 .... 127 E7
Tudor Rd. Welw AL6 .... 89 B3
Tudor Rd. Whea AL4 .... 108 C8
Tudor Rise. Hod EN10 .... 134 E2
Tudor Way. Hert SG14 .... 113 A7
Tudor Way. Ric WD3 .... 165 A2
Tudor Way. Wa Aby EN9 .... 163 D6
Tudor Wlk. Watf WD2 .... 154 D2
Tuffnells Way. Harp AL5 .... 85 D4
Tunfield Rd. Hod EN11 .... 135 A8
Tunnel Wood Cl. Watf WD1 .... 153 F2
Tunnel Wood Rd. Watf WD1 .... 153 F2
Tunnmeade. Harl CM20 .... 118 A1
Turf La. Gra SG4 .... 36 B4
Turkey St. Enf EN1,EN3 .... 162 C2
Turkey Street Sta. Enf 162 C2
Turmore Dale. Wel G C AL8 .... 110 C5
Turn Braemar. Heml H HP2 .... 105 B1
Turnberry Ctr. Sth Ox WD1 .... 175 C7
Turnberry Dr. Bri Wd AL2 .... 140 E1
Turner Cl. Stev SG2 .... 36 C2
Turner Rd. Bus WD2 .... 168 C5
Turners Cl. Bram SG14 .... 91 E4
Turners Cl. Harp AL5 .... 86 C4
Turners Ct. Ches EN8 .... 162 D8
Turners Hill. Ches EN8 .... 148 D1
Turners Hill. Heml H HP2 .... 124 E2
Turners Orch. Chor WD3 .... 164 D4
Turners Rd N. Luton LU2 .... 46 A2
Turners Rd S. Luton LU2 .... 46 A2
Turnford Sch. Ches 148 E3
Turnford Villas. Ches EN10 .... 148 F5
Turnpike Dr. Luton LU3 .... 31 C1
Turnpike Gn. Heml H HP2 .... 124 F7
Turnpike La. Ick SG5 .... 21 E3
Turnstones The. Watf WD2 .... 154 E3
Turpin's Rise. Royst SG8 .... 7 D5
Turpin's Rise. Stev SG2 .... 50 F1
Turpin's Way. Bal SG7 .... 23 F7
Turpins Chase. Welw AL6 .... 89 F7
Turpins Cl. Hert SG14 .... 112 F6
Turpins Ride. Welw AL6 .... 89 F7
Tuxford Cl. Bor WD6 .... 156 E1
Tweed Cl. Berk HP4 .... 122 B5
Twelve Acres. Wel G C AL7 .... 110 E4
Twelve Leys. Wing HP22 .... 60 B3
Twickenham Gdns. Har HA3 .... 176 F3
Twigden Ct. Luton LU3 .... 44 E5
Twinwoods. Stev SG1 .... 50 F4
Twist The. Wigg HP23 .... 100 D4
Twitchell The. Bal SG7 .... 23 F8
Two Acres. Wel G C AL7 .... 110 E4
Two Beeches. Heml H HP2 .... 124 F8
Two Dells La. Ash Gr HP5 .... 136 A4
Two Oaks Dr. Welw AL6 .... 90 C6
Two Waters Jun Mix Inf Sch.
  Heml H 138 D6
Two Waters Rd. Heml H HP3 .... 124 C1
Two Waters Rd. Heml H HP3 .... 138 D5
Twyford Bsns Ctr The. Bis St 77 A5
Twyford Bury La. Bis St CM22 .... 77 A5
Twyford Cl. Bis St CM23 .... 77 A5
Twyford Dr. Luton LU2 .... 46 D1
Twyford Gdns. Bis St CM23 .... 76 F4
Twyford Rd. Bis St CM23 .... 77 A5
Twyford Rd. St Alb AL4 .... 128 D7
Tye End. Stev SG2 .... 69 B8
Tyfield Cl. Ches EN8 .... 148 C1
Tylers Cl. Kin L WD4 .... 138 F3
Tylers Cswy. New St SG13 .... 132 C1
Tylers. Harp AL5 .... 86 D1
Tylers Hill Rd. Bot HP5 .... 150 B4
Tylers Mead. Luton LU2 .... 45 E5
Tylers Way. Radl WD2 .... 168 E4
Tylers Wood. Welw AL6 .... 90 C6
Tylersfield. Abb L WD5 .... 154 A8
Tynedale. Lon C AL2 .... 142 F4
Tynemouth Dr. Enf EN1 .... 162 A1
Typleden Cl. Heml H HP2 .... 124 D5
Tysoe Ave. Enf EN3 .... 162 F2
Tythe Rd. Luton LU4 .... 44 C8
Tyttenhanger Gn. Coln H AL1 .... 142 D4

Uckfield Rd. Enf EN3 .... 162 D2
Ufford Cl. Har HA3 .... 176 B3
Ufford Rd. Har HA3 .... 176 B3
Ullswater Rd. Heml H HP3 .... 125 C1

Underacres Cl. Heml H HP2 .... 125 A4
Underhill Inf Sch. Barn 171 E4
Underhill Jun Sch. Barn 171 E4
Underwood Rd. Stev SG1 .... 36 C2
Union Gn. Heml H HP2 .... 124 D4
Union St. Barn EN5 .... 171 E6
Union St. Luton LU1 .... 63 E6
Union Terr. Bun SG9 .... 40 E7
United States International
   University Sch. Bus 167 F5
Unity Rd. Enf EN3 .... 162 D2
University Cl. Bus WD2 .... 168 A5
University of Hertfordshire. Hat 129 F3
University of Hertfordshire
   (Hertford Campus). Hert 113 A4
Unwin Cl. Letw SG6 .... 22 E4
Unwin Pl. Stev SG2 .... 51 C3
Unwin Rd. Stev SG2 .... 51 C3
Updale Cl. Pot B EN6 .... 158 E6
Upland Dr. Bro Pk AL9 .... 145 B6
Uplands Ave. Hit SG4 .... 35 B6
Uplands. Brag SG11 .... 55 F6
Uplands. Cro Gr WD3 .... 165 F3
Uplands. Luton LU3 .... 44 D8
Uplands. Stev SG2 .... 51 D7
Uplands The. Bri Wd AL2 .... 140 E1
Uplands The. Harp AL5 .... 107 A4
Uplands. Ware SG12 .... 93 F2
Uplands. Wel G C AL8 .... 89 C2
Upper Ashlyns Rd. Berk HP4 .... 122 B3
Upper Barn. Heml H HP3 .... 138 F8
Upper Clabdens. Ware SG12 .... 93 F2
Upper Culver Rd. St Alb AL1 .... 127 F5
Upper Dagnall St. St Alb AL3 .... 127 D3
Upper George St. Luton LU1 .... 63 D7
Upper Gn. Tewin AL6 .... 90 D3
Upper Green Rd. Tewin AL6 .... 90 E2
Upper Hall Pk. Berk HP4 .... 122 E2
Upper Heath Rd. St Alb AL1 .... 127 F5
Upper Highway. Abb L WD5 .... 153 D6
Upper Hill Rise. Ric WD3 .... 165 B3
Upper Hitch. Sth Ox WD1 .... 167 E1
Upper Icknield Way. Ald LU7 .... 80 E1
Upper Icknield Way. Ast Cl HP22 ... 99 A3
Upper Icknield Way. Tri HP23 .... 100 D8
Upper King St. Royst SG8 .... 7 D6
Upper Lattimore Rd. St Alb AL1 .... 127 E3
Upper Marlborough Rd.
   St Alb AL1 .... 127 E3
Upper Marsh La. Hod EN11 .... 135 A5
Upper Maylins. Letw SG6 .... 23 C3
Upper Paddock Rd. Watf WD1 ...... 167 E3
Upper Pk. Harl CM20 .... 117 B1
Upper Sales. Heml H HP1 .... 123 F2
Upper Sean. Stev SG2 .... 51 A3
Upper Shott. Wel G C AL7 .... 111 A7
Upper Shott. Ham St EN7 .... 147 F5
Upper Station Rd. Radl WD7 .... 156 A4
Upper Tail. Sth Ox WD1 .... 175 E7
Upper Tilehouse St. Hit SG5 .... 34 E7
Upperfield Rd. Wel G C AL7 .... 110 F5
Upperstone Cl. Stot SG5 .... 11 F6
Upshire Rd. Wa Aby EN9 .... 163 F7
Upton Ave. St Alb AL3 .... 127 D4
Upton Cl. Luton LU2 .... 45 D6
Upton Cl. Pk St AL2 .... 141 D6
Upton Lodge Cl. Bus WD2 .... 168 C2
Upton Rd. Watf WD1 .... 167 B6
Upwell Rd. Luton LU2 .... 46 B2
Uranus Rd. Heml H HP2 .... 124 F5
Urban Rd. Bis St CM23 .... 77 B7
Uxbridge Rd. Ric WD3 .... 173 A8
Uxbridge Road (Harrow Weald).
   Stan HA3 .... 176 D3
Uxbridge Road (Hatch End).
   Pnr HA5 .... 175 F3
Uxbridge Road (Pinner). Pnr HA5 . 175 D2
Uxbridge Road (Stanmore).
   Stan HA7 .... 176 F4

Vadis Cl. Luton LU3 .... 44 E7
Vale Ave. Bor WD6 .... 170 B4
Vale Cl. Harp AL5 .... 85 D4
Vale Ct. Whea AL4 .... 108 D7
Vale Rd. Watf WD2 .... 167 E4
Valence Dr. Ches EN7 .... 148 A4
Valency Cl. Mo Pk HA6 .... 174 F6
Valerian Way. Stev SG2 .... 51 D8
Valerie Cl. St Alb AL1 .... 128 B3
Valeside. Hert SG14 .... 113 A6
Vallans Cl. Ware SG12 .... 93 D3
Vallansgate. Stev SG2 .... 51 B1
Valley Cl. Hert SG13 .... 113 D5
Valley Cl. Pnr HA5 .... 175 B1
Valley Cl. Stu LU6 .... 82 B4
Valley Cl. Wa Aby EN9 .... 163 C7
Valley Cl. Ware SG12 .... 93 B2
Valley Cl. Whip LU6 .... 81 E7
Valley Gn. Heml H HP2 .... 105 B1
Valley Gn The. Wel G C AL8 .... 110 C7
Valley La. Fla AL3 .... 83 A1
Valley Rd. Berk HP4 .... 121 F6
Valley Rd. Cod SG4 .... 67 F1
Valley Rd. Letw SG6 .... 22 D7
Valley Rd. Ric WD3 .... 165 B3
Valley Rd. St Alb AL3 .... 127 F7
Valley Rd. Stu LU6 .... 82 B4
Valley Rd. Wel G C AL8 .... 110 B6
Valley Rise. Royst SG8 .... 7 E6
Valley Rise. Watf WD2 .... 154 B6
Valley Rise. Whea AL4 .... 86 F2
Valley The. Whit SG4 .... 66 E7
Valley View. Barn EN5 .... 171 E3
Valley View. Gofs O EN7 .... 147 C3
Valley Way. Stev SG2 .... 51 A3
Valley Wlk. Cro Gr WD3 .... 166 C4
Valleyside. Heml H HP1 .... 123 F3
Vanda Cres. St Alb AL1 .... 127 F2
Vantorts Cl. Saw CM21 .... 97 E2
Vantorts Rd. Saw CM21 .... 97 E2
Vardon Rd. Stev SG1 .... 50 F8
Varna Cl. Luton LU3 .... 45 A3
Varney Cl. Ham St EN7 .... 148 A4
Varney Cl. Heml H HP1 .... 124 A3
Varney Rd. Heml H HP1 .... 123 F3
Vaughan Mead. Red AL3 .... 106 A4

Vaughan Rd. Harp AL5 .... 86 B1
Vaughan Rd. Stot SG5 .... 11 E7
Vauxhall Rd. Heml H HP2 .... 125 B3
Vauxhall Rd. Luton LU1 .... 64 B5
Vauxhall Way. Luton LU2 .... 46 B2
Vega Cres. Mo Pk HA6 .... 175 A6 1
Vega Rd. Bus WD2 .... 168 C2
Velizy Ave. Harl CM20 .... 117 D1
Venetia Rd. Luton LU2 .... 46 A4
Ventnor Gdns. Luton LU3 .... 45 A7
Ventura Pk. Lon C AL2 .... 141 F2
Venus Hill. Bov HP3 .... 151 A8
Ver Rd. Red AL3 .... 106 C6
Ver Rd. St Alb AL3 .... 127 C3
Vera Ct. Watf WD1 .... 167 D2
Vera La. Welw AL6 .... 90 B4
Verdure Cl. Bri Wd WD2 .... 154 E7
Verity Way. Stev SG1 .... 51 B8
Verlam Sch. St Alb 128 A5
Verney Cl. Berk HP4 .... 121 F5
Verney Cl. Tri HP23 .... 100 C5
Vernon Ave. Enf EN3 .... 162 E3
Vernon Dr. Hare UB9 .... 173 C2
Vernon Rd. Luton LU1 .... 63 C8
Vernon Rd. Watf WD1 .... 167 A4
Vernon's Cl. St Alb AL1 .... 127 E2
Veronica House. Wel G C AL7 ...... 111 A6
Verulam Gdns. Luton LU3 .... 44 F7
Verulam Golf Course. St Alb 127 F1
Verulam Rd. Hit SG5 .... 34 F8
Verulam Rd. St Alb AL3 .... 127 C4
Verwood Rd. Har HA2 .... 176 C1
Vespers Cl. Dun LU4 .... 44 A2
Vesta Ave. St Alb AL1 .... 141 C6
Veysey Cl. Heml H HP1 .... 124 B1
Viaduct Rd. Ware SG12 .... 114 E8
Viaduct Way. Wel G C AL7 .... 89 F2
Vian Ave. Enf EN3 .... 162 E4
Vicarage Cl. Arl SG15 .... 11 A1
Vicarage Cl. Bis St CM23 .... 76 F7 3
Vicarage Cl. Heml H HP1 .... 124 C2
Vicarage Cl. Nort EN6 .... 145 F1
Vicarage Cl. Shil SG5 .... 19 D3
Vicarage Cl. St Alb AL1 .... 141 C8
Vicarage Cl. Stand SG11 .... 55 E2
Vicarage Cswy. Hert H SG13 .... 114 B4
Vicarage Gdns. Fla AL3 .... 84 B1
Vicarage Gdns. Mars HP23 .... 80 A2
Vicarage Gdns. Pot En HP4 .... 123 B7
Vicarage La. Bov HP3 .... 137 B4
Vicarage La. Kin L WD4 .... 138 F2
Vicarage La. Pit LU7 .... 80 F5
Vicarage La. Stap SG14 .... 92 B2
Vicarage La. Bun SG9 .... 40 E8
Vicarage Rd. Mars HP23 .... 80 A2
Vicarage Rd. Pit LU7 .... 80 D3
Vicarage Rd. Pot En HP4 .... 123 A7
Vicarage Rd. Ware SG12 .... 93 E1
Vicarage Rd. Watf WD1 .... 167 A4
Vicarage Rd. Wigg HP23 .... 100 D1
Vicarage Road Prec. Watf WD1 .... 167 B5
Vicarage St. Luton LU1 .... 63 F7
Vicarage Wood. Harl CM20 .... 118 A1
Vicerons Pl. Bis St CM23 .... 76 D4
Victoria C of E Sch. Berk 122 C4
Victoria Cl. Ric WD3 .... 165 D2
Victoria Cl. Stev SG1 .... 50 D7
Victoria Dr. Stot SG5 .... 12 A5
Victoria La. Barn EN5 .... 171 F5
Victoria Pl. Heml H HP2 .... 124 D3
Victoria Rd. Berk HP4 .... 122 C4
Victoria Rd. Bus WD2 .... 168 B1
Victoria Rd. Harp AL5 .... 86 B1
Victoria Rd. Wa Aby EN9 .... 163 C5
Victoria Rd. Watf WD2 .... 154 B1
Victoria St. Luton LU1 .... 63 E6
Victoria St. St Alb AL1 .... 127 E3
Victoria St. Stev SG1 .... 50 D7
Victoria The. Hit SG5 .... 34 D8
Victors Way. Barn EN5 .... 171 F6
Victory Rd. Berk HP4 .... 122 A5
View Point. Stev SG1 .... 50 A5
View Rd. Pot B EN6 .... 159 C7
Vigors Croft. Hat AL10 .... 129 F4
Villa Ct. Luton LU2 .... 63 D8 6
Villa Rd. Luton LU2 .... 63 D8
Village Cl. St Alb AL4 .... 128 D7
Village St. Lan SG4 .... 49 F1
Villiers Cres. St Alb AL4 .... 128 D6
Villiers Rd. Watf WD1 .... 167 E3
Villiers Rd. Hert SG13 .... 113 E6
Villiers-Sur-Marne Ave.
   Bis St CM23 .... 76 D4
Vincent Cl. Ches EN8 .... 148 E3
Vincent Ct. Norwd HA6 .... 174 F2
Vincent. Letw SG6 .... 23 C4
Vincent Rd. Luton LU4 .... 44 D5
Vincenzo Cl. Wel G AL9 .... 144 C3
Vine Cl. Wel G C AL8 .... 110 C7
Vine Gr. East CM20 .... 117 E5
Vines The. Stot SG5 .... 11 F5
Vineyard The. Ware SG12 .... 94 A2
Vineyard The. Wel G C AL8 .... 110 C8
Vineyards Rd. Cuf EN6 .... 146 B2
Vinters Ave. Stev SG1 .... 50 F5
Violet Ave. Enf EN2 .... 161 D1
Violet Way. Ric WD3 .... 165 C5
Violets La. Fur P SG9 .... 43 B5
Virgil Dr. Hod EN10 .... 148 F8
Virginia Cl. Luton LU2 .... 45 F3
Viscount Cl. Luton LU3 .... 45 A5
Vivian Cl. Watf WD1 .... 167 A1
Vivian Gdns. Watf WD1 .... 167 A1
Vixen Dr. Hert SG13 .... 114 A6
Vyse Cl. Barn EN5 .... 171 C5

Wacketts. Ham St EN7 .... 148 A4
Waddesdon Cl. Luton LU2 .... 46 D2
Waddington Rd. St Alb AL3 .... 127 D3 1
Wade The. Wel G C AL7 .... 111 A3
Wades The. Hat AL10 .... 130 A2
Wadesmill Rd. Ton SG14 .... 92 D3
Wadham Rd. Wstle SG12 .... 92 D7
Wadhurst Ave. Luton LU3 .... 45 C4
Wadley Cl. Heml H HP2 .... 124 F2 1

Wadnall Way. Welw SG3 .... 68 F3
Waggon Rd. Had W EN4 .... 159 E2
Waggoners Rd. Ware SG12 .... 93 D2 4
Wagon Rd. Pot B EN4 .... 159 B2
Wagon Way. Ric WD3 .... 165 C6
Wain Cl. Pot B EN6 .... 145 B2
Wakefield Wlk. Ches EN8 .... 162 E4
Walcot Ave. Luton LU2 .... 46 B1
Waldeck Rd. Luton LU1,LU3 .... 63 C8
Waldegrave Pk. Harp AL5 .... 86 D1
Walden End. Stev SG1 .... 50 E4
Walden Pl. Wel G C AL8 .... 110 D8
Walden Rd. Wel G C AL8 .... 110 D8
Waleran Cl. Stan HA7 .... 176 F4
Waleys Cl. Luton LU3 .... 44 E8
Walfords Cl. Harl CM17 .... 118 C3
Walk The. Pot B EN6 .... 159 B7
Walkern Jun Mix Inf Sch. Walk 52 A3
Walkern Rd. Ben SG2 .... 52 A3
Walkern Rd. Ben SG2 .... 52 D5
Walkern Rd. Stev SG1 .... 50 D8
Walkern Rd. Wat St SG14 .... 70 D5
Walkers Cl. Harp AL5 .... 107 C7
Walkers' Ct. Bal SG7 .... 23 F8
Walkers Rd. Harp AL5 .... 107 B7
Wall Hall. Radl 155 B3
Wallace Way. Hit SG4 .... 22 A2
Waller Ave. Luton LU3,LU4 .... 44 F2
Waller Dr. Norwd HA6 .... 175 A2
Waller Street Mall. Luton LU1 ...... 63 E7
Waller's Cl. Gt Ch SG8 .... 9 F2
Wallers Rd. Hod EN11 .... 115 B1
Wallingford Wlk. St Alb AL1 .... 141 D8
Wallington Rd. Bal SG7 .... 13 D1
Wallington Rd. Clo SG7 .... 13 D1
Walnut Ave. Bal SG7 .... 24 A4
Walnut Cl. Chis AL2 .... 141 B4
Walnut Cl. Hit SG4 .... 35 B4
Walnut Cl. Luton LU2 .... 46 B4
Walnut Cl. Muc H SG10 .... 74 F7
Walnut Cl. Stot SG5 .... 11 F6
Walnut Cotts. Saw CM21 .... 97 E3
Walnut Ct. Wel G C AL7 .... 110 E3
Walnut Dr. Bis St CM23 .... 76 D3
Walnut Gn. Bus WD2 .... 167 F7
Walnut Gr. Heml H HP2 .... 124 D3
Walnut Gr. Wel G C AL7 .... 110 E3
Walnut House. Wel G C AL7 .... 110 F3
Walnut Tree Ave. Saw CM21 .... 97 E4
Walnut Tree Cl. Ast SG2 .... 51 D5
Walnut Tree Cl. Ches EN8 .... 162 D8
Walnut Tree Cl. Hod EN11 .... 135 A6
Walnut Tree Cres. Saw CM21 .... 97 E3
Walnut Tree La. Far CM23 .... 58 E4
Walnut Tree Rd. Pirt SG5 .... 20 D3
Walnut Tree Wlk. Gt Am SG12 .... 114 E6
Walnut Way. Ick SG5 .... 21 F1
Walpole Cl. Pnr HA5 .... 176 A4
Walpole Ct. Stev SG2 .... 69 C7
Walsh Cl. Hit SG5 .... 34 D7
Walsham Cl. Stev SG2 .... 69 C7
Walshford Way. Bor WD6 .... 157 A1
Walsingham Cl. Hat AL10 .... 129 F6
Walsingham Cl. Luton LU2 .... 45 D7
Walsingham Way. Lon C AL2 .... 142 C4
Walsworth Rd. Hit SG4 .... 35 A8
Waltham Cross Sta. Ches 162 F5
Waltham Holy Cross City
   Jun & Inf Sch. Wa Aby 163 D6
Waltham Rd. Hit SG4 .... 34 F6 6
Waltham Rd. Lo Naz EN9 .... 149 F5
Walton Gdns. Wa Aby EN9 .... 163 B6
Walton Rd. Hod EN11 .... 135 C8
Walton Rd. Ware SG12 .... 114 D8
Walton Rd. Watf WD2 .... 167 E5
Walton St. St Alb AL1 .... 127 F5
Walverns Cl. Watf WD1 .... 167 C3
Wandon Cl. Luton LU2 .... 46 C4
Wannions Cl. Bov HP3 .... 136 A1
Wansford Pk. Bor WD6 .... 170 E5
Warburton Cl. Stan HA3 .... 176 D4
Ward Cl. Ham St EN7 .... 148 A4
Ward Cl. Ware SG12 .... 93 C2
Ward Cres. Bis St CM23 .... 76 E6
Warden Hill Cl. Luton LU2 .... 45 C8
Warden Hill Gdns. Luton LU2 .... 45 C8
Warden Hill Inf Sch. Luton 45 C7
Warden Hill Jun Sch. Luton 45 C7
Warden Hill Rd. Luton LU2 .... 45 C8
Wardown Cres. Luton LU2 .... 45 E2
Wardown Ct. Luton LU3 .... 45 D2
Wardown House (Luton
   Museum & Art Gallery). Luton . 45 D2
Ware Coll. Ware 114 D8
Ware Park Rd. Hert SG14 .... 113 B8
Ware Rd. Gt Am SG13 .... 115 A2
Ware Rd. Hod EN11 .... 115 A4
Ware Rd. Sac SG12 .... 71 C3
Ware Rd. Ton SG12 .... 92 F6
Ware Rd. SG12,SG14 .... 71 C3
Ware Rd. Widf SG12 .... 95 D4
Ware St Catherine's
   Jun Mix & Inf Sch. Ware 93 B2
Ware Sta. Ware 114 D8
Wareham's La. Hert SG14 .... 113 C5
Warenford Way. Bor WD6 .... 170 A8
Wareside CE Prim Sch. Wars 94 E3
Wareside. Heml H HP2 .... 105 A1
Warham Rd. Har HA3 .... 176 F1
Warmark Rd. Heml H HP1 .... 123 E5
Warminster Cl. Luton LU2 .... 46 C5
Warneford Pl. Watf WD1 .... 167 E3
Warner Rd. Ware SG12 .... 114 D8
Warners Ave. Hod EN11 .... 134 F4
Warners Cl. Stev SG2 .... 51 C3
Warners End Rd. Heml H HP1 ..... 124 B3
Warren Cl. Hat AL10 .... 130 B8
Warren Cl. Letw SG6 .... 22 D7
Warren Dale. Wel G C AL8 .... 89 D1
Warren Dr The. Nwml E LU1 .... 64 C1
Warren Gr. Bor WD6 .... 170 D5
Warren La. Clo SG7 .... 24 D7
Warren La. Cotrd SG9 .... 39 B6

Warren La. Stan HA7 .... 176 F8
Warren Park Rd. Hert SG14 .... 113 D7
Warren Pl. Hert SG14 .... 113 D6 14
Warren Rd. Bus WD2 .... 168 D1
Warren Rd. Luton LU1 .... 62 F8
Warren Rd. St Alb AL1 .... 141 C7
Warren Terr. Hert SG14 .... 113 D8
Warren The. Harp AL5 .... 107 A6
Warren The. Radl WD7 .... 156 B6
Warren The. Royst SG8 .... 7 B7
Warren Way. Welw AL6 .... 89 A8
Warrenfield Cl. Ches EN7 .... 162 A8
Warrengate La. Pot B EN6 .... 158 C8
Warrengate Rd. Wel G AL9 .... 144 C4
Warrensgreen La. Wes SG4 .... 37 D5
Warton Gn. Luton LU2 .... 46 E2
Warwick Ave. Cuf EN6 .... 146 D4
Warwick Cl. Bus WD2 .... 168 C2
Warwick Cl. Cuf EN6 .... 146 D4
Warwick Cl. Hert SG13 .... 113 C4
Warwick Cl. Luton LU4 .... 63 C8
Warwick Dr. Ches EN8 .... 148 D3
Warwick Rd. Bor WD6 .... 170 D6
Warwick Rd E. Luton LU4 .... 63 B8
Warwick Rd. Enf EN3 .... 162 F2
Warwick Rd. St Alb AL1 .... 127 F5
Warwick Rd. Stev SG2 .... 51 C6
Warwick Rd W. Luton LU4 .... 63 B8
Warwick Way. Cro Gr WD3 .... 166 C5
Wash La. Pot B EN6 .... 158 C4
Wash La. Pot B EN6 .... 158 C5
Wash The. Fur P SG9 .... 43 D5
Wash The. Hert SG14 .... 113 D6
Washington Ave. Heml H HP2 ...... 124 E8
Watchlytes Jun Mix & Inf Sch.
   Wel G C 111 C6
Watchlytes. Wel G C AL7 .... 111 C6
Watchmead. Wel G C AL7 .... 110 A6
Water End. Pot En HP4 .... 123 C7
Water La. Abb L WD4 .... 139 B2
Water La. Berk HP4 .... 122 C4
Water La. Bis St CM23 .... 76 D3
Water La. Bov HP3 .... 137 B1
Water La. Hert SG14 .... 113 C5
Water La. Hit SG5 .... 21 F1
Water La. St M CM24 .... 59 E6
Water La. Watf WD1 .... 167 D5
Waterbeach. Wel G C AL7 .... 111 D6
Watercress Cl. Ast SG2 .... 51 D5
Waterdale. Hert SG13 .... 113 C4
Waterdell La. St Ipp SG4 .... 35 A2
Waterend La. Red AL3 .... 106 B5
Waterfield. Wel G C AL7 .... 111 B7
Waterfields Way. Watf WD1 .... 167 E5
Waterford Gn. Wel G C AL7 .... 111 A7
Watergate The. Sth Ox WD1 .... 175 D8
Waterhouse Gate. St Alb AL1 ...... 127 D3
Waterhouse St. Heml H HP1 .... 124 C2
Waterhouse The. Heml H HP1 ..... 124 C2
Waterloo La. Hol SG5 .... 21 A6
Waterlow Mews. L Wym SG4 .... 35 E3
Waterman Cl. Watf WD1 .... 167 B3
Watermark Way. Hert SG13 .... 113 F6
Watermead Rd. Luton LU3 .... 44 F6
Watermill Ind Est. Bun 40 E6
Watermill La. Hert SG14 .... 113 D8
Waterside. Berk HP4 .... 122 C4
Waterside Cl. Kin L UB5 .... 139 B2
Waterside. Lon C AL2 .... 142 E4
Waterside Pl. Sheer CM21 .... 98 A2
Waterside. Sta M CM24 .... 59 E6
Waterside. Wel G C AL7 .... 90 B1
Waterslade Gn. Luton LU3 .... 45 B6
Watersplash Ct. Lon C AL2 .... 142 F4
Watery La. Hat AL3 .... 84 E3
Watery La. Hat AL10 .... 129 E4
Watery La. Mars HP23 .... 79 F5
Watford Arches Ret Pk. Watf 167 D4
Watford By-Pass. Stan WD6 .... 169 F7
Watford Central Prim Sch. Watf ... 167 C5
Watford Coll. Watf 167 D6
Watford County Ct. Watf 167 C5
Watford Enterprise Ctr. Watf 166 E3
Watford Field Jun Mix & Inf Sch.
   Watf 167 D4
Watford Fields Rd. Watf WD1 ...... 167 C4
Watford Football Gd. Watf 167 B4
Watford General Hospl
   (Shrodells Wing). Watf 167 B4
Watford Gram Sch. Watf 166 F5
Watford Gram Sch for Girls. Watf 167 B5
Watford Heath. Watf WD1 .... 167 D2
Watford High Street Sta. Watf 167 C5
Watford North Sta. Watf 154 C2
Watford Rd. Abb L WD4 .... 153 C6
Watford Rd. Chis AL2 .... 141 A6
Watford Rd. Cro Gr WD3 .... 166 B3
Watford Rd. Elst WD6 .... 169 C3
Watford Rd. Kin L WD4 .... 139 A1
Watford Rd. Mo Pk HA6 .... 175 A4
Watford Rd. Radl WD7 .... 155 F4
Watford Rd. St Alb AL1 .... 141 A6
Watford Sch of Art & Design.
   Watf 154 B1
Watford Sch of Music. Watf 154 A1
Watford Sta. Watf 166 F6
Watford Stadium Sta. Watf 167 A3
Watling Cl. Heml H HP2 .... 124 E6 1
Watling Ct. Bor WD6 .... 169 D3
Watling Knoll. Radl WD7 .... 155 F6
Watling St. Pk St AL2 .... 141 D6
Watling St. St Alb AL1 .... 141 C8
Watling View Sch. St Alb 141 D7
Watling View. St Alb AL1 .... 141 D7
Watson Ave. St Alb AL1 .... 127 F6
Watson's Wlk. St Alb AL1 .... 127 E2
Watton at Stone Prim Sch. Wat St 70 D3
Watton at Stone Sta. Wat St 70 D3
Watton Rd. Kneb SG3 .... 69 A5
Watton Rd. Ware SG12 .... 93 C2
Watton Rd. Wat St SG3 .... 70 B2
Watts Cl. L Had SG11 .... 57 C2
Waulud Inf Sch. Luton 44 E7

Waulud Jun Sch. Luton 44 E7
Waulud's Bank Dr. Luton LU3 .... 44 E7
Wavell Cl. Ches EN8 .... 148 E4
Wavell Rd. St Alb AL1 .... 128 C2
Waveney. Heml H HP2 .... 124 F8
Waveney Rd. Harp AL5 .... 85 F8
Waverley Cl. Stev SG2 .... 69 A8
Waverley Gdns. Norwd HA6 .... 175 C2
Waverley Rd. St Alb AL3 .... 127 D5
Waxwell Cl. Pnr HA5 .... 175 D1
Waxwell La. Pnr HA5 .... 175 D1
Wayre St. Harl CM17 .... 118 C4
Wayre The. Harl CM17 .... 118 C4
Waysbrook. Letw SG6 .... 23 B5
Wayside Ave. Bus WD2 .... 168 D3
Wayside. Chipf WD4 .... 138 B1
Wayside. Pot B EN6 .... 159 B7
Wayside. Shen WD7 .... 156 D6
Wayside. The. Heml H HP3 .... 125 C8
Waysmeet. Letw SG6 .... 23 B3
Waytemore Rd. Bis St CM23 .... 76 E6
Weald Coll (Annexe). Har 176 E2
Weald Fst Sch. Har 176 F1
Weald La. Har HA3 .... 176 D2
Weald Mid Sch. Har 176 F1
Weald Rise. Har HA3 .... 176 F2
Wealdwood Gdns. Pnr HA5 .... 176 B4
Weall Gn. Watf WD2 .... 154 B7
Weardale Ct. Barn EN5 .... 171 C4
Weatherby Rd. Luton LU4 .... 44 D2
Weavers Rd. Tri HP23 .... 99 E4
Weavers Way. Bal SG7 .... 24 A8
Webb Cl. Letw SG6 .... 23 C5
Webb Rise. Stev SG1 .... 50 F7
Webber Cl. Elst WD6 .... 169 D3
Wedgewood Cl. Norwd HA6 .... 174 C4
Wedgewood Pk. Stev SG1 .... 37 C2
Wedgwood Ct. Stev SG1 .... 37 C2
Wedgwood Way. Stev SG1 .... 37 C2
Wedmore Rd. Hit SG4 .... 35 A6
Wedon Way. Byg SG7 .... 13 D1
Weedon Cl. Henlw SG16 .... 10 C5
Weighton Rd. Har HA3 .... 176 D2
Welbeck Cl. Bor WD6 .... 170 A6
Welbeck Rise. Harp AL5 .... 107 D6
Welbury Ave. Luton LU3 .... 45 C7
Welch Pl. Pnr HA5 .... 175 C2
Welclose St. St Alb AL3 .... 127 C3
Welcote Dr. Norwd HA6 .... 174 D4
Weldon Cl. Luton LU2 .... 46 E1
Welham Cl. Wel G AL9 .... 144 C7
Welham Green Sta. Wel G 144 D8
Welham Manor. Wel G AL9 .... 144 C7
Well App. Barn EN5 .... 171 C4
Well Croft. Heml H HP1 .... 124 B4
Well End Rd. Bor WD6 .... 157 D1
Well Garth. Wel G C AL7 .... 110 E5
Well Gn. Bram SG14 .... 91 C4
Well La. Harl CM19 .... 117 A1
Well La. Men LU7 .... 61 B8
Well Rd. Barn EN5 .... 171 C4
Well Rd. Nort EN6 .... 145 E2
Well-Row. Bay SG13 .... 132 F6
Wellands. Hat AL10 .... 130 A7
Wellbrook Mews. Tri HP23 .... 100 B6
Wellcroft. Wel G C AL7 .... 111 A4
Wellcroft. Pit HP1 .... 80 F5
Wellcroft Rd. Wel G C AL7 .... 111 A4
Wellen Rise. Heml H HP3 .... 138 E8
Wellers Gr. Ches EN7 .... 148 A3
Wellesley Ave. Mo Pk HA6 .... 174 F5
Wellesley Cres. Pot B EN6 .... 158 E6
Wellfield Cl. Hat AL10 .... 130 A6
Wellfield Cl. Stev SG1 .... 37 B1
Wellfield Rd. Hat AL10 .... 130 A7
Wellfield Wood Jun Mix Sch. Stev 37 A2
Wellgate Rd. Luton LU4 .... 44 D2
Wellhouse Cl. Luton LU1 .... 63 A7
Wellhouse La. Barn EN5 .... 171 D5
Wellingham Ave. Hit SG5 .... 21 D1
Wellington Ave. Pnr HA5 .... 175 F2
Wellington Dr. Wel G C AL7 .... 111 C6
Wellington Pl. Knee SG8 .... 2 B5
Wellington Rd. Lon C AL2 .... 142 D5
Wellington Rd. Pnr HA5 .... 175 C2
Wellington Rd. St Alb AL1 .... 128 B2
Wellington Rd. Stev SG1 .... 51 C5
Wellington Rd. Watf WD1 .... 167 B7
Wellington St. Hert SG14 .... 113 B7
Wellington St. Luton LU1 .... 63 D7
Wells Cl. Harp AL5 .... 85 E4
Wells Cl. St Alb AL3 .... 127 C4
Wells Yd. Ware SG12 .... 93 D1 8
Wells Yd. Watf WD1 .... 167 B6
Wellside Cl. Barn EN5 .... 171 C5
Wellstones. Watf WD1 .... 167 B5
Wellswood Cl. Heml H HP2 .... 125 B4
Welsummer Way. Ches EN8 .... 148 D3
Weltmore Rd. Luton LU3 .... 44 F6
Welwyn By Pass Rd. Welw AL6 ...... 89 F7
Welwyn Cl. Heml H HP2 .... 124 F7
Welwyn Garden City Sta. Wel G C 110 D7
Welwyn North Sta. Welw 89 F3
Welwyn Rd. Hert SG14 .... 112 F7
Wendover Cl. Harp AL5 .... 86 D1
Wendover Cl. St Alb AL4 .... 128 C8
Wendover Ct. Welw AL6 .... 89 C8
Wendover Dr. Welw AL6 .... 89 C8
Wendover Way. Bus WD2 .... 168 C3
Wendover Way. Luton LU2 .... 45 F3
Wengeo La. Ware SG12 .... 93 B2
Wenham Ct. Walk SG2 .... 52 B8
Wenlock Jun Sch. Luton 64 B8
Wenlock St. Luton LU2 .... 63 E8
Wensley Cl. Harp AL5 .... 107 D6
Wensley Dale. Luton LU2 .... 45 E1
Wensleydale. Heml H HP2 .... 124 F6
Wensum Way. Ric WD3 .... 165 D1
Wentbridge Path. Bor WD6 .... 157 A1
Wentworth Ave. Bor WD6 .... 169 F4
Wentworth Cl. Barn EN5 .... 171 E6
Wentworth Cl. Pot B EN6 .... 159 A8
Wentworth Dr. Bis St CM23 .... 76 D6
Wentworth Rd. Barn EN5 .... 171 D6
Wentworth Rd. Hert SG13 .... 113 C3

Wenwell Cl. Ast Cl HP22 ...... 99 A3
Wesley Cl. Arl SG15 ...... 11 A4
Wesley Cl. Gofs O EN7 ...... 147 C3
Wesley Rd. Mark AL3 ...... 83 E5
Wessex Ct. Barn EN5 ...... 171 D5
Wessex Dr. Pnr HA5 ...... 175 E3
West Alley. Hit SG5 ...... 34 E7 3
West Ave. Bal SG7 ...... 23 E8
West Ave. Chis AL2 ...... 141 B6
West Burrowfield. Wel G C AL7 ...... 110 D4
West Chantry. Har HA3 ...... 176 B2
West Cl. Barn EN5 ...... 171 B4
West Cl. Hit SG4 ...... 22 B1
West Cl. Hod EN11 ...... 135 A8
West Cl. Stev SG1 ...... 50 F5
West Comm. Harp AL5 ...... 107 B6
West Comm. Red AL3 ...... 106 A4
West Common Cl. Harp AL5 ...... 107 B5
West Common Gr. Harp AL5 ...... 107 B5
West Common Way. Harp AL5 ...... 107 A4
West Ct. Saw CM21 ...... 97 E3
West Dene. Gt Gd HP2 ...... 104 A8
West Dr. Arl SG15 ...... 11 B4
West Dr. Stan HA3 ...... 176 A3
West Dr. Watf WD2 ...... 154 B3
West Drive Gdns. Stan HA3 ...... 176 D4
West End. Ashw SG7 ...... 4 C3
West End La. Barn EN5 ...... 171 D5
West End La. Ess AL9 ...... 131 D6
West End Rd. Bric EN7 ...... 147 F8
West End Rd. Ched LU7 ...... 79 F7
West Herts Coll Watford Campus. Watf 167 A6
West Herts Golf Course. Sar 166 C7
West Hill. Hit SG5 ...... 34 D7
West Hill Rd. Hod EN11 ...... 134 F4
West Hill Rd. Luton LU1 ...... 63 E5
West Hyde La. C St P SL9 ...... 172 A4
West La. Gt Of SG5 ...... 33 C2
West La. Pirt SG5 ...... 20 D5
West Lieth. Tri HP23 ...... 99 F1
West Mead. Wel G C AL7 ...... 111 B3
West Passage. Tri HP23 ...... 100 A3
West Rd. Berk HP4 ...... 122 A5
West Rd. Bis St CM23 ...... 76 E6
West Rd. H Wy CM21 ...... 97 C3
West Rd. Harl CM20 ...... 118 A4
West Rd. Saw CM21 ...... 97 C3
West Rd. Sta M CM24 ...... 59 E6
West Reach. Stev SG2 ...... 50 F2
West Riding. Bri Wd AL2 ...... 140 F1
West Riding. Tewin AL6 ...... 90 D5
West Side. Ches EN10 ...... 148 E6
West St. Hert SG13 ...... 113 C5
West St. Lily LU2 ...... 32 D1
West St. Ware SG12 ...... 93 D1
West St. Watf WD1 ...... 167 B7
West Valley Rd. Heml H HP3 ...... 138 D7
West View Gdns. Elst WD6 ...... 169 D3
West View. Hat AL10 ...... 130 A7
West View. Letw SG6 ...... 22 E5
West View Rd. St Alb AL3 ...... 127 D4
West Watford Sta. Watf 166 F4
West Way. Harp AL5 ...... 86 C2
West Way. Ric WD3 ...... 165 B1
West Way. Wa Aby EN9 ...... 163 B2
West Ways. Norwd HA6 ...... 175 A1
Westall Cl. Hert SG13 ...... 113 C5
Westall Mews. Hert SG13 ...... 113 C5
Westbourne Mews. St Alb AL1 ...... 127 D3
Westbourne Rd. Luton LU4 ...... 45 B1
Westbrook Cl. Ste Mo SG8 ...... 5 B8
Westbrook Hay (Sch). Heml H 137 D7
Westbury Cl. Hit SG5 ...... 34 D8
Westbury Gdns. Luton LU2 ...... 45 E3
Westbury Pl. Letw SG6 ...... 22 E5
Westbury Prim Sch. Letw 22 E5
Westbury Rd. Mo Pk HA6 ...... 174 E7
Westbury Rd. Watf WD1 ...... 167 B4
Westbush Cl. Hod EN11 ...... 114 F1
Westcott. Wel G C AL7 ...... 111 D7
Westcroft Cl. Enf EN3 ...... 162 C1
Westcroft Cl. Hod EN10 ...... 135 A4
Westell Cl. Bal SG7 ...... 24 A8
Westerdale. Heml H HP2 ...... 124 E6
Westerdale. Luton LU4 ...... 44 B4
Western Ave. Henlw SG16 ...... 10 B3
Western Cl. Letw SG6 ...... 11 E1
Western House Hosp. Ware 93 E2
Western Rd. Lo Naz EN9 ...... 135 E1
Western Rd. Luton LU1 ...... 63 D6
Western Rd. Tri HP23 ...... 99 F3
Western Terr. Hod EN11 ...... 115 B1
Western Way. Letw SG6 ...... 11 F1
Westfield Ave. Harp AL5 ...... 86 A3
Westfield Cl. Watf WD2 ...... 154 D1
Westfield Cl. Bis St CM23 ...... 76 E8
Westfield Cl. Ches EN8 ...... 162 F8
Westfield Cl. Hit SG5 ...... 34 D7
Westfield Ct. St Alb AL3 ...... 141 A8
Westfield Cty Prim Sch. Berk 121 F5
Westfield Cty Prim Sch. Hod 134 F7
Westfield Dr. Harp AL5 ...... 86 B4
Westfield. Hat AL9 ...... 144 F8
Westfield La. Hit SG5 ...... 34 D7
Westfield Pk. Pnr HA5 ...... 175 F3
Westfield Pl. Harp AL5 ...... 86 B4
Westfield Rd. Bis St CM23 ...... 76 E8
Westfield Rd. Harp AL5 ...... 86 B4
Westfield Rd. Hert SG14 ...... 113 C8
Westfield Rd. Hod EN11 ...... 134 F7
Westfield Rd. Nthch HP4 ...... 121 E6
Westfield Sch. Watf 166 F3
Westfield. Wel G C AL7 ...... 111 A7
Westfield Wlk. Ches EN8 ...... 162 F8
Westfields. St Alb AL3 ...... 141 A8
Westgate. Stev SG1 ...... 50 D5
Westholm. Letw SG6 ...... 23 A8
Westholme. Letw SG6 ...... 22 F8
Westland Dr. Bro Pk AL9 ...... 144 E4
Westland Rd. Watf WD1 ...... 167 B7
Westlea Ave. Watf WD2 ...... 154 E4
Westlea Cl. Hod EN10 ...... 148 F8
Westlea Rd. Hod EN10 ...... 148 F8
Westlecote Gdns. Luton LU2 ...... 45 A7
Westly Wood. Wel G C AL7 ...... 111 A7
Westmade Cl. Ches EN8 ...... 148 B2
Westmill La. Ick SG5 ...... 21 C3
Westmill Rd. Hit SG5 ...... 21 D1
Westmill Rd. Thun SG12 ...... 93 A3

Westminster Ct. St Alb AL1 ...... 127 C1
Westmorland Ave. Luton LU3 ...... 44 F5
Weston Ave. Royst SG8 ...... 7 C7
Weston Ct. Pot B EN6 ...... 158 F7
Weston Jun Mix Inf Sch. Wes 24 C1
Weston Rd. Stev SG1 ...... 36 E1
Weston Way. Bal SG7 ...... 23 E7
Westray. Heml H HP3 ...... 125 C1
Westridge Cl. Heml H HP1 ...... 123 F3
Westview Ct. Elst WD6 ...... 169 D3
Westview Rise. Heml H HP2 ...... 124 D4
Westway. Luton LU2 ...... 46 C4
Westwick Cl. Heml H HP2 ...... 125 E2
Westwick Pl. Watf WD2 ...... 154 C5
Westwick Row. Heml H HP2 ...... 125 E2
Westwood Ave. Hit SG4 ...... 35 A6
Westwood Cl. Pot B EN6 ...... 145 A1
Wetherby Cl. Stev SG1 ...... 51 C8
Wetherby Rd. Bor WD6 ...... 169 E8
Wetherby Rd. Enf EN2 ...... 161 C1
Wetherfield. Sta M CM24 ...... 59 D7
Wetherly Cl. Harl CM17 ...... 118 F4
Wetherne Link. Luton LU4 ...... 44 C5
Wexham Cl. Luton LU3 ...... 44 E8
Weybourne Cl. Harp AL5 ...... 86 D2
Weybourne Dr. Luton LU2 ...... 45 C7
Weymouth St. Heml H HP3 ...... 138 D7
Weyver Ct. St Alb AL1 ...... 127 E4
Whaley Rd. Pot B EN6 ...... 159 C6
Wharf La. Nthch HP4 ...... 121 C8
Wharf La. Ric WD3 ...... 165 E1
Wharf Rd. Bis St CM23 ...... 76 F6
Wharf Rd. Heml H HP1 ...... 124 B1
Wharf Rd. Hod EN10 ...... 148 F8
Wharf Row. Ast Cl HP22 ...... 99 B4
Wharfdale. Luton LU4 ...... 44 C5
Wharfedale. Heml H HP2 ...... 124 E6
Wheat Cl. St Alb AL4 ...... 128 A7
Wheat Croft. Bis St CM23 ...... 76 E4
Wheat Hill. Letw SG6 ...... 22 F8
Wheatbarn. Wel G C AL7 ...... 111 B7
Wheatcotes. Welw SG3 ...... 69 C1
Wheatcroft. Ches EN7 ...... 148 A4
Wheatcroft Jun Mix Inf Sch. Hert 114 A7
Wheatfield Ave. Harp AL5 ...... 107 A5
Wheatfield Cres. Royst SG8 ...... 7 E6
Wheatfield. Hat AL10 ...... 130 B6
Wheatfield. Heml H HP2 ...... 124 D5
Wheatfields. Harp AL5 ...... 107 A4
Wheatfields. Harl CM17 ...... 118 C6
Wheatfields Inf Sch. St Alb 128 B7
Wheatfields Jun Mix Inf Sch. St Alb 128 B7
Wheathampstead Rd. Harp AL5 ...... 107 E8
Wheathampstead Rd. Whea AL4 ...... 108 A8
Wheathampstead Sch. Whea 108 C7
Wheatlands. Stev SG2 ...... 51 C7
Wheatley Cl. Saw CM21 ...... 97 C1
Wheatley Cl. Wel G C AL7 ...... 111 A4
Wheatley Rd. Wel G C AL7 ...... 111 A4
Wheatleys. St Alb AL4 ...... 128 C5
Wheatlock Mead. Red AL3 ...... 106 A5
Wheatsheaf Dr. Ware SG12 ...... 93 B3
Wheatsheaf Rd. Hun SG12 ...... 95 D1
Wheelers Cl. Lo Naz EN9 ...... 135 F1
Wheelers La. Heml H HP3 ...... 124 E1
Wheelright Cl. Bus WD2 ...... 168 A8
Whempstead La. Wat St SG12 ...... 71 B6
Whempstead Rd. Wat St SG12 ...... 71 B7
Whetstone Cl. Welw AL6 ...... 89 E8
Whinbush Gr. Hit SG5 ...... 34 F8
Whinbush Rd. Hit SG5 ...... 34 F8
Whippendell Hill. Chipf WD4 ...... 138 C1
Whippendell Rd. Watf WD1 ...... 166 F4
Whipperley Ct. Luton LU1 ...... 63 C5
Whipperley Inf Sch. Luton 63 A6
Whipperley Ring. Luton LU1 ...... 63 A6
Whipperley Way. Luton LU1 ...... 63 B5
Whipsnade Park Golf Course. Whip 81 E5
Whipsnade Wildlife Animal Pk. Whip 81 F7
Whisper Wood. Ric WD3 ...... 165 B6
Whisperwood Cl. Har HA3 ...... 176 E3
Whit Hern Ct. Ches EN8 ...... 148 C1
Whitby Rd. Luton LU3 ...... 45 C1
White Bear. Sta M CM24 ...... 59 E8
White Craig Cl. Pnr HA5 ...... 176 A5
White Crofts. Stot SG5 ...... 11 F6
White Gate Gdns. Har HA3 ...... 176 F3
White Hart Cl. Bun SG9 ...... 40 E8
White Hart Dr. Heml H HP2 ...... 124 F2
White Hart Rd. Heml H HP2 ...... 125 A2
White Hart St. Heml H HP11 ...... 138 D7
White Hedge Dr. St Alb AL3 ...... 127 C5
White Hill. Ash Gr HP5 ...... 136 C7
White Hill. Fla AL3 ...... 105 B8
White Hill. Heml H HP1 ...... 123 F7
White Hill. Ric WD3 ...... 174 A4
White Hill. Walk SG2 ...... 38 C2
White Hill. Welw AL6 ...... 89 A3
White Horse La. Lon C AL2 ...... 142 C4
White Horse La. Welw AL6 ...... 90 C7
White House The. Ches EN8 ...... 148 B2
White La. St Ipp SG4 ...... 49 C7
White Orchards. Barn N20 ...... 171 F1
White Post Field. Saw CM21 ...... 97 D2
White Shack La. Sar WD3 ...... 152 F2
White Stubbs La. Brick EN10 ...... 133 C2
White Stubbs La. New St SG13 ...... 133 C2
White Way The. Stev SG2 ...... 51 C7
Whitebarns. Fur P SG9 ...... 43 A5
Whitebarns La. Fur P SG9 ...... 43 A6
Whitebeam Cl. Ham St EN7 ...... 147 E5
Whitebeams. Chis AL2 ...... 141 C3
Whitebeams. Hat AL10 ...... 130 A2
Whitebroom Rd. Heml H HP1 ...... 123 E5
Whitechurch Cl. Luton LU2 ...... 46 D2
Whitechurch Gdns. Letw SG6 ...... 23 C3
Whitecroft Rd. Luton LU2 ...... 64 A8
Whitecroft. St Alb AL1 ...... 142 B8
Whitefield Ave. Luton LU3 ...... 44 C7
Whitefield House. Hat AL10 ...... 130 A7
Whitefield Inf Sch. Luton 44 E8
Whitefield Jun Sch. Luton 44 E8
Whitefields Rd. Ches EN8 ...... 148 C3
Whitefriars Ave. Har HA3 ...... 176 E1
Whitefriars Centre Coll. Har 176 D1
Whitefriars Dr. Har HA3 ...... 176 E1
Whitefriars Fst & Mid Sch. Har 176 E1
Whitefriars Trad Est. Har 176 D1

Whitegale Cl. Hit SG4 ...... 35 A6
Whitegates Cl. Cro Gr WD3 ...... 166 A5
Whitehall Cl. Lo Naz EN9 ...... 135 E1
Whitehall Coll. Bis St 58 E1
Whitehall Jun Mix Inf Sch. Bis St 35 A5
Whitehall La. Bis St CM23 ...... 58 F1
Whitehall Rd. Bis St CM23 ...... 58 E1
Whitehall Village. Bis St CM23 ...... 58 E1
Whitehands Cl. Hod EN11 ...... 134 F6
Whiteheart Cross. Bov HP3 ...... 136 F3
Whitehicks. Letw SG6 ...... 12 A1
Whitehill Ave. Luton LU1 ...... 63 D5
Whitehill Cotts. Welw AL6 ...... 89 A3
Whitehill Ct. Berk HP4 ...... 122 D5
Whitehill Rd. Hit SG4 ...... 35 A6
Whitehorse St. Bark SG8 ...... 17 D4
Whitehorse St. Bal SG7 ...... 23 F8
Whitehorse Vale. Luton LU3 ...... 31 A1
Whitehouse Ave. Bor WD6 ...... 170 B5
Whitehouse La. Bri Wd EN2 ...... 140 C4
Whitehurst Ave. Hit SG5 ...... 21 F1
Whitelands Ave. Chor WD3 ...... 164 C5
Whiteleaf Rd. Heml H HP3 ...... 138 C8
Whiteley Cl. Dan En SG12 ...... 71 E7
Whiteley La. Buck SG9 ...... 27 C8
Whitesmead Rd. Stev SG1 ...... 50 E7
Whitestone Wlk. Heml H HP1 ...... 124 A6
Whitethorn La. Letw SG6 ...... 23 A4
Whitethorn Way. Luton LU1 ...... 63 A6
Whitethorn. Wel G C AL7 ...... 111 B5
Whitewaites. Harl CM20 ...... 117 E1
Whiteway. Letw SG6 ...... 23 C4
Whitewaybottom La. Kim SG4 ...... 66 A3
Whitewebbs La. Enf EN2 ...... 161 F4
Whitewebbs Pk. Cre H 161 D4
Whitewebbs Rd. Cre H EN2 ...... 161 C4
Whitewood Rd. Berk HP4 ...... 122 A4
Whitfield Way. Ric WD3 ...... 164 F1
Whitings Cl. Harp AL5 ...... 86 D4
Whitings Hill Jun Mix & Inf Sch. Barn 171 C4
Whitings Rd. Barn EN5 ...... 171 C4
Whitlars Dr. Kin L WD4 ...... 138 F3
Whitley Cl. Abb L WD5 ...... 154 A7
Whitley Gn. Luton LU2 ...... 46 D2
Whitley Rd. Hod EN11 ...... 135 B8
Whitmores Wood. Heml H HP2 ...... 125 B4
Whitney Dr. Stev SG1 ...... 36 C1
Whittingham Cl. Luton LU2 ...... 46 F1
Whittingstall Rd. Hod EN11 ...... 135 B8
Whittington La. Stev SG1 ...... 50 E4
Whittington Way. Bis St CM23 ...... 76 F3
Whittle Cl. Henlw SG16 ...... 10 B4
Whittlesea Cl. Har HA3 ...... 176 C3
Whittlesea Path. Har HA3 ...... 176 C2
Whittlesea Rd. Har HA3 ...... 176 C3
Whittlesea Sch. Har 176 C3
Whitwell Cl. Luton LU3 ...... 45 B8
Whitwell Rd. Watf WD2 ...... 154 D4
Whitworth Jones Ave. Henlw 10 C5
Whitworth Rd. Stev SG1 ...... 37 B3
Whomerley Rd. Stev SG1 ...... 50 E4
Whydale Rd. Royst SG8 ...... 7 E5
Whytingham Rd. Tri HP23 ...... 100 C4
Wick Ave. Whea AL4 ...... 108 D8
Wick Hill. Ken Co LU6 ...... 82 F8
Wick Rd. Wigg HP23 ...... 120 D8
Wick The. Hert SG14 ...... 92 C1
Wicken Fields. Ware SG12 ...... 93 C3
Wickets The. Luton LU2 ...... 45 E1
Wickfield Cl. Welw SG3 ...... 69 A2
Wickham Cl. Hare UB9 ...... 173 D2
Wickham Rd. Har HA3 ...... 176 D1
Wickham Way. Stansl SG11 ...... 55 E3
Wickhams Wharf. Ware SG12 ...... 93 E1
Wicklands Rd. Hun SG12 ...... 116 D8
Wickmere Cl. Luton LU2 ...... 45 C7
Wickstead Ave. Luton LU4 ...... 44 E4
Wickwood Ct. St Alb AL1 ...... 128 B5
Widbury Gdns. Ware SG12 ...... 93 F1
Widbury Hill. Ware SG12 ...... 93 F1
Widford Jun Mix & Inf Sch. Widf 95 D4
Widford Rd. Hun SG12 ...... 95 D4
Widford Rd. Wel G C AL7 ...... 111 B6
Widford Terr. Heml H HP2 ...... 105 A1
Widgeon Way. Watf WD2 ...... 154 E4
Widmore Dr. Heml H HP2 ...... 125 A5
Wieland Rd. Norwd HA6 ...... 175 A3
Wiggenhall Rd. Watf WD1 ...... 167 C4
Wiggington Bottom. Wigg HP23 ...... 120 E8
Wigmore La. Luton LU2 ...... 46 D3
Wigmore Park Ctr. Luton 46 E1
Wigmore Prim Sch. Luton 46 E2
Wigmores N. Wel G C AL8 ...... 110 D7
Wigram Way. Stev SG2 ...... 51 B3
Wilbury Cl. Letw SG6 ...... 22 C7
Wilbury Hills Rd. Letw SG6 ...... 22 C7
Wilbury Jun Mix Sch. Letw 22 D6
Wilbury Lodge. Barn EN5 ...... 171 B5
Wilbury Rd. Letw SG6 ...... 22 E8
Wilbury Way. Hit SG4 ...... 22 A3
Wilcot Ave. Watf WD1 ...... 167 E2
Wilcox Cl. Bor WD6 ...... 170 C8
Wild Cherry Dr. Luton LU1 ...... 63 D5
Wild March Ct. Enf EN8 ...... 162 C4
Wild Oaks Cl. Norwd HA6 ...... 174 F4
Wilderness The. Berk HP4 ...... 122 C4
Wildwood Ave. Bri Wd AL2 ...... 140 F1
Wildwood La. Stev SG1 ...... 50 B4
Wildwood. Norwd HA6 ...... 174 D4
Wilford Cl. Norwd HA6 ...... 174 D3
Wilga Rd. Welw AL6 ...... 89 B5
Wilkin's Green La. Coln H AL4 ...... 129 C4
Wilkins Gr. Wel G C AL8 ...... 110 D5
Willenhall Cl. Luton LU3 ...... 45 A7
William Austin Sch. Luton 45 C4
William Covell Cl. Enf EN2 ...... 160 F1
William Ct. Heml H HP3 ...... 138 D7
William Pl. Stev SG2 ...... 51 A3
William Ransom Sch The (Jun Mix & Inf). Hit 35 B7
William St. Berk HP4 ...... 122 D4
William St. Luton LU1 ...... 45 E1
William St. Mark AL3 ...... 83 E5
William St. Watf WD2 ...... 167 D6
Williams Way. Radl WD7 ...... 156 C4

Williamson St. Luton LU1 ...... 63 E7
Williamson Way. Ric WD3 ...... 165 A1
Willian Church Rd. Letw SG6 ...... 23 A2
Willian Rd. Gt Wy SG4 ...... 35 F7
Willian Rd. Hit SG4,SG6 ...... 22 D1
Willian Way. Bal SG7 ...... 23 E6
Willian Way. Letw SG6 ...... 23 A3
Willingale Cl. Wa Aby EN9 ...... 163 D7
Williton Rd. Luton LU2 ...... 46 C2
Willoughby Cl. Hod EN10 ...... 134 E2
Willoughby Rd. Harp AL5 ...... 86 B4
Willoughby Way. Hit SG4 ...... 35 A6
Willow Cl. Bis St CM23 ...... 76 E8
Willow Cl. Gt Ho SG9 ...... 42 A8
Willow Cl. Ham St EN7 ...... 147 E5
Willow Cl. Reed SG8 ...... 16 D5
Willow Cnr. Bay SG13 ...... 132 F5
Willow Cres. St Alb AL4 ...... 128 C3
Willow Ct. Har HA3 ...... 176 F2
Willow Ct. Luton LU3 ...... 44 E5
Willow Dean. Pnr HA5 ...... 175 D1
Willow Dene. Bus WD2 ...... 168 A2
Willow Dr. Barn EN5 ...... 171 E5
Willow Edge. Kin L WD4 ...... 139 A2
Willow End. Norwd HA6 ...... 175 A4
Willow Gn. Bor WD6 ...... 170 D4
Willow Gr. Wel G C AL8 ...... 89 D3
Willow La. Hit SG5 ...... 34 D6
Willow La. Watf WD1 ...... 167 A4
Willow Mead. Saw CM21 ...... 97 E2
Willow Springs. Bis St CM23 ...... 76 D8
Willow Way. Chis AL2 ...... 141 A4
Willow Way. Harp AL5 ...... 86 C4
Willow Way. Hat AL10 ...... 129 F2
Willow Way. Heml H HP1 ...... 124 B5
Willow Way. Luton LU3 ...... 44 E5
Willow Way. Pot B EN6 ...... 159 B6
Willow Way. Radl WD7 ...... 155 E3
Willow Wlk. Welw AL6 ...... 89 C8
Willowby Ct. Lon C AL2 ...... 142 D5
Willowdene. Ches EN8 ...... 148 C4
Willowfield Sch. Cad 62 F4
Willowgate Trad Est. Luton 44 B8
Willowmead. Hert SG14 ...... 113 B5
Willows Cl. Pnr HA5 ...... 175 C1
Willows Link. Stev SG2 ...... 69 A8
Willows The. Bus SG9 ...... 40 D8
Willows The. Heml H HP2 ...... 125 B5
Willows The. Hit SG4 ...... 35 A5
Willows The. Ric WD3 ...... 173 A8
Willows The. St Alb AL1 ...... 142 B7
Willows The. Stev SG2 ...... 51 A1
Willows The. Watf WD1 ...... 167 B2
Willowside. Lon C AL2 ...... 142 E4
Willowside Way. Royst SG8 ...... 7 C8
Wilsden Rd. Stev SG1 ...... 36 F1
Wilshere Ave. St Alb AL1 ...... 127 C1
Wilshere Cres. Hit SG4 ...... 35 C8
Wilshere Rd. Welw AL6 ...... 89 A5
Wilshere-Dacre (Sch Jun Mix). Hit 34 F8
Wilsmere Dr. Har HA3 ...... 176 E3
Wilson Cl. Stev SG1 ...... 36 D1
Wilsons La. Ashw SG7 ...... 4 C4
Wilstone Dr. St Alb AL4 ...... 128 C8
Wilton Cl. Bis St CM23 ...... 77 B7
Wilton Cres. Hert SG13 ...... 113 C4
Wilton Rd. Hit SG5 ...... 21 E1
Wilton Way. Hert SG13 ...... 113 C4
Wiltshire Rd. Stev SG2 ...... 51 A4
Wimborne Cl. Saw CM21 ...... 97 D2
Wimborne Gr. Watf WD1 ...... 153 E2
Wimborne Rd. Luton LU1 ...... 63 B8
Wimple Rd. Dun LU4 ...... 44 A2
Winch Cl. Cod SG4 ...... 88 F8
Winch St. Luton LU2 ...... 45 F1
Winchdells. Heml H HP3 ...... 139 A8
Winches Farm Dr. St Alb AL4 ...... 128 D3
Winchester Cl. Bis St CM23 ...... 76 D4
Winchester Cl. Stev SG1 ...... 37 B2
Winchester House. St Alb AL3 ...... 127 C2
Winchester Rd. Norwd HA6 ...... 174 F1
Winchester Way. Cro Gr WD3 ...... 166 B4
Winchfield Way. Ric WD3 ...... 165 C2
Windermere Ave. St Alb AL1 ...... 128 B1
Windermere Cl. Chor WD3 ...... 164 D4
Windermere Cl. Heml H HP3 ...... 125 C2
Windermere Cres. Luton LU3 ...... 44 F5
Windermere Jun Mix Inf Sch. St Alb 128 B1
Windhill. Bis St CM23 ...... 76 E7
Windhill Old Rd. Bis St CM23 ...... 76 E7
Windhill. Wel G C AL7 ...... 111 A7
Winding Hill. Muc H SG10 ...... 75 A4
Winding Shot. Heml H HP1 ...... 124 A4
Winding Shott. Bram SG14 ...... 91 C4
Windmill Ave. St Alb AL4 ...... 128 C4
Windmill Cl. Bark SG8 ...... 17 C5
Windmill Cl. Pit LU7 ...... 80 F5
Windmill Cl. Wa Aby EN9 ...... 163 D5
Windmill Dr. Cro Gr WD3 ...... 165 F3
Windmill Field. Ware SG12 ...... 114 D8
Windmill Fields. Harl CM17 ...... 118 F4
Windmill Hill. Bun SG9 ...... 40 F6
Windmill Hill. Chipf WD4 ...... 151 F7
Windmill La. Bus WD2 ...... 168 E1
Windmill La. Ches EN8 ...... 148 E1
Windmill La. Edg EN5 ...... 170 F3
Windmill Rd. Bre Gr SG4 ...... 47 D2
Windmill Rd. Heml H HP2 ...... 124 E2
Windmill Rd. Luton LU1 ...... 63 F6
Windmill Rd. Mark AL3 ...... 84 B6
Windmill St. Bus WD2 ...... 168 E1
Windmill Way. Muc H SG10 ...... 74 E1
Windmill Way. Tri HP23 ...... 99 F4
Windmills. Dan En SG12 ...... 71 E8
Windmore Ave. Pot B EN6 ...... 158 C8
Windridge Cl. St Alb AL3 ...... 127 A1
Winds End Cl. Heml H HP2 ...... 125 A5
Windsor Cl. Bor WD6 ...... 170 A8
Windsor Cl. Chor WD3 ...... 137 A3
Windsor Cl. Ches EN7 ...... 148 A1
Windsor Cl. Heml H HP3 ...... 138 D7
Windsor Cl. Norwd HA6 ...... 175 A1
Windsor Cl. Stev SG2 ...... 69 B7
Windsor Cl. Welw AL6 ...... 89 D3
Windsor Ct. Kin L WD4 ...... 139 A2
Windsor Dr. St Alb AL1 ...... 128 A3
Windsor Gdns. Bis St CM23 ...... 76 C2
Windsor Rd. Barn EN5 ...... 171 E3

Windsor Rd. Enf EN3 ...... 162 D3
Windsor Rd. Har HA3 ...... 176 D2
Windsor Rd. Royst SG8 ...... 7 F6
Windsor Rd. Watf WD2 ...... 154 C1
Windsor Rd. Welw AL6 ...... 89 B3
Windsor St. Luton LU1 ...... 63 D6
Windsor Way. Ric WD3 ...... 165 A1
Windsor Wlk. Luton LU1 ...... 63 D6
Windsor Wood. Wa Aby EN9 ...... 163 E6
Windward Cl. Enf EN3 ...... 162 D4
Windy Rise. Dan En SG12 ...... 71 F7
Winford Dr. Hod EN10 ...... 134 F1
Wingate Gdns. Welw AL6 ...... 89 B5
Wingate Rd. Luton LU4 ...... 44 F2
Wingrave C of E Combd Sch. Wing 60 A3
Wingrave Rd. Tri HP23 ...... 100 B6
Wingrave Rd. Wils HP23 ...... 79 D1
Winifred House (Conv Hospl for Children). Edg 170 F3
Winifred Rd. Heml H HP3 ...... 138 D7
Winkfield Cl. Dun LU4 ...... 44 B1
Winnington Rd. Enf EN3 ...... 162 C2
Winsdon Rd. Luton LU1 ...... 63 D6
Winslow Cl. Luton LU3 ...... 45 C4
Winslow Rd. Wing HP22 ...... 60 B3
Winston Cl. Har HA3 ...... 176 F4
Winston Cl. Hit SG5 ...... 34 D7
Winston Ct. Har HA3 ...... 176 B3
Winston Gdns. Berk HP4 ...... 121 F4
Winston Way. Pot B EN6 ...... 159 A6
Winstre Rd. Bor WD6 ...... 170 A8
Winters La. Walk SG2 ...... 38 C1
Winterscroft Rd. Hod EN11 ...... 134 F7
Winton App. Cro Gr WD3 ...... 166 C4
Winton Cl. Letw SG6 ...... 23 C8
Winton Cl. Luton LU2 ...... 45 C4
Winton Cres. Cro Gr WD3 ...... 166 B4
Winton Dr. Cro Gr WD3 ...... 166 C4
Winton Dr. Ware SG12 ...... 93 F1
Wisden Rd. Stev SG1 ...... 36 F1
Wiseman Cl. Luton LU2 ...... 45 E7
Wisemans Gdns. Saw CM21 ...... 97 C1
Wistlea Cres. Coln H AL4 ...... 129 B1
Wistow Rd. Luton LU3 ...... 45 A6
Witchford. Wel G C AL7 ...... 111 D6
Withy Cl. Luton LU4 ...... 44 B4
Withy Pl. Chis AL2 ...... 141 C3
Witney Cl. Pnr HA5 ...... 175 F4
Witsend. Bric SG13 ...... 113 E1
Witter Ave. Ick SG5 ...... 21 E4
Wiveton Cl. Luton LU2 ...... 45 D7
Woburn Ave. Bis St CM23 ...... 76 C7
Woburn Cl. Bus WD2 ...... 168 C3
Woburn Cl. Stev SG2 ...... 69 C7
Woburn Ct. Luton LU4 ...... 44 D5
Wodecroft Rd. Luton LU3 ...... 45 A6
Wodson Park Sports & L Ctr. Ware 93 F4
Wolfsburg Ct. Luton LU4 ...... 44 C5
Wolsey Ave. Gofs O EN7 ...... 147 F2
Wolsey House. Kin L WD4 ...... 139 A2
Wolsey Mansions. Mo Pk HA6 ...... 174 C7
Wolsey Rd. Heml H HP2 ...... 124 D7
Wolsey Rd. Mo Pk HA6 ...... 174 D7
Wolston Cl. Luton LU1 ...... 63 C7
Wolves Mere. Welw SG3 ...... 69 A2
Wolvescroft. Welw SG3 ...... 69 A2
Wood Cl. Hat AL10 ...... 130 B5
Wood Comm. Hat AL10 ...... 130 B8
Wood Cres. Heml H HP3 ...... 124 E1
Wood Dr. Stev SG2 ...... 51 B2
Wood End. Chis AL2 ...... 141 C4
Wood End Cl. Heml H HP2 ...... 125 C4
Wood End Hill. Harp AL5 ...... 85 D3
Wood End Inf Sch. Harp 85 D3
Wood End Jun Mix Sch. Harp 85 D3
Wood End La. Fla AL3 ...... 104 E8
Wood End Rd. Harp AL5 ...... 85 D3
Wood Farm Rd. Heml H HP2 ...... 124 E2
Wood Green Cl. Luton LU2 ...... 46 B3
Wood Green Rd. Luton LU2 ...... 46 C5
Wood Green Way. Ches EN8 ...... 162 E8
Wood La. Heml H HP2 ...... 124 D2
Wood La. Mee SG9 ...... 30 A6
Wood Lane End. Heml H HP2 ...... 125 B4
Wood St. Barn EN5 ...... 171 D5
Wood St. Luton LU1 ...... 63 F6
Wood Vale. Hat AL10 ...... 130 B5
Wood View. Cuf EN6 ...... 146 E4
Wood View. Heml H HP1 ...... 124 B5
Woodacre Dr. Welw AL6 ...... 90 A8
Woodbine Gr. Enf EN2 ...... 161 C4
Woodbridge Cl. Luton LU4 ...... 44 E4
Woodbrook Gdns. Wa Aby EN9 ...... 163 E6
Woodbury Hill. Luton LU2 ...... 45 E2
Woodcock Hill. Ric WD3 ...... 173 E4
Woodcock Hill. Sand AL4 ...... 108 E1
Woodcock Rd. Luton LU1 ...... 63 A7
Woodcock Rd. Stev SG2 ...... 51 B2
Woodcote Cl. Ches EN8 ...... 148 C1
Woodcote House. Hit SG4 ...... 34 F7 1
Woodcroft Ave. Sta Ab SG12 ...... 115 C4
Woodcroft. Hit SG5 ...... 34 E5
Woodfall Ave. Barn EN5 ...... 171 F4
Woodfield Ave. Mo Pk HA6 ...... 174 E6
Woodfield Cl. Sta M CM24 ...... 59 E6
Woodfield Dr. Heml H HP3 ...... 125 D1
Woodfield Gdns. Heml H HP3 ...... 125 D1
Woodfield La. Hat AL9 ...... 145 E8
Woodfield Rd. Radl WD7 ...... 156 A3
Woodfield Rd. Stev SG1 ...... 36 D1
Woodfield Rd. Wel G C AL7 ...... 110 F6
Woodfield Rise. Bus WD2 ...... 168 C2
Woodfield Sch. Heml H 125 C1
Woodfield Terr. Sta M CM24 ...... 59 D4
Woodfields. Sta M CM24 ...... 59 D4
Woodford Cres. Pnr HA5 ...... 175 B1
Woodford Rd. Watf WD1 ...... 167 C5
Woodforde Cl. Ashw SG7 ...... 4 A4
Woodgate Cres. Norwd HA6 ...... 175 A4
Woodgate. Watf WD2 ...... 154 B6
Woodgrange Cl. Har HA3 ...... 176 F3
Woodhall Ave. Pnr HA5 ...... 175 E2
Woodhall Cl. Hert SG14 ...... 113 C8

Woodhall Ct. Wel G C AL7 .... 110 E5
Woodhall Dr. Pnr HA5 .... 175 E2
Woodhall Gate. Pnr HA5 .... 175 D2
Woodhall Gr. Bis St CM23 .... 76 D6
Woodhall Jun Mix & Inf Schs.
 Sth Ox 175 E6
Woodhall La. Heml H HP2 .... 124 E4
Woodhall La. Shen WD7 .... 156 F4
Woodhall La. Sth Ox WD1 .... 175 E6
Woodhall La. Wel G C AL7 .... 110 E4
Woodham Way. Gt Am SG12 .... 115 C4
Woodhouse Eaves. Mo Pk HA6 .... 175 A5
Woodhurst Ave. Watf WD2 .... 154 D4
Woodhurst. Letw SG6 .... 22 F8
Woodland Ave. Heml H HP1 .... 124 B2
Woodland Ave. Luton LU3 .... 45 B2
Woodland Cl. Heml H HP1 .... 124 B2
Woodland Cl. Tri HP23 .... 99 F2
Woodland Dr. St Alb AL4 .... 128 C4
Woodland Dr. Watf WD1 .... 166 F8
Woodland La. Chor WD3 .... 164 D6
Woodland Mount. Hert SG13 ...... 113 F6
Woodland Pl. Heml H HP1 .... 124 B2
Woodland Rd. Hert H SG13 .... 114 C3
Woodland Rd. Map Cr WD3 .... 172 D5
Woodland Rise. Wel G C AL8 ...... 110 C8
Woodland Rise. Whip LU6 .... 82 B7
Woodland Way. Bal SG7 .... 23 F6
Woodland Way. Gofs O EN7 .... 147 B3
Woodland Way. Stev SG2 .... 51 A1
Woodland Way. Welw AL6 .... 90 A7
Woodlands Ave. Berk HP4 .... 122 D3
Woodlands. Bis St CM23 .... 77 C8
Woodlands. Bro Pk AL9 .... 145 B4
Woodlands. Chis AL2 .... 141 C4
Woodlands Cl. Bor WD6 .... 170 B5
Woodlands Cl. Hod EN11 .... 135 A5
Woodlands Dr. Abb L WD4 .... 139 C3
Woodlands Dr. Hod EN11 .... 135 A4
Woodlands. Harp AL5 .... 85 E3
Woodlands Meade. Wes SG4 ...... 37 B8
Woodlands. Radl WD7 .... 156 A5
Woodlands Rd. Abb L WD4 .... 139 A4
Woodlands Rd. Enf EN2 .... 161 D1
Woodlands Rd. Hert SG13 .... 113 F6
Woodlands Rd. Thun SG12 .... 93 D6
Woodlands Rd. Watf WD2 .... 167 E4

Woodlands. Royst SG8 .... 7 E6
Woodlands Sch. Bor 170 A8
Woodlea. Chis AL2 .... 141 A6
Woodlea Gr. Norwd HA6 .... 174 C4
Woodley Rd. Ware SG12 .... 93 F2
Woodleys. Harl CM20 .... 118 A1
Woodman Rd. Heml H HP3 .... 124 E1 2
Woodmere Ave. Bus WD2 .... 154 E1
Woodmere. Luton LU3 .... 31 A1
Woodmill Mews. Hod EN11 .... 135 B8
Woodpecker Cl. Bus WD2 .... 168 C1
Woodpecker Cl. Har HA3 .... 176 F2
Woodpecker Cl. Hat AL10 .... 129 F2
Woodridge Way. Norwd HA6 ...... 174 E4
Woodridings Ave. Pnr HA5 .... 175 F2
Woodridings Cl. Pnr HA5 .... 175 F3
Woods Ave. Hat AL10 .... 130 B4
Woods Pl. Tri HP22 .... 100 A3
Woods The. Radl WD7 .... 156 B5
Woods The. Sth Ox HA6 .... 175 A5
Woodshots Meadow. Watf WD1 .. 166 D4
Woodside. Bis St CM23 .... 77 D8
Woodside. Bor WD6 .... 169 F5
Woodside Farm & Wild Fowl Park.
 Mark 84 A8
Woodside. Hert H SG13 .... 114 C2
Woodside House. Wel G C AL8 .... 110 C7
Woodside Ind Pk. Letw 23 B7
Woodside Jun Mix Inf Sch.
 Gofs O 147 B2
Woodside La. Hat AL9 .... 131 A1
Woodside Pl. Hat AL9 .... 131 B2
Woodside Rd. Abb L WD5 .... 154 B8
Woodside Rd. Bri Wd AL2 .... 140 F2
Woodside Rd. Cad LU1 .... 63 B3
Woodside Rd. Welw AL6 .... 89 F3
Woodside. Watf WD2 .... 154 A3
Woodstock Cl. Hert H SG13 .... 114 B4
Woodstock Rd. Bus WD2 .... 168 F2
Woodstock Rd. Hod EN10 .... 134 E4
Woodstock Rd N. St Alb AL1 ...... 128 B4
Woodstock Rd S. St Alb AL1 ...... 128 B3
Woodstock. Welw SG3 .... 68 F3
Woodville Court Mews.
 Watf WD1 .... 167 A7
Woodville Ct. Watf WD1 .... 167 A7
Woodville Pl. Hert SG14 .... 113 B8
Woodward Gdns. Har HA7 .... 176 F3
Woodway. Watf WD1 .... 167 C2
Woodwicks. Map Cr WD3 .... 172 D5

Woolenwick Prim Schs. Stev 50 B6
Woolgrove Ct. Hit SG4 .... 22 B1
Woolgrove Rd. Hit SG4 .... 22 B1
Woolgrove Sch. Letw 23 D5
Woollam Cres. St Alb AL3 .... 127 C7
Woollams. Red AL3 .... 106 A4
Woollard St. Wa Aby EN9 .... 163 C5
Woolmans Cl. Hod EN10 .... 134 F1
Woolmer Cl. Bor WD6 .... 157 A1
Woolmer Dr. Heml H HP2 .... 125 C3
Woolmer Green C of E Sch. Welw .. 69 A1
Woolmers La. Hertng SG14 .... 112 B2
Woolmers Way. Stev SG1 .... 50 C6
Woolsgrove Ct. Royst SG8 .... 7 E5
Woolston Ave. Letw SG6 .... 23 A4
Wootton Cl. Luton LU3 .... 45 B7
Wootton Dr. Heml H HP2 .... 124 F8
Worboys Ct. Gu M SG8 .... 1 F5
Worcester Rd. Hat AL10 .... 129 F6
Worcesters Ave. Enf EN1 .... 162 A1
Worcesters Prim Sch. Enf 161 F1
Wordsworth Cl. Royst SG8 .... 2 D1
Wordsworth Rd. Dun LU4 .... 44 A2
Wordsworth Rd. Harp AL5 .... 86 A3
Works Rd. Letw SG6 .... 23 C7
Worley Rd. St Alb AL3 .... 127 D4
Wormley Lodge Cl. Hod EN10 .... 148 F8
Wormley Prim Sch. Hod 148 E8
Worsted La. Gt Ho SG9 .... 41 E7
Wortham Rd. Royst SG8 .... 7 E4
Wortham Way. Stev SG2 .... 51 B3
Wraglins The. Bis St CM23 .... 77 B5
Wratten Cl. Hit SG5 .... 34 E6
Wratten Rd E. Hit SG5 .... 34 E6
Wratten Rd W. Hit SG5 .... 34 E6
Wrayfields. Stot SG5 .... 12 B8
Wren Cl. Kim SG4 .... 66 B1
Wren Cl. Luton LU2 .... 46 C6
Wren Cl. Stev SG2 .... 51 B6
Wren Cres. Bus WD2 .... 168 C1
Wren Wood. Wel G C AL7 .... 111 B7
Wrenbrook Rd. Bis St CM23 ...... 76 F6
Wrensfield. Heml H HP1 .... 124 B3
Wrestlers Cl. Hat AL10 .... 130 C7
Wrexham Terr. Royst SG8 .... 7 D7
Wright Cl. Whea AL4 .... 108 E7
Wright's Bldgs. Watf WD1 .... 167 B7
Wrights Green La. L Hal CM22 .... 98 D7
Wrights Meadow. Walk SG2 .... 52 B8
Wrights Orch. Ast SG2 .... 51 E2
Wrotham Park. Pot B 158 E3

Wrotham Rd. Barn EN5 .... 171 E7
Wroxham Ave. Heml H HP3 .... 124 D1
Wroxham Gdns. Cre H EN2 .... 161 B4
Wroxham Gdns. Pot B EN6 .... 158 D8
Wroxham Jun Mix Inf Sch. Pot B . 158 D8
Wroxham Way. Harp AL5 .... 86 C3
Wulfrath Way. Ware SG12 .... 93 C3
Wulwards Cl. Luton LU1 .... 63 B6
Wulwards Ct. Luton LU1 .... 63 B6
Wyatt Cl. Bus WD2 .... 168 E2
Wyatt Cl. Ick SG5 .... 21 D4
Wyatt's Cl. Chor WD3 .... 165 A6
Wyatt's Rd. Chor WD3 .... 165 A6
Wyburn Ave. Barn EN5 .... 171 F6
Wych Elm. Harl CM20 .... 117 C1
Wych Elm La. Welw AL6 .... 68 F2
Wych Elms. Chis AL2 .... 141 B3
Wychdell. Stev SG2 .... 69 C8
Wychford Dr. Saw CM21 .... 97 C1
Wychwood Ave. Luton LU2 .... 45 E3
Wychwood Way. Norwd HA6 ..... 174 F3
Wycklond Cl. Stot SG5 .... 11 E6
Wycliffe Cl. Luton LU3 .... 45 C6
Wycliffe Ct. Abb L WD5 .... 153 E7
Wycombe Way. Luton LU3 .... 45 C8
Wycombe Way. St Alb AL4 .... 128 B6
Wyddial Gn. Wel G C AL7 .... 111 B6
Wyddial Rd. Bun SG9 .... 40 E8
Wyedale. Lon C AL2 .... 142 F4
Wykeham Rise. Barn N20 .... 171 E1
Wyken Cl. Luton LU3 .... 45 A7
Wyldwood Cl. Harl CM17 .... 118 C6
Wyllyotts Cl. Pot B EN6 .... 158 F7
Wyllyotts Pl. Pot B EN6 .... 158 F7
Wylo Dr. Edge EN5 .... 171 A3
Wymondley Cl. Hit SG4 .... 35 A7
Wymondley Jun Mix Inf Sch.
 L Wym 35 E4
Wymondley Rd. Hit SG4 .... 35 B6
Wymondley Rd. Letw SG4 .... 23 A1
Wynchgate. Har HA3 .... 176 E3
Wynchlands Cres. St Alb AL4 ..... 128 D3
Wynd Arcade The. Letw SG6 ...... 22 F6
Wyndham Rd. Dun LU4 .... 44 C2
Wyndhams End. Wel G C AL7 .... 110 F2
Wynlie Gdns. Pnr HA5 .... 175 B1
Wynn Cl. Bal SG7 .... 13 A1
Wyrley Dell. Letw SG6 .... 23 A3
Wyton. Wel G C AL7 .... 111 D6
Wyvern Cl. Luton LU4 .... 44 E3

Yardley Ave. Pit LU7 .... 80 D4
Yardley Ct. Harp AL5 .... 86 B1 7
Yardley. Letw SG6 .... 23 C4
Yarmouth Rd. Stev SG1 .... 50 A7
Yarmouth Rd. Watf WD2 .... 154 C1
Yately Cl. Luton LU2 .... 45 D7
Yeatman House. Watf WD2 .... 154 B3
Yeats Cl. Royst SG8 .... 2 D1
Yeomanry Dr. Bal SG7 .... 13 A1
Yeomans Ave. Harp AL5 .... 85 D3
Yeomans Cl. Bis St CM23 .... 76 D6
Yeomans Dr. Ast SG2 .... 51 E2
Yeomans Ride. Heml H HP2 ...... 105 A1
Yeovil Rd. Luton LU2 .... 46 B2
Yew Cl. Ham St EN7 .... 147 E4
Yew Gr. Wel G C AL7 .... 111 C5
Yew Tree Cl. Bot HP5 .... 136 A1
Yew Tree Ct. Pit LU7 .... 80 E5
Yew Tree Ct. Bov HP3 .... 137 B3
Yew Tree Ct. Heml H HP1 .... 124 A1
Yew Tree Pl. Bis St CM23 .... 76 F8
Yew Wlk. Hod EN11 .... 135 A5
Yewlands. Hod EN11 .... 135 A5
Yewlands. Saw CM21 .... 97 F1
Yews Ave. Enf EN1 .... 162 B3
Yewtree End. Chis AL2 .... 141 B4
York Cl. Kin L WD4 .... 139 A2
York Cres. Bor WD6 .... 170 D7
York House. St Alb AL3 .... 127 C2
York Mead Jun Mix Inf Sch.
 Cro Gr 166 A4
York Rd. Ches EN8 .... 162 E6
York Rd. Hit SG5 .... 34 E8
York Rd. Norwd HA6 .... 175 A1
York Rd. St Alb AL1 .... 127 F4
York Rd. Stev SG1 .... 36 F1
York Rd. Watf WD1 .... 167 C4
York Terr. Enf EN2 .... 161 C1
York Way. Heml H HP2 .... 124 E2
York Way. Royst SG8 .... 7 B8
York Way. Wel G C AL6 .... 89 C3
Yorke Rd. Cro Gr WD3 .... 166 A3
Youngfield Rd. Heml H HP1 ...... 123 F4
Youngs Rise. Wel G C AL8 .... 110 C6
Youngsbury La. Thun SG12 ...... 93 E8
Yule Cl. Bri Wd AL2 .... 140 F1

Zambesi Rd. Bis St CM23 .... 77 A5

STREET ATLASES ORDER FORM

All Street Atlases contain Ordnance Survey mapping and provide the perfect solution for the driver who needs comprehensive, detailed regional mapping in a choice of compact and easy-to-use formats. They are indispensable and are ideal for use in the car, the home or the office.

The series is available from all good bookshops or by mail order direct from the publisher. Before placing your order, please check by telephone that the complete range of titles are available. Payment can be made in the following ways:

By phone Phone your order through on our special Credit Card Hotline on 01733 371999 (Fax: 01733 370585). Speak to our customer service team during office hours (9am to 5pm) or leave a message on the answering machine, quoting your full credit card number plus expiry date and your full name and address.

By post Simply fill out the order form (you may photocopy it) and send it to: Reed Books Direct, 43 Stapledon Road, Orton Southgate, Peterborough PE2 6TD.

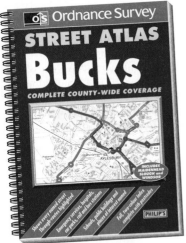

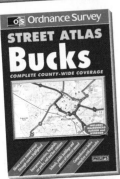

NEW COLOUR EDITIONS

	HARDBACK	SPIRAL	POCKET	£ Total
	Quantity @ £10.99 each	Quantity @ £8.99 each	Quantity @ £4.99 each	£ Total
BERKSHIRE	☐ 0 540 06170 0	☐ 0 540 06172 7	☐ 0 540 06173 5	➤
	Quantity @ £10.99 each	Quantity @ £8.99 each	Quantity @ £3.99 each	£ Total
MERSEYSIDE	☐ 0 540 06480 7	☐ 0 540 06481 5	☐ 0 540 06482 3	➤
	Quantity @ £12.99 each	Quantity @ £8.99 each	Quantity @ £4.99 each	£ Total
SURREY	☐ 0 540 06435 1	☐ 0 540 06436 X	☐ 0 540 06438 6	➤
	Quantity @ £12.99 each	Quantity @ £9.99 each	Quantity @ £4.99 each	£ Total
BUCKINGHAMSHIRE	☐ 0 540 07466 7	☐ 0 540 07467 5	☐ 0 540 07468 3	➤
DURHAM	☐ 0 540 06365 7	☐ 0 540 06366 5	☐ 0 540 06367 3	➤
HERTFORDSHIRE	☐ 0 540 06174 3	☐ 0 540 06175 1	☐ 0 540 06176 X	➤
EAST KENT	☐ 0 540 07483 7	☐ 0 540 07276 1	☐ 0 540 07287 7	➤
WEST KENT	☐ 0 540 07366 0	☐ 0 540 07367 9	☐ 0 540 07369 5	➤
GREATER MANCHESTER	☐ 0 540 06485 8	☐ 0 540 06486 6	☐ 0 540 06487 4	➤
EAST SUSSEX	☐ 0 540 07306 7	☐ 0 540 07307 5	☐ 0 540 07312 1	➤
WEST SUSSEX	☐ 0 540 07319 9	☐ 0 540 07323 7	☐ 0 540 07327 X	➤
TYNE AND WEAR	☐ 0 540 06370 3	☐ 0 540 06371 1	☐ 0 540 06372 X	➤
SOUTH YORKSHIRE	☐ 0 540 06330 4	☐ 0 540 06331 2	☐ 0 540 06332 0	➤
WEST YORKSHIRE	☐ 0 540 06329 0	☐ 0 540 06327 4	☐ 0 540 06328 2	➤
	Quantity @ £14.99 each	Quantity @ £9.99 each	Quantity @ £4.99 each	£ Total
LANCASHIRE	☐ 0 540 06440 8	☐ 0 540 06441 6	☐ 0 540 06443 2	➤

STREET ATLASES ORDER FORM

BLACK AND WHITE EDITIONS

	HARDBACK Quantity @ £12.99 each	SOFTBACK Quantity @ £9.99 each	POCKET Quantity @ £4.99 each	£ Total
BRISTOL AND AVON	☐ 0 540 06140 9	☐ 0 540 06141 7	☐ 0 540 06142 5	➤ ☐
CARDIFF, SWANSEA & GLAMORGAN	☐ 0 540 06186 7	☐ 0 540 06187 5	☐ 0 540 06207 3	➤ ☐
CHESHIRE	☐ 0 540 06143 3	☐ 0 540 06144 1	☐ 0 540 06145 X	➤ ☐
DERBYSHIRE	☐ 0 540 06137 9	☐ 0 540 06138 7	☐ 0 540 06139 5	➤ ☐
EDINBURGH & East Central Scotland	☐ 0 540 06180 8	☐ 0 540 06181 6	☐ 0 540 06182 4	➤ ☐
EAST ESSEX	☐ 0 540 05848 3	☐ 0 540 05866 1	☐ 0 540 05850 5	➤ ☐
GLASGOW & West Central Scotland	☐ 0 540 06183 2	☐ 0 540 06184 0	☐ 0 540 06185 9	➤ ☐
NORTH HAMPSHIRE	☐ 0 540 05852 1	☐ 0 540 05853 X	☐ 0 540 05854 8	➤ ☐
SOUTH HAMPSHIRE	☐ 0 540 05855 6	☐ 0 540 05856 4	☐ 0 540 05857 2	➤ ☐
NOTTINGHAMSHIRE	☐ 0 540 05858 0	☐ 0 540 05859 9	☐ 0 540 05860 2	➤ ☐
OXFORDSHIRE	☐ 0 540 05986 2	☐ 0 540 05987 0	☐ 0 540 05988 9	➤ ☐
STAFFORDSHIRE	☐ 0 540 06134 4	☐ 0 540 06135 2	☐ 0 540 06136 0	➤ ☐
	Quantity @ £12.99 each	Quantity @ £8.99 each	Quantity @ £4.99 each	£ Total
WEST ESSEX	☐ 0 540 05849 1	☐ 0 540 05867 X	☐ 0 540 05851 3	➤ ☐
	Quantity @ £10.99 each	Quantity @ £8.99 each	Quantity @ £4.99 each	£ Total
WARWICKSHIRE	☐ 0 540 05642 1	—	—	➤ ☐

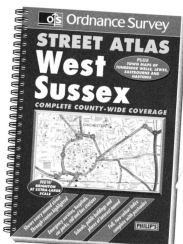

Post to: **Reed Books Direct,
43 Stapledon Road, Orton
Southgate, Peterborough**
PE2 6TD

◆ Free postage and packing

◆ All available titles will
normally be dispatched
within 5 working days of
receipt of order but please
allow up to 28 days for
delivery

☐ Please tick this box if you
do not wish your name to be
used by other carefully
selected organisations that
may wish to send you
information about other
products and services

Registered Office: Michelin
House, 81 Fulham Road,
London sw3 6RB.
Registered in England
number:1974080

I enclose a cheque / postal order, for a **total** of ☐

made payable to *Reed Book Services,* or please debit my

☐ Access ☐ American Express ☐ Visa ☐ Diners

account by ☐

Account no
☐☐☐☐ ☐☐☐☐ ☐☐☐☐ ☐☐☐☐

Expiry date ☐☐ ☐☐

Signature...

Name...

Address...

....

....

....POSTCODE